SOURCES
OF
WORLD HISTORY

Sources of World History

Readings for World Civilization
Volume II

Mark A. Kishlansky, Editor
Harvard University

with the assistance of
Susan Lindsey Lively
Harvard University

HarperCollinsCollegePublishers

Acquisitions Editor: Bruce Borland
Developmental Editor: Carol Einhorn
Project Editor: Marina Vaynshteyn
Design Supervisor: Mary McDonnell
Cover Design: Mary McDonnell
Cover Illustration: Detail of "La Guelaguetza" by Alfredo Ramos Martinez (1932). Bryce R. Bannatyne Gallery, Santa Monica, CA.
Photo Researcher: Sandy Schneider
Production Manager: Laura Chavoen
Manufacturing Manager: Willie Lane
Compositor: LaToya Wigfall
Printer and Binder: R. R. Donnelley & Sons Company
Cover Printer: The Lehigh Press, Inc.

Sources of World History: Readings for World Civilization, Volume II
Copyright © 1995 by HarperCollins College Publishers

Library of Congress Cataloging-in-Publication Data
Sources of world history : readings for world civilization / Mark A. Kishlansky, editor, with the assistance of Susan Lindsey Lively.
     p.   cm.
     ISBN 0-06-501034-5 (v. 1). —ISBN 0-06-501035-3 (v. 2)
     1. History—Sources.   I. Kishlansky, Mark A.   II. Lively, Susan Lindsey.
D5.S68 1993
909—dc20   93-30336
          CIP

94 95 96   9 8 7 6 5 4 3 2 1

Contents

VOLUME II

PART IV   THE WORLD OF TRAVELERS AND TRADERS

Monarchy and Revolution

The New Science

Empires of Goods

Travelers to the East and West

PART V INDUSTRIALISM AND IMPERIALISM

The Industrial Revolution in Britain

Critiquing Industrial Society

PART VI THE MODERN WORLD

World War I

Struggles for National Liberation

The Japanese Miracle

Toward the Future

Preface

Sources of World History is a collection of documents designed to supplement textbooks and lectures in the teaching of world civilization. The use of primary materials is an essential component of the study of history. By hearing the voices of the past students come to realize both the similarities and differences between their society and previous ones. In witnessing others ponder the same questions that rouse their own curiosity, students feel a connection between the past and the present. Moreover, by observing the ways in which such questions and experiences are worked out and described they come to an understanding and respect for the integrity of other cultures. By confronting the materials of the past, students exercise an imagination that is at the heart of the teaching and learning of history.

Historical sources are the building blocks from which instructor and textbook writer have ultimately constructed their accounts and their explanations of world historical development. It is essential that even beginning students learn that the past does not come to us prepackaged, but is formed by historians who exercise their own imaginations on primary materials. Historical thinking involves examining the ideas of others, understanding past experiences on others' terms, and recognizing other points of view. This process makes everyone, student and instructor alike, a historian.

I have observed a number of principles in selecting the materials for this collection, which is designed for beginning-level college students. I believe strongly in the value of primary sources and feel that they should be made as accessible to contemporary students as possible. Thus I have preferred to use up-to-date translations of many texts despite the costliness of acquiring their rights. Many of the late nineteenth century translations that are commonly used in source books present texts that are syntactically too complex for modern students to comprehend easily. I have also chosen to present longer selections than is usual in books of this type. Unlike works that contain snippets of hundreds of documents, *Sources of World History* presents a sizable amount of a small number of sources. It therefore allows students to gain a deeper feeling for authors and texts and to concentrate their energies and resources. No selection is so long that it cannot be easily read at a sitting and none so short as to defy recall. Each selection raises a significant issue around which classroom discussion can take place or to which lectures can refer. Some may even stimulate students to seek out the complete original works.

Two other principles lie behind the selections I have made. The first is that a steady diet of even the world's greatest thinkers is unpalatable without other varieties of social and cultural materials. For this reason I have tried to leaven the mass of intellectual history with materials that draw on social conditions or common experiences in past eras. These should not only aid students in making connections between past and present but should also introduce them to the varieties of materials from which history is re-created. Second, I have been especially concerned to recover the voices or highlight the experiences of those who are not always adequately represented in surveys of world civilization. The explosion of work in social history, in the history of the family, and in the history of women has made possible the inclusion of materials here that were barely discovered a decade ago. While this effort can be clearly seen in the materials chosen for the modern sections, it is also apparent in the selections made from more traditional older documents.

By providing longer selections and by expanding the scope of the materials to be incorporated I have necessarily been compelled to make some hard choices. There exists a superabundance of materials that demand inclusion in a collection such as this. I have tried to find representative examples of the works of each of the major civilization complexes, Asia, Africa, Latin America, and the Islamic world as well as the central works of Western civilization. This poses very difficult problems of balance, equity, and accessibility. Since early African and Latin American civilizations were oral cultures, they have necessarily left fewer documentary artifacts, despite the richness of their cultures. Much of what is known comes to us through the eyes of travelers or through the memory of later representatives of these cultures. I have included many such documents along with cautions about how to use them. I have also included Western views of Asia in an effort to raise questions of a comparative and cross-cultural nature. Having so few documents for so many civilizations necessarily raises questions of selection. It is my conviction that it is the experience of using primary materials—rather than the primary materials that are used—that is vital. Thus I have tried to provide a balance among constitutional documents, political theory, philosophy, imaginative literature, and social description. In all cases I have made the pedagogical value of the specific texts the prime consideration, selecting for significance, readability, and variety.

The feature How to Read a Document is designed to introduce students to a disciplined approach of working with primary sources and to encourage them to use their imaginations in their historical studies. No brief introduction pretends to be authoritative, and there are many other strategies and questions that can be adopted in training students to become critical readers. It is hoped that this introduction will remove some of the barriers that usually exist between student and source by walking them through a single exercise with a document in front of them. Any disciplined approach to source materials will sensitize students to the construction of historical documents, their content and meaning, and the ways in which they relate to modern experience. Individual instructors will easily be able to improve upon the example offered here.

A number of individuals helped to stimulate my thinking about the selection of sources. For their thoughtful critiques of the manuscript, I would like to thank: Philip Crow, North Harris Community College; Jonathan Goldstein, West Georgia College; Joseph Gowaskie, Rider College; Fred Krebs, Johnson County Community College; Ray Lorantas, Drexel University; Peter Mellini, Sonoma State University; Stephen Morillo, Wabash College; Kerry Spiers, University of Louisville; Alexander Sydorenko, Arkansas State University; David White, Appalachian State University. I would especially like to thank Eric McGeer, R. Bin Wong, Ann Waltner, Leroy Vail, and Mark Wasserman. Carol Einhorn, Bruce Borland, and Betty Slack of HarperCollins made this work possible. My greatest debt is to Susan Lindsey Lively for her assistance in compiling these texts. Her discipline helped keep me going as we sifted through hundreds of possible selections and her common sense tempered our final choices.

Mark A. Kishlansky

How to Read a Document

Do you remember the first time you ever used a road map? After struggling to unfold it and get the right side up and the right way around you were then confronted by an astonishing amount of information. You could calculate the distance between places, from towns to cities, or cities to cities, even the distance between exits on the toll roads. You could observe relative population density and categorize large and small places. You could even judge the quality of roads. But most likely, you used that map to help you figure out how to get from one place to another, how to find the best route for the trip you were taking.

To make the map tell you that, you had to know how to ask the right questions. It all seems so obvious now—you put one finger on the place where you were and another on the place to which you wanted to go and then you found the best and most direct route between them. In order to do something as simple as this, there are a lot of assumptions that you made about the map. First, you assumed that the map is directionally oriented, north at the top, east to the right, south and west opposite. Second, you assumed that the map is in scale, that the distance between places on the map is proportional to their distances in reality. Third, you assumed that intersections on the map were intersections on the ground, that the two roads that appear to cross on paper actually do cross in reality. These assumptions make possible the answer to your initial question. Of course, if any of them were not true you would have found out soon enough.

Learning to read a historical document is much like learning to read a map. It is important to ask the right questions and to make the right assumptions. But unlike the real voyage that the map makes possible, the voyage made with a historical document is one of the imagination. You will have to learn to test your assumptions and to sharpen your ability to ask questions before you can have any confidence that you are on the right road. Like anything else, this is a matter of concentration and practice. You will have to discipline yourself to ask and answer questions about the document on the first level before you pose questions on higher levels. At the beginning you will be asking questions that you can answer directly; by the end you will be asking questions that will give full play to your imagination and your skills as a historian. Let us consider an example.

Read the following selection slowly and carefully.

1   Ye emperors, kings, dukes, marquises, earls, and knights, and all other people
2   desirous of knowing the diversities of the races of mankind, as well as the
3   diversities of kingdoms, provinces, and regions of all parts of the East, read
4   through this book, and ye will find in it the greatest and most marvellous char-
5   acteristics of the peoples especially of Armenia, Persia, India, and Tartary, as
6   they are severally related in the present work by Marco Polo, a wise and
7   learned citizen of Venice, who states distinctly what things he saw and what
8   things he heard from others. For this book will be a truthful one.

9   Kublai, who is styled grand khan, or lord of lords, is of the middle stature, that
10   is, neither tall nor short; his limbs are well formed, and in his whole figure
11   there is a just proportion. His complexion is fair, and occasionally suffused
12   with red, like the bright tint of the rose, which adds much grace to his coun-
13   tenance. His eyes are black and handsome, his nose is well shaped and promi-
14   nent. He has four wives of the first rank, who are esteemed legitimate, and the
15   eldest born son of any one of these succeeds to the empire, upon the decease
16   of the grand khan. They bear equally the title of empress, and have their sep-
17   arate courts. None of them have fewer than three hundred young female
18   attendants of great beauty, together with a multitude of youths as pages, and
19   other eunuchs, as well as ladies of the bedchamber; so that the number of per-
20   sons belonging to each of their respective courts amounts to ten thousand.
21   Besides these, he has many concubines provided for his use, from a province
22   of Tartary named Ungut, having a city of the same name, the inhabitants of
23   which are distinguished for beauty of features and fairness of complexion.
24   Thither the grand khan sends his officers every second year, or oftener, as it
25   may happen to be his pleasure, who collect for him, to the number of four or
26   five hundred, or more, of the handsomest of the young women, according to
27   the estimation of beauty communicated to them in their instructions. . . .
28   Upon their arrival in his presence, he causes a new examination to be made by
29   a different set of inspectors, and from amongst them a further selection takes
30   place, when thirty or forty are retained for his own chamber. . . . These, in the
31   first instance, are committed separately to the care of the wives of certain of
32   the nobles, whose duty it is to observe them attentively during the course of
33   the night, in order to ascertain that they have not any concealed imperfec-
34   tions, that they sleep tranquilly, do not snore, have sweet breath, and are free
35   from unpleasant scent in any part of the body. Having undergone this rigor-
36   ous scrutiny, they are divided into parties of five, one of which parties attends
37   during three days and three nights, in his majesty's interior apartment, where
38   they are to perform every service that is required of them, and he does with
39   them as he likes. The remainder of them, whose value had been estimated at
40   an inferior rate, are assigned to the different lords of the household, . . . in this
41   manner he provides for them all amongst his nobility. It may be asked whether
42   the people of the province do not feel themselves aggrieved in having their
43   daughters thus forcibly taken from them by the sovereign? Certainly not; but,
44   on the contrary, they regard it as a favour and an honour done to them; and
45   those who are the fathers of handsome children feel highly gratified by his
46   condescending to make choice of their daughters.

47   The grand khan usually resides during three months of the year, namely,
48   December, January, and February, in the great city of Kanbalu, situated towards
49   the north-eastern extremity of the province of Cathay; and here, on the south-
50   ern side of the new city, is the site of his vast palace, the form and dimensions
51   of which are as follows. In the first place is a square enclosed with a wall and
52   deep ditch; each side of the square being eight miles in length, and having at
53   an equal distance from each extremity an entrance-gate, for the concourse of
54   people resorting thither from all quarters. Within this enclosure there is, on
55   the four sides, an open space one mile in breadth, where the troops are sta-
56   tioned; and this is bounded by a second wall, enclosing a square of six miles,
57   having three gates on the south side, and three on the north, the middle por-
58   tal of each being larger than the other two, and always kept shut, excepting on
59   the occasions of the emperor's entrance or departure. . . . Within these walls,
60   which constitute the boundary of four miles, stands the palace of the grand
61   khan, the most extensive that has ever yet been known. It reaches from the
62   northern to the southern wall, leaving only a vacant space (or court), where
63   persons of rank and the military guards pass and repass. It has no upper floor,
64   but the roof is very lofty. The paved foundation or platform on which it stands
65   is raised ten spans above the level of the ground, and a wall of marble, two
66   paces wide, is built on all sides, to the level of this pavement, within the line of
67   which the palace is erected; so that the wall, extending beyond the ground plan
68   of the building, and encompassing the whole, serves as a terrace, where those
69   who walk on it are visible from without. Along the exterior edge of the wall is a
70   handsome balustrade, with pillars, which the people are allowed to approach.
71   The sides of the great halls and the apartments are ornamented with dragons
72   in carved work and gilt, figures of warriors, of birds, and of beasts, with repre-
73   sentations of battles. The inside of the roof is contrived in such a manner that
74   nothing besides gilding and painting presents itself to the eye. On each of the
75   four sides of the palace there is a grand flight of marble steps, by which you
76   ascend from the level of the ground to the wall of marble which surrounds the
77   building, and which constitute the approach to the palace itself. The grand hall
78   is extremely long and wide, and admits of dinners being there served to great
79   multitudes of people. The palace contains a number of separate chambers, all
80   highly beautiful, and so admirably disposed that it seems impossible to suggest
81   any improvement to the system of their arrangement. The exterior of the roof
82   is adorned with a variety of colours, red, green, azure, and violet, and the sort
83   of covering is so strong as to last for many years. The glazing of the windows is
84   so well wrought and so delicate as to have the transparency of crystal. In the
85   rear of the body of the palace there are large buildings containing several
86   apartments, where is deposited the private property of the monarch, or his
87   treasure in gold and silver bullion, precious stones, and pearls, and also his ves-
88   sels of gold and silver plate. Here are likewise the apartments of his wives and
89   concubines; and in this retired situation he despatches business with conve-
90   nience, being free from every kind of interruption.

      Now what sense can we make out of all of that? You have just read a his-
torical document, a selection from *The Travels of Marco Polo, The Venetian*. It was

written in 1298, while Marco Polo was in prison, and was based on his own observations during 17 years of travel in Asia. Marco Polo was born into a Venetian merchant family. His father and elder brothers had made an earlier trip into Asia where they had met the Grand Khan. Marco accompanied his brothers on their return trip. During his stay he was favored with free passage throughout the khan's dominions and on his return to Venice he was required to tell and retell the stories of his journey. After commanding a ship in an unsuccessful war against Genoa, Marco Polo was captured and imprisoned. It was during this time that he sorted through the many notations that he had made in Asia and composed the tale of his travels.

In order to understand this document we are going to need to ask and answer a series of questions about it. Let us start at the beginning with a number of questions that we might designate Level One questions.

LEVEL ONE

The first set of questions that need to be addressed are those for which you should be able to find concrete answers. The answers to these questions will give you the basic information you need to begin the process of interpretation. Although Level One questions are seemingly straightforward, they contain important implications for deeper interpretation. If you do not consciously ask these questions, you will deprive yourself of some of the most important evidence there is for understanding documents. Train yourself to underline or highlight the information that will allow you to answer the following questions.

1. Who wrote this document?

In the first place, we need to know how this document came to be created. In the case of *The Travels of Marco Polo, The Venetian* we know that the document was written by Marco Polo (**line 6**), who was an Italian merchant. This document is thus the work of a single author written from his own point of view. What is especially important to remember is that Marco Polo was an outsider, describing a society that was not his own. His account of China in the thirteenth century was an account of a European's impressions of China. We will need to learn as much as we can about the "author" of a document to help us answer more complicated questions.

2. Who is the intended audience?

The audience of a document will tell us much about the document's language, about the amount of knowledge that the writer is assuming, even sometimes about the best form for the document to take. There can be more than one audience intended by the writer. *The Travels of Marco Polo, The Venetian* was written in the thirteenth century, and therefore was not written for "publication" in the conventional sense of the word. In fact, *The Travels* was not published for centuries after composition. But Marco Polo obviously intended his work to be read by others, and it was circulated in manuscript and repeated orally. His preface was addressed to "emperors, kings, dukes, marquises, earls, and knights" (**line 1**), a rather distinguished audience. But his real audience was his own countrymen to whom he was describing a foreign place in terms they would understand. Notice, for example, how he describes the khan's complexion, "like the bright tint of the rose" (**line 12**).

3. What is the story line?

The final Level One question has to do with the content of the document. We now know enough about it in a general way to pay attention to what it actually says. To answer this question you might want to take some notes while you are reading or underline the important parts in your text. The story here seems to be simple. Marco Polo is impressed with the splendor of the court of the grand khan and especially with the way in which he finds his wives and concubines. Polygamy is interesting to a European viewing a non-Western society and Marco Polo describes it in a way that will titillate his anticipated audience. He also makes it believable, explaining why parents would volunteer their daughters (**lines 44–45**). He is also impressed with the size of everything that surrounds the Grand Khan. If each of his wives had a retinue of 10,000 (**line 20**) their courts alone would be more populous than the entire city of Venice.

LEVEL TWO

If Level One questions allow you to identify the nature of the document and its author, Level Two questions allow you to probe behind the essential facts. Now that you know who wrote the document, to whom it is addressed, and what it is about, you can begin to try to understand it. Since your goal is to learn what this document means, first in its historical context and then in your current context, you now want to study it from a more detached point of view, to be less accepting of "facts" and more critical in the questions you pose. At the first level, the document controlled you; at the second level, you will begin to control the document.

1. Why was this document written?

Understanding the purpose of a historical document is critical to analyzing the strategies that the author employs within it. A document intended to convince will employ logic; a document intended to entertain will employ fancy; a document attempting to motivate will employ emotional appeals. In order to find these strategies we must first know what purpose the document was intended to serve. Travelers' tales generally have two interrelated purposes, first, to impress upon one culture the differences to be found in another, and second to show people their own culture in a new light. Marco Polo is genuinely impressed with the opulence and power of the khan but he is also impressed by the way that the khan provides for his nobles, how he rewards those who have been faithful to him (**lines 40–41**). As the member of an elite merchant family, Marco Polo was concerned that the Venetian doge reward those faithful to him, especially those who might be temporarily imprisoned.

2. What type of document is this?

The form of a document is vital to its purpose. We would expect a telephone book to be alphabetized, a poem to be in meter, and a work of philosophy to be in prose. Here we have a traveler's account and its style and language is employed to create wonder and admiration in its readers. To do this the author needs to provide detailed description that is visually arresting yet sufficiently concrete to be persuasive. This is especially difficult when describing customs as alien to Venetians as those practiced at the court of the grand khan. In order to be believed, the traveler has to overcome the natural skepticism of his audience. During his lifetime, Marco Polo was nicknamed "Marco Millione" (Marco Millions) because people thought he exaggerated the numbers of the Chinese population and the extent of the khan's wealth.

3. What are the basic assumptions made in this document?

All documents make assumptions that are bound up with their intended audience, with the form in which they are written, and with their purpose. Some of the assumptions that are at work in this selection from *The Travels of Marco Polo, The Venetian* relate to the way in which a state is ruled. Marco Polo describes the khan and his court as if government in China were organized in the same way that government in Italy was. Thus the khan can be understood as a sort of pope or doge. Similarly, Marco Polo assumes that his readers will admire great wealth and large quantities of things. He takes pains to describe things as beautiful, great, wide, and large (**lines 52–81**).

LEVEL THREE

So far, you have been asking questions of your document that the document itself can answer. Sometimes it is more difficult to know who composed a document or who was the intended audience than it has been with *The Travels of Marco Polo, The Venetian*. Sometimes you have to guess at the purpose of the document, but essentially Level One and Level Two questions have direct answers. Once you have learned to ask them, you will have a great deal of information about the historical document at your disposal. You will then be able to think historically, that is, to pose your own questions about the past and to use the material the document presents you to find answers. In Level Three, you will exercise your critical imagination, probing the material and developing your own assessment of its value. Level Three questions will not always have definite answers; in fact, they are the kind of questions that arouse disagreement and debate and that make for lively classroom discussion.

1. Can I believe this document?

If they are successful, documents designed to persuade, to recount events, or to motivate people to act must be believable to their audience. But for the critical historical reader, it is that very believability that must be in question. Every author has a point of view and exposing the assumptions of the document is an essential task for the reader. We must treat all claims skeptically (even while admiring audacity, rhetorical tricks, and clever comparisons). One question we certainly want to ask is, "Is this a likely story?" Do the parents of daughters destined for concubinage at court really believe that it is a sign of good fortune? Do all officers sent by the khan really perform their duties speedily and efficiently? Is there really a wall 8 miles square around the city that contains the khan's palace (**line 52**)? Testing the credibility of a document means looking at it from the other side. What would most impress a subject of the khan about his own society? What would most impress him about Venice?

2. What can I learn about the society that produced this document?

All documents unintentionally reveal things about their authors and about their age. It is the things that are embedded in the very language, structure, and assumptions of the document that can tell us the most about the historical period or event that we are studying. This is centrally important in studying a travel account. We must ask ourselves both what we can learn about China in the late thirteenth century and what we can learn about Venice. Marco Polo is acting as a double filter, running Chinese customs through his own European expectations and then explaining them to Europeans through his expectation of what they will believe and what they will reject. He is also telling us, indirectly, about the things that Venetians would find unusual and wonderful and therefore by contrast what they would find commonplace. We can learn many things about both Chinese and Venetian society by reading into this document rather than by simply reading it.

3. What does this document mean to me?

So what? What does *The Travels of Marco Polo, The Venetian,* written almost 700 years ago, have to do with you? Other than the practical problem of passing your exams and getting your degree, why should you be concerned with historical documents and what can you learn from them? Only you can answer that question. But you will not be able to answer it until you have asked it. You should demand the meaning of each document you read. What it meant to the historical actors—authors, audience, and society—and what it means to our own society. In light of *The Travels of Marco Polo,* how would you go about describing an alien society to your generation? How would you go about appreciating an alien culture? Look around your classroom and ask yourself how often you represent yourself to members of other cultures and how often you have to understand the assumptions of other cultures to understand your classmates.

Now that you have seen how to unfold the map of a historical document, you must get used to asking these questions by yourself. The temptation will be great to jump from Level One to Level Three, to start in the middle, or to pose the questions in no sequence at all. After all, you probably have a ready-made answer to the question, "What does this document mean to me?" If you develop the discipline of asking all your questions in the proper order, however, you will soon find that you are able to gain command of a document on a single reading and that the complicated names and facts that ordinarily would confuse you will easily settle into a pattern around one or another of your questions. After a few weeks, reread these pages and ask yourself how careful you have been to maintain the discipline of posing historical questions. Think also about how much more comfortable you now feel about reading and discussing historical documents.

PART IV

The World of Travelers and Traders

Monarchy and Revolution

Portrait of James I by Van Somer.

·79·

James I
True Law of a Free Monarchy
(1598)

James VI of Scotland (1567–1625), who also reigned as James I of England from 1603 to 1621, was the product of the ill-fated love affair between Mary, Queen of Scots, and Henry, Lord Darnley. He was raised as a Presbyterian by the Protestant lords who declared that Mary had vacated the throne of Scotland. James fancied himself a theologian and scholar and wrote a number of works on both scholarly and popular issues, including an attack upon the use of tobacco. He became king of England at the death of Elizabeth I in 1603 and ruled there for over 20 years. He was considered generous to a fault, but his rough Scottish speech and manner came in for more than its fair share of criticism.

While still king of Scotland, James composed the *True Law of a Free Monarchy* for the instruction of his subjects. It is one of the clearest statements of both the powers and restrictions placed upon a divine right monarch.

THE TREW LAW OF FREE MONARCHIES: OR THE RECIPROCK AND MUTUALL DUETIE BETWIXT A FREE KING AND HIS NATURALL SUBJECTS

As there is not a thing so necessarie to be knowne by the people of any land, next the knowledge of their God, as the right knowledge of their alleageance, according to the forme of governement established among them, especially in a *Monarchie* (which forme of government, as resembling the Divinitie, approacheth nearest to perfection, as all the learned and wise men from the beginning have agreed upon; Unitie being the perfection of all things,) So hath the ignorance, and (which is worse) the seduced opinion of the multitude blinded by them, who thinke themselves able to teach and instruct the ignorants, procured the wracke and overthrow of sundry flourishing Common-wealths; and heaped heavy calamities, threatning utter

destruction upon others. And the smiling successe, that unlawfull rebellions have oftentimes had against Princes in ages past (such hath bene the misery, and iniquitie of the time) hath by way of practise strengthened many in their errour: albeit there cannot be a more deceiveable argument; then to judge by the justnesse of the cause by the event thereof; as hereafter shall be proved more at length. And among others, no Commonwealth, that ever hath bene since the beginning, hath had greater need of the trew knowledge of this ground, then this our so long disordered, and distracted Common-wealth hath: the misknowledge hereof being the onely spring, from whence have flowed so many endlesse calamities, miseries, and confusions, as is better felt by many, then the cause thereof well knowne, and deeply considered. The naturall zeale therefore, that I beare to this my native countrie, with the great pittie I have to see the so-long disturbance thereof for lacke of the trew knowledge of this ground (as I have said before) hath compelled me at last to breake silence, to discharge my conscience to you my deare country men herein, that knowing the ground from whence these your many endlesse troubles have proceeded, as well as ye have already too-long tasted the bitter fruites thereof, ye may by knowledge, and eschewing of the cause escape, and divert the lamentable effects that ever necessarily follow thereupon. I have chosen then onely to set downe in this short Treatise, the trew grounds of the mutuall deutie, and alleageance betwixt a free and absolute *Monarche,* and his people.

First then, I will set downe the trew grounds, whereupon I am to build, out of the Scriptures, since *Monarchie* is the trew paterne of Divinitie, as I have already said: next, from the fundamental Lawes of our owne Kingdome, which nearest must concerne us: thirdly, from the law of Nature, by divers similitudes drawne out of the same.

By the Law of Nature the King becomes a naturall Father to all his Lieges at his Coronation: And as the Father of his fatherly duty is bound to care for the nourishing, education, and vertuous government of his children; even so is the king bound to care for all his subjects. As all the toile and paine that the father can take for his children, will be thought light and well bestowed by him, so that the effect thereof redound to their profite and weale; so ought the Prince to doe towards his people. As the kindly father ought to foresee all inconvenients and dangers that may arise towards his children, and though with the hazard of his owne person presse to prevent the same; so ought the King towards his people. As the fathers wrath and correction upon any of his children that offendeth, ought to be by a fatherly chastisement seasoned with pitie, as long as there is any hope of amendment in them; so ought the King towards any of his Lieges that offend in that measure. And shortly, as the Fathers chiefe joy ought to be in procuring his childrens welfare, rejoycing at their weale, sorrowing and pitying at their evill,

to hazard for their safetie, travell for their rest, wake for their sleepe; and in a word, to thinke that his earthly felicitie and life standeth and liveth more in them, nor in himselfe; so ought a good Prince thinke of his people.

As to the other branch of this mutuall and reciprock band, is the duety and alleageance that the Lieges owe to their King: the ground whereof, I take out of the words of *Samuel,* dited by Gods Spirit, when God had given him commandement to heare the peoples voice in choosing and annointing them a King. And because that place of Scripture being well understood, is so pertinent for our purpose, I have insert herein the very words of the Text.

10   So *Samuel* tolde all the wordes of the Lord unto the people that asked a King of him.

11   And he said, this shall be the maner of the King that shall raigne over you: he will take your sonnes, and appoint them to his Charets, and to be his horsemen, and some shall runne before his Charet.

12   Also, hee will make them his captaines over thousands, and captaines over fifties, and to eare his ground, and to reape his harvest, and to make instruments of warre and the things that serve for his charets:

13   Hee will also take your daughters, and make them Apothicaries, and Cookes, and Bakers.

14   And hee will take your fields, and your vineyards, and your best Olive trees, and give them to his servants.

15   And he will take the tenth of your seed, and of your Vineyards, and give it to his Eunuches, and to his servants.

16   And he will take your men servants, and your maid-servants, and the chiefe of your young men, and your asses, and put them to his worke.

17   He will take the tenth of your sheepe: and ye shall be his servants.

18   And ye shall cry out at that day, because of your King, whom ye have chosen you: and the Lord God will not heare you at that day.

19   But the people would not heare the voice of *Samuel,* but did say: Nay, but there shalbe a King over us.

20   And we also will be all like other Nations, and our King shall judge us, and goe out before us, and fight our battels.

As likewise, although I have said, a good king will frame all his actions to be according to the Law; yet is hee not bound thereto but of his good will, and for good example-giving to his subjects: For as in the law of abstaining from eating of flesh in *Lenton,* the king will, for examples sake, make his owne house to observe the Law; yet no man will thinke he needs to take a licence to eate flesh. And although by our Lawes, the bearing and wearing of hag-buts, and pistolets be forbidden, yet no man can find any fault in the King, for causing his traine use them in any raide upon the Borderers, or other malefactours or rebellious subjects. So as I have alreadie said, a good King, although hee be above the Law, will subject and frame his actions thereto, for examples sake to his subjects, and of his owne free-will, but not as subject or bound thereto.

And the agreement of the Law of nature in this our ground with the Lawes and constitutions of God, and man, already alledged, will by two similitudes easily appeare. The King towards his people is rightly compared to a father of children, and to a head of a body composed of divers members: For as fathers, the good Princes, and Magistrates of the people of God acknowledged themselves to their subjects. And for all other well ruled Common-wealths, the stile of *Pater patriae* was ever, and is commonly used to Kings. And the proper office of a King towards his Subjects, agrees very wel with the office of the head towards the body, and all members thereof: For from the head, being the seate of Judgement, proceedeth the care and foresight of guiding,

and preventing all evill that may come to the body or any part thereof. The head cares for the body, so doeth the King for his people. As the discourse and direction flowes from the head, and the execution according thereunto belongs to the rest of the members, every one according to their office: so it is betwixt a wise Prince, and his people. As the judgement comming from the head may not onely imploy the members, every one in their owne office, as long as they are able for it; but likewise in case any of them be affected with any infirmitie must care and provide for their remedy, in-case it be curable, and if otherwise, gar cut them off for feare of infecting of the rest: even so is it betwixt the Prince, and his people. And as there is ever hope of curing any diseased member by the direction of the head, as long as it is whole; but by the contrary, if it be troubled, all the members are partakers of that paine, so is it betwixt the Prince and his people.

And now first for the fathers part (whose naturall love to his children I described in the first part of this my discourse, speaking of the dutie that Kings owe to their Subjects) consider, I pray you what duetie his children owe to him, & whether upon any pretext whatsoever, it wil not be thought monstrous and unnaturall to his sons, to rise up against him, to control him at their appetite, and when they thinke good to sley him, or to cut him off, and adopt to themselves any other they please in his roome: Or can any pretence of wickednes or rigor on his part be a just excuse for his children to put hand into him? And although wee see by the course of nature, that love useth to descend more than to ascend, in case it were trew, that the father hated and wronged the children never so much, will any man, endued with the least sponke of reason, thinke it lawfull for them to meet him with the line? Yea, suppose the father were furiously following his sonnes with a drawn sword, is it lawfull for them to turne and strike againe, or make any resistance but by flight? I thinke surely, if there were no more but the example of bruit beasts & unreasonable creatures, it may serve well enough to qualifie and prove this my argument. We read often the pietie that the Storkes have to their olde and decayed parents: And generally wee know, that there are many sorts of beasts and fowles, that with violence and many bloody strokes will beat and banish their yong ones from them, how soone they perceive them to be able to fend themselves; but wee never read or heard of any resistance on their part, except among the vipers; which prooves such persons, as ought to be reasonable creatures, and yet unnaturally follow this example, to be endued with their viperous nature.

And it is here likewise to be noted, that the duty and alleageance, which the people sweareth to their prince, is not only bound to themselves, but likewise to their lawfull heires and posterity, the lineall succession of crowns being begun among the people of God, and happily continued in divers christian common-wealths: So as no objection either of heresie, or whatsoever private statute or law may free the people from their oathgiving to their king, and his succession, established by the old fundamentall lawes of the kingdom: For, as hee is their heritable over-lord, and so by birth, not by any right in the coronation, commeth to his crowne; it is a like unlawful (the crowne ever standing full) to displace him that succeedeth thereto, as to eject the former: For at the very moment of the expiring of the king reigning, the nearest and lawful heire entreth in his place: And so to refuse him, or intrude another, is not to holde out uncomming in, but to expell and put out their righteous King. And I trust at this time whole *France* acknowledgeth the superstitious rebellion of the liguers, who upon pretence of heresie, by force of armes held so long out, to the great desolation of their whole countrey, their native and righteous king from possessing of his owne crowne and naturall kingdome.

Not that by all this former discourse of mine, and Apologie for kings, I meane that whatsoever errors and intollerable abominations a sovereigne prince commit, hee ought to escape all punishment, as if thereby the world were only ordained for kings, & they without controlment to turne it upside down at their pleasure: but by the contrary, by remitting them to God (who is their onely ordinary Judge) I remit them to the sorest and sharpest schoolmaster that can be devised for them: for the further a king is preferred by God above all other ranks & degrees of men, and the higher that his seat is above theirs, the greater is his obligation to his maker. And therfore in case he forget himselfe (his unthankfulness being in the same measure of height) the sadder and sharper will his correction be; and according to the greatnes of the height he is in, the weight of his fall wil recompense the same: for the further that any person is obliged to God, his offence becomes and growes so much the greater, then it would be in any other. *Joves* thunderclaps light oftner and sorer upon the high & stately oakes, then on the low and supple willow trees: and the highest bench is sliddriest to sit upon. Neither is it ever heard that any king forgets himselfe towards God, or in his vocation; but God with the greatnesse of the plague revengeth the greatnes of his ingratitude: Neither thinke I by the force and argument of this my discourse so to perswade the people, that none will hereafter be raised up, and rebell against wicked Princes. But remitting to the justice and providence of God to stirre up such scourges as pleaseth him, for punishment of wicked kings (who made the very vermine and filthy dust of the earth to bridle the insolencie of proud *Pharaoh*) my onely purpose and intention in this treatise is to perswade, as farre as lieth in me, by these sure and infallible grounds, all such good Christian readers, as beare not onely the naked name of a Christian, but kith the fruites thereof in their daily forme of life, to keep their hearts and hands free from such monstrous and unnaturall rebellions, whensoever the wickednesse of a Prince shall procure the same at Gods hands: that, when it shall please God to cast such scourges of princes, and instruments of his fury in the fire, ye may stand up with cleane handes, and unspotted consciences, having prooved your selves in all your actions trew Christians toward God, and dutifull subjects towards your King, having remitted the judgement and punishment of all his wrongs to him, whom to onely of right it appertaineth.

But craving at God, and hoping that God shall continue his blessing with us, in not sending such fearefull desolation, I heartily wish our kings behaviour so to be, and continue among us, as our God in earth, and loving Father, endued with such properties as I described a King in the first part of this Treatise. And that ye (my deare countreymen, and charitable readers) may presse by all means to procure the prosperitie and welfare of your King; that as hee must on the one part thinke all his earthly felicitie and happinesse grounded upon your weale, caring more for himselfe for your sake then for his owne, thinking himselfe onely ordained for your weale; such holy and happy emulation may arise betwixt him and you, as his care for your quietnes, and your care for his honour and preservation, may in all your actions daily strive together, that the Land may thinke themselves blessed with such a King, and the king may thinke himselfe most happy in ruling over so loving and obedient subjects.

1. How is a king's power limited, according to James?

2. James's mother and predecessor on the Scottish throne, Queen Mary, was overthrown and driven into exile. How is this fact reflected in the king's political views?

3. Why is a strong monarchy the best form of government?

4. What are the two main metaphors James employs in describing a king's power? How do they differ from modern political images such as the "ship of state"?

5. Although James, of course, has an interest in arguing for a powerful monarchy, how would such a government be advantageous to a king's subjects?

·80·

Philippe Duplessis-Mornay
A Defense of Liberty Against Tyrants
(1579)

Philippe Duplessis-Mornay (1549–1623), a French nobleman of Huguenot extraction, entered the service of Henry of Navarre, the leading Huguenot prince, and became his chief advisor by 1573. Duplessis-Mornay took up arms during the Wars of Religion and was captured by Catholic forces. He avoided paying a ruinous fine by escaping in disguise and making his way back to the Huguenot lines. He continued in his role as advisor to the new king, Henry IV, but broke with him when Henry publicly converted to Catholicism. Duplessis-Mornay died in obscurity in 1623.

A *Defense of Liberty* was the most influential of Duplessis-Mornay's many writings. Though there remains some controversy over whether it was written alone or in collaboration, *Defense* was the first Huguenot tract that attempted to justify resistance to lawful authority. It is a seminal work in the history of resistance theory.

FIRST QUESTIONS: MUST SUBJECTS OBEY PRINCES WHO ISSUE ORDERS COUNTER TO THE LAW OF GOD?

At first sight this question might appear to waste our time to no purpose because it seems to call the most evident axiom of Christianity into doubt as if it were still controversial, although it has been corroborated by so many testimonies of sacred Scripture, so many examples accumulated over the centuries, and the pyres of so many pious martyrs. What other reason, it might be asked, could explain the willingness of the pious to undergo such extraordinary suffering if not their conviction that God is to be obeyed simply and absolutely, kings, however, only so long as they do not issue orders counter to the law of God? How else are we to understand the apostolic precept to obey God rather than men? And since God's will alone is always just, whereas the will of anybody else can be unjust at any time, who could doubt that only the former is to be obeyed without exception, but the latter always with reservations?

There are, however, many princes nowadays who boast the name of Christ, yet dare to arrogate an immense power that most assuredly does not depend from God. There are also many adulators who worship them as gods on earth, and many others seized by fear, or else coerced by force, who either really believe that obedience is never to be denied to princes or at least wish to seem to believe it. The vice of our times indeed appears to be that nothing is so firm that it could not be uprooted, nothing so certain that it could not be disputed, and nothing so sacred that it could not be violated. Therefore I am afraid that anyone carefully weighing the matter will consider this question to be not only far

from useless, but even absolutely necessary, especially in our century. . . .

The question then is whether subjects are obliged to obey kings whose orders are in conflict with the law of God. Who of the two, in other words, is rather to be obeyed, God or the king? If an answer can be given for the king, whose power is deemed the greatest of all, the same answer will apply to other magistrates.

In short, we see that kings are invested with their kingdoms by God in almost the same manner in which vassals are invested with their fiefs by their superior lords, and that they are deprived of their benefices for the same reasons. Therefore we must on all counts conclude that the former are in an almost identical place as the latter and that all kings are vassals of God. Having said this, our question is easily finished. For if God occupies the place of a superior lord, and the king that of a vassal, who will not declare that one should rather obey the lord than the vassal? If God commands this, and the king the other, who will consider someone refusing to obey the king as a rebel? Who will not on the contrary condemn it as rebellion if he fails to obey God promptly or if he obeys the king instead? And finally, if the king calls us to this choice and God to that, who will not declare that we must desert the king in order to fight for God? Thus we are not only not obliged to obey a king who orders something against the law of God, but we even commit rebellion if we do obey him, in no other way than a landholder does who fights for a senior vassal against the king, or who prefers to obey the edict of the inferior rather than the superior, of the vicar rather than the prince, and of the minister rather than the king. . . .

MAY PRIVATE INDIVIDUALS RESIST WITH ARMS?

It only remains to deal with private persons. First of all, individuals as such are not bound by the covenant that is established between God and the people as a whole, that they should be God's people. For just as what is owed to a community is not owed to individuals, so individuals do not owe what the community owes. Furthermore they have none of the duties of office. The obligation to serve God depends upon the position to which one has been called. Private individuals, however, have no power, perform no magistracy, have no dominion and no power of punishment. God did not give the sword to private persons and therefore does not require them to use it. To private persons it is said: "Put thy sword into its scabbard"; to magistrates, however: "You do not bear the sword in vain." The former are guilty if they draw the sword, the latter are guilty of grave negligence unless they draw it when necessary.

But, you may ask, is there no covenant between God and the individuals at all, as there is between God and the community? No covenant with private persons as with magistrates? What could then be the purpose of circumcision and baptism? Why else is this sacred covenant mentioned over and over again in Scripture? Of course there is a covenant, but of a wholly different sort. For just as all the subjects of a just prince in general, of whatever rank they may be, are obliged to obey him, but only some of them have a special obligation, for example in the form of a magistracy, to take care that the others will be obedient, too, so all human beings in general are indeed obliged to serve God, but only some of them have taken on a greater burden along with their higher position so that, if they neglect their duty, they are responsible up to a point for the guilt of the rest. Kings, the community, and magistrates who have received the sword from the community must take care that the body of the church is governed according to the rite. Individuals, however, have no other function than to be members of that church. The former must pay heed that the temple of the lord is not polluted and does not collapse, but is safe from all internal corruption and external injury; the latter only that their body, which is the temple of God, is not impure, so that God's spirit can live in it. "Whosoever shall destroy God's temple, which you are," says Paul, "him shall God destroy." This is the reason why the former have been given a sword that can be fastened to their belts, whereas only the sword of the spirit has been entrusted to the latter, that is, the word of the lord with which Paul girds all Christians against the devil's attack.

What then shall private individuals do when the king urges impious rites upon them? If the nobles with authority from the entire people, or at least their own magistrates, oppose themselves to the king, they shall obey, follow, and assist the pious striving of the pious with all of their might as soldiers of God. If the nobles and magistrates applaud a raging king, however, or if at least they fail to resist him, the advice of Christ should be taken to heart: they should withdraw to another city. But if there is nowhere to escape to, they should rather forsake their lives than God, rather let themselves be crucified than, as the apostle says, crucify Christ once again. Do not, says our lord, fear those who can only kill the body, a lesson that has been taught to us by his own example as well as that of the apostles and innumerable pious martyrs.

Is no private person at all then permitted to resist with arms? But what about Moses, who led Israel out of Egypt against the will of Pharaoh? What about Ehud, who killed king Eglon of Moab and liberated Israel from the yoke of the Moabites after their rule had already lasted for eighteen years, when they might have seemed to acquire a right to the kingdom? And what about Jehu, who killed king Jehoram, for whom he himself had used to fight, who destroyed the line of Ahab and killed all the worshipers of Baal? Were they not private persons? As such you may of course consider them as private persons because they were not equipped with power in the normal way. But since we know them to have been called by extraordinary means, God himself, so to speak, evidently girding them with their swords, we may regard them not only as more than mere private persons, but also as placed above anyone equipped with power by ordinary means. The vocation of Moses is confirmed by an express word of God and by the most obvious signs. Ehud is explicitly said to have been incited by God to kill the tyrant and save Israel. And Jehu, anointed at the command of the prophet Elijah, was ordered to destroy the line of Ahab, although the leading people had greeted him as the king earlier on. The same can be shown for all others like them who can be adduced from Scripture.

But when God has spoken neither himself nor through prophets out of the ordinary, we must be especially sober and circumspect. If someone arrogates authority by reason of divine inspiration, he must find out whether he is not rather swelled up with arrogance, does not confuse God with himself, and creates his great spirits out of himself, lest he should conceive vanity and beget a lie. And the people, although they may be desiring to fight under the sign of Christ, must find out whether they are not perhaps fighting to their own great damage. I do not say that the same God who is sending us Pharaohs and Ahabs in this century does not occasionally also inspire liberators in an extraordinary way. His justice and his mercy have certainly never waned. But when external signs are lacking, we must at least recognize the inner ones by their effects, a mind devoid of all ambition, true and fervid zeal, good conscience, and knowledge, too, lest someone misled by error should serve false gods or being driven mad by ambition should serve himself rather than the true God.

Third Question: Is It Permitted to Resist a Prince Who Oppresses or Destroys the Commonwealth? To What Extent, by Whom, in What Fashion, and by What Right?

Kings Are Created by the People

We have previously shown that it is God who sets up kings, gives them their kingdoms, and chooses them. Now we add that it is the people who constitute kings, deliver them their kingdoms, and approve their election by vote. God wanted it to be like that so that, next to himself, the kings would receive all of their authority and power from the people. That is why they should devote all of their care, thought, and energy to the good of the people, but should not deem themselves to have been raised above the rest by some natural preeminence, as men are raised above sheep and cattle. They should rather remember that they have been born to exactly the same lot as all other human beings and that they have been raised from the earth to their rank by the votes of the people, as if by shoulders on which the burdens of the commonwealth may later for the greater part fall back again. . . .

In general, since no one is born as a king, can turn himself into a king, or is able to rule without a people, whereas the people can very well exist on their own before there are kings, all kings were obviously first created by the people. Although the sons and nephews of kings may seem to have turned their kingdoms into hereditary possessions by imitating their fathers' virtues, and although the power of free election seems to have vanished in certain regions, it thus remains the custom in all well-established kingdoms that children do not succeed to their fathers until they are constituted by the people, as if they had had no claims upon the throne at all. They are not born to their fathers as heirs of a family property, but are only considered kings as soon as those who represent the people's majesty have invested them with the kingdom through scepter and crown. Even in Christian kingdoms that are nowadays said to descend by hereditary succession there are obvious traces of this fact. In France, Spain, England, and other countries it thus is the custom that kings are inaugurated and put in possession of the kingdom, so to speak, by the estates of the realm, the peers, the patricians, and the magnates who represent the community of the people.

The Nature of Tyranny

So far we have described a king. Now we shall describe tyrants a little more accurately. We have said that a king is someone legitimately ruling over a kingdom conveyed to him by inheritance or election and properly committed to his care. It follows that a tyrant, is the direct opposite of a king, is someone who has either usurped power by force or fraud or who governs a kingdom that has been freely conveyed to him against human and divine law and persists in administering it in violation of the laws and pacts to which he has bound himself by oath. A single individual may of course fall into both kinds of tyranny at the same time. The former is commonly called a tyrant without title, the latter a tyrant by conduct. It can, however, also happen that someone governs justly over a kingdom that he has occupied by force, or governs unjustly over a kingdom legally conveyed to him. In that case, since kingship is a matter of right rather than of heredity, a function rather than a possession, someone administering his office badly is worthier of being called a tyrant than someone who has not entered his office in the proper way. . . .

Natural law, first of all, teaches us to preserve and protect our lives and liberty, without which life can hardly be lived, against all violence and injury. This is what nature has instilled in dogs against wolves, bulls against lions, doves against hawks, and chickens against kites. So much the more in man against man, if man becomes a wolf to man. Hence no doubt is permitted whether one should fight back, for nature herself is fighting here.

In addition there is the law of peoples, which distinguishes between countries, fixes limits and sets up borders that everybody is obliged to defend against foreign enemies. Hence it is just as permissible to resist Alexander if he mounts an enormous fleet in order to invade a people over which he has no rights and from which he has suffered no harm as it is to resist the pirate Diomedes if he raids the sea with but a single ship. Under such circumstances Alexander out-

does Diomedes, not by his greater right, but merely by his greater impunity. One may also resist Alexander's devastation of a region as though he were a vagabond stealing a cloak, and resist an enemy putting a city under siege as though he were a burglar breaking into a house.

Above all there is civil law, by which all human societies are constituted according to particular laws, so that each of them is governed by its own laws. Some societies are ruled by one man, others by several, and still others by all; some reject government by women, others accept it; some elect kings from a specific line, others do not; and so on. If anyone should try to break this law by force or fraud, all are obliged to resist him, because he violates society, to which everything is owed, and undermines the foundations of the fatherland, to which we are bound by nature, laws, and sacred oaths. If we neglect to resist him, we are truly traitors of our fatherland, deserters of human society, and contemners of law. Since the laws of nature, of peoples, and civil law all command us to take up arms against tyrants of that kind, no reason at all can be offered to dissuade a tyrant at all times. Since a man does not govern other men as a god, as men do with oxen, but rather as a human being born to the same lot as they, it is not only presumptuous of a prince to mistreat human beings as though they were brutes, but also iniquitous of the people to look for a god in their prince, and a divinity in his fallible nature. If the prince, however, overturns the commonwealth on purpose, if he unabashedly demolishes the laws, if he cares not a bit about promises, conventions, justice, and piety, if he becomes an enemy to his people, and finally if he exercises all or the most important tyrannical skills that we have mentioned, then he can really be judged a tyrant, that is (although there was a time when that word had more pleasant connotations) an enemy of God and man. . . .

1. Duplessis-Mornay was a Protestant living under the rule of a Roman Catholic. How might his status affect his political theory?

2. How might a monarch, like King James, argue against Duplessis-Mornay's theories?

3. How are the powers of a king limited?

4. Under what circumstances is resistance to a lawful ruler allowable? Who may offer resistance?

5. Absolute monarchs maintain that they received their authority from God. How does Duplessis-Mornay think monarchs get their power?

·81·

Sir William Clarke
The Putney Debates
(1647)

*T*his debate between the leaders of the New Model Army and a group of soldiers and civilians is one of the most remarkable in English history for the stark contrast in the positions of the antagonists; for the eloquence of the appeals to natural, civil, and divine law; and as expressions of the underlying themes of English political theory.

Among the main speakers, Henry Ireton (1611–1651), son-in-law of Oliver Cromwell, was commissary-general of cavalry in the Army and one of its chief political strategists. From a modest landed background in Nottinghamshire, Ireton served under Parliament until his death in Ireland in 1653.

Thomas Rainsborough (given as Rainborow in the following selection), whose immortal speech "the smallest hee in England" has always marked him out as a champion of the common man, was, in fact, the son of a wealthy naval officer. He was colonel of a regiment of infantry in the New Model Army.

John Wildman (1623–1693) was only 24 when he came to Putney and is the most likely candidate for the authorship of the Agreement of the People, which precipitated the debate. Wildman was to have a remarkable career over the course of the seventeenth century, sitting in Parliament under Charles II and holding the office of postmaster general.

The debates took place over a four-day period at the end of October 1647. They were recorded, in a shorthand cipher, by William Clarke, Secretary of the Army. Clarke's notes were hastily made, parts of important speeches are missing, and the cipher was not transcribed for over five years. Clarke's manuscript was not discovered until the end of the nineteenth century.

The Paper called the Agreement read: The first article is, "That the people of England, being at this day very unequally distributed by Counties, Cities, and Burroughs, for the election of their Deputies in Parliament ought to be more indifferently proportioned, according to the number of the Inhabitants; the circumstances whereof, for number, place, and manner, are to be set down before the end of this present Parliament."

COMMISSARY IRETON. The exception that lies in itt is this. Itt is said: "The people of England" etc. . . . they are to bee distributed "according to the number of the inhabitants;" and this doth make mee thinke that the meaning is, that every man that is an inhabitant is to bee equally consider'd, and to have an equall voice in the election of the representors, those persons that are for the Generall Representative; and if that bee the meaning then I have something to say against itt.

MR. PETTY, a soldier. Wee judge that all inhabitants that have nott lost their birthright should have an equall voice in Elections.

COL. RAINBOROW. I desir'd that those that had engaged in itt [should speak] for really I thinke that the poorest hee that is in England hath a life to live as the greatest hee; and therefore truly, Sir, I thinke itt's cleare, that every man that is to live under a Government ought first by his owne consent to putt himself under that Governement; and I doe thinke that the poorest man in England is nott att all bound in a stricte sence to that Governement that hee hath not had a voice to putt himself under; and I am confident that when I have heard the reasons against itt, somethinge will bee said to answer those reasons, insoemuch that I should doubt whether he was an Englishman or noe that should doubt of these thinges.

COMMISSARY IRETON. That's [the meaning of] this ["according to the number of the inhabitants."]

Give mee leave to tell you, that if you make this the rule I thinke you must flie for refuge to an absolute naturall Right, and you must deny all Civill Right; and I am sure itt will come to that in the consequence. For my parte I thinke itt is noe right att all. I thinke that noe person hath a right to an interest or share in the disposing or determining of the affaires of the Kingdome, and in chusing those that shall determine what lawes wee shall bee rul'd by heere, noe person hath a right to this, that hath nott a permanent fixed interest in this Kingedome; and those persons together are properly the Represented of this Kingedome, and consequentile are to make uppe the Representors of this Kingedome, who taken together doe comprehend whatsoever is of reall or permanent interest in the Kingedome. And I am sure I cannott tell what otherwise any man can say why a forraigner coming in amongst us—or as many as will coming in amongst us, or by force or otherwise setling themselves heere, or att least by our permission having a being heere—why they should nott as well lay claime to itt as any other. Wee talke of birthright. Truly [by] birthright there is thus much claime. Men may justly have by birthright, by their very being borne in England, that wee should nott seclude them out of England, that wee should nott refuse to give them aire, and place, and ground, and the freedome of the high wayes and other thinges, to live amongst us; nott [to] any man that is borne heere, though by his birth there come nothing att all to him that is parte of the permanent interest of this Kingedome. That I thinke is due to a man by birth. Butt that by a man's being borne heere hee shall have a share in that power that shall dispose of the lands heere, and of all thinges heere, I doe nott thinke itt a sufficient ground. I am sure if wee looke uppon that which is the utmost within man's view of what was originally the constitution of this Kingedome, [if wee] looke uppon that which is most radicall and fundamentall, and which if you take away there is noe man hath any land, any goods, [or] any civill interest, that is this: that those that chuse the Representors for the making of Lawes by which this State and Kingedome are to bee govern'd, are the persons who taken together doe comprehend the locall interest of this Kingedome; that is, the persons in whome all land lies, and those in Corporations in whome all trading lies. This is the most fundamentall Constitution of this Kingedome, which if you doe nott allow you allow none att all. This Constitution hath limitted and determined itt that onely those shall have voices in Elections. Itt is true as was said by a Gentleman neere mee, the meanest man in England ought to have [a voice in the election of the government he lives under]. . . . I say this, that those that have the meanest locall interest, that man that hath butt fourty shillinges a yeare, hee hath as great voice in the Election of a Knight for the shire as hee that hath ten thousand a yeare or more.

COL. RAINBOROW. Truly, Sir, I am of the same opinion I was; and am resolved to keepe itt till I know reason why I should nott. Therfore I say, that either itt must bee the law of God or the law of man that must prohibite the meanest man in the Kingedome to have this benefitt as well as the greatest. I doe nott finde any thinge in the law of God, that a Lord shall chuse 20 Burgesses, and a Gentleman butt two, or a poore man shall chuse none. I finde noe such thing in the law of nature, nor in the law of nations. Butt I doe finde, that all Englishmen must bee subject to English lawes, and I doe verily believe, that there is noe man butt will say, that the foundation of all law lies in the people, and if [it lie] in the people, I am to seeke for this exemption. And truly I have thought something [else], in what a miserable distressed condition would many a man that hath fought for the Parliament in this quarrell bee? I will bee bound to say, that many a man whose zeale and affection to God and this Kingedome hath carried him forth in this cause hath soe spent his estate that in the way the State, the Army are going hee shall nott hold uppe his head; and when his estate is lost, and nott worth 40s. a yeare, a man shall nott have any interest; and there are many other wayes by which estates men have doe fall to decay, if that bee the rule which God in his providence does use. A man when hee hath an estate hath an interest in making lawes, when hee hath none, hee hath noe power in itt. Soe that a man cannott loose that which hee hath for the maintenance of his family, butt hee must loose that which God and nature hath given him. Therfore I doe [think]

and am still of the same opinion; that every man born in England cannot, ought nott, neither by the law of God nor the law of nature, to bee exempted from the choice of those who are to make lawes, for him to live under, and for him, for ought I know, to loose his life under. Therfore I thinke there can bee noe great sticke in this.

COMMISSARY GEN. IRETON. All the maine thinge that I speake for is because I would have an eye to propertie. I hope wee doe nott come to contend for victorie, butt lett every man consider with himself that hee doe nott goe that way to take away all propertie. For heere is the case of the most fundamentall parte of the Constitution of the Kingedome, which if you take away, you take away all by that. Heere are men of this and this qualitie are determined to bee the Electors of men to the Parliament, and they are all those who have any permanent interest in the Kingedome, and who taken together doe comprehend the whole interest of the Kingedome. I meane by permanent, locall, that is nott anywhere else. As for instance; hee that hath a freehold, and that freehold cannott bee removed out of the Kingedome; and soe there's a [freeman of a] Corporation, a place which hath the priviledge of a markett and trading, which if you should allow to all places equallie, I doe nott see how you could preserve any peace in the Kingedome, and that is the reason why in the Constitution wee have but some few markett townes. Now those people [that have freeholds] and those that are the freemen of Corporations, were look't upon by the former Constitution to comprehend the permanent interest of the Kingdom. For [firstly] hee that hath his livelihood by his trade, and by his freedome of trading in such a Corporation which hee cannott exercise in another, hee is tied to that place, his livelihood depends uppon itt. And secondly, that man hath an interest, hath a permanent interest there, uppon which hee may live, and live a freeman without dependance. These Constitutions this Kingedome hath look't att. Now I wish wee may all consider of what right you will challenge, that all the people should have right to Elections. Is itt by the right of nature? If you will hold forth that as your ground, then I thinke you must deny all property too, and this is my reason. For thus: by the same right of nature, whatever itt bee that you pretend, by which you can say, "one man hath an equall right with another to the chusing of him that shall governe him"—by the same right of nature, hee hath an equal right in any goods hee sees: meate, drinke, cloathes, to take and use them for his sustenance. Hee hath a freedome to the land, [to take] the ground, to exercise itt, till itt; he hath the [same] freedome to any thinge that any one doth account himself to have any propriety in.

COL. RAINBOROW. To the thinge itt self propertie. I would faine know how itt comes to bee the propertie [of some men, and not of others]. As for estates, and those kinde of thinges, and other thinges that belonge to men, itt will bee granted that they are propertie; butt I deny that that is a propertie, to a Lord, to a Gentleman, to any man more then another in the Kingdome of England. Iff itt bee a propertie, itt is a propertie by a law; neither doe I thinke, that there is very little propertie in this thinge by the law of the land, because I thinke that the law of the land in that thinge is the most tyrannicall law under heaven, and I would faine know what wee have fought for, and this is the old law of England and that which inslaves the people of England that they should bee bound by lawes in which they have noe voice att all.

MR. PETTY. For this [argument] that itt destroyes all right [to property] that every Englishman that is an inhabitant of England should chuse and have a choice in the Representatives, I suppose itt is [on the contrary] the onely meanes to preserve all propertie. For I judge every man is naturally free; and I judge the reason why men when they were in soe great numbers [chose representatives was] that every man could nott give his voice; and therefore men agreed to come into some forme of Governement that they who were chosen might preserve propertie. I would faine know, if we were to begin a Governement, [whether you would say] 'you have nott 40s. a yeare, therfore you shall not have a voice'. Wheras before there was a Governement every

man had such a choice, and afterwards for this very cause they did chuse Representatives, and putt themselves into formes of Governement that they may preserve propertie, and therfore itt is nott to destroy itt [to give every man a choice].

COL. RICH, a Cavalry officer. I confesse [there is weight in] that objection that the Commissary Generall last insisted uppon; for you have five to one in the Kingedome that have noe permanent interest. Some men [have] ten, some twenty servants, some more, some lesse. If the Master and servant shall bee equall Electors, then clearlie those that have noe interest in the Kingedome will make itt their interest to chuse those that have noe interest. Itt may happen, that the majority may by law, nott in a confusion, destroy propertie; there may bee a law enacted, that there shall bee an equality of goods and estate. I thinke that either of the extreames may be urg'd to inconveniencie. That is, men that have noe interest as to Estate should have no interest as to Election.

COL. RAINBOROW. I should nott have spoken againe. I thinke itt is a fine guilded pill, butt there is much danger and itt may seeme to some, that there is some kinde of remedy, I thinke that wee are better as wee are. That the poore shall chuse many, still the people are in the same case, are over voted still. And therfore truly, Sir, I should desire to goe close to the businesse; and the thinge that I am unsatisfied in is how itt comes about that there is such a propriety in some freeborne Englishmen, and nott [in] others.

COM. COWLING, an officer of the General Staff. Whether the younger sonne have nott as much right to the Inheritance as the eldest?

COM. GEN. IRETON. Will you decide itt by the light of nature?

COM. COWLING. Why Election was only 40s a yeare, which was more then 40£ a yeare now, the reason was [this], that the Commons of England were overpowr'd by the Lords, who had abundance of vassalls, butt that they might still make their lawes good against incroaching prerogatives, therefore they did exclude all slaves. Now the case is nott soe; all slaves have bought their freedomes. They are more free that in the common wealth are more beneficiall. There are men in the country . . . there is a tanner in Stanes worth 3000£, and another in Reading worth 3 horseskins.

COM. GEN. IRETON. In the beginning of your speech you seeme to acknowledge [that] by law, by civill Constitution, the propriety of having voices in Election was fixt in certaine persons. Soe then your exception of your argument does nott prove that by civill constitution they have noe such propriety, butt your arguement does acknowledge [that] by civil [constitution they have such] propriety. You argue against this law, that this law is nott good.

MR. WILDMAN. Unlesse I bee very much mistaken wee are very much deviated from the first Question. Instead of following the first proposition to inquire what is just, I conceive wee looke to prophesies, and looke to what may bee the event, and judge of the justnesse of a thinge by the consequence. I desire wee may recall [ourselves to the question] whether itt bee right or noe. I conceive all that hath bin said against itt will be reduc't to this and another reason; that itt is against a fundamental law, [and] that every person ought to have a permanent interest, because itt is nott fitt that those should chuse Parliaments that have noe lands to bee disposed of by Parliament.

COM. GEN. IRETON. If you will take itt by the way, itt is not fitt that the Representees should chuse the Representors, or the persons who shall make the law in the Kingedome, who have nott a permanent fix't interest in the Kingedome.

MR. WILDMAN. Sir I doe soe take itt; and I conceive that that is brought in for the same reason, that forraigners might come to have a voice in our Elections as well as the native Inhabitants.

COM. GEN. IRETON. That is uppon supposition that these should bee all Inhabitants.

MR. WILDMAN. Every person in England hath as cleere a right to Elect his Representative as the greatest person in England. I conceive that's the undeniable maxime of Governement: that all governement is in the free consent of the people. If [so], then uppon that account, there is noe person that is under a just Governement, or hath justly his owne, unlesse hee by his owne free

consent bee putt under that Governement. This hee cannott bee unlesse hee bee consenting to itt, and therfore according to this maxime there is never a person in England [but ought to have a voice in elections]. And therfore I should humbly move, that if the Question bee stated—which would soonest bringe thinges to an issue—itt might rather bee this: whether any person can justly bee bound by law, who doth nott give his consent that such persons shall make lawes for him?

COM. GEN. IRETON. Lett the Question bee soe; whether a man can bee bound to any law that hee doth nott consent to? And I shall tell you, that hee may and ought to bee [bound to a law] that hee doth nott give a consent to, nor doth nott chuse any [to consent to], and I will make itt cleare. If a forraigner come within this Kingedome, if that stranger will have libertie [to dwell here] who hath noe local interest heere—hee is a man itt's true, hath aire that by nature wee must nott expell our Coasts, give him noe being amongst us, nor kill him because hee comes uppon our land, comes uppe our streame, arrives att our shoare. Itt is a peece of hospitality, of humanity, to receive that man amongst us. Butt if that man bee received to a being amongst us I thinke that man may very well bee content to submitt himself to the law of the land: that is, the law that is made by those people that have a property, a fixt property, in the land.

COL. RAINBOROW. Sir I see, that itt is impossible to have liberty butt all propertie must be taken away. If itt be laid downe for a rule, and if you will say itt, itt must bee soe. But I would faine know what the souldier hath fought for all this while? Hee hath fought to inslave himself, to give power to men of riches, men of estates, to make him a perpetuall slave.

COM. GEN. IRETON. I tell you what the souldier of the Kingedome hath fought for. First, the danger that wee stood in was, that one man's will must bee a law. The people of the Kingedome must have this right att least, that they should nott bee concluded [but] by the Representative of those that had the interest of the Kingedome. Some men fought in this, because they were imediately concern'd and engag'd in itt. Other men who had noe other interest in the Kingedome butt this, that they should have the benefitt of those lawes made by the Representative, yett [fought] that they should have the benefitt of this Representative. They thought itt was better to bee concluded by the common consent of those that were fix't men and setled men that had the interest of this Kingedome [in them], and from that way [said they] I shall know a law and have a certainty. Every man that was borne in itt that hath a freedome is a denizon, hee was capable of trading to gett money and to gett estates by, and therfore this man I thinke had a great deale of reason to build uppe such a foundation of interest to himself: that is, that the will of one man should not bee a law, butt that the law of this Kingedome should bee by a choice of persons to represent, and that choice to bee made by the generality of the Kingedome. Heere was a right that induced men to fight, and those men that had this interest, though this bee nott the utmost interest that other men have, yett they had some interest.

1. What is the radical view of equality expressed in the debate by people like Colonel Rainsborough, and how is this view justified?

2. What is the conservative response to the radical view?

3. Although the sides in the debate disagree about who should choose representatives in Parliament, they do share some political assumptions. What are they?

4. How do the views expressed in the debate differ from the political theories expounded by James I in his *True Law of a Free Monarchy*?

5. This debate was never officially published, and we know what was said only through Clarke's rough notes. How might this affect our understanding of what went on at Putney?

·82·

Duc de Saint-Simon
Memoirs
(1694–1723)

Louis de Rouvroy, Duke of Saint-Simon (1675–1755), led a privileged life at the very heart of the French absolute state. A godson of Louis XIV, Saint-Simon was brought up in Versailles in the shadow of the Sun King. Although he served briefly as an ambassador and as an officer in the French army, Saint-

Simon never carved out a place for himself in either government service or court life. He tended to blame Louis XIV for his failures, but his record of achievement in the next reign was equally unimpressive. He died bitter and resentful in 1755.

Saint-Simon is remembered only for his voluminous *Memoirs* from which much of our knowledge of the day-to-day life at the court of Versailles derives. He began keeping them when he was 19 and continued on into middle age; the *Memoirs* show his talent for observation, particularly of social detail, and his ear for the latest court gossip. His character sketches, such as the one of Louis XIV, which is presented here, always unearth the darker side of the subject under study. There is always as much of Saint-Simon in his portrayals as there is of the people he is describing.

I shall pass over the stormy period of Louis XIV's minority. At twenty-three years of age he entered the great world as King, under the most favourable auspices. His ministers were the most skilful in all Europe; his generals the best; his Court was filled with illustrious and clever men, formed during the troubles which had followed the death of Louis XIII.

Louis XIV was made for a brilliant Court. In the midst of other men, his figure, his courage, his grace, his beauty, his grand mien, even the tone of his voice and the majestic and natural charm of all his person, distinguished him till his death as the King Bee, and showed that if he had only been born a simple private gentleman, he would equally have excelled in fêtes, pleasures, and gallantry, and would have had the greatest success in love. The intrigues and adventures which early in life he had been engaged in— when the Comtesse de Soissons lodged at the Tuileries, as superintendent of the Queen's household, and was the centre figure of the Court roup—had exercised an unfortunate influence upon him: he received those impressions with which he could never after successfully struggle. From this time, intellect, education, nobility of sentiment, and high principle, in others, became objects of suspicion to him, and soon of hatred. The more he advanced in years the more this sentiment was confirmed in him.

He wished to reign by himself. His jealousy on this point unceasingly became weakness. He reigned, indeed, in little things; the great he could never reach: even in the former, too, he was often governed. The superior ability of his early ministers and his early generals soon wearied him. He liked nobody to be in any way superior to him. Thus he chose his ministers, not for their knowledge, but for their ignorance; not for their capacity, but for their want of it. He liked to form them, as he said; liked to teach them even the most trifling things. It was the same with his generals. He took credit to himself for instructing them; wished it to be thought that from his cabinet he commanded and directed all his armies. Naturally fond of trifles, he unceasingly occupied himself with the most petty details of his troops, his household, his mansions; would even instruct his cooks, who received, like novices, lessons they had known by heart for years. This vanity, this unmeasured and unreasonable love of admiration, was his ruin. His ministers, his generals, his mistresses, his courtiers, soon perceived his weakness. They praised him with emulation and spoiled him. Praises, or to say truth, flattery, pleased him to such an extent, that the coarsest was well received, the vilest even better relished. It was the sole means by which you could approach him. Those whom he liked owed his affection for

Louis XIV and members of his family, Largillière, 1710.

them, to their untiring flatteries. This is what gave his ministers so much authority, and the opportunities they had for adulating him, of attributing everything to him, and of pretending to learn everything from him. Suppleness, meanness, an admiring, dependent, cringing manner—above all, an air of nothingness—were the sole means of pleasing him.

This poison spread. It spread, too, to an incredible extent, in a prince who, although of intellect beneath mediocrity, was not utterly without sense, and who had had some experience. Without voice or musical knowledge, he use to sing, in private, the passages of the opera

prologues that were fullest of his praises! He was drowned in vanity; and so deeply, that at his public suppers—all the Court present, musicians also—he would hum these self-same praises between his teeth, when the music they were set to was played!

And yet, it must be admitted, he might have done better. Though his intellect, as I have said, was beneath mediocrity, it was capable of being formed. He loved glory, was fond of order and regularity; was by disposition prudent, moderate, discreet, master of his movements and his tongue. Will it be believed? He was also by disposition good and just! God had sufficiently gifted him to enable him to be a good King; perhaps even *a tolerably great King!* All the evil came to him from elsewhere. His early education was so neglected that nobody dared approach his apartment. He has often been heard to speak of those times with bitterness, and even to relate that, one evening he was found in the basin of the Palais Royale garden fountain, into which he had fallen! He was scarcely taught how to read or write, and remained so ignorant, that the most familiar historical and other facts were utterly unknown to him! He fell, accordingly, and sometimes even in public, into the grossest absurdities.

It was his vanity, his desire for glory, that led him, soon after the death of the King of Spain, to make that event the pretext for war; in spite of renunciations so recently made, so carefully stipulated, in the marriage contract. He marched into Flanders; his conquests there were rapid; the passage of the Rhine was admirable; the triple alliance of England, Sweden, and Holland only animated him. In the midst of winter he took Franche-Comté, by restoring which at the peace of Aix-la-Chapelle, he preserved his conquests in Flanders. All was flourishing then in the state. Riches everywhere. Colbert had placed the finances, the navy, commerce, manufactures, letters even, upon the highest point; and this age, like that of Augustus, produced in abundance illustrious men of all kinds—even those illustrious only in pleasures.

Thus, we see this monarch grand, rich, conquering, the arbiter of Europe; feared and admired as long as the ministers and captains existed who really deserved the name. When they were no more, the machine kept moving some time by impulsion, and from their influence. But soon afterwards we saw beneath the surface; faults and errors were multiplied, and decay came on with giant strides; without, however, opening the eyes of that despotic master, so anxious to do everything and direct everything himself, and who seemed to indemnify himself for disdain abroad by increasing fear and trembling at home.

So much for the reign of this vain-glorious monarch.

Let me touch now upon some other incidents in his career, and upon some points in his character.

He early showed a disinclination for Paris. The troubles that had taken place there during the minority made him regard the place as dangerous; he wished, too, to render himself venerable by hiding himself from the eyes of the multitude; all these considerations fixed him at St. Germains soon after the death of the Queen, his mother. It was to that place he began to attract the world by fêtes and gallantries, and by making it felt that he wished to be often seen.

His love for Madame de la Vallière, which was at first kept secret, occasioned frequent excursions to Versailles, then a little card castle, which had been built by Louis XIII—annoyed, and his suite still more so, at being frequently obliged to sleep in a wretched inn there, after he had been out hunting in the forest of Saint Leger. That monarch rarely slept at Versailles more than one night, and then from necessity; the King, his son, slept there, so that he might be more in private with his mistress, pleasures unknown to the hero and just man, worthy son of Saint Louis, who built the little château.

These excursions of Louis XIV by degrees gave birth to those immense buildings he erected at Versailles; and their convenience for a numerous court, so different from the apartments at St. Germains, led him to take up his abode there entirely shortly after the death of the Queen. He built an infinite number of apartments, which were asked for by those who wished to pay their court to him; whereas at St. Germains nearly everybody was obliged to lodge in the town, and the few who found accommodation at the château were strangely inconvenienced.

The frequent fêtes, the private promenades at Versailles, the journeys, were means on which the King seized in order to distinguish or mortify the courtiers, and thus render them more assiduous in pleasing him. He felt that of real favours he had not enough to bestow; in order to keep up the spirit of devotion, he therefore unceasingly invented all sorts of ideal ones, little preferences and petty distinctions, which answered his purpose as well.

He was exceedingly jealous of the attention paid him. Not only did he notice the presence of the most distinguished courtiers, but those of inferior degree also. He looked to the right and to the left, not only upon rising but upon going to bed, at his meals, in passing through his apartments, or his gardens of Versailles, where alone the courtiers were allowed to follow him; he saw and noticed everybody; not one escaped him, not even those who hoped to remain unnoticed. He marked well all absentees from the court, found out the reason of their absence, and never lost an opportunity of acting towards them as the occasion might seem to justify. With some of the courtiers (the most distinguished), it was a demerit not to make the court their ordinary abode; with others it was a fault to come but rarely; for those who never or scarcely ever came it was certain disgrace. When their names were in any way mentioned, "I do not know them," the King would reply haughtily. Those who presented themselves but seldom were thus characterised: "They are people I never see"; these decrees were irrevocable. He could not bear people who liked Paris.

Louis XIV took great pains to be well informed of all that passed everywhere; in the public places, in the private houses, in society and familiar intercourse. His spies and tell-tales were infinite. He had them of all species; many who were ignorant that their information reached him; others who knew it; others who wrote to him direct, sending their letters through channels he indicated; and all these letters were seen by him alone, and always before

everything else; others who sometimes spoke to him secretly in his cabinet, entering by the back stairs. These unknown means ruined an infinite number of people of all classes, who never could discover the cause; often ruined them very unjustly; for the King, once prejudiced, never altered his opinion, or so rarely, that nothing was more rare. He had, too, another fault, very dangerous for others and often for himself, since it deprived him of good subjects. He had an excellent memory; in this way, that if he saw a man who, twenty years before, perhaps, had in some manner offended him, he did not forget the man, though he might forget the offence. This was enough, however, to exclude the person from all favour. The representations of a minister, of a general, of his confessor even, could not move the King. He would not yield.

The most cruel means by which the King was informed of what was passing—for many years before anybody knew it—was that of opening letters. The promptitude and dexterity with which they were opened passes understanding. He saw extracts from all the letters in which there were passages that the chiefs of the post-office, and then the minister who governed it, thought ought to go before him; entire letters, too, were sent to him, when their contents seemed to justify the sending. Thus the chiefs of the post, nay, the principal clerks were in a position to suppose what they pleased and against whom they pleased. A word of contempt against the King or the government, a joke, a detached phrase, was enough. It is incredible how many people, justly or unjustly, were more or less ruined, always without resource, without trial, and without knowing why. The secret was impenetrable; for nothing ever cost the King less than profound silence and dissimulation.

1. What qualities did Saint-Simon admire in Louis XIV?

2. To what does Saint-Simon attribute Louis's early successes?

3. Judging from Saint-Simon's description of courtly life, what did a courtier need to get along?

4. On balance, Saint-Simon believed Louis to have been a failure. Why?

5. What sort of a picture does Saint-Simon present of the workings of the absolutist state?

The New Science

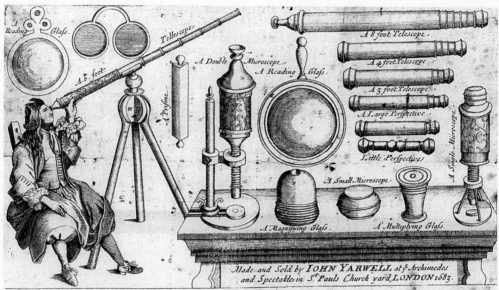

Made-and Sold by IOHN YARWELL at ý Archimedes
and Spectacles in St Pauls Church yard, LONDON 1683.

All the above named Instruments as Telescopes of all lengths, Microscopes single and double, Perspectives great and small
Reding Glasses of all Sizes, Magnifying Glasses, Multiplying Glasses, Triangular Prisms, Speaking Trumpetts, Spectacles fitted
to all ages, And all other sorts of Glasses, both Concave and Convex.

This seventeenth-century trade card advertises many of the fashionable scientific objects being made
in London at that time.

·83·

Galileo Galilei
The Two New Sciences
(1638)

*B*orn in Florence and educated in Padua, Galileo Galilei (1564–1642) was one of the greatest of all of the seventeenth-century scientists. His early studies of motion led him to accept the basic theories of Copernicus, the Polish astronomer who postulated that the earth was a planet that revolved around the sun. Galileo perfected the first telescope, and with it he was able to identify the moons of Jupiter and describe the lunar surface. At first Galileo was prohibited from publishing his findings, but in 1632 he received a license for the publication of *A Dialogue Between the Two Great Systems of the World,* a tract that took the form of a debate between an adherent of the old Aristotelian system and a convert to the new Copernican one. Galileo was subsequently arrested by the Inquisition, tried, condemned, and forced to recant his Copernican views.

Five years later, while under house arrest, Galileo smuggled his most important scientific work, *The Two New Sciences,* out of Italy to Holland, where it was published. *The Two New Sciences* is presented in the form of a fictitious discussion between Galileo and two companions who act as a foil for his positions. These excerpts show the development of his theory of inertia, one of the crucial discoveries of the new scientists.

SAGREDO.   I have always considered it to be an idle notion of the common people that in these and similar frameworks one cannot reason from the small to the large, because many mechanical devices succeed on a small scale that cannot exist in great size. Now, all reasonings about mechanics have their foundations in geometry, in which I do not see that largeness and smallness make large circles, triangles, cylinders, cones, or any other figures [or] solids subject to properties different from those of small ones; hence if the large scaffolding is built with every member proportional to its counterpart in the smaller one, and if the smaller is sound and stable under the use for which it is designed, I fail to see why the larger should not also be proof against adverse and destructive shocks that it may encounter.

SALVATI.   Here you must note how conclusions that are true may seem improbable at a first glance, and yet when only some small thing is pointed out, they cast off their concealing cloaks and, thus naked and simple, gladly show off their secrets. For who does not see that a horse falling from a height of three or four braccia will break its bones, while a dog falling from the same height, or a cat from eight or ten, or even more, will suffer no harm? Thus a cricket might fall without damage from a tower, or an ant from the moon. Small children remain unhurt in falls that would break the legs, or the heads, of their elders. And just as smaller animals are proportionately stronger or more robust than larger ones, so smaller plants will sustain themselves better. I think you both know that if an oak were two hundred feet high, it could not support branches spread out similarly to those of an oak of average size. Only by a miracle could nature form a horse the size of twenty horses, or a giant ten times the height of a man—unless she greatly altered the proportions of the members, especially those of the skeleton, thickening the bones far beyond their ordinary symmetry.

Similarly, to believe that in artificial machines the large and small are equally practicable and durable is a manifest error. Thus, for example, small spires, little columns, and other solid shapes can be safely extended or heightened without risk of breaking them, whereas very large ones will go to pieces at any adverse accident, or for no more cause than that of their own weight.

I SAY THAT THAT MOTION IS EQUABLY OR UNIFORMLY ACCELERATED WHICH, ABANDONING REST, ADDS ON TO ITSELF EQUAL MOMENTA OF SWIFTNESS IN EQUAL TIMES.

SAGREDO.   Just as it would be unreasonable for me to oppose this, or any other definition whatever assigned by any author, all [definitions] being arbitrary, so I may, without offence, doubt whether this definition, conceived and assumed in the abstract, is adapted to, suitable for, and verified in the kind of accelerated motion that heavy bodies in fact employ in falling naturally. And since it seems that the Author promises us that what he has defined is the natural motion of heavy bodies, I should like to hear you remove certain doubts that disturb my mind, so that I can then apply myself with better attention to the propositions that are expected, and their demonstrations.

SALVATI.   It will be good for you and Simplicio to propound the difficulties, which I imagine will be the same ones that occurred to me when I first saw this treatise, and that our Author himself put to rest for me in our discussions, or that I removed for myself by thinking them out.

SAGREDO.   I picture to myself a heavy body falling. It leaves from rest; that is, from the deprivation of any speed whatever, and enters into motion in which it goes accelerating according to the ratio of increase of time from its first instant of motion. It will have obtained, for example, eight degrees of speed in eight pulse-beats, of which at the fourth beat it will have gained four; at the second [beat], two; and at the first, one. Now, time being infinitely divisible, what follows from this? The speed being always diminished in this ratio, there will be no degree of speed, however small (or we might say, "no degree of slowness, however great"), such that the moveable will not be found to have this [at some time] after its departure from infinite slowness, that is, from rest. Thus if the degree of speed that it had at four beats of time were such that, maintaining this uniformly, it would run two miles in one hour, while with the degree of speed that it had at the second beat it would have made one mile an hour, it must be said that in instants of time closer and closer to the first [instant] of its moving from rest, it would be found to be so slow that, continuing to move with this slowness, it would not pass a mile in an hour, nor in a day, nor in a year, nor in a thousand [years], and it would not pass even one span in some still longer time. Such events I find very hard to accommodate in my imagination, when our senses show us that a heavy body in falling arrives immediately at a very great speed.

SALVATI.   This is one of the difficulties that gave me pause at the outset; but not long afterward I removed it, and its removal was effected by the same experience that presently sustains it for you.

You say that it appears to you that experience shows the heavy body, having hardly left from rest, entering into a very considerable speed; and I say that this same experience makes it clear to us that the first impetuses of the falling body, however heavy it may be, are very slow indeed. Place a heavy body on some yielding material, and leave it until it has pressed as much as it can with its mere weight. It is obvious that if you now raise it one or two braccia, and then let it fall on the same material, it will make a new pressure on impact, greater than it made by its weight alone. This effect will be caused by the falling moveable in conjunction with the speed gained in fall, and will be greater and greater according as the height is greater from which the impact is made; that is, according as the speed of the striking body is greater. The amount of speed of a falling body, then, we can estimate without error from the quality and quantity of its impact.

But tell me, gentlemen: if you let a sledge fall on a pole from a height of four braccia, and it drives this, say, four inches into the ground, and will drive it much less from a height of two braccia, and still less from a height of one, and less yet from a span only; if finally it is raised but a single inch, how much more will it accomplish than if it were placed on top [of the pole] without striking it at all? Certainly very little. And its effect would be quite imperceptible if it were lifted only the thickness of a leaf. Now, since the effect of impact is governed by the speed of a given percussent, who can doubt that its motion is very slow and minimal when its action is imperceptible? You now see how great is the force of truth, when the same experience that seemed to prove one thing at first glance assures us of the contrary when it is better considered.

But without restricting ourselves to this experience, though no doubt it is quite conclusive, it seems to me not difficult to penetrate this truth by simple reasoning. We have a heavy stone, held in the air at rest. It is freed from support and set at liberty; being heavier than air, it goes falling downward, not with uniform motion, but slowly at first and continually accelerated thereafter. Now, since speed may be increased or diminished *in infinitum*, what argument can persuade me that this moveable, departing from infinite slowness (which is rest), enters immediately into a speed of ten degrees rather than into one of four, or into the latter before a speed of two, or one, or one-half, or one one-hundredth? Or, in short, into all the lesser [degrees] *in infinitum?*

Please hear me out. I believe you would not hesitate to grant me that the acquisition of degrees of speed by the stone falling from the state of rest may occur in the same order as the diminution and loss of those same degrees when, driven by impelling force, the stone is hurled upward to the same height. But if that is

so, I do not see how it can be supposed that in the diminution of speed in the ascending stone, consuming the whole speed, the stone can arrive at rest before passing through every degree of slowness.

SIMPLICIO.   But if the degrees of greater and greater tardity are infinite, it will never consume them all, and this rising heavy body will never come to rest, but will move forever while always slowing down—something that is not seen to happen.

SALVATI.   This would be so, Simplicio, if the moveable were to hold itself for any time in each degree; but it merely passes there, without remaining beyond an instant. And since in any finite time [*temp quanto*], however small, there are infinitely many instants, there are enough to correspond to the infinitely many degrees of diminished speed. It is obvious that this rising heavy body does not persist for any finite time in any one degree of speed, for if any finite time is assigned, and if the moveable had the same degree of speed at the first instant of that time and also at the last, then it could likewise be driven upward with this latter degree [of speed] through as much space [again], just as it was carried from the first [instant] to the second; and at the same rate it would pass from the second to a third, and finally, it would continue its uniform motion *in infinitum.*

SIMPLICIO.   Truly, I should be one of those who concede that the falling heavy body *vires acquirat eundo* [acquires force in going], the speed increasing in the ratio of the space, while the momentum of the same percussent is doubled when it comes from double height, appear to me as propositions to be granted without repugnance or controversy.

SALVATI.   And yet they are as false and impossible as [it is] that motion should be made instantaneously, and here is a very clear proof of it. When speeds have the same ratio as the spaces passed or to be passed, those spaces come to be passed in equal times, if therefore the speeds with which the falling body passed the space of four braccia were the doubles of the speeds with which it passed the first two braccia, as one space is double the other space, then the times of those passages are equal; but for the same moveable to pass the four braccia and the two in the same time cannot take place except in instantaneous motion. But we see that the falling heavy body makes its motion in time, and passes the two braccia in less [time] than the four; therefore it is false that its speed increases as the space.

The other proposition is shown to be false with the same clarity. For that which strikes being the same body, the difference and momenta of the impacts must be determined only by the difference of the speeds; if therefore the percussent coming from a double height delivers a blow of double momentum, it must strike with double speed; but double speed passes the double space in the same time, and we see the time of descent to be longer from the greater height.

SAGREDO.   Too evident and too easy is this [reasoning] with which you make hidden conclusions manifest. This great facility renders the conclusions less prized than when they were under seeming contradiction. I think that people generally will little esteem ideas gained with so little trouble, in comparison with those over which long and unresolvable altercations are waged.

SALVATI.   Things would not be so bad if men who show with great brevity and clarity the fallacies of propositions that have commonly been held to be true by people in general received only such bearable injury as scorn in place of thanks. What is truly unpleasant and annoying is a certain other attitude that some people habitually take. Claiming, in the same studies, at least parity with anyone that exists, these men see that the conclusions they have been putting forth as true are later exposed by someone else, and shown to be false by short and easy reasoning. I shall not call their reaction envy, which then usually transforms itself into rage and hatred against those who reveal such fallacies, but I do say that they are goaded by a desire to maintain inveterate errors rather than to permit newly discovered truths to be accepted. This desire sometimes induces them to write in contradiction to those truths of which they themselves are only too aware in their own hearts, merely to keep down the reputations of other men in the estimation of the common herd of little understanding. I have heard from our Academician not a few such false conclusions, accepted as true and [yet] easy to refute; and I have kept a record of some of these.

1.   How was scientific argument carried on in Galileo's time? How does it differ from modern scientific debate?

2.   What sort of basic knowledge does Galileo's treatise assume?

3.   Why do people fall into erroneous beliefs about what goes on around them?

4.   Galileo was one of the most distinguished practitioners of the scientific method. How is this revealed in the dialogue?

5.   How do others react to the discoveries of scientists such as Galileo? Why?

·84·

René Descartes
Discourse on Method
(1637)

*R*ené Descartes (1596–1650) was the son of a French provincial lawyer and judge. He was schooled by the Jesuits and attended university at Poitiers, where he took a degree in canon law. Although his father expected that young René would follow in his footsteps, Descartes decided, instead, to see the world. He enlisted in the military and fought in the Thirty Years' War in Germany. But mostly he continued his mathematical studies and contemplated. One night in an army camp he had a dream of devising a universal intellectual system. He moved to Holland in 1628 and spent most of the rest of his life there, writing and studying. Descartes became an international figure after the publication of his *Discourse on Method*. He died in 1650 while in residence at the Swedish court.

The system Descartes presents in *Discourse on Method* combines the rigorous principles of reasoning found in mathematics with the central problems of moral philosophy. He propounds the view that all the universe is either matter or mind; this dualist idea tries to reconcile the new science and traditional authorities such as the Church.

Good sense is of all things in the world the most equitably distributed; for everyone thinks himself so amply provided with it, that even those most difficult to please in everything else do not commonly desire more of it than they already have. It is not likely that in this respect we are all of us deceived; it is rather to be taken as testifying that the power of judging well and of distinguishing between the true and the false, which, properly speaking, is what is called good sense, or reason, is by nature equal in all men; and that the diversity of our opinions is not due to some men being endowed with a larger share of reason than others, but solely to this, that our thoughts proceed along different paths, and that we are, therefore, not attending to the same things. For to be possessed of good mental powers is not of itself enough; what is all-important is that we employ them rightly. The greatest minds,

capable as they are of the greatest virtues, are also capable of the greatest vices; and those who proceed very slowly may make much greater progress, provided they keep to the straight road, than those who, while they run, digress from it.

For myself, I have never supposed my mind to be in any way more perfect than that of the average man; on the contrary, I have often wished I could think as quickly, image as accurately and distinctly, or remember as fully and readily as some others. Beyond these I know of no other qualities making for the perfection of the mind; for as to reason, or sense, inasmuch as it is that alone which renders us men, and distinguishes us from the brutes, I am disposed to believe that it is complete in each one of us; and in this I am following the common opinion of those philosophers who say that differences of

Portrait of Descartes by Frans Hals.

more and less hold in respect only of *accidents,* and not in respect of the *forms,* or natures, of the *individuals* of the same *species.*

Thus my present design is not to teach a method which everyone ought to follow for the right conduct of his reason, but only to show in what manner I have endeavored to conduct my own. Those who undertake to give precepts ought to regard themselves as wiser than those for whom they prescribe; and if they prove to be in the least degree lacking, they have to bear the blame. But in putting forward this piece of writing merely as a history, or, if you prefer so to regard it, as a fable, in which, among some examples worthy of imitation, there will also, perhaps, be found others we should be well advised not to follow, I hope that it will be of use to some without being harmful to anyone, and that all will welcome my plain-speaking. . . .

I came to believe that the four following rules would be found sufficient, always provided I took the firm and unswerving resolve never in a single instance to fail in observing them.

The first was to accept nothing as true which I did not evidently know to be such, that is to say, scrupulously to avoid precipitance and prejudice, and in the judgments I passed to include nothing additional to what had presented itself to my mind so clearly and so distinctly that I could have no occasion for doubting it.

The second, to divide each of the difficulties I examined into as many parts as may be required for its adequate solution.

The third, to arrange my thoughts in order, beginning with things the simplest and easiest to know, so that I may then ascend little by little, as it were step by step, to the knowledge of the more complex, and, in doing so, to assign an order of thought even to those objects which are not of themselves in any such order of precedence.

And the last, in all cases to make enumerations so complete, and reviews so general, that I should be assured of omitting nothing.

I then proceeded to consider, in a general manner, what is requisite to the truth and certainty of a proposition. Having found one—*I think, therefore I am*—which I knew to be true and certain, I thought that I ought also to know in what this certainty consists; and having noted that in this proposition nothing assures me of its truth save only that I see very clearly that in order to think it is necessary to be, I judged that I could take as being a general rule, that the things we apprehend very clearly and distinctly are true— bearing in mind, however, that there is some difficulty in rightly determining which are those we apprehend distinctly.

Reflecting in accordance with this rule on the fact that I doubted, and that consequently my being was not entirely perfect (seeing clearly, as I did, that it is a greater perfection to know than to doubt), I resolved to inquire whence I had learned to think of something more perfect than I myself was; and I saw clearly that it must proceed from some nature that was indeed more perfect. As to the thoughts I had of other things outside me, such as the heavens, the Earth, light, heat and a thousand others, I had not any such difficulty in knowing whence they came. Remarking nothing in them which seemed to render them superior to myself, I could believe that, if they were true, they were dependencies of my nature in so far as my nature had a certain perfection; and that if they were not true, I received them from nothing, that is to say, that they were in me in so far as I was in some respects lacking in perfection. But this latter suggestion could not be made in respect of the idea of a being more perfect than myself, since receiving the idea from nothing is a thing manifestly impossible. And since it is no less contradictory that the more perfect should result from, and depend on, the less perfect than that something should proceed from nothing, it is equally impossible I should receive it from myself. Thus we are committed to the conclusion that it has been placed in me by a nature which is veritably more perfect than I am, and which has indeed within itself all the perfections of which I have any idea, that is to say, in a single word, that is God. And since some perfections other than those I myself possess were known to me, I further concluded that I was not the only being in existence. There must of necessity exist some other more perfect being upon whom I was dependent, and from whom I had received all that I had. For if I alone had existed, independently of all else, in such wise that I had from myself all the perfection, however small in amount, through which I participated in the perfections of Divine Existence, I should have been able, for the same reason, to have from myself the whole surplus of perfections which I know to be lacking to me, and so could of myself have been infinite, eternal, immutable, omniscient, all-powerful—in short, have been able to possess all the perfections that I could discern as being in God.

Consequently, in order to know the nature of God (in extension of the above reasonings in proof of His existence) so far as my own nature allows of my doing so, I had only to consider in respect of all the things of which I found in myself any idea, whether the possession of them was or was not a perfection; thereby I was at once assured that none of those which showed any imperfection was in Him, and that all the others

were—just as I had learned that doubt, inconstancy, sadness and such like, could not be in Him, seeing that I myself should have been very glad to be free from them. In addition to these latter I had ideas of things which are sensible and corporeal. For although I might suppose that I was dreaming, and that all I saw or imaged was false, I yet could not deny that the ideas of them were indeed in my thought. But because I had already very clearly discerned in myself that the intelligent is distinct from the corporeal, and since I had also observed that all composition witnesses to dependence and that dependence is manifestly a defect, I therefore judged that it could not be a perfection in God to be composed of two natures, and that He was not so compounded. At the same time I likewise concluded that if there be in the world any bodies, or even any intelligences or other natures, which are not wholly perfect, their being must depend on His power in such a way that without Him they could not subsist for a single moment.

I then set myself to look for other truths, and having directed my attention to the object dealt with by geometers, which I took to be a continuous body, a space indefinitely extended in length, breadth, height and depth, which allowed of diverse shapes and sizes, and of their being moved or transposed in all sorts of ways (for all this the geometers take as being in the object of their studies), I perused some of their simple demonstrations; and while noting that the great certitude which by common consent is accorded to them is founded solely upon this that they are apprehended as evident, in conformity with the rule above stated, I likewise noted that there is nothing at all in them which assures me of the existence of their object. Taking, for instance, a triangle, while I saw that its three angles must be equal to two right angles, I did not on this account see anything which could assure me that anywhere in the world a triangle existed. On the other hand, on reverting to the examination of the idea of a Perfect Being, I found that existence is comprised in the idea precisely in the way in which it is comprised in the idea of a triangle that its three angles are equal to two right angles, or in that of a sphere that all its parts are equally distant from its center, and indeed even more evidently; and that in consequence it is at least as certain that God, who is this Perfect Being, is or exists, as any demonstration of geometry can possibly be.

The reason why many are persuaded that there is difficulty in knowing this truth, as also in knowing what their soul is, is that they never raise their minds above the things of sense, and that they are so accustomed to consider nothing except what they can image (a mode of thinking restricted to material things), that whatever is not imageable seems to them not intelligible. Even the philosophers in their schools do so, as is sufficiently manifest from their holding as a maxim that there is nothing in the understanding which was not previously in the senses, where, however, it is certain, the ideas of God and of the rational soul have never been. Those who employ their power of imagery to comprehend these ideas behave, as it seems to me, exactly as if in order to hear sounds or smell odors they sought to avail themselves of their eyes—unless, indeed, there is this difference, that the sense of sight does not afford any less truth than do hearing and smell. In any case, neither our imagination nor our senses can ever assure us of anything whatsoever save so far as our understanding intervenes.

Finally, if there still be men who are not sufficiently persuaded of the existence of God and of their soul by the reasons which I have cited, I would have them know that all the other things which they think to be more assured, as that they have a body and that there are stars and an Earth, and such like things, are less certain. For though the moral assurance we have of these things is such that there is an appearance of extravagance in professing to doubt of their existence, yet none the less when it is a metaphysical certitude that is in question, no one, unless he is devoid of reason, can deny that we do have sufficient ground for not being entirely assured, namely, in the fact that, as we are aware, we can, when asleep, image ourselves as possessed of a different body and as seeing stars and another Earth, without there being any such things. For how do we know that the thoughts which come in dreams are more likely to be false than those we experience when awake? Are not the former no less vivid and detailed than the latter? The ablest minds may treat of this question at whatever length they please, but I do not believe that they will be able to find any reason sufficient to remove this doubt, unless and until they presuppose the existence of God. For, to begin with, even the maxim which a short time ago I adopted as a rule, viz., that the things we cognize very clearly and very distinctly are all true, is reliable only because God is or exists, because He is a Perfect Being, and because all that is in us comes from Him. Thereupon it follows that our ideas or notions, as being of real things, and as coming from God, must in so far as they are clear and distinct be to that extent true. So that, though quite often we have ideas which contain some falsity, this can only be in the case of those in which there is some confusion or obscurity, i.e., owing to their participation, in this respect, in nothingness; or, in other words, that in us they are thus confused because we are not wholly perfect. And it is evident that it is not less repugnant that the falsity or imperfection, in so far as it is such, should proceed from God, than that truth or perfection should proceed from nothing. If, however, we did not know that whatever in us is real and true comes from a Being perfect and infinite, our ideas, however clear and distinct, would yield us no ground of assurance that they had the perfection of being true.

1.   How is Descartes's philosophy affected by the ideals of new science?

2.   What are the four main principles of Descartes's method?

3. What does "I think, therefore I am" mean? How does Descartes prove the truth of this proposition?

4. How does Descartes know that God exists?

5. What sort of God does Descartes describe?

Empires of Goods

"View of Broad Quay, Bristol," c. 1735, artist unknown.

·85·

The Rise and Decline of Flora

(ca. 1637)

*T*he Netherlands was one of the most densely populated parts of Europe; despite its poor soil and wet climate, it was able to take advantage of its strategic location to become the leading trading nation of the world in the seventeenth century. Dutch merchants organized complicated exchanges that allowed them to acquire commodities from one place that were needed in another and thus to accrue the profit of trade rather than manufacture. Amsterdam became the greatest financial and commercial center in Europe. It was here that the first bank was established in 1609, and that techniques for trading bonds and bills of exchange were perfected.

Occasionally, the frenzy for trade led to wild speculations as in the great Tulip Bubble of 1636–1637. Here a market in tulip futures arose, with people selling anticipated new tulip bulbs from the next year's crop. Because no one knew how many new tulips there would be, buyers bid up prices and sellers sold many more bulbs than could possibly be delivered. In 1637 the bubble burst, and tulip shares became nearly worthless. *The Rise and Decline of Flora* explores the attractions and dangers of speculative investments in the seventeenth century.

WAERMONDT. God grant you a fine day, Gaergoedt, my special friend. How are things with you?

GAERGOEDT. Everything is fine for me and the Florists. Our lives are a joy and we are quite satisfied. But come in, we'll talk a bit together by the fire.

WAERMONDT. Thank you, I'm on my way to someone else's.

GAERGOEDT. Oh no, you're not in that much of a hurry. I have something I must tell you, and I'll let you go when you want.

WAERMONDT. Well, if you want me to, I will.

GAERGOEDT. Sit down there, my friend. Come, Anneken, bring wood and turf, I must talk a little with my old friend. Where have you been all this time? Give me the bottle of brandy, or do you want Spanish wine, or a good French wine to drink, or a draught of good beer?

WAERMONDT. You're offering so many things that I don't know how to choose among them.

GAERGOEDT. We Florists have everything we need now, for a little flower pays for it all.

WAERMONDT. If you are paid as well as you hope, that's fine, but many a plowman has high hopes when he sows his grain and all he reaps is stubble.

GAERGOEDT. No, this is too sure a business for that. Come now, have a drink, here's one for you.

WAERMONDT. Thank you, I'll repay you in kind. But what expensive bottle is this?

GAERGOEDT. Everything comes from noble Flora. I was at the brandy distiller's just now; I offered him a little flower and took this full bottle for it. That is what I usually do; I get my meat, my bacon, my wine, for nothing, as much as I need for this whole year.

WAERMONDT.   If you can earn a profit so easily, that is a good business. The storekeepers and workpeople are all complaining about high costs and little work. The merchants complain about the great damage they suffer from pirates at sea and from the great storms which ruin their cargoes or cause their total loss.

GAERGOEDT.   I could talk about such things too, but now that I have gone into the flower business, I have only made profits, and let me tell you, I have made more than sixty thousand guilders in a space of four months—but don't tell anyone.

WAERMONDT.   Well, that's a big profit. Have you received it all?

GAERGOEDT.   Oh no, but I have letters from the buyers in their own hand.

WAERMONDT.   That's enough. You almost make me ready to invest a little too.

GAERGOEDT.   If you've a mind to, I'll sell you a small shipment, and since you're a good man and my special old friend, the price will be fifty guilders less than for anybody else, and let me add that if you don't make [250 guilders] on it within a month, I'll make up the difference myself.

WAERMONDT.   What kind of sales talk are you giving me? If I owned this supply, how would I get rid of it? Would people come to me or would I have to go to them?

GAERGOEDT.   I'll tell you. You have to go to a tavern. I'll name a few, for I know hardly any without a "club." Go in and ask if there are any florists. When you go to their room, some will quack like a duck because you're a newcomer, and some will say, "There's a new whore in the brothel," and such things. But you mustn't let it disturb you, they'll stop. They put your name on a slate and then the board goes around. That is, everyone in the club must send the board to anyone whose name is on the slate, and he asks for an offer. You must not put up your own goods for auction, even if you have a bit more than you're able to carry. But if you drop a word that you have something, someone will want them and drag them away from you; otherwise you'll receive the board. When the boards are given out, each seller and buyer picks a "man." The

seller goes to his "man" first and if his wares are worth, say, a hundred, he demands two hundred; then the buyer comes to the "man" and when he hears the asking price, he becomes angry and offers as much less as you demanded more. The "men" establish the price; everyone receives a figure on his board. The men announce the price, and if you are satisfied with it, you leave your figure on the board and if the buyer and seller both leave their figures, then a sale has been made. But on the other hand, if the figures are erased, the sale is off. And if a person leaves his figure on his board only the other party who has erased his is written down for a payment to the club. In some places it's two pennies, in others three, or five, or even six. And if a sale is made, then the seller gives a half penny for each guilder, but only three guilders if the sale is 120 guilders or more, not even if it is over a thousand guilders.

WAERMONDT.   What do they do with this money?

GAERGOEDT.   They have to drink, don't they? They pay for tobacco, beer, wine, fuel, light, and make contributions to the poor and to the girls too.

WAERMONDT.   Enough is gotten for all that?

GAERGOEDT.   Yes, often the sales of wine bring in even more than that. Several times I brought more money home than I took to the tavern, and I had eaten and drunk wine, beer, tobacco, all kinds of fine foods, fish, meat, even poultry and rabbits, and sweet pastries too, from morning until three or four o'clock in the night.

WAERMONDT.   It's smart to be that kind of a guest.

GAERGOEDT.   Well, I made a good profit too; I took in some six or seven "triplets," for I did twelve thousand guilder's worth of business and the "triplets" kept falling like drops of water off a thatched roof after it has rained.

WAERMONDT.   I've never heard stories the likes of this. But will it go on?

GAERGOEDT.   If it lasts a year or two or three, that's enough for me.

WAERMONDT.   I'm afraid that the Florists will find that in the end, Flora, whose name they bear and was a whore in Rome, will deceive them. You must have read her story.

GAERGOEDT.   No, I haven't! Please tell me about it.

WAERMONDT.   In the time of the Romans this Flora was a harlot whose beauty and pleasant talk, proud looks and graceful manner won her many lovers including such important men as Roman senators, who came to visit her. Her great conquests and the gifts they brought made her proud and haughty.

GAERGOEDT.   Well, what you tell me is to the advantage of the Florists, for Flora became rich and so will the Florists. . . .

WAERMONDT.   You don't understand what I mean. Flora made out well, but not the Florists who followed her, although they all lived on hope. And I fear that the same will happen with you and that you will lose in this business of yours the fine piece of property which your fathers earned by so many hours of long work and anxiety. Would it not have been better for you to have stuck to your own trade? . . .

WAERMONDT.   It's almost noon, I'd better go home and see what I've got to do there. I'll take your books with me.

GAERGOEDT.   Come, sit a little while and be my guest. My wife should be back from market soon with some fish. What can be keeping her so long? She must be doing business again. When I am out, she often buys and sells more than four or five thousand guilder's worth. Sit, maybe she'll bring us some news.

WAERMONDT.   I'm sorry, my friend, I cannot stay now. I must go home; I left some people there waiting for me. Good day, my friend.

GAERGOEDT.   When shall I expect you again, so that I can go over the books?

WAERMONDT.   At exactly two o'clock.

GAERGOEDT.   That's fine, I'll wait. Goodbye. I wonder where my wife has been for so long? She knows that I'm home. Doesn't she like me any more? I don't know what to think. Isn't that she coming there? Yes, it is. I'll wait for her inside. Well, my little Christina, how are things? Where have you been so long? You could have

sent the fish home as soon as the fishwife cleaned it. I had hoped to have a guest dine with us.

CHRISTINA.   Darling, I have no fish. I heard the quail sing such a wonderful song that I had no taste for fish. Come inside, I have something to tell you.

GAERGOEDT.   I still think that your sister is not with child. She has run around so much with that fellow that either one of their friends has died or they are through. You know what I mean. I don't know what to think.

CHRISTINA.   That's not what I'm talking about. I was visiting our niece Anneken, who told me that the Florists are in a panic. Some goods are going for less than half that what they brought the same evening.

GAERGOEDT.   Oh, I hope not.

CHRISTINA.   The time for hoping is past. Everything I've told you is true. . . .

GAERGOEDT.   Well, wife, don't be too worried, for it isn't as bad as you say. I've got a chance. Someone is coming this afternoon to whom I hope to make a good sale. I must get rid of some of my stock, for too much is on hand. But he won't know that. Of course, he is a good, special old acquaintance, but everyone must look for himself, for in business it is better to see a brother in trouble, not to speak of an acquaintance, than oneself. . . .

ANNEKEN.   Madame, the clock has struck two.

CHRISTINA.   I'll stay a quarter of an hour for your sake, my dear, but I really cannot stay after that, for my heart aches with what I've just told you. I must go out and find out what is happening.

GAERGOEDT.   That's not worth the trouble to go out for. I'll hear soon enough when I go to the club in the evening, for everything that happens in the city is talked over. Anneken, Anneken, someone is knocking. Let him in.

ANNEKEN.   It is the man who was here this morning.

GAERGOEDT.   Let him in.

WAERMONDT.   Good day, my friend Gaergoedt, and you too, Christina.

CHRISTINA. Come and sit her by my husband. I have to go out. Anneken, it's cold outside, bring some wood and open a small jug of wine.

WAERMONDT. There's no need to do that, I won't be long.

GAERGOEDT. Stay as long as you'd like. Come and sit down.

CHRISTINA. Goodbye, husband, goodbye, friend Waermondt. Have a good chat.

WAERMONDT. Goodbye. I went over your books for the flower business quickly and went to my cousin to discuss what it would be best for me to do. He advised me to wait a few days and see how things come out. There is no buying now, so that I am afraid I cannot take anything on now.

1. What does the growth of financial speculation in Holland illustrate about the seventeenth-century Dutch economy?

2. Waermondt is no speculator; what does he think of the flower phenomenon? How does his friend react to his skepticism?

3. What seems to be the prevailing Dutch attitude toward money and profit?

4. How does the flower market work?

5. What are the motives behind the speculation? Do you feel the speculators' behavior is ethical?

·86·

Thomas Mun
England's Treasure by Foreign Trade
(1664)

Thomas Mun (1571–1641) was born into a successful London merchant family. His stepfather was a member of the powerful East India Company, as was one of his elder brothers. Mun appears to have traded for a time in the Mediterranean, but in 1615 he became a director of the East India Company. His first economic writings in the 1620s, when a severe depression in trade raised commodity prices, were a defense of overseas trade in general and of the East India Company in particular. Mun argued that the export of precious metals increased rather than decreased the nation's wealth. He continued to serve the East India Company until his death.

England's Treasure was probably written in 1630 but was not published until 1664. It repeated many of Mun's arguments on the balance of trade and the ways in which a nation slowly increased its wealth. Mun's work was influential for over a century after his death and was a central reference point for Adam Smith, who regarded it as the classic statement of mercantilist doctrine.

THE QUALITIES WHICH ARE REQUIRED IN A PERFECT MERCHANT OF FORRAIGN TRADE

The love and service of our Country consisteth not so much in the knowledge of those duties which are to be performed by others, as in the skilful practice of that which is done by our selves; and therefore (my Son) it is now fit that I say something of the Merchant, which I hope in due time shall be thy Vocation: Yet herein are my thoughts free from all Ambition, although I rank thee in a place of so high estimation; for the Merchant is worthily called *The Steward of the Kingdoms Stock*, by way of Commerce with other Nations; a work of no less *Reputation* than *Trust*, which ought to be performed with great skill and conscience, that so the private gain may ever accompany the publique good. And because the nobleness of this Profession may the better stir up thy desires and endeavours to obtain those abilities which may effect it worthily, I will briefly set down the excellent qualities which are required in a perfect Merchant.

1.   He ought to be a good Penman, a good Arithmetician, and a good Accomptant, by that noble order of *Debtor* and *Creditor*, which is used onely amongst Merchants; also to be expert in the order and form of *Charter-parties, Bills of Lading, Invoyces, Contracts, Bills of Exchange*, and *Policies of Ensurance.*

2.   He ought to know the Measures, Weights, and Monies of all forraign Countries, especially where we have Trade, & the Monies not onely by their several denominations, but also by their intrinsique values in weight & fineness, compared with the Standard of this Kingdom, without which he cannot well direct his affaires.

3.   He ought to know the Customs, Tolls, Taxes, Impositions, Conducts and other charges upon all manner of Merchandize exported or imported to and from the said Forraign Countries.

4.   He ought to know in what several commodities each Country abounds, and what be the wares which they want, and how and from whence they are furnished with the same.

5.   He ought to understand, and to be a diligent observer of the rates of Exchanges by Bills, from one State to another, whereby he may the better direct his affairs, and remit over and receive home his Monies to the most advantage possible.

6.   He ought to know what goods are prohibited to be exported or imported in the said forraign Countreys, lest otherwise he should incur great danger and loss in the ordering of his affairs.

7.   He ought to know upon what rates and conditions to fraight his Ships, and ensure his adventures from one Countrey to another, and to be well acquainted with the laws, orders and customes of the Ensurance office both here and beyond the Seas, in the many accidents which may happen upon the damage or loss of Ships or goods, or both these.

8.   He ought to have knowledge in the goodness and in the prices of all the several materials which are required for the building and repairing of Ships, and the divers workmanships of the same, as also for the Masts, Tackling, Cordage, Ordnance, Victuals, Munition, and Provisions of many kinds; together with the ordinary wages of *Commanders, Officers*, and *Mariners*, all which concern the Merchant as he is an Owner of Ships.

9.   He ought (by the divers occasions which happen sometimes in the buying and sell-

ing of one commodity and sometimes in another) to have indifferent if not perfect knowledge in all manner of Merchandize or wares, which is to be as it were a man of all occupations and trades.

10.   He ought by his voyaging on the Seas to become skilful in the Art of Navigation.

11.   He ought, as he is a Traveller, and sometimes abiding in forraign Countreys, to attain to the speaking of divers Languages, and to be a diligent observer of the ordinary Revenues and expences of forraign Princes, together with their strength both by Sea and Land, their laws, customes, policies, manners, religions, arts, and the like; to be able to give account thereof in all occasions for the good of his Countrey.

12.   Lastly, although there be no necessity that such a Merchant should be a great Scholar; yet is it (at least) required, that in his youth he learn the Latine tongue, which will the better enable him in all the rest of his endeavours.

THE MEANS TO ENRICH THIS KINGDOM, AND TO ENCREASE OUR TREASURE

Although a Kingdom may be enriched by gifts received, or by purchase taken from some other Nations, yet these are things uncertain and of small consideration when they happen. The ordinary means therefore to increase our wealth and treasure is by *Forraign Trade,* wherein wee must ever observe this rule; to sell more to strangers yearly than wee consume of theirs in value. For suppose that when this Kingdom is plentifully served with the Cloth, Lead, Tinn, Iron, Fish and other native commodities, we doe yearly export the overplus to forraign Countreys to the value of twenty two hundred thousand pounds; by which means we are enabled beyond the Seas to buy and bring in forraign wares for our use and Consumptions, to the value of twenty hundred thousand pounds: By this order duly kept in our trading, we may rest assured that the Kingdom shall be enriched yearly two hundred

thousand pounds, which must be brought to us in so much Treasure; because that part of our stock which is not returned to us in wares must necessarily be brought home in treasure.

THE EXPORTATION OF OUR MONEYS IN TRADE OF MERCHANDIZE IS A MEANS TO ENCREASE OUR TREASURE

This Position is so contrary to the common opinion, that it will require many and strong arguments to prove it before it can be accepted of the Multitude, who bitterly exclaim when they see any monies carried out of the Realm; affirming thereupon that wee have absolutely lost so much Treasure, and that this is an act directly against the long continued laws made and confirmed by the wisdom of this Kingdom in the High Court of Parliament, and that many places, nay *Spain* it self which is the Fountain of Mony, forbids the exportation thereof, some cases only excepted.

First, I will take that for granted which no man of judgement will deny, that we have no other means to get Treasure but by forraign trade, for Mines wee have none which do afford it, and how this mony is gotten in the managing of our said Trade I have already shewed, that it is done by making our commodities which are exported yearly to over ballance in value the forraign wares which we consume; so that it resteth only to shew how our moneys may be added to our commodities, and being jointly exported may so much the more encrease our Treasure.

Wee have already supposed our yearly consumptions of forraign wares to be for the value of twenty hundred thousand pounds, and our exportations to exceed that two hundred thousand pounds, which sum wee have thereupon affirmed is brought to us in treasure to ballance the accompt. But now if we add three hundred thousand pounds more in ready mony unto our former exportations in wares, what profit can we have (will some men say) although by this means we should bring in so much ready mony more than wee did before, seeing that wee have carried out the like value.

To this the answer is, that when wee have prepared our exportations of wares, and sent out as much of everything as wee can spare or vent abroad: It is not therefore said that then we should add our money thereunto to fetch in the more mony immediately, but rather first to enlarge our trade by enabling us to bring in more forraign wares, which being sent out again will in due time much encrease our Treasure.

For although in this manner wee do yearly multiply our importations to the maintenance of more Shipping and Mariners, improvement of His Majesties Customs and other benefits: yet our consumption of those forraign wares is no more than it was before; so that all the said encrease of commodities brought in by the means of our ready mony sent out as is afore written, doth in the end become an exportation unto us of a far greater value than our said moneys were.

The answer is (keeping our first ground) that if our consumption of forraign wares be no more yearly than is already supposed, and that our exportations be so mightily encreased by this manner of Trading with ready money, as is before declared: It is not then possible but that all the over ballance or difference should return either in mony or in such wares as we must export again, which, as is already plainly shewed will be still a greater means to encrease our Treasure.

For it is in the stock of the Kingdom as in the estates of private men, who having store of wares, doe not therefore say that they will not venture out or trade with their mony (for this were ridiculous) but do also turn that into wares, whereby they multiply their Mony, and so by a continual and orderly change of one into the other grow rich, and when they please turn all their estates into Treasure; for they that have Wares cannot want money.

Neither is it said that Mony is the Life of Trade, as if it could not subsist without the same; for we know that there was great trading by way of commutation or barter when there was little mony stirring in the world. The *Italians* and some other Nations have such remedies against this want, that it can neither decay nor hinder their trade, for they transfer bills of debt, and

have Banks both publick and private, wherein they do assign their credits from one to another daily for very great sums with ease and satisfaction by writings only, whilst in the mean time the Mass of Treasure which gave foundation to these credits is employed in Forraign Trade as a Merchandize, and by the said means they have little other use of money in those countreys more than for their ordinary expences. It is not therefore the keeping of our mony in the Kingdom, but the necessity and use of our wares in forraign Countries, and our want of their commodities that causeth the vent and consumption of all sides, which makes a quick and ample Trade. If wee were once poor, and now having gained some store of mony by trade with resolution to keep it still in the Realm; shall this cause other Nations to spend more of our commodities than formerly they have done, whereby we might say that our trade is Quickned and Enlarged? no verily, it will produce no such good effect: but rather according to the alteration of times by their true causes wee may expect the contrary; for all men do consent that plenty of mony in a Kingdom doth make the native commodities dearer, which as it is to the profit of some private men in their revenues, so is it directly against the benefit of the Publique in the quantity of the trade; for as plenty of mony makes wares dearer, so dear wares decline their use and consumption.

There is yet an objection or two as weak as all the rest: that is, if wee trade with our Mony wee shall issue out the less wares; as if a man should say, those Countreys which heretofore had occasion to consume our Cloth, Lead, Tin, Iron, Fish, and the like, shall now make use of our monies in the place of those necessaries, which were most absurd to affirm, or that the Merchant had not rather carry out wares by which there is ever some gains expected, than to export money which is still but the same without any encrease.

But on the contrary there are many Countreys which may yield us very profitable trade for our mony, which otherwise afford us no trade at all, because they have no use of our wares, as namely the *East Indies* for one in the first beginning thereof, although since by industry in our commerce with those Nations we have brought them into the use of much of our Lead, Cloth, Tin, and other things, which is a good addition to the former vent of our commodities.

Again, some men have alleged that those Countries which permit mony to be carried out, do it because they have few or no wares to trade withall: but wee have great store of commodities, and therefore their action ought not to be our example.

To this the answer is briefly, that if we have such a quantity of wares as doth fully provide us of all things needful from beyond the seas: why should we then doubt that our monys sent out in trade, must not necessarily come back again in treasure; together with the great gains which it may procure in such manner as is before set down? And on the other side, if those Nations which send out their monies do it because they have but few wares of their own, how come they then to have so much Treasure as we ever see in those places which suffer it freely to be exported at all times and by whomsoever? I answer, *Even by trading with their Moneys;* for by what other means can they get it, having no Mines of Gold or Silver?

Thus may we plainly see, that when this weighty business is duly considered in his end, as all our humane actions ought well to be weighed, it is found much contrary to that which most men esteem thereof, because they search no further than the beginning of the work, which misinforms their judgments, and leads them into error: For if we only behold the actions of the husbandman in the seed-time when he casteth away much good corn into the ground, we will rather accompt him a mad man than a husbandman: but when we consider his labours in the harvest which is the end of his endeavours, we find the worth and plentiful encrease of his actions.

1. Even beyond the period when Mun wrote, trade was often considered to be a disreputable occupation. What is Mun's view of the importance of the merchant?

2. Mun gives a long list of the qualities of a good merchant. How are they different from what is required to succeed in business today?

3. How does a nation enrich itself?

4. The common economic argument of Mun's time was that exporting gold and silver coin to pay for imports was wrong. Mun disagrees. Why?

5. How does Mun's position as a merchant affect the presentation of his case?

·87·

Adam Smith
The Wealth of Nations
(1776)

Adam Smith (1723–1790) was the most important representative of the eighteenth-century Scottish enlightenment. Though his father was a customs official, the younger Smith trained for a university career from an early age. Having entered Glasgow University in 1737 at a period when it was one of the leading European centers of learning, he studied moral philosophy and was judged so proficient in his subject that 15 years later he was appointed to the chair of moral philosophy there. His interests turned to law and economics, and he began to formulate the principles that were to underlie his greatest work, *The Wealth of Nations*. Smith subsequently resigned his academic post to travel and lead a quiet life. He died in Edinburgh in 1790.

The Wealth of Nations is one of the classics of Western economic theory. In it, Smith postulates self-interest as the principal motivation of economic activity and demonstrates how a free marketplace enhances economic exchange among self-interested traders. Smith's views remain central to modern capitalist organization and doctrine.

OF THE NATURAL AND MARKET PRICE OF COMMODITIES

There is in every society or neighbourhood an ordinary or average rate both of wages and profit in every different employment of labour and stock. This rate is naturally regulated, as I shall show hereafter, partly by the general circum-

stances of the society, their riches or poverty, their advancing, stationary, or declining condition; and partly by the particular nature of each employment.

There is likewise in every society or neighbourhood an ordinary or average rate of *rent*, which is regulated too, as I shall show hereafter, partly by the general circumstances of the society or neighbourhood in which the land is situated, and partly by the natural or improved fertility of the land.

These ordinary or average rates may be called the natural rates of wages, profit, and rent, at the time and place in which they commonly prevail.

When the price of any commodity is neither more nor less than what is sufficient to pay the rent of the land, the wages of the labour, and the profits of the stock employed in raising, preparing, and bringing to market, according to their natural rates, the commodity is then sold for what may be called its natural price.

The commodity is then sold precisely for what it is worth, or for what it really costs the person who brings it to market; for though in common language what is called the prime cost of any commodity does not comprehend the profit of the person who is to sell it again, yet if he sells it at a price which does not allow him the ordinary rate of profit in his neighbourhood, he is evidently a loser by the trade; since by employing his stock in some other way he might have made that profit. His profit, besides, is his revenue, the

Engraving of Adam Smith by James Tassie, 1787.

proper fund of his subsistence. As, while he is preparing and bringing the goods to market, he advances to his workmen their wages, or their subsistence; so he advances to himself, in the same manner, his own subsistence, which is generally suitable to the profit which he may reasonably expect from the sale of his goods. Unless they yield him this profit, therefore, they do not repay him what they may very properly be said to have really cost him.

Though the price, therefore, which leaves him this profit is not always the lowest at which a dealer may sometimes sell his goods, it is the lowest at which he is likely to sell them for any considerable time; at least where there is perfect liberty, or where he may change his trade as often as he pleases.

The actual price at which any commodity is commonly sold is called its market price. It may either be above, or below, or exactly the same with its natural price.

The market price of every particular commodity is regulated by the proportion between the quantity which is actually brought to market, and the demand of those who are willing to pay the natural price of the commodity, or the whole value of the rent, labour, and profit which must be paid in order to bring it thither. Such people may be called the effectual demanders, and their demand the effectual demand; since it may be sufficient to effectuate the bringing of the commodity to market. It is different from the absolute demand. A very poor man may be said in some sense to have a demand for a coach and six; he might like to have it; but his demand is not an effectual demand, as the commodity can never be brought to market in order to satisfy it.

When the quantity of any commodity which is brought to market falls short of the effectual demand, all those who are willing to pay the whole value of the rent, wages, and profit which must be paid in order to bring it thither, cannot be supplied with the quantity which they want. Rather than want it altogether, some of them will be willing to give more. A competition will immediately begin among them, and the market price will rise more or less above the natural price,

according as either the greatness of the deficiency, or the wealth and wanton luxury of the competitors, happen to animate more or less the eagerness of the competition. Among competitors of equal wealth and luxury the same deficiency will generally occasion a more or less eager competition, according as the acquisition of the commodity happens to be of more or less importance to them. Hence the exorbitant price of the necessaries of life during the blockade of a town or in a famine.

When the quantity brought to market exceeds the effectual demand, it cannot be all sold to those who are willing to pay the whole value of the rent, wages, and profit which must be paid in order to bring it thither. Some part must be sold to those who are willing to pay less, and the low price which they give for it must reduce the price of the whole. The market price will sink more or less below the natural price, according as the greatness of the excess increases more or less the competition of the sellers, or according as it happens to be more or less important to them to get immediately rid of the commodity. The same excess in the importation of perishable, will occasion a much greater competition than in that of durable commodities; in the importation of oranges, for example, than in that of old iron.

When the quantity brought to market is just sufficient to supply the effectual demand and no more, the market price naturally comes to be either exactly, or as nearly as can be judged of, the same with the natural price. The whole quantity upon land can be disposed of for this price, and cannot be disposed of for more. The competition of the different dealers obliges them all to accept of this price, but does not oblige them to accept of less.

The quantity of every commodity brought to market naturally suits itself to the effectual demand. It is the interest of all those who employ their land, labour, or stock in bringing any commodity to market, that the quantity never should exceed the effectual demand; and it is the interest of all other people that it never should fall short of that demand.

If at any time it exceeds the effectual demand, some of the component parts of its price must be paid below their natural rate. If it is rent, the interest of the landlords will immediately prompt them to withdraw a part of their land; and if it is wages or profit, the interest of the labourers in the one case, and of their employers in the other, will prompt them to withdraw a part of their labour or stock from this employment. The quantity brought to market will soon be no more than sufficient to supply the effectual demand. All the different parts of its price will rise to their natural rate, and the whole price to its natural price.

If, on the contrary, the quantity brought to market should at any time fall short of the effectual demand, some of the component parts of its price must rise above their natural rate. If it is rent, the interest of all other landlords will naturally prompt them to prepare more land for the raising of this commodity; if it is wages or profit, the interest of all other labourers and dealers will soon prompt them to employ more labour and stock in preparing and bringing it to market. The quantity brought thither will soon be sufficient to supply the effectual demand. All the different parts of its price will soon sink to their natural rate, and the whole price to its natural price.

But in some employments the same quantity of industry will in different years produce very different quantities of commodities; while in others it will produce always the same, or very nearly the same. The same number of labourers in husbandry will, in different years, produce very different quantities of corn, wine, oil, hops, &c. But the same number of spinners and weavers will every year produce the same or very nearly the same quantity of linen and woollen cloth. It is only the average produce of the one species of industry which can be suited in any respect to the effectual demand; and as its actual produce is frequently much greater and frequently much less than its average produce, the quantity of the commodities brought to market will sometimes exceed a good deal, and sometimes fall short a good deal, of the effectual

demand. Even though that demand therefore should continue always the same, their market price will be liable to great fluctuations, will sometimes fall a good deal below, and sometimes rise a good deal above their natural price. In the other species of industry, the produce of equal quantities of labour being always the same or very nearly the same, it can be more exactly suited to the effectual demand. While that demand continues the same, therefore, the market price of the commodities is likely to do so too, and to be either altogether, or as nearly as can be judged of, the same with the natural price. That the price of linen and woollen cloth is liable neither to such frequent nor to such great variations as the price of corn, every man's experience will inform him. The price of the one species of commodities varies only with the variations in the demand: that of the other varies, not only with the variations in the demand, but with the much greater and more frequent variations in the quantity of what is brought to market in order to supply that demand.

But though the market price of every particular commodity is in this manner continually gravitating, if one may say so, towards the natural price, yet sometimes particular accidents, sometimes natural causes, and sometimes particular regulations of policy, may, in many commodities, keep up the market price for a long time together a good deal above the natural price.

When by an increase in the effectual demand the market price of some particular commodity happens to rise a good deal above the natural price, those who employ their stocks in supplying that market are generally careful to conceal this change. If it was commonly known, their great profit would tempt so many new rivals to employ their stocks in the same way, that, the effectual demand being fully supplied, the market price would soon be reduced to the natural price, and perhaps for some time even below it. If the market is at a great distance from the residence of those who supply it, they may sometimes be able to keep the secret for several years together, and may so long enjoy their extraordinary profits without any new rivals. Secrets of this kind, however, it must be acknowledged, can seldom be long kept; and the extraordinary profit can last very little longer than they are kept.

A monopoly granted either to an individual or to a trading company has the same effect as a secret in trade or manufactures. The monopolists, by keeping the market constantly understocked, by never fully supplying the effectual demand, sell their commodities much above the natural price, and raise their emoluments, whether they consist in wages or profit, greatly above their natural rate.

The price of monopoly is upon every occasion the highest which can be got. The natural price, or the price of free competition, on the contrary, is the lowest which can be taken, not upon every occasion, indeed, but for any considerable time together. The one is upon every occasion the highest which can be squeezed out of the buyers, or which, it is supposed, they will consent to give: the other is the lowest which the sellers can commonly afford to take and at the same time continue their business.

The exclusive privileges of corporations, statutes of apprenticeship, and all those laws which restrain in particular employments the competition to a smaller number than might otherwise go into them, have the same tendency, though in a less degree. They are a sort of enlarged monopolies, and may frequently, for ages together, and in whole classes of employments, keep up the market price of particular commodities above the natural price, and maintain both the wages of the labour and the profits of the stock employed about them somewhat above their natural rate.

Such enhancements of the market price may last as long as the regulations of policy which give occasion to them.

The market price of any particular commodity, though it may continue long above, can seldom continue long below its natural price. Whatever part of it was paid below the natural rate, the persons whose interest it affected would immediately feel the loss, and would immediately withdraw either so much land, or so much labour, or so much stock, from being employed about it, that the quantity brought to market would soon be no more than sufficient to supply the effectual demand. Its market price, therefore, would soon rise to the natural price. This at least would be the case where there was perfect liberty.

1. What is the difference between what Smith defines as the natural price of an item and its market price?

2. How do supply and demand regulate the market?

3. How might merchants manipulate the price of commodities?

4. What is Smith's view of the regulation of markets? What, according to him, is the impact of such regulation?

5. Smith's work has often been pointed to as a masterful statement of the positive nature of free enterprise. What do you think that free enterprise means for Smith?

The Balance of Power in Europe

This engraving by Le Mire is called "The Cake of the Kings: First Partition of Poland, 1773." The monarchs of Russia, Austria, and Prussia join in carving up Poland. The Polish king is clutching his tottering crown.

·88·
Catherine the Great
Memoirs
(ca. 1755)

Catherine II, the Great, who ruled from 1762–1796, was born in Germany in 1729 and married into the Russian royal family. Her marriage was a total disaster, as her husband neglected both his wife and his princely responsibilities. When he finally inherited the throne in 1762, he was so unpopular that Catherine led a coup against him and had herself proclaimed empress. Catherine was considered an "enlightened despot," who ruled with near absolute power, employing the latest philosophical and scientific thinking to improve the lives of their subjects. She is forever linked with Peter the Great (1682–1725) and the transformation of Russia into one of the great European powers.

While Catherine left many important political documents, including a new codification of Russian laws, she wrote a rather remarkable history of her early life as well. It is difficult to establish when her *Memoirs* were begun; they break off abruptly in the 1750s. The *Memoirs* reveal a private side of Catherine and are unusually graphic in their treatment of her childhood and youth.

I was born on April 21st, 1729 (forty-two years ago) at Stettin in Pomerania. I was told later that, a son having been more desired, my arrival as the first-born had given rise to some disappointment. My father, however, showed more satisfaction at the event than all the rest of the entourage. My mother almost died in bringing me into the world and it took her nineteen irksome weeks to recover.

My wet-nurse was the wife of a Prussian soldier; she was only nineteen, gay and pretty. I was placed in the care of a lady who was the widow of a certain Herr von Hohendorf and acted as companion to my mother.

I was told that the lady showed so little sense in her treatment of me that I developed an unaccountable obstinacy. She also showed little sense regarding my mother and was soon dismissed. She was very abrupt and fond of raising her voice; she succeeded so well in her method that I never did as I was told unless the order was repeated at least three times and very loudly.

My father, whom I saw very seldom, considered me to be an angel, my mother did not bother much about me. She had had, eighteen months after my birth, a son whom she passionately loved, whereas I was merely tolerated and often repulsed with violence and temper, not always with justice. I was aware of all this, but not always able to understand what I really felt about it.

At the age of seven I was suddenly seized with a violent cough. It was the custom that we should kneel every night and every morning to say our prayers. One night as I knelt and prayed I began to cough so violently that the strain caused me to fall on my left side, and I had such sharp pains in my chest that they almost took my breath away.

Finally, after much suffering, I was well enough to get up and it was discovered, as they started to put on my clothes, that I had in the meantime assumed the shape of the letter Z; my right shoulder was much higher than the left, the backbone running in a zigzag and the left side falling in. The women who attended me, also my mother's women, whom they consulted, decided to break the news to my father and my mother. The first step undertaken was to swear everybody to secrecy concerning my condition. My parents were distressed to see one of their children lame, the other a cripple. Finally after consulting several experts in strict confidence, it was decided to summon a specialist in matters of dislocation.

They searched for one in vain; they were loath to ask the only man who knew anything about it, as he was the local hangman. For a long time they hesitated. Finally, under a pledge of great secrecy, he was called in. This man, after examining me, ordered that every morning at six, a girl should come to me on an empty stomach and rub my shoulder and backbone with her saliva. Then he proceeded to fabricate a sort of frame, which I never removed day or night except when changing my underclothes, and every other day he came to examine me in the morning. Besides this he made me wear a large black ribbon which went under the neck, crossed the right shoulder round the right arm, and was fastened at the back. I do not know whether it was because of all these remedies or that I was not meant to become a cripple, but after eighteen months I began to show signs of straightening out. I was ten or eleven when I was at last allowed to discard this more cumbersome framework.

At the age of seven all my dolls and other toys were taken away, and I was told that I was now a big girl and therefore it was no longer suitable that I should have them. I had never liked dolls, and found a way of making a plaything out of anything, my hands, a handkerchief, all served that purpose. The trend of my life went on as before and this deprivation of toys must have

been a mere question of etiquette, as no one interfered with me in my games.

I began to grow taller and the extreme ugliness with which I was afflicted was beginning to disappear when I went to visit the future King of Sweden, my uncle, then Bishop of Lübeck.

I do not know if I was actually ugly as a child, but I know that I was so often told that I was and that because of this I should try to acquire wit and other merits that until the age of fourteen or fifteen I was convinced that I was a regular ugly duckling and tried much more to acquire these other virtues than rely upon my face. It is true that I have seen a portrait of myself painted when I was ten, excessively ugly—if it was a good likeness, then I was not being deceived.

The Grand Duke had shown some interest in me during my illness and continued to do so after I recovered. While he seemed to like me, I cannot say that I either liked or disliked him. I was taught to obey and it was my mother's business to see about my marriage, but to tell the truth I believe that the Crown of Russia attracted me more than his person. He was sixteen, quite good-looking before the pox, but small and infantile, talking of nothing but soldiers and toys. I listened politely and often yawned, but did not interrupt him and as he thought that he had to speak to me and referred only to the things which amused him, he enjoyed talking to me for long periods of time. Many people took this for affection, especially those who desired our marriage, but in fact we never used the language of tenderness. It was not for me to begin, for modesty and pride would have prevented me from doing so even if I had had any tender feelings for him; as for him, he had never even thought of it, which did not greatly incline me in his favour. Young girls may be as well brought up as you could wish, but they like sweet nonsense, especially from those whom they can hear it without blushing.

The next day, St. Peter's Day, when my betrothal was to be celebrated, the Empress's portrait framed in diamonds was brought to me early in the morning, and shortly afterwards the portrait of the Grand Duke, also encircled with diamonds. Soon after, he came to take me to the Empress who, wearing her crown and Imperial mantle, proceeded on her way under a canopy of massive silver, carried by eight major-generals and followed by the Grand Duke and myself. After me came my mother, the Princess of Homburg, and the other ladies according to their rank.

Towards St. Peter's Day the whole Court returned from Peterhof to town. I remember that on the eve of that feast I suddenly had the fancy to have all my ladies and maids sleeping in my room. For that purpose I had my mattress as well as theirs stretched out on the floor and that is how we spent the night, but before we went to sleep we had a prolonged discussion on the difference between the sexes.

I am certain that most of us were extremely innocent; for myself I can testify that though I was more than sixteen years old, I had no idea what this difference was; I went so far as to promise my women to question my mother the next morning about; they agreed that I should do so and we went to sleep. Next day I put the question to my mother and was severely scolded.

At last all the preparations for my wedding were almost completed and the day was fixed for August 21st of this year 1745. In vain did the doctors point out to the Empress that the delicate Grand Duke, who had only just recovered from a severe illness, had not yet reached puberty and that it would be wise to wait another few years.

The nearer my wedding-day approached, the more despondent did I become, and often found myself crying without quite knowing why; I tried to conceal my tears as much as I could, but my women, who were constantly with me, could not help noticing my distress and tried to divert me. On the eve of the 21st we moved from the Summer to the Winter Palace. Until then I had lived in the stone building in the Summer Place which gives on to the Fontanka behind the pavilion of Peter I. In the evening my mother came to my rooms. We had a long and friendly

talk, she exhorted me concerning my future duties, we cried a little together and parted very tenderly.

On the day of the ceremony I rose at 6 a.m. At eight the Empress ordered me to her apartments where I was to be dressed. I found a dressing-table prepared in her State bedroom and her Court ladies were already there. First came the hair-dressing and my valet was busy curling my forelock when the Empress came in. I rose to kiss her hand; as soon as she had embraced me, she began to scold my valet and forbade him to curl my fringe.

She wanted my hair to be flat in front because the jewels would not stay on my head if the forelock was curled. Having said this, she left the room. My man, who was obdurate, would not give up his curled forelock. He persuaded Countess Rumiantsev who herself affected curly hair and did not care for smooth dressing, to speak to the Empress in favour of the forelock. After the Countess had gone three or four journeys between the Empress and my valet, while I remained an impartial spectator of what was going on, the Empress sent word, not without anger, that he could do as he wished.

When my hair was dressed, the Empress came to place the Grand Ducal crown on my head and told me I could wear as many jewels as I wanted, both hers and mine. She left the room and the Court ladies continued dressing me in my mother's presence. My dress was of a silver moiré, embroidered in silver on all the hems, and of a terrible weight.

I would have been ready to like my new husband had he been capable of affection or willing to show any. But in the very first days of our marriage I came to a sad conclusion about him. I said to myself: 'If you allow yourself to love that man, you will be the unhappiest creature on this earth; with your temperament you will expect some response whereas this man scarcely looks at you, talks of nothing but dolls or such things, and pays more attention to any other woman than yourself; you are too proud to complain, therefore, attention, please, and keep on a leash any affection you might feel for this gentleman; you have yourself to think about, my dear girl.' This first scar made upon my impressionable heart remained with me for ever; never did this firm resolution leave my noddle, but I took good care not to tell anybody that I had resolved never to love without restraint a man who would not return this love in full; such was my disposition that my heart would have belonged entirely and without reserve to a husband who loved only me and who would not have subjected me to taunts as this one did.

I have always considered jealousy, suspicion, mistrust, and all that follows them as the greatest misery, and maintained that it depended on the husband whether his wife loved him; if a woman has a kind heart and gentle disposition, a husband's courtesy and good nature would soon win her.

1. If Catherine's case may be taken as typical, what was childhood like for a member of a royal family in the eighteenth century?

2. Why did Catherine marry the heir to the Russian throne? What was her relationship with her husband like?

3. A memoir tells the story of an individual's life, but an author is always in a position to shape the story. How might Catherine have used her own memoir to justify her later coup against her husband?

4. Royal marriages were acts of state, not private affairs. Did Catherine appear to realize this when she married?

5. What sort of impression does Catherine's memoir make upon you? What sort of a person do you think the empress was?

·89·

Maria Theresa
Testament
(1749–1750)

Maria Theresa (1717–1780) was one of the most capable of all of the Habsburgs who ruled the Holy Roman Empire. After the death of her only brother, Maria's father, Emperor Charles VI, promulgated the Pragmatic Sanction, which allowed a woman to rule the empire (though not to take the title emperor). Maria Theresa came into this inheritance at the age of 23 and was immediately embroiled in warfare that aimed at dismembering her territories. She confounded the sages of Europe by rallying her people and repelling a Prussian invasion.

Her *Testament* details the reforms she initiated in her states. It is written mostly as an apologetic history, assessing praise and blame and casting her own actions in the best possible light, but it also shows flashes of her dynamic personality and shrewd political abilities.

Instructions drawn up out of motherly solicitude for the especial benefit of my posterity. I have thought well to divide these in sections according to their importance.

The first describes the situation of the Monarchy, both internal and international, as I found it when I began my reign.

The second, the abuses which gradually crept into the said Monarchy under my predecessors.

The third, the measures introduced during the nine difficult years of the recent war, and the reasons which induced me to take them.

The fourth, the changes effected after the conclusion of general peace in the internal constitution of the Ministries and the Provinces, in accordance with the system established for the preservation of the Monarchy.

The fifth, the benefit that will accrue to my posterity from this reorganization, this being the only means of consolidating the Monarchy and perserving it for my posterity.

The sixth, the necessity of maintaining the institutions so established, to avert ruin, and what maxims my successors must follow to achieve this end.

From the outset I decided and made it my principle, for my own inner guidance, to apply myself, with a pure mind and instant prayer to God, to put aside all secondary considerations, arrogance, ambition, or other passions, having on many occasions examined myself in respect of these things, and to undertake the business of government incumbent on me quietly and resolutely—a principle that has, indeed, been the one guidance which saved me, with God's help, in my great need, and made me follow the resolutions taken by me, making it ever my chief maxim in all I did and left undone to trust only in God, Whose almighty hand singled me out for

this position without move or desire of my own and Who would therefore also make me worthy through my conduct, principles, and intentions to fulfill properly the tasks laid on me, and thus to call down and preserve His almighty protection for myself and those He has set under me, which truth I had held daily before my eyes and maturely considered that my duty was not to myself personally but only to the public.

After I had each time well tested my intentions by this principle, I afterwards undertook each enterprise with great determination and strong resolution, and was consequently tranquil in my spirit in the greatest extremity as though the issue did not affect me personally at all; and with the same tranquillity and pleasure, had Divine Providence so disposed, I would instantly have laid down the whole government and left it to the enemies who so beset me, had I believed that in so doing I would be doing my duty or promoting the best welfare of my lands, which two points have always been my chief maxims. And dearly as I love my family and children, so that I spare no effort, trouble, care, or labor for their sakes, yet I would always have put the general welfare of my dominions above them had I been convinced in my conscience that I should do this or that their welfare demanded it, seeing that I am the general and first mother of the said dominions.

I found myself in this situation, without money, without credit, without army, without experience and knowledge of my own and finally, also without any counsel, because each one of them at first wanted to wait and see what way things would develop.

In the first, difficult years of my reign it was quite impossible for me personally to investigate the conditions and resources of the Provinces, so that I was obliged to follow my Ministers' advice not to ask any more help from the Provinces, either in money or men, especially since the Ministers constantly pretended that any such demands would make my reign deeply detested at its very outset. Consequently, there was no money to mobilize the few regiments earmarked for use against Prussia. And when I found myself forced to ask for this purpose for some hundreds of thousands as loans or urgent grants in aid from private persons, I could not but see that the big men, and even the Ministers themselves, were plainly trying to spare their own pockets.

I have described the defects and abuses of the Constitution then in effect, and felt myself the more compelled to abolish it, because Divine Providence had shown me clearly that the measures essential for the preservation of the Monarchy could not be combined with these old institutions, nor put into effect while they existed.

Each one of my Ministers readily agreed that if the Crown and scepter were to be preserved, it was most necessary to keep a standing force of over 100,000 men, and consequently indispensable to bring a new system and order into the extreme confusion into which the finances had fallen.

To this end, I instructed the Ministers to put their views to me in writing, and to work out such a system as speedily as possible. When, however, no constructive idea emerged, my repeated reminders notwithstanding, and when I saw that the Ministers were more inclined to spread themselves in controversy and argument than genuinely to take the problem in hand—urgent as it was—that the work dragged on and on, and that no one was willing, or able, to attack the problem seriously, then, however, by the especial intervention and Providence of God, and to the salvation of these lands, I became acquainted with Count Haugwitz.

He was truly sent to me by Providence, for to break the deadlock I needed such a man, honorable, disinterested, without predispositions, and with neither ambition nor hangers-on, who supported what was good because he saw it to be good, of magnanimous disinterestedness and

attachment to his Monarch, unprejudiced, with great capacity and industry and untiring diligence, not afraid to come into the open or to draw on himself the unjust hatred of interested parties.

Difficulties came with the three Inner Austrian Provinces. All the Austrian Provinces, but particularly these three, had managed their affairs in so irresponsible and unbusinesslike a fashion that the Court—that is, the Chancelleries of the day—had allowed them to accumulate a so-called domestic debt of twenty-four million, the interest on which amounted to 200,000 gulden. It was the financial weakness of these lands that involved them in this big debt, and was also the reason why the quotas allocated to them were regarded in advance as impossibly high, and in certain cases could really be regarded as such.

The Estates' persistent representations that the burdens were too heavy for them, which were not without their force, although the fault lay in their own unbusinesslike methods, naturally led me to make provision for a better and more equitable management of the local finances. And I must insist that it is generally true that the prime cause of the decay of my Hereditary Lands lies in the overgreat freedom the Estates had gradually usurped; for the Estates seldom behaved justly, their Presidents usually simply doing as their predecessors had done and furthering their private advantages, while refusing or rejecting any help that justice demanded should be given to the poor oppressed classes, and thus as a rule letting one Estate oppress another.

The final purpose of most of the so-called prerogatives of the Estates was simply to secure an arbitrary free hand for some of their members, who claimed an inordinate authority over the rest.

It was formerly the easier for all this to go on because the said overpowerful members of the Estates, who usually made common cause with the Ministers in charge of the Provinces, generally had in their hands the fortunes, both of the

Crown and of the Estates themselves, and thus disposed of them according to their pleasure, for which very reason the Ministers here in Vienna gave every support to the prerogatives which brought them so much advantage.

And although the result was only detriment to the public interest, yet the Estates insisted on these prerogatives the more stubbornly because most of them failed to understand the position and easily allowed themselves to be hoodwinked by these their own representatives.

Neither do I myself wish, nor do I advise my successors, to encroach on the useful and legitimate privileges of the Estates, seeing that the welfare of my dominions is inexpressibly dear to me, and I cannot repeat often enough that if I had found their privileges so clear, or if they had conducted the administration more justly than I or the Crown, I should not merely not have hesitated to submit and abrogate my authority entirely to them, I should rather myself have diminished and renounced or limited it for my successors, because I should always have placed the welfare and prosperity of the Provinces before my own or that of my family and children.

But neither my own interest nor that of my successors, and least of all the public interest, can be sacrificed to illegitimate abuses which have taken root with the connivance of the Ministers; wherefore such alleged privileges as are founded on abuse and an evil tradition should not be confirmed without extreme caution and careful consideration, and I have often observed that Crown rights which have fallen into desuetude through the connivance of the Ministers are questioned with the object of tying the Monarch's hands in these respects also; this applies above all to the supervision of the Estates' domestic funds and the management of them, and also to the equalization and adjustment of taxation, which should be conscientiously undertaken in the interest of justice and of the general welfare.

In order to put all this on a firm and lasting foundation, I found myself forced to depart from the old, traditional Constitution, with the detrimental qualities which it had acquired, and to enact such new measures as could be harmonized with the new system.

1. How does Maria Theresa's *Testament* differ in style and content from Catherine the Great's *Memoirs?*

2. What problems did Maria Theresa face when she came to the throne?

3. Maria Theresa was one of the so-called enlightened despots of the eighteenth century. How do enlightenment and despotism manifest themselves in her *Testament?*

4. What stood in the way of reform in Maria Theresa's Austria?

5. Maria Theresa approaches her task with a set of political assumptions common among European rulers of the early modern period. What are these assumptions, and how are they reflected in her *Testament?*

·90·

Thomas Jefferson
The Declaration of Independence
(1776)

*T*homas Jefferson (1743–1826) was born into one of Virginia's most prominent families. With wide-ranging interests—from architecture to education to politics—he spent most of his early life on his plantation studying the wisdom of the past. Jefferson had an abiding interest in politics and first served in the Virginia colonial assembly. In 1775 he was named a delegate to the Second Continental Congress, where he quickly distinguished himself as a speaker and writer. During the American Revolution he served as governor of Virginia, was the first secretary of state in the Washington government, was vice-president, and in 1801 was elected president of the United States. After his retirement from public life, he founded the University of Virginia in 1819. He is today regarded as one of the greatest of all American thinkers.

Jefferson wrote *The Declaration of Independence* at the request of the Continental Congress. This document was at once a succinct statement of liberal principles and a brilliant piece of political propaganda. The *Declaration* is one of the central documents in the history of democratic government.

IN CONGRESS, JULY 4, 1776.

The unanimous Declaration of the Thirteen United States of America.

When in the Course of human events, it becomes necessary for one people to dissolve the political bands which have connected them with another, and to assume among the Powers of the earth, the separate and equal station to which the Laws of Nature and of Nature's God entitle them, a decent respect to the opinions of mankind requires that they should declare the causes which impel them to the separation.

We hold these truths to be self-evident, that all men are created equal, that they are endowed by their Creator with certain unalienable Rights, that among these are Life, Liberty and the pursuit of Happiness. That to secure these rights, Governments are instituted among Men, deriving their just powers from the consent of the governed, That whenever any Form of Government becomes destructive of these ends, it is the Right of the People to alter or to abolish it, and to institute new Government, laying its foundation on such principles and organizing its powers in such form, as to them shall seem most likely to effect their Safety and Happiness. Prudence, indeed, will dictate that Governments long established should not be changed for light and transient causes; and accordingly all experience hath shown, that mankind are more disposed to suffer, while evils are sufferable, than to right themselves by abolishing the forms to which they are

"The Declaration of Independence" painted by John Trumbull (1756–1843).

accustomed. But when a long train of abuses and usurpations, pursuing invariably the same Object, evinces a design to reduce them under absolute Despotism, it is their right, it is their duty to throw off such Government, and to provide new Guards for their future security. Such has been the patient sufferance of these Colonies; and such is now the necessity which constrains them to alter their former Systems of Government. The history of the present King of Great Britain is a history of repeated injuries and usurpations, all having in direct object the establishment of an absolute Tyranny over these States. To prove this, let Facts be submitted to a candid world.

He has refused his Assent to Laws, the most wholesome and necessary for the public good.

He has forbidden his Governors to pass Laws of immediate and pressing importance, unless suspended in their operation till his Assent should be obtained; and when so suspended, he has utterly neglected to attend to them.

He has refused to pass other Laws for the accommodation of large districts of people, unless those people would relinquish the right of Representation in the Legislature, a right inestimable to them and formidable to tyrants only.

He has called together legislative bodies at places unusual, uncomfortable, and distant from the depository of their Public Records, for the sole purpose of fatiguing them into compliance with his measures.

He has dissolved Representative Houses repeatedly, for opposing with manly firmness his invasions on the rights of the people.

He has refused for a long time, after such dissolutions to cause others to be elected; whereby the Legislative Powers, incapable of Annihilation, have returned to the People at large for their exercise; the State remaining in the mean time exposed to all the dangers of invasion from without, and convulsions within.

He has endeavoured to prevent the population of these States; for that purpose obstructing the Laws for Naturalization of Foreigners; refusing to pass others to encourage their migrations hither, and raising the conditions of new Appropriations of Lands.

He has obstructed the Administration of Justice, by refusing his Assent to Laws for establishing Judiciary Powers.

He has made Judges dependent on his Will alone, for the tenure of their offices, and the amount and payment of their salaries.

He has erected a multitude of New Offices, and sent hither swarms of Officers to harass our People, and eat out their substance.

He has kept among us, in times of peace, Standing Armies without the Consent of our legislatures.

He has affected to render the Military independent of and superior to the Civil Power.

He has combined with others to subject us to a jurisdiction foreign to our constitution, and unacknowledged by our laws; giving his Assent to their Acts of pretended Legislation:

For quartering large bodies of armed troops among us:

For protecting them, by a mock Trial, from Punishment for any Murders which they should commit on the Inhabitants of these States:

For cutting off our Trade with all parts of the world:

For imposing taxes on us without our Consent:

For depriving us in many cases, of the benefits of Trial by Jury:

For transporting us beyond Seas to be tried for pretended offences:

For abolishing the free System of English Laws in a neighboring Province, establishing therein an Arbitrary government, and enlarging its Boundaries so as to render it at once an example and fit instrument for introducing the same absolute rule into these Colonies:

For taking away our Charters, abolishing our most valuable Laws, and altering fundamentally the Forms of our Governments:

For suspending our own Legislatures, and declaring themselves invested with Power to legislate for us in all cases whatsoever.

He has abdicated Government here, by declaring us out of his Protection and waging War against us.

He has plundered our seas, ravaged our Coasts, burnt our towns, and destroyed the lives of our people.

He is at this time transporting large armies of foreign mercenaries to compleat the works of death, desolation and tyranny, already begun with circumstances of Cruelty & Perfidy scarcely paralleled in the most barbarous ages, and totally unworthy the Head of a civilized nation.

He has constrained our fellow Citizens taken Captive on the high Seas to bear Arms against their Country, to become the executioners of their friends and Brethren, or to fall themselves by their Hands.

He has excited domestic insurrections amongst us, and has endeavoured to bring on the inhabitants of our frontiers, the merciless Indian Savages, whose known rule of warfare, is an undistinguished destruction of all ages, sexes and conditions.

In every stage of these Oppressions We have Petitioned for Redress in the most humble terms: Our repeated Petitions have been answered only be repeated injury. A Prince, whose character is thus marked by every act which may define a Tyrant, is unfit to be the ruler of a free People.

Nor have We been wanting in attention to our British brethren. We have warned them from time to time of attempts by their legislature to extend an unwarrantable jurisdiction over us. We have reminded them of the circumstances of our emigration and settlement here. We have appealed to their native justice and magnanimity and we have conjured them by the ties of our common kindred to disavow these usurpations, which would inevitably interrupt our connections and correspondence. They too have been deaf to the voice of justice and of consanguinity. We must, therefore, acquiesce in the necessity which denounces our Separation, and hold them, as we hold the rest of mankind, Enemies in War, in Peace Friends.

We, therefore, the Representatives of the united States of America, in General Congress, Assembled, appealing to the Supreme Judge of the world for the rectitude of our intentions, do, in the Name, and by Authority of the good People of these Colonies, solemnly publish and declare, That these United Colonies are, and of Right ought to be Free and Independent States; that they are Absolved from all allegiance to the British Crown, and that all political connection between them and the State of Great Britain, is and ought to be totally dissolved; and that as Free and Independent States, they have full power to levy War, conclude Peace, contract Alliances, establish Commerce, and to do all other Acts and Things which Independent States may of right do. And for the support of the Declaration, with a firm reliance on the Protection of Divine Providence, we mutually pledge to each other our Lives, our Fortunes and our sacred Honor.

1. *The Declaration of Independence* is a statement of political principles—what are they?

2. The *Declaration* was meant to be a piece of political propaganda as well as political philosophy. How is this reflected in the document?

3. Why does Jefferson single out George III as the principal villain in his story?

4. Jefferson's argument was very persuasive for many people, but there were also those who remained unconvinced. Can you construct an argument against his case?

5. The *Declaration*'s ultimate goal is the achievement of the public welfare. This was also the aim of enlightened despots such as Maria Theresa. Would Jefferson and Maria Theresa agree about what the "public good" was? How would their means to this common end differ?

·91·

Viscount Bolingbroke
The Idea of a Patriot King
(1749)

*H*enry St. John, Viscount Bolingbroke (1678–1751), was the son of a prominent English gentleman. His social position and talents marked him for advancement in politics, and he entered Parliament before the age of 25. Queen Anne appointed him secretary of war in 1706, in which capacity he became one of England's most important political figures. After a brief spell out of office, Bolingbroke returned as secretary of state in 1710. Bolingbroke opposed the Hanoverian succession and was dismissed from office and impeached by the government of George I. He fled to France in 1715 and devoted himself to pleasure and writing. He was as famous for his extravagant lifestyle as he was for his books. He was welcomed back to England in 1723 and became a foe of Sir Robert Walpole and the Whigs.

The Idea of a Patriot King, written in 1738 and published 11 years later, was addressed to George II's eldest son, Prince Frederick; but in fact its greatest influence was upon George III and his chief minister, the Earl of Bute. Bolingbroke argued against the rule of parties, urging the patriot king to put the national interest ahead of all others.

Now we are subject, by the constitution of human nature, and therefore by the will of the Author of this and every other nature, to two laws. One given immediately to all men by God, the same to all, and obligatory alike on all. The other given to man by man; and therefore not the same to all, nor obligatory alike on all: founded indeed on the same principles, but varied by different applications of them to times, to characters, and to a number which may be reckoned infinite, of other circumstances. By the first you see, that I mean the universal law of reason; and by the second the particular law, or constitution of laws, by which every distinct community has chosen to be governed.

The obligation of submission to both, is discoverable by so clear and so simple a use of our intellectual faculties, that it may be said properly enough to be *revealed to us by God;* and though *both* these laws cannot be said properly to be given by Him, yet our obligation to submit to the *civil* law is a principal paragraph in the *natural* law, which he has most manifestly given us. In truth we can no more doubt of the obligations of both these laws, than of the existence of the lawgiver. As supreme lord over all his works, his *general* providence regards immediately the *great commonwealth* of mankind; but then, as supreme Lord likewise, his authority gives a sanction to the *particular bodies* of law which are made under it. The law of *nature* is the law of *all* his subjects: the constitutions of *particular* governments are like the *bylaws* of cities, or the appropriated customs of provinces. It follows, therefore, that he who breaks the *laws of his country* resists the *ordinance of God,* that is, the law of his nature. God has instituted neither monarchy, nor aristocracy, nor democracy, nor mixed government: but though God has instituted no particular form of government among men, yet by the general laws of his kingdom, he exacts our obedience to the laws of those communities to which each of us is attached by birth, or to which we may be attached by a subsequent and lawful engagement.

From such plain, unrefined, and therefore I suppose true reasoning, the *just authority* of *kings,* and the *due obedience* of *subjects,* may be deduced with the utmost certainty. And surely it is far better for kings themselves to have their authority thus founded on principles incontestible, and on fair deductions from them, than on the chimeras of madmen, or, what has been more common, the sophisms of knaves. A *human right,* that cannot be controverted, is preferable surely to a *pretended divine right,* which every man must believe implicitly, as few will do, or not believe at all.

But the principles we have laid down do not stop here. A divine right in kings is to be deduced evidently from them. A divine right to govern *well,* and conformably to the constitution at the head of which they are placed. A divine right to govern *ill,* is an absurdity: to assert it is blasphemy. A people may choose, or hereditary succession may raise, a *bad* prince to the throne; but a *good* king alone can derive his right to govern from *God.* The reason is plain: good government alone can be in the divine intention. God has made us to desire happiness; he has made our happiness dependent on society; and the happiness of society dependent on good or bad government. His intention therefore was, that government should be *good.*

This is essential to his wisdom; for wisdom consists surely in proportioning means to ends: therefore it cannot be said without absurd impiety, that he confers a right to oppose his intention.

The office of kings is then of *right divine,* and their persons are to be reputed *sacred.* As *men,* they have no such *right,* no such sacredness belonging to them: as *kings* they have both, unless they forfeit them. Reverence for government obliges to reverence governors, who, for the sake of it, are raised above the level of other men: but reverence for governors, independently of government, any further than reverence would be due to their virtues if they were private men, is preposterous, and repugnant to common sense. The spring from which this legal reverence, for so I may call it, arises, is *national,* not *personal.*

All this is as true of *elective,* as it is of *hereditary* monarchs; though the scriblers for tyranny, under the name of monarchy, would have us believe that there is something more august, and more sacred in one than the other. They are sacred *alike,* and this attribute is to be ascribed, or not ascribed to them, as they answer, or do not answer, the *Ends* of their institution. But there is another comparison to be made, in which a great and most important dissimilitude will be found between hereditary and elective monarchy. Nothing can be more absurd, in pure *speculation,* than an hereditary right in any mortal to govern other men: and yet, in *practice,* nothing can be more absurd than to have a king to choose at every vacancy of a throne. We draw at a *lottery* indeed in one case, where there are many chances to lose, and few to gain. But have we much more advantage of this kind in the other? I think not.

To conclude this head therefore, I think a *limited monarchy* the best of governments, so I think an *hereditary monarchy* the best of monarchies. I said a *limited monarchy;* for an *unlimited monarchy,* wherein arbitrary will, which is in truth no rule, is however the sole rule, or stands instead of all rule of government, is so great an absurdity, both in reason unformed or uninformed by experience, that it seems a government fitter for savages than for civilized people.

But I think it proper to explain a little more what I mean, when I say a *limited* monarchy, that I may leave nothing untouched which ought to be taken into consideration by us, when we attempt to fix our ideas of a Patriot King.

Among many reasons which determine me to prefer *monarchy* to every form of government, this is a principal one. When monarchy is the essential form, it may be more easily and more usefully *tempered* with *aristocracy* or *democracy,* or both, than either of them, when they are the essential forms, can be *tempered* with *monarchy.* It seems to me, that the introduction of a real permanent monarchical power, or any thing more than the pageantry of it, into either of these, must destroy them and extinguish them, as a great light extinguishes a less. Whereas it may easily be shewn, and the true form of our government will demonstrate, without seeking any other example, that very considerable *aristocratical* and *democratical powers* may be grafted on a *monarchical stock,* without diminishing the lustre, or restraining the power and authority of the prince, enough to alter in any degree the essential form.

A great difference is made in nature, and therefore the distinction should be always preserved in our notions, between two things that we are apt to confound in speculation, as they have been confounded in practice, *legislative* and *monarchical power.* There must be an absolute, unlimited, and uncontrollable power lodged *somewhere* in every government; but to constitute monarchy, or the government of a single person, it is not necessary that this power should be lodged in the monarch *alone.* It is no more necessary that he should exclusively and independently establish the rule of his government, than it is, that he should govern without any rule at all: and this surely will be thought reasonable by no man.

The *good of the people* is the ultimate and true *end* of government. Governors are therefore appointed for *this end,* and the civil constitution which appoints them, and invests them with their power, is determined to do so by the *law of nature* and *reason,* which has determined the *end* of government, and which admits this *form* of government as the proper means of arriving at it. Now the greatest good of a people is their liberty: and in the case here referred to, the people

has judged it so, and provided for it accordingly. *Liberty* is to the collective body, what *health* is to every individual body. Without *health* no pleasure can be tasted by man: without *liberty* no happiness can be enjoyed by *society.* The obligation, therefore, to defend and maintain the freedom of such constitutions, will appear most sacred to a Patriot King.

Kings who have weak understandings, bad hearts, and strong prejudices, and all these, as it often happens, inflamed by their passions, and rendered incurable by their self-conceit and presumption; such kings are apt to imagine, and they conduct themselves so as to make many of their subjects imagine, that the king and the people in free governments are *rival powers,* who stand in *competition* with one another, who have *different interests,* and must of course have different *views:* that the *rights* and *privileges* of the people are so many *spoils* taken from the *right* and *prerogative* of the crown; and that the rules and laws, made for the exercise and security of the former, are so many *diminutions* of their dignity, and *restraints* on their power.

A Patriot King will see all this in a far different, and much truer light. The constitution will be considered by him as *one law,* consisting of *two tables,* containing the rule of his government, and the measure of his subjects obedience; or as *one system,* composed of *different parts* and *powers,* but all duly proportioned to one another, and conspiring by their harmony to the perfection of the whole. He will make one, and *but one* distinction between his rights, and those of his people: he will look on his to be a *trust,* and theirs a *property,* He will discern, that he can have a right to no more than is trusted to him by the constitution: and that his people, who had an original right to the *whole* by the law of nature, can have the sole indefeasible right to *any part;* and really have such a right to *that part* which they have reserved to themselves. In fine, the *constitution* will be reverenced by him as the *law of God* and of *man;* the *force* of which binds the king as *much* as the meanest subject, and the *reason* of which binds him *much more.*

1. What is the duty of a subject to his government?

2. How does Bolingbroke modify the old idea of divine right monarchy?

3. What is the importance of liberty in a state, according to Bolingbroke?

4. What is a patriot king?

5. Bolingbroke wrote after long experience in the service of a constitutional monarchy, in which power was shared by the king and parliament, and contested between political parties. How might this experience have affected the assumptions the author made about the workings of the constitution?

Asia Alone

Official court painting of the emperor Kang Hsi (1661–1722).

·92·

Yamamoto Tsunetomo
Hagakure (The Book of the Samurai)

(1716)

Yamamoto Tsunetomo (1659–1720) was a scribe to the samurai Nabeshima Mitsushige, a provincial governor of the Tokugawa. Yamamoto's father had served the same family, but it was not until he was 20 that Yamamoto secured his position. In his youth he was deeply influenced by a Zen Buddhist monk and a Confucian scholar, whose traditions merged in the cult of the samurai that Yamamoto was to perpetuate. He served Mitsushige until his master's death in 1700. He was prohibited from performing the ritual suicide that was still common when one's retainer died. Instead he became a Buddhist priest. Nothing is known of the rest of his life.

The Book of the Samurai was dictated by Yamamoto to his own scribe. It contains the accumulated wisdom of three generations of the Nabeshima family, and reflects the changed circumstances of the warrior class after the end of Japan's century of civil war. Mitsushige had never fought in battle and his most vital pursuits were literary rather than martial, but the codes of the samurai, which were passed from generation to generation, were central to his life and to Yamamoto's dictates.

Although it stands to reason that a samurai should be mindful of the Way of the Samurai, it would seem that we are all negligent. Consequently, if someone were to ask, "What is the true meaning of the Way of the Samurai?" the person who would be able to answer promptly is rare. This is because it has not been established in one's mind beforehand. From this, one's unmindfulness of the Way can be known.

Negligence is an extreme thing.

The Way of the Samurai is found in death. When it comes to either/or, there is only the quick choice of death. It is not particularly difficult. Be determined and advance. To say that dying without reaching one's aim is to die a dog's death is the frivolous way of sophisticates. When pressed with the choice of life or death, it is not necessary to gain one's aim.

We all want to live. And in large part we make our logic according to what we like. But not having attained our aim and continuing to live is cowardice. This is a thin dangerous line. To die without gaining one's aim *is* a dog's death and fanaticism. But there is no shame in this. This is the substance of the Way of the Samurai. If by setting one's heart right every morning and evening, one is able to live as though his body were already dead, he gains freedom in the Way. His whole life will be without blame, and he will succeed in his calling.

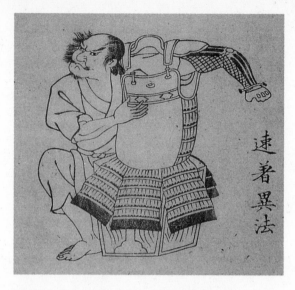

Woodcut illustration from the Tanki Yoryaku *(a horseman's armor-wearing manual) by Masahiro Mura.*

A man is a good retainer to the extent that he earnestly places importance in his master. This is the highest sort of retainer. If one is born into a prominent family that goes back for generations, it is sufficient to deeply consider the matter of obligation to one's ancestors, to lay down one's body and mind, and to earnestly esteem one's master. It is further good fortune if, more than this, one has wisdom and talent and can use them appropriately. But even a person who is good for nothing and exceedingly clumsy will be a reliable retainer if only he has the determination to think earnestly of his master. Having only wisdom and talent is the lowest tier of usefulness.

According to their nature, there are both people who have quick intelligence, and those who must withdraw and take time to think things over. Looking into this thoroughly, if one thinks selflessly and adheres to the four vows of the Nabeshima samurai, surprising wisdom will occur regardless of the high or low points of one's nature.

People think that they can clear up profound matters if they consider them deeply, but they exercise perverse thoughts and come to no good because they do their reflecting with only self-interest at the center.

It is difficult for a fool's habits to change to selflessness. In confronting a matter, however, if at first you leave it alone, fix the four vows in your heart, exclude self-interest, and make an effort, you will not go far from your mark.

Because we do most things relying only on our own sagacity we become self-interested, turn our backs on reason, and things do not turn out well. As seen by other people this is sordid, weak, narrow and inefficient. When one is not capable of true intelligence, it is good to consult with someone of good sense. An advisor will fulfill the Way when he makes a decision by selfless and frank intelligence because he is not personally involved. This way of doing things will certainly be seen by others as being strongly rooted. It is, for example, like a large tree with many roots. One man's intelligence is like a tree that has been simply stuck in the ground.

Being a retainer is nothing other than being a supporter of one's lord, entrusting matters of good and evil to him, and renouncing self-interest. If there are but two or three men of this type, the fief will be secure.

If one looks at the world when affairs are going smoothly, there are many who go about putting in their appearance, being useful by their wisdom, discrimination and artfulness. However, if the lord should retire or go into seclusion, there are many who will quickly turn their backs on him and ingratiate themselves to the man of the day. Such a thing is unpleasant even to think about. Men of high position, low position, deep wisdom and artfulness all feel that *they* are the ones who are working righteously, but when it comes to the point of throwing away one's life for his lord, all get weak in the knees. This is rather disgraceful. The fact that a useless person often becomes a matchless warrior at such times is because he has already given up his life and has become one with his lord. . . .

Loyalty is said to be important in the pledge between lord and retainer. Though it may seem unobtainable, it is right before your eyes. If you once set yourself to it, you will become a superb retainer at that very moment.

To give a person one's opinion and correct his faults is an important thing. It is compassionate and comes first in matters of service. But the way of doing this is extremely difficult. To discover the good and bad points of a person is an easy thing, and to give an opinion concerning them is easy, too. For the most part, people think that they are being kind by saying the things that others find distasteful or difficult to say. But if it is not received well, they think that there is nothing more to be done. This is completely worthless. It is the same as bringing shame to a person by slandering him. It is nothing more than getting it off one's chest.

To give a person an opinion one must first judge well whether that person is of the disposition to receive it or not. One must become close with him and make sure that he continually trusts one's word. Approaching subjects that are dear to him, seek the best way to speak and to be well understood. Judge the occasion, and determine whether it is better by letter or at the time of leave-taking. Praise his good points and use every device to encourage him, perhaps by talking about one's own faults without touching on his, but so that they will occur to him. Have him receive this in the way that a man would drink water when his throat is dry, and it will be an opinion that will correct faults.

This is extremely difficult. If a person's fault is a habit of some years prior, by and large it won't be remedied. I have had this experience myself. To be intimate with all one's comrades,

correcting each other's faults, and being of one mind to be of use to the master is the great compassion of a retainer. By bringing shame to a person, how could one expect to make him a better man?

It is bad taste to yawn in front of people. When one unexpectedly has to yawn, if he rubs his forehead in an upward direction, the sensation will stop. If that does not work, he can lick his lips while keeping his mouth closed, or simply hide it with his hand or his sleeve in such a way that no one will know what he is doing. It is the same with sneezing. One will appear foolish. There are other things besides these about which a person should use care and training.

Every morning one should first do reverence to his master and parents and then to his patron deities and guardian Buddhas. If he will only make his master first in importance, his parents will rejoice and the gods and Buddhas will give their assent. For a warrior there is nothing other than thinking of his master. If one creates this resolution within himself, he will always be mindful of the master's person and will not depart from him even for a moment.

Moreover, a woman should consider her husband first, just as he considers his master first.

There are two things that will blemish a retainer, and these are riches and honor. If one but remains in strained circumstances, he will not be marred.

Once there was a certain man who was very clever, but it was his character to always see the negative points of his jobs. In such a way, one will be useless. If one does not get it into his head from the very beginning that the world is full of unseemly situations, for the most part his demeanor will be poor and he will not be believed by others. And if one is not believed by others, no matter how good a person he may be, he will not have the essence of a good person. This can also be considered as a blemish.

There was a man who said, "Such and such a person has a violent disposition, but this is what I said right to his face. . . ." This was an unbecoming thing to say, and it was said simply because he wanted to be known as a rough fellow. It was rather low, and it can be seen that he was still rather immature. It is because a samurai has correct manners that he is admired. Speaking of other people in this way is no different from an exchange between low class spearmen. It is vulgar.

---

1. Why was *The Book of the Samurai* written?

2. Characterize the relationship between a samurai and his retainer.

3. Why are there instructions on how to suppress a yawn in *The Book of the Samurai?*

4. What is a samurai supposed to think about death? about wisdom? about good manners?

·93·

Honda Toshiaki
A Secret Plan for Managing the Country
(1798)

*H*onda Toshiaki (1744–1821) was born in northwestern Japan, the second son of a samurai who had killed a man and moved his family to escape detection. Honda was educated in Edo, where he studied mathematics and astronomy, but he continued to be strongly influenced by his northern origins. He was first a schoolmaster and was credited with introducing Western scientific ideas about astronomy and mathematics to Japan. He taught himself Dutch and made a number of translations of Dutch scientific works. Ultimately, Honda served as a government official with special responsibility for foreign affairs. His writings were known only to a small group of intimates and only became popular a century later. Nothing is known of his personal life other than that he married and had a daughter.

A Secret Plan for Managing the Country is Honda's most important work. It sets out a program for improving the Japanese economy. He advocates Western techniques and emphasizes Western exploitation of mineral resources in enriching Japan. Honda also proposes a series of social welfare programs, including a family allowance of rice for children, designed to stimulate economic growth and alleviate the misery of Japanese farming families. Although he is economically radical, Honda is socially conservative. He argues for the preservation of the traditional Japanese social hierarchy.

I am a subject, and other men are likewise subjects. Being thus of the same condition, our opinions might also be the same. This, however, is not the case, and I therefore cannot do otherwise than to discuss mine.

Can it be that anyone born in Japan would fail to think of what is beneficial to his country, or rejoice in Japan's misfortunes and begrudge her good fortune? Rather it should be in the nature of every person born in Japan to share in the joy at his country's good fortune and the desire to promote it, as well as in the sorrow over her ill fortune and the desire to prevent it. Not only is this not true of present-day customs, however, but if ever there is anything which looks as if it will prove advantageous for the country and the people, there are always envious and wicked people who come forward to destroy it. It is the way of the world that good things are always weak, and bad ones strong, so that in the end the good cannot be accomplished. It is just like the fact that it is difficult to become wealthy and easy to remain poor. If one honestly seeks to discover whose fault it is that this situation has arisen, a few moments of silent thought will assuredly yield the answer.

We should be grateful that for the first time in the history of Japan the country is as peaceful as it now is. The people rejoice in the benefits of this fortunate condition, and the expression 'the joys of good government' might well be used of these times. It is thus entirely to be expected that the population should show a tendency to increase in numbers steadily. There will then be insufficient food to supply the nation's wants unless food production increases in direct proportion to this growth of the population. For this reason, the entire land of Japan must be developed, even the waste areas and remote mountain-regions, and converted into farmland which can produce grain and fruit. If these measures prove inadequate and there is still not enough food to meet the needs of the people, some of them will starve in years of poor harvest or famine. Since most of those who starve will be farmers, the amount of farm produce will be still further reduced, and there will be disturbances in the country.

When the entire population is fed by the farmers and society is maintained along the class lines of samurai, farmers, artisans, merchants and idlers, there is stability, and the nation is peaceful. But if many of the farmers, who are the foundation of the nation, die of starvation, the stability is upset and calamities of every sort arise. If such trouble is suppressed in one place, it boils up in another; if put down in that place, it is felt in still another. These disorders arise because of poverty. Far-reaching consideration must therefore be given to the matter.

The chief object of such study should be how to keep from hindering the natural increase in numbers of the four classes of society. Towards this end, the four imperative needs should be made the prime consideration of the government. When the country is thus ruled, there will be no obstacles to increase, and the population will multiply and flourish. There will then no longer be widespread abandonment of good farmland such as now takes place. On the contrary, the amount of land under cultivation would increase, and with it the prosperity of the nation. If, mistakenly, the country is not governed in accordance with the four imperative needs, the unsuitability of these other policies to the well-being of the nation results in the steady increase of wasteland and its attendant disasters. Of such events there are numerous examples in both ancient and modern history.

The four imperative needs are so called because they represent the four things which are most urgently required at present: that is, (1) gunpowder, (2) metals, (3) shipping and (4) colonisation. I have divided the four and will discuss each of them below.

GUNPOWDER

Gunpowder is of great use to a nation in times of peace as well as in war. For example, when conditions do not permit the use of river craft to ship goods, and the produce of a locality lies rotting on the ground as a result, the situation may best be alleviated by making the river usable by boats and thus enabling the produce to be transported to areas where it is needed. There may be rocks and boulders which form rapids in the rivers. These cannot be removed by human labour, but if gunpowder is used, the obstructions can be blasted and easily removed. A channel will then be open, permitting river craft to pass through taking products from one region to another.

It is impossible to complete any major construction undertaking without the use of gunpowder. That is why the European nations consider it to be a product of the greatest value and importance to their countries and make many uses of it. . . .

METALS

There are gold, silver, copper, iron and lead mines scattered throughout the country, but in spite of their great numbers, they are all abandoned and yield no profit. . . .

It is a basic part of a ruler's duties as parent to the people to ensure that these articles of permanent worth are transmitted in perpetuity by the noble families. Another duty of the ruler is to insist that the miners be treated with consideration at all times, for the mining of precious metals involves long hours of work in caves. If a ruler is lax in this matter, he will be no better than a speculator out for profit, which is contrary to the calling of a ruler. The ruler's duty to the nation requires him to secure profit for the nation regardless of the expenses involved. . . .

The capitals of France, Spain, England and Holland have become thriving places. There are reasons for their prosperity which I shall attempt to explain by using the example of one of them. France long ago became the first country to manufacture cannon, and she also invented the method of making gunpowder for military use. This gave her supremacy over her neighbouring countries. She afterwards used her inventions against those countries which were at war, thus compelling them to cease fighting. This was the great achievement of France. No matter how well-equipped a nation might be, even if it possessed mighty fortresses of steel, when French cannons were brought to bear against them or French privateers attacked, not only would its fortresses fall, but very few of its people would be left to tell the tale. Thus, for fear of loss of human life France has not yet transmitted her inventions to other countries.

Europe was first with all other important inventions as well. Because astronomy, calendar-making and mathematics are considered the ruler's business, the European kings are well-versed in matters of celestial and terrestrial principles, and instruct the common people in them. Thus even among the lower classes one finds great men who show great ability in their particular fields. The Europeans have as a result been able to establish industries with which the rest of the world is unfamiliar. It is for this reason that all the treasures of the world are said to be attracted to Europe. There is no place in the world to compare with Europe. It may be wondered in what way this supremacy was achieved. In the first place, the European nations have behind them a history of five to six thousand years. In this period they have delved deep into the beauties of the arts, have divined the foundations of government, and have established a system based on a thorough examination of those factors which naturally make a nation prosperous. Because of their proficiency in mathematics they have excelled also in astronomy, calendar-making and surveying. They have elaborated laws of navigation so that there is nothing simpler for them than to sail the oceans of the world. . . .

Since Japan is a maritime nation, shipping and trade should be the chief concern of the ruler. Ships should be sent to all countries to obtain products needed for national consumption and to bring precious metals to Japan. A maritime nation is equipped with the means to increase her national strength.

Everything depends entirely on the course of action adopted. If it is a good one, the outstand-ing men of the country will come forward to serve the ruler and demonstrate their loyalty. The precious metals of the country will gravitate towards the ruler and circulate as he chooses. The people will all seek to be perfectly loyal to the ruler, and will direct their faithful attentions towards him. Everyone will sincerely desire to help the programme. Since there will be no opposition to the government, there will be few criminals. When the country is ruled by force against the will of the people, many in their hearts will oppose this compulsion and become criminals. All these blessings depend on finding men who are talented and able, and who are versed in the laws of Heaven, earth and man. If the rulers are lacking in these talents, the people will not have faith in their decrees.

The above secret programme may seem like outspoken criticism of the government because it goes down to the origins of contemporary practices and openly discusses their merits and demerits. This is a matter of which I am deeply afraid. However, if in consideration of that fear I wrote with deference and reverence, the important principles might appear shallow, and so I have recorded my thoughts plainly even at the risk of having spoken in a manner unbefitting my status.

1. Why does Honda concentrate on the peaceful uses of gunpowder?

2. What is the importance of trade to Honda?

3. Why does Honda think that the study of the arts has led to European supremacy? Do you agree?

4. How does Honda define the obligations of a ruler?

·94·
Ferdinand Verbiest
Letter from China
(1683)

F erdinand Verbiest (1623–1688) was a Flemish missionary and astronomer who served at the court of the Manchu emperor K'ang-hsi (1661–1722). Although K'ang-hsi's father had put his Jesuit missionaries to death, the young emperor was particularly impressed with Father Verbiest, who made a crucial readjustment of the Chinese calendar. Verbiest instructed the emperor in astronomy and mathematics, learning the Tartar language to do so, and was allowed considerable access to the court. Verbiest accompanied K'ang-hsi on two military expeditions into the south, where pockets of resistance remained against the Manchu dynasty, which itself had recently usurped power. Owing to his mathematical skill, Verbiest was ultimately able to determine the exact location of the Chinese-Russian border.

The excerpt printed here is from Verbiest's account of his second voyage into the Crimea with Emperor K'ang-hsi. It is a letter written from China to Jesuit officials in Europe. Verbiest's description of the emperor and his entourage is one of the best portraits of the early Manchus. His wonder at the Great Wall of China is still shared today.

Letter of Father Ferdinand Verbiest, sent from Pekin, the capital of China, to Europe; concerning a Second Journey which he made with the Emperor of China, beyond the great Chinese Wall into Tartary.

The emperor of China, on the 6th of July, A.D. 1683, being the thirtieth year of his life, with the queen, his grandmother, and a great attendance, to the amount of 60,000 persons and 100,000 horses, commenced a journey to West Tartary, having expressed a special desire that I should accompany him, together with one of the two fathers my colleagues at my selection. I accordingly selected Philip Grimaldi, as being the older, and specially accomplished in the sciences. The causes of this journey were several. The first was, to keep the military during peace in constant movement and practice, to fit it for the exigencies of war. For this motive the emperor, in this same year (having made a levy from all his provinces of his best troops), returning to Pekin, after having established a solid peace throughout the vast empire of China, resolved in his council to make annually three such expeditions, each at a certain season, in the which he might, on the pretext of the chase and of practising his soldiers in the pursuit of stags, wild boars, and tigers, procure an image and representation of war with human enemies and rebels, and a rehearsal of conflicts which might thereafter ensue. He had in view at the least to prevent for his soldiers, and especially his Tartar troops, that infection of Chinese luxury and corruption which might otherwise naturally ensue from the idleness of peace. And, in fact, this fashion in which the emperor went forth to the chase, had all the form and appearance of a royal progress to war; for he went attended by 100,000 horses and more than 60,000 men, all armed with bow and arrows and sabre, and divided into troops and companies, and with all the military accompaniments of banners and music. In the chase these surrounded mountains and forests in a wide circuit, like those who invest a town to be besieged; in which they observed the process pursued by the Western Tartars in their great hunts. The army, again, is divided into an advanced, a centre, and a rear-guard, and into wings right and left. The command of each of these bodies is committed to officers of eminence, and to members of the imperial house.

Inasmuch, however, as this expedition was planned for a march of more than seventy days (the emperor being on each day from morning till evening devoted to the chase), and all the provisions, and baggage, and other heavy impediments had to be conveyed over continual ascents and descents, partly on waggons, partly on camels, mules, and horses, the labours and difficulties of each day's march are not to be described. For in the whole of this West Tartary (West Tartary is not to be understood as relative to China, which is itself west of it, but with relation to the more Eastern Tartary) nothing is met with but mountain and valley. It has no towns, and no villages, no, not even a house. All its inhabitants live as herdsmen under tents or hovels, which they convey from valley to valley when they move in search of fresh and better pasture for their herds, which consist solely of oxen, sheep, and horses; for of pigs, dogs, geese, and other animals, which abound among an agricultural peasantry, they have none. I say that they possess nothing but these cattle, which graze the uncultivated soil.

These Tartars are a slothful people, and little disposed to any toil, even to that of the chase. They neither sow nor reap, nor plough nor harrow. They live for the most part on milk, cheese, and flesh. They make a certain wine which resembles our brandy, and which they delight to swallow to repletion, till they fling themselves

down and are reduced, soul and body, to the condition of the very cattle.

They hold, meanwhile, their priests, called lamas, in great veneration, and in this respect are distinguished from some neighbouring Tartar tribes, who practise no religious observances, or next to none, and live as Atheists.

Both being equally slaves, and bound to the service of their lords, are on this account difficult of conversion to our faith; following the nod of the latter, in matters of religion, like the cattle, which follow where they are led, not where they choose to go.

In this manner did the emperor lead his troops a march of many days, through such desert districts, over ridges of mountains almost linked with each other, over many acclivities, beyond measure steep and far removed from the ordinary track. He followed the chase every day, riding in advance of the troops, often under a blazing sun, sometimes in heavy rain. Many who had taken part in the campaigns of preceding years, openly confessed to me that they had never, in actual war, endured such hardships as in this factitious campaign. Thus the emperor fully compassed his primary object, that of inuring his troops.

It appears, however, that another motive for the expedition was, the political object of keeping these Western Tartars in obedience, and checking the plots and intrigues of their councils. This was one reason for the magnitude of the force, and the imperial pomp with which the emperor penetrated their country. For this he conveyed also thither some pieces of cannon. . . . These he occasionally caused to be discharged in the winding valleys, in which the reverberation from the cliffs added to the effect of those thundering salutes with which the emperor's movements from his palace in Pekin are usually attended; and which, as also the accompanying music of trumpets, drums, and copper cymbals, were now employed on the occasions of the emperor's marching, or at meal times, to dazzle and fill the eyes and ears of the barbarous tribes. For the Chinese empire has, from remote times, feared no enemy so much as these Tartars, who, starting from this Eastern district, encompass Northern and Western China with a countless multitude of tribes, to repel the invasion, or, so to speak, the inundation of which, former emperors constructed the great Wall. I had four times passed over and personally inspected that work. In truth, the seven wonders of the world condensed into one, could not be compared with it. That which I have seen with my own eyes of it, far exceeds all report of it which has yet reached Europe.

There are two circumstances which exalt this work to the skies. The first is, that it is carried not alone over level places, but in many places over the highest summits of the mountains from east to west, and follows all the acclivities; towers of a lasting construction rising high into the air, at intervals of two bow-shots apart. On our return we ascertained by our instruments the height of a portion of the Wall above the horizon at 1037 geometrical feet.

We might well wonder how the builders could draw to such a height, up the steepest places, from the lowest valleys, which are destitute themselves of water, such a quantity of stones, lime, water, etc.

The other circumstance is, that the Wall should be carried, not with one, but with a variety of curves, following all the prominences of the mountain; so that it may be considered not a single, but a triple Wall, which protects the whole Tartarian frontier of China.

The emperor has divided the immeasurable districts of West Tartary into forty-eight provinces, and has made them all subject and tributary; and thus may this sovereign of the Chinese and of both Tartaries, be justly named as the greatest and mightiest monarch and sole ruler in the world; as one who has incorporated into one body so many districts and nations under one authority, without the interposition of any other prince. He may, I say, be named, as the monarch most essentially and most singularly worthy of the name, for this reason, that he of all rulers the most by himself governs so vast a multitude of men; for what is most remarkable in him and distinctive from all others, is that from the beginning of his reign to this present day since he took the helm of government, he has never permitted any one to govern for him or in his place, nor allowed any one, whether of the princes of the realm, or of the kolaos, or other authorities who may be familiar with him, or who enjoy his favour and are near his heart, more than others to dispose of or settle any public matter by their own separate deliberation. Nay, not within the innermost recesses of the palace has he ever so condescended to any of the eunuchs or the youth of the court, his contemporaries with whom he had been brought up from infancy, as to allow any one of them to act on his own behalf in public matters; facts which are altogether singular, and may be regarded as miracles in this kind of government, when the practice of his predecessors is taken into consideration.

This emperor chastises offenders of the highest as well as lowest class with marvellous impartiality, according to their misdeeds, depriving them of rank and dignity. He himself, after considering the proceedings and sentences of the Imperial Council or the Courts of Law, determines and directs the issue. On this account men of all ranks and dignities whatsoever, even the nearest to him in blood, stand in his presence with the deepest awe, and recognize him as sole ruler.

As a point which concerns ourselves and our objects, I must refer to my former observations on the Tartar priests or lamas, that these, by reason of the policy pursued in the government of the Tartaries, have easy access to the princes and dignitaries, a circumstance which makes the introduction of our faith among these people the more difficult. These priests have much influence with the queen-mother, who sprung from West Tartary, and has attained the age of fifty, and they have for many years past enjoyed her warm affection.

Inasmuch as this queen is held in great consideration by the emperor, and knows well from these priests that we are strong opponents of the superstition to which she clings, it is a wonder, nay a miracle, at the least a singular proof of God's power and providence, that the emperor should have hitherto treated us with such benignity and with familiarity and honour, even beyond these lamas themselves.

The third and last cause of this expedition was that the emperor wished to consult the condition of his health; for experience had taught him, that while he remained at Pekin his health from various annoyances often failed him, which he hoped by his present movement and change of life to provide against, and even to gain strength. . . .

It may be added that by this movement he with the queen-mother avoided the summer heat, which in the dog-days at Pekin is tremendous. For in this part of Tartary not only is the air very cooling, but wintry, especially at night, so that the inhabitants not only wear woollens, but betake themselves to furs and peltry for clothing. The cause of this is the mountainous character of the country and its elevation, such that for five days' journey we were constantly traversing high ridges, and climbing higher and higher.

The emperor desired to know how much this mountain was elevated above the level of Pekin, from which capital it is about three hundred miles distant, and commanded us to devise some means of measuring the difference. We therefore on our return, after measuring the heights and distances of more than one hundred summits, found that the horizon, or rather the circular level of Pekin was three thousand geometrical paces lower than the highest ridge or top of this mountain.

Several petty kings of West Tartary came in to see the emperor from distances of three and even five hundred Italian miles, with their sons and kinsmen. They all saluted us with great demonstration of good will, which they evinced openly by looks and gestures of hand and body. For many of them could speak no language but their own, which is different from that of the East Tartars. Some also had formerly been presented to us at Pekin, and some had visited our church there.

One day as we were arriving at the town which was the end and object of our journey, we met towards dusk a very old prince, who was returning from the emperor's tents, and on our appearance halted with all his attendants, which was very numerous, and asked, through an interpreter, which of us was Nau Hoay Gi? One of our followers pointing me out with voice and gesture, he approached us with much appearance of pleasure and benignity, and said, "I have long since heard of your name; are you well?" He approached father Grimaldi with the like demeanour, and asked how he was? From this conduct we derived some hope that at some time or other our worship might find access to these secular princes, especially should some of our scientific brethren find means to open the door of such access by pleasing exhibitions of knowledge, and if the people could be cajoled by presents.

The emperor throughout our whole journey exhibited to us a benevolence and attention, such as, in truth, he displayed to no one else, not even of the princes or his own kinsmen, and this both in word and deed in presence of the whole army.

One day as the emperor fell in with us in an extensive valley, while we were employed in a scientific operation for ascertaining the height and distance of certain mountains, he halted with all his court and escort, and while still at some distance, shouted out in the Chinese tongue, "Hao mo?" that is, are you well? He then asked some questions in the Tartar language as to the heights of the mountains, which I answered in the same. He then turned to his attendants and spoke much in our praise, all which his uncle, who was present, reported to me that evening.

The same goodwill he showed us on many other occasions, to wit, in frequently sending us dishes from his own table to our tent, in the sight of all his grandees. He even ordered us sometimes to be entertained in his own tent. Sometimes when he knew we were abstaining from flesh, he would send us dishes suited to our wants. For he well knew our habits of keeping fast days, and would often ask whether the day were a fast day or not.

His eldest son, following the example of his father, showed us similar goodwill. Once having hurt his shoulder by a fall from his horse, he was obliged to remain still for ten days, which we also did with the greater part of the army. On this occasion, his father being far absent with the chase, he almost every day, and often twice a-day, at midday and evening, sent to our huts dishes from his own table.

This constant benevolence of the emperor is so much the more to be ascribed to the special favour and providence of God, because to others, and even to the princes of his blood, he is very mutable and unstable in his disposition.

1. Why did the emperor of China make this journey?

2. Why was Verbiest in China?

3. Characterize the relationship between Verbiest and the emperor.

4. Why did Verbiest think K'ang-hsi was a great emperor? Do you agree?

·95·

Wu Ching-tzu
The Scholars
(1750)

Wu Ching-tzu (1701–1754) came from a distinguished but declining Chinese family. His father held minor government posts, but was dismissed from his last one after a quarrel with a superior. When his father he died in 1724, Wu inherited a middling-sized estate, which he then proceeded to run into the ground. He sat for several of the examinations to enter state service, but did not achieve the high rank necessary for an official career. After he lost all of his land, he moved to Nanking, where he lived from charity and the small income that could be made from writing. His father's and his own experiences with the Chinese civil service embittered Wu and his writings have a keen satirical edge when discussing these subjects.

Wu Ching-tzu was the pioneer of the Chinese satirical tradition. *The Scholars* was written over more than a decade. It was at first intended for the amusement of Wu's friends and was circulated in portions of self-contained stories. It was not published until nearly 20 years after Wu's death. Though *The Scholars* is a satirical novel, it was based closely on Wu's own experiences and its characters were modeled upon people he knew. It thus provides a valuable portrait of eighteenth-century village life.

PROVINCIAL GRADUATE WANG MEETS A FELLOW CANDIDATE IN A VILLAGE SCHOOL; CHOU CHIN PASSES THE EXAMINATION IN HIS OLD AGE

In Hsueh Market, a village of Wen-shang county, Shantung, there lived over a hundred families, all of whom worked on the land. At the entrance to the village was a Kuan-yin Temple with three halls and a dozen empty rooms. Its back door overlooked the river. Peasants from all around contributed to the upkeep of this temple, and only one monk lived there. Here the villagers would come to discuss public business.

It was the last year of the Cheng-hua period of the Ming Dynasty, when the country was prosperous. One year, on the eighth of the first month, just after New Year, some of the villagers met in the temple to discuss the dragon lantern dance which is held on the fifteenth. At breakfast time the man who usually took the lead, Shen Hsiang-fu, walked in, followed by seven or eight others. In the main hall they bowed to Buddha, and the monk came to wish them a happy New Year. As soon as they had returned his greeting, Shen reproved him.

"Monk! At New Year you should burn more incense before Buddha! Gracious Heaven! You've been pocketing money from all sides, and you ought to spend a little of it. Come here, all of you, and take a look at this lamp: it's only half filled with oil." Then, pointing to an old man who was better dressed than most: "Not to mention others, Mr. Hsün alone sent you fifty catties of oil on New Year's Eve. But you are using it all for your cooking, instead of for the glory of Buddha."

The monk apologized profusely when Shen had finished. Then he fetched a pewter kettle, put in a handful of tea leaves, filled the kettle with water, boiled it over the fire and poured out tea for them. Old Mr. Hsün was the first to speak.

"How much do we each have to pay for the lantern dance in the temple this year?" he asked.

"Wait till my relative comes," said Shen. "We'll discuss it together."

As they were speaking, a man walked in. He had red-rimmed eyes, a swarthy face, and sparse, dingy whiskers. His cap was cocked to one side, his blue cloth gown was greasy as an oil vat, and he carried a donkey switch in one hand. Making a casual gesture of greeting to the company, he plumped himself down in the seat of honour. This was Hsia, the new village head for Hsueh Market.

Sitting there in the seat of honour, he shouted: "Monk! Take my donkey to the manger in the back yard, unsaddle it, and give it plenty of hay. After my business here I have to go to a feast with Bailiff Huang of the county yamen." Having given these orders, he hoisted one foot on to the bench, and started massaging the small of his back with his fists, saying, "I envy you farmers these days. This New Year I've got invitations from everybody in the magistrate's yamen, literally everybody! And I have to go to wish them all the season's greetings. I trot about on this donkey to the county seat and back until my head reels. And this damned beast stumbled on the road and threw me, so that my backside is still sore."

"On the third I prepared a small dinner for you," said Shen. "I suppose it was because you were so busy that you didn't come."

"You don't have to remind me," said Village Head Hsia. "Since New Year, for the last seven or eight days, what free time have I had? Even if I had two mouths, I couldn't get through all the eating. Take Bailiff Huang, who's invited me today. He's a man who can talk face to face with the magistrate. And since he honours me like this, wouldn't he be offended if I didn't go?"

"I heard that Bailiff Huang had been sent out on some business for the magistrate since the beginning of the year," said Shen. "He has no brothers or sons, so who will act as host?"

"You don't understand," said Hsia. "Today's feast is given by Constable Li. His own rooms are small, so he is using Bailiff Huang's house."

Eventually they started discussing the dragon lanterns. "I'm tired of managing it for you," said Village Head Hsia. "I took the lead every year in the past, and everyone wrote down what contribution he would make, and then failed to pay up. Heaven knows how much I had to pay to make good the deficit. Besides, all the officials in the yamen are preparing lanterns this year, and I shall have too much to watch. What time do I have to look at the lanterns in the village? Still, since you've mentioned it, I shall make a contribution. Choose someone to be responsible. A man like Mr. Hsün, who has broad lands and plenty of grain, should be asked to give more. Let each family pay its share, and you'll get the thing going." Nobody dared disagree. They immediately came down on Mr. Hsün for half the money, and made up the rest between them. In this way they raised two or three taels of silver, a record of the contributors being made.

The monk then brought out tea, sugar wafers, dates, melon seeds, dried beancurd, chestnuts, and assorted sweets. He spread two tables, and invited Village Head Hsia to sit at the head. Then he poured out tea for them.

"The children are growing up," said Shen, "and this year we must find them a teacher. This temple can be used as a school."

The others agreed.

"There are a lot of families who have sons who should be in school," said one of them. "For instance, Mr. Shen's son is Village Head Hsia's son-in-law. Hsia is always getting notices from the magistrate, so he needs someone who can read. But the best thing would be to find a teacher from the county seat."

"A teacher?" said the village head. "I can think of one. You know who? He's in our yamen, and he used to teach in chief accountant Ku's house. His name is Chou Chin. He's over sixty. The former magistrate placed him first on the list of county candidates, but he's never yet been able to pass the prefectural examination. Mr. Ku employed him as tutor for his son for three years; and his son passed the examination last year, at the same time as Mei Chiu from our village. The day that young Ku was welcomed back from the school he wore a scholar's cap and a broad red silk sash, and rode a horse from the magistrate's stable, while all the gongs and trumpets sounded. When he reached the door of his house, I and the other yamen officials offered him wine in the street. Then Mr. Chou was asked over. Mr. Ku toasted his son's teacher three times and invited him to sit in the seat of honour. Mr. Chou chose as entertainment the opera about Liang Hao, who won the first place in the palace examination when he was eighty; and Mr. Ku was not at all pleased. But then the opera showed how Liang Hao's pupil won the same distinction at seventeen or eighteen, and Mr. Ku knew that it was a compliment to his son. That made him feel better. If you want a teacher, I'll invite Mr. Chou for you." All the villagers approved. When they had finished their tea the monk brought in some beef noodles, and after eating these they went home.

The next day, sure enough, Village Head Hsia spoke to Chou Chin. His salary would be twelve taels of silver a year, and it was arranged that he should eat with the monk, whom he would pay two cents a day. It was settled that he should come after the Lantern Festival, and begin teaching on the twentieth.

On the sixteenth the villagers sent in contributions to Shen Hsiang-fu, who prepared a feast for the new teacher to which he also invited Mei Chiu, the new scholar of the village. Mei Chiu arrived early, wearing his new square cap, but

Chou Chin did not turn up till nearly noon. When dogs started barking outside, Shen Hsiang-fu went out to welcome the guest; and the villagers stared as Chou Chin came in. He was wearing an old felt cap, a tattered grey silk gown, the right sleeve and seat of which were in shreds, and a pair of shabby red silk slippers. He had a thin, dark face, and a white beard. Shen escorted him in, and only then did Mei Chiu rise slowly to greet him.

"Who is this gentleman?" asked Chou.

They told him, "He is Mr. Mei, our village scholar."

When Chou Chin heard this, he declared it would be presumptuous on his part to allow Mei to bow to him. And although Mei Chiu said, "Today is different," he still refused.

"You are older than he is," said the villagers. "You had better not insist."

But Mei Chiu rounded on them, "You people don't understand the rule of our school. Those who have passed the prefectural examination are considered senior to those who have not, regardless of age. But today happens to be exceptional, and Mr. Chou must still be honoured."

[Ming Dynasty scholars called all those who passed the prefectural examination "classmates," and those who only qualified for this examination "juniors." A young man in his teens who passed was considered senior to an unsuccessful candidate, even if the latter were eighty years old. It was like the case of a concubine. A woman is called "new wife" when she marries, and later "mistress"; but a concubine remains "new wife" even when her hair is white.]

Since Mei Chiu spoke like this, Chou Chin did not insist on being polite, but let Mei Chiu bow to him. When all the others had greeted him too, they sat down. Mei and Chou were the only two to have dates in their tea cups—all the others had plain green tea. After they had drunk their tea two tables were laid, and Chou Chin was invited to take the seat of honour, Mei Chiu the second place. Then the others sat down in order of seniority, and wine was poured. Chou Chin, cup in hand, thanked the villagers and drained his cup. On each table were eight or nine dishes—pig's head, chicken, carp, tripe, liver, and other dishes. At the signal to begin, they fell to with their chopsticks, like a whirlwind scattering wisps of cloud. And half the food had gone before they noticed that Chou Chin had not eaten a bite.

"Why aren't you eating anything?" asked Shen. "Surely we haven't offended you the very first day?" He selected some choice morsels and put them on the teacher's plate.

But Chou Chin stopped him and said, "I must explain—I am having a long fast."

"How thoughtless we have been!" exclaimed his hosts. "May we ask why you are fasting?"

"On account of a vow I made before the shrine of Buddha when my mother was ill," said Chou Chin. "I have been abstaining from meat now for more than ten years."

"Your fasting reminds me of a joke I heard the other day from Mr. Ku in the county town," said Mei Chiu. "It is a one character to seven character verse about a teacher." The villagers put down their chopsticks to listen, while he recited:

A
Foolish scholar
Fasted so long,
Whiskers covered his cheeks;
Neglecting to study the classics,
He left pen and paper aside.
He'll come without being invited next year.

After this recitation he said, "A learned man like Mr. Chou here is certainly not foolish." Then, putting his hand over his mouth to hide a smile, he added, "But he should become a scholar soon, and the description of the fasting and the whiskers is true to life." He gave a loud guffaw, and everybody laughed with him, while Chou Chin did not know which way to look.

Shen Hsiang-fu hastily filled a cup with wine and said, "Mr. Mei should drink a cup of wine. Mr. Chou was the teacher in Mr. Ku's house."

"I didn't know that," said Mei Chiu. "I should certainly drink a cup to apologize. But this joke was not against Mr. Chou. It was about a scholar. However, this fasting is a good thing. I have an uncle who never ate meat either. But after he passed the prefectural examination his patron sent him some sacrificial meat, and my grandmother said, 'If you don't eat this, Confucius will be angry, and some terrible calamity may happen. At the very least, he will make you fall sick.' So my uncle stopped fasting. Now, Mr. Chou, you are bound to pass the examination this autumn. Then you will be offered sacrificial meat, and I'm sure you will stop fasting."

They all said this was a lucky omen, and drank a toast to congratulate Chou Chin in advance, until the poor man's face turned a mottled red and white, and he could barely stammer out his thanks as he took the wine cup. Soup was carried in from the kitchen with a big dish of dumplings and a plate of fried cakes. They assured Chou Chin that there was no animal fat in the cakes, and pressed him to eat some. But he was afraid the soup was unclean, and asked for tea instead.

While they were eating the dessert, someone asked Shen, "Where is the village head today? Why hasn't he come to welcome Mr. Chou?"

"He has gone to a feast with Constable Li," said Shen.

"These last few years, under the new magistrate, Mr. Li has done very well," said someone else. "In one year he must make about a thousand taels of silver. But he is too fond of gambling. It's a pity he's not like Bailiff Huang. Bailiff Huang used to play too, but later he turned over a new leaf and was able to build a house just like a palace—it is very grand."

"Since your relative became the village head," said Mr. Hsün to Shen Hsiang-fu, "he's been in luck. Another year or two, and I suppose he will be like Bailiff Huang."

"He's not doing badly," said Shen. "But it'll be several years before his dream of catching up with Bailiff Huang comes true."

With his mouth full of cake, Mr. Mei put in: "There *is* something in dreams." And turning to Chou Chin he asked: "Mr. Chou, these past years, during the examinations, what dreams have you had?"

"None at all," replied Chou Chin.

"I was fortunate," said Mei Chiu. "Last year on New Year's Day, I dreamed that I was on a very high mountain. The sun in the sky was directly above me, but suddenly it fell down on my head! Sweating with fright, I woke up and rubbed my head, and it still seemed hot. I didn't understand then what the dream meant, but later it came true!"

By this time all the cakes were finished, and they had another round of drinks. By then it was time to light the lamps, and Mei Chiu and all the others went home, while Shen Hsiang-fu produced blue bedding and escorted Mr. Chou to the temple to sleep, where he settled with the monk that the two empty rooms at the back should be used for the school.

When the day came to start school, Shen Hsiang-fu and the other villagers took their sons, large and small, to pay their respects to the teacher; and Chou Chin taught them. That evening, when he opened the envelopes containing their school fees, he found there was one-tenth of a tael of silver from the Hsün family with an extra eight cents for tea, while the others had given only three or four cents or a dozen coppers apiece; so altogether he had not enough for one month's food. He gave what he had to the monk, however, promising to settle his account later.

The children were a wild lot. The moment Chou Chin took his eyes off them, they would slip outside to play hopscotch or kick balls. They were up to mischief every day, yet he had to sit there patiently and teach them.

Soon more than two months had passed and it began to grow warm. One day after lunch, Chou Chin opened the back gate and went out to stroll on the river bank. It was a small country place, with some peach trees and willows beside the stream, their pink and green beautifully intermingled. Chou Chin enjoyed the scenery until it began to drizzle. Then he went back to his doorway to watch the rain falling on the river and mist shrouding the distant trees, making them look even lovelier. The rain was beginning to fall more heavily when a boat came downstream—a small craft with a matting roof which could not keep out the wet. As it approached the bank, he saw a man sitting in the middle of the boat and two servants in the stern, while in the bow were two hampers. They reached the bank and the man ordered the boatman to moor the boat, then stepped ashore followed by his servants. He was wearing a scholar's cap, a sapphire-blue gown and black slippers with white soles. His beard was combed into three tufts, and he looked a little over thirty. Coming to the temple gate he nodded to Chou Chin, then entered saying to himself, "This seems to be a school."

"Yes," said Chou Chin, accompanying him in and greeting him.

"And you, I suppose, are the teacher?"

"That is correct."

"How is it we don't see the monk?" the stranger asked his servants.

But just then the monk hurried in, saying, "Please take a seat, Mr. Wang, and I'll make tea for you." Then he told Chou Chin, "This is Mr. Wang Hui, a new provincial scholar. Please sit down and keep him company while I go to make tea."

The newcomer showed no false modesty. When the servants drew up a bench he promptly sat himself down in the place of honour of it, leaving the teacher to take a lower seat.

"What is your name?" he demanded.

Knowing that this man was a provincial scholar, Chou Chin replied, "Your pupil is called Chou."

"Where did you teach before?"

"In the family of Mr. Ku of the county yamen."

"Aren't you the man who came first in that test which my patron, Mr. Pai, supervised? He said that you were teaching in Mr. Ku's family. That's right. That's right."

"Do you know my former employer, Mr. Ku, sir?"

"Mr. Ku is one of the secretaries in our office. He is one of my sworn brothers too."

Presently the monk brought in tea, and when they had drunk it Chou Chin said, "I read your examination essay over and over again, sir. The last two paragraphs were particularly fine."

"Those two paragraphs were not by me."

"You are too modest, sir. Who else could have written them?"

"Although not by me, they were not by anybody else either," said the scholar. "It was the first day of the examination, on the ninth, getting on for dusk; but I had still not finished the first essay, and I said to myself, 'Usually I write very quickly. What makes me so slow today?' As I was racking my brains, I dozed off on the desk. Then I saw five green-faced men leaping into the cell. One of them made a mark on my head with a big brush which he had in his hand, then darted away. Then a man in a gauze cap, red robe, and golden belt came in, who shook me and said, 'Mr. Wang, please get up!' I woke up, trembling, bathed in icy sweat, and taking the pen into my hand began to write without knowing what I was doing. From this one can see that there *are* spirits in the examination school. When I made this statement to the chief examiner, he said that I ought to pass the very highest examination."

He was speaking with great gusto, when a small boy came in with a written exercise. Chou Chin told him to put it down, but Wang Hui said, "You go ahead and correct it. I have other things to see to." Then the teacher went to his desk while Wang Hui said to his servants, "Since it is dark and the rain has not stopped, bring the hampers here and tell the monk to cook a peck of rice. Order the boatman to wait. I shall leave tomorrow morning." He told Chou Chin, "I have just come back from visiting the graves of my ancestors, and did not expect to run into rain. I shall spend the night here."

While he was speaking, he caught sight of the name Hsün Mei on the little boy's exercise, and gave an involuntary start. He pursed his lips and his face was a study, but Chou Chin could not very well question him. When Chou Chin had finished correcting the exercise and sat down again as before, Wang Hui asked, "How old is that boy?"

"Seven."

"Did he start school this year? Did you choose that name for him?"

"I didn't choose the name. At the beginning of the term his father asked the new village scholar, Mei Chiu, to choose a name for him. And Mr. Mei said, 'My own name seems to be an auspicious one, so I will give it to him and hope that he will turn out like me.'"

"This is certainly a joke," said Wang Hui with a short laugh. "On the first day of this year I dreamed that I was looking at the list of metropolitan examination results. My name was on it—that goes without saying. But the third name was that of another man from Wen-shang county called Hsün Mei, and I wondered at this, since there was no provincial scholar from my county called Hsün. Fancy it's turning out to be this little student's name! As if I could be on the same list as he!" He burst out laughing, then went on, "It's obvious that dreams are unreliable. Fame and achievement depend upon study, not upon any supernatural forces."

"Some dreams do come true, though," said Chou Chin. "The day that I arrived here, Mr. Mei told me that one New Year's Day he dreamed that a great red sun fell on his head, and that year, sure enough, he passed the prefectural examination."

"That doesn't prove anything," retorted Wang Hui. "Suppose he does pass the prefectural examination and have a sun falling on his head—what about me? I have passed the provincial examination. Shouldn't the whole sky fall on my head?"

As they were chatting, lights were brought in, and the servants spread the desk with wine, rice, chicken, fish, duck, and pork. Wang Hui fell to, without inviting Chou Chin to join him; and when Wang Hui had finished, the monk sent up the teacher's rice with one dish of cabbage and a jug of hot water. When Chou Chin had eaten, they both went to bed. The next day the weather cleared. Wang Hui got up, washed and dressed, bade Chou Chin a casual goodbye, and went away in his boat, leaving the schoolroom floor so littered with chicken, duck, and fish bones, and melon seed shells, that it took Chou Chin a whole morning to clear them all away, and the sweeping made him dizzy.

When the villagers heard about Wang Hui's dream that Mr. Hsün's son would pass the metropolitan examination in the same year as himself, most of them thought it a great joke, and Hsün Mei's classmates took to calling him Dr. Hsün. But their fathers and elder brothers were annoyed. Out of spite, they went to congratulate Mr. Hsün on being the father of a metropolitan graduate, until he was so angry he could hardly speak.

Shen Hsiang-fu told the villagers secretly, "Mr. Wang could never have said such a thing. It's all made up by that fellow Chou. He saw that the Hsün family was the only one in the village with money, so he spun this yarn to flatter them, in the hope that they would send him more food during festivals. Only the other day I heard that the Hsüns sent some dried bean curd to the temple; and they have often sent him dumplings and cakes too. Depend on it, this is the reason."

Everyone was indignant, and Chou Chin's position became precarious. But since he had been introduced by the village head, they could not dismiss him; and he went on teaching as best he could for a year. At the end of that time, however, Village Head Hsia also became convinced that the teacher was a fool, because Chou Chin did not come often enough to flatter him. So Hsia allowed the villagers to dismiss him.

Having lost his job, Chou Chin went home. He was extremely hard up. One day his brother-in-law, Chin Yin-yu, came to see him and said, "Don't take offence at what I say, brother. But all this study doesn't seem to be getting you anywhere, and a bad job is better than none. How long can you go on like this—neither fish, flesh, nor fowl? I am going to the provincial capital with some other merchants to buy goods, and we need someone to keep accounts. Why don't you come with us? You are all on your own, and in our group you won't want for food or clothes."

"Even if a paralytic falls into a well, he can be no worse off than before," thought Chou Chin. "It can't hurt me to go." So he consented.

Chin chose an auspicious day, and they set off with a party of merchants to the provincial capital, where they stayed in a merchants' guild. Since Chou Chin had nothing to do, he strolled through the streets until he saw a group of workmen who said that they were going to repair the examination school. He followed them to the gate of the school and wanted to go in, but the gateman cracked his whip and drove him away.

That evening he told his brother-in-law how much he wanted to look over the examination school, and Chin had to tip the gateman to get him in. Some of the other merchants decided to go too, and asked the guild head to act as their guide. This time they simply sailed through the gate of the school, because the gateman, whose palm had been greased, made no attempt to stop them. When they reached the Dragon Gate, the guild head pointed to it, and said, "This is the gate for Scholars." They went into a corridor with examination cells on both sides, and the guild head told them, "This is Number One. You can go in and have a look." Chou Chin went in, and when he saw the desk set there so neatly, tears started to his eyes. He gave a long sigh, knocked his head against the desk, and slipped to the ground unconscious.

1. Characterize village life in eighteenth-century China.

2. What role do the prefectural examinations play in the lives of the people portrayed in *The Scholars*?

3. What does the passage tell us about the social position of scholars in eighteenth-century China?

4. *The Scholars* is famous for its social satire. How is this literary device used in this passage? For what purpose?

The European Enlightenment

Voltaire presiding over a repast with philosophers, in a drawing by Hubert (eighteenth century).

·96·
Voltaire
Candide
(1759)

*F*rançois-Marie Arouet, called Voltaire (1694–1778), was born into a middle-class Parisian family. His wit sharpened by a Jesuit education, Voltaire
abandoned the study of law and became a writer of plays and poetry, most with
classical themes. He ran into trouble when he turned a critical eye on the
French government and the Roman Catholic church. After a short imprisonment in the Bastille for his opinions, he was forced into exile in England,
where he came to admire the English constitution. He returned to France,
where his growing reputation as an enlightened thinker resulted in a wide correspondence with European monarchs and intellectuals. He was patronized
by Catherine the Great of Russia and lived briefly at the Prussian court. Eventually settling in Switzerland with his mistress, he spent his later years writing
on religion, science, and culture.

Candide is Voltaire's most famous work, said to have been written over a
weekend. It was enormously popular and went through 12 editions in its first
year in print. The fictional story of the travels of a naïve youth, *Candide* satirizes
philosophical optimism and takes on religious bigotry and tyranny. It was condemned by both Catholic and Protestant religious authorities.

1. HOW CANDIDE WAS BROUGHT UP IN A FINE CASTLE, AND HOW HE WAS EXPELLED THEREFROM

In Westphalia, in the castle of My Lord the Baron
of Thunder-ten-tronckh, there was a young man
whom nature had endowed with the gentlest of
characters. His face bespoke his soul. His judgment was rather sound and his mind of the simplest; this is the reason, I think, why he was named
Candide. The old servants of the house suspected
that he was the son of My Lord the Baron's sister
and of a good and honorable gentleman of the
neighborhood whom the lady never would marry
because he could prove only seventy-one quarter-
ings and the rest of his genealogical tree had
been lost by the injuries of time.

My Lord the Baron was one of the most powerful lords in Westphalia, for his castle had a
door and windows. His great hall was even
adorned with a piece of tapestry. All the dogs of
his stable yards formed a pack of hounds when
necessary; his grooms were his huntsmen; the village vicar was his Grand Almoner. They all called
him My Lord, and they laughed at the stories he
told.

My Lady the Baroness, who weighed about
three hundred and fifty pounds, attracted very
great consideration by that fact, and did the honors of the house with a dignity that made her
even more respectable. Her daughter Cunégonde, aged seventeen, was rosy-complexioned,
fresh, plump, appetizing. The Baron's son
appeared in all respects worthy of his father. The

tutor Pangloss was the oracle of the house, and little Candide listened to his lessons with all the candor of his age and character.

Pangloss taught metaphysico-theologo-cosmolo-nigology. He proved admirably that there is no effect without a cause and that, in this best of all possible worlds, My Lord the Baron's castle was the finest of castles, and My Lady the best of all possible Baronesses.

"It is demonstrated," he said, "that things cannot be otherwise, for, everything being made for an end, everything is necessarily for the best end. Note that noses were made to wear spectacles, and so we have spectacles. Legs were visibly instituted to be breeched, and we have breeches. Stones were formed to be cut and to make into castles; so My Lord has a very handsome castle; the greatest baron in the province should be the best housed; and, pigs being made to be eaten, we eat pork all year round: consequently, those who have asserted that all is well have said a foolish thing; they should have said that all is for the best."

Candide listened attentively and believed innocently; for he thought Mademoiselle Cunégonde extremely beautiful, though he never made bold to tell her so. He concluded that after the happiness of being born Baron of Thunder-ten-tronckh, the second degree of happiness was to be Mademoiselle Cunégonde; the third, to see her every day; and the fourth, to listen to Doctor Pangloss, the greatest philosopher in the province and consequently in the whole world.

One day Cunégonde, walking near the castle in the little wood they called The Park, saw in the bushes Doctor Pangloss giving a lesson in experimental physics to her mother's chambermaid, a very pretty and very docile little brunette. Since Mademoiselle Cunégonde had much inclination for the science, she observed breathlessly the repeated experiments of which she was a witness; she clearly saw the Doctor's sufficient reason, the effects and the causes, and returned home all agitated, all pensive, all filled with the desire to be learned, thinking that she might well be the sufficient reason of young Candide, who might equally well be hers.

She met Candide on the way back to the castle, and blushed; Candide blushed too; she said good morning to him in a faltering voice; and Candide spoke to her without knowing what he was saying. The next day, after dinner, as everyone was leaving the table, Cunégonde and Candide found themselves behind a screen; Cunégonde dropped her handkerchief, Candide picked it up, she innocently took his hand, the young man innocently kissed the young lady's hand with a very special vivacity, sensibility, and grace; their lips met, their eyes glowed, their knees trembled, their hands wandered. My Lord the Baron of Thunder-ten-tronckh passed near the screen and, seeing this cause and this effect, expelled Candide from the castle with great kicks in the behind; Cunégonde swooned; she was slapped in the face by My Lady the Baroness as soon as she had come to herself; and all was in consternation in the finest and most agreeable of all possible castles.

29. How Candide Found Cunégonde and the Old Woman Again

While Candide, the Baron, Pangloss, Martin, and Cacambo were relating their adventures, reasoning on the contingent or noncontingent events of this universe, arguing about effects and causes, moral and physical evil, free will and necessity, and the consolations that may be experienced when one is in the galleys in Turkey, they landed on the shore of Propontis at the house of the prince of Transylvania. The first objects that met their eyes were Cunégonde and the old woman, who were spreading out towels on lines to dry.

The Baron paled at this sight. The tender lover Candide, on seeing his fair Cunégonde dark-skinned, eyes bloodshot, flat-bosomed, cheeks wrinkled, arms red and rough, recoiled three steps in horror, and then advanced out of good manners. She embraced Candide and her brother; they embraced the old woman; Candide ransomed them both.

There was a little farm in the neighborhood; the old woman proposed to Candide that he buy it while waiting for the entire group to enjoy a better destiny. Cunégonde did not know that she had grown ugly, no one had told her so; she reminded Candide of his promises in so positive a tone that the good Candide did not refuse her. So he notified the Baron that he was going to marry his sister.

"I shall never endure," said the Baron, "such baseness on her part and such insolence on yours; no one shall ever reproach me with that infamy; my sister's children would not be able to enter the chapters* of Germany. No, never shall my sister marry anyone but a baron of the Empire."

Cunégonde threw herself at his feet and bathed them with tears; he was inflexible.

"You maddest of madmen," said Candide, "I rescued you from the galleys, I paid your ransom, I paid your sister's too; she was washing dishes here, she is ugly, I am kind enough to make her my wife, and you still presume to oppose it; I would kill you again if I heeded my anger."

"You may kill me again," said the Baron, "but you shall not marry my sister while I am alive."

30. CONCLUSION

At the bottom of his heart, Candide had no desire to marry Cunégonde. But the Baron's extreme impertinence determined him to clinch the marriage, and Cunégonde urged him on so eagerly that he could not retract. He consulted Pangloss, Martin, and the faithful Cacambo. Pangloss composed a fine memoir by which he proved that the Baron had no rights over his sister, and that according to all the laws of the Empire she could make a left-handed marriage† with Candide. Martin's judgement was to throw the Baron in the sea; Cacambo decided that he

*Knightly assemblies.

†A morganatic marriage, giving no equality to the party of lower rank.

should be returned to the Levantine captain and put back in the galleys, after which he would be sent by the first ship to the Father General in Rome. The plan was considered very good; the old woman approved it; they said nothing about it to his sister; for a little money the thing was carried out, and they had the pleasure of trapping a Jesuit and punishing the pride of a German Baron.

It was quite natural to imagine that after so many disasters Candide, married to his mistress and living with the philosopher Pangloss, the philosopher Martin, the prudent Cacambo, and the old woman, moreover having brought back so many diamonds from the land of the ancient Incas, would lead the most pleasant life in the world. But he was so cheated that he had nothing left but his little farm; his wife, becoming uglier every day, became shrewish and intolerable; the old woman was an invalid and was even more bad-humored than Cunégonde. Cacambo, who worked in the garden and who went and sold vegetables at Constantinople, was worn out with work and cursed his destiny. Pangloss was in despair at not shining in some university in Germany. As for Martin, he was firmly persuaded that a man is equally badly off anywhere; he took things patiently.

In the neighborhood there was a very famous dervish who was considered the best philosopher in Turkey; they went to consult him; Pangloss was the spokesman and said to him: "Master, we have come to ask you to tell us why such a strange animal as man was ever created."

"What are you meddling in?" said the dervish. "Is that your business?"

"But, Reverend Father," said Candide, "there is a horrible amount of evil on earth."

"What does it matter," said the dervish, "whether there is evil or good? When His Highness sends a ship to Egypt, is he bothered about whether the mice in the ship are comfortable or not?"

"Then what should we do?" said Pangloss.

"Hold your tongue," said the dervish.

"I flattered myself," said Pangloss, "that you and I would reason a bit together about effects and causes, the best of all possible worlds, the origin of evil, the nature of the soul, and preestablished harmony." At these words the dervish shut the door in their faces.

During this conversation the news had gone round that in Constantinople they had just strangled two viziers of the Divan and the mufti and impaled several of their friends. This catastrophe caused a great stir everywhere for a few hours. Pangloss, Candide, and Martin, returning to the little farm, came upon a good old man enjoying the fresh air by his door under a bower of orange trees. Pangloss, whose curiosity was as great as his love of reasoning, asked him the name of the mufti who had just been strangled.

"I know nothing about it," replied the good man, "and I have never known the name of any mufti or any vizier. I am entirely ignorant of the adventure that you are telling me about; I presume that in general those who meddle with public affairs sometimes perish miserably, and that they deserve it; but I never inquire what is going on in Constantinople; I content myself with sending there for sale the fruits of the garden that I cultivate."

Having said these words, he had the strangers come into his house; his two daughters and his two sons presented them with several kinds of sherbets which they made themselves, Turkish cream flavored with candied citron peel, oranges, lemons, limes, pineapples, pistachios, and Mocha coffee that had not been mixed with the bad coffee from Batavia and the West Indies. After which the two daughters of this good Moslem perfumed the beards of Candide, Pangloss, and Martin.

"You must have a vast and magnificent estate?" said Candide to the Turk.

"I have only twenty acres," replied the Turk; "I cultivate them with my children; work keeps away three great evils: boredom, vice, and need."

As Candide went back to this farm, he reflected deeply on the Turk's remarks. He said to Pangloss and Martin: "That good old man seems to me to have made himself a life far preferable to that of the six Kings with whom we had the honor of having supper."

"Great eminence," said Pangloss, "is very dangerous, according to the report of all philosophers. For after all Eglon, King of the Moabites, was assassinated by Ehud; Absalom was hanged by his hair and pierced with three darts; King Nadab son of Jeroboam was killed by Baasha, King Elah by Zimri, Ahaziah by Jehu, Athaliah by Jehoiada; Kings Jehoiakim, Jeconiah, and Zedekiah became slaves. You know how Croesus perished, Astyages, Darius, Dionysius of Syracuse, Pyrrhus, Perseus, Hannibal, Jugurtha, Ariovistus, Caesar, Pompey, Nero, Otho, Vitellius, Domitian, Richard II of England, Edward II, Henry VI, Richard III, Mary Stuart, Charles I, the three Henrys of France, the Emperor Henry IV? You know. . . ."

"I also know," said Candide, "that we must cultivate our garden."

"You are right," said Pangloss, "for when man was put in the Garden of Eden, he was put there *ut operaretur eum,* to work; which proves that man was not born for rest."

"Let us work without reasoning," said Martin, "it is the only way to make life endurable."

All the little society entered into this laudable plan; each one began to exercise his talents. The little piece of land produced much. True, Cunégonde was very ugly; but she became an excellent pastry cook; Paquette embroidered; the old woman took care of the linen. No one, not even Friar Giroflée, failed to perform some service; he was a very good carpenter, and even became an honorable man; and Pangloss sometimes said to Candide: "All events are linked together in the best of all possible worlds; for after all, if you had not been expelled from a fine castle with great kicks in the backside for love of Mademoiselle Cunégonde, if you had not been subjected to the Inquisition, if you had not traveled about America on foot, if you had not given the Baron a great blow with your sword, if you had not lost all your sheep from the good country of Eldorado, you would not be here eating candied citrons and pistachios."

"That is well said," replied Candide, "but we must cultivate our garden."

1. What seems to be Voltaire's opinion of the nobility?

2. Voltaire satirized the philosophy of his time with his description of Pangloss's opinions. What is the tutor's philosophy? How does he support what he says?

3. Characterize Voltaire's philosophy. Is he pessimistic or optimistic?

4. Why do you think *Candide* was such a popular book in its time? People of different classes read the story, and it appealed to them all. Why? Do you think that everyone came away with the same message?

5. How, in the end, do Candide and his friends resolve their questions about the meaning of life?

·97·

Jean-Jacques Rousseau
The Social Contract
(1762)

*J*ean-Jacques Rousseau (1712–1778) was born in Geneva and was raised by his unstable father. Alternately neglected and overprotected, Rousseau received little formal education and was eventually apprenticed to an engraver. He escaped from service and traveled throughout Europe before settling in Paris, where he began writing. He was taken up by the leaders of the salons, the fashionable meetings of French intellectuals, and gained wide popularity for his writings on educational and social issues. Living in constant motion, fearing both his friends and enemies, he finally settled down and married his long-time mistress.

The Social Contract is Rousseau's most significant political work. Despite his own experiences, he had an optimistic view of human nature. He believed that people were essentially good, and that government was formed by them to provide the greatest possible amount of personal freedom. His ideas were central to many of the reforms of the French Revolution.

THE SOCIAL COMPACT

I suppose man arrived at a point where obstacles, which prejudice his preservation in the state of nature, outweigh, by their resistance, the force which each individual can employ to maintain himself in this condition. Then the primitive state can no longer exist; and mankind would perish did it not change its way of life.

Now, as men cannot engender new forces, but can only unite and direct those which exist, they have no other means of preservation than to form by aggregation a sum of forces which could prevail against resistance, and to put them in play by a single motive and make them act in concert.

This sum of forces can be established only by the concurrence of many; but the strength and liberty of each man being the primary instruments of his preservation, how can he pledge them without injury to himself and without neglecting the care which he owes to himself? This difficulty as related to my subject may be stated as follows: "To find a form of association which shall defend and protect with the public force the person and property of each associate, and by means of which each, uniting with all, shall obey however only himself, and remain as free as before." Such is the fundamental problem of which the *Social Contract* gives the solution.

The clauses of this contract are so determined by the nature of the act, that the least modification would render them vain and of no effect; so that, although they may, perhaps, never have been formally enunciated, they are everywhere the same, everywhere tacitly admitted and recognized until, the social compact being violated, each enters again into his first rights and resumes his natural liberty, thereby losing the conventional liberty for which he renounced it.

These clauses, clearly understood, may be reduced to one: that is the total alienation of each associate with all his rights to the entire community, for, first, each giving himself entire-ly, the condition is the same for all, and the conditions being the same for all, no one has an interest in making it onerous for the others.

Further, the alienation being without reserve, the union is as complete as it can be, and no associate has anything to claim: for, if some rights remained to individuals, as there would be no common superior who could decide between them and the public, each, being in some points his own judge, would soon profess to be so in everything: the state of nature would exist, and the association would necessarily become tyrannical and useless.

Finally, each giving himself to all, gives himself to none; and as there is not an associate over whom he does not acquire the same right as is ceded, an equivalent is gained for all that is lost, and more force to keep what he has.

If, then, we remove from the social contract all that is not of its essence, it will be reduced to the following terms: "Each of us gives in common his person and all his force under the supreme direction of the general will; and we receive each member as an indivisible part of the whole."

Immediately, instead of the individual person of each contracting party, this act of association produces a moral and collective body, composed of as many members as the assembly has votes, which receives from this same act its unity—its common being, its life and its will. This public personage, thus formed by the union of all the others, formerly took the name of the city, and now takes that of republic or body politic. This is called the *state* by its members when it is passive; the *sovereign* when it is active; and a *power* when comparing it to its equals. With regard to the associates, they take collectively the name *people*, and call themselves individually *citizens*, as participating in the sovereign authority, and *subjects*, as submitted to the laws of the state. But these terms are often confounded and are taken one for the other. It is enough to know how to distinguish them when they are employed with all precision.

SIGNS OF A GOOD GOVERNMENT

When it is asked positively which is the best government, a question is asked which is unanswerable as it is indeterminate; or, if you will, it has as many good answers as there are combinations possible in the absolute and relative positions of peoples.

But if it be asked by what sign it may be known whether a given people is well or ill governed, it would be another thing, and the question of fact could be answered.

However, it is not answered because each wishes to answer it in his own way. Subjects vaunt public tranquility; citizens, individual liberty; one prefers the safety of property, and the other that of the person; one thinks that the best government is the most severe, the other maintains that it is the most gentle; this one wishes that crimes be punished, and that one that they be prevented; one finds it delightful to be feared by his neighbors, another prefers to be unknown to them; one is content when money circulates, another requires that the people have bread. Even were an agreement reached upon these and similar points, would an advance be made? Moral qualities lacking exact measurements—if an agreement were reached as to the sign, how could it be reached as to the estimate to be put upon them?

As for me, I am always astonished that so simple a sign fails to be recognized, or that such bad faith prevails that it is not acknowledged. What is the *object* of political association? The preservation and prosperity of its members. And what is the surest sign that they are preserved and prospered? It is their number and population. Do not look elsewhere for this much disputed sign. Other things being equal, the government under which—without outside means, without naturalization, without colonies—the citizens increase and multiply most, is invariably the best. That under which a people diminishes and perishes is the worst. Statisticians, it is now your affair; count, measure, compare.

THE GENERAL WILL IS INDESTRUCTIBLE

As long as men united together look upon themselves as a single body, they have but one will relating to the common preservation and general welfare. Then all the energies of the state are vigorous and simple; its maxims are clear and luminous; there are no mixed contradictory interests; the common prosperity shows itself everywhere, and requires only good sense to be appreciated. Peace, union, and equality are enemies of political subtleties. Upright, honest men are difficult to deceive, because of their simplicity; decoys and pretexts do not impose upon them, they are not cunning enough to be dupes. When we see among the happiest people in the world troops of peasants regulating the affairs of state under an oak, and conducting themselves wisely, can we help despising the refinements of other nations, who make themselves illustrious and miserable with so much art and mystery?

A state thus governed has need of few laws; and, in proportion as it becomes necessary to promulgate new ones this necessity will be universally recognized. The first to propose them will say only what all have already felt, and it requires neither intrigues nor eloquence to cause to become laws what each has already resolved upon, as soon as he can be sure that others will do likewise.

But when the social knot begins to relax, and the state to weaken, when individual interests commence to be felt, and small societies to influence the great, the common interest changes and finds opponents: unanimity no longer rules in the suffrages; the general will is no longer the will of all; contradictions and debates arise, and the best counsel does not prevail without dispute.

Finally, when the state, near its fall, exists only by a vain and illusory form; when the social tie is broken in all hearts; when the vilest interests flaunt boldly in the sacred name of the public welfare, then the general will becomes silent; all being guided by secret motives think no more like citizens than if the state had never existed. Iniquitous decrees are passed falsely under the name of the law, which have for object individual interests only.

Does it follow that the general will is annihilated or corrupted? No; it is always constant, inalterable, and pure; but it is subordinated to others which overbalance it. Each in detaching his interest from the common interest, sees that he cannot separate it entirely; but his part of the public misfortune seems nothing to him compared to the exclusive good which he thinks he has appropriated to himself. This particular good excepted, he desires the general well-being for his own interest as strongly as any other. Even in selling his vote for money he has not extinguished in himself the general will—he eludes it.

The fault which he commits is in evading the question and answering something which has not been asked him; instead of saying by his vote, "It is advantageous to the state," he says, "It is advantageous to such a man or party that such or such counsel prevail." The law of public order in assemblies is not so much to maintain the general will there, as to see that it is always interrogated and always answers.

I should have here many reflections to make upon the simple right to vote upon each act of sovereignty, a right which nothing can take from citizens, and upon the right to think, to propose, to divide, to discuss, which the government has always taken great care to allow only to its members; but this important matter will require a separate treatise, and I cannot consider it fully here.

1. What is the fundamental problem the social contract is meant to solve?

2. What are the signs of good government?

3. How do Rousseau's assumptions about how a society is organized differ from the assumptions of earlier theorists like Machiavelli or Richelieu?

4. Rousseau has much to say about the general will. What is it, and how do we know what it is?

5. Rousseau's view of human nature colors his political views. How does his general optimism affect his work? What assumptions does he make about human nature?

·98·

Cesare Beccaria
On Crimes and Punishments
(1764)

Cesare Beccaria (1738–1794) came from an aristocratic family in northern Italy. He received the standard legal education of the day and became a doctor of laws in 1758. In Milan at the time resided a group of enlightened intellectuals who called themselves the "academy of fists"; they were social reformers who were dedicated to overthrowing bigotry and narrow-mindedness. Beccaria's work on legal reform grew out of their inspiration and his commitment to an improved legal system. His proposals made him famous throughout Europe, and he was appointed to high office in Milan where he served for the rest of his life.

On Crimes and Punishments had an enormous impact on European law. The first systematic treatment of crime and punishment to be published, it opened debate on such controversial issues as the use of torture to extract confessions and the use of capital punishment to deter offenders. Law codes were reformed in light of Beccaria's principles and entire schools of legal and social reform, especially the English Utilitarians, took their inspiration from it.

If we glance at the pages of history, we will find that laws, which surely are, or ought to be, compacts of free men, have been, for the most part, a mere tool of the passions of some, or have arisen from an accidental and temporary need. Never have they been dictated by a dispassionate student of human nature who might, by bringing the actions of a multitude of men into focus, consider them from this single point of view; the *greatest happiness shared by the greatest number.* Happy are those few nations that have not waited for the slow succession of coincidence and human vicissitude to force some little turn for the better after the limit of evil has been reached, but have facilitated the intermediate progress by means of good laws.

Model used to build the first guillotine during the French Revolution.

IMPRISONMENT

An error no less common that it is contrary to the purpose of association—which is assurance of personal security—is that of allowing a magistrate charged with administering the laws to be free to imprison a citizen at his own pleasure, to deprive an enemy of liberty on frivolous pretexts, and to leave a friend unpunished notwithstanding the clearest evidences of his guilt. Detention in prison is a punishment which, unlike every other, must of necessity precede conviction for crime, but this distinctive character does not remove the other which is essential—namely, that only the law determines the cases in which a man is to suffer punishment. It pertains to the law, therefore, to indicate what evidences of crime justify detention of the accused, his subjection to investigation and punishment. A man's notoriety, his flight, his nonjudicial confession, the confession of an accomplice, threats and the constant enmity of the injured person, the manifest fact of the crime, and similar evidences, are proofs sufficient to justify imprisonment of a citizen. But these proofs must be determined by the law, not by judges, whose decrees are always contrary to political liberty when they are not particular applications of a general maxim included in the public code. When punishments have become more moderate, when squalor and hunger have been removed from prisons, when pity and mercy have forced a way through barred doors, overmastering the inexorable and obdurate ministers of justice, then may the laws be content with slighter evidences as grounds for imprisonment.

A man accused of a crime, who has been imprisoned and acquitted, ought not to be branded with infamy. How many Romans accused of very great crimes, and then found innocent, were revered by the populace and honored with public offices! For what reason, then, is the fate of an innocent person so apt to be different in our time? It seems to be because, in the present system of criminal law, the idea of power and arrogance prevails over that of justice, because accused and convicted are thrown indiscriminately into the same cell, because imprisonment is rather the torment than the confinement of the accused, and because the internal power that protects the laws and the external power that defends the throne and nation are separated when they ought to be united. By means of the common sanction of the laws, the former [internal power] would be combined with judicial authority, without, however, passing directly under its sway; the glory that attends the pomp and ceremony of a military corps would remove infamy, which, like all popular sentiments, is more attached to the manner than to the thing itself, as is proved by the fact that military prisons are, according to the common opinion, less disgraceful than the civil. Still discernible in our people, in their customs and laws, which always lag several ages behind the

actual enlightened thought of a nation—still discernible are the barbaric impressions and savage notions of those people of the North who hunted down our forefathers.

THE DEATH PENALTY

This useless prodigality of torments, which has never made men better, has prompted me to examine whether death is really useful and just in a well-organized government.

What manner of right can men attribute to themselves to slaughter their fellow beings? Certainly not that from which sovereignty and the laws derive. These are nothing but the sum of the least portions of the private liberty of each person; they represent the general will, which is the aggregate of particular wills. Was there ever a man who can have wished to leave to other men the choice of killing him? Is it conceivable that the least sacrifice of each person's liberty should include sacrifice of the greatest of all goods, life? And if that were the case, how could such a principle be reconciled with the other, that man is not entitled to take his own life? He must be, if he can surrender that right to others or to society as a whole.

The punishment of death, therefore, is not a right, for I have demonstrated that it cannot be such; but it is the war of a nation against a citizen whose destruction it judges to be necessary or useful. If, then, I can show that death is neither useful nor necessary I shall have gained the cause of humanity.

There are only two possible motives for believing that the death of a citizen is necessary. The first: when it is evident that even if deprived of liberty he still has connections and power such as endanger the security of the nation—when, that is, his existence can produce a dangerous revolution in the established form of government. The death of a citizen thus becomes necessary when a nation is recovering or losing its liberty or, in time of anarchy, when disorders themselves take the place of laws. But while the laws reign tranquilly, in a form of government

enjoying the consent of the entire nation, well
defended externally and internally by force, and
by opinion, which is perhaps even more efficacious than force, where executive power is
lodged with the true sovereign alone, where
riches purchase pleasures and not authority. I
see no necessity for destroying a citizen, except if
his death were the only real way of restraining
others from committing crimes; this is the second motive for believing that the death penalty
may be just and necessary.

It is not the intensity of punishment that has
the greatest effect on the human spirit, but its
duration, for our sensibility is more easily and
more permanently affected by slight but repeated impressions than by a powerful but momentary action. The sway of habit is universal over
every sentient being; as man speaks and walks
and satisfies his needs by its aid, so the ideas of
morality come to be stamped upon the mind
only by long and repeated impressions. It is not
the terrible yet momentary spectacle of the
death of a wretch, but the long and painful
example of a man deprived of liberty, who, having become a beast of burden, recompenses with
his labors the society he has offended, which is
the strongest curb against crimes. That efficacious idea—efficacious, because very often
repeated to ourselves—"I myself shall be
reduced to so long and miserable a condition if I
commit a similar misdeed" is far more potent
than the idea of death, which men envision
always at an obsure distance.

The death penalty becomes for the majority
a spectacle and for some others an object of compassion mixed with disdain; these two sentiments
rather than the salutary fear which the laws pretend to inspire occupy the spirits of the spectators. But in moderate and prolonged punishments the dominant sentiment is the latter,
because it is the only one. The limit which the
legislator ought to fix on the rigor of punishments would seem to be determined by the sentiment of compassion itself, when it begins to
prevail over every other in the hearts of those

who are the witnesses of punishment, inflicted
for their sake rather than for the criminal's.

For a punishment to be just it should consist
of only such gradations of intensity as suffice to
deter men from committing crimes. Now, the
person does not exist who, reflecting upon it,
could choose for himself total and perpetual
loss of personal liberty, no matter how advantageous a crime might seem to be. Thus the intensity of the punishment of a life sentence of servitude, in place of the death penalty, has in it what
suffices to deter any determined spirit. It has, let
me add, even more. Many men are able to look
calmly and with firmness upon death—some
from fanaticism, some from vanity, which almost
always accompanies man even beyond the tomb,
some from a final and desperate attempt either
to live no longer or to escape their misery. But
neither fanaticism nor vanity can subsist among
fetters or chains, under the rod, under the yoke,
in a cage of iron, where the desperate wretch
does not end his woes but merely begins them.
Our spirit resists violence and extreme but
momentary pains more easily than it does time
and incessant weariness, for it can, so to speak,
collect itself for a moment to repel the first, but
the vigor of its elasticity does not suffice to resist
the long and repeated action of the second.

If one were to cite against me the example of
all the ages and of almost all the nations that
have applied the death penalty to certain crimes,
my reply would be that the example reduced
itself to nothing in the face of truth, against
which there is no prescription; that the history of
men leaves us with the impression of a vast sea of
errors, among which, at great intervals, some
rare and hardly intelligible truths appear to float
on the surface. Human sacrifices were once common to almost all nations, yet who will dare to
defend them? That only a few societies, and for a
short time only, have abstained from applying
the death penalty, stands in my favor rather than
against me, for that conforms with the usual lot
of great truths; which are about as long-lasting as
a lightning flash in comparison with the long

dark night that envelops mankind. The happy time has not yet arrived in which truth shall be the portion of the greatest number, as error has heretofore been. And from this universal law those truths only have been exempted which Infinite Wisdom has chosen to distinguish from others by revealing them.

1. What should be the basic underlying principle of a law, according to Beccaria?

2. Beccaria condemns the contemporary form of sentencing individuals. What is wrong with it, and how would he change it?

3. What is Beccaria's opinion of the death penalty?

4. *On Crimes and Punishments* argues that capital punishment is not a deterrent. Why? What is a better deterrent?

5. *On Crimes and Punishments* is a work of the Enlightenment. Thinking about some of the other documents of the same period, what general characteristics do they seem to share?

· 99 ·

Marquis de Condorcet
Progress of the Human Mind
(1793)

Marie-Jean-Antoine Nicholas de Caritat, Marquis de Condorcet (1743–1794), was the eldest son of an old French noble family. Trained as a mathematician, he wrote a number of technical treatises early in his career and contributed to the great French encyclopedia. Condorcet was a member of a small circle of French philosophers and scientists who popularized the Enlightenment. Although he held a government post as inspector general of the Royal Mint, Condorcet was an enthusiastic supporter of the French Revolution and became secretary of the revolutionary Legislative Assembly. Interested in educational reform, he drafted a plan for the founding of free public schools. He also supported the creation of the Republic but opposed the execution of Louis XVI. Condorcet's moderate stand compromised him with the radical Jacobins, and he was arrested and became a fugitive in 1793. He was eventually caught after a dramatic chase and died in prison.

Condorcet wrote the *Progress of the Human Mind* while he was in hiding. He believed that although humans begin as savages, humanity is steadily progressing toward a state of perfection. Enlightened education is critically important to this progress, while monarchy and religion stand in its way. This work is one of the most important contemporary statements of Enlightenment belief.

THE FUTURE PROGRESS OF THE HUMAN MIND

If man can, with almost complete assurance, predict phenomena when he knows their laws, and if, even when he does not, he can still, with great expectation of success, forecast the future on the basis of his experience of the past, why, then, should it be regarded as a fantastic undertaking to sketch, with some pretence to truth, the future destiny of man on the basis of his history? The sole foundation for belief in the natural sciences is this idea, that the general laws directing the phenomena of the universe, known or unknown, are necessary and constant. Why should this principle be any less true for the development of the intellectual and moral faculties of man than for the other operations of nature? Since beliefs founded on past experience of like conditions provided the only rule of conduct for the wisest of men, why should the philosopher be forbidden to base his conjectures on these same foundations, so long as he does not attribute to them a certainty superior to that warranted by the number, the constancy, and the accuracy of his observations?

Our hopes for the future condition of the human race can be subsumed under three important heads: the abolition of inequality between nations, the progress of equality within each nation, and the true perfection of mankind. Will all nations one day attain that state of civilization which the most enlightened, the freest and the least burdened by prejudices, such as the French and the Anglo-Americans, have attained already? Will the vast gulf that separates these peoples from the slavery of nations under the rule of monarchs, from the barbarism of African tribes, from the ignorance of savages, little by little disappear?

If we glance at the state of the world today we see first of all that in Europe the principles of the French constitution are already those of all enlightened men. We see them too widely propagated, too seriously professed, for priests and despots to prevent their gradual penetration even into the hovels of their slaves; there they will soon awaken in these slaves the remnants of their common sense and inspire them with that smouldering indignation which not even constant humiliation and fear can smother in the soul of the oppressed.

The time will therefore come when the sun will shine only on free men who know no other master but their reason; when tyrants and slaves, priests and their stupid or hypocritical instruments will exist only in works of history and on the stage; and when we shall think of them only to pity their victims and their dupes; to maintain ourselves in a state of vigilance by thinking on their excesses; and to learn how to recognize and so to destroy, by force of reason, the first seeds of tyranny and superstition, should they ever dare to reappear amongst us.

In looking at the history of societies we shall have had occasion to observe that there is often a great difference between the rights that the law allows its citizens and the rights that they actually enjoy, and, again, between the equality established by political codes and that which in fact exists amongst individuals; and we shall have noticed that these differences were one of the principal causes of the destruction of freedom in the Ancient republics, of the storms that troubled them, and of the weakness that delivered them over to foreign tyrants.

These differences have three main causes: inequality in wealth; inequality in status between the man whose means of subsistence are hereditary and the man whose means are dependent on the length of his life, or, rather, on that part of his life in which he is capable of work; and, finally, inequality in education.

We therefore need to show that these three sorts of real inequality must constantly diminish without however disappearing altogether: for they are the result of natural and necessary causes which it would be foolish and dangerous to wish to eradicate; and one could not even attempt to bring about the entire disappearance of their effects without introducing even more fecund sources of inequality, without striking more direct and more fatal blows at the rights of man.

With all this progress in industry and welfare which establishes a happier proportion between men's talents and their needs, each successive generation will have larger possessions, either as a result of this progress or through the preservation of the products of industry; and so, as a consequence of the physical constitution of the human race, the number of people will increase.

There is another kind of progress within the sciences that is no less important; and that is the perfection of scientific language which is at present so vague and obscure. This improvement could be responsible for making the sciences genuinely popular, even in their first rudiments. Genius can triumph over the inexactitude of language as over other obstacles and can recognize the truth through the strange mask that hides or disguises it. But how can someone with only a limited amount of leisure to devote to his education master and retain even the simplest truths if they are distorted by an imprecise language? The fewer the ideas that he is able to acquire and combine, the more necessary is it that they should be precise and exact. He has no fund of knowledge stored up in his mind which he can draw upon to protect himself from error, and his understanding, not being strengthened and refined by long practice, cannot catch such feeble rays of light as manage to penetrate the obscurities, the ambiguities of an imperfect and perverted language.

Once people are enlightened they will know that they have the right to dispose of their own life and wealth as they choose; they will gradually learn to regard war as the most dreadful of scourges, the most terrible of crimes. The first wars to disappear will be those into which usurpers have forced their subjects in defence of their pretended hereditary rights.

Nations will learn that they cannot conquer other nations without losing their own liberty; that permanent confederations are their only means of preserving their independence; and that they should seek not power but security. Gradually mercantile prejudices will fade away: and a false sense of commercial interest will lose the fearful power it once had of drenching the earth in blood and of ruining nations under pretext of enriching them. When at last the nations come to agree on the principles of politics and morality, when in their own better interests they invite foreigners to share equally in all the benefits men enjoy either through the bounty of nature or by their own industry, then all the causes that produce and perpetuate national animosities and poison national relations will disappear one by one; and nothing will remain to encourage or even to arouse the fury of war.

1.   How does Condorcet try to predict the future of mankind?

2.   What stands in the way of progress? How will these obstacles be overcome?

3.   In Condorcet's future world, will there be inequality among individuals?

4. What role does education play in Condorcet's vision?

5. How realistic do you think Condorcet was when he wrote his book?

·100·

Montesquieu
Spirit of the Laws
(1748)

Charles-Louis, Baron de Montesquieu (1689–1755), was one of the most important political philosophers of the Enlightenment. He received a legal education and at the age of 27 became an officer in the French law courts. His provincial post was an important one, but he was attracted by life in the capital and soon moved to Paris. Once there, he threw himself into Parisian social and intellectual life. He won considerable fame as a wit, publishing several works of satire. Influenced by English models, he embarked upon a course of study on the nature of government and politics which resulted in his most important work, *Spirit of the Laws*. Though his work brought him great fame outside of France, Montesquieu remained a modest, good-humored man. He died quietly in Paris in 1755.

Spirit of the Laws was one of the most celebrated books of its time. Montesquieu spent 14 years writing it, and he produced a careful analysis of the origins of government and politics. The book had great impact throughout the West; among its contributions was the principle of separation of powers, now enshrined in the U.S. Constitution.

OF THE NATURE OF THE THREE DIFFERENT GOVERNMENTS

There are three species of government; *republican, monarchical,* and *despotic.* In order to discover their nature, it is sufficient to recollect the common notion, which supposes three definitions or rather three facts, that the *republican* government is that in which the body or only a part of the people is possessed of the supreme power: monarchy that in which a single person governs but by fixed and established laws: a despotic government, that in which a single person directs every thing by his own will and caprice.

This is what I call the nature of each government; we must examine now which are those laws that follow this nature directly, and consequently are the first fundamental laws.

OF THE REPUBLICAN GOVERNMENT AND THE LAWS RELATIVE TO DEMOCRACY

When the body of the people in a republic are possessed of the supreme power, this is called a *democracy*.

In a democracy the people are in some respect the sovereign, and in others the subject.

There can be no sovereign but by suffrages, which are their own will; and the sovereign's will is the sovereign himself. The laws therefore which establish the right of suffrage, are fundamental to this government. In fact, it is as important to regulate in a republic, in what manner, by whom, to whom, and concerning what, suffrages are to be given, as it is in a monarchy to know who is the prince and after what manner he ought to govern.

It is an essential point to fix the number of citizens that are to form the public assemblies; otherwise it might be uncertain whether the whole body or only a part of the people have voted.

The people in whom the supreme power resides, ought to do of themselves whatever conveniently they can; and what they cannot well do, they must commit to the management of ministers.

The ministers are not properly theirs, unless they have the nomination of them: it is therefore a fundamental maxim in this government, that the people should choose their ministers, that is, their magistrates.

The people are extremely well qualified for choosing those whom they are to entrust with part of their authority. They can tell when a person has been often in battle, and has had particular success; they are therefore very capable of electing a general. They can tell when a judge is assiduous in his office, when he gives general satisfaction, and has never been charged with bribery. These are all facts of which they can

have better information in a public forum, than a monarch in his palace. But are they able to manage an affair, to find out and make a proper use of places, occasions, moments? No, this is beyond their capacity.

The law which determines the manner of giving the suffrages is likewise fundamental in a democracy. It is a question of some importance, whether the suffrages ought to be public or secret. Cicero observes, that the laws which rendered them secret towards the close of the republic, were the cause of its decline. But as this is differently practiced in different republics, I shall offer here my thoughts concerning this subject.

The people's suffrages ought doubtless to be public; and this should be considered as a fundamental law of democracy. The lower sort of people ought to be directed by those of higher rank, and restrained within bounds by the gravity of certain personages. Hence by rendering the suffrages secret in the Roman republic all was lost; it was no longer possible to direct a populace that sought its own destruction.

It is likewise a fundamental law in democracies, that the people should have the sole power to enact laws. And yet there are a thousand occasions on which it is necessary the senate should have a power of decreeing; nay it is frequently proper to make some trial of a law before it is established. The constitution of Rome and Athens were extremely wise. The decrees of the senate had the force of laws for the space of a year, and did not become perpetual till they were ratified by the consent of the people.

OF THE RELATION OF LAWS TO THE NATURE OF MONARCHICAL GOVERNMENT

The intermediate, subordinate, and dependent powers, constitute the nature of monarchical government, that is, of that in which a single person governs by fundamental laws. I said, *intermediate, subordinate,* and *dependent powers*. In fact, in monarchies the prince is the source of all power political and civil. These fundamental laws necessarily suppose the intermediate channels through which the power flows: for if there be only the momentary and capricious will of a single person to govern the state, nothing can be fixed, and, of course there can be no fundamental law.

The most natural, intermediate and subordinate power is that of the nobility. This in some measure seems to be essential to a monarchy, whose fundamental maxim is, *no monarch, no nobility; no nobility, no monarch;* but there may be a despotic prince.

There are men who have endeavoured in some countries in Europe to abolish all the jurisdiction of the nobility; not perceiving that they were driving at the very thing that was done by the parliament of *England.* Abolish the privileges of the lords, of the clergy, and of the cities in a monarchy, and you will soon have a popular state, or else an arbitrary government.

Though the ecclesiastic power is so dangerous in a republic, yet it is extremely proper in a monarchy, especially of the absolute kind. What would become of *Spain* and *Portugal* since the subversion of their laws, were it not for this only barrier against the torrent of arbitrary power? A barrier that is always useful when there is no other: for as a despotic government is productive of the most frightful calamities to human nature, the very evil that restrains it, is beneficial to the subject.

OF THE CONDITION OR STATE OF WOMEN IN DIFFERENT GOVERNMENTS

In monarchies women are subject to very little restraint, because as the distinction of ranks calls them to court, they repair thither in order to assume that spirit of liberty, which is the only one there tolerated. The aspiring courtier avails himself of their charms and passions, in order to advance his fortune; and as their weakness admits not of pride, but of vanity: luxury constantly attends them.

In despotic governments women do not introduce, but are themselves an object of luxury. They must be here in a state of the most rigorous servitude. Every one follows the spirit of the government, and adopts in his own family the customs he sees elsewhere established. As the laws are very severe and executed on the spot, they are afraid lest the liberty of women should involve them in dangers. Their quarrels, indiscretions, repugnancies, jealousies, piques, and that art, in fine, which little souls have of interesting great ones, would be attended there with fatal consequences.

In republics women are free by the laws, and constrained by manners; luxury is banished from thence, and with it corruption and vice.

OF THE CORRUPTION OF THE PRINCIPLE OF DEMOCRACY

The principle of democracy is corrupted, not only when the spirit of equality is extinct, but likewise when they fall into a spirit of extreme equality, and when every citizen wants to be upon a level with those he has chosen to command him. Then the people, incapable of bearing the very power they have entrusted, want to do every thing of themselves, to debate for the senate, to execute for the magistrate, and to strip the judges.

When this is the case, virtue can no longer subsist in the republic. The people want to exercise the functions of the magistrates; who cease to be revered. The deliberations of the senate are slighted; all respect is then laid aside for the senators, and consequently for old age. If respect ceases for old age, it will cease also for parents; deference to husbands will be likewise thrown off, and submission to masters. This licentiousness will soon captivate the mind; and the restraint of command be as fatiguing as that of obedience. Wives, children, slaves, will shake off all subjection. No longer will there be any such thing as manners, order, or virtue.

Democracy hath therefore two excesses to avoid, the spirit of inequality which leads to aristocracy or monarchy; and the spirit of extreme equality, which leads to despotic power, as the latter is completed by conquest.

OF THE CORRUPTION OF THE PRINCIPLE OF MONARCHY

As democracies are destroyed when the people despoil the senate, magistrates and judges of their functions; so monarchies are corrupted when the prince insensibly deprives societies of their prerogatives, or cities of their privileges. In the first case the multitude usurp a despotic power; in the second it is usurped by a single person.

Monarchy is destroyed, when a prince thinks he shows a greater exertion of power in changing than in conforming to the order of things; when he deprives some of his subjects of their hereditary employments to bestow them arbitrarily upon others, and when he is fonder of being guided by his fancy than by his judgment.

Monarchy is destroyed when the prince directing every thing entirely to himself, calls that state to his capital, the capital to his court, and the court to his own person.

Monarchy is destroyed in fine, when the prince mistakes his authority, his situation, and the love of his people; and when he is not fully persuaded that a monarch ought to think himself secure, as a despotic prince ought to think himself in danger.

The principle of monarchy is corrupted, when the first dignities are marks of the first servitude, when the great men are stripped of popular respect, and rendered the low tools of arbitrary power.

It is still more corrupted, when honor is set up in contradiction to honors, and when men are capable of being loaded at the very same time with infamy and dignities.

1. What are the three types of government?

2. Montesquieu attaches a great deal of importance to the vote in a republic but argues against secrecy of the ballot. Why?

3. Where does power reside in a monarchy?

4. What prevents a king from becoming a tyrant in a monarchical state?

5. How does the status of women vary under the three different forms of government?

6. Both monarchy and democracy, according to Montesquieu, are subject to decay. What are the special pitfalls each faces?

The French Revolution

In this 1792 drawing by Gerard, the National Assembly demands that Louis XVI order his guards to stop firing on the Parisians who are storming the palace.

·101·
Abbé de Sieyès
What Is the Third Estate?
(1789)

*E*mmanuel-Joseph Sieyès (1748–1836) came from a middle-class family in provincial France. Son of a notary, he studied at the Sorbonne, and sought a career in the Church, where his talents caused him to rise rapidly in the Catholic hierarchy. Nevertheless, he found that his modest origins hampered his career. Sieyès saw in the French Revolution an opportunity to end the noble privilege that had blighted his own prospects. He championed the interests of the commoners—the third estate—and achieved considerable fame and political influence as a result. He was elected to the National Assembly and voted for the execution of the king. Sieyès's political effectiveness dwindled, however, because of his quarrelsome personality. He did remain at the center of the turbulent events of the 1790s and was instrumental in planning the coup that brought Napoleon Bonaparte to power in 1799. Ironically, Napoleon rewarded him with a title of nobility, and thereafter Sieyès faded into the background. Exiled from France for 15 years after Napoleon's fall, Sieyès did not return to Paris until he was near the end of his days.

What Is the Third Estate? a pamphlet published in January 1789, posed one of the central questions of the Revolution. In it, Sieyès argued that only the underprivileged majority of the nation had the right to reform the French constitution. Government did not belong to the king—it was the prerogative of the people.

The plan of this pamphlet is very simple. We have three questions to ask:

1. What is the third estate? Everything.
2. What has it been heretofore in the political order? Nothing.
3. What does it demand? To become something therein.

We shall see if the answers are correct. Then we shall examine the measures that have been tried and those which must be taken in order that the third estate may in fact become *something*. Thus we shall state:

4. What the ministers have *attempted,* and what the privileged classes themselves *propose* in it favor.
5. What *ought* to have been done.
6. Finally, what *remains* to be done in order that the third estate may take its rightful place.

THE THIRD ESTATE IS A COMPLETE NATION

What are the essentials of national existence and prosperity? *Private* enterprise and *public* functions.

This 1789 engraving contrasts the costumes representing the three Estates in prerevolutionary France.

Private enterprise may be divided into four classes: 1st. Since earth and water furnish the raw material for man's needs, the first class will comprise all families engaged in agricultural pursuits. 2nd. Between the original sale of materials and their consumption or use, further workmanship, more or less manifold, adds to these materials a second value, more or less compounded. Human industry thus succeeds in perfecting the benefits of nature and in increasing the gross produce twofold, tenfold, one hundredfold in value. Such is the work of the second class. 3rd. Between production and consumption, as well as among the different degrees of production, a group of intermediate agents, useful to producers as well as to consumers, comes into being; these are the dealers and merchants. . . . 4th. In addition to these three classes of industrious and useful citizens concerned with goods for consumption and use, a society needs many private undertakings and endeavors which are *directly* useful or agreeable to the *individual.* The fourth class includes from the most distinguished scientific and liberal professions to the least esteemed domestic services. Such are the labors which sustain society. Who performs them? The third estate.

Public functions likewise under present circumstances may be classified under four well known headings: the Sword, the Robe, the Church, and the Administration. It is unnecessary to discuss them in detail in order to demonstrate that the third estate everywhere constitutes nineteen-twentieths of them, except that it is burdened with all that is really arduous, with all the tasks that the privileged order refuses to perform. Only the lucrative and honorary positions are held by members of the privileged order. . . . nevertheless they have dared lay the order of the third estate under an interdict. They have said to it: "Whatever be your services, whatever your talents, you shall go thus far and no farther. It is not fitting that you be honored.". . .

It suffices here to have revealed that the alleged utility of a privileged order to public service is only a chimera; that without it, all that is arduous in such service is performed by the third estate; that without it, the higher positions would be infinitely better filled; that they naturally ought to be the lot of and reward for talents and recognized services; and that if the privileged classes have succeeded in usurping all the lucrative and honorary positions, it is both an odious injustice to the majority of citizens and a treason to the commonwealth.

Who, then, would dare to say that the third estate has not within itself all that is necessary to constitute a complete nation? It is the strong and robust man whose one arm remains enchained. If the privileged order were abolished, the nation would not be something less but something more. Thus, what is the third estate? Everything; but an everything shackled and oppressed. What would it be without the privileged order? Everything; but an everything free and flourishing. Nothing can progress without it; everything would proceed infinitely better without the others. It is not sufficient to have demonstrated that the privileged classes, far from being useful to the nation, can only enfeeble and injure it; it is necessary, moreover, to prove that the nobility does not belong to the social organization at all; that, indeed, it may be a *burden* upon the nation, but that it would not know how to constitute a part thereof.

The third estate, then, comprises everything appertaining to the nation; and whatever is not the third estate may not be regarded as being of the nation. What is the third estate? Everything!

WHAT HAS THE THIRD ESTATE BEEN HERETOFORE? NOTHING

We shall examine neither the state of servitude in which the people has suffered so long, nor that of constraint and humiliation in which it is still confined. Its civil status has changed; it must change still more; it is indeed impossible that the nation as a whole, or that even any order in particular, may become free if the third estate is not. Freedom is not the consequence of privileges, but of the rights appertaining to all. The third estate must be understood to mean the mass of the citizens belonging to the common order. Legalized privilege in any form deviates from the common order, constitutes an exception to the common law, and, consequently, does not apper-

tain to the third estate at all. We repeat, a common law and a common representation are what constitute *one nation*. It is only too true that one is *nothing* in France when one has only the protection of the common law; if one does not possess some privilege, one must resign oneself to enduring contempt, injury, and vexations of every sort. . . .

But here we have to consider the order of the third estate less in its civil status than in its relation with the constitution. Let us examine its position in the Estates General.

Who have been its so-called representatives? The ennobled or those privileged for a period of years. These false deputies have not even been always freely elected by the people. Sometimes in the Estates General, and almost always in the provincial Estates, the representation of the people has been regarded as a perquisite of certain posts of offices. Add to this appalling truth that, in one manner or another, all branches of the executive power also have fallen to the caste which furnishes the Church, the Robe, and the Sword. A sort of spirit of brotherhood causes the nobles to prefer themselves . . . to the rest of the nation. Usurpation is complete; in truth, they reign.

. . . [I]t is a great error to believe that France is subject to a monarchical régime.

. . . It is the court, and not the monarch, that has reigned. It is the court that makes and unmakes, appoints and discharges ministers, creates and dispenses positions, etc. And what is the court if not the head of this immense aristocracy which overruns all parts of France; which through its members attains all and everywhere does whatever is essential in all parts of the commonwealth? . . .

Let us sum up: the third estate has not heretofore had real representatives in the Estates General. Thus its political rights are null.

WHAT DOES THE THIRD ESTATE DEMAND? TO BECOME SOMETHING

. . . The true petitions of this order may be appreciated only through the authentic claims

directed to the government by the large munici-
palities of the kingdom. What is indicated therein? That the people wishes to be *something,* and,
in truth, the very least that is possible. It wishes to
have real representatives in the Estates General,
that is to say, deputies *drawn from its order,* who
are competent to be interpreters of its will and
defenders of its interests. But what will it avail it
to be present at the Estates General if the pre-
dominating interest there is contrary to its own!
Its presence would only consecrate the oppression of which it would be the eternal victim.
Thus, it is indeed certain that it cannot come to
vote at the Estates General unless it is to have in
that body *an influence at least equal to that of the
privileged classes;* and it demands a number of
representatives equal to that of the first two
orders together. Finally, this equality of representation would become completely illusory if
every chamber voted separately. The third estate
demands, then, that votes be taken *by head and
not by order.* This is the essence of those claims so
alarming to the privileged classes, because they
believed that thereby the reform of abuses would
become inevitable. The real intention of the
third estate is to have an influence in the Estates
General equal to that of the privileged classes. I
repeat, can it ask less? And is it not clear that if its
influence therein is less than equality, it cannot
be expected to emerge from its political nullity
and become *something?*

But what is indeed unfortunate is that the
three articles constituting the demand of the
third estate are insufficient to give it this equality
of influence which it cannot, in reality, do without. In vain will it obtain an equal number of representatives drawn from its order; the influence
of the privileged classes will establish itself and
dominate even in the sanctuary of the third
estate. . . .

Besides the influence of the aristocracy . . .
there is the influence of property. This is natural. I do not proscribe it at all; but one must agree
that it is still all to the advantage of the privileged
classes. . . . The more one considers this matter,
the more obvious the insufficiency of the three
demands of the third estate becomes. But finally,

such as they are, they have been vigorously
attacked. Let us examine the pretexts for this
hostility.

[Sieyès then proceeds to this examination by
analyzing the three demands under the
headings: 1. That the representation of the
third estate be chosen only among citizens
who really belong to the third estate; 2. That
its deputies be equal in number to those of
the two privileged orders; 3. That the Estates
General vote not by order, but by head. In
discussing the third demand he makes the
following comment.]

I have only one observation to make. Obviously there are abuses in France; these abuses
are profitable to someone; they are scarcely
advantageous to the third estate—indeed, they
are injurious to it in particular. Now I ask if, in
this state of affairs, it is possible to destroy any
abuse so long as those who profit therefrom control the *veto?* All justice would be powerless; it
would be necessary to rely entirely on the sheer
generosity of the privileged classes. Would that
be your idea of what constitutes the social order?

WHAT OUGHT TO HAVE BEEN DONE—
BASIC PRINCIPLES

In every free nation—and every nation ought to
be free—there is only one way to terminate differences which arise over the constitution.
Recourse must be had not to the notables, but to
the nation itself. If we lack a constitution we must
make one; the nation alone has that right. If we
have a constitution, as some persist in maintaining, and if, according thereto, the national
assembly is divided, as they claim, into three dep-
utations of three orders of citizens, one cannot,
at all events, avoid seeing that one of these
orders possesses so strong a claim that further
progress cannot be made without giving it consideration. But who has the right to settle such
disputes?

1st, Where shall we find the nation? Where it
is; in the 40,000 parishes which comprise all the
territory, all the inhabitants, and all the tribu-

taries of the commonwealth; there, without a doubt, is the nation. A territorial division should have been indicated to facilitate the means of resolving itself into *arrondissements* of from twenty to thirty parishes for the first deputies. According to a similar plan, the *arrondissements* would have formed provinces, and these would have sent real, special representatives to the capital, with special power to decide on the constitution of the Estates General.

But, you will say, if the majority of citizens had named special representatives, what would have become of the distinction of the three orders? What would have become of privileges? They would have become what they deserve to be. . . .

As we see it, the privileged classes have good reasons for confounding ideas and principles in this matter. Today they will support with intrepidity the contrary of what they advocated six months ago. Then there was only one cry in France: we had no constitution at all and we were demanding the formation of one.

Today not only do we have a constitution, but, if one believes the privileged classes, it comprises two excellent and unassailable provisions.

The first [of these] is the division of citizens by order; the second is equality of influence for each and every order in the formation of the national will. Already we have sufficiently proved that even if all these things composed our constitution, the nation could always alter them. The nature of this *equality* of influence on the national will, which would be attributed to each order, remains to be examined more particularly. We shall see that no idea could be more absurd, and that no nation can show anything similar in its constitution. . . .

If, then, the French constitution supposedly provides that 200,000 or 300,000 individuals out of 26,000,000 citizens constitute two-thirds of the common will, what to reply if not to affirm that two and two make five?

Individual wills are the sole elements of the general will. The majority may not be deprived of the right to concur in it, nor may ten wills be decreed worth only one against ten others that

are worth thirty. These are contradictions in terms, veritable absurdities.

It is useless to talk reason if, for a single instant, this first principle, that the general will is the opinion of the majority and not of the minority, is abandoned. By the same token, it may be decided that the will of one alone will be called the majority, and there is no longer need for either Estates General or national will, etc. . . . for if one will can equal ten, why should it not be worth one hundred, one million, twenty-six millions?

WHAT REMAINS TO BE DONE. DEVELOPMENT OF SOME PRINCIPLES

The time is past when the three orders, thinking only of defending themselves from ministerial despotism, were ready to unite against the common enemy. . . .

The third estate awaits, to no purpose, the meeting of all classes, the restitution of its political rights, and the plenitude of its civil rights; the fear of seeing abuses reformed alarms the first two orders far more than the desire for liberty inspires them. Between liberty and some odious privileges, they have chosen the latter. Their soul is identified with the favors of servitude. Today they dread this Estates General which but lately they invoked so ardently. All is well with them; they no longer complain, except of the spirit of innovation. They no longer lack anything; fear has given them a constitution.

The third estate must perceive in the trend of opinions and circumstances that it can hope for nothing except from its own enlightenment and courage. Reason and justice are in its favor; . . . there is no longer time to work for the conciliation of parties. What accord can be anticipated between the energy of the oppressed and the rage of the oppressors?

They have dared pronounce the word secession. They have menaced the King and the people. Well! Good God! How fortunate for the nation if this so desirable secession might be made permanently! How easy it would be to dispense with the privileged classes! How difficult to induce them to be citizens!

It is certain, then, that only nonprivileged members are capable of being electors and deputies to the national assembly. The wishes of the third estate will always be good for the major- ity of citizens, those of the privileged classes would always be bad. . . . The third estate, there- fore, is sufficient for whatever one may expect from a national assembly; it alone, then, is capa- ble of procuring all the advantages that may rea- sonably be expected from the Estates General.

1. Sieyès wrote to persuade readers of the justice of his cause. How effective is his work? What must such a work accomplish to succeed?

2. What is the position of the Third Estate under the old régime?

3. What is the part of the privileged classes in France, according to Sieyès?

4. How does Sieyès propose to enfranchise the Third Estate?

5. If Sieyès's argument for reform were accepted, what would the new French constitution be like?

·102·

The Declaration of the Rights of Man
(1789)

and *The Declaration of the Rights of Woman*
(1791)

*T*he Declaration of the Rights of Man *was one of the earliest and most impor- tant political documents of the French Revolution. The National Assem- bly, having just overthrown the ancient régime, decided to secure the Revolu- tion with a declaration of principle.* The Declaration *was heavily influenced by transatlantic examples. The English Bill of Rights was one model, but more important were the statements of rights in the American state constitutions. These were quickly translated into French and had considerable influence upon the members of the Assembly.* The Declaration of the Rights of Man *is a brief but powerful statement of the central themes of the revolution: Liberty, Equal- ity, and Fraternity.*

The political and intellectual ferment of the Revolution also gave rise to a new assertiveness by some French women. Olympe de Gouges, the daughter of a provincial butcher, was one who felt that the declaration of 1789 did not go far enough. In 1791, dissatisfied with the unequal position women continued to hold in spite of the Revolution, she wrote *The Declaration of the Rights of Woman,* and addressed it to the queen, rather than to Louis XVI or the National Assembly. In it, de Gouges demanded political and social rights for women.

DECLARATION OF THE RIGHTS OF MAN AND OF THE CITIZEN

The representatives of the French people, organized as a National Assembly, believing that the ignorance, neglect, or contempt of the rights of man are the sole cause of public calamities and of the corruption of governments, have determined to set forth in a solemn declaration the natural, inalienable, and sacred rights of man, in order that this declaration, being constantly before all the members of the social body, shall remind them continually of their rights and duties; in order that the acts of the legislative power, as well as those of the executive power, may be compared at any moment with the objects and purposes of all political institutions and may thus be more respected; and, lastly, in order that the grievances of the citizens, based hereafter upon simple and incontestable principles, shall tend to the maintenance of the constitution and redound to the happiness of all. Therefore the National Assembly recognizes and proclaims, in the presence and under the auspices of the Supreme Being, the following rights of man and of the citizen:

1. Men are born and remain free and equal in rights. Social distinctions may be founded only upon the general good.

2. The aim of all political association is the preservation of the natural and imprescriptible rights of man. These rights are liberty, property, security, and resistance to oppression.

3. The principle of all sovereignty resides essentially in the nation. No body nor individual may exercise any authority which does not proceed directly from the nation.

4. Liberty consists in the freedom to do everything which injures no one else; hence the exercise of the natural rights of each man has no limits except those which assure to the other members of the society the enjoyment of the same rights. These limits can only be determined by law.

5. Law can only prohibit such actions as are hurtful to society. Nothing may be prevented which is not forbidden by law, and no one may be forced to do anything not provided for by law.

6. Law is the expression of the general will. Every citizen has a right to participate personally, or through his representative, in its formation. It must be the same for all, whether it protects or punishes. All citizens, being equal in the eyes of the law, are equally eligible to all dignities and to all public positions and occupations, according to their abilities, and without distinction except that of their virtues and talents.

7. No person shall be accused, arrested, or imprisoned except in the cases and according to the forms prescribed by law. Any one soliciting, transmitting, executing, or causing to be executed, any arbitrary order, shall be punished. But any citizen summoned or arrested in virtue of the law shall submit without delay, as resistance constitutes an offense.

8. The law shall provide for such punishments only as are strictly and obviously necessary, and no one shall suffer punishment except it be legally inflicted in virtue of a law passed and promulgated before the commission of the offense.

9. As all persons are held innocent until they shall have been declared guilty, if arrest shall be deemed indispensable, all harshness not

essential to the securing of the prisoner's person shall be severely repressed by law.

10.   No one shall be disquieted on account of his opinions, including his religious views, provided their manifestation does not disturb the public order established by law.

11.   The free communication of ideas and opinions is one of the most precious of the rights of man. Every citizen may, accordingly, speak, write, and print with freedom, but shall be responsible for such abuses of this freedom as shall be defined by law.

12.   The security of the rights of man and of the citizen requires public military forces. These forces are, therefore, established for the good of all and not for the personal advantage of those to whom they shall be intrusted.

13.   A common contribution is essential for the maintenance of the public forces and for the cost of administration. This should be equitably distributed among all the citizens in proportion to their means.

14.   All the citizens have a right to decide, either personally or by their representatives, as to the necessity of the public contribution; to grant this freely; to know to what uses it is put; and to fix the proportion, the mode of assessment and of collection and the duration of the taxes.

15.   Society has the right to require of every public agent an account of his administration.

16.   A society in which the observance of the law is not assured, nor the separation of powers defined, has no constitution at all.

17.   Since property is an inviolable and sacred right, no one shall be deprived thereof except where public necessity, legally determined, shall clearly demand it, and then only on condition that the owner shall have been previously and equitably indemnified.

DECLARATION OF THE RIGHTS OF WOMAN AND THE FEMALE CITIZEN

Man, are you capable of being just? It is a woman who poses the question; you will not deprive her of that right at least. Tell me, what gives you sovereign empire to oppress my sex? Your strength? Your talents? Observe the Creator in his wisdom; survey in all her grandeur that nature with whom you seem to want to be in harmony, and give me, if you dare, an example of this tyrannical empire. Go back to animals, consult the elements, study plants, finally glance at all the modifications of organic matter, and surrender to the evidence when I offer you the means; search, probe, and distinguish, if you can, the sexes in the administration of nature. Everywhere you will find them mingled; everywhere they cooperate in harmonious togetherness in this immortal masterpiece.

Man alone has raised his exceptional circumstances to a principle. Bizarre, blind, bloated with science and degenerated—in a century of enlightenment and wisdom—into the crassest ignorance, he wants to command as a despot a sex which is in full possession of its intellectual faculties; he pretends to enjoy the Revolution and to claim his rights to equality in order to say nothing more about it.

Declaration of the Rights of Woman and the Female Citizen

For the National Assembly to decree in its last sessions, or in those of the next legislature:

Preamble

Mothers, daughters, sisters [and] representatives of the nation demand to be constituted into a national assembly. Believing that ignorance, omission, or scorn for the rights of woman are the only causes of public misfortunes and of the corruption of governments, [the women] have resolved to set forth in a solemn declaration the natural, inalienable, and sacred rights of woman in order that this declaration, constantly exposed before all the members of the society, will ceaselessly remind them of their rights and duties; in order that the authoritative acts of women and the authoritative acts of men may be at any moment compared with and respectful of the purpose of all political institutions; and in order that citizens' demands, henceforth based on simple and incontestable principles, will always support the constitution, good morals, and the happiness of all.

Consequently, the sex that is as superior in beauty as it is in courage during the sufferings of maternity recognizes and declares in the presence and under the auspices of the Supreme Being, the following Rights of Woman and of Female Citizens.

Article I

Woman is born free and lives equal to man in her rights. Social distinctions can be based only on the common utility.

Article II

The purpose of any political association is the conservation of the natural and imprescriptible rights of woman and man; these rights are liberty, property, security, and especially resistance to oppression.

Article III

The principle of all sovereignty rests essentially with the nation, which is nothing but the union of woman and man; no body and no individual can exercise any authority which does not come expressly from it [the nation].

Article IV

Liberty and justice consist of restoring all that belongs to others; thus, the only limits on the exercise of the natural rights of woman are perpetual male tyranny; these limits are to be reformed by the laws of nature and reason.

Article V

Laws of nature and reason proscribe all acts harmful to society; everything which is not prohibited by these wise and divine laws cannot be prevented, and no one can be constrained to do what they do not command.

Article VI

The law must be the expression of the general will; all female and male citizens must contribute either personally or through their representatives to its formation; it must be the same for all: male and female citizens, being equal in the eyes of the law, must be equally admitted to all honors, positions, and public employment according to their capacity and without other distinctions besides those of their virtues and talents.

Article VII

No woman is an exception; she is accused, arrested, and detained in cases determined by law. Women, like men, obey this rigorous law.

Article VIII

The law must establish only those penalties that are strictly and obviously necessary, and no one can be punished except by virtue of a law established and promulgated prior to the crime and legally applicable to women.

Article IX

Once any woman is declared guilty, complete rigor is [to be] exercised by the law.

Article X

No one is to be disquieted for his very basic opinions; woman has the right to mount the scaffold; she must equally have the right to mount the rostrum, provided that her demonstrations do not disturb the legally established public order.

Article XI

The free communication of thoughts and opinions is one of the most precious rights of woman, since that liberty assures the recognition of children by their fathers. Any female citizen thus may say freely, I am the mother of a child which belongs to you, without being forced by a barbarous prejudice to hide the truth; [an exception may be made] to respond to the abuse of this liberty in cases determined by the law.

Article XII

The guarantee of the rights of woman and the female citizen implies a major benefit; this guarantee must be instituted for the advantage of all, and not for the particular benefit of those to whom it is entrusted.

Article XIII

For the support of the public force and the expenses of administration, the contributions of woman and man are equal; she shares all the duties [*corvées*] and all the painful tasks; therefore, she must have the same share in the distribution of positions, employment, offices, honors and jobs [*industrie*].

Article XIV

Female and male citizens have the right to verify, either by themselves or through their representatives, the necessity of the public contribution. This can only apply to women if they are granted an equal share, not only of wealth, but also of public administration, and in the determination of the proportion, the base, the collection, and the duration of the tax.

Article XV

The collectivity of women, joined for tax purposes to the aggregate of men, has the right to demand an accounting of his administration from any public agent.

Article XVI

No society has a constitution without the guarantee of rights and the separation of powers; the constitution is null if the majority of individuals comprising the nation have not cooperated in drafting it.

Article XVII

Property belongs to both sexes whether united or separate; for each it is an inviolable and sacred right; no one can be deprived of it, since it is the true patrimony of nature, unless the legally determined public need obviously dictates it, and then only with a just and prior indemnity.

Postscript

Woman, wake up; the tocsin of reason is being heard throughout the whole universe; discover your rights. The powerful empire of nature is no longer surrounded by prejudice, fanaticism, superstition, and lies. The flame of truth has dispersed all the clouds of folly and usurpation. Enslaved man has multiplied his strength and needs recourse to yours to break his chains. Having become free, he has become unjust to his companion. Oh, women, women! When will you cease to be blind? What advantage have you received from the Revolution? A more pronounced scorn, a more marked disdain. In the centuries of corruption you ruled only over the weakness of men. The reclamation of your patrimony, based on the wise decrees of nature—what have you to dread from such a fine undertaking?

1. Where does sovereignty lie according to the National Assembly?

2. What rights do citizens have under *The Declaration of the Rights of Man*?

3. What is the status of personal property in the Assembly's view?

4. How is *The Declaration of the Rights of Man* similar to the position expressed by other eighteenth-century political thinkers, such as Jefferson and Rousseau?

5. Compare the *Rights of Man* with the *Rights of Woman*. How are they different? How are they alike?

6. What have women achieved in the Revolution, according to de Gouges?

·103·

Edmund Burke
Reflections on the Revolution in France
(1790)

*E*dmund Burke (1729–1797) came from the Anglo-Irish gentry. He received a legal education but was always more interested in politics and political theory than the practice of law. Burke entered the House of Commons in 1765, where he remained for almost 30 years. In the 1770s, Burke favored conciliation with the American colonies and argued for a less oppressive government in Ireland. Despite these liberal views, however, he is generally characterized as a conservative political thinker. The French Revolution deeply alarmed him, and he spent much of the rest of his life warning of its dangers.

Reflections is the most important expression of Burke's opposition to revolution. He wrote in defense of tradition and hierarchy in society. Burke believed that the institutions of his day owed much to the wisdom of past generations and that to overthrow them in favor of a new theory or speculation was as dangerous as it was foolish. Burke's conservative arguments against radical change have become vital to conservative thought everywhere.

You might, if you pleased, have profited of our example, and have given to your recovered freedom a correspondent dignity. Your privileges, though discontinued, were not lost to memory. Your constitution, it is true, whilst you were out of possession, suffered waste and dilapidation; but you possessed in some parts the walls, and in all the foundations of a noble and venerable castle. You might have repaired those walls; you might have built on those old foundations. Your constitution was suspended before it was perfected; but you had the elements of a constitution very nearly as good as could be wished.

You had all these advantages in your ancient states; but you chose to act as if you had never been moulded into civil society, and had everything to begin anew. You began ill, because you began by despising every thing that belonged to you. You set up your trade without a capital. If the last generations of your country appeared without much lustre in your eyes, you might have passed them by, and derived your claims from a more early race of ancestors. Under a pious predilection to those ancestors, your imaginations would have realized in them a standard of virtue and wisdom, beyond the vulgar practice of the hour: and you would have risen with the example to whose imitation you aspired. Respecting your forefathers, you would have been taught to respect yourselves. You would not have chosen to consider the French as a people of yesterday, as a nation of low-born servile wretches until the emancipating year of 1789. In order to furnish, at the expense of your honour, an excuse to your apologists here for several enormities of yours, you would not have been content to be represented as a gang of Maroon slaves, suddenly broke loose from the house of bondage, and therefore to be pardoned for your abuse of the liberty to which you were not accustomed and ill fitted.

By following wise examples you would have given new examples of wisdom to the world. You would have rendered the cause of liberty venerable in the eyes of every worthy mind in every nation. You would have shamed despotism from the earth, by showing that freedom was not only reconcilable, but as, when well disciplined it is, auxiliary to law. You would have had an unoppressive but a productive revenue. You would have had a flourishing commerce to feed it. You would have had a free constitution; a potent monarchy; a disciplined army; a reformed and venerated clergy; a mitigated but spirited nobility, to lead your virtue, not to overlay it; you would have had a liberal order of commons, to emulate and to recruit that nobility; you would have had

a protected, satisfied, laborious, and obedient people, taught to seek and to recognize the happiness that is to be found by virtue in all conditions; in which consists the true moral equality of mankind, and not in that monstrous fiction, which, by inspiring false ideas and vain expectations into men destined to travel in the obscure walk of laborious life, serves only to aggravate and embitter that real inequality, which it never can remove; and which the order of civil life establishes as much for the benefit of those whom it must leave in an humble state, as those whom it is able to exalt to a condition more splendid, but not more happy. You had a smooth and easy career of felicity and glory laid open to you, beyond any thing recorded in the history of the world; but you have shewn that difficulty is good for man.

Compute your gains: see what is got by those extravagant and presumptuous speculations which have taught your leaders to despise all their predecessors, and all their contemporaries, and even to despise themselves, until the moment in which they became truly despicable. By following those false lights, France has bought undisguised calamities at a higher price than any nation has purchased the most unequivocal blessings! France has bought poverty by crime! France has not sacrificed her virtue to her interest; but she has abandoned her interest, that she might prostitute her virtue. All other nations have begun the fabric of a new government, or the reformation of an old, by establishing originally, or by enforcing with greater exactness some rites or other of religion. All other people have laid the foundations of civil freedom in severe manners, and a system of a more austere and masculine morality. France, when she let loose the reins of regal authority, doubled the licence, of a ferocious dissoluteness in manners, and of an insolent irreligion in opinions and practices; and has extended through all ranks of life, as if she were communicating some privilege, or laying open some secluded benefit, all the unhappy corruptions that usually were the disease of wealth and power. This is one of the new principles of equality in France.

This was unnatural. The rest is in order. They have found their punishment in their success. Laws overturned; tribunals subverted; industry without vigour; commerce expiring; the revenue unpaid, yet the people impoverished; a church pillaged, and a state not relieved; civil and military anarchy made the constitution of the kingdom; every thing human and divine sacrificed to the idol of public credit, and national bankruptcy the consequence; and to crown all, the paper securities of new, precarious, tottering power, the discredited paper securities of impoverished fraud, and beggared rapine, held out as a currency for the support of an empire, in lieu of the two great recognized species that represent the lasting conventional credit of mankind, which disappeared and hid themselves in the earth from whence they came, when the principle of property, whose creatures and representatives they are, was systematically subverted.

Were all these dreadful things necessary? were they the inevitable results of the desperate struggle of determined patriots, compelled to wade through blood and tumult, to the quiet shore of a tranquil and prosperous liberty? No! nothing like it. The fresh ruins of France, which shock our feelings wherever we can turn our eyes, are not the devastation of civil war; they are the sad but instructive monuments of rash and ignorant counsel in time of profound peace. They are the display of inconsiderate and presumptuous, because unresisted and irresistible authority. The persons who have thus squandered away the precious treasure of their crimes, the persons who have made this prodigal and wild waste of public evils (the last stake reserved for the ultimate ransom of the state) have met in their progress with little, or rather with no opposition at all.

When men of rank sacrifice all ideas of dignity to an ambition without a distinct object, and work with low instruments and for low ends, the whole composition becomes low and base. Does not something like this now appear in France? Does it not produce something ignoble and inglorious? A kind of meanness in all the preva-

lent policy? A tendency in all that is done to lower along with individuals all the dignity and importance of the state? Other revolutions have been conducted by persons, who whilst they attempted or effected changes in the commonwealth, sanctified their ambition by advancing the dignity of the people whose peace they troubled. They had long views. They aimed at the rule, not at the destruction of their country. They were men of great civil, and great military talents, and if not for the terror, the ornament of their age.

It is said, that twenty-four millions ought to prevail over two hundred thousand. True; if the constitution of a kingdom be a problem of arithmetic. This sort of discourse does well enough with the lamp-post for its second: to men who *may* reason calmly, it is ridiculous. The will of the many, and their interest, must very often differ; and great will be the difference when they make an evil choice. A government of five hundred country attornies and obscure curates is not good for twenty-four millions of men, though it were chosen by eight and forty millions; nor is it the better for being guided by a dozen of persons of quality, who have betrayed their trust in order to obtain that power.

In France you are now in the crisis of a revolution, and in the transit from one form of government to another—you cannot see that character of men exactly in the same situation in which we see it in this country. With us it is militant; with you it is triumphant; and you know how it can act when its power is commensurate to its will. The worst of these politics of revolution is this; they temper and harden the breast, in order to prepare it for the desperate strokes which are sometimes used in extreme occasions. But as these occasions may never arrive, the mind receives a gratuitous taint; and the moral sentiments suffer not a little, when no political purpose is served by the depravation. This sort of people are so taken up with their theories about the rights of man, that they have totally forgot his nature. Without opening one new avenue to the understanding, they have succeeded in stopping up those that lead to the heart.

1. What, according to Burke, did the French do when they overthrew their monarchy? What was their attitude toward the past?

2. What is Burke's view of equality in society?

3. What has been the result of the Revolution, according to Burke? Why has it failed?

4. How do you think Burke, as an Englishman, was influenced by his own nation's constitution?

5. Burke argues that representative democracy is not the best way to run a state. What is wrong with it?

Travelers to the East and West

Japanese woodcut of a Russian, a Chinese, and a Dutchman, early nineteenth century.

·104·

John Ovington

A Voyage to Surat in the Year 1689

(1696)

John Ovington (1653–1731) was an English minister who took a post as a ship's chaplain with the East India Company. He was born in Yorkshire and educated at Trinity College Dublin and Cambridge University. He probably had difficulty obtaining a living as a parish clergyman, for he was already in his thirties when he decided to serve aboard ship. His first journey, to the east coast of Africa and then to India, was made in 1689. He stayed some time in Bombay, which was controlled by the East India Company, and then moved on to Surat, where he lived for two years as a chaplain to the English trading factory. While in Surat, Ovington observed the power of the Moguls and the nature of their commercial empire.

Ovington returned to England to write his *Voyage to Surat*, which was an instant success and helped advance his career. He was one of the early advocates of tea-drinking, writing *The Nature and Quality of Tea* to promote its benefits. Ovington was ultimately made a royal chaplain and received a living in Kent, where he served until his death in 1731.

THE CITY OF SURAT, AND ITS INHABITANTS

The City of Surat lies in 21 degrees, and some odd minutes of north latitude. It is by Ptolomy called Muziris, and is situated upon a river ten or twelve miles distant from the sea. The name of the river is Tapy, or Tindy, which rises from the mountain of Deccan, and from thence falls down through Brampore, and by Meanders from Surat glides down gently into the ocean. . . . Its greatest strength is in the castle, which commands not only the ships and boats in the river, but likewise guards the city by land.

The castle is built towards the south-west part of the city, having a river to defend it on one side, and a ditch on the other. It is built square, and fortified at each corner with a large tower, containing various lodgings, and furnished with all conveniences fit for accommodating the gov-

ernor, and has several cannons mounted upon the walls.

The entrance into the city is by six or seven gates, where are centinels fixed continually, requiring an account, upon the least suspicion, of all that enter in, or pass out of the city.

The houses are many of them fair and stately, though unproportionable to the wealth of the inhabitants, who are always concerned to conceal their riches, and therefore never exceed in any luxurious furniture, lest it should prove too powerful a temptation to the avarice of the Mogul. They are flat roofed, or rather made a little shelving, after the manner of the buildings in Spain and Portugal, covered with tiles, and the walls are made of brick or stone. The windows are without glass, and kept open for the convenience of the fresh air; and the floors both of the lower and upper stories are all terrassed to make them cool. But the poorer sort, and such as inhabit the skirts of the city, live much meaner, in houses, whose walls are only bamboos at a foot distance, with reeds wove through them; and their covering is only cajan, or palm-leaves of trees, which gives them the common name of cajan-houses.

The streets are some too narrow, but in many places of a convenient breadth; and in an evening, especially near the bazar, or market-place, are more populous than any part of London; and so much thronged, that it is not very easy to pass through the multitude of Bannians and other merchants that expose their goods. For here they stand with their silks and stuffs in their hands, or upon their heads, to invite such as pass by to come and buy them.

In the midst of the city is a spacious vacant place, called castle-green, because of its nearness to the castle, on which are laid all sorts of goods in the open air, both day and night, excepting the mussoun time. And here the English, French, and Dutch, with the natives, place their bales, and prepare them as loadings for their ships.

The governor of the castle is appointed by the Mogul; and his authority seldom stretches beyond the space of three years, in all which time he is a real prisoner under the appearance of a high commander, and under a severe and strict engagement never to pass without the walls of his castle; but to be continually upon his guard, in a constant readiness for any emergence or sur-prize, all the time he is in the government.

Surat is reckoned the most famed emporium of the Indian Empire, where all commodities are vendible, though they never were there seen before. The very curiosity of them will engage the expectation of the purchaser to sell them again with some advantage, and will be apt to invite some other by their novelty, as they did him, to venture upon them. And the river is very commodious for the importation of foreign goods, which are brought up to the city in hoys and yachts, and country boats, with great conve-nience and expedition. And not only from

Europe, but from China, Persia, Arabia, and other remote parts of India, ships unload abun-dance of all kinds of goods, for the ornament of the city, as well as enriching of the port.

It is renowned for traffick through all Asia, both for rich silks, such as atlasses, cuttanees, soofeys, culgars, allajars, velvets, taffaties, and sattins; and for zarbafts from Persia; and the abundance of pearls that are brought hither from the Persian Gulph; but likewise for dia-monds, rubies, saphires, topazes, and other stones of splendor and esteem, which are vendible here in great quantities: and for aggats, cornelians, nigganees, desks, scrutores, and boxes neatly polished and embellished, which may be purchased here at very reasonable rates.

Goods are brought to Surat from Agra, their cap-ital city, from Delhi, Broach, Ahmedabad, and other cities noted for particular commodities, which are sold off in great quantities to the Euro-peans, Turks, Arabians, Persians, and Armeni-ans, who above any of the rest travel the farthest, spread themselves in all parts of Asia, as well as Europe, and are as universal merchants as any in the world. . . .

Besides their governor of the castle of Surat, who is always confined a prisoner within its walls, there is another of the city, to whose manage-ment and care is committed the trust of all civil affairs. He receives addresses from the principal merchants and men of note, and all applications of moment from the inhabitants are made to him. He generally keeps at home for dispatching the business of his master, or the people under his care; and if he goes abroad, he sometimes takes the air upon an elephant, seated in a chair of state upon his back; and besides the keeper of the beast, carries along with him a peon, or ser-vant to fan him, and drive away the busy flies and troublesome mosquitoes: This is done with the hair of a horse's tail fastened to the end of a small stick of a foot length, a very homely fan, but yet the only one in esteem with the grandees, and even the emperor himself. To maintain the dignity of his post and station, he maintains several large elephants, and keeps in constant pay and readiness many soldiers, both horse and foot, to guard his person at home and abroad, and to be ready for his dispatches.

He does not peremptorily arbitrate in cases of moment, but when any matter of consequence is brought before him, he seldom determines it without the consultation and concurrence of other officers of the city, the cogy, the vacanavish, and catoual.

The cogy is a person skilled in the municipal laws, acts as judge, and is consulted in matters relating to the civil customs of the empire.

The vacanavish is the Mogul's public intelligencer, and is employed in giving a weekly account from Surat to the court of India, of all occurrences here of truth and moment.

Next to him, and somewhat like him, is another officer called the harcarrah, who harkens to all kind of news, whether true or false, listens to everything that happens, whether of moment or of no account, and reports to the great Mogul whatever is done or spoke of; but with so soft a pen, that nothing may offend, considering the profound veneration due to such a powerful prince, whose frowns are mortal.

The catoual is another officer in the city, somewhat resembling a justice of the peace, in endeavouring the suppression of all enormities in the city. For which reason he is obliged to ride the streets for prevention of disorder, thrice in the night, at 9, 12, and 3 o'clock, till 5 in the morning, at which hours the drums beat, and a large long copper trumpet sounds aloud. The catoual is always attended with several peons and soldiers armed with swords, lances, bows and arrows, and some with a very dreadful weapon, a rod of iron about a cubit's length, with a large ball of iron at the end, which is able with ease to dash out the brains, or break and shatter the bones at once. When he meets with a person guilty of petty irregularities, or some trivial offence, he confines him for some time; but if his

misdemeanour be more notorious, he must smart for it by a chawbuck, or bastinado.

Though this city is frequented by a conflux of several nations, and peopled by abundance of foreigners as well as natives, whose mixed concourse and mutual conversations might be apt to raise tumults and disputes, yet they very rarely happen, so much as to cause even a slight punishment. And for capital inflictions, there are seldom criminals so daring as to merit or incur the guilt of them. . . .

. . . The Moors are allowed a precedence to all the rest because of their religion, which is the same with that of their prince, and for this reason they are advanced to the most eminent stations of honour and trust; and appointed governors of provinces, and are entrusted with the principal military, as well as civil employments. . . .

As the Mahometan principles indulge an extraordinary liberty for women, so are they nice in the innocent allowance of wine, and strictly prohibit the tasting of strong liquor. The Moors therefore here, as in other kingdoms, practise the use of concubines, according as their fortunes and abilities can reach towards their maintenance; by which means they fancy not only an impunity to themselves, but something of merit, by propagating the number and increase of the faithful.

Yet though they are under a severe restraint from the juice of the grape, they are not debarred the eating of rich and delicate food, nor from dressing it with such store of spice and high cordial ingredients, as mightily invigorate their spirits, warm their stomachs, and inflame the vital heat. Cloves and ambergrese, cinnamon and other fragrant oriental spices, do often help to compound their dishes of pilau, and other meats that are in use among them, in the families of men of fortune and estates. Some of whom, notwithstanding their Prophet, through whose prohibition they are restrained from wine, will yet privately be as licentious therein, as other persons who are allowed to drink it with moderation. . . .

The Moors with a very rigid and avowed abstinence, observe every year one month, a fast, which they term the Ramezan; during which time they are so severely abstemious, that they stretch not their hands to either bread or water, till the sun be set, and the stars appear; no, not the youths of 12 or 13 years of age. Which makes the penance so much the more rigorous and troublesome, in that a draught of water in those warm parching climates is so very necessary, and so refreshing to such as are ready to faint with thirst. . . .

The language of the Moors is different from that of the ancient original inhabitants of India, but is obliged to these gentiles for its characters. For though the Moors dialect is peculiar to themselves, yet is it destitute of letters to express it; and therefore in all their writings in their mother tongue, they borrow their letters from the heathens, or from the Persians, or other nations. The court language is Persian, which obtains with all the honourable omrahs, and with all persons of ingenuity and polite conversation through the empire, which creates an ambition of dressing their speech as well as writing in that favourite style. For foreign languages in Asia, as well as Europe, invade the use of the mother tongue with princes, and their ministers of state; as here the Persian prevails; in Persia the Ottoman language; and at the august port the Arabian tongue.

It is observable that the introduction of a language concurs towards completing the conquest of a nation; which yet the Moguls have not been able to effect in India, neither totally to reduce the old natives to a cheerful undisturbed compliance with the government: But a potent raja is tempted to raise new factions now and then to disturb the affairs of the Mogul, and give diversion to his army. And zealous of the tradition of their ancestors, maintain not only their own tongue, but as much as possible their ancient customs and opinions, and start new objections against their present state, the better to assert their primitive liberty again; and the ancient possession of those kingdoms, which their progenitors for so many ages by immemorial custom had formerly retained.

1.   Characterize Surat in the seventeenth century.

2.   Why were the Moors the most eminent people in the city?

3.   What is Ovington's attitude to the religious practices of the Moors?

4.   How strong was the Moguls' control over the city?

·105·
Hsieh Ch'ing kao
The Hai-Lu
(1783–1797)

Wwhile there are many travelogues in which Europeans describe the new cultures they encountered during their travels abroad, there are far fewer accounts of Europe by non-Western observers. Even as late as the end of the eighteenth century, well-informed Chinese only knew what they had been told of Europe by European travelers to China. Thus *The Hai-Lu* of Hsieh Ch'ing kao is an important travel account, which reverses the conventional viewpoint. Hsieh Ch'ing kao traveled throughout Western Europe during a 14-year period between 1783 and 1797. He worked, presumably as an able-bodied seamen, on a Chinese merchant ship.

Hsieh Ch'ing kao (1765–1822) was illiterate and went blind during the course of his travels. Thus the places he had seen were deeply etched in his memory. Toward the end of his life, he dictated his account to one of the local schoolboys. While it is possible that he traveled to America, as his excerpt suggests, it is more likely that he heard tales of the invention of the steamship rather than saw one.

Portugal (called Ta-hsi-yang, or Pu-lu-chi-shih) ". . . has a climate colder than that of Fukien and Kwangtung. Her chief seaport [*Lisbon*] faces the south and is protected by two forts manned by 2000 soldiers and equipped with about four or five hundred cannons. Whenever any ship calls at the port, it is first examined by officials to see whether there is any case of smallpox on board. If there is not, the ship is permitted to enter; otherwise, the ship must wait outside the harbor until all traces of the disease have disappeared. Places of importance are seven in all: Lisbon, Coimbra, Guarda, Vizeu, Villa Real, A-la-chia [?], and Chaves. All these towns are densely settled, garrisoned by heavy forces, and are connected by good land and water routes.

"The people are white in color, and are fond of cleanliness. As to the dress, the men usually wear trousers and short upper clothes, both very much tight-fitting. On special occasions, another piece is worn over the shirt, short in the front and long in the back, just like the wings of a cicada. Women also wear short and tight-fitting upper clothes, but instead of trousers they wear skirts which are sometimes eight or nine folds deep. Among the poor this is made of cotton; among the rich, silk. When rich women go out they often wear a veil made of fine black silk. Both men and women wear leather shoes.

"Monogamy is the prevailing practice. It is only when either the husband or wife has died that the other may remarry. The family of the prospective bridegroom takes particular pains to find out the size of the bride's dowry before marrying her. Marriages between persons of the same surname are permitted but they are prohibited between children of the same parents. All marriages must receive the sanction of the Church, and it is only after the priest has pronounced his benediction on the couple that a marriage is considered concluded. The marriage ceremonies usually take place in the church.

"Religion plays a dominant part in the lives of these people. Whenever anyone would commit a crime, he would go to the priest in the church and confess his sins and repent, after which he would be absolved by the priest. The priest is strictly forbidden to tell others what he has heard; he would be hanged if he did so. When a king ascends the throne, he does not take a new reign title, but follows the Christian calendar. There are also womenfolk who withdraw from the world and live apart in convents.

"The king of the country is called *li—rei*. His eldest son is called *li-fan-tieh* [*l'infante*]; his other sons, *pi-lin-hsi-pi* [*principes*]; his daughters, *pi-lin-so-shih* [*princezas*]. The Prime Minister is called *kan-tieh* [*conde*]; the commander-in-chief of the army, *ma-la-chi-tsa* [*marquesado*]. . . . These officers are usually selected from among the leading citizens of the local community. In order to assist the local officials in their administration of affairs, the home government usually sends out a military official to each region. If the possession is a large one, then three or four officials are sent. If any problem arises, a conference is held of the four local officials and the two central officials from home to decide on the solution and this solution must be in conformity with local customs and habits."

Spain ". . . is said to be north-northwest of Portugal and could be reached by sailing in that direction for about eight or nine days from Portugal [*one of Hsieh's mistakes in indicating direction.*] The area of this country is larger than that of Portugal; the people are fierce and wicked. Catholicism is the main religion. Its products are gold, silver, copper, iron, wine, glass, and watches, etc. The silver dollars used in China are manufactured in this country."

England ". . . is located southwest [sic] of France and could be reached by sailing north from St. Helena for about two months. It is a sparsely settled island, separated from the mainland, with a large number of rich families. The dwelling houses have more than one story. Maritime commerce is one of the chief occupations of the English, and wherever there is a region in which profits could be reaped by trading, these people strive for them, with the result that their commercial vessels are to be seen on the seven seas. Commercial traders are to be found all over the country. Male inhabitants from the ages of fifteen to sixty are conscripted into the service of the king as soldiers. Moreover, a large foreign mercenary army is also maintained. Consequently, although the country is small, it has such a large military force that foreign nations are afraid of it.

"Near the sea is Lun-lun [*London*], which is one of the largest cities in the country. In this city is a fine system of waterworks. From the river, which flows through the city, water is raised by means of revolving wheels, installed at three different places, and poured into pipes which carry it to all parts of the city. Anyone desirous of securing water would just have to lay a pipe between his house and the water mains, and water would be available. The water tax for each family is calculated on the number of persons in that family.

"Men and women all wear white ordinarily; for mourning, however, black is used. The army wears a red uniform. Women wear long dresses that sweep the floor, with the upper part tight and the lower part loose. At the waist is a tight belt with a buckle. Whenever there is a celebration of festive occasion, then some young and beautiful girls would be asked to sing and dance to the accompaniment of music. Girls of rich and noble families start to learn these arts when they are very young.

"Whenever English ships meet on the ocean a ship in dire straits, they must rescue all persons on the ill-fated ship, feed and clothe them, and then provide them with sufficient funds to take them back to their native lands. Any captains neglecting to perform such a task would be liable to punishment.

"Among the minerals produced here are gold, silver, copper, tin, and iron. Manufactured articles include tin plate, cotton and woolen goods, clocks, watches, wine, and glass."

Sweden ". . . can be reached by sailing about ten days or more from Holland and about six or seven days from England. The inhabitants of the country are more honest and simple than the English. Her trading vessels carry a blue flag with a white cross. Northwest of Sweden . . . and on the same island and connected with it by land routes is Yung-li-ma-lu-chia [*Denmark, which then included the present Norway*]. The people here have a slightly larger and stronger physique than the Swedes and their customs and habits are similar to those in Sweden. This is the country whose ships fly the yellow flag in Canton.

"*Mieh-li-kan* [*America*] is a small isolated island in the middle of the ocean. It could be reached by sailing west for about ten days from England. Formerly it was part of England but now is an independent country, although the customs and practices of the two countries still remain alike. This land is called Hua-ch'i by the Cantonese. [*Hua-ch'i, "Flowery Flag," refers to the United States flag flown from the ships.*]

"Minerals found in the country include gold, silver, copper, iron, lead, and tin. Manufactured products include tin plate, glass, snuff, wine, woolen and cotton goods. Water transportation in this country is done by means of boats which have wheels on the side and a fire engine in the center. When a strong fire is generated, the wheels are set in motion, thereby propelling the boat forward. The construction of such a boat is clever and ingenious, and other countries are following the example."

1. What aspects of each country did Hsieh think it was most important to record?

2. Why is it likely that Hsieh never visited America?

3. Do you think that Hsieh's subsequent blindness affected his account?

4. What does this excerpt tell us about Hsieh's own culture?

· 106 ·

Vasilii Galovnin
Memoirs of a Captivity in Japan
(1811–1813)

*F*rom the middle of the seventeenth century, Japan was closed to the ships of all foreigners. The Tokugawa emperors deliberately isolated their nation and enforced their policy ruthlessly. All foreigners who attempted to land on Japanese territory were warned off, and those who actually did land were imprisoned. Because of the proximity of Russia, however, it occasionally happened that either Japanese or Russians were shipwrecked on each other's shores. When, at the end of the eighteenth century, a Russian vessel landed in

Japan to repatriate stranded Japanese fishermen, they were informed that henceforth any Russian who harbored in Japan for any purpose would be imprisoned. This was the fate that awaited Captain Vasilii Galovnin in 1811 when he landed on one of the Kurile Islands held by Japan.

Galovnin was held in captivity for three years (1811–1813). During that time he was able to observe and analyze Japanese society. Unlike many Westerners, he was less interested in the differences between Japan and his native land and more interested in understanding what he saw. Thus his accounts of Japanese cities and social customs are among the most valuable that have survived. The following excerpt describes the Japanese caste system as Galovnin understood it.

The inhabitants of Japan are divided into eight classes:

1. Damjo [daimyō], or reigning princes.
2. Chadamodo [hatamoto], or nobility.
3. Bonzes, or priests.
4. Soldiers.
5. Merchants.
6. Mechanics.
7. Peasants and laborers.
8. Slaves.

First Class.—The reigning princes do not all enjoy the same rights and privileges: some have greater or smaller advantages above the others, founded on conventions and agreements. . . . These privileges are different not only in things of consequence, but they even extend to the most insignificant circumstances of etiquette and ceremony. Some princes, for instance, have the right to use saddle cloths of beaver skin when they ride on horseback; others have them of panther skins, etc. But the greatest privilege of them all consists in their governing their principalities as independent sovereigns, as far as the general laws of the empire allow, and as is consistent with the welfare of the other parts of the empire.

The dignity of all the reigning princes is hereditary, and properly always belongs to the eldest son; but a laudable and useful ambition in the princes, to have only worthy successors, frequently causes them to break through this rule. If the eldest son is incapable of supplying the place of his father, the ablest of the younger sons obtains the right of succeeding him. It not unfrequently happens that a prince, induced by the incapacity of all his children, deprives them of the succession, and adopts the most worthy of the younger sons of another prince, has him educated under his own eye, and leaves him his title and his possessions. The consequence of this measure is that the reigning princes, in Japan, are almost always sensible men, well versed in public affairs: hence, too, they are so formidable to the emperors, as they can always restrain his power within the due bounds.

Second Class.—The nobility, also, enjoy very important privileges in Japan. All the places in the second council, or senate, all the important offices of state, and the posts of governors in the imperial provinces, are filled up entirely from their body alone. If a war breaks out, the commanding generals are chosen from among the reigning princes or the nobility. Every noble family has a particular distinction, and the right to keep a train of honor, which is made use of by the eldest of the family. The nobility is also hereditary, and descends to the eldest son, or, according to the will of the father, to the most worthy. If the father judges his legitimate unworthy of this dignity, he may adopt a son from another family; hence, a good-for-nothing nobleman is a rare phenomenon, which only the too great love of a father for an unworthy son can render possible.

Third Class.—The ecclesiastics, who consist of priests and monks, are very numerous in Japan, and divided into several classes, which have their particular privileges in the different sects: the principal of them are not indeed sanctioned by the laws, but enjoyed by the ecclesiastics among all nations: I mean idleness and luxury, at the expense of others.

Fourth Class.—In the class of soldiers, the higher military officers must not be included, because in Japan these are chosen out of the nobility, or another class, and such as have already filled public offices in the civil departments. Everybody who is in the service of the emperor or the princes must learn the art of war, that he may be fit, in case of war, to be employed against the enemy. As the Japanese consider war merely as a temporary concern, they will not dedicate their whole lives to the service. Besides, the situation of the empire, and the pacific policy of the government, often make it impossible for a whole series of generations, from the grandfather to the great-grandson, to serve their country in this line. Every Japanese of distinction, therefore, endeavors to obtain a civil appointment, and learns besides the art of war, in order, in case of need, to command the troops which are in garrison in the fortresses, or are distributed in other places to maintain order and tranquility among the people.

The profession of the inferior military officers, and of the privates, is hereditary, and therefore they form a distinct class. No soldier, however old or weak, obtains his discharge till he can bring a son to supply his place, who must have already thoroughly learned everything belonging to the service. The boys are capable of bearing arms at the age of fifteen. If a soldier has more than one son, he is at liberty to dedicate all of them, or only one, to the military profession; but as in Japan the service is easy, and the maintenance good, soldiers generally let all their sons follow the profession and serve themselves till their death. If a soldier has no sons, he may adopt one, educate him, and let him supply his place. The laws allow both the soldiers and the

other classes to adopt three children, but if these die, no more can be adopted, as it is presumed to be against the will of the gods.

The military profession is held in great honor in Japan. The common people, and even the merchants, give the soldiers in conversation the title of *sama* (sir) and show them all possible respect. I have spoken before of the privileges which the Imperial soldiers possess above those of the princes: Europeans who have visited Japan have always taken the common soldiers for people invested with high offices; and this is very natural, because when European ships arrive they generally put on rich silk dresses, embroidered with gold and silver, receive the Europeans proudly, and remain sitting, and smoke tobacco while they speak with them. At the beginning of our imprisonment we were in the same error: we believed that the Japanese feared us greatly, since they appointed officers to guard us. But when we became better acquainted with these supposed officers, we found that they were soldiers. . . .

All the soldiers have the right to wear a saber and dagger, like the first officers of the empire. In almost every village are two or three soldiers, whose business it is to preserve order, and to keep a watchful eye on the police officers. To deprive a soldier . . . of his profession is the greatest punishment that can be inflicted on him. The oldest soldier, or subaltern officer, who was on guard over us when we escaped was degraded, but afterwards obtained the rank of a common soldier again: during this time he suffered his hair, beard, and nails to grow, and showed in this manner his profound affliction. The Japanese soldiers have such a sense of honor that they frequently fight duels with each other in consequence of being affronted.

Fifth Class.—The class of merchants, in Japan, is very extensive and rich, but not held in honor. The merchants have not the right to bear arms: but though their profession is not respected, their wealth is; for this, as in Europe, supplies the place of talents and dignity and attains privileges and honorable places. The Japanese told us that their officers of state and men of rank behaved themselves outwardly with great haughtiness to the merchants, but, in private, are very familiar with the rich merchants and are often under great obligations to them. We had with us, for some time, a young officer who was the son of a rich merchant, and who, as the Japanese said, owed his rank not to his own merit but to his father's gold: thus, though the laws do not favor the mercantile profession, yet its wealth raises it; for even in Japan, where the laws are so rigorously enforced, they are often outweighed by the influence of gold.

Sixth Class.—The Japanese seem not yet to be acquainted with the difference between mechanics and artists; therefore the architect and the carpenter, the sculptor and the brazier, etc., belong, among them, to one class: their rights and privileges are almost the same as those of the merchants, except those which the latter acquire by their riches.

Seventh Class.—The peasants and laborers are the last class of the free inhabitants of Japan. In this class are included all those who go into the service of others to gain their livelihood; for Japan is so populous, that everybody who possesses the smallest piece of land does not cultivate it himself, but hires persons who are quite indigent to do it for him. We had soldiers among our guards who possessed gardens, and paid laborers to cultivate them; they themselves went hunting in their leisure hours and sold the game they had caught. In this class they also reckon sailors, whom the Japanese call Fäkscho-Sschto [hyakushō no hito], i.e., "laborers." The lower classes in general are denominated by the Madsino-Sschto [machi no hito], literally translated, "people who carry on their business in the streets."

Eighth Class.—The last class of the inhabitants of Japan are slaves; they are descended from the prisoners taken in ancient times in China, Korea, etc., and from children who were sold by their parents as slaves, from poverty and inability to bring them up. This trade in children is still carried on; but the law to make prisoners slaves has been also abolished since the time that the Christian religion was extirpated: at present prisoners are kept in confinement for life, as one of the most ancient laws prescribes; by this means the Japanese have the advantage that the prisoners cannot communicate their religion or their manners to the people. The slaves are entirely in the power of their masters.

I could not learn from our Japanese acquaintance to what class the civil officers, who are not nobles, the physicians, the literati, and the younger children of the nobles belonged? They told us that these persons were respected in the state, had titles suitable to their rank, but formed no particular class. The literati and physicians wear a saber and a dagger, like all persons in office, and are on an intimate footing with them: but the Japanese could not tell us whether they possess a civil rank or any dignity answerable to it; we only heard that the eldest among the two hundred physicians of the temporal emperor was equal in rank with the governor of Matsumae.

The commercial spirit of the Japanese is visible in all the towns and villages. In almost every house there is a shop, for more or less important goods; and, as we see in England the magnificent magazine of a jeweler next door to an oyster shop, so we see here a rich silk merchant and a mender of straw shoes live and carry on their business close to each other. In their regard to order, the Japanese very much resemble the English; they love cleanliness and the greatest accuracy. All goods have in Japan, as in England, little printed bills, on which are noted the price, the use, and the name of the article, the name of the maker, or manufactory, and often something in their praise. Even tobacco, pomatum, tooth powder, and other trifles are wrapped up in papers, on which a notice of the quality and the price is printed. In packing up goods, they observe the same order as in Europe. Rice and other grain they pack in sacks made of straw. They have no casks for liquids; but keep them, as Sotschio [shōchū], Sagi [sake], Soja [shōyu], etc. in tubs which hold three or four pailfuls.

These tubs have only wooden hoops, and are broader above than below; in the top board there is a small hole, generally square. The best kind of sagi is kept in large earthen jars. Stuffs of all kinds, tea, etc., are packed up in chests. Silk goods are laid in pieces, in separate chests which are made of very thin boards, and have an inscription indicating the article, the name of the maker, the measure, and the quality.

1. How would you characterize the society described by Galovnin?

2. Do slaves exist in this society?

3. Why do you think Galovnin's description of the merchants is so significant?

4. Why was Galovnin confused by how people like physicians and the younger children of nobles fit into Japan's class system?

·107·

Joseph Crassons de Medeuil
Notes on the French Slave Trade
(1784–1785)

*T*he African slave trade began with the first Portuguese excursions into Africa and continued for centuries. Few Europeans settled in Africa, therefore the trade was organized through African tribes, which took slaves from among their rivals and held them until European slave traders arrived to exchange arms and manufactured goods for black Africans. All of the European nations participated in the slave trade, although outside of Portugal there were few blacks enslaved in Europe. Rather, the trade was used to provide plantation workers for the New World. The slave trade reached its height in the eighteenth century, when the demand for slaves in North America and the West Indies was greatest. After that, both the natural increase of the transplanted slaves and the political movement for abolition of the slave trade depressed demand.

The following account was written by a French sea captain who spent time on the East African coast and who believed that the slave trade could be made more efficient through better organization and the application of rigorous mercantile principles.

Almost the whole of the East Coast of Africa is unknown to us. The detailed maps of Mr. D'Apris [Jean Baptist Nicolas Denis d'Après de Mannevillette] are not accurate. The mapping of the coast line seems to have been done in a haphazard manner and [a] number of islands and reefs known to certain navigators are not marked on these maps.

We only have approximate knowledge of the coast from the Cape of Good Hope to Cape Corrientes. Even in this stretch several bays are still unknown to us, in particular the Bay of Lourenço Marques. This bay merits the most careful attention.

From Cape Corrientes to Cape Natal the coast looks most inviting and attractive. It is presumably thickly populated if one can judge by the number of fires visible along it.

The coast, from Cape Corrientes to Cape Delgado and in particular as far as the Angoxa Islands, is very sparsely inhabited and little known. The Portuguese have always made a mystery of this section. We are assured that they have trading posts on all the rivers, including the Quilimani, stretching fifty miles inland.

The stretch between Mozambique and Ibo is fairly thickly populated. It is there we go in search of our blacks. We trade for them at Kerimba, Ibo and Mozambique, small islands detached from the coast and inaccurately marked on the map.

From Cape Delgado to Kilwa the coast is inhabited only by Moors and Arabs who take from it a prodigious number of blacks (*in margin:* inferior to those of Kilwa but which they bring there to sell to us), particularly from the river Mongallo, a little-known river which flows through fertile and thickly populated country stretching a long way inland.

This stretch of country is entirely unknown to us, the approach to it is very difficult and we rarely go there.

From Kilwa to Mafia, a large and lovely island which is at the moment engaged in making itself independent of the King of Kilwa, the sea, according to the map, appears to be without hazards and easily navigable. But there is a mass of islands which occupies a space of more than ten leagues and notably the island of Songo Songo, which is thickly populated. Here M. Crassons bargained for blacks and food supplies in 1754. This island is six leagues from the mainland. The channel is from twelve to fifteen cubits deep.

The Islands of Zanzibar are well known. It was among them that the vessel *St. Pierre,* carrying a rich cargo of *piastres,* and commanded by M. Maurice [M. Morice of the preceding passage] was lost. The vessel had been equipped in Mauritius. (*Marginal note:* There is [in Zanzibar] a fortress which belongs to the Imam of Muscat, to whom the Moors and Arabs of Mombasa, Pate and Barawa pay dues. The whole of the remaining part of this coast as far as the entrance to the Red Sea itself ought to be better known to us.) He escaped to Kilwa with the remains of his fortune. This man was a surgeon and he rendered such valuable services that the King of Kilwa treated him with friendliness and wanted to settle him in his domains. For the sum of 4,000 *piastres* he ceded to him the northern portion of Kilwa in which is situated the ancient Portuguese citadel. It is very favourably situated as it commands the northern channel which has a depth of fifteen to twenty-two cubits. Death put an end to M. Morice's progress. He was mourned for and is still spoken of with tenderness and veneration. The original of this deed of sale was sent to Mauritius. The counterpart is in the possession of the son of the former minister Bwana Muhammad by name, leader of the religion of Kilwa and whose father was our friend.

A COMMUNICATION PRESENTED TO M. DE CURT, ROYAL COMMISSIONER, TO MAKE TO MONSEIGNEUR LE MARÉCHAL DE CASTRIES, MINISTER OF THE NAVY

Kilwa.

Let it be known that the Seigneur Joseph Crassons de Medeuil, a captain in the merchant navy, who has served in the wars of 1758 and 1778, sometimes as a pilot and sometimes as an auxiliary officer in His Majesty's ships, and who has recently come from India, feels it his duty to report to His Excellency the Marshal on what he has seen and done during his voyages along the East Coast of Africa in his ship *La Créolle,* and particularly in the port of Kilwa situated in latitude nine degrees and a few minutes south. He went thither on two occasions to trade for blacks and found this island friendly disposed towards establishing this type of trade in a manner likely to commend itself to the Ministry, which appears to wish to engage in it, since it has had time to study and to take note of the size and safety of this port for the accommodation of a very great number of ships and even of fighting fleets. In view of the type of slaves obtainable in this area and the qualities of the piece of land adjacent to this great bay, which has been released by the king whom they call sultan, and also in view of the fact that the great majority of the natives are disposed to be friendly to us, ardently desiring as they do to be able to enjoy and share in the protection of France and to make an effective treaty of alliance with us, a letter was composed in a general assembly held for this purpose, addressed to the king, asking for his protection and for a guarantee against all foreign invasion, particularly against the Arabs and the Portuguese who are the two neighbours most likely to give them trouble; in the said address made to His Majesty they offer to hand over a part of the island on its North Coast in which is situated the fort formerly belonging to the Portuguese and from which they were driven out by the present king's [of Kilwa] father, with immediate possession of the same piece of land which was formerly purchased by M. Maurice, a Frenchman who died in the said place, with permission to build there a fortress, to plant our flag, to have sole exclusive right to the trade in negroes and in all other such materials and products as may suit us; that in the said fortress we may have as many soldiers as we find necessary and establish everywhere on the coast and in the interior the trading centres required for purposes of cultivation. They even offer to maintain 200 men and in order to do so to divide with the officer who is

given command of the fort the six *piastres* which they levy on each captive. The above document, with which I have been entrusted, I put into the hands of the Governor on my arrival in Pondichéry.

FURTHERMORE

While we were busy with the King or Sultan of Kilwa drawing up the above-mentioned document, an armed corvette arrived at the said place carrying the son of the Imam of Muscat, who is a pretender to the Government of the town and to the succession of the Estates of his father, who died about three or four years ago, but this son was despoiled of his inheritance by another brother, whose faction is the more powerful; in consequence the former fled from Muscat to come and collect supporters on this coast from Zanzibar, Pate, Mombasa, Barawa, as far as the island of Socotra, which is almost entirely inhabited by Moors and Arabs who are in sympathy with his cause; and he being anxious to be able to take possession again of Muscat and seeing the zeal of the Sultan or Kilwa in invoking the protection of France, has joined him and made a special request on his behalf, offering and promising full satisfaction of France's commercial needs on the seas and in the ports of Arabia and the Persian Gulf and a fort and a counting house at Muscat under the [French] flag. Further he undertakes to pay and reimburse all expenses which might arise in this connexion and he is eager to come to France in person to ask for these things. He even wished to buy my ship but found it too small as he was purposing at that time to attack the fortress of Zanzibar (whose commander had been appointed by his brother) and was levying troops in Kilwa; for his enterprise I had offered him everything at my disposal, two twenty-four inch cannon, twenty guns, powder, bullets and money. He did not see fit to accept these, assuring me that he would make himself master by the force of persuasion alone and of the respect that these people generally have for their chiefs. As he had always treated me with the greatest deference and with all the marks of open friendship we parted with a desire to meet again. In consequence I promised to come in person to submit his request to the attention of the Ministry, and on his part he gave me a passport signed by himself and bearing his seal with which I can present myself at any of the Arab ports belonging to his faction with a very strong recommendation that I should be served, protected and welcomed as he would be himself, whose envoy I am. This is the sole motive of my journey to Paris, having sought in this negotiation only to procure for the king and the nation such things as might be useful, to extend the glory and importance of his protection; to extend our trade and our sea routes which are too restricted in this area and in which we could develop our trade and influence very profitably.

CONCERNING THE PORT OF KILWA

This Port is well placed particularly for doing damage in time of war to English warships on their way to India as it is situated at the Northern exit of the Mozambique Channel.

The Port is vast and safe and can hold a prodigious number of ships. The timber there is of good quality and appearance and is easily worked and plentiful. Water might be a little less plentiful because the inhabitants have only the number of wells necessary to them on the island. But it must be possible to find water in the neighbouring rivers of which there are five in as much as a ship of 200 tons could go up some of them to a distance of more than ten leagues, the sea is fifteen feet deep and I have been inland with my *pirogue* for more than eleven leagues. I found two delightful springs and there must be others, seeing that the river ends up in two charming mountains; in the two passes there is enough water for the largest-vessels, it being at its shallowest fourteen fathoms deep. The country is superb and pleasing once one has extricated oneself from the forests of half submerged trees

called Mangroves. Judging from the ruins of stone-built houses, which can be seen not only on the island of Kilwa but also on the southern side of the pass, it appears that this was once a very important town and that it must have had a big trade; at Kilwa one can see the whole of a big mosque built in stone whose arches are very well constructed. Within the last three years a pagoda which stood at the southern extremity, and which was very curious looking, fell. Finally, this country produces millet, indigo, superb cotton, silkier even than the cotton produced on the Ile de Bourbon, sugar cane, gums in abundance, brown cowries of the second sort which are currency at Jiddah and in Dahomey, besides elephant ivory which is very common, as are elephants, and lastly negroes—superb specimens if they are selected with care. This selection we cannot make ourselves, being at the discretion of the traders, who are now aware of our needs and who know that it is absolutely essential for us to sail at a given season in order to round the Cape of Good Hope. In addition to competition amongst ourselves the expeditions have never been properly thought out and always left to chance, and so it happens that three or four ships find themselves in the same place and crowd each other out. This would not happen if there were a properly organized body and the expeditions were planned to fit in with the seasons and the quantity of cargo and the means of using up surplus also planned, since it is not the business of seamen to concern themselves with correspondence and administration. To my knowledge, the trading that has been done in this port for the last three years, without counting traders not personally known to me, is as follows:

La Pintade	Capt		600 blacks	
La Victoire	” La Touche	224	”	1st voyage
Les bons amis	” Beguet	336	”	
La Samaritaine	” Herpin	254	”	
La Créolle	” Crassons	176	”	
La Victoire	” La Touche			
	3rd voyage 230	690	”	In his three voyages
[omitted]	” Berton	233	”	

La Grande Victoire	"	Michel	289	"
La Thémis	"	Bertau	450	"
La Grande Victoire	"	Michel	289	"
La Créolle	"	Crassons	211	"
La Thémis 2nd voyage	"	Bertau	480	"
La Grande Victoire	"	Rouillard	250	"
			4,193	"

A total, to my knowledge, of 4,193, and certainly there must have been more in three years.

It is clear that if this number of captives, i.e. 4,193, who were traded for at least in this period of three years, cost forty *piastres* each, this represents a sum of 167,720 *piastres,* raised for the most part from the Ile de France and from Bourbon, or from France direct. It is therefore important not only to safeguard this trade but also to find a way of spending rather fewer *piastres,* which would be quite possible if one considers that the *piastres* which we give them for their captives do not remain long in their hands and that they almost immediately give them to the Moors and Arabs who provide them with their needs which are rice, millet, lambs, tunics, shirts, carpets, needles, swords, shoes, and silk materials for dresses and linings. The Arabs obtain most of these things from Surat, and why should we not get them direct from there ourselves? We should make the profit they make, and we should employ men and ships and we should keep a good number of our *piastres* which would remain in the Ile de France and in Bourbon; more certainly still, if privately owned ships from Europe or these islands could not go to the coast of Mozambique and if ships belonging to a private company sent out from Europe could participate in this trade only by means of *piastres* taken to Kilwa, it can be estimated how much we have paid into the hands of the Portuguese at Mozambique, Kerimba and . . . [omitted: Ibo] where they make us pay fifty or sixty *piastres* each for them. This does not include presents and tiresome vexations. What need is there to give our money to the Portuguese, when we have the means to operate among ourselves and when we can use our own industry and keep our money? I have heard for a long time talk of establishing a settlement or trading post in Madagascar. Truly, seeing the number of idle hands we have and the great number of poor and needy and foundlings in our almshouses it is surprising that we have not yet considered this plan, at least as far as that part of the island which we have most visited over a long period is concerned, and also, in certain ports which are particularly well situated, trading posts could be established without straining the resources of the State.

1. Do you think that the natives of Kilwa were ardent for a treaty with France?

2. Why did the Sultan of Kilwa reject the French offer of arms?

3. What is Captain Crassons de Medeuil's analysis of the French slave trade?

4. What was the author's purpose in making these observations about Africa?

·108·
Vaclav (Remedius) Prutky
Travels in Ethiopia and
Other Countries

(1751)

Vaclav (Remedius) Prutky (1717–1770) was born in Bohemia, of Czech descent. He studied medicine at the University of Prague and then took holy orders as a Franciscan. After learning Arabic, he was sent to Egypt in 1750 and in the following year he led a mission into Ethiopia, which continued into the Middle East. Prutky took copious notes during his travels, but he was clearly unprepared for encounters with non-Europeans, and most of what he wrote condemned the customs and habits of the indigenous peoples he encountered.

Prutky's description of his stay in Mocha is valuable for its account of what had become a world market for the exchange of coffee. Prutky clearly shows how European traders competed for the coffee crops and how Arab merchants manipulated their control of this valuable crop. Until the Dutch succeeded in cultivating coffee on the island of Java, Mocha coffee was the luxury drink of the wealthiest Europeans.

From such a description of the intense heat one would expect that the population would be black of skin, but as colouring is due to natural causes and not to the sun's heat, as I explained of the Abyssinians, the people of Mocha, and of Arabia Felix, Deserta, and the neighbouring area, are neither black nor white but dark-complexioned from the sunshine. They are usually seen in public with a covering round their loins and private parts, though the noblemen wear long shifts, as in Gidda, except in the time of high winds. They are more honest than other Mahometans and better disposed to Christians, and when the European traders entrust to the camel-drivers their bags full of money, unsealed, with which to buy coffee, the journey of four days to Beit Facky passes in complete security, and no case is ever known of any loss, even from highwaymen. On the other hand the dwellers in the Red Sea port are frauds and deceivers, and dishonest in business transactions. The Mochan merchants generally take possession of the merchandize brought by the Europeans without making any payment, but with the obligation to pay within two or three months, when they honestly discharge their debt in money or coffee. Sometimes the Dola or governor pilfers merchandize in his own or the king's name, and then makes difficulties over payment, denying knowledge of the goods when asked to pay and refusing payment. During my visit it happened to the English that a just debt on the king's part of 30,000 patacas was repudiated, and the more wary Dutch seldom or never give delivery of goods except against payment in cash.

The cities and towns of this kingdom seem to be well enough built after the Turkish fashion, though they fail by some way to reach the European standard of order: the principal ones are Mohab, Sanaa, Mocha, Beit Facky, Hodide, Alzevit. Of these Mocha is the chief trade centre on the shore of the Red Sea, with a good harbour which is safe only while the great heat lasts, as already recounted, and unsafe when the winds get up, whereupon all ships must set sail or face the risk of shipwreck. It boasts two forts, poorly provided with cannon, which guard the two horns of the city like the horns of the moon. Except during the windy season, countless trading vessels are to be seen at anchor, which have put in from all parts of the world to buy coffee. With few exceptions the houses are built of stone, three or at least two stories high, but all of them gloomy within from lack of glass in the windows, in default of which the squared apertures are protected by bars; these however have to be treated with caution by many householders on account of the fires that often break out, because many houses being partly built of straw are out of spite set on fire by the soldiery, thus exposing the city to the risk of fire and to damage from thieves and robbers. Only houses built of stone, with high walls, are safe from fire, apart from the combustible nature of the window bars, which are often made of wood. It is on account of this and other dangers that stone houses fetch a high price, a small enough building selling for 2,000 patacas: European strangers, who all for greater safety choose stone dwelling houses, have to pay exorbitant prices for them. My colleague and I, while awaiting our passage to India, lodged in the house of a Mahometan holy man named Prevdo, and for a miserable dark cell with no window paid each week one Roman scudo, because while the European ships from India are in port lodging houses fetch a high price, this season being called in Arabic *musa,* or market time. Each European trader is compelled to contract for his lodging for a whole year, and even when only one month of the year remains he still has to pay for the whole year; nor do they permit

another merchant to live with him in the same house without his paying the same price again, and indeed if the merchant departs after only one month, and his associate wishes to continue the tenancy, a further rental payment in advance is again extorted.

The season of musa or market begins in January, when the Dutch ships come from Batavia, the English from Madras and Bombay, the French from *Ponticheri* and Bengal, the Portuguese from Goa, and numbers of other ships from Europe, including Flanders: many Indian ships put in as well, of heathen ownership, and though in times past they employed navigators or captains from Europe, they have now become instructed in this lore and sail their ships on their own, to the Christian traders' great loss. From Surat, from Diu and from other ports do they come, all intent to buy coffee for the more valuable silver currency of Spanish patacas, which the Arabs value above all other coins, or of imperial dollars, since gold coins, of whatever currency, rapidly depreciate from their intrinsic value when subject to the arbitrary caprices of Arab taxation. The patacas and dollars are divided up into pieces, and small change is struck from them, this process bringing much profit to the ruler, who strikes a coin known as the comassi, equivalent in value to the German kreutzer, just as in Cairo the para or medinus is coined. One pataca is exchanged for seventy or sometimes eighty comassi, and with Arab dishonesty the authorities arbitrarily increase or decrease the number of comassi, and defraud the European traders thereby: at one time the pataca is exchanged only for fifteen or twenty comassi, while at other times the governor orders a depreciation of the currency. . . .

Only the Dutch, more astute than the others, trade in spices, cinnamon, carroway, nutmeg, flower of mace, pepper, benzoin a transparent scented gum found in the forests of the Indies, sugar, steel, iron, camphor, thick cloth, ebony, ivory, beautiful Chinese porcelain, Spanish sticks, the so-called reed of India, and excellent aromatic oils: for each of these the Arabs are eager buyers and cluster round them like flies, paying the Dutch whatever they like to ask. The heathen and idolaters from India, and indeed the English traders, bring in fine cloths, sashes or waistbands that can be wound into turbans, the cloth called baft, a fine stuff much used by Europeans for gloves, muslin, Indian silks and bombazine of excellent weave, cotton, rice, corn, arrack, a very potent spirit, distilled at least three times, which burns like fire, as well as Indian pepper; along with a variety of European goods these are much to the Arabs' liking, so that the traders, after loading their ships with coffee, myrrh, Socotran aloes and a number of small trifles, depart with the balance of their receipts in the form of cash.

Now that the Arabs realise the truth about their coffee, that no better is available anywhere else, they have vastly increased its price. On the other hand no Arab is able to enter into contracts to buy or sell, all trade being carried on by middlemen, called by the Dutch *mackelar,* who are idolatrous Bagnians stemming from Diu, and who, as so often happens to the Jews in Europe, live separated from their wives and assist each other in all brotherliness: keen men of business and extremely hard working, they sell and resell goods to the Europeans and the Turks, and, plying their trade of mackelar they deceive and defraud those not of their own caste, growing rich without difficulty, whereupon with a full purse they return to their own land.

Everyone who brings goods in for sale is taxed, the natives at five per cent and the Europeans at five and a half, while if the stranger is an Indian by birth the Mahometans skin him to the bone, taxing his merchandize as the fancy takes them, but mostly at ten per cent. Europeans are treated most courteously, and when a ship's captain puts in to the harbour his national flag is flown, he is accorded a military escort with a military band, and conducted on horseback to the palace of the Dola or governor, throwing alms to the populace on the way; the Dola presents him with a caftan or robe of honour, sometimes even with a fine horse, although under the system of restitution and reciprocity the Dola receives back in gifts three times what he gives. Similar honours are paid to the Indian captains, their escort of janissaries continuously discharging their firearms, and on entering the governor's house saluting them with three cheers, a practice which on returning they punctiliously repeat. Although Mahometans elsewhere regard Christians as their enemies, the Mochans are better disposed towards them; the population includes a few Jews, and countless Bagnians who are idolaters.

The English and Dutch traders maintain a permanent factory, and though their expenses are great their profit is even greater. Over a three-year period three officers of the company are stationed at Mocha, guarded night and day by eight soldiers: for food alone their monthly expenses are at least five hundred patacas, for water ten patacas, the Mochan water being fetid and wormy and necessitating its importation from ten leagues off at a place called *Musa:* for a few green vegetables or lettuce, which have to be brought in from a mile off, they pay a pataca, and every small delicacy involves them in great expense, so that the maintenance of these three Europeans costs 700 patacas per month. Notwithstanding these costs, in their three-year tour of duty they turn a profit of at least 80,000 patacas for themselves, quite apart from the profits earned for the trading company; not that this is their own salary paid to them by the East India company, but the return from their own private trading, especially in coffee, by which they enrich themselves. If the price charged to the company for every pound of coffee be raised by one kreutzer, enormous sums of money accrue, which they appropriate to themselves as the just reward of their labour. If this be the product of Dutch and English theology, yet they are assured of the unspoken support of their superiors, who in times past as the servants of this great company walked the same road and acquired riches for themselves. When subordinates are posted to such places as Mocha, they are charged to be accurate and industrious in the performance of their duties; secondly to maintain the honour, credit and glory of the company; and thirdly not to neglect their own interests. They live therefore in great splendour, with an escort of soldiers when one of the three leaves the building, a number of attendant slaves, and a servant to hold an umbrella over his head: when the principal of the three walks abroad he is accompanied by six armed soldiers and a corporal, and whenever he enters or leaves any house all six soldiers discharge their weapons thrice, to emphasize his importance by this truly regal respect.

Europeans here indulge heavily in *punch* made of arrack or very strong spirit of Pataira. The fermented juice of the cocoa-palm, mixed with rice and sugar, is distilled at least three times to produce a very potent spirit, to which the English are particularly addicted. Their recipe is as follows: to one measure of heated arrack put an equal measure of water, add lemon juice, sugar and nutmeg, and mix thoroughly, throwing in a piece of toasted bread to counteract the flavour of the water. This they drink by day and by night, their drunken slumbers are elegant to behold, and many perish miserably from the burning heat of the climate.

1. Why does Prutky find the honesty of the Mochan merchants so surprising?

2. What is the nature of exchange in Mocha? Is it efficient?

3. What does Prutky think of the hospitality of the governor of Mocha toward the great European merchants?

4. What is Prutky's attitude toward the members of the Dutch and English East India companies? Why?

·109·

Olaudah Equiano
The Interesting Narrative of the Life of Olaudah Equiano
(1789)

*O*laudah Equiano (1745–1797) was an Ibo (Eboe) tribesman from what is now Nigeria. When he was 10 years old he and his sister were captured by African slavers and removed from their village. They were ultimately sold to white slave traders and shipped to the West Indies. He was given the name Gustavus Vasa (after the great Swedish king of the seventeenth century) by his master, a British soldier, and that is how he referred to himself for the rest of his life. Equiano accompanied his master in infantry battles in Canada and naval expeditions on the Mediterranean. Equiano visited England several times, first in company with his master and then as a vocal opponent of slavery.

His autobiography provides a unique viewpoint from which to view both Africa and Europe. Though he lived in Africa only during his boyhood, everything he knew about Europe he learned within the context of his African experiences. The selection reprinted here relates his memories of childhood among the Ibo.

MY EARLY LIFE IN EBOE

That part of Africa known by the name of Guinea to which the trade for slaves is carried on extends along the coast above 3,400 miles, from the Senegal to Angola, and includes a variety of kingdoms. Of these the most considerable is the kingdom of Benin, both as to extent and wealth, the richness and cultivation of the soil, the

Olaudah Equiano.

power of its king, and the number and warlike disposition of the inhabitants. . . . This kingdom is divided into many provinces or districts, in one of the most remote and fertile of which, called Eboe, I was born in the year 1745, situated in a charming fruitful vale, named Essaka. The distance of this province from the capital of **Benin** and the sea coast must be very considerable, for I had never heard of white men or Europeans, nor of the sea, and our subjection to the king of Benin was little more than nominal; for every transaction of the government, as far as my slender observation extended, was conducted by the chiefs or elders of the place. The manners and government of a people who have little commerce with other countries are generally very simple, and the history of what passes in one family or village may serve as a specimen of a nation. My father was one of those elders or chiefs I have spoken of and was styled Embrenché, a term as I remember importing the highest distinction, and signifying in our language a *mark* of grandeur. This mark is conferred on the person entitled to it by cutting the skin across at the top of the forehead and drawing it down to the eyebrows, and while it is in this situation applying a warm hand and rubbing it until it shrinks up into a thick *weal* across the lower part of the forehead. Most of the judges and senators were thus marked; my father had long borne it. I had seen it conferred on one of my brothers, and I was also *destined* to receive it by my parents. Those Embrenché or chief men decided disputes and punished crimes, for which purpose they always assembled together. The proceedings were generally short, and in most cases the law of retaliation prevailed. I remember a man was brought before my father and the other judges for kidnapping a boy, and although he was the son of a chief or senator, he was condemned to make recompense by a man or woman slave. Adultery, however, was sometimes punished with slavery or death, a punishment which I believe is inflicted on it throughout most of the nations of Africa, so sacred among them is the honour of the marriage bed and so jealous are they of the fidelity of their wives. Of this I recollect an instance—a woman was convicted before the judges of adultery, and delivered over, as the custom was, to her husband, to be punished. Accordingly he determined to put her to death: but it being found just before her execution that she had an infant at her breast, and no woman being prevailed on to perform the part of a nurse, she was spared on account of the child. The men however do not preserve the same constancy to their wives which they expect from them, for they indulge in a plurality, though seldom in more than two. Their mode of marriage is thus: both parties are usually betrothed when young by their parents, (though I have known the males to betroth themselves). On this occasion a feast is prepared, and the bride and bridegroom stand up in the midst of all their friends who are assembled for the purpose, while he declares she is thenceforth to be looked upon as his wife, and that no other person is to pay any addresses to her. This is also immediately proclaimed in the vicinity, on which the bride retires from the assembly. Some time after she is brought home to her husband, and then another feast is made to which the relations of both parties are invited: her parents then deliver her to the bridegroom accompanied with a number of blessings, and at the same time they tie round her waist a cotton string of the thickness of a goose-quill, which none but married women are permitted to wear: she is now considered as completely his wife, and at this time the dowry is given to the new married pair, which generally consists of portions of land, slaves, and cattle, household goods, and implements of husbandry. These are offered by the friends of both

parties, besides which the parents of the bridegroom present gifts to those of the bride, whose property she is looked upon before marriage; but after it she is esteemed the sole property of her husband. The ceremony being now ended, the festival begins, which is celebrated with bonfires and loud acclamations of joy accompanied with music and dancing.

We are almost a nation of dancers, musicians, and poets. Thus every great event such as a triumphant return from battle or other cause of public rejoicing is celebrated in public dances, which are accompanied with songs and music suited to the occasion. The assembly is separated into four divisions, which dance either apart or in succession, and each with a character peculiar to itself. The first division contains the married men, who in their dances frequently exhibit feats of arms and the representation of a battle. To these succeed the married women, who dance in the second division. The young men occupy the third and the maidens the fourth. Each represents some interesting scene of real life, such as a great achievement, domestic employment, a pathetic story, or some rural sport, and as the subject is generally founded on some recent event it is therefore ever new. This gives our dances a spirit and variety which I have scarcely seen elsewhere. We have many musical instruments, particularly drums of different kinds, a piece of music which resembles a guitar, and another much like a stickado. These last are chiefly used by betrothed virgins who play on them on all grand festivals.

As our manners are simple, our luxuries are few. The dress of both sexes is nearly the same. It generally consists of a long piece of calico or muslin, wrapped loosely round the body somewhat in the form of a highland plaid. This is usually dyed blue, which is our favourite colour. It is extracted from a berry and is brighter and richer than any I have seen in Europe. Besides this our women of distinction wear golden ornaments, which they dispose with some profusion on their arms and legs. When our women are not employed with the men in tillage, their usual occupation is spinning and weaving cotton, which they afterwards dye and make into garments. They also manufacture earthen vessels, of which we have many kinds. Among the rest tobacco pipes, made after the same fashion and used in the same manner, as those in Turkey.

Our manner of living is entirely plain, for as yet the natives are unacquainted with those refinements in cookery which debauch the taste: bullocks, goats, and poultry, supply the greatest part of their food. These constitute likewise the principal wealth of the country and the chief articles of its commerce. The flesh is usually stewed in a pan; to make it savoury we sometimes use also pepper and other spices, and we have salt made of wood ashes. Our vegetables are mostly plantains, eadas, yams, beans, and Indian corn. The head of the family usually eats alone; his wives and slaves have also their separate tables. Before we taste food we always wash our hands: indeed our cleanliness on all occasions is extreme, but on this it is an indispensable ceremony. After washing, libation is made by pouring out a small portion of the drink on the floor, and tossing a small quantity of the food in a certain place for the spirits of departed relations, which the natives suppose to preside over their conduct and guard them from evil. They are totally unacquainted with strong or spirituous liquors, and their principal beverage is palm wine. . . .

Our land is uncommonly rich and fruitful, and produces all kinds of vegetables in great abundance. We have plenty of Indian corn, and vast quantities of cotton and tobacco. Our pineapples grow without culture; they are about the size of the largest sugar-loaf and finely flavoured. We have also spices of different kinds, particularly pepper, and a variety of delicious fruits which I have never seen in Europe, together with gums of various kinds and honey in abundance. All our industry is exerted to improve those blessings of nature. Agriculture is our chief employment, and everyone, even the children and women, are engaged in it. Thus we are all habituated to labour from our earliest years. Everyone

contributes something to the common stock, and as we are unacquainted with idleness we have no beggars. . . . Deformity is indeed unknown amongst us, I mean that of shape. Numbers of the natives of Eboe now in London might be brought in support of this assertion, for in regard to complexion, ideas of beauty are wholly relative. I remember while in Africa to have seen three negro children who were tawny, and another quite white, who were universally regarded by myself and the natives in general, as far as related to their complexions, as deformed. . . .

Our tillage is exercised in a large plain or common, some hours walk from our dwellings, and all the neighbours resort thither in a body. They use no beasts of husbandry, and their only instruments are hoes, axes, shovels, and beaks, or pointed iron to dig with. Sometimes we are visited by locusts, which come in large clouds so as to darken the air and destroy our harvest. This however happens rarely, but when it does a famine is produced by it. . . . This common is often the theatre of war, and therefore when our people go out to till their land they not only go in a body but generally take their arms with them for fear of a surprise, and when they apprehend an invasion they guard the avenues to their dwellings by driving sticks into the ground, which are so sharp at one end as to pierce the foot and are generally dipped in poison. From what I can recollect of these battles, they appear to have been irruptions of one little state or district on the other to obtain prisoners or booty. Perhaps they were incited to this by those traders who brought the European goods I mentioned amongst us. Such a mode of obtaining slaves in Africa is common, and I believe more are procured this way and by kidnapping than any other. When a trader wants slaves he applies to a chief for them and tempts him with his wares. It is not extraordinary if on this occasion he yields to the temptation with as little firmness, and accepts the price of his fellow creatures liberty with as little reluctance as the enlightened merchant. Accordingly he falls on his neighbours and a desperate battle ensues. If he prevails and takes prisoners, he gratifies his avarice by selling them; but if his party be vanquished and he falls into the hands of the enemy, he is put to death: for as he has been known to foment their quarrels it is thought dangerous to let him survive, and no ransom can save him, though all other prisoners may be redeemed. We have fire-arms, bows and arrows, broad two-edged swords and javelins: we have shields also which cover a man from head to foot. All are taught the use of these weapons; even our women are warriors and march boldly out to fight along with the men. . . . Those prisoners which were not sold or redeemed we kept as slaves: but how different was their condition from that of the slaves in the West Indies! With us they do no more work than other members of the community, even their master; their food, clothing and lodging were nearly the same as theirs, (except that they were not permitted to eat with those who were freeborn), and there was scarce any other difference between them than a superior degree of importance which the head of a family possesses in our state, and that authority which, as such, he exercises over every part of his household. Some of these slaves have even slaves under them as their own property and for their own use.

As to religion, the natives believe that there is one Creator of all things and that he lives in the sun and is girded round with a belt that he may never eat or drink; but according to some he smokes a pipe, which is our own favourite luxury. They believe he governs events, especially our deaths or captivity, but as for the doctrine of eternity, I do not remember to have ever heard of it: some however believe in the transmigration of souls in a certain degree. Those spirits which are not transmigrated, such as their dear friends or relations, they believe always attend them and guard them from the bad spirits or their foes. For this reason they always before eating, as I have observed, put some small portion of the meat and pour some of their drink, on the ground for them, and they often make oblations of the blood of beasts or fowls at their graves. I was very fond of my mother and almost constantly with her. When she went to make these oblations at her mother's tomb, which was a kind of small solitary thatched house, I sometimes attended her. There she made her libations and spent most of the night in cries and lamentations. I have been often extremely terrified on these occasions. The loneliness of the place, the darkness of the night, and the ceremony of libation, naturally awful and gloomy, were heightened by my mother's lamentations; and these, concurring with the doleful cries of birds by which these places were frequented, gave an inexpressible terror to the scene.

1. Why do the Ibo practice self-mutilation?

2. Is Equiano's memory of Ibo sexual practices likely to be accurate? What does he think of the double standard?

3. What is the nature of the hierarchy that is portrayed in Ibo dances?

4. What is Equiano's attitude toward slavery? Why are some forms more acceptable than others?

·110·
Abul Hassan
Journal at the Court of King George III
(1809–1810)

Mizra Abul Hassan Kahn (1776–1846) was the first Persian ambassador to visit England in two centuries. He was born into a high-ranking family with powerful connections at the Iranian court. His father was a royal minister and his uncle was the most powerful officer in Iran until he incurred the displeasure of the shah in 1801 and was boiled in oil. For some years Abul Hassan himself was an exile. He made a pilgrimage to Mecca and then lived for three years in India. He was finally welcomed home and ultimately appointed ambassador to Great Britain in order to negotiate the Anglo-Persian trade treaty of 1810.

While in London, Abul Hassan kept a journal, hoping that it would be useful for future Iranian diplomats. In 1809 he was the sensation of the London social scene and he reports his popularity with the same wide-eyed wonder as he does his diplomatic achievements. He was the first Iranian made a Freemason in England. After much effort he finally achieved both a personal audience with King George III and the treaty with England. Abul Hassan became the foreign minister to two successive shahs of Iran before his death in 1846.

In the special coach, and my companions in theirs, travelled with the speed of lightning towards London. We came to a great river, greater even than the Shatt al-Arab, and over its width loomed a mountain as tall as Demavand. On closer observation this turned out to be a bridge built by some master of technology with great ingenuity. Its columns and arches rivalled those of the Tagh-i Khosrow, and we saw that ships could easily pass under them. We crossed the bridge, and in the distance the city came into view. Then, suddenly, rain fell from the clouds, darkening the bright day, and we felt no inclination to move from our seats.

The fast coach stopped at a magnificent house and the sentries standing at the door ran forward, removing their hats as a sign of respect. As they say: 'Alight, the honour is mine but the house is thine.' We entered a porch with lofty columns and found ourselves in a palace. Truly it is a wondrous house: one sitting-room is hung with tall mirrors to reflect the trees and mountain slopes of the surrounding countryside. We delighted in making a tour of the splendid edifice; but the army of sleep made a surprise attack on the army of consciousness and we were forced to take some rest.

I opened my eyes to banquet tables lavishly laid with every kind of delicacy: a variety of roast meats, preserves and confections. Each of my companions had been given a place at table appropriate to his rank, and behind each one an agile servant with the face of a *houri* stood in attendance.

I was truly vexed that there had been no *isteqbal*, no official welcome, from the inhabitants of the city, because of the severe rain.

WEDNESDAY, 6 DECEMBER

This morning Mr Morier and my other travelling companions came to greet me in my new residence. They told me that today, by Royal decree, the Marquis Wellesley was appointed Minister for Foreign Affairs: his responsibilities include the making and breaking of treaties of friendship with other countries. That greatest of great ministers, Councillor and Secretary of State, pillar among pillars of the nation, is a former Governor of Calcutta (which is the chief city of India) and has lately been charged by the King with an embassy to Spain. He returned to the capital only a few days ago. Endowed with every gift, the Marquis Wellesley is well versed in the literature of Hind, Rum and Farang, and is fluent in the idioms of Arabic, Turkish and Persian. Never before in England, indeed in the whole world, has there been a well-born minister of such tact and authority, such a paragon of perfection.

Mr Morier said to me: 'The King has appointed Sir Gore Ouseley, a gentleman of high station, a Baronet (that is to say, a nobleman of high rank), to be your host, your *mehmandar*. But as his house is outside London, some distance away, he was unable to wait upon you last night. He begged me to carry out in his stead any wishes your Excellency might have.'

At this moment Lord Radstock, the husband of Mr Morier's maternal aunt, came to call on me. And while we were becoming acquainted, it was announced that Sir Gore Ouseley, Bart, had arrived at the house. When my eye fell upon him, I had the feeling that I had known him for years. 'A friend knows the voice of a friend.'

When he pronounced the official courtesies on behalf of the King and Prime Minister, he spoke so eloquently that my heart was touched

and my spirits utterly transformed. I was made conscious of his high rank and authority and I felt as if I were conversing with an Iranian friend. Then, with flattering words and a sweet tongue, he told me he had been appointed by the King to act as my host. His Persian is so fluent that I doubted he was truly an Englishman! I thought to myself:

> He was the dearest soul, so I was told.
> I saw him—and it's true, a thousandfold.

While talking together it became apparent that not only does he know Persian; he is also familiar with the languages of Hind, Rum and Bengal, of France, Italy and Greece. And so learned is he about all religions that each sect considers him one of their own and conceals none of its mysteries from him. I thought to myself: What if God would make it his destiny to be Ambassador to Iran; what if the King of England, because of my friendship with the man, would appoint him to the Court of the Sultan of Sultans (may God perpetuate his reign) in order to maintain and strengthen the ties between our two Governments?

Sir Gore Ouseley offered so many apologies on behalf of the King and the Prime Minister that I became quite embarrassed. Thereafter I felt no desire for the companionship of anyone else. It is the good fortune of His Majesty the Shahanshah, the Hope of the Incomparable God the Creator, that such a man has become my companion, to make my days content.

I learned that the King had today, as is his custom every Wednesday, travelled in state from Windsor, some six *farsakhs* away, to hold a Council at his magnificent Palace in London, which his Ministers and Councillors are required to attend. Each one takes his place according to rank and the current business of the Kingdom is deliberated. Today, the seals of the Minister for Foreign Affairs, a position of the highest rank, were bestowed on the Marquis Wellesley.

Because of the cold and the dark, our gathering was lit by a blaze of candles in crystal chandeliers and candelabra of gold and silver. The eye was dazzled by the reflection of light in the mirrors, which greatly increased their brilliance. Yet again I pondered on the wonders of the universe and the marvels of science.

The King's Deputy Master of the Ceremonies came to call on me. When I remarked on the use of so many thousands of candles during the day, he said we would not see the sun for another four months!

THURSDAY, 7 DECEMBER

Towards evening Sir Gore Ouseley arrived. He told me that his family arrived in town today, so he may now devote himself with an easy heart to acting as my companion and sympathetic support. 'It is no secret,' he said, 'that a *mehmandar*, like a powerful minister, may authorize expenses for an ambassador from the time of his arrival and throughout his stay in the capital.' And so, said he:

We are at your service; what is your command?

I replied: '*Alhamdolillah valmenah!* Thanks to God's grace and the bounty of the Government of his Majesty the Shahanshah, I come well stocked with provisions, and lack no necessities. So, it is a matter for your discretion. However, I would be pleased to have live animals and game birds for my servants to slaughter, as well as rice and other dry cereals. Otherwise, I lack for nothing.'

While we were talking, a note was delivered from the Master of the Ceremonies asking for a translation of the *farman* from the Sultan of Iran to King George III. I said: 'Your Ambassador in Iran has already translated it and sent a copy to the Prime Minister. For my part, it is impossible for me to unseal the *farman* except to deliver it into the hands of the English King at his Court, as is fitting and proper between governments.'

Sir Gore Ouseley replied: 'As you were to carry the original, Sir Harford Jones sent only a summary copy of its contents to the Prime Minister—so you must not blame the Ministers.'

I was indeed angry; but, bowing to the *farman,* from which all justice flows, I removed the seals from the casket and fully acquainted him with its contents, penned with the customary eloquence. After perusing the letter, he reproached Sir Harford Jones exceedingly for his inaccurate reporting.

I announced that I would be patient for no more than four days: on the fifth I must meet with the English King to carry out my mission of good will.

Sir Gore Ouseley answered: 'But, my dear friend, you must understand English customs. The Ambassador from Istanbul has been waiting for three months now; and envoys from other countries—from India and Africa, as well as from Russia and other countries of Europe—are finding it more or less impossible to secure an audience. You are not yet rested from the rigours of the voyage. You have not even left the house to visit the city or walk in the pleasure-gardens of London.'

'But,' I insisted, 'until I have seen your King, I shall not set foot outside this house.'

TUESDAY, 19 DECEMBER

Sir Gore Ouseley said: 'It has been arranged that a Royal coach will be sent for you to ride in tomorrow. When you reach the entrance to the Palace, one of the King's sons, accompanied by many noblemen and soldiers, will meet you and conduct you to the presence of the King with honour and respect.'

'But,' I said, 'until I receive a letter written in the Minister's hand and with the King's seal, detailing the facts of the King's illness and advanced years and the long distance from the Royal residence to the capital, I will not set foot in the coach. On the first day, Mr Perceval, the Prime Minister, promised to write a letter under the King's seal, explaining that the delay in my audience in no way reflected on the Shah's Majesty, but was necessitated by the reasons stated. Unless my request is granted, my situation is impossible.'

Sir Gore Ouseley then went out to explain the situation to the Prime Minister, who agreed to write the letter and to sign it himself—its truth attested by the seal of the exalted King of England.

WEDNESDAY, 20 DECEMBER

The King's Master of the Ceremonies, accompanied by a troop of soldiers and officials of the English Court, brought the special coach—drawn by six bay horses in matching harness—to the entrance of my house. Sir Gore Ouseley also arrived, having just left the Prime Minister; he brought the good news that the letter had been written. 'Thank God!' he said and, composing himself, mounted the coach. Four of my own attendants also got in and we set off for the Palace.

The streets were lined on all sides with men and women; and from the splendid palaces where beautiful, sunny-faced girls were sitting to watch, came whistles and shouts of 'Hurrah! Hurrah!' I asked the meaning of this uproar and of the word 'hurrah'. I was told it is a word used by the English in moments of joy and happiness: when an ambassador goes to meet the King, all the people shout 'Hurrah!' as a mark of honour and respect.

Snow began to fall heavily, pitching a white tent over the streets and avenues and house-tops, delaying our arrival at the Palace.

Finally we reached a spacious square with colonnades. Nearby, at one side of the square, was a vast pool; and massive trees were planted—like worshippers with arms raised in prayer. Streams of water ran in channels. Truly, it was a marvellous sight!

The coach stopped at the door of the Palace and I and my companions got out and entered the building. From all sides officials of the King's Government greeted me with courtesy. I was conducted to a waiting-room on the ground floor; and, finding the room unpleasant, I asked the reason for the delay. The Minister for Foreign Affairs came in and said that the King was being robed and we must wait a little. 'The letter explaining the delay in your audience is ready sealed,' he said; and, reaching into his breast pocket, he drew it out and handed it to me. Then he left us, returning after a while to say the time had come. Sir Gore Ouseley and I followed him up to the first floor of the building.

We entered a small gilded room where the King was standing alone. I did not recognize him, and Sir Gore Ouseley said: 'My dear friend, this is the King.' After carrying out the formalities due to so great and powerful a monarch, I took his Majesty the Shah's letter—in its gold case—and placed it myself in the hands of the English King. The King received the letter with great respect and handed it to the Prime Minister.

The King did me the honour of enquiring after his Majesty the Shahanshah's health, and of expressing his appreciation for his assistance in the overthrow of Zaman Shah's Government.

I replied: 'The Shah has done everything required by his affection and friendship for you: in return, he asks that—just as you helped the Sultan of Turkey to liberate Egypt from the armies of the French—you will do even better now and assist in liberating the city of Tiflis from Russian occupation. This would further strengthen our amity and friendship.'

. . . The King said that he would do his best; and, God willing, as a result of the firm friendship between our two governments, the enemy would be repulsed—assuredly their expulsion from Tiflis would be even more successful than the Egyptian affair.

After this, he spoke in English to the Prime Minister, praising me with compliments worthy of a King: 'Until today we have seen no ambassador from any monarch so young and so learned: it betokens the good fortune of the Government and the great glory of the Shah of Iran.' The King praised Sir Gore Ouseley's Persian highly, and gave us leave to depart with eloquent instructions to my *mehmandar*. On leaving the Audience Chamber, we met a group of Nobles in Court Dress waiting to enter. My companions and I then mounted the carriage provided for us and went home.

1. What do Abul Hassan's observations about England tell us about his own country?

2. What was diplomacy like in the early nineteenth century?

3. Why was Abul Hassan so impressed with Sir Gore Ouseley?

4. Why was Abul Hassan so interested in having an audience with the king of England?

PART V

Industrialism and Imperialism

The Industrial Revolution in Britain

Sketches of coal mines in Northumberland and Durham by T. H. Hair, 1839.

·111·

Arthur Young
Political Arithmetic

(1774)

*A*rthur Young (1741–1820) originally intended to pursue a career as a merchant but eventually became a farmer. Although he was never a financial success, Young was a tireless promoter of the use of new scientific and technological methods in farming. He edited an agricultural journal and wrote constantly on the subject. His writings did much to convert British farmers to more efficient techniques; eventually he was appointed to the newly established Board of Agriculture. Young traveled throughout Europe studying agricultural methods and comparing European techniques to English ones.

Political Arithmetic, one of Young's most important works, deals with both economics and politics. Concentrating on agriculture and trade, subjects on which he was an acknowledged expert, Young propounded his views on the connections among a free citizen, a free market, and free trade. His arguments for efficiency and productivity conflicted with the views of those who saw other dimensions to economic activity. His opponent in this selection was Dr. Richard Price (1723–1791), a well-known social and political reformer.

LIBERTY

The advance which the agriculture of this country has made, is owing primarily to the excellency of our constitution—to that general liberty which is diffused among all ranks of the people, and which ensures the legal possessions of every man from the hand of violence and power: This is the original and animating soul that enlivens the husbandry of *Britain.* But it is not owing to this alone that we have attained to an high degree of excellence; other causes also have operated, and very powerful ones, for freedom alone will not do, as we see by *Scotland,* where the constitution is the same, but agriculture abundantly different. This we see also in *Ireland.* Our farmers, and all the people employed by them, enjoy that general freedom and security which is the birthright, I will not say of *Britons,* but of all

mankind. The operations of a correct and spirited agriculture require considerable expence; the returns of which are some years before they come in; such a business, above most others, requires every favour that legislation can shew: A great degree of security of possession is necessary in such a case, not only from the effects of arbitrary power, but also from all oppressions that the nobility, gentry, and wealthy landlords can throw upon their tenants. An *English* farmer, with a lease, is as independent of his landlord, as the landlord is of the farmer; and if he has no lease, we may be sure he is favoured in the rent proportionably to such circumstance. This general liberty, which our farmers enjoy in common with the rest of their fellow subjects, it must be evident, to all attentive observers, cannot fail of being of the highest consequence to the promotion of good husbandry. It is impossible to enter into a full explanation of all the advantages they receive under this general head; which, in fact, is of all others the greatest encouragement, not only to agriculture, but equally so to arts, manufactures, commerce, and, in a word, every species of industry in the state.

SIZE OF FARMS

A statesman, in his ideas of improving the agriculture of his country, ought to give a perfect freedom to landlords and tenants, the one in letting their estates in whatever sized farms they please, and the other in hiring them. But there are writers that will give very different advice, who will assert, that instead of giving such entire liberty, both landlords and tenants ought to be restrained in the circumstance of rendering farms great—since it is supposed that great farms are pernicious to population, and raise the prices of provisions too high. Now as listening to such ideas would in any legislature be a most mischievous circumstance, it is necessary to offer a few general reasons to shew the necessity of giving perfect liberty in this respect.

A considerable farmer, with a greater proportioned wealth than the smaller occupier, is able to work greater improvements in his business, and experience tells us, that this is constantly the case; he can build, hedge, ditch, plant, plough, harrow, drain, manure, hoe, weed, and, in a word, execute every operation of his business, better and more effectually than a little farmer: In the same manner as a wealthy manufacturer always works greater improvements in a fabric than a poor one. He also employs better cattle, and uses better implements; he purchases more manures, and adopts more improvements; all very important objects in making the soil yield its utmost produce. The raising greater crops of every sort, so far increases the solid public wealth of the kingdom; himself, his landlord, and the nation are the richer for the size of his farm; his wealth is raised by those improvements which are most of them

wrought by an increase of labour; he employs more hands in proportion than the little tenant, consequently he promotes population more powerfully; for in every branch of industry *employment is the soul of population.* Thus he employs more people and he creates more wealth, which again sets more hands to work, and in the whole of his course does more effectual service to his country. The gentlemen who maintain a contrary opinion must virtually assert that good husbandry is pernicious, bad husbandry beneficial; a position which I leave them to meditate on.

Dr. *Price* has the following observation:— "Let a tract of ground be supposed in the hands of a multitude of little proprietors and tenants who maintain themselves and families by the produce of the ground they occupy, by sheep kept on a common, by poultry, hogs, &c. and who therefore have little occasion to purchase any of the means of subsistence. If this land gets into the hands of a few great farmers, the consequence must be, that the little farmers will be converted into a body of men who earn their subsistence by working for others, and who will be under a necessity of going to market for all they want: And subsistence in this way being difficult, families of children will become burthens, marriage will be avoided, and population will decline. At the same time perhaps there will be more labour because there will be more compulsion to it. More bread will be consumed, and therefore more corn grown; because there will be less ability of going to the price of other food. Parishes likewise will be more loaded, because the number of poor will be greater. And towns and manufactures will increase, because more will be driven to them in quest of places and employments. This is the way in which the engrossing of farms naturally operates: And this is the way in which for many years it has been actually operating in this kingdom."

It is a very barren disquisition to enquire into the different means of promoting population, without we previously shew that the increase of people will be of any use comparable to the evils that will attend it. The Doctor sets out with the idea that the minute sub-division of landed property is favourable to population: It may be so. But what would a nation of cottagers do for their defence? They would become the prey of the first invader: they are to have neither manufactures nor commerce; for, says he, a flourishing commerce whilst it flatters may be destroying. What does this mean but proscribing it? For we must take men's sentiments in their tendency, and not admit the ideal measure and degree of trade and luxury which they will allow, as if it was in human power to say to wealth, So far shalt thou go, and no farther. This nation of cottagers therefore must pay all taxes, which we may suppose sufficiently productive to support the magnificence of a shepherd king— no army—no fleet—no wars—What has such a situation to do with the state of the modern world! If the author says it is extravagant to carry his idea so far, I reply, such a supposition shews the necessity of limits—shews that we must have something else in a modern state than the cultivators of seven jugers. If this is admitted, how far is the exception to go? Who is to lay down the line of division, and say, Here propriety ends— there excess begins? In a word, the great fact proved by this argument is, that you must give up a degree of population in favour of more important objects—that is, you must admit commerce and wealth—This must be admitted—I desire no other concession: your whole system at once tumbles about your ears. My politics of classing national wealth before population, needs no exception—it sets population at defiance—Yours of giving populousness the first rank, necessitates you to call in a superior to your assistance—and like all superior powers called to the support of the weaker, it destroys their independence.

But to proceed: the Doctor says, when the land is got into few hands, the little farmers must become labourers: Certainly; and in that state are just as useful to the nation as in their former. But, says he, subsistence then being dif-

ficult, they will not marry: So marriage, in a given state, thrives in proportion to the ability of maintaining families. In the back country of *America,* where every child is 50 acres to the father, and the wife 100—where there is no society beyond the cottage, and where a woman is necessary almost to the existence of a man—I admit this. In a modern *European* state, I deny it: I appeal to every man's observation for telling him that celibacy is more common among the wealthy than the poor—and that the classes least able to support a family, marry more readily than the rich. At the same time, says the Doctor, there will be more labour: then I reply, there is every thing we want, for labour is the valuable effect of population. In a great farm there is but one idle person, in a small one there is the same. Sure, therefore, the supernumerary farmers are a mere burthen to the state; and idea applicable to every one who stands in the place of a labourer without performing his office, but consumes those products that ought to go to market.

There is one argument I have heard in conversation against large farms, which appears more specious than any to be found against them in Dr. *Price.* It is said, that large farms are in fact machines in agriculture, which enable the cultivators of the soil to do that with few hands which before they did with many; resembling a stocking-loom, for instance, which enables the master manufacturer to turn off half his hands, and yet make more stockings than ever. A lively argument, but false in almost every particular; indeed the resemblance holds no farther than the capacity of performing in some operations much more with ten men in one farm, than with the same number divided among the five farms; of which there can be no doubt: But I appeal to all persons conversant in husbandry, if this holds true through one-tenth of the labour of a farm; witness ploughing, harrowing, sowing, digging, mowing, reaping, threshing, hedging, ditching, and an hundred other articles in which one man, separately taken, performs the full tenth of ten men collected. The saving of labour is but in few articles, such as carting hay or corn; carting dung or marl; keeping sheep, &c.

But take the comparison in another light. Who dungs most? Who brings most manure from towns? Who digs most chalk, clay or marl? Who cultivates most turnips? Which hoes them best? Which plants most peas, beans, potatoes, &c. in rows for hand-hoeing? Who digs most drains? Who digs the largest and deepest ditches? Which gives the soil the most numerous, deep and effective ploughings? Which brought into culture the most waste land? Who in all this, and many things more, expends most labour in proportion to their acres, the great or the little farmers? That any man who pretends to know wheat from barley should assert so preposterous an idea as the *poorer* occupier to be the *best* cultivator, is not a little astonishing. Nothing appears to me so reasonable as the contrary; and when I compared the population of 250 different-sized farms, the fact turned out as every one might suppose.

As to the change of the consumption from meat to bread, it is perfectly harmless—for I know no good in one being consumed more than in another, as long as meat is dear enough to induce the farmers to keep proper stocks of cattle for manure. But it is a little extraordinary if the consumption of meat declines so much, that the price should continue so high. Farther, towns and manufactures will increase—This is a great misfortune in the Doctor's political creed—but I would recommend him, if he will hold national wealth in contempt, to consider manufactures in that most beautiful idea of Mr. *Hume's—a storehouse of labour for the public:* those hands which are employed in these fabrics yield a surplus always at the service of government— but what navies, what armies are recruited from farmers? The people employed in raising food must be tied to the soil, and so we every where see them. The fewer employed (consistently with good husbandry) the better; for then the less product is intercepted before it reaches the markets, and you may have so many the more for manufacturers, sailors and soldiers.

1. How does government affect the agricultural economy?

2. Young argues that farmers should be free to farm as much land as they choose. What is the argument in favor of small farms? How does Young reply to it?

3. Dr. Price maintains that a growing population is at the heart of national well-being; Young argues that national wealth is more important. What is the difference?

4. Young has been criticized for ignoring the needs of the poor. Would you agree?

5. The author reveals a number of assumptions about what makes a nation important and powerful. What are these? Do they apply today?

·112·
Samuel Smiles
Self-Help
(1859)

Samuel Smiles (1812–1904) was born in Scotland, one of eleven children. His father died when he was a child, and Smiles was forced to learn first-hand the value of hard work and independence. Although he was trained as a doctor, he moved to England where he gave up his medical practice for journalism. Ultimately, Smiles came to edit the *Leeds Times,* a newspaper that championed radical reform. He believed in the benefits of science and progress and stood squarely behind such liberal values as free trade and private enterprise; most of all, he was an advocate of self-reliance. He wrote several books, all promoting and titled after the Victorian values he most cherished: *Character* (1871), *Thrift* (1875), and *Duty* (1880).

Smiles' most successful book was *Self-Help.* The examples of successful English manufacturers, such as Josiah Wedgwood, captured the interest of government leaders and the imagination of the urban middle classes. *Self-Help* was translated not only into the major European languages, but also into Turkish, Arabic, and Japanese, and was a worldwide best-seller.

Josiah Wedgwood was one of those indefatigable men who from time to time spring from the ranks of the common people, and by their energetic character not only practically educate the working population in habits of industry, but by the example of diligence and perseverance which they set before them, largely influence the public activity in all directions, and contribute in a great degree to form the national character. He was, like Arkwright, the youngest of a family of thirteen children. His grandfather and granduncle were both potters, as was also his father, who died when he was a mere boy, leaving him a patrimony of twenty pounds. He had learned to read and write at the village school; but on the death of his father he was taken from it and set to work as a "thrower" in a small pottery carried on by his elder brother. There he began life, his working life, to use his own words, "at the lowest round of the ladder," when only eleven years old. He was shortly after seized by an attack of virulent smallpox, from the effects of which he suffered during the rest of his life, for it was followed by a disease in the right knee, which recurred at frequent intervals, and was only got rid of by the amputation of the limb many years later. Mr. Gladstone, in his eloquent eulogy on Wedgwood recently delivered at Burslem, well observed that the disease from which he suffered was not improbably the occasion of his subsequent excellence. "It prevented him from growing up to be the active, vigorous English workman, possessed of all his limbs, and knowing right well the use of them; but it put him upon considering whether, as he could not be that, he might not be something else, and something greater. It sent his mind inward; it drove him to meditate upon the laws and secrets of his art.

The result was, that he arrived at a perception and a grasp of them which might, perhaps, have been envied, certainly have been owned, by an Athenian potter."

When he had completed his apprenticeship with his brother, Josiah joined partnership with another workman, and carried on a small business in making knife-hafts, boxes, and sundry articles for domestic use. Another partnership followed, when he proceeded to make melon table-plates, green pickle leaves, candlesticks, snuff-boxes, and such like articles; but he made comparatively little progress until he began business on his own account at Burslem in the year 1759. There he diligently pursued his calling, introducing new articles to the trade, and gradually extending his business. What he chiefly aimed at was to manufacture cream-colored ware of a better quality than was then produced in Staffordshire as regarded shape, color, glaze and durability. To understand the subject thoroughly, he devoted his leisure to the study of chemistry; and he made numerous experiments on fluxes, glazes, and various sorts of clay. Being a close inquirer and accurate observer, he noticed that a certain earth containing silica, which was black before calcination, became white after exposure to the heat of a furnace. This fact, observed and pondered on, led to the idea of mixing silica with the red powder of the potteries, and to the discovery that the mixture becomes white when calcined. He had but to cover this material with a vitrification of transparent glaze to obtain one of the most important products of fictile art—that which, under the name of English earthenware, was to attain the greatest commercial value and become of the most extensive utility.

Wedgwood was for some time much troubled by his furnaces, though nothing like to the same extent that Palissy was; and he overcame his difficulties in the same way—by repeated experiments and unfaltering perseverance. His first attempts at making porcelain for table use were a succession of disastrous failures—the labors of months being often destroyed in a day.

It was only after a long series of trials, in the course of which he lost time, money and labor, that he arrived at the proper sort of glaze to be used; but he would not be denied, and at last he conquered success through patience. The improvement of pottery became his passion, and was never lost sight of for a moment. Even when he had mastered his difficulties, and become a prosperous man—manufacturing white stone ware and cream-colored ware in large quantities for home and foreign use—he went forward perfecting his manufactures, until, his example extending in all directions, the action of the entire district was stimulated, and a great branch of British industry was eventually established on firm foundations. He aimed throughout at the highest excellence, declaring his determination "to give over manufacturing any article, whatsoever it might be, rather than to degrade it."

Wedgwood was cordially helped by many persons of rank and influence; for, working in the truest spirit, he readily commanded the help and encouragement of other true workers. He made for Queen Charlotte the first royal table-service of English manufacture, of the kind afterward called "queen's-ware," and was appointed Royal Potter: a title which he prized more than if he had been made a baron. Valuable sets of porcelain were intrusted to him for imitation, in which he succeeded to admiration. Sir William Hamilton lent him specimens of ancient art from Herculaneum, of which he produced accurate and beautiful copies. The Duchess of Portland outbid him for the Barberini Vase when that article was offered for sale. He bid as high as seventeen hundred guineas for it: her grace secured it for eighteen hundred; but when she learned Wedgwood's object she at once generously lent him the vase to copy. He produced fifty copies at a cost of about £2,500, and his expenses were not covered by their sale; but he gained his object, which was to show that whatever had been done, that English skill and energy could and would accomplish.

Wedgwood called to his aid the crucible of the chemist, the knowledge of the antiquary, and the skill of the artist. He found out Flaxman when a youth, and while he liberally nurtured his genius, drew from him a large number of beautiful designs for his pottery and porcelain; converting them by his manufacture into objects of taste and excellence, and thus making them instrumental in the diffusion of classical art among the people. By careful experiment and study he was even enabled to rediscover the art of painting on porcelain or earthenware vases and similar articles—an art practiced by the ancient Etruscans, but which had been lost since the time of Pliny. He distinguished himself by his own contributions to science; and his name is still identified with the pyrometer which he invented. He was an indefatigable supporter of all measures of public utility; and the construction of the Trent and Mersey Canal, which completed the navigable communication between the eastern and western sides of the island, was mainly due to his public-spirited exertions, allied to the engineering skill of Brindley. The road accommodation of the district being of an execrable character, he planned and executed a turnpike-road through the potteries, ten miles in length. The reputation he achieved was such that his works at Burslem, and subsequently those at Etruria, which he founded and built, became a point of attraction to distinguished visitors from all parts of Europe.

The result of Wedgwood's labors was, that the manufacture of pottery, which he found in the very lowest condition, became one of the staples of England; and instead of importing what we needed for home use from abroad, we became large exporters to other countries, supplying them with earthenware even in the face of enormous prohibitory duties on articles of British produce. Wedgwood gave evidence as to his manufactures before Parliament in 1785, only some thirty years after he had begun his operations; from which it appeared, that instead of providing only casual employment to a small number of inefficient and badly remunerated

workmen, about 20,000 persons then derived their bread directly from the manufacture of earthenware, without taking into account the increased numbers to which it gave employment in coal-mines, and in the carrying trade by land and sea, and the stimulus which it gave to employment in many ways in various parts of the country. Yet, important as had been the advances made in his time, Mr. Wedgwood was of opinion that the manufacture was but in its infancy, and that the improvements which he had effected were of but small amount compared with those to which the art was capable of attaining, through the continued industry and growing intelligence of the manufacturers, and the natural facilities and political advantages enjoyed by Great Britain; an opinion which has been fully borne out by the progress which has since been effected in this important branch of industry. In 1852 not fewer than 84,000,000 pieces of pottery were exported from England to other countries, besides what were made for home use. But it is not merely the quantity and value of the produce that is entitled to consideration, but the improvement of the condition of the population by whom this great branch of industry is conducted. When Wedgwood began his labors, the Staffordshire district was only in a half-civilized state. The people were poor, uncultivated, and few in number. When Wedgwood's manufacture was firmly established, there was found employment at good wages for three times the number of population; while their moral advancement had kept pace with their material improvement.

Men such as these are fairly entitled to take rank as the Industrial Heroes of the civilized world. Their patient self-reliance amid trials and difficulties, their courage and perseverance in the pursuit of worthy objects, are not less heroic of their kind than the bravery and devotion of the soldier and the sailor, whose duty and pride it is heroically to defend what these valiant leaders of industry have so heroically achieved.

1. What qualities does Smiles admire most in a person?

2. Josiah Wedgwood became one of the most successful manufacturers of his time. What were the principal factors behind his rise?

3. Smiles' account of Wedgwood's success reveals something about early Victorian views about formal education and practical experience. Which was more important?

4. What was Wedgwood's contribution to the British economy?

5. From whose point of view is *Self-Help* written? How might Smiles' account have been different if he were writing from the perspective of one of Wedgwood's employees or a member of the titled aristocracy?

·113·

Sir Edwin Chadwick
Inquiry into the Condition of the Poor

(1842)

Sir Edwin Chadwick (1800–1890) was one of the most active of all nine-teenth-century social reformers in Britain. Born in the industrial north, he saw the effects of the new industrialization on both people and the environment. He made public health issues his own specialty and advocated a wide range of health reforms. He worked first as an investigator for the Royal Commission that examined the effectiveness of the Poor Laws and later rose to become its secretary. His work led to the creation of a Board of Health and to one of the first Public Health Acts in European history. Local authorities were required to improve sewerage, roads, and housing and to appoint local medical examiners.

Chadwick compiled his *Inquiry into the Condition of the Poor* for the use of the British government. He documented the unsafe and unhealthy conditions of Britain's working poor and pressed for parliamentary reform. It was this report and his constant agitation that led to the Public Health Act (1848).

The evils arising from the bad ventilation of places of work will probably be most distinctly brought to view, by the consideration of the evidence as to its effects on one particular class of workpeople.

The frequency of cases of early deaths, and orphanage, and widowhood amongst one class of labourers, the journeymen tailors, led me to make some inquiries as to the causes affecting them; and I submit the following evidence for peculiar consideration, as an illustration of the operation of one predominant cause; bad ventilation or overcrowding, and the consequences on the moral habits, the loss of healthful existence and happiness to the labourer, the loss of profit to the employer, and of produce to the community, and the loss in expenditure for the relief of the destitution, which original cause (the bad ventilation) we have high scientific authority for stating to be easily and economically controllable.

Mr. Thomas Brownlow, tailor, aged 52:

"It is stated that you have been a journeyman tailor, and now work for yourself. At what description of places have you worked?—I have always worked at the largest places in London; one part of my time I worked at Messrs. Allen's, of Old Bond-street where I worked eight years; at another part of my time I worked at Messrs. Stultze's, in Clifford-street, where I worked four years. At Messrs. Allen's they had then from 80 to 100 men at work; at Messrs. Stultze's they had, when I worked there, about 250 men.

"Will you describe the places of work, and the effects manifested in the health of the workmen?—The place in which we used to work at Messrs. Allen's was a room where 80 men worked together. It was a room about 16 or 18 yards long, and 7 or 8 yards wide, lighted with skylights; the men were close together, nearly knee to knee. In summer time the heat of the men and the heat of the irons made the room 20 or 30 degrees higher than the heat outside; the heat was then most suffocating, especially after the candles were lighted. I have known young men, tailors from the country, faint away in the shop from the excessive heat and closeness; per-

sons, working-men, coming into the shop to see some of the men, used to complain of the heat, and also of the smell as intolerable; the smell occasioned by the heat of the irons and the various breaths of the men really was at times intolerable. The men sat as loosely as they possibly could, and the perspiration ran from them from the heat and the closeness. It is of frequent occurrence in such workshops that light suits of clothes are spoiled from the perspiration of the hand, and the dust and flue which arises darkening the work. I have seen £40 or £50 worth of work spoiled in the course of the summer season from this cause.

"In what condition are these work-places in winter?—They are more unhealthy in winter, as the heat from the candles and the closeness is much greater. Any cold currents of air which come in give annoyance to those who are sitting near the draught. There is continued squabbling as to the windows being opened; those who are near the windows, and who do not feel the heat so much as the men near the stoves, objecting to their being opened. The oldest, who had been inured to the heat, did not like the cold, and generally prevailed in keeping out the cold or the fresh air. Such has been the state of the atmosphere, that in the very coldest nights large thick tallow candles (quarter of a pound candles) have melted and fallen over from the heat.

"What was the effect of this state of the work-places upon the habits of the work-men?—It had a very depressing effect on the energies; that was the general complaint of those who came into it. Many could not stay out the hours, and went away earlier. Those who were not accustomed to the places generally lost appetite. The natural effect of the depression was, that we had recourse to drink as a stimulant. We went into the shop at six o'clock in the morning; but at seven o'clock, when orders for the breakfast were called for, gin was brought in, and the common allowance was half-a-quartern. The younger hands did not begin with gin.

"Was gin the first thing taken before any solid food was taken?—Yes, and the breakfast was very light; those who took gin generally took only half-a-pint of tea and half a twopenny loaf as breakfast.

"When again was liquor brought in?—At eleven o'clock.

"What was taken then?—Some took beer, some took gin again. In a general way, they took a pint of porter at eleven o'clock. It was seldom the men took more than the half-quartern of gin.

"When again was liquor brought in?—At three o'clock, when some took beer and some gin, just the same as in the morning. At five o'clock the beer and gin came in again, and was usually taken in the same quantities. At seven o'clock the shop was closed.

"After work was there any drinking?—Yes; nearly all the young men went to the public-house, and some of the others.

"What were the wages they received?—Six-pence per hour, which, at the full work, made 6s. a-day, or 36s. a-week.

"Did they make any reserves from this amount of wages?—No; very few had anything for themselves at the end of the week.

"How much of the habit of drinking was produced by the state of the work-place?—I should say the greater part of it; because when men work by themselves, or only two or three together, in cooler and less close places, there is scarcely any drinking between times. Nearly all this drinking proceeds from the large shops, where the men are crowded together in close rooms: it is the same in the shops in the country, as well as those in the town. In a rural place, the tailor, where he works by himself, or with only two or three together, takes very little of the fer-mented liquor or spirits which the men feel themselves under a sort of necessity for doing in towns. The closer the ventilation of the place of work, the worse are the habits of the men work-ing in them.

"You referred to the practice of one large shop where you worked some time since; was that the general practice, and has there been no alteration?—It was and is now the general prac-tice. Of late, since coffee has become cheaper, somewhat more of coffee and less of beer has

been bought in; but there is as much gin now brought in between times, and sometimes more.

"What would be the effect of an alteration of the place of work—a ventilation which would give them a better atmosphere?—It would, with-out doubt, have an immediately beneficial effect on the habits. It might not cure those who have got into the habit of drinking; but the men would certainly drink less, and the younger ones would not be led into the habit so forcibly as they are.

"What is the general effect of this state of things upon the health of the men exposed to them?—Great numbers of them die of consump-tion. 'A decline' is the general disease of which they die. By their own rules, a man at 50 years of age is superannuated, and is thought not to be fit to do a full day's work.

"What was the average of the ages of men at work at such shops as those you have worked at?—Thirty-two, or thereabouts.

"In such shops were there many superannu-ated men, or men above 50 years of age?—Very few. Amongst the tailors employed in the shops, I should say there were not 10 men in the hun-dred above 50 years of age.

"When they die, what becomes of their wid-ows and children, as they seldom make any reserve of wages?—No provision is made for the families; nothing is heard of them, and, if they cannot provide for themselves, they must go upon the parish.

"Are these habits created by the closeness of the rooms, attended by carelessness as to their mode of living elsewhere?—I think not as to their lodgings. The English and Scotch tailors are more careful as to their places of lodging, and prefer sleeping in an open place. The men, however, who take their pint of porter and their pipe of tobacco in a public-house after their hours of work, take it at a place which is some-times as crowded as a shop. Here the single men will stay until bedtime.

"Are gin and beer the only stimulants which you conceive are taken in consequence of the want of ventilation and the state of the place of work when crowded?—No: snuff is very much taken as a stimulant; the men think snuff has a beneficial effect on the eyes. After going into these close shops from the open air, the first sensation experienced is frequently a sensation of drowsiness, then a sort of itching or uneasiness at the eye, then a dimness of the sight. Some men of the strongest sight will complain of this dimness; all eyes are affected much in a similar manner. Snuff is much used as a stimulant to awaken them up; smoking in the shops is not approved of, though it is much attempted; and the journeymen tailors of the large shops are in general great smokers at the public-houses.

"Do the tailors from villages take snuff or smoke as well as drink so much as the tailors in the large shops in the towns?—They neither take so much snuff nor tobacco, nor so much of any of the stimulants, as are taken by the workmen in the crowded shops of the towns.

"Do their eyes fail them as soon?—No, certainly not.

"With the tailors, is it the eye that fails first?—Yes; after long hours of work the first thing complained of by the tailors is that the eyes fail; the sight becomes dim, and a sort of mist comes between them and their work.

"Judging from your own practical experience, how long do you conceive that a man would work in well-ventilated or uncrowded room, as compared with a close, crowded, ill-ventilated room?—I think it would make a difference of two hours in the day to a man. He would, for example, be able, in an uncrowded or well-ventilated room, to do his twelve hours' work in the twelve hours; whereas in the close-crowded room he would not do more than ten hours' work in the twelve."

The following is the account given by a miner himself of the lodging-places:

William Eddy, one of the miners, states:

"I went to work in Greenside four years. Our lodging-rooms were such as not to be fit for a swine to live in. In one house there was 16 bedsteads in the room up stairs, and 50 occupied these beds at the same time. We could not always get all in together, but we got in when we could. Often three at a time in the bed, and one at the foot. I have several times had to get out of bed, and sit up all night to make room for my little brothers, who were there as washers. There was not a single flag or board on the lower floor, and there were pools of water 12 inches deep. You might have taken a coal-rake and raked off the dirt and potatoe peelings six inches deep. At one time we had not a single coal. After I had been there two years, rules were laid down, and two men were appointed by the master to clean the house up stairs twice a week. The lower apartment was to be cleaned twice a day. Then the shop floor was boarded, and two tables were placed in the shop. After that two more shops were fitted up, but the increase of workmen more than kept up with the increased accommodation. The breathing at night when all were in bed was dreadful. The workmen received more harm from the sleeping-places than from the work. There was one pane of glass which we could open, but it was close to a bed-head.

"The mines at Greenside were well ventilated, and in that respect there was nothing to complain of.

"In the winter time the icicles came through the roof, and within 12 inches of the people sleeping in bed. During a thaw, water dropped plentifully into the beds. In the upper beds the person sleeping next to the wall cannot raise his head or change his shirt."

Joseph Eddy, another workman, states:

"I consider the lodging-shops more injurious to the health of the miners than their work itself. So many sleeping in the same room, so many breaths, so much stour arising from their working-clothes, so much perspiration from the men themselves, it is impossible to be comfortable. Two miners occupy one bed, sometimes three. The beds are shaken once a week on the Monday morning, when the miners come. Some miners make their beds every night. The rooms are in general very dirty, being never washed, and very seldom swept, not over once a month.

There is no ventilation, so that the air is very close at night."

The evidence already given will, to some extent, have furnished answers to the question—how far the physical evils by which the health, and strength, and morals of the labouring classes are depressed may be removed, or can reasonably be expected to be removed by private and voluntary exertions. I now submit for consideration the facts which serve to show how far the aid of the legislature, and of administrative arrangements are requisite for the attainment of the objects in question.

It will have been perceived, that the first great remedies, external arrangements, *i.e.,* efficient drainage, sewerage and cleansing of towns, come within the acknowledged province of the legislature. Public opinion has of late required legislative interference for the regulation of some points of the internal economy of certain places of work, and the appointment of special agents to protect young children engaged in certain classes of manufactures from mental deterioration from the privation of the advantages of education, and from permanent bodily deterioration from an excess of labour beyond their strength. Claims are now before Parliament for an extension of the like remedies to other classes of children and to young persons, who are deemed to be in the same need of protection.

The legislature has interfered to put an end to one description of employment which was deemed afflicting and degrading, *i.e.,* that of climbing-boys for sweeping chimneys, and to force a better means of performing by machinery the same work. It will be seen that it has been the policy of the legislature to interfere for the public protection by regulating the structure of private dwellings to prevent the extension of fires; and the common law has also interposed to protect the public health by preventing overcrowding in private tenements. The legislature has recently interfered to direct the poorer description of tenements in the metropolis to be properly cleansed. On considering the evidence before given with relation to the effects of different classes of buildings, the suggestion immediately arises as to the extent to which it is practicable to protect the health of the labouring classes by measures for the amendment of existing buildings, and for the regulation of new buildings in towns in the great proportion of cases where neither private benevolence nor enlightened views can be expected to prevail extensively.

It will have been perceived how much of the existing evils originate from the defects of the external arrangements for drainage, and for cleansing, and for obtaining supplies of water. Until these are completed, therefore, the force of the evils arising from the construction of the houses could scarcely be ascertained.

1. How did the condition of the poor affect the rest of nineteenth-century British society?

2. What were the main problems faced by workers in the tailoring trade?

3. Miners were given lodging by their employers when they were on the job. What were these places like?

4. How did workers cope with the conditions in industry?

5. Many people argued that Parliament had no right to interfere in the areas of working conditions and public health. How does Chadwick respond to that charge?

6. Chadwick's aim was to convince Parliament of the need for legislative reform of working conditions. Is his case persuasive? How might he have manipulated the outcome to achieve his goal?

·114·

Friedrich Engels
The Condition of the Working Class in England

(1845)

*F*riedrich Engels (1820–1895) was a historian, philosopher, and lifelong collaborator of Karl Marx. His father was a German industrialist with whom he had a tempestuous relationship: the more his father pushed him into business, the more strongly the younger Engels inclined toward socialism. As a youth he joined a number of German socialist organizations even while serving his apprenticeship in industry. For a time he joined the Prussian army. Moving to Berlin in the 1840s, Engels attended university lectures and imbibed the heady atmosphere of political radicalism. There he met Marx and the two became close friends. In 1842 Engels moved to England where his father owned an interest in a cotton mill. There he worked as a businessman by day and a sociological inquirer by night. He entered the homes of working people, questioned them about the conditions of their employment, and observed their diet and their health.

From these studies came *The Condition of the Working Class in England,* a scathing attack upon English industrial capitalism. Engels describes the lives of the poor workers in pitiless detail, exposing the horror of the conditions in which they worked. His observations did not differ much from those of the English parliamentary commission that had been officially charged with the task, but his conclusions were starkly different. He believed that no possible reform could be undertaken that would successfully improve the lives of poor workers. The only solution was the overthrow of the capitalist system.

That a class which lives under the conditions already sketched and is so ill-provided with the most necessary means of subsistence, cannot be healthy and can reach no advanced age, is self-evident. Let us review the circumstances once more with especial reference to the health of the workers. The centralisation of population in great cities exercises of itself an unfavourable influence; the atmosphere of London can never be so pure, so rich in oxygen, as the air of the country; two and a half-million pairs of lungs, two hundred and fifty thousand fires, crowded upon an area three to four miles square, consume an enormous amount of oxygen, which is replaced with difficulty, because the method of building cities in itself impedes ventilation. The carbonic acid gas, engendered by respiration and fire, remains in the streets by reason of its specific gravity, and the chief air current passes over the roofs of the city. The lungs of the inhabitants fail to receive the due supply of oxygen, and the consequence is mental and physical lassitude and low vitality. For this reason, the dwellers in cities are far less exposed to acute,

This illustration by Gustave Doré appeared in The Condition of the Working Class in England *by Friedrich Engels. Small and cramped industrial working-class houses with their tiny, walled backyards are framed by railway lines.*

and especially to inflammatory, affections than rural populations, who live in a free, normal atmosphere; but they suffer the more from chronic afflictions. And if life in large cities is, in itself, injurious to health, how great must be the harmful influence of an abnormal atmosphere in the working-people's quarters, where, as we have seen, everything combines to poison the air. In the country, it may, perhaps, be comparatively innoxious to keep a dung-heap adjoining one's dwelling, because the air has free ingress from all sides; but in the midst of a large town, among closely built lanes and courts that shut out all movement of the atmosphere, the case is different. All putrefying vegetable and animal substances give off gases decidedly injurious to health, and if these gases have no free way of escape, they inevitably poison the atmosphere. The filth and stagnant pools of the working-people's quarters in the great cities have, therefore, the worst effect upon the public health, because they produce precisely those gases which engender disease; so, too, the exhalations from contaminated streams. But this is by no means all. The manner in which the great multitude of the poor is treated by society to-day is revolting. They are drawn into the large cities where they breathe a poorer atmosphere than in the country; they are relegated to districts which, by reason of the method of construction, are worse ventilated than any others; they are deprived of all means of cleanliness, of water itself, since pipes are laid only when paid for, and the rivers so polluted that they are useless for such purposes, they are obliged to throw all offal and garbage, all dirty water, often all disgusting drainage and excrement into the streets, being without other means of disposing of them; they are thus compelled to infect the region of their own dwellings. Nor is this enough. All conceivable evils are heaped upon the heads of the poor. If the population of great cities is too dense in general, it is they in particular who are packed into the least space. As though the vitiated atmosphere of the streets were not enough, they are penned in dozens into single rooms, so that the air which they breathe at night is enough in itself to stifle them. They are given damp dwellings, cellar dens that are not waterproof from below, or garrets that leak from above. Their houses are so built that the clammy air cannot escape. They are supplied bad, tattered, or rotten clothing, adulterated and indigestible food. They are exposed to the most exciting changes of mental condition, the most violent vibrations between hope and fear; they are hunted like game, and not permitted to attain peace of mind and quiet enjoyment of life. They are deprived of all enjoyments except that of sexual indulgence and drunkenness, are worked every day to the point of complete exhaustion of their mental and physical energies, and are thus constantly spurred on to the maddest excess in the only two enjoyments at their command. And if they surmount all this, they fall victims to want of work in a crisis when all the little is taken from them that had hitherto been vouchsafed them.

How is it possible, under such conditions, for the lower class to be healthy and long lived? What else can be expected than an excessive mortality, an unbroken series of epidemics, a progressive deterioration in the physique of the working population. Let us see how the facts stand.

That the dwellings of the workers in the worst portions of the cities, together with the other conditions of life of this class, engender numerous diseases, is attested on all sides. The article already quoted from the *Artisan* asserts with perfect truth, that lung diseases must be the inevitable consequence of such conditions, and that, indeed, cases of this kind are disproportionately frequent in this class. That the bad air of London, and especially of the working-people's districts, is in the highest degree favourable to the development of consumption, the hectic appearance of great numbers of persons sufficiently indicates. If one roams the streets a little in the early morning, when the multitudes are on their way to their work, one is amazed at the number of persons who look wholly or half-consumptive. Even in Manchester the people have not the same appearance; these pale, lank, narrow-chested, hollow-eyed ghosts, whom one passes at every step, these languid, flabby faces, incapable of the slightest energetic expression, I have seen in such startling numbers only in London, though consumption carries off a horde of victims annually in the factory towns of the North. In competition with consumption stands typhus, to say nothing of scarlet fever, a disease which brings most frightful devastation into the ranks of the working-class. Typhus, that universally diffused affliction, is attributed by the official report on the sanitary condition of the working-class, directly to the bad state of the dwellings in the matters of ventilation, drainage, and cleanliness. This report, compiled, it must not be forgotten, by the leading physicians of England from the testimony of other physicians, asserts that a single ill-ventilated court, a single blind alley without drainage, is enough to engender fever, and usually does engender it, especially if the inhabitants are greatly crowded. This fever has the same character almost everywhere, and develops in nearly every case into specific typhus. It is to be found in the working-people's quarters of all great towns and cities, and in single ill-built, ill-kept streets of smaller places, though it naturally seeks out single victims in better district also. In London it has now prevailed for a considerable time; its extraordinary violence in the year 1837 gave rise to the report already referred to.

When one remembers under what conditions the working-people live, when one thinks how crowded their dwellings are, how every nook and corner swarms with human beings, how sick and well sleep in the same room, in the same bed, the only wonder is that a contagious disease like this fever does not spread yet farther. And when one reflects how little medical assistance the sick have at command, how many are without any medical advice whatsoever, and ignorant of the most ordinary precautionary measures, the mortality seems actually small. Dr. Alison, who has made a careful study of this disease, attributes it directly to the want and the wretched condition of the poor, as in the report already quoted. He asserts that privations and the insufficient satisfaction of vital needs are what prepare the frame for contagion and make the epidemic widespread and terrible. He proves that a period of privation, a commercial crisis or a bad harvest, has each time produced the typhus epidemic in Ireland as in Scotland, and that the fury of the plague has fallen almost exclusively on the working-class. It is a noteworthy fact, that according to his testimony, the majority of persons who perish by typhus are fathers of families, precisely the persons who can least be spared by those dependent upon them; and several Irish physicians whom he quotes bear the same testimony.

Another category of diseases arises directly from the food rather than the dwellings of the workers. The food of the labourer, indigestible enough in itself, is utterly unfit for young children, and he has neither means nor time to get his children more suitable food. Moreover, the custom of giving children spirits, and even opium is very general; and these two influences, with the rest of the conditions of life prejudicial to bodily development, give rise to the most diverse affections of the digestive organs, leaving life-long traces behind them. Nearly all workers have stomachs more or less weak, and are yet forced to adhere to the diet which is the root of the evil. How should they know what is to blame for it? And if they knew, how could they obtain a more suitable regimen so long as they cannot adopt a different way of living and are not better educated?

The employment of the wife dissolves the family utterly and of necessity, and this dissolution, in our present society, which is based upon the family, brings the most demoralizing consequences for parents as well as children. A mother who has no time to trouble herself about her child, to perform the most ordinary loving services for it during its first year, who scarcely indeed sees it, can be no real mother to the child, must inevitably grow indifferent to it, treat it unlovingly like a stranger. The children who grow up under such conditions are utterly ruined for later family life, can never feel at home in the family which they themselves found, because they have always been accustomed to isolation, and they contribute therefore to the already general undermining of the family in the working-class. A similar dissolution of the family is brought about by the employment of the children. When they get on far enough to earn more than they cost their parents from week to week, they begin to pay the parents a fixed sum for board and lodging, and keep the rest for themselves. This often happens from the fourteenth or fifteenth year. In a word, the children emancipate themselves, and regard the paternal dwelling as a lodging-house, which they often exchange for another, as suits them.

In many cases the family is not wholly dissolved by the employment of the wife, but turned upside down. The wife supports the family, the husband sits at home, tends the children, sweeps the room and cooks. This case happens very frequently; in Manchester alone, many hundred such men could be cited, condemned to domestic occupations. It is easy to imagine the wrath aroused among the working-men by this reversal of all relations within the family, while the other social conditions remain unchanged. There lies before me a letter from an English working-man, Robert Pounder, Baron's Buildings, Wood-house, Moorside, in Leeds (the bourgeoisie may hunt him up there; I give the exact address for the purpose), written by him to Oastler:

He relates how another working-man, being on tramp, came to St. Helens, in Lancashire, and there looked up an old friend. He found him in a miserable, damp cellar, scarcely furnished; and when my poor friend went in, there sat poor Jack near the fire, and what did he, think you? why he sat and mended his wife's stockings with the bod-kin; and as soon as he saw his old friend at the door-post, he tried to hide them. But Joe, that is my friend's name, had seen it, and said: "Jack, what the devil art thou doing? Where is the mis-sus? Why, is that thy work?" and poor Jack was ashamed, and said: "No, I know this is not my work but my poor missus is i' th' factory; she has to leave at half-past five and works till eight at night, and then she is so knocked up that she cannot do aught when she gets home, so I have to do everything for her what I can, for I have no work, nor had any for more nor three years, and I shall never have any more work while I live;" and then he wept a big tear. Jack again said: "There is work enough for women folks and chil-dren hereabouts, but none for men; thou mayest sooner find a hundred pound on the road than work for men—but I should never have believed that either thou or any one else would have seen me mending my wife's stockings, for it is bad work. But she can hardly stand on her feet; I am afraid she will be laid up, and then I don't know what is to become of us, for it's a good bit that she has been the man in the house and I the woman; it is bad work, Joe;" and he cried bitterly, and said, "It has not been always so." "No," said Joe; "but when thou hadn't no work, how hast thou not shifted?" "I'll tell thee, Joe, as well as I can, but it was bad enough; thou knowest when I got married I had work plenty, and thou knows I was not lazy." "No, that thou wert not." "And we

had a good furnished house, and Mary need not go to work. I could work for the two of us; but now the world is upside down. Mary has to work and I have to stop at home, mind the childer, sweep and wash, bake and mend; and, when the poor woman comes home at night, she is knocked up. Thou knows, Joe, it's hard for one that was used different." "Yes, boy, it is hard." And then Jack began to cry again, and he wished he had never married, and that he had never been born; but he had never thought, when he wed Mary, that it would come to this. "I have often cried over it," said Jack. Now when Joe heard this, he told me that he had cursed and damned the factories, and the masters, and the Government, with all the curses that he had learned while he was in the factory from a child.

Can any one imagine a more insane state of things than that described in this letter? And yet this condition, which unsexes the man and takes from the woman all womanliness without being able to bestow upon the man true womanliness, or the woman true manliness—this condition which degrades, in the most shameful way, both sexes, and, through them, Humanity, is the last result of our much-praised civilization, the final achievement of all the efforts and struggles of hundreds of generations to improve their own situation and that of their posterity. We must either despair of mankind, and its aims and efforts, when we see all our labour and toil result in such a mockery, or we must admit that human society has hitherto sought salvation in a false direction; we must admit that so total a reversal of the position of the sexes can have come to pass only because the sexes have been placed in a false position from the beginning. If the reign of the wife over the husband, as inevitably brought about by the factory system, is inhuman, the pristine rule of the husband over the wife must have been inhuman too. If the wife can now base her supremacy upon the fact that she supplies the greater part, nay, the whole of the common possession, the necessary inference is that this community of possession is no true and rational one, since one member of the family boasts offensively of contributing the greater share. If the family of our present society is being thus dissolved, this dissolution merely shows that, at bottom, the binding tie of this family was not family affection, but private interest lurking under the cloak of a pretended community of possessions.

1. What is Engels's view of the urban life of the poor?

2. What impact does the factory system have upon women and children, according to Engels?

3. What are Engels's assumptions about the way a family ought to function? How does working-class life conflict with those assumptions?

4. Whom does Engels's blame for the terrible conditions workers endure in Britain?

5. Both Engels and Edwin Chadwick, in his report for Parliament, are concerned about the poor. How do their accounts differ?

Critiquing Industrial Society

Chartists marching with their Great Petition to the House of Commons in 1842.

·115·

John Stuart Mill
On Liberty
(1859)

John Stuart Mill (1806–1873) was trained from infancy to be a philosopher and reformer in the tradition of the Benthamites. When he was only 3, young John Stuart's father, one of the original Utilitarians, began the boy's education, teaching him languages and classics. At the age of 17 Mill entered the service of the East India Company, where he rose to the important post of chief examiner. While with the East India Company he wrote a number of works on social and economic questions and edited the *London Review*. When the company was dissolved in 1858, Mill turned to writing full time. His own philosophy moved away from that of his father's, becoming more idealistic as time passed. In 1865 he was elected to Parliament, where he voted with the radicals and advocated the extension of the franchise to women. He died in France in 1873.

On Liberty was the product of many years of thought about the nature of freedom. Mill advocated individual rights over those of the state and carefully delineated personal and social liberty.

The object of this Essay is to assert one very simple principle, as entitled to govern absolutely the dealings of society with the individual in the way of compulsion and control, whether the means used be physical force in the form of legal penalties, or the moral coercion of public opinion. That principle is, that the sole end for which mankind are warranted, individually or collectively, in interfering with the liberty of action of any of their number, is self-protection. That the only purpose for which power can be rightfully exercised over any member of a civilized community, against his will, is to prevent harm to others. His own good, either physical or moral, is not a sufficient warrant. He cannot rightfully be compelled to do or forbear because it will be better for him to do so, because it will make him happier, because, in the opinions of others, to do so would be wise, or even right. These are good reasons for remonstrating with him, or reasoning with him, or persuading him, or entreating him, but not for compelling him, or visiting him with any evil in case he do otherwise. To justify that, the conduct from which it is desired to deter him must be calculated to produce evil to some one else. The only part of the conduct of any one, for which he is amenable to society, is that which concerns others. In the part which merely concerns himself, his independence is, of right, absolute. Over himself, over his own body and mind, the individual is sovereign.

This, then, is the appropriate region of human liberty. It comprises, first, the inward domain of consciousness; demanding liberty of conscience, in the most comprehensive sense; liberty of thought and feeling; absolute freedom of opinion and sentiment on all subjects, practical or speculative, scientific, moral, or theologi-

Portrait of English philosopher and economist John Stuart Mill (1806–1873).

cal. The liberty of expressing and publishing opinions may seem to fall under a different principle, since it belongs to that part of the conduct of an individual which concerns other people; but, being almost of as much importance as the liberty of thought itself, and resting in great part on the same reasons, is practically inseparable from it. Secondly, the principle requires liberty of tastes and pursuits; of framing the plan of our life to suit our own character; of doing as we like, subject to such consequences as may follow: without impediment from our fellow creatures, so long as what we do does not harm them, even though they should think our conduct foolish, perverse, or wrong. Thirdly, from this liberty of each individual, follows the liberty, within the

same limits, of combination among individuals; freedom to unite, for any purpose not involving harm to others; the persons combining being supposed to be of full age, and not forced or deceived.

No society in which these liberties are not, on the whole, respected, is free, whatever may be its form of government; and none is completely free in which they do not exist absolute and unqualified. The only freedom which deserves the name, is that of pursuing our own good in our own way, so long as we do not attempt to deprive others of theirs, or impede their efforts to obtain it. Each is the proper guardian of his own health, whether bodily, or mental and spiritual. Mankind are greater gainers by suffering each other to live as seems good to themselves, than by compelling each to live as seems good to the rest.

Apart from the peculiar tenets of individual thinkers, there is also in the world at large an increasing inclination to stretch unduly the powers of society over the individual, both by the force of opinion and even by that of legislation: and as the tendency of all the changes taking place in the world is to strengthen society, and diminish the power of the individual, this encroachment is not one of the evils which tend spontaneously to disappear, but, on the contrary, to grow more and more formidable. The disposition of mankind, whether as rulers or as fellow-citizens, to impose their own opinions and inclinations as a rule of conduct on others, is so energetically supported by some of the best and by some of the worst feelings incident to human nature, that it is hardly ever kept under restraint by anything but want of power; and as the power is not declining, but growing, unless a strong barrier of moral conviction can be raised against the mischief, we must expect, in the present circumstances of the world, to see it increase.

OF INDIVIDUALITY

No one pretends that actions should be as free as opinions. On the contrary, even opinions lose their immunity, when the circumstances in

which they are expressed are such as to constitute their expression a positive instigation to
some mischievous act. An opinion that corn-
dealers are starvers of the poor, or that private
property is robbery, ought to be unmolested
when simply circulated through the press, but
may justly incur punishment when delivered
orally to an excited mob assembled before the
house of a corn-dealer, or when handed about
among the same mob in the form of a placard.
Acts, of whatever kind, which, without justifiable
cause, do harm to others, may be, and in the
more important cases absolutely require to be,
controlled by the unfavourable sentiments, and,
when needful, by the active interference of
mankind. The liberty of the individual must be
thus far limited; he must not make himself a nui-
sance to other people. But if he refrains from
molesting others in what concerns them, and
merely acts according to his own inclination and
judgment in things which concern himself, the
same reasons which show that opinion should be
free, prove also that he should be allowed, without molestation, to carry his opinions into practice at his own cost. That mankind are not infallible; that their truths, for the most part, are only
half-truths; that unity of opinion, unless resulting from the fullest and freest comparison of
opposite opinions, is not desirable, and diversity
not an evil, but a good, until mankind are much
more capable than at present of recognizing all
sides of the truth, are principles applicable to
men's modes of action, not less than to their
opinions. As it is useful that while mankind are
imperfect there should be different opinions, so
is it that there should be different experiments
of living; that free scope should be given to varieties of character, short of injury of others; and
that the worth of different modes of life should
be proved practically, when any one thinks fit to
try them. It is desirable, in short, that in things
which do not primarily concern others, individuality should assert itself. Where, not the person's
own character, but the traditions or customs of
other people are the rule of conduct, there is
wanting one of the principal ingredients of
human happiness, and quite the chief ingredi-
ent of individual and social progress.

In maintaining this principle, the greatest
difficulty to be encountered does not lie in the
appreciation of means towards an acknowledged
end, but in the indifference of persons in general to the end itself. If it were felt that the free
development of individuality is one of the leading essentials of well-being; that it is not only a
coordinate element with all that is designated by
the terms of civilization, instruction, education,
culture, but is itself a necessary part and condition of all those things; there would be no danger that liberty should be under-valued, and the
adjustment of the boundaries between it and
social control would present no extraordinary
difficulty. But the evil is, that individual spontaneity is hardly recognized by the common
modes of thinking, as having any intrinsic worth,
or deserving any regard on its own account. The
majority, being satisfied with the ways of
mankind as they now are (for it is they who make
them what they are), cannot comprehend why
those ways should not be good enough for everybody; and what is more, spontaneity forms no
part of the ideal of the majority of moral and
social reformers, but is rather looked on with
jealousy, as a troublesome and perhaps rebellious obstruction to the general acceptance of
what these reformers, in their own judgment,
think would be best for mankind.

LIMITS TO THE AUTHORITY OF SOCIETY

What, then, is the rightful limit to the sovereignty of the individual over himself? Where does the
authority of society begin? How much of human
life should be assigned to individuality, and how
much to society?

Each will receive its proper share, if each has
that which more particularly concerns it. To individuality should belong the part of life in which it
is chiefly the individual that is interested; to society, the part which chiefly interests society.

Though society is not founded on a contract, and though no good purpose is answered
by inventing a contract in order to deduce social
obligations from it, every one who receives the
protection of society owes a return for the benefit, and the fact of living in society renders it

indispensable that each should be bound to observe a certain line of conduct towards the rest. This conduct consists, first, in not injuring the interests of one another; or rather certain interests, which, either by express legal provision or by tacit understanding, ought to be considered as rights; and secondly, in each person's bearing his share (to be fixed on some equitable principle) of the labours and sacrifices incurred for defending the society or its members from injury and molestation. These conditions society is justified in enforcing, at all costs to those who endeavor to withhold fulfillment. Nor is this all that society may do. The acts of an individual may be hurtful to others, or wanting in due consideration for their welfare, without going the length of violating any of their constituted rights. The offender may then be justly punished by opinion, though not by law. As soon as any part of a person's conduct affects prejudicially the interests of others, society has jurisdiction over it, and the question whether the general welfare will or will not be promoted by interfering with it, becomes open to discussion. But there is no room for entertaining any such question when a person's conduct affects the interests of no persons besides himself, or needs not affect them unless they like (all the persons concerned being of full age, and the ordinary amount of understanding). In all such cases there should be perfect freedom, legal and social, to do the action and stand the consequences.

It would be a great misunderstanding of this doctrine, to suppose that it is one of selfish indif

ference, which pretends that human beings have no business with each other's conduct in life, and that they should not concern themselves about the well-doing or well-being of one another, unless their own interest is involved. Instead of any diminution, there is need of a great increase of disinterested exertion to promote the good of others. But disinterested benevolence can find other instruments to persuade people to their good, than whips and scourges, either of the literal or the metaphorical sort. I am the last person to undervalue the self-regarding virtues; they are only second in importance, if even second, to the social. It is equally the business of education to cultivate both. But even education works by conviction and persuasion as well as by compulsion, and it is by the former only that, when the period of education is past, the self-regarding virtues should be inculcated. Human beings owe to each other help to distinguish the better from the worse, and encouragement to choose the former and avoid the latter. They should be for ever stimulating each other to increase exercise of their higher faculties, and increased direction of their feelings and aims towards wise instead of foolish, elevating instead of degrading, objects and contemplations. But neither one person, nor any number of persons, is warranted in saying to another human creature of ripe years, that he shall not do with his life for his own benefit what he chooses to do with it.

1. When is society justified in restricting liberty?

2. What conditions must be satisfied before Mill would describe a society as truly free?

3. How might Mill respond to the arguments of reformers who demand state intervention in the economy and society?

4. How does Mill distinguish between the sort of liberty that is allowable and that which is not?

5. Mill saw his vision of freedom as beneficial, but others criticized it as unrealistic and even inhumane. Why?

·116·
Pierre Proudhon
What Is Property?
(1840)

*P*ierre Joseph Proudhon (1809–1865), a radical French socialist, achieved fame as an advocate of anarchy as a political system. Proudhon's political ideas were colored by his upbringing as the son of a poor and irresponsible peasant. Forced to leave school at an early age, Proudhon began his career as a printer's apprentice. He learned to read and write on the job. As his interests became more political, he became a writer and journalist. Proudhon scandalized France with his declaration that "Property is theft" and was subjected to constant political harassment after the publication of *What Is Property?* His newspaper, *Representative of the People,* was closed down, and he was jailed for several years before being exiled. He returned to France after being pardoned by Napoleon III and in his last years became an influential leader of the Parisian working class.

What Is Property? was Proudhon's first and most important book. Proudhon believed that anarchy—a radical individualism in which there was no room for the state—was the only logical solution to social inequality and injustice.

From the right of the strongest springs the exploitation of man by man, or bondage; usury, or the tribute levied upon the conquered by the conqueror; and the whole numerous family of taxes, duties, monarchical prerogatives, house-rents, farm-rents, &c.; in one word—property.

Force was followed by artifice, the second manifestation of justice; from artifice sprang the profits of manufacturers, commerce, and banking, mercantile frauds, and pretensions which are honored with the beautiful names of *talent* and *genius,* but which ought to be regarded as the last degree of knavery and deception; and, finally, all sorts of social inequalities.

In those forms of robbery which are prohibited by law, force and artifice are employed alone and undisguised; in the authorized forms, they conceal themselves within a useful product, which they use as a tool to plunder their victim.

The direct use of violence and stratagem was early and universally condemned; but no nation has yet got rid of that kind of robbery which acts through talent, labor, and possession, and which is the source of all the dilemmas of casuistry and the innumerable contradictions of jurisprudence.

The right of force and the right of artifice—glorified by the rhapsodists in the poems of the "Iliad" and the "Odyssey"—inspired the legislation of the Greeks and Romans, from which they passed into our morals and codes. Christianity has not changed at all. The Gospel should not be blamed, because the priests, as stupid as the legists, have been unable either to expound or to understand it. The ignorance of councils and popes upon all questions of morality is equal to that of the market-place and the money-changers; and it is this utter ignorance of right, justice, and society, which is killing the Church, and discrediting its teachings for ever. The infidelity of the Roman Church and other Christian churches is flagrant; all have disregarded the precept of Jesus; all have erred in moral and doctrinal points; all are guilty of teaching false and absurd dogmas, which lead straight to wickedness and murder. Let it ask pardon of God and men,—this church which called itself infallible, and which has grown so corrupt in morals; let its reformed sisters humble themselves, . . . and the people, undeceived, but still religious and merciful, will begin to think.

The development of right has followed the same order, in its various expressions, that property has in its forms. Every where we see justice driving robbery before it and confining it within narrower and narrower limits. Hitherto the victories of justice over injustice, and of equality over inequality, have been won by instinct and the simple force of things; but the final triumph of our social nature will be due to our reason, or else we shall fall back into feudal chaos. Either this glorious height is reserved for our intelligence, or this miserable depth for our baseness.

The second effect of property is despotism. Now, since despotism is inseparably connected with the idea of legitimate authority, in explaining the natural causes of the first, the principle of the second will appear.

What is to be the form of government in the future? I hear some of my younger readers reply: "Why, how can you ask such a question? You are a republican." "A republican! Yes; but that word specifies nothing. *Res publica;* that is, the public thing. Now, whoever is interested in public affairs—no matter under what form of government—may call himself a republican. Even kings are republicans."—"Well! you are a democrat?"—"No."—"What! you would have a monarchy."—"No."—"A constitutionalist?"—"God forbid!"—"You are then an aristocrat?"—"Not at all."—"You want a mixed government?"—"Still less."—"What are you, then?"—"I am an anarchist."

"Oh! I understand you; you speak satirically. This is a hit at the government."—"By no means.

I have just given you my serious and well-considered profession of faith. Although a firm friend of order, I am (in the full force of the term) an anarchist. Listen to me."

By means of self-instruction and the acquisition of ideas, man acquires the idea of *science*—that is, of a system of knowledge in harmony with the reality of things, and inferred from observation. He searches for the science, or the system, of inanimate bodies—the system of organic bodies, the system of the human mind, and the system of the universe: why should he not also search for the system of society? But, having reached this height, he comprehends that political truth, or the science of politics, exists quite independently of the will of sovereigns, the opinion of majorities, and popular beliefs—that kings, ministers, magistrates, and nations, as wills, have no connection with the science, and are worthy of no consideration. He comprehends, at the same time, that, if man is born a sociable being, the authority of his father over him ceases on the day when, his mind being formed and his education finished, he becomes the associate of his father; that his true chief and his king is the demonstrated truth; that politics is a science, not a stratagem; and that the function of the legislator is reduced, in the last analysis, to the methodical search for truth.

Thus, in a given society, the authority of man over man is inversely proportional to the stage of intellectual development which that society has reached; and the probable duration of that authority can be calculated from the more or less general desire for a true government—that is, for a scientific government. And just as the right of force and the right of artifice retreat before the steady advance of justice, and must finally be extinguished in equality, so the sovereignty of the will yields to the sovereignty of the reason, and must at least be lost in scientific socialism. Property and royalty have been crumbling to pieces ever since the world began. As man seeks justice in equality, so society seeks order in anarchy.

Anarchy—the absence of a master, of a sovereign—such is the form of government to which we are every day approximating, and which our accustomed habit of taking man for our rule, and his will for law, leads us to regard as the height of disorder and the expression of chaos. The story is told, that a citizen of Paris in the seventeenth century having heard it said that in Venice there was no king, the good man could not recover from his astonishment, and nearly died from laughter at the mere mention of so ridiculous a thing. So strong is our prejudice. The most advanced among us are those who wish the greatest possible number of sovereigns. Soon, undoubtedly, some one will say, "Everybody is king." But, when he has spoken, I will say, in my turn, "Nobody is king; we are, whether we will or no, associated." Every question of domestic politics must be decided by departmental statistics; every question of foreign politics is an affair of international statistics. The science of government rightly belongs to one of the sections of the Academy of Sciences, whose permanent secretary is necessarily prime minister; and, since every citizen may address a memoir to the Academy, every citizen is a legislator. But, as the opinion of no one is of any value until its truth has been proven, no one can substitute his will for reason—nobody is king.

All questions of legislation and politics are matters of science, not of opinion. The legislative power belongs only to the reason, methodically recognized and demonstrated. To attribute to any power whatever the right of veto or of sanction, is the last degree of tyranny. Justice and legality are two things as independent of our approval as is mathematical truth. To compel, they need only to be known; to be known, they need only to be considered and studied. What, then, is the nation, if it is not the sovereign—if it is not the source of the legislative power? The nation is the guardian of the law—the nation is the *executive power*. Every citizen may assert: "This is true; that is just"; but his opinion controls no one but himself. That the truth which he proclaims may become a law, it must be recognized. Now, what is it to recognize a law? It is to verify a mathematical or a metaphysical calculation; it is to repeat an experiment, to observe a phenomenon, to establish a fact. Only the nation has the right to say, "Be it known and decreed."

I confess that this is an overturning of received ideas, and that I seem to be attempting to revolutionize our political system; but I beg the reader to consider that, having begun with a paradox, I must, if I reason correctly, meet with paradoxes at every step, and must end with paradoxes. For the rest, I do not see how the liberty of citizens would be endangered by entrusting to their hands, instead of the pen of the legislator, the sword of the law. The executive power, belonging properly to the will, cannot be confided to too many proxies. That is the true sovereignty of the nation.

The proprietor, the robber, the hero, the sovereign—for all these titles are synonymous—imposes his will as law, and suffers neither contradiction nor control; that is, he pretends to be the legislative and the executive power at once. Accordingly, the substitution of the scientific and true law for the royal will is accomplished only by a terrible struggle; and this constant substitution is, after property, the most potent element in history, the most prolific source of political disturbances. Examples are too numerous and too striking to require enumeration.

The old civilization has run its race; a new sun is rising, and will soon renew the face of the earth. Let the present generation perish, let the old prevaricators die in the desert! The holy earth shall not cover their bones. Young man, exasperated by the corruption of the age, and absorbed in your zeal for justice! If your country is dear to you, and if you have the interests of humanity at heart, have the courage to espouse the cause of liberty! Cast off your old selfishness, and plunge into the rising flood of popular equality! There your regenerate soul will acquire new life and vigor; your enervated genius will recover unconquerable energy; and your heart, perhaps already withered, will be rejuvenated! Every thing will wear a different look to your illuminated vision; new sentiments will engender new ideas within you; religion, morality, poetry, art, language will appear before you in nobler and fairer forms; and thenceforth, sure of your faith, and thoughtfully enthusiastic, you will hail the dawn of universal regeneration!

And you, sad victims of an odious law! You, whom a jesting world despoils and outrages! You, whose labor has always been fruitless, and whose rest has been without hope, take courage! Your tears are numbered! The fathers have sown in affliction, the children shall reap in rejoicings!

O God of liberty! God of equality! Thou who didst place in my heart the sentiment of justice, before my reason could comprehend it, hear my ardent prayer! Thou hast dictated all that I have written; Thou hast shaped my thought; Thou hast directed my studies; Thou hast weaned my mind from curiosity and my heart from attachment, that I might publish Thy truth to the mas-

ter and the slave. I have spoken with what force and talent Thou hast given me: it is Thine to finish the work. Thou knowest whether I seek my welfare or Thy glory, O God of liberty! Ah! perish my memory, and let humanity be free! Let me see from my obscurity the people at last instructed; let noble teachers enlighten them; let generous spirits guide them! Abridge, if possible, the time of our trial; stifle pride and avarice in equality; annihilate this love of glory which enslaves us; teach these poor children that in the bosom of liberty there are neither heroes nor great men! Inspire the powerful man, the rich man, him whose name my lips shall never pronounce in Thy presence, with a horror of his crimes; let him be the first to apply for admission to the redeemed society; let the promptness of his repentance be the ground of his forgiveness! Then, great and small, wise and foolish, rich and

1. Why does Proudhon maintain that property is theft?

2. What is the author's solution for the problems of his age?

3. Politics, Proudhon argues, is a science, not an art. What does he mean?

4. What will anarchy bring to society? What will this new society look like?

5. What is Proudhon trying to do in his work? Is he offering a practical blueprint for society?

·117·

The Great Charter

(1842)

The Great Charter was a petition from a broad-based movement for political and social reform that dominated British politics in the 1840s. The Chartists were a loose confederation of middle-class shopkeepers, tradesmen, artisans, and all varieties of workers. They demanded political reform of the franchise and the process of parliamentary elections. Chartism was both a popular and a national movement, joining together Irish and Scottish reformers with English ones. Its greatest leader was the Irishman Feargus O'Connor.

The Charter delivered to the House of Commons in 1842 contained over 3 million signatures. In 1848 an effort was made to double that number and to bring over half a million people to London for its presentation. In the end, only 50,000 appeared, and as economic prosperity returned to England after 1848, Chartism diminished in importance. Though the major points of the Charter were not achieved, the agitation was important to the many franchise reforms that followed.

THE PEOPLE'S CHARTER—PETITION

[A Petition from the working classes throughout the kingdom, of the presentation of which Mr. Thomas Duncombe had previously given notice, was brought down to the House, by a procession consisting of a vast multitude. Its bulk was so great, that the doors were not wide enough to admit it, and it was necessary to unroll it, to carry it into the House. When unrolled, it spread over a great part of the floor and rose above the level of the Table.]

Mr. T. Duncombe, in presenting it to the House, said,—Looking at the vast proportions of this petition—looking, too, at the importance attaching to it, not only from the matter it contains, but from the millions who have signed it, I am quite satisfied, that if I were to ask the House to relax the rules which it has laid down to govern the presentation of petitions, it would grant me the indulgence; but as I have given notice of a motion for tomorrow, that the petition should be taken into the serious consideration of the House, and that those who have signed it, should by their counsel and agents, be heard at the Bar of your House, in support of the allegations which the petition contains, I shall not ask the House to grant me that indulgence, but will keep myself strictly within the limits which have been laid down for the presentation of all petitions. I beg respectfully to offer to the acceptance of this House, a petition signed by 3,315,752 of the industrious classes of this country. The petition proceeds from those upon whose toil, upon whose industry, upon whose affection, and upon whose attachment, I may

say, every institution, every law, nay, even the very Government, and the whole property and commerce of the country depend. These persons now most respectfully come before you, to state the manifold grievances under which they are suffering. . . .

The petition was read by the Clerk, as follows:

TO THE HONOURABLE THE COMMONS OF
GREAT BRITAIN AND IRELAND,
IN PARLIAMENT ASSEMBLED.

"The petition of the undersigned people of the United Kingdom,

"Sheweth—That Government originated from, was designed to protect the freedom and promote the happiness of, and ought to be responsible to, the whole people.

"That the only authority on which any body of men can make laws and govern society, is delegation from the people.

"That as Government was designed for the benefit and protection of, and must be obeyed and supported by all, therefore all should be equally represented.

"That any form of Government which fails to effect the purposes for which it was designed, and does not fully and completely represent the whole people, who are compelled to pay taxes to its support and obey the laws resolved upon by it, is unconstitutional, tyrannical, and ought to be amended or resisted.

"That your honourable House, as at present constituted, has not been elected by, and acts irresponsibly of, the people; and hitherto has only represented parties, and benefitted the few, regardless of the miseries, grievances, and petitions of the many. Your honourable House has enacted laws contrary to the expressed wishes of the people, and by unconstitutional means enforced obedience to them, thereby creating an unbearable depotism on the one hand, and degrading slavery on the other.

"That if your honourable House is of opinion that the people of Great Britain and Ireland ought not to be fully represented, your petitioners pray that such opinion may be unequivocally made known, that the people may fully understand what they can or cannot expect from your honourable House; because if such be the decision of your honourable House, your petitioners are of opinion that where representation is denied, taxation ought to be resisted.

"That your petitioners instance, in proof of their assertion, that your honourable House has not been elected by the people; that the population of Great Britain and Ireland is the present time about twenty-six millions of persons; and that yet, out of this number, little more than nine hundred thousand have been permitted to vote in the recent election of representatives to make laws to govern the whole.

"That the existing state of representation is not only extremely limited and unjust, but unequally divided, and gives preponderating influence to the landed, and monied interests, to the utter ruin of the small-trading and labouring classes.

"That bribery, intimidation, corruption, perjury, and riot, prevail at all parliamentary elections, to an extent best understood by the Members of your honourable House.

"That your petitioners complain that they are enormously taxed to pay the interest of what is termed the national debt, a debt amounting at present to £800,000,000, being only a portion of the enormous amount expended in cruel and expensive wars for the suppression of all liberty, by men not authorised by the people, and who, consequently, had no right to tax posterity for the outrages committed by them upon mankind. And your petitioners loudly complain of the augmentation of that debt, after twenty-

six years of almost uninterrupted peace, and whilst poverty and discontent rage over the land.

"That taxation, both general and local, is at this time too enormous to be borne; and in the opinion of your petitioner is contrary to the spirit of the Bill of Rights, wherein it is clearly expressed that no subject shall be compelled to contribute to any tax, talliage, or aid, unless imposed by common consent in Parliament.

"That in England, Ireland, Scotland, and Wales, thousands of people are dying from actual want; and your petitioners, whilst sensible that poverty is the great exciting cause of crime, view with mingled astonishment and alarm the ill provision made for the poor, the aged, and infirm; and likewise perceive, with feelings of indignation, the determination of your honourable House to continue the Poor-law Bill in operation, notwithstanding the many proofs which have been afforded by sad experience of the unconstitutional principle of that bill, of its unchristian character, and of the cruel and murderous effects produced upon the wages of working men, and the lives of the subjects of this realm."

"That your petitioners conceive that bill to be contrary to all previous statutes, opposed to the spirit of the constitution, and an actual violation of the precepts of the Christian religion; and, therefore, your petitioners look with apprehension to the results which may flow from its continuance.

"That your petitioners would direct the attention of your honourable House to the great disparity existing between the wages of the producing millions, and the salaries of those whose comparative usefulness ought to be questioned, where riches and luxury prevail amongst the rulers, and poverty and starvation amongst the ruled.

"That your petitioners, with all due respect and loyalty, would compare the daily income of the Sovereign Majesty with that of thousands of the working men of this nation; and whilst your petitioners have learned that her Majesty receives daily for her private use the sum of £164 17s. 10d., they have also ascertained that many thousands of the families of the labourers are only in the receipt of 3 3/4*d.* per head per day.

"That your petitioners have also learned that his royal Highness Prince Albert receives each day the sum of £104 2*s.,* whilst thousands have to exist upon 3*d.* per head per day.

"That your petitioners have also heard with astonishment, that the King of Hanover daily receives £57 10*s.* whilst thousands of the taxpayers of this empire live upon 2 3/4*d.* per head per day.

"That your petitioners have, with pain and regret, also learned that the Archbishop of Canterbury is daily in the receipt of £52 10*s.* per day, whilst thousands of the poor have to maintain their families upon an income not exceeding 2*d.* per head per day.

"That notwithstanding the wretched and unparalleled condition of the people, your honourable House has manifested no disposition to curtail the expenses of the State, to diminish taxation, or promote general prosperity.

"That unless immediate remedial measures be adopted, your petitioners fear the increasing distress of the people will lead to results fearful to contemplate; because your petitioners can produce evidence of the gradual decline of wages, at the same time that the constant increase of the national burdens must be apparent to all.

"That your petitioners know that it is the undoubted constitutional right of the people, to meet freely, when, how, and where they choose, in public places, peaceably, in the day, to discuss their grievances, and political or other subjects, or for the purpose of framing discussing, or passing any vote, petition, or remonstrance, upon any subject whatsoever.

"That your petitioners complain that the right has unconstitutionally been infringed; and 500 well disposed persons have been arrested, excessive bail demanded, tried by packed juries, sentenced to imprisonment, and treated as felons of the worst description.

"That an unconstitutional police force is distributed all over the country, at enormous cost, to prevent the due exercise of the people's rights. And your petitioners are of opinion that the Poor-law Bastilles and the police stations, being co-existent, have originated from the same cause, viz., the increased desire on the part of the irresponsible few to oppress and starve the many.

"That your petitioners complain that the hours of labour, particularly of the factory workers, are protracted beyond the limits of human endurance, and that the wages earned, after unnatural application to toil in heated and unhealthy workshops, are inadequate to sustain the bodily strength, and supply those comforts which are so imperative after an excessive waste of physical energy.

"That your petitioners also direct the attention of your honourable House to the starvation wages of the agricultural labourer, and view with horror and indignation the paltry income of those whose toil gives being to the staple food of this people.

"That your petitioners believe all men have a right to worship God as may appear best to their consciences, and that no legislative enactments should interfere between man and his Creator.

"That your petitioners maintain that it is the inherent, indubitable, and constitutional right, founded upon the ancient practice of the realm of England, and supported by well approved statutes, of every male inhabitant of the United Kingdom, he being of age and of sound mind, non-convict of crime, and not confined under any judicial process, to exercise the elective franchise in the choice of Members to serve in the Commons House of Parliament.

"That your petitioners can prove, that by the ancient customs and statutes of this realm, Parliament should be held once in each year.

"That your petitioners maintain that Members elected to serve in Parliament ought to be the servants of the people, and should, at short and stated intervals, return to their constituencies, to ascertain if their conduct is approved of, and to give the people power to reject all who have not acted honestly and justly.

"That your petitioners complain that possession of property is made the test of men's qualification to sit in Parliament.

"That your petitioners can give proof that such qualification is irrational, unnecessary, and not in accordance with the ancient usages of England.

"That your petitioners complain, that by influence, patronage, and intimidation, there is at present no purity of election; and your petitioners contend for the right of voting by ballot.

"That your petitioners complain that seats in your honourable House are sought for at a most extravagant rate of expense; which proves an enormous degree of fraud and corruption.

"That your petitioners, therefore, contend, that to put an end to secret political traffic, all representatives should be paid a limited amount for their services.

"That your petitioners complain of the inequality of representation; and contend for the division of the country into equal electoral districts.

"That your petitioners, therefore, exercising their just constitutional right, demand that your honourable House do remedy the many gross and manifest evils of which your petitioners complain, do immediately, without alteration, deduction, or addition, pass into a law the document entitled, 'The People's Charter,' which embraces the representation of male adults, vote by ballot, annual Parliaments, no property qualification, payment of members, and equal electoral districts.

"And that your petitioners, desiring to promote the peace of the United Kingdom, security of property, and prosperity of commerce, seriously and earnestly press this, their petition, on the attention of your honourable House.

1. The presentation of the Great Charter to Parliament was meant to make a powerful impression upon the British people. What message do you think the presentation conveyed?

2. The petition's name was meant to echo the famous Magna Carta of the thirteenth century. Why? Why would reformers choose to make their point with a petition?

3. What is the political philosophy of the Chartists? What, according to them, makes a government legitimate?

4. How does the Charter propose to reform the British government?

5. Many people thought the Charter was a revolutionary document. Would you agree?

·118·

Karl Marx and
Friedrich Engels
Communist Manifesto

(1848)

*K*arl Marx (1818–1883) was born in Prussia, the son of a lawyer and public official. He was trained as a philosopher and received a doctorate in 1841. It was his interest in history and public law, however, that led him to become a social reformer. Marx worked as a journalist, writing for liberal and radical papers in Germany, France, and Belgium. He became a supporter of the French socialist movement and began a lifelong collaboration with Friedrich Engels. By the 1850s Marx was working on his sustained analysis of the capitalist system, which resulted in the publication of his three-volume work *Das Kapital* (*Capital*) (1867–1894). He died in London in 1883.

The *Communist Manifesto* is one of the definitive documents of modern political organization. With it, the Communist movement, which would ultimately result in the Russian Revolution, was generated. Marx and Engels wrote the *Manifesto* as a platform for the Communist League, an international workers' organization that they had joined the previous year. The *Manifesto* was both a statement of belief and a resounding call to action.

BOURGEOIS AND PROLETARIANS

The history of all hitherto existing society is the history of class struggles.

Freeman and slave, patrician and plebeian, lord and serf, guildmaster and journeyman, in a word, oppressor and oppressed, stood in constant opposition to one another, carried on an uninterrupted, now hidden, now open fight, a fight that each time ended, either in a revolutionary reconstitution of society at large, or in the common ruin of the contending classes.

In the earlier epochs of history, we find almost everywhere a complicated arrangement of society into various orders, a manifold grada-

tion of social rank. In ancient Rome we have patricians, knights, plebeians, slaves; in the Middle Ages, feudal lords, vassals, guildmasters, journeyman, apprentices, serfs; in almost all of these classes, again, subordinate gradations.

The modern bourgeois society that has sprouted from the ruins of feudal society, has not done away with class antagonisms. It has but established new classes, new conditions of oppression, new forms of struggle in place of the old ones.

Our epoch, the epoch of the bourgeoisie, possesses, however, this distinctive feature: It has simplified the class antagonisms. Society as a whole is more and more splitting up into two great hostile camps into two great classes directly facing each other—bourgeoisie and proletariat.

PROLETARIANS AND COMMUNISTS

The immediate aim of the Communists is the same as that of all the other proletarian parties; Formation of the proletariat into a class, overthrow of bourgeois supremacy, conquest of political power by the proletariat.

The distinguishing feature of Communism is not the abolition of property generally, but the abolition of bourgeois property. But modern bourgeois private property is the final and most complete expression of the system of producing and appropriating products that is based on class antagonisms, on the exploitation of the many by the few.

In this sense, the theory of the Communists may be summed up in the single sentence: abolition of private property.

We Communists have been reproached with the desire of abolishing the right of personally acquiring property as the fruit of man's own labour, which property is alleged to be the groundwork of all personal freedom, activity and independence.

Hard-won, self-acquired, self-earned property! Do you mean the property of the petty artisan and of the small peasant, a form of property that preceded the bourgeois form? There is no need to abolish that; the development of industry has to a great extent already destroyed it, and is still destroying it daily.

Or do you mean modern bourgeois private property?

But does wage-labour create any property for the labourer? Not a bit. It creates capital, *i.e.,* that kind of property which exploits wage-labour, and which cannot increase except upon condition of begetting a new supply of wage-labour for fresh exploitation. Property, in its present form, is based on the antagonism of capital and wage-labour. Let us examine both sides of this antagonism.

To be a capitalist, is to have not only a purely personal, but a social *status* in production. Capital is a collective product, and only by the united action of many members, nay, in the last resort, only by the united action of all members of society, can it be set in motion.

Capital is therefore not a personal, it is a social, power.

When, therefore, capital is converted into common property, into the property of all members of society, personal property is not thereby transformed into social property. It is only the social character of the property that is changed. It loses its class character.

Let us now take wage-labour.

The average price of wage-labour is the minimum wage, *i.e.,* that quantum of the means of subsistence which is absolutely requisite to keep the labourer in bare existence as a labourer. What, therefore, the wage-labourer appropriates by means of his labour, merely suffices to prolong and reproduce a bare existence. We by no means intend to abolish this personal appropriation of the products of labour, an appropriation that is made for the maintenance and reproduction of human life, and that leaves no surplus wherewith to command the labour of others. All that we want to do away with is the miserable character of this appropriation, under which the labourer lives merely to increase capital, and is allowed to live only insofar as the interest of the ruling class requires it.

In bourgeois society, living labour is but a means to increase accumulated labour. In Communist society, accumulated labour is but a means to widen, to enrich, to promote the existence of the labourer.

In bourgeois society, therefore, the past dominates the present; in Communist society, the present dominates the past. In bourgeois society capital is independent and has individuality, while the living person is dependent and has no individuality.

And the abolition of this state of things is called by the bourgeois, abolition of individuality and freedom! And rightly so. The abolition of bourgeois individuality, bourgeois independence, and bourgeois freedom is undoubtedly aimed at.

By freedom is meant, under the present bourgeois conditions of production, free trade, free selling and buying.

But if selling and buying disappears, free selling and buying disappears also. This talk about free selling and buying, and all the other "brave words" of our bourgeois about freedom in general, have a meaning, if any, only in contrast with restricted selling and buying, with the fettered traders of the Middle Ages, but have no meaning when opposed to the Communist abolition of buying and selling, of the bourgeois conditions of production, and of the bourgeoisie itself.

You are horrified at our intending to do away with private property. But in your existing society, private property is already done away with for nine-tenths of the population; its existence for the few is solely due to its non-existence in the hands of those nine-tenths. You reproach us, therefore, with intending to do away with a form of property, the necessary condition for whose existence is the non-existence of any property for the immense majority of society.

In a word, you reproach us with intending to do away with your property. Precisely so; that is just what we intend.

From the moment when labour can no longer be converted into capital, money, or rent, into a social power capable of being monopolised, *i.e.,* from the moment when individual property can no longer be transformed into bourgeois property, into capital, from that moment, you say, individuality vanishes.

You must, therefore, confess that by "individual" you mean no other person than the bourgeois, than the middle class owner of property. This person must, indeed, be swept out of the way, and made impossible.

But you Communists would introduce community of women, screams the whole bourgeoisie in chorus.

The bourgeois sees his wife as a mere instrument of production. He hears that the instruments of production are to be exploited in common, and, naturally, can come to no other conclusion that the lot of being common to all will likewise fall to the woman.

He has not even a suspicion that the real point aimed at is to do away with the status of women as mere instruments of production.

For the rest, nothing is more ridiculous than the virtuous indignation of our bourgeois at the community of women which, they pretend, is to be openly and officially established by the Communists. The Communists have no need to introduce community of women; it has existed almost from time immemorial.

Our bourgeois, not content with having the wives and daughters of their proletarians at their disposal, not to speak of common prostitutes, take the greatest pleasure in seducing each other's wives.

Bourgeois marriage is in reality a system of wives in common and thus, at the most, what the Communists might possibly be reproached with is that they desire to introduce, in substitution for a hypocritically concealed, an openly legalised community of women. For the rest, it is self-evident, that the abolition of the present system of production must bring with it the abolition of the community of women springing from that system, *i.e.,* of prostitution both public and private.

The Communists are further reproached with desiring to abolish countries and nationality.

The workingmen have no country. We cannot take from them what they have not got. Since the proletariat must first of all acquire political supremacy, must rise to be the leading class of the nation, must constitute itself *the* nation, it is, so far, itself national, though not in the bourgeois sense of the word.

National differences and antagonisms between peoples are vanishing gradually from day to day, owing to the development of the bourgeoisie, to freedom of commerce, to the world market, to uniformity in the mode of production and in the conditions of life corresponding thereto.

The supremacy of the proletariat will cause them to vanish still faster. United action, of the leading civilised countries at least, is one of the first conditions for the emancipation of the proletariat.

In proportion as the exploitation of one individual by another is put an end to, the exploitation of one nation by another will also be put an end to. In proportion as the antagonism between classes within the nation vanishes, the hostility of one nation to another will come to an end.

"Undoubtedly," it will be said, "religion, moral, philosophical and juridical ideas have been modified in the course of historical development. But religion, morality, philosophy, political science, and law, constantly survived this change."

"There are, besides, eternal truths, such as Freedom, Justice, etc., that are common to all states of society. But Communism abolishes eternal truths, it abolishes all religion, and all morality, instead of constituting them on a new basis; it therefore acts in contradiction to all past historical experience."

What does this accusation reduce itself to? The history of all past society has consisted in the development of class antagonisms, antagonisms that assumed different forms at different epochs.

But whatever form they may have taken, one fact is common to all past ages, *viz.*, the exploitation of one part of society by the other. No wonder, then, that the social consciousness of past ages, despite all the multiplicity and variety it displays, moves within certain common forms, or general ideas, which cannot completely vanish except with the total disappearance of class antagonisms.

The Communist revolution is the most radical rupture with traditional property relations; no wonder that its development involves the most radical rupture with traditional ideas.

The Communists disdain to conceal their views and aims. They openly declare that their ends can be attained only by the forcible overthrow of all existing social conditions. Let the ruling classes tremble at a Communist revolution. The proletarians have nothing to lose but their chains. They have a world to win.

Workingmen of all countries, unite!

---

1. In the Marxist view, what has been the course of history? What was the state of politics when the *Manifesto* was composed?

2. What is the Communist party's relation to the working class?

3. What is the party's goal? How will this end be achieved?

4. Marx and Engels scoffed at those who denounced communism as inimical to freedom. Why? What is freedom, according to the *Manifesto*?

5. Why would the nation-state disappear under communism?

·119·
Charles Darwin
The Origin of Species
(1859)

*C*harles Darwin (1809–1882), the pioneer of the biological theory of evolution, was born into a prominent middle-class English family. His grandfather was Josiah Wedgwood, whose ceramic potteries were celebrated by Samuel Smiles. Darwin was not a distinguished student and failed at both medical and divinity studies. By chance in 1832 he was signed on to a naval expedition whose purpose was to catalog plant and animal life in South America and the Pacific. During the voyage Darwin became an accomplished naturalist. His observations led him to the theory of natural selection, adaptation, and eventually to evolution itself. He published a number of volumes based on his discoveries while at sea and worked secretly to provide a convincing explanation of his theory of evolution. After the publication of *The Origin of Species* he became a celebrated scientific figure in Britain. On his death in 1882 he was buried in Westminster Abbey.

The Origin of Species is one of the seminal works of modern biology. It was immediately controversial, both among scientists and the educated public. When Darwin extended his theory of evolution to humans in *The Descent of Man* (1871), he invited a storm of protest from leaders of the Anglican church. Evolutionary theory remains a topic of discussion to this day.

STRUGGLE FOR EXISTENCE

Before entering on the subject of this chapter, I must make a few preliminary remarks, to show how the struggle for existence bears on Natural Selection. It has been seen in the last chapter that amongst organic beings in a state of nature there is some individual variability: indeed I am not aware that this has ever been disputed. It is immaterial for us whether a multitude of doubtful forms be called species or sub-species or varieties; what rank, for instance, the two or three hundred doubtful forms of British plants are entitled to hold, if the existence of any well-marked varieties be admitted. But the mere existence of individual variability and of some few well-marked varieties, though necessary as the foundation for the work, helps us but little in understanding how species arise in nature. How have all those exquisite adaptations of one part of the organisation to another part, and to the conditions of life, and of one organic being to another being, been perfected? We see these beautiful co-adaptations most plainly in the woodpecker and the mistletoe; and only a little less plainly in the humblest parasite which clings to the hairs of a quadruped or feathers of a bird; in the structure of the beetle which dives through the water: in the plumed seed which is wafted by the gentlest breeze; in short, we see beautiful adaptations everywhere and in every part of the organic world.

Again, it may be asked, how is it that varieties, which I have called incipient species, become ultimately converted into good and distinct species, which in most cases obviously differ from each other far more than do the varieties of the same species? How do those groups of species, which constitute what are called distinct genera, and which differ from each other more than do the species of the same genus, arise? All these results, as we shall more fully see in the next chapter, follow from the struggle for life. Owing to this struggle, variations, however slight, and from whatever cause proceeding, if they be in any degree profitable to the individuals of a species, in their infinitely complex relations to other organic beings and to their physical conditions of life, will tend to the preservation of such individuals, and will generally be inherited by the offspring. The offspring, also, will thus have a better chance of surviving, for, of the many individuals of any species which are periodically born, but a small number can survive. I have called this principle, by which each slight variation, if useful, is preserved, by the term Natural Selection, in order to mark its relation to man's power of selection. But the expression often used by Mr. Herbert Spencer of the Survival of the Fittest is more accurate, and is sometimes equally convenient. We have seen that man by selection can certainly produce great results, and can adapt organic beings to his own uses, through the accumulation of slight but useful variations, given to him by the hand of Nature. But Natural Selection, as we shall hereafter see, is a power incessantly ready for action, and is as immeasurably superior to man's feeble efforts, as the works of Nature are to those of Art.

Nothing is easier than to admit in words the truth of the universal struggle for life, or more difficult—at least I have found it so—than constantly to bear this conclusion in mind. Yet unless it be thoroughly ingrained in the mind, the whole economy of nature, with every fact on distribution, rarity, abundance, extinction, and variation, will be dimly seen or quite misunderstood. We behold the face of nature bright with gladness, we often see superabundance of food; we do not see or we forget, that the birds which are idly singing round us mostly live on insects or seeds, and are thus constantly destroying life; or we forget how largely these songsters, or their eggs, or their nestlings, are destroyed by birds and beasts of prey; we do not always bear in mind, that, though food may be now superabundant, it is not so at all seasons of each recurring year.

The Term, Struggle for Existence, Used in a Large Sense

I should premise that I use this term in a large and metaphorical sense including dependence of one being on another, and including (which is more important) not only the life of the individual, but success in leaving progeny. Two canine animals, in a time of dearth, may be truly said to struggle with each other which shall get food and live. But a plant on the edge of a desert is said to struggle for life against the drought, though more properly it should be said to be dependent on the moisture. A plant which annually produces a thousand seeds, of which only one on an average comes to maturity, may be more truly said to struggle with the plants of the same and other kinds which already clothe the ground. The mistletoe is dependent on the apple and a few other trees, but can only in a far-fetched sense be said to struggle with these trees, for, if too many of these parasites grow on the same tree, it languishes and dies. But several seedling mistletoes, growing close together on the same branch, may more truly be said to struggle with each other. As the mistletoe is disseminated by birds, its existence depends on them; and it may metaphorically be said to struggle with other fruit-bearing plants, in tempting the birds to devour and thus disseminate its seeds. In these several senses, which pass into each other, I use for convenience' sake the general term of Struggle for Existence.

Geometrical Ratio of Increase

A struggle for existence inevitably follows from the high rate at which all organic beings tend to increase. Every being, which during its natural lifetime produces several eggs or seeds, must suffer destruction during some period of its life, and during some season or occasional year, otherwise, on the principle of geometrical increase, its numbers would quickly become so inordinately great that no country could support the product. Hence, as more individuals are produced than can possibly survive, there must in every case be a struggle for existence, either one individual with another of the same species, or with the individuals of distinct species, or with the physical conditions of life. It is the doctrine of Malthus applied with manifold force to the whole animal and vegetable kingdoms; for in this case there can be no artificial increase of food, and no prudential restraint from marriage. Although some species may be now increasing, more or less rapidly, in numbers, all cannot do so, for the world would not hold them.

There is no exception to the rule that every organic being naturally increases at so high a rate, that, if not destroyed, the earth would soon be covered by the progeny of a single pair. Even slow-breeding man has doubled in twenty-five years, and at this rate, in less than a thousand years, there would literally not be standing-room for his progeny. Linnaeus has calculated that if an annual plant produced only two seeds—and there is no plant so unproductive as this—and their seedlings next year produced two, and so on, then in twenty years there would be a million plants. The elephant is reckoned the slowest breeder of all known animals, and I have taken some pains to estimate its probable minimum rate of natural increase; it will be safest to assume that it begins breeding when thirty years old, and goes on breeding till ninety years old, bringing forth six young in the interval, and surviving till one hundred years old; if this be so, after a period of from 740 to 750 years there would be nearly nineteen million elephants alive, descended from the first pair.

NATURAL SELECTION OR THE SURVIVAL OF THE FITTEST

How will the struggle for existence, briefly discussed in the last chapter, act in regard to variation? Can the principle of selection, which we have seen is so potent in the hands of man, apply under nature? I think we shall see that it can act most efficiently. Let the endless number of slight variations and individual differences occurring in our domestic productions, and, in a lesser degree, in those under nature, be borne in mind; as well as the strength of the hereditary tendency. Under domestication, it may be truly said that the whole organization becomes in some degree plastic. But the variability, which we almost universally meet with in our domestic productions, is not directly produced, as Hooker and Asa Gray have well remarked, by man; he can neither originate varieties, nor prevent their occurrence; he can only preserve and accumulate such as do occur. Unintentionally he exposes organic beings to new and changing conditions of life, and variability ensues; but similar changes of conditions might and do occur under nature. Let it also be borne in mind how infinitely complex and close-fitting are the mutual relations of all organic beings to each other and to their physical conditions of life; and consequently what infinitely varied diversities of structure might be of use to each being under changing conditions of life. Can it, then, be thought improbable, seeing that variations useful to man have undoubtedly occurred, that other variations useful in some way to each being in the great and complex battle of life, should occur in the course of many successive generations? If such do occur, can we doubt (remembering that many more individuals are born than can possibly survive) that individuals having any advantage, however slight, over others, would have the best chance of surviving and of procreating their kind? On the other hand, we may feel sure that any variation in the least degree injurious would be rigidly destroyed. This preservation of favourable individual differences and variations, and the destruction of those which are injurious, I have called Natural Selection, or the Survival of the Fittest. Variations neither useful nor injurious would not be affected by natural selection, and would be left either a fluctuating element, as perhaps we see in certain polymorphic species, or would ultimately become fixed, owing to the nature of the organism and the nature of the conditions.

We shall best understand the probable course of natural selection by taking the case of a country undergoing some slight physical change, for instance, of climate. The proportional numbers of its inhabitants will almost immediately undergo a change, and some species will probably become extinct. We may conclude, from what we have seen of the intimate and complex manner in which the inhabitants of each country are bound together, that any change in the numerical proportions of the inhabitants, independently of the change of climate itself, would seriously affect the others. If the country were open on its borders, new forms would certainly immigrate, and this would likewise seriously disturb the relations of some of the former inhabitants. Let it be remembered how powerful the influence of a single introduced tree or mammal has been shown to be. But in the case of an island, or of a country partly surrounded by barriers, into which new and better adapted forms could not freely enter, we should then have places in the economy of nature which would assuredly be better filled up, if some of the original inhabitants were in some manner modified; for, had the area been open to immigration, these same places would have been seized on by intruders. In such cases, slight modifications, which in any way favoured the individuals of any species, by better adapting them to their altered conditions, would tend to be preserved; and natural selection would have free scope for the work of improvement.

We have good reason to believe, as shown in the first chapter, that changes in the conditions of life give a tendency to increased variability; and in the foregoing cases the conditions have changed, and this would manifestly be favourable to natural selection, by affording a better chance of the occurrence of profitable variations. Unless such occur, natural selection can do nothing. Under the term of "variations," it must never be forgotten that mere individual differences are included. As man can produce a great result with his domestic animals and plants by adding up in any given direction individual differences, so could natural selection, but far more easily, from having incomparably longer time for action. Nor do I believe that any great physical change, as of climate, or any unusual degree of isolation to check immigration, is necessary in order that new and unoccupied places should be left, for natural selection to fill up by improving some of the varying inhabitants. For as all the inhabitants of each country are struggling together with nicely balanced forces, extremely slight modifications in the structure or habits of one species would often give it an advantage over others; and still further modifications of the same kind would often still further increase the advantage, as long as the species continued under the same conditions of life and profited by similar means of subsistence and defense. No country can be named in which all the native inhabitants are now so perfectly adapted to each other and to the physical conditions under which they live, that none of them could be still better adapted or improved; for in all countries, the natives have been so far conquered by naturalised productions, that they have allowed some foreigners to take firm possession of the land. And as foreigners have thus in every country beaten some of the natives, we may safely conclude that the natives might have been modified with advantage, so as to have better resisted the intruders.

As man can produce, and certainly has produced, a great result by his methodical and unconscious means of selection, what may not natural selection effect? Man can act only on external and visible characters: Nature, if I may be allowed to personify the natural preservation or survival of the fittest, cares nothing for appearances, except in so far as they are useful to any being. She can act on every internal organ, on every shade of constitutional difference, on the whole machinery of life. Man selects only for his own good: Nature only for that of the being which she tends. Every selected character is fully exercised by her, as is implied by the fact of their selection. Man keeps the natives of many climates in the same country; he seldom exercises each selected character in some peculiar and fitting manner; he feeds a long and a short beaked pigeon on the same food; he does not exercise a long-backed or long-legged quadruped in any peculiar manner; he exposes sheep with long and short wool to the same climate. He does not allow the most vigorous males to struggle for the females. He does not rigidly destroy all inferior animals, but protects during each varying season, as far as lies in his power, all his productions. He often begins his selection by some half-monstrous form; or at least by some modification prominent enough to catch the eye or to be plainly useful to him. Under nature, the slightest differences of structure or constitution may well turn the nicely-balanced scale in the struggle for life, and so be preserved. How fleeting are the wishes and efforts of man! how short his time! and consequently how poor will be his results, compared with those accumulated by Nature during whole geological periods! Can we wonder, then, that Nature's productions should be far "truer" in character than man's productions; that they should be infinitely better adapted to the most complex conditions of life, and should plainly bear the stamp of far higher workmanship?

Illustrations of the Action of Natural Selection, or the Survival of the Fittest

In order to make it clear how, as I believe, natural selection acts, I must beg permission to give one or two imaginary illustrations. Let us take the case of a wolf, which preys on various animals, securing some by craft, some by strength, and some by fleetness; and let us suppose that the fleetest prey, a deer for instance, had from any change in the country increased in numbers, or that other prey had decreased in numbers, during that season of the year when the wolf was hardest pressed for food. Under such circumstances the swiftest and slimmest wolves would have the best chance of surviving, and so be preserved or selected—provided always that they retained strength to master their prey at this or some other period of the year, when they were compelled to prey on other animals. I can see no more reason to doubt that this would be the result, than that man should be able to improve

the fleetness of his greyhounds by careful and methodical selection, or by that kind of unconscious selection which follows from each man trying to keep the best dogs without any thought of modifying the breed.

It may be worthwhile to give another and more complex illustration of the action of natural selection. Certain plants excrete sweet juice, apparently for the sake of eliminating something injurious from the sap; this is effected, for instance, by glands at the base of the stipules in some Leguminosæ, and at the backs of the leaves of the common laurel. This juice, though small in quantity, is greedily sought by insects; but their visits do not in any way benefit the plant. Now, let us suppose that the juice or nectar was excreted from the inside of the flowers of a certain number of plants of any species. Insects in seeking the nectar would get dusted with pollen, and would often transport it from one flower to another. The flowers of two distinct individuals of the same species would thus get crossed; and the act of crossing, as can be fully proved, gives rise to vigorous seedlings, which consequently would have the best chance of flourishing and surviving. The plants which produced flowers with the largest glands or nectaries, excreting most nectar, would oftenest be visited by insects, and would oftenest be crossed; and so in the long-run would gain the upper hand and form a local variety. The flowers, also, which had their stamens and pistils placed, in relation to the size and habits of the particular insect which visited them, so as to favour in any degree the transportal of the pollen, would likewise be favoured. We might have taken the case of insects visiting flowers for the sake of collecting pollen instead of nectar; and as pollen is formed for the sole purpose of fertilisation, its destruction appears to be a simple loss to the plant; yet if a little pollen were carried, at first occasionally and then habitually, by the pollen-devouring insects from flower to flower, and a cross thus effected, although nine-tenths of the pollen were destroyed, it might still be a great gain to the plant to be thus robbed; and the individuals which produced more and more pollen, and had larger anthers, would be selected.

1. What is natural selection? How does it work and what purpose does it serve?

2. What sort of picture does Darwin give of nature?

3. Darwin talks about a struggle for existence. What does he mean?

4. Why, according to Darwin, is nature better at selection than people when they practice selective breeding?

5. Darwin's work caused a great deal of controversy in his own time and continues to do so today. Why?

·120·

Sigmund Freud
The Interpretation of Dreams
(1899)

Sigmund Freud (1856–1939) was an Austrian medical doctor whose work forms the basis of the discipline of psychology. Born in a provincial town in what was then Austria, Freud came from an assimilated middle-class Jewish family. He studied medicine at the University of Vienna, and after graduation decided to specialize in psychiatry. Opening his own practice, Freud began to work on the theories that were to make him a household name. In the 1890s he developed the technique that he labeled psychoanalysis, introducing a number of terms that have passed into common parlance, including ego, id, and Oedipus complex. He also pioneered work on the unconscious. Freud lived in Vienna until it was occupied by Hitler's troops in 1938. He fled to London where he died the following year.

Freud's best known and most important work was *The Interpretation of Dreams*, in which he uncovered the ways in which the unconscious operates and posited the now familiar theory of dreams as wish-fulfillment.

I am proposing to show that dreams are capable of interpretation; and any contributions to the solution of the problem which have already been discussed will emerge only as possible by-products in the accomplishment of my special task. On the hypothesis that dreams are susceptible of interpretation, I at once find myself in disagreement with the prevailing doctrine of dreams—in fact, with all the theories of dreams, excepting only that of Scherner, for "to interpret a dream" is to specify its "meaning," to replace it by something which takes its position in the concatenation of our psychic activities as a link of definite importance and value. But, as we have seen, the scientific theories of the dream leave no room for a problem of dream-interpretation; since, in the first place, according to these theories, dreaming is not a psychic activity at all, but a somatic process which makes itself known to the psychic apparatus by means of symbols. Lay opinion has always been opposed to these theories. It asserts its privilege of proceeding illogically, and although it admits that dreams are incomprehensible and absurd, it cannot summon up the courage to deny that dreams have any significance. Led by a dim intuition, it seems rather to assume that dreams have a meaning, albeit a hidden one; that they are intended as a substitute for some other thought-process, and that we have only to disclose this substitute correctly in order to discover the hidden meaning of the dream.

The unscientific world, therefore, has always endeavored to "interpret" dreams, and by applying one or the other of two essentially different methods. The first of these envisages the dream-content as a whole, and seeks to replace it by another content, which is intelligible and in certain respects analogous. This is symbolic dream-interpretation; and of course it goes to pieces at the very outset in the case of those dreams which are not only unintelligible but confused. The construction which the biblical Joseph placed upon the dream of Pharaoh furnishes an example of this method. The seven fat kine, after which came seven lean ones that devoured the former, were a symbolic substitute for seven years of famine in the land of Egypt, which according to the prediction were to consume all the surplus that seven fruitful years had produced. Most of the artificial dreams contrived by the poets are intended for some such symbolic interpretation, for they reproduce the thought conceived by the poet in a guise not unlike the disguise which we are wont to find in our dreams.

The idea that the dream concerns itself chiefly with the future, whose form it surmises in advance—a relic of the prophetic significance with which dreams were once invested—now becomes the motive for translating into the future the meaning of the dream which has been found by means of symbolic interpretation.

A demonstration of the manner in which one arrives at such a symbolic interpretation can-

not, of course, be given. Success remains a matter of ingenious conjecture, of direct intuition, and for this reason dream-interpretation has naturally been elevated into an art which seems to depend upon extraordinary gifts. The second of the two popular methods of dream-interpretation entirely abandons such claims. It might be described as the "cipher method," since it treats the dream as a kind of secret code in which every sign is translated into another sign of known meaning, according to an established key. For example, I have dreamt of a letter, and also of a funeral or the like; I consult a "dream-book," and I find that "letter" is to be translated by "vexation" and "funeral" by "engagement." It now remains to establish a connection, which I am again to assume as pertaining to the future, by means of the rigmarole which I have deciphered.

An ancient and stubbornly retained popular belief seems to have come nearer to the truth of the matter than the opinion of modern science. I must insist that the dream actually does possess a meaning, and that a scientific method of dream-interpretation is possible.

When, after passing through a narrow defile, one suddenly reaches a height beyond which the ways part and a rich prospect lies outspread in different directions, it is well to stop for a moment and consider whither one shall turn next. We are in somewhat the same position after we have mastered this first interpretation of a dream. We find ourselves standing in the light of a sudden discovery. The dream is not comparable to the irregular sounds of a musical instrument, which, instead of being played by the hand of a musician, is struck by some external force; the dream is not meaningless, not absurd, does not presuppose that one part of our store of ideas is dormant while another part begins to awake. It is a perfectly valid psychic phenomenon, actually a wish-fulfilment; it may be enrolled in the continuity of the intelligible psychic activities of the waking state; it is built up by a highly complicated intellectual activity. But at the very moment when we are about to rejoice in this discovery a host of problems besets us. If the dream, as this theory defines it, represents a fulfilled wish, what is the cause of the striking and unfamiliar manner in which this fulfilment is expressed?

It is easy to show that the wish-fulfilment in dreams is often undisguised and easy to recognize, so that one may wonder why the language of dreams has not long since been understood. There is, for example, a dream which I can evoke as often as I please, experimentally, as it were. If, in the evening, I eat anchovies, olives, or other strongly salted foods, I am thirsty at night, and therefore I wake. The waking, however, is preceded by a dream, which has always the same content, namely, that I am drinking. I am drinking long draughts of water; it tastes as delicious as only a cool drink can taste when one's throat is parched; and then I wake, and find that I have an actual desire to drink. The cause of this dream is thirst, which I perceive when I wake. From this sensation arises the wish to drink, and the dream shows me this wish as fulfilled. It thereby serves a function, the nature of which I soon surmise. I sleep well, and am not accustomed to being waked by a bodily need. If I succeed in appeasing my thirst by means of the dream that I am drinking, I need not wake up in order to satisfy that thirst. It is thus a *dream of convenience*. The dream takes the place of action, as elsewhere in life.

If I now declare that wish-fulfilment is the meaning of *every* dream, so that there cannot be any dreams other than wish-dreams, I know beforehand that I shall meet with the most emphatic contradiction. Nevertheless, it is not difficult to parry these objections. It is merely necessary to observe that our doctrine is not based upon the estimates of the obvious dream-content but relates to the thought-content, which, in the course of interpretation, is found to lie behind the dream. Let us compare and contrast the *manifest* and the *latent dream-content*. It is true that here are dreams the manifest content of which is of the most painful nature. But has anyone ever tried to interpret these dreams—to dis-

cover their latent thought-content? If not, the two objections to our doctrine are no longer valid; for there is always the possibility that even our painful and terrifying dreams may, upon interpretation, prove to be wish-fulfilments.

She puts a candle into a candlestick; but the candle is broken, so that it does not stand up. The girls at school say she is clumsy; but she replies that it is not her fault.

Here, too, there is an actual occasion for the dream; the day before she had actually put a candle into a candlestick; but this one was not broken. An obvious symbolism has here been employed. The candle is an object which excites the female genitals; its being broken, so that it does not stand upright, signifies impotence on the man's part (*it is not her fault*). But does this young woman, carefully brought up, and a stranger to all obscenity, know of such an application of the candle? By chance she is able to tell how she came by this information. While paddling a canoe on the Rhine, a boat passed her which contained some students, who were singing rapturously, or rather yelling: "When the Queen of Sweden, behind closed shutters, with the candles of Apollo. . . ."

She does not hear or else understand the last word. Her husband was asked to give her the required explanation. These verses are then replaced in the dream-content by the innocent recollection of a task which she once performed *clumsily* at her boarding-school, because of the *closed shutters*. The connection between the theme of masturbation and that of impotence is clear enough. "Apollo" in the latent dream-content connects this dream with an earlier one in which the virgin Pallas figured. All this is obviously not innocent.

THE DREAM-WORK

All other previous attempts to solve the problems of dreams have concerned themselves directly with the manifest dream-content as it is retained in the memory. They have sought to obtain an interpretation of the dream from this content, or, if they dispensed with an interpretation, to base their conclusions concerning the dream on the evidence provided by this content. We, however, are confronted by a different set of data; for us a new psychic material interposes itself between the dream-content and the results of our investigations: the *latent* dream-content, or dream-thoughts, which are obtained only by our method. We develop the solution of the dream from this latent content, and not from the manifest dream-content. We are thus confronted with a new problem, an entirely novel task—that of examining and tracing the relations between the latent dream-thoughts and the manifest dream-content, and the processes by which the latter has grown out of the former.

The dream-thoughts and the dream-content present themselves as two descriptions of the same content in two different languages; or, to put it more clearly, the dream-content appears to us as a translation of the dream-thoughts into another mode of expression, whose symbols and laws of composition we must learn by comparing the origin with the translation. The dream-thoughts we can understand without further trouble the moment we have ascertained them. The dream-content is, as it were, presented in hieroglyphics, whose symbols must be translated, one by one, into the language of the dream-thoughts.

And what of the value of dreams in regard to our knowledge of the future? That, of course, is quite out of the question. One would like to substitute the words: "in regard to our knowledge of the past." For in every sense a dream has its origin in the past. The ancient belief that dreams reveal the future is not indeed entirely devoid of truth. By representing a wish as fulfilled the dream certainly leads us into the future; but this future, which the dreamer accepts as his present, has been shaped in the likeness of the past by the indestructible wish.

1. What are the popular types of dream interpretation?

2. How does Freud's method of interpreting dreams differ from previous techniques?

3. What, according to Freud, is a dream? Why do we have them?

4. Why are dreams important?

5. Freud criticized traditional dream interpretation as unscientific, yet his own methods have been questioned. How might Freud's own experience and circumstances have affected his theories?

Controlling Latin America

"Simon Bolivar at the Battle of Araure," by Tito Salas.

·121·
Simon Bolivar
Jamaican Letter
(1815)

Simon Bolivar (1783–1830) is known throughout Latin America as "El Libertador" ("The Liberator"). He was the son of a Venezuelan nobleman and grew up surrounded by great wealth. After the death of his parents, Bolivar was sent to Spain to finish his education and to find a suitable spouse. He returned to Venezuela in 1807 when Napoleon's conquest of Spain loosened the Spanish hold on its New World colonies. Venezuela declared its independence in 1811 but its war against Spain was a long and bloody one. Bolivar assumed leadership of the revolution, first in Venezuela and then in New Granada, a large territory comprised of what is modern-day Colombia, Ecuador, Peru, and Bolivia. In 1819 Bolivar's army defeated the Spanish forces in a portion of New Granada and he declared the liberated territory the Republic of Colombia. The fighting against Spain continued for another six years before upper Peru was finally won. The territory was renamed Bolivia in his honor.

Bolivar's *Jamaican Letter* is one of his most famous political manifestoes. Its optimistic outlook is all the more remarkable in that it was written at the low point of the struggle against Spain. Having failed to attract support from either Europe or the United States, Bolivar was in exile in Jamaica appealing for support. The ideas he expressed here for the reorganization of the states of Latin America were ones that he attempted to put into practice during his years of power as president of Peru, Colombia, and Bolivia.

It is difficult to foresee the future fate of the New World, to set down its political principles, or to prophesy what manner of government it will adopt. Every conjecture relative to America's future is, I feel, pure speculation. When mankind was in its infancy, steeped in uncertainty, ignorance, and error, was it possible to foresee what system it would adopt for its preservation? Who could venture to say that a certain nation would be a republic or a monarchy; this nation great, that nation small? To my way of thinking, such is our own situation. We are a young people. We inhabit a world apart, separated by broad seas. We are young in the ways of almost all the arts and sciences, although, in a certain manner, we are old in the ways of civilized society. I look upon the present state of America as similar to that of Rome after its fall. Each part of Rome adopted a political system conforming to its interest and situation or was led by the individual ambitions of certain chiefs, dynasties, or associations. But this important difference exists: those dispersed parts later reestablished their ancient nations, subject to the changes imposed by circumstances or events. But we scarcely retain a vestige of what once was;

Simon Bolivar.

we are, moreover, neither Indian nor European, but a species midway between the legitimate proprietors of this country and the Spanish usurpers. In short, though Americans by birth we derive our rights from Europe, and we have to assert these rights against the rights of the natives, and at the same time we must defend ourselves against the invaders. This places us in a most extraordinary and involved situation. Notwithstanding that it is a type of divination to predict the result of the political course which America is pursuing, I shall venture some conjectures which, of course, are colored by my enthusiasm and dictated by rational desires rather than by reasoned calculations.

The rôle of the inhabitants of the American hemisphere has for centuries been purely passive. Politically they were non-existent. We are still in a position lower than slavery, and therefore it is more difficult for us to rise to the enjoyment of freedom. Permit me these transgressions in order to establish the issue. States are slaves because of either the nature or the misuse of their constitutions; a people is therefore enslaved when the government, by its nature or its vices, infringes on and usurps the rights of the citizen or subject. Applying these principles, we find that America was denied not only its freedom but even an active and effective tyranny. Let me explain. Under absolutism there are no recognized limits to the exercise of governmental powers. The will of the great sultan, khan, bey, and other despotic rulers is the supreme law, carried out more or less arbitrarily by the lesser pashas, khans, and satraps of Turkey and Persia, who have an organized system of oppression in which inferiors participate according to the authority vested in them. To them is entrusted the administration of civil, military, political, religious, and tax matters. But, after all is said and done, the rulers of Ispahan are Persians; the viziers of the Grand Turk are Turks; and the sultans of Tartary are Tartars. China does not bring its military leaders and scholars from the land of Genghis Khan, her conqueror, notwithstanding that the Chinese of today are the lineal descendants of those who were reduced to subjection by the ancestors of the present-day Tartars.

How different is our situation! We have been harassed by a conduct which has not only deprived us of our rights but has kept us in a sort of permanent infancy with regard to public affairs. If we could at least have managed our domestic affairs and our internal administration, we could have acquainted ourselves with the processes and mechanics of public affairs. We should also have enjoyed a personal consideration, thereby commanding a certain unconscious respect from the people, which is so necessary to preserve amidst revolutions. That is why I say we have even been deprived of an active tyranny, since we have not been permitted to exercise its functions.

Americans today, and perhaps to a greater extent than ever before, who live within the Spanish system occupy a position in society no better than that of serfs destined for labor, or at best they have no more status than that of mere consumers. Yet even this status is surrounded with galling restrictions, such as being forbidden to grow European crops, or to store products which are royal monopolies, or to establish factories of a type the Peninsula itself does not possess. To this add the exclusive trading privileges, even in articles of prime necessity, and the barriers between American provinces, designed to prevent all exchange of trade, traffic, and understanding. In short, do you wish to know what our future held?—simply the cultivation of the fields of indigo, grain, coffee, sugar cane, cacao, and cotton; cattle raising on the broad plains; hunting wild game in the jungles; digging in the earth to mine its gold—but even these limitations could never satisfy the greed of Spain.

So negative was our existence that I can find nothing comparable in any other civilized society, examine as I may the entire history of time and the politics of all nations. Is it not an outrage and a violation of human rights to expect a land so splendidly endowed, so vast, rich, and populous, to remain merely passive?

As I have just explained, we were cut off and, as it were, removed from the world in relation to the science of government and administration of the state. We were never viceroys or governors, save in the rarest of instances; seldom archbishops and bishops; diplomats never; as military men, only subordinates; as nobles, without royal privileges. In brief, we were neither magistrates nor financiers and seldom merchants—all in flagrant contradiction to our institutions.

It is harder, Montesquieu has written, to release a nation from servitude than to enslave a free nation. This truth is proven by the annals of all times, which reveal that most free nations have been put under the yoke, but very few enslaved nations have recovered their liberty. Despite the convictions of history, South Americans have made efforts to obtain liberal, even perfect, institutions, doubtless out of that instinct to aspire to the greatest possible happiness, which, common to all men, is bound to follow in civil societies founded on the principles of justice, liberty, and equality. But are we capable of maintaining in proper balance the difficult charge of a republic? Is it conceivable that a newly emancipated people can soar to the heights of liberty, and, unlike Icarus, neither have its wings melt nor fall into an abyss? Such a marvel is inconceivable and without precedent. There is no reasonable probability to bolster our hopes.

More than anyone, I desire to see America fashioned into the greatest nation in the world, greatest not so much by virtue of her area and wealth as by her freedom and glory. Although I seek perfection for the government of my country, I cannot persuade myself that the New World can, at the moment, be organized as a great republic. Since it is impossible, I dare not desire it; yet much less do I desire to have all America a monarchy because this plan is not only impracticable but also impossible. Wrongs now existing could not be righted, and our emancipation would be fruitless. The American states need the care of paternal governments to heal the sores and wounds of despotism and war. The parent country, for example, might be Mexico, the only country fitted for the position by her intrinsic strength, and without such power there can be no parent country. Let us assume it were to be the Isthmus of Panamá, the most central point of this vast continent. Would not all parts continue in their lethargy and even in their present disorder? For a single government to infuse life into the New World; to put into use all the resources for public prosperity; to improve, educate, and perfect the New World, that government would have to possess the authority of a god, much less the knowledge and virtues of mankind.

From the foregoing, we can draw these conclusions: The American provinces are fighting for their freedom, and they will ultimately succeed. Some provinces as a matter of course will form federal and some central republics; the larger areas will inevitably establish monarchies, some of which will fare so badly that they will disintegrate in either present or future revolutions. To consolidate a great monarchy will be no easy task, but it will be utterly impossible to consolidate a great republic.

It is a grandiose idea to think of consolidating the New World into a single nation, united by pacts into a single bond. It is reasoned that, as these parts have a common origin, language, customs, and religion, they ought to have a single government to permit the newly formed states to unite in a confederation. But this is not possible. Actually, America is separated by climatic differences, geographic diversity, conflicting interests, and dissimilar characteristics. How beautiful it would be if the Isthmus of Panamá could be for us what the Isthmus of Corinth was for the Greeks! Would to God that some day we may have the good fortune to convene there an august assembly of representatives of republics, kingdoms, and empires to deliberate upon the high interests of peace and war with the nations of the other three-quarters of the globe. This type of organization may come to pass in some

happier period of our regeneration. But any other plan, such as that of Abbé St. Pierre, who in laudable delirium conceived the idea of assembling a European congress to decide the fate and interests of those nations, would be meaningless.

Among the popular and representative systems, I do not favor the federal system. It is over-perfect, and it demands political virtues and talents far superior to our own. For the same reason I reject a monarchy that is part aristocracy and part democracy, although with such a government England has achieved much fortune and splendor. Since it is not possible for us to select the most perfect and complete form of government, let us avoid falling into demagogic anarchy or monocratic tyranny. These opposite extremes would only wreck us on similar reefs of misfortune and dishonor; hence, we must seek a mean between them. I say: Do not adopt the best system of government, but the one that is most likely to succeed.

1. How does Bolivar describe the situation of the present leaders of Latin America?

2. What, in Bolivar's view, is a form of tyranny worse than slavery?

3. What is the intended audience of this document? Why does Bolivar adopt the tone he does?

4. What does Bolivar believe to be the best form of government? What form of government does he think will be adopted in Latin America?

·122·

The Monroe Doctrine

(1823)

James Monroe (1758–1831) was the fifth president of the United States. He came to office at the time that the major European states had agreed to act in concert to maintain a balance of power. This balance was threatened by rebellions within Spain's South American colonies. Monroe feared that the

European states would intervene militarily, threatening the security of the United States. On December 2, 1823, President Monroe delivered an address to the U.S. Congress in which he enunciated his foreign policy objectives. This speech outlined what ultimately came to be known as the Monroe Doctrine.

The Monroe Doctrine, which denied European powers the right to intervene in the affairs of the states of the Western hemisphere, was not immediately effective. In 1833 Britain occupied the Falkland Islands, and it was only with the aid of the British navy that the United States could keep France from intervening in South America. It was not until the 1880s that the Monroe Doctrine became an official part of American policy and then it was used not to keep Europe out of South America, but rather to justify the U.S. government's right to police the affairs of the states of Latin America.

Washington, *December 2, 1823.*
Fellow-Citizens of the Senate and House of Repre-
sentatives:

Many important subjects will claim your attention during the present session, of which I shall endeavor to give, in aid of your deliberations, a just idea in this communication. I undertake this duty with diffidence, from the vast extent of the interests on which I have to treat and of their great importance to every portion of our Union. I enter on it with zeal from a thorough conviction that there never was a period since the establishment of our Revolution when, regarding the condition of the civilized world and its bearing on us, there was greater necessity for devotion in the public servants to their respective duties, or for virtue, patriotism, and union in our constituents.

Meeting in you a new Congress, I deem it proper to present this view of public affairs in greater detail than might otherwise be necessary. I do it, however, with peculiar satisfaction, from a knowledge that in this respect I shall comply more fully with the sound principles of our Government. The people being with us exclusively the sovereign, it is indispensable that full information be laid before them on all important subjects, to enable them to exercise that high power with complete effect. If kept in the dark, they must be incompetent to it. We are all liable to error, and those who are engaged in the man-

agement of public affairs are more subject to excitement and to be led astray by their particular interests and passions than the great body of our constituents, who, living at home in the pursuit of their ordinary avocations, are calm but deeply interested spectators of events and of the conduct of those who are parties to them. To the people every department of the Government and every individual in each are responsible, and the more full their information the better they can judge of the wisdom of the policy pursued and of the conduct of each in regard to it. From their dispassionate judgment much aid may always be obtained, while their approbation will form the greatest incentive and most gratifying reward for virtuous actions, and the dread of their censure the best security against the abuse of their confidence. Their interests in all vital questions are the same, and the bond, by sentiment as well as by interest, will be proportionably strengthened as they are better informed of the real state of public affairs, especially in difficult conjunctures. It is by such knowledge that local prejudices and jealousies are surmounted, and that a national policy, extending its fostering care and protection to all the great interests of our Union, is formed and steadily adhered to.

A precise knowledge of our relations with foreign powers as respects our negotiations and transactions with each is thought to be particularly necessary. . . .

In compliance with a resolution of the House of Representatives adopted at their last session, instructions have been given to all the ministers of the United States accredited to the powers of Europe and America to propose the proscription of the African slave trade by classing it under the denomination, and inflicting on its perpetrators the punishment, of piracy. Should this proposal be acceded to, it is not doubted that this odious and criminal practice will be promptly and entirely suppressed. It is earnestly hoped that it will be acceded to, from the firm belief that it is the most effectual expedient that can be adopted for the purpose.

At the commencement of the recent war between France and Spain it was declared by the French Government that it would grant no commissions to privateers, and that neither the commerce of Spain herself nor of neutral nations should be molested by the naval force of France, except in the breach of a lawful blockade. This declaration, which appears to have been faithfully carried into effect, concurring with principles proclaimed and cherished by the United States from the first establishment of their independence, suggested the hope that the time had arrived when the proposal for adopting it as a permanent and invariable rule in all future maritime wars might meet the favorable consideration of the great European powers. Instructions have accordingly been given to our ministers with France, Russia, and Great Britain to make those proposals to their respective Governments, and when the friends of humanity reflect on the essential amelioration to the condition of the human race which would result from the abolition of private war on the sea and on the great facility by which it might be accomplished, requiring only the consent of a few sovereigns, an earnest hope is indulged that these overtures will meet with an attention animated by the spirit in which they were made, and that they will ultimately be successful.

The ministers who were appointed to the Republics of Colombia and Buenos Ayres during the last session of Congress proceeded shortly afterwards to their destinations. Of their arrival there official intelligence has not yet been received. The minister appointed to the Republic of Chile will sail in a few days. An early appointment will also be made to Mexico. A minister has been received from Colombia, and the other Governments have been informed that ministers, or diplomatic agents of inferior grade, would be received from each, accordingly as they might prefer the one or the other.

It was stated at the commencement of the last session that a great effort was then making in Spain and Portugal to improve the condition of the people of those countries, and that it appeared to be conducted with extraordinary moderation. It need scarcely be remarked that the result has been so far very different from what was then anticipated. Of events in that quarter of the globe, with which we have so much intercourse and from which we derive our origin, we have always been anxious and interested spectators.

The citizens of the United States cherish sentiments the most friendly in favor of the liberty and happiness of their fellow-men on that side of the Atlantic. In the wars of the European powers in matters relating to themselves we have never taken any part, nor does it comport with our policy so to do. It is only when our rights are invaded or seriously menaced that we resent injuries or make preparation for our defense. With the movements in this hemisphere we are of necessity more immediately connected, and by causes which must be obvious to all enlightened and impartial observers. The political system of the allied powers is essentially different in this respect from that of America. This difference proceeds from that which exists in their respective Governments; and to the defense of our own, which has been achieved by the loss of so much blood and treasure, and matured by the wisdom of their most enlightened citizens, and under which we have enjoyed unexampled felicity, this whole nation is devoted. We owe it, therefore, to candor and to the amicable relations existing between the United States and those powers to declare that we should consider any attempt on their part to extend their system to any portion of this hemisphere as dangerous to our peace and safety. With the existing colonies or dependencies of any European power we have not interfered and shall not interfere. But with the Governments who have declared their independence and maintained it, and whose independence we have, on great consideration and on just principles, acknowledged, we could not view any interposition for the purpose of oppressing them, or controlling in any other manner their destiny, by any European power in any other light than as the manifestation of an unfriendly disposition toward the United States. In the war between those new Governments and Spain we declared our neutrality at the time of their recognition, and to this we have adhered, and shall continue to adhere, provided no change shall occur which, in the judgment of the competent authorities of this Government, shall make a corresponding change on the part of the United States indispensable to their security.

The late events in Spain and Portugal shew that Europe is still unsettled. Of this important fact no stronger proof can be adduced than that the allied powers should have thought it proper, on any principle satisfactory to themselves, to have interposed by force in the internal concerns of Spain. To what extent such interposition may be carried, on the same principle, is a question in which all independent powers whose governments differ from theirs are interested, even those most remote, and surely none more so than the United States.

Our policy in regard to Europe, which was adopted at an early stage of the wars which have so long agitated that quarter of the globe, nevertheless remains the same, which is, not to interfere in the internal concerns of any of its powers; to consider the government *de facto* as the legitimate government for us; to cultivate friendly relations with it, and to preserve those relations by a frank, firm, and manly policy, meeting in all instances the just claims of every power, submitting to injuries from none. But in regard to those continents circumstances are eminently and conspicuously different. It is impossible that the allied powers should extend their political system to any portion of either continent without endangering our peace and happiness; nor can anyone believe that our southern brethren, if left to themselves, would adopt it of their own accord. It is equally impossible, therefore, that we should behold such interposition in any form with indifference. If we look to the comparative strength and resources of Spain and those new Governments, and their distance from each other, it must be obvious that she can never subdue them. It is still the true policy of the United States to leave the parties to themselves, in the hope that other powers will pursue the same course.

If we compare the present condition of our Union with its actual state at the close of our Revolution, the history of the world furnishes no example of a progress in improvement in all the important circumstances which constitute the happiness of a nation which bears any resemblance to it. At the first epoch our population did not exceed 3,000,000. By the last census it amounted to about 10,000,000, and, what is more extraordinary, it is almost altogether native, for the immigration from other countries has been inconsiderable. At the first epoch half the territory within our acknowledged limits was uninhabited and a wilderness. Since then new territory has been acquired of vast extent, comprising within it many rivers, particularly the Mississippi, the navigation of which to the ocean was of the highest importance to the original States. Over this territory our population has expanded in every direction, and new States have been established almost equal in number to those which formed the first bond of our Union. This expansion of our population and accession of new States to our Union have had the happiest effect on all its highest interests. That it has eminently augmented our resources and added to our strength and respectability as a power is admitted by all. But it is not in these important circumstances only that this happy effect is felt. It is manifest that by enlarging the basis of our system and increasing the number of States the system itself has been greatly strengthened in both its branches. Consolidation and disunion have thereby been rendered equally impracticable. Each Government, confiding in its own strength, has less to apprehend from the other, and in consequence each, enjoying a greater freedom of action, is rendered more efficient for all the purposes for which it was instituted. It is unnecessary to treat here of the vast improvement made in the system itself by the adoption of this Constitution and of its happy effect in elevating the character and in protecting the rights of the nation as well as of individuals. To what, then, do we owe these blessings? It is known to all that we derive them from the excellence of our institutions. Ought we not, then, to adopt every measure which may be necessary to perpetuate them?

James Monroe.

1. Why did Monroe choose this time to present his policy?

2. Why did the United States feel threatened by the unrest in South America?

3. Does Monroe sympathize with the South American revolutionary movements?

4. What does Monroe hope to achieve through his policy?

·123·

Two Views of Porfirio Díaz
(1910–1912)

*P*orfirio Díaz (1830–1915) was the Mexican president most associated with modernization and centralization following that country's independence. Part Indian and of a poor background, Díaz at first thought of becoming a Roman Catholic priest. But the outbreak of the Mexican War led him to enlist; he rose to be a brilliant and successful general. He fought against French power and ultimately led one of the armies that secured Mexican independence. But Díaz became disillusioned with the new regime that he had helped install and he led a series of coups until one finally succeeded in 1876. For the next 34 years he ruled Mexico with an iron hand and much success. The benchmark of Díaz's rule was centralization and the reorganization of the

Mexican economy. He made it easier for foreign investors to profit in Mexico, leading both to the building of the Mexican railroads and a hatred of outside profiteers. Although Díaz was continually reelected under the provisions of the Constitution, he did not allow political opposition. When Francisco Madero ran against him in 1910, he was abused by Díaz supporters and arrested. Madero led a military coup against Díaz and ousted him.

The following selections present two different views of the Díaz regime. The first, by Francisco Madero, was his presidential platform of 1910, issued before his arrest. The second was written by an exiled opponent of Díaz, Luis Para y Pardo.

THE PRESIDENTIAL PLATFORM OF 1910

A popular maxim said, "Mexico is the mother of foreigners and the stepmother of Mexicans." This saying, which passed from mouth to mouth and even appeared in books by foreigners, summed up in a few words the financial, administrative, domestic, and foreign policies of General Díaz. And nothing explains better why, while foreign countries showered decorations on Díaz and his sons, nephews, kinsmen, and lackeys and exalted him as the greatest statesman of Latin America, the Mexican people, outside the circle of his adoring favorites, heaped curses on him and waited impatiently for death to snatch him from the Presidency of the Republic or for some man to arise and topple him from his pinnacle of power. . . .

The object of every national government is to improve the social and political condition of its people. A good government does not reject foreign aid, for that would be absurd and even impossible in the present state of civilization, but it insists that this cooperation always be subordinated to the national interest. Immigration is only desirable when the immigrant represents a civilizing force and joins his interests to those of the country in which he makes his residence.

Only colonial governments of the worst type have for their sole object the unrestrained, senseless, and disorderly exploitation of the national resources for the benefit of foreigners and the enslavement or extermination of the natives. The government of General Díaz belongs in this unhappy category. . . .

The dazzling prosperity of the Díaz era was due in very large part to the exploitation of certain resources—of minerals, above all—on a greater scale than ever before. The export of these commodities, as well as that of certain tropical products in great demand abroad, increased in an astounding way. In only twenty years of Díaz' rule the export of minerals rose from a value of 36 million pesos (in 1890) to more than 111 million (in 1910). In the same period the export of henequen increased from a value of less than 6 million to more than 20 million pesos, and the export of other tropical products, such as fine woods, tobacco, coffee, etc., also rose sharply.

But aside from henequen, coffee, and some other products of particular regions, this prosperity was based on the exploitation of exhaustible resources owed by foreigners who did not even reside in Mexico. The lion's share of the 120 million pesos of exported minerals went into dividends for foreign stockholders; only the extremely low wages paid to the workers remained in the country. As in colonial times, ships sailed from Mexico with treasure drawn from the bowels of the earth by enslaved Indians, for the benefit of foreign masters who never set eyes on the places where those riches were produced.

As in colonial times, around these mines arose populous and hastily built centers. But again as in colonial times, the day had to come when the veins would be exhausted and the people would depart with empty purses, leaving only skeleton cities, vast cities of the dead like Zacatecas, Guanajuato, Taxco, that retain only the vestiges of their ancient splendor.

The same happened with our agricultural exports, except for henequen and coffee. . . . As concerns the exploitation of the fine woods, it is well known that it was carried on in such a destructive way that whole forests were ravaged without seeding a single useful plant in the looted soil.

Meanwhile agricultural production for the internal market, the cultivation of the grains on which our people live, remained stationary or even declined in relation to the population; year after year it was necessary to import North American corn and wheat to fill the needs of the internal market.

Equally dismal are the statistics for industry: There were 123 textile factories in 1893; eighteen years later the number was 146. And only the fact that the textile industry, almost entirely monopolized by Spaniards and Frenchmen, enjoyed privileges that closed the door to similar foreign articles and compelled the people to buy high-priced articles of inferior quality, made this achievement possible. The tobacco and liquor industries, on the other hand, advanced by leaps and bounds. There were 41 factories manufacturing cigarettes and cigars in 1893; in 1909 their number had increased to 437—that is, ten times. The production of rum reached 43 million liters in 1909.

The panegyrists of General Díaz proclaim his greatness as an administrator. They base their claim above all on the construction of more than 20,000 kilometers of railroads. I have already explained the open-handed generosity of Díaz in granting concessions to American capitalists for the construction of railroads. Each of these concessions was a gift, made directly to the capitalist involved or through the mediation of some favorite that he had bribed. All Mexico knows that many families owe their present wealth to concessions secured from General Díaz and sold to foreign capitalists. In the ministry of communications there were employees who defrauded the state of millions of pesos, taking bribes from individuals who obtained concessions and subventions for the construction of railways. It is no mystery that many of those roads were not constructed with the aim of favoring commerce or of meeting the needs of particular regions. . . .

The official statistics maintain a profound silence concerning the nationality of the directors of the mining companies, the great agricultural enterprises, and of the manufacturing industries of Mexico. But everyone knows that more than 75 per cent of them are foreign; as for the railroads, their foreign character is so marked that English has been the official language of the majority of lines.

In order to explain and justify this situation, which became so acute during the rule of General Díaz that it caused almost a crisis of "antiforeignism," some say that our lack of enterprise, our apathy, and our ignorance render us unfit to exploit our own resources, and that these must inevitably pass into the hands of foreigners.

I do not deny that from lack of education and on account of the social conditions in our country the Mexican people suffers from such defects. Nor do I make the mistake of attributing this state of affairs to General Díaz, or of demanding that he explain why the national character did not experience a radical change under his rule.

But this is not the only reason that Mexico is absolutely dominated by foreigners at present; furthermore, the government of General Díaz made not the slightest effort to keep the foreign invasion within the limits of fair dealing and the national interest. The monopolization of business by foreigners would have been legitimate and beneficial for the country if it had been the result of free competition between the natives and the immigrants—if the latter, through their capital and their spirit of enterprise, employed within just and legal limits, had emerged victorious. . . .

But for every property legitimately acquired, for every dollar, or franc, or mark, or pound sterling invested in enterprises that yielded benefits to the country, how many monopolies, servitudes, ruinous and truly iniquitous contracts did the government of General Díaz not leave behind it!

Not apathy and ignorance but tyranny deprived the Mexicans of the possession and exploitation of their own resources. If a Mexican sought the grant of a waterfall, a forest, a piece of land, a mine, or a deposit of coal or oil, his petition had to be supported and endorsed by some minion of the President who secured at an exorbitant price the favor of having the matter attended to with fair dispatch. Frequently the Mexican, having purchased in this manner the services of public officials, would receive a round "No" for an answer; and in a little while he would see in the Official Daily the announcement that the favor he was applying for had been graciously granted—to none other than the person whose intercession he had sought!

And if this happened to Mexicans on a social level close to that of the privileged class, what must have been the condition of laborers, small farmers, and artisans! Pity the unhappy peasant who, loving the soil he had inherited from his forefathers and seized with a sudden passion for progress, undertook to irrigate his inheritance, to buy machines and use fertilizers, and who by means of patient and painful effort succeeded in obtaining the best yields and in attracting the attention of the neighborhood to his land! From that moment was awakened the rapacity of the *jefe político,* of the military commander, of the secretary of the state government, or of the curate, canon, or archbishop, who would not rest until they had despoiled him of his property; and if he defended it with the admirable tenacity with which the Indian defends his land, he would land in the barracks, condemned to the slavery of the soldier-convict, or a group of soldiers would take him out of jail and shoot him in the back while on the march.

Governmental expenditures during the thirty-five years' reign of Don Porfirio amounted to more, much more, than 2 billion pesos. This vast sum was entirely at his disposal; it was tribute paid by the country that General Díaz could have invested in bettering the social condition of Mexico. But of this immense sum of money not a cent was ever invested in irrigating or fertilizing the land on which 12,000,000 Indians passed their lives in struggle for a handful of grain with which to sate their hunger. Nor was any part of it used to bring to these people—the largest social class, the only class devoted to the cultivation of the soil—some notion of justice or some education that would enable them to take a step toward civilization. Not the least effort was made to liberate the rural population from the slavery that made its life almost intolerable. Calling itself paternal, his government made not the slightest effort to rescue this enormous mass of people from the clutches of alcoholism, which a rapacious masterclass injected into the veins of the people the better to ensure its domination.

That is why at the end of those thirty-five years the rural population of Mexico continues under a régime of true slavery, receiving a daily wage of a few cents, sunk in ignorance, without hope of redemption. And since the monopolies have greatly raised the cost of living, the situation of the people in general is much worse than when General Díaz rose to power. Above that great oppressed mass arose a wealthy, brutal, splendid caste—but when has the wealth of a master-class served any other purpose than to oppress and degrade the serfs? Has it ever served to liberate them?

ARE WE READY FOR DEMOCRACY?

Thinking carefully over our past, re-reading our history, we find episodes so surprising, actions so heroic, Mexicans so great, so magnanimous that they appeared on our national soil in such good time to save the Fatherland that we seemed to see the hand of Providence which guides us toward our great destinies. All our history has a certain seal of greatness which impresses one, and not even the very Dictatorship of General Díaz fails to have it. After all, our present President has been able to carry to an end a colossal work and he had surrounded himself with such prestige abroad and even in the country that he has built a very high pedestal on the crest of which shines his bronzed figure, always serene, always tranquil, and with his gaze fixed on the great destinies of the Fatherland.

General Díaz has not been a common despot and history tells us of very few men who have used absolute power with so much moderation. The work of General Díaz has consisted in erasing the deep hatreds which earlier divided Mexicans. Although this program was rather limited in the beginning, it has come to put down such deep roots in the national soil to such an extent that its flourishing growth in our country seems assured. General Díaz, with his iron hand, has ended our turbulent and restless spirit. Now that we have the necessary calm and that we understand how desirable is the rule of law, now certainly we are prepared to come together peacefully at the electoral urns in order to deposit our votes.

Undoubtedly, the principal obstacle in our country for implanting democratic practices in our country has been militarism which recognizes no law other than brute force.... Consequently, this element will be the principal difficulty which the people will encounter in order to make use of their electoral rights.

Let us see how it will be possible to overcome this obstacle. Immediately one understands that General Díaz, who owes his power to his victorious sword, will hardly permit that such power be taken away from him while his sword preserves his prestige. This idea is in the national consciousness, and everybody is of the opinion that it is better to wait until General Díaz disappears from the scene, even though this situation should be prolonged for some years more, provided the soil of the Republic be not stained again with the blood of brothers. The result is that there is nobody who is animated to promote any democratic movement, because the opinion prevails that it will fail roundly if, indeed, it does not face greater dangers.

It would not be difficult to wait some few years more in order to make use of our democratic rights if this would be due to happen when General Díaz should abandon this world, because no matter how healthy and regulated may be the life that he leads, it cannot be prolonged much longer. We have indicated also that it is an error to believe that things will happen in that way and that the most probable thing is that it will happen in that way and that the present state of things will be aggravated. In view of this obstacle, what decision to make? What will be the remedy for the present situation?

The remedy consists in waging a constant struggle until the first change of functionaries is brought about through democratic methods. If the Nation comes to organize itself strongly into political parties, at last it will see to it that its rights are respected. Once the first triumph has been won, it will have set a precedent, and above all, an administration which owes its power to the law and to the people will always be respectful with them and will obey its mandates.

In order to obtain this first triumph many other factors can make a contribution. Seeing the Nation so strong through means of the organization of political parties, some of the Governors or of the Presidents will give way through fear of public opinion or because they also have caught the contagion of democratic ideas and they wish to make themselves great by means of a magnanimous act.

Above all, one must remember that whatever advantage, whatever concession, whatever conquest obtained through democratic practices will be an enduring thing, while a triumph, no matter how important it may be when obtained with arms, will do no more than aggravate our domestic situation without figuring on the dangers of an intervention which, although we do not think it so probable as do many other news men, that does not mean that we ought not to take it into consideration.

Recapitulating what we have said. . . , we find that the Mexican people have been slandered on saying that they are not ready for democracy, and the one element which is not ready is the present government whose power is based on force and, therefore, it considers this item as the supreme law. We have arrived at a rating in which all the Nation respects the law. Now all that is lacking is that the General Díaz, and those who surround him, should respect it in order that the Nation should be able to enter fully into the exercise of its rights so that the constitutional regime should be re-established in substance.

If General Díaz should come to give the tremendous example of respecting the law and the national will in the next electoral contest, he would have set a precedent which none of his successors would dare to break, and then he would have crowned his work of national pacification, consolidating it with the prestige of law, with the majesty of the national will, with the prestige which such magnanimous action would give to him.

One cannot imagine that this may be so difficult. Up to now, in dealing with presidential elections, the Nation has given very few signs that it does not wish that General Díaz should continue at the forefront of its destinies, and that tacit sentiment he may very well take as approbation of all his actions. For this reason, we repeat that now is not the time to judge it. Let us hope that he observes such conduct in the next electoral campaign. Everything makes us suppose that there will be a contest because the people commence to perceive the danger which it runs if it continues as an impassive observer of those events instead of assuming its own sovereignty.

Therefore, if we are convinced that the Mexican people is ready for democracy and that it is indispensable that it begin to exercise its rights, let us see in what way it will be able to organize its forces.

Afterward, we shall study the probable attitude of the present administration, facing the people, perfectly organized.

1. Compare the two assessments of Díaz and his administration.

2. What did the two authors hope to achieve by writing their analyses?

3. Why do you think that the two documents have such different tones?

4. Which author has more hope for Mexico's future? On what grounds?

Eastern Europe

Woodcut depicting Russian serfs after their emancipation by Alexander.

·124·

Alexander II and Prince Kropotkin
The Emancipation of the Serfs
(1861)

*A*lexander II (1818–1881) became emperor of Russia upon the death of his father, Nicholas I. Unlike his rigidly conservative father, Alexander was determined to use his autocratic power to reform Russia. He instituted a series of educational and administrative reforms and worked to simplify the legal system. Convinced of the importance of economic modernization, Alexander encouraged the building of railroads. He also did much to improve Russia's inadequate banking system. He was most famous, however, for his decision to free the serfs. Bound to their land and masters, Russian serfs were little better than slaves. Convinced that serfdom stood in the way of economic advance and relying upon his God-given authority as emperor, Alexander abolished the institution. Hailed as the "Tsar Liberator" and beloved by his people, Alexander ironically was assassinated by terrorists demanding even greater social reforms.

In a speech before the State Council in 1861, Alexander confronted reluctant aristocrats with the inevitability of his decision. Prince Peter Kropotkin (1842–1921) was one of the young nobles who had a firsthand view of the impact of the emancipation. In his later years, Kropotkin was a famous revolutionary and anarchist, but in 1861 he was a student in the exclusive Corps of Pages, a school for the sons of the aristocracy. In his memoirs he gave an eyewitness account of the events following the tsar's proclamation.

ALEXANDER'S ADDRESS IN THE STATE COUNCIL, JANUARY 28, 1861

The matter of the liberation of the serfs, which has been submitted for the consideration of the State Council, I consider to be a vital question for Russia, upon which will depend the development of her strength and power. I am sure that all of you, gentlemen, are just as convinced as I am of the benefits and necessity of this measure. I have another conviction, which is that this mat-

ter cannot be postponed; therefore I demand that the State Council finish with it in the first half of February so that it can be announced before the start of work in the fields; . . . I repeat—and this is my absolute will—that this matter should be finished right away.

For four years now it has dragged on and has been arousing various fears and anticipations among both the estate owners and the peasants. Any further delay could be disastrous to the state. I cannot help being surprised and happy, and I am sure all of you are happy, at the trust and calm shown by our good people in this matter. Although the apprehensions of the nobility are to a certain extent understandable, for the closest and material interests of each are involved, notwithstanding all this, I have not forgotten and shall never forget that the approach to the matter was made on the initiative of the nobility itself, and I am happy to be able to be a witness to this before posterity. In my private conversations with the *guberniia* marshals of the nobility, and during my travels about Russia, when receiving the nobility, I did not conceal the trend of my thoughts and opinions on the question that occupies us all and said everywhere that this transformation cannot take place without certain sacrifices on their part and that all my efforts consist in making these sacrifices as little weighty and burdensome as possible for the nobility. I hope, gentlemen, that on inspection of the drafts presented to the State Council, you will assure yourselves that all that can be done for the protection of the interests of the nobility has been done; if on the other hand you find it necessary in any way to alter or to add to the present work, then I am ready to receive your comments; but I ask you only not to forget that the basis of the whole work must be the improvement of the life of the peasants—an improvement not in words alone or on paper but in actual fact.

Before proceeding to a detailed examination of this draft itself, I would like to trace briefly the historical background of this affair. You are acquainted with the origin of serfdom. Formerly it did not exist among us; this law was established by autocratic power and only autocratic power can abolish it, and that is my sincere will.

My predecessors felt all the evils of serfdom and continually endeavored, if not to destroy it completely, to work toward the gradual limitation of the arbitrary power of the estate owners. . . . My late father [Nicholas I] was continuously occupied with the thought of freeing the serfs. Sympathizing completely with this thought, already in 1856, before the coronation, while in Moscow I called the attention of the leaders of the nobility of the Moscow *guberniia* to the necessity for them to occupy themselves with improving the life of the serfs, adding that serfdom could not continue forever and that it would therefore be better if the transformation took place from above rather than from below. . . .

The Editorial Commissions worked for a year and seven months and, notwithstanding all the reproaches, perhaps partly just, to which the commissions were exposed, they finished their work conscientiously and presented it to the Main Committee. The Main Committee, under the chairmanship of my brother [Grand Duke Konstantin Nikolaevich], toiled with indefatigable energy and zeal. I consider it my duty to thank all the members of the committee, especially my brother, for their conscientious labors in this matter.

There may be various views on the draft presented, and I am willing to listen to all the different opinions. But I have the right to demand one thing from you: that you, putting aside all personal interests, act not like estate owners but like imperial statesmen invested with my trust. Approaching this important matter I have not concealed from myself all those difficulties that awaited us and I do not conceal then now; but, firmly believing in the grace of God and being convinced to the sacredness of this matter, I trust that God will not abandon us but will bless us to finish it for the future prosperity of our beloved fatherland. . . .

KROPOTKIN'S MEMOIR

We went to the parade; and when all the military performances were over, Alexander II, remaining on horseback, loudly called out, "The officers to me!" They gathered round him, and he began, in a loud voice, a speech about the great event of the day.

"The officers . . . the representatives of the nobility in the army"—these scraps of sentences reached our ears—"an end has been put to centuries of injustice . . . I expect sacrifices from the nobility . . . the loyal nobility will gather round the throne" . . . and so on. Enthusiastic hurrahs resounded amongst the officers as he ended.

We ran rather than marched back on our way to the corps, hurrying to be in time for the Italian opera, of which the last performance in the season was to be given that afternoon; some manifestation was sure to take place then. Our military attire was flung off with great haste, and several of us dashed, lightfooted, to the sixth-story gallery. The house was crowded.

During the first entr'acte the smoking-room of the opera filled with excited young men, who all talked to one another, whether acquainted or not. We planned at once to return to the hall, and to sing, with the whole public in a mass choir, the hymn "God Save the Tsar."

However, sounds of music reached our ears, and we all hurried back to the hall. The band of the opera was already playing the hymn, which was drowned immediately in enthusiastic hurrahs coming from all parts of the hall. I saw Bavéri, the conductor of the band, waving his stick, but not a sound could be heard from the powerful band. Then Bavéri stopped, but the hurrahs continued. I saw the stick waved again in the air; I saw the fiddle-bows moving, and musicians blowing the brass instruments, but again the sound of voices overwhelmed the band. Bavéri began conducting the hymn once more, and it was only by the end of that third repetition that isolated sounds of brass instruments pierced through the clamor of human voices.

The same enthusiasm was in the streets. Crowds of peasants and educated men stood in front of the palace, shouting hurrahs, and the Tsar could not appear without being followed by demonstrative crowds running after his carriage. Herzen was right when, two years later, as Alexander was drowning the Polish insurrection in blood, and "Muravioff the Hanger" was stran-gling it on the scaffold, he wrote, "Alexander Nikolaevich, why did you not die on that day? Your name would have been transmitted in history as that of a hero."

Where were the uprisings which had been predicted by the champions of slavery? Conditions more indefinite than those which had been created by the Polozhenie (the emancipation law) could not have been invented. If anything could have provoked revolts, it was precisely the perplexing vagueness of the conditions created by the new law. And yet, except in two places where there were insurrections, and a very few other spots where small disturbances entirely due to misunderstandings and immediately appeased took place, Russia remained quiet—more quiet than ever. With their usual good sense, the peasants had understood that serfdom was done away with, that "freedom had come," and they accepted the conditions imposed upon them, although these conditions were very heavy.

I was in Nikolskoye [a Kropotkin estate in the Kaluga *guberniia*] in August 1861, and again in the summer of 1862, and I was struck with the quiet, intelligent way in which the peasants had accepted the new conditions.

They knew perfectly well how difficult it would be to pay the redemption tax for the land, which was in reality an indemnity to the nobles in lieu of the obligations of serfdom. But they so much valued the abolition of their personal enslavement that they accepted the ruinous charges—not without murmuring, but as a hard necessity—the moment that personal freedom was obtained.

When I saw our Nikolskoye peasants, fifteen months after the liberation, I could not but admire them. Their inborn good nature and softness remained with them, but all traces of servility had disappeared. They talked to their masters as equals talk to equals, as if they never had stood in different relations. Besides, such men came out from among them as could make a stand for their rights.

1. Judging from the tsar's speech to his council, what sort of generalizations might you make about the monarch's power in the Russian state?

2. What appears to be the chief obstacle in the way of liberating the serfs? How does Alexander handle this problem?

3. How was the tsar's act received in Saint Petersburg?

4. What was the reaction of the peasants to their liberation?

·125·

Otto von Bismarck
Professorial Politics
(1863)

*O*tto von Bismarck (1815–1898) was one of the most successful statesmen of the nineteenth century. His political and diplomatic talents made possible the unification of Germany under the leadership of Prussia. Born into a minor aristocratic family, Bismarck was prepared for a legal career and began working as an officer of the courts. During the upheavals of 1848, Bismarck emerged as an inflexible champion of conservatism. He attracted the favorable notice of the king, who sent him to the Federal Diet as a representative from Prussia. Bismarck ultimately rose to become prime minister, a post he held for 30 years. His goal was the unification of the diverse German states under Prussian leadership; this he accomplished through diplomacy and war. In 1871 he became the first chancellor of Germany.

Although Bismarck was called upon to make many speeches, he was a relatively poor speaker. In the selection here, from a speech to the Prussian Parliament, Bismarck expresses his contempt for professorial politics.

PROFESSORIAL POLITICS

December 21, 1863

The conception which the previous speaker has of the politics of Europe reminds me of a man from the plains who is on his first journey to the mountains. When he sees a huge elevation loom up before him, nothing seems easier than to climb it. He does not even think that he will need a guide, for the mountain is in plain sight, and the road to it apparently without obstacles. But

German Otto von Bismarck (1815–1898) was known as the Iron Chancellor.

when he starts, he soon comes upon ravines and crevasses which not even the best of speeches will help him to cross. The gentleman comforted us concerning similar obstacles in the path of politics by saying things like these: "It is well known that Russia can do nothing at present; it does not appear that Austria will take a contrary step; England knows very well that her interests are counselling peace; and finally, France will not act against her national principles." If we should believe these assurances, and think more highly of the estimate which the gentleman has made of the politics of Europe than of our own official judgment, and should thereby drive Prussia to an isolated and humiliating position, could we then excuse ourselves by saying, "We could see the danger coming, but we trusted the speaker, thinking he knew probably more than we"? If

this is impossible, how can we attach to the remarks of the speaker the weight which he wishes us to attach to them?

For all official positions, those of the judges for instance, and even those of the subalterns in the army, we require examinations and a practical knowledge—difficult examinations. But high politics—oh, any one can practise them who feels himself called upon to do so. Nothing is easier than to make endless assertions in this field of conjectures and to cast caution to the winds. You know that one must write a whole book to controvert one erroneous thought, and he who voiced the error remains unconvinced. It is a dangerous and far-spread mistake which assumes that a naïve intuition will reveal to the political dilettante what remains hidden from the wisdom of the expert.

I do not at all deny the familiarity of the previous speaker with political theories. But he has wandered from the field of theory into that of practice. He has announced with complete assurance to me and to this assembly what each European cabinet will probably do in this concrete case. These are the very things which, I believe, I must know better than he. This belief I have expressed. The previous speaker has referred to his activity in theoretical politics as a professor through many years. If the gentleman had served even one year in practical politics, possibly as a bureau chief in the ministry of foreign affairs, he would not have said what he said today from the speaker's desk. And his advice, after this one year of practical training, would be of greater value to me than if he had been active, even more years than he says, as a professor on the lecture platform.

I shall take the liberty of referring with one more word to the reproaches, often occurring in the press and also in the Reichstag, that I had frequently and abruptly changed my views. Well, I am not one of those who at any time of their life have believed, or believe today, that they can learn no more. If a man says to me: "Twenty years ago you held the same opinion as I; I still hold it, but you have changed your views," I reply: "You see, I was as clever twenty years ago as you are today. Today I know more, I have learned things in these twenty years." But, gentlemen, I will not even rely on the justice of the remark that the man who does not learn also fails to progress and cannot keep abreast of his time. People are falling behind when they remain rooted in the position they occupied years ago. However, I do not at all intend to excuse myself with such observations, for *I have always had one compass only, one lode-star by which I have steered: Salus Publica, the welfare of the State.* Possibly I have often acted rashly and hastily since I first began my career, but whenever I had time to think I have always acted according to the question, "What is useful, advantageous, and right for my fatherland, and—as long as this was only Prussia—for my dynasty, and today—for the German nation?" I have never been a theorist. The systems which bind and separate parties are for me of secondary importance. The nation comes first, its position in the world and its independence, and above all our organization along lines which will make it possible for us to draw the free breath of a great nation.

Everything else, liberal, reactionary, or conservative constitution—gentlemen, I freely confess, all this I consider in second place. It is the luxury of furnishing the house, when the house is firmly established. In the interest of the country I can parley now with one person, now with another in purely party questions. Theories I barter away cheaply. First let us build a structure secure on the outside and firmly knit on the inside, and protected by the ties of a national union. After that, when you ask my advice about furnishing the house with more or less liberal constitutional fittings, you may perhaps hear me say, "Ah well, I have no preconceived ideas. Make your suggestions, and, when the sovereign whom I serve agrees, you will find no objections on principle on my part." It can be done thus, and again thus. There are many roads leading to Rome. There are times when one should govern liberally, and times when one should govern autocratically. Everything changes. Nothing is eternal in these matters. But of the structure of the German empire and the union of the German nation I demand that they be free and unassailable, with not only a passing field fortification on one side. I have given to its creation and growth my entire strength from the very beginning. And if you point to a single moment when I have not steered by this direction of the compass-needle, you may perhaps prove that I have erred, but you cannot prove that I have for one moment lost sight of the national goal.

1. What is Bismarck's view of politics? Who is best suited for making political decisions?

2. What appear to be Bismarck's main political principles? What does he believe in?

3. Bismarck has been described as the Iron Chancellor. Does his speech lend credence to that view?

4. What occupies a higher place in Bismarck's thought: the German nation or the German people? Is there a difference between the two?

Imperialism

THE RHODES COLOSSUS
STRIDING FROM CAPE TOWN TO CAIRO.

An 1812 cartoon from Punch *captures the dream of empire builder Cecil Rhodes for British domination of Africa from "Cape to Cairo."*

·126·
J. A. Hobson
Imperialism
(1902)

J. A. Hobson (1858–1940) was the son of a prosperous English newspaper owner. He inherited his father's liberalism as well as his considerable fortune. Hobson graduated from Oxford University and began a career in politics and journalism. His chief interests were economic and social reform. He became an important figure in the progressive circles that were making themselves felt in early twentieth-century politics. He opposed the erosion of civil liberties brought on by World War I; after the war he joined the Labor party, where he remained an influential figure, especially active in the creation of the League of Nations.

Imperialism was one of Hobson's most important works and one that has become a benchmark of the subject. The author had observed the British imperial system firsthand in South Africa and had fought against it from the beginning. He was one of the first to link imperialism's social and economic effects with its cultural effects and to argue the case that imperialism corrupted both rulers and ruled.

I

If Imperialism may no longer be regarded as a blind inevitable destiny, is it certain that imperial expansion as a deliberately chosen line of public policy can be stopped?

We have seen that it is motived, not by the interests of the nation as a whole, but by those of certain classes, who impose the policy upon the nation for their own advantage. The amalgam of economic and political forces which exercises this pressure has been submitted to close analysis. But will the detection of this confederacy of vicious forces destroy or any wise abate their operative power? For this power is a natural outcome of an unsound theory in our foreign policy. Put into plain language, the theory is this, that any British subject choosing, for his own private pleasure or profit, to venture his person or his property in the territory of a foreign State can

call upon this nation to protect or avenge him in case he or his property is injured either by the Government or by any inhabitant of this foreign State. Now this is a perilous doctrine. It places the entire military, political, and financial resources of this nation at the beck and call of any missionary society which considers it has a peculiar duty to attack the religious sentiments or observances of some savage people, or of some reckless explorer who choose just those spots of earth known to be inhabited by hostile peoples ignorant of British power; the speculative trader or the mining prospector gravitates naturally towards dangerous and unexplored countries, where the gains of a successful venture will be quick and large. All these men, missionaries, travellers, sportsmen, scientists, traders, in no proper sense the accredited representatives of this country, but actuated by private personal motives, are at Liberty to call upon the

British nation to spend millions of money and thousands of lives to defend them against risks which the nation has not sanctioned. It is only right to add that unscrupulous statesmen have deliberately utilised these insidious methods of encroachment, seizing upon every alleged outrage inflicted on these private adventurers or marauders as a pretext for a punitive expedition which results in the British flag waving over some new tract of territory. Thus the most reckless and irresponsible individual members of our nation are permitted to direct our foreign policy. Now that we have some four hundred million British subjects, any one of whom in theory or in practice may call upon the British arms to extricate him from the results of this private folly, the prospects of a genuine *pax Britannica* are not particularly bright.

But those sporadic risks, grave though they have sometimes proved, are insignificant when compared with the dangers associated with modern methods of international capitalism and finance. It is not long since industry was virtually restricted by political boundaries, the economic intercourse of nations being almost wholly confined to commercial exchanges of goods. The recent habit of investing capital in a foreign country has now grown to such an extent that the well-to-do and politically powerful classes in Great Britain to-day derive a large and ever larger proportion of their incomes from capital invested outside the British Empire. This growing stake of our wealthy classes in countries over which they have no political control is a revolutionary force in modern politics; it means a constantly growing tendency to use their political power as citizens of this State to interfere with the political condition of those States where they have an industrial stake.

II

Analysis of Imperialism, with its natural supports, militarism, oligarchy, bureaucracy, protection, concentration of capital and violent trade fluctuations, has marked it out as the supreme danger of modern national States. The power of the imperialist forces within the nation to use the national resources for their private gain, by operating the instrument of the State, can only be overthrown by the establishment of a genuine democracy, the direction of public policy by the people for the people through representatives over whom they exercise a real control. Whether this or any other nation is yet competent for such a democracy may well be matter of grave doubt, but until and unless the external policy of a nation is "broad-based upon a people's will" there appears little hope of remedy. The scare of a great recent war may for a brief time check the confidence of these conspirators against the commonwealth, and cause them to hold their hands, but the financial forces freshly generated will demand new outlets, and will utilise the same political alliances and the same social, religious, and philanthropic supports in their pressure for new enterprises. The circumstances of each new imperialist exploit differ from those of all preceding ones: whatever ingenuity is requisite for the perversion of the public intelligence, or the inflammation of the public sentiment, will be forthcoming.

The chief economic source of Imperialism has been found in the inequality of industrial opportunities by which a favoured class accumulates superfluous elements of income which, in their search for profitable investments press ever farther afield: the influence on State policy of these investors and their financial managers secures a national alliance of other vested interests which are threatened by movements of social reform: the adoption of Imperialism thus serves the double purpose of securing private material benefits for favoured classes of investors and traders at the public cost, while sustaining the general cause of conservatism by diverting public energy and interest from domestic agitation to external employment.

To term Imperialism a national policy is an impudent falsehood: the interests of the nation are opposed to every act of this expansive policy. Every enlargement of Great Britain in the tropics is a distinct enfeeblement of true British nationalism. Indeed, Imperialism is commended in some quarters for this very reason, that by breaking the narrow bounds of nationalities it facilitates and forwards internationalism. There are even those who favour or condone the forcible suppression of small nationalities by larger ones under the impulse of Imperialism, because they imagine that this is the natural approach to a world-federation and eternal peace. A falser view of political evolution it is difficult to conceive.

The claim that an imperial State forcibly subjugating other peoples and their lands does so for the purpose of rendering services to the conquered equal to those which she exacts is notoriously false: she neither intends equivalent services nor is capable of rendering them, and the pretence that such benefits to the governed form a leading motive or result of Imperialism implies a degree of moral or intellectual obliquity so

grave as itself to form a new peril for any nation fostering so false a notion of the nature of its conduct. "Let the motive be in the deed, not in the event," says a Persian proverb.

Imperialism is a depraved choice of national life, imposed by self-seeking interests which appeal to the lusts of quantitative acquisitiveness and of forceful domination surviving in a nation from early centuries of animal struggle for existence. Its adoption as a policy implies a deliberate renunciation of that cultivation of the higher inner qualities which for a nation as for an individual constitutes the ascendency of reason over brute impulse. It is the besetting sin of all successful States, and its penalty is unalterable in the order of nature.

1. What, according to Hobson, is the main thrust of British foreign policy? What is wrong with that policy?

2. Why is imperialism dangerous?

3. Who benefits most from imperialism, according to Hobson?

4. Some imperialists claimed that expansion was in the interests of colonial subjects as well as the mother country. How does Hobson respond to this argument?

5. How might a dedicated imperialist answer Hobson's criticisms?

·127·

Cecil Rhodes
Confession of Faith
(1877)

Cecil Rhodes (1853–1902) was one of the greatest of all of the European empire builders. He left his mark on the continent of Africa with the De Beers diamond mines and founded the white-dominated state of Rhodesia (now Zimbabwe). Rhodes was a sickly child who went to South Africa in hope of improving his health. Once there, he became caught up in diamond fever. He began by forming partnerships and staking claims. By 1891 he owned 90 percent of all the diamond-producing mines in South Africa. His investments in gold mines were equally lucrative, and he became one of the richest men in the world. Rhodes was heavily involved in British political policy in South Africa and was forced to resign his offices after the abortive Jameson Raid. He died in 1902, leaving most of his fortune to philanthropic projects, including the establishment of the Rhodes scholarships that send American and German students to England.

Rhodes's *Confession of Faith* is in the form of a final testament. It expounds his views on racial supremacy, religion, and imperialism.

It often strikes a man to inquire what is the chief good in life; to one the thought comes that it is a happy marriage, to another great wealth, and as each seizes on his idea, for that he more or less works for the rest of his existence. To myself thinking over the same question the wish came to render myself useful to my country. I then asked myself how could I and after reviewing the various methods I have felt that at the present day we are actually limiting our children and perhaps bringing into the world half the human beings we might owing to the lack of country for them to inhabit that if we had retained America there would at this moment be millions more of English living. I contend that we are the finest race in the world and that the more of the world we inhabit the better it is for the human race. Just fancy those parts that are at present inhabited by the most despicable specimens of human beings what an alteration there would be if they were brought under Anglo-Saxon influence, look again at the extra employment a new country added to our dominions gives. I contend that every acre added to our territory means in the future birth to some more of the English race who otherwise would not be brought into existence. Added to this the absorption of the greater portion of the world under our rule simply means the end of all wars, at this moment had we not lost America I believe we could have stopped the Russian-Turkish way by merely refusing money and supplies. Having these ideas what scheme could we think of to forward this object. I look into history and I read the story of the Jesuits I see what they were able to

do in a bad cause and I might say under bad leaders.

The idea gleaming and dancing before one's eyes like a will-of-the-wisp at last frames itself into a plan. Why should we not form a secret society with but one object the furtherance of the British Empire and the bringing of the whole uncivilised world under British rule for the recovery of the United States for the making the Anglo-Saxon race but one Empire. What a dream, but yet it is probable, it is possible. I once heard it argued by a fellow in my own college, I am sorry to own it by an Englishman, that it was a good thing for us that we have lost the United States. There are some subjects on which there can be no arguments, and to an Englishman this is one of them, but even from an American's point of view just picture what they have lost, look at their government, are not the frauds that yearly come before the public view a disgrace to any country and especially their's which is the finest in the world. Would they have occurred had they remained under English rule great as they have become how infinitely greater they would have been with the softening and elevating influences of English rule, think of those countless 1000's of Englishmen that during the last 100 years would have crossed the Atlantic and settled and populated the United States. Would they have not made without any prejudice a finer country of it than the low class Irish and German emigrants? All this we have lost and that country loses owing to whom? Owing to two or three ignorant pig-headed statesmen of the last century, at their door lies the blame. Do you ever feel mad? do you ever feel murderous? I think I do with those men. I bring facts to prove my assertion. Does an English father when his sons wish to emigrate ever think of suggesting emigration to a country under another flag, never—it would seem a disgrace to suggest such a thing I think that we all think that poverty is better under our own flag than wealth under a foreign one.

Put your mind into another train of thought. Fancy Australia discovered and colonised under the French flag, what would it mean merely several millions of English unborn that at present exist we learn from the past and to form our future. We learn from having lost to cling to what we possess. We know the size of the world we know the total extent. Africa is still lying ready for us it is our duty to take it. It is our duty to seize every opportunity of acquiring more territory and we should keep this one idea steadily before our eyes that more territory simply means more of the Anglo-Saxon race more of the best the most human, most honourable race the world possesses.

To forward such a scheme what a splendid help a secret society would be a society not openly acknowledged but who would work in secret for such an object.

I contend that there are at the present moment numbers of the ablest men in the world who would devote their whole lives to it. I often think what a loss to the English nation in some respects the abolition of the Rotten Borough System has been. What thought strikes a man entering the House of Commons, the assembly that rules the whole world? I think it is the mediocrity of the men but what is the cause. It is simply—an assembly of wealth of men whose lives have been spent in the accumulation of money and whose time has been too much engaged to be able to spare any for the study of past history. And yet in the hands of such men rest our destinies. Do men like the great Pitt, and Burke and Sheridan not now exist. I contend they do. There are men now living [who] live and die unused, unemployed. What has been the main cause of the success of the Romish Church? The fact that every

enthusiast, call it if you like every madman finds employment in it. Let us form the same kind of society a Church for the extension of the British Empire. A society which should have its members in every part of the British Empire working with one object and one idea we should have its members placed at our universities and our schools and should watch the English youth passing through their hands just one perhaps in every thousand would have the mind and feelings for such an object, he should be tried in every way, he should be tested whether he is endurant, possessed of eloquence, disregardful of the petty details of life, and if found to be such, then elected and bound by oath to serve for the rest of his life in his Country. He should then be supported if without means by the Society and sent to that part of the Empire where it was felt he was needed.

Take another case, let us fancy a man who finds himself his own master with ample means on attaining his majority whether he puts the question directly to himself or not, still like the old story of virtue and vice in the Memorabilia a fight goes on in him as to what he should do. Take if he plunges into dissipation there is nothing too reckless he does not attempt but after a time his life palls on him, he mentally says this is not good enough, he changes his life, he reforms, he travels, he thinks now I have found the chief good in life, the novelty wears off, and he tires, to change again, he goes into the far interior after the wild game he thinks at last I've found that in life of which I cannot tire, again he is disappointed. He returns he thinks is there nothing I can do in life? Here I am with means, with a good house, with everything that is to be envied and yet I am not happy I am tired of life[;] to such a man the Society should go, should test, and should finally show him the greatness of the scheme and list him as a member.

Take one more case of the younger son with high thoughts, high aspirations, endowed by nature with all the faculties to make a great man, and with the sole wish in life to serve his Country but he lacks two things the means and the opportunity, ever troubled by a sort of inward deity urging him on to high and noble deeds, he is compelled to pass his time in some occupation which furnishes him with mere existence, he lives unhappily and dies miserably. Such men as these the Society should search out and use for the furtherance of their object.

In every Colonial legislature the Society should attempt to have its members prepared at all times to vote or speak and advocate the closer union of England and the colonies, to crush all disloyalty and every movement for the severance of our Empire. The Society should inspire and even own portions of the press for the press rules the mind of the people. The Society should always be searching for members who might by their position in the world by their energies or character forward the object but the ballot and test for admittance should be severe.

Once make it common and it fails. Take a man of great wealth who is bereft of his children perhaps having his mind soured by some bitter disappointment who shuts himself up separate from his neighbours and makes up his mind to a miserable existence. To such men as these the society should go gradually disclose the greatness of their scheme and entreat him to throw in his life and property with them for this object. I think that there are thousands now existing who would eagerly grasp at the opportunity. Such are the heads of my scheme.

For fear that death might cut me off before the time for attempting its development I leave all my worldly goods in trust to S. G. Shippard and the Secretary for the Colonies at the time of my death to try to form such a Society with such an object.

1. What was Rhodes's life's goal, according to his testament?

2. What reasons does Rhodes give for supporting imperial expansion?

3. How does Rhodes propose to advance Anglo-Saxon world domination?

4. What role would the native peoples in new colonies play once Anglo-Saxon rule was established?

5. The confession was written for posterity and was not published until after Rhodes's death. What sort of impression do you think Rhodes wanted to create with this document?

·128·

Rudyard Kipling
The White Man's Burden

(1899)

Rudyard Kipling (1865–1936) was one of the most celebrated authors of the era. Born in India the son of a civil servant, his life was tied up from the beginning with the British Empire. His parents sent him to England to attend boarding school, where he was lonely and unhappy. As soon as he could, he returned to India to write novels and stories, including *The Jungle Book* (1894–1895) and *Kim* (1901). He won the Nobel Prize for Literature in 1907. Kipling's patriotism was placed in the service of the state during World War I, though the battlefield death of his only son affected him deeply.

Kipling's work stresses imperial themes; "The White Man's Burden" (1899) is a succinct summary of his view on the duties of empire. It was actually addressed to Americans after their victory in the Spanish-American War.

Take up the White Man's burden—
   Send forth the best ye breed—
Go bind your sons to exile
   To serve your captives' need;
To wait in heavy harness,
   On fluttered folk and wild—
Your new-caught, sullen peoples,
   Half-devil and half-child.

Take up the White Man's burden—
   In patience to abide,
To veil the threat of terror
   And check the show of pride;
By open speech and simple,
   An hundred times made plain,
To seek another's profit,
   And work another's gain.

Take up the White Man's burden—
   The savage wars of peace—
Fill full the mouth of Famine
   And bid the sickness cease;
And when your goal is nearest
   The end for others sought,
Watch Sloth and heathen Folly
   Bring all your hope to nought.

Take up the White Man's burden—
   No tawdry rule of kings,
But toil of serf and sweeper—
   The tale of common things.

The ports ye shall not enter,
   The roads ye shall not tread,
Go make them with your living,
   And mark them with your dead.

Take up the White Man's burden—
   And reap his old reward:
The blame of those ye better,
   The hate of those ye guard—
The cry of hosts ye humour
   (Ah, slowly!) toward the light:—
"Why brought ye us from bondage,
   "Our loved Egyptian night?"

Take up the White Man's burden—
   Ye dare not stoop to less—
Nor call too loud on Freedom
   To cloak your weariness;
By all ye cry or whisper,
   By all ye leave or do,
The silent, sullen peoples
   Shall weigh your Gods and you.

Take up the White Man's burden—
   Have done with childish days—
The lightly proffered laurel,
   The easy, ungrudged praise.
Comes now, to search your manhood
   Through all the thankless years,
Cold, edged with dear-bought wisdom,
   The judgment of your peers!

1. What is the "white man's burden"? What are the responsibilities of the imperialist toward his subjects?

2. How do colonial subjects repay their masters, according to Kipling?

3. What assumptions does Kipling make about other peoples?

4. Compare Kipling's view of race with Rhodes's. Are they alike or different?

·129·

George Orwell
Shooting an Elephant
(1936)

George Orwell (1903–1950) is the pseudonym of Eric Blair, who was born into a civil servant's household in India. Though the family had relatively high social status, neither parent had much of an income. Orwell had to make his way by his wits, eventually earning a scholarship at Eton, one of the most prestigious English schools. Although he distinguished himself intellectually, Orwell shunned an academic career and instead enlisted in the Burmese police force. His firsthand experiences with British imperialism shocked him deeply, and he began a lifelong identification with the underprivileged and outcasts of society. Returning to England, Orwell began to write for a living, surviving mostly on fees from journalism and a small income from novels. It was not until the very end of his life that he achieved fame and financial security. His last two novels, *Animal Farm* (1945) and *Nineteen Eighty-Four* (1949), have become classics. He died of tuberculosis in 1950.

"Shooting an Elephant" is largely autobiographical in content. It is a story at once simple and complex about rulers and ruled, domination and subordination, freedom and responsibility.

In Moulmein, in Lower Burma, I was hated by large numbers of people—the only time in my life that I have been important enough for this to happen to me. I was sub-divisional police officer of the town, and in an aimless, petty kind of way anti-European feeling was very bitter. No one had the guts to raise a riot, but if a European woman went through the bazaars alone somebody would probably spit betel juice over her dress. As a police officer I was an obvious target

*George Orwell was the pseudonym of English author
Eric Blair (1903–1950).*

and was baited whenever it seemed safe to do so.
When a nimble Burman tripped me up on the
football field and the referee (another Burman)
looked the other way, the crowd yelled with
hideous laughter. This happened more than
once. In the end the sneering yellow faces of
young men that met me everywhere, the insults
hooted after me when I was at a safe distance, got
badly on my nerves. The young Buddhist priests
were the worst of all. There were several thousands of them in the town and none of them
seemed to have anything to do except stand on
street corners and jeer at Europeans.

All this was perplexing and upsetting. For at
that time I had already made up my mind that
imperialism was an evil thing and the sooner I
chucked up my job and got out of it the better.
Theoretically—and secretly, of course—I was all
for the Burmese and all against their oppressors,
the British. As for the job I was doing, I hated it
more bitterly than I can perhaps make clear. In a
job like that you see the dirty work of Empire at
close quarters. The wretched prisoners huddling
in the stinking cages of the lock-ups, the grey,

cowed faces of the long-term convicts, the
scarred buttocks of the men who had been
flogged with bamboos—all these oppressed me
with an intolerable sense of guilt. But I could get
nothing into perspective. I was young and ill-
educated and I had had to think out my problems in the utter silence that is imposed on every
Englishman in the East. I did not even know that
the British Empire is dying, still less did I know
that it is a great deal better than the younger
empires that are going to supplant it. All I knew
was that I was stuck between my hatred of the
empire I served and my rage against the evil-spir-
ited little beasts who tried to make my job impossible. With one part of my mind I thought of the
British Raj as an unbreakable tyranny, as something clamped down, *in saecula saeculorum,* upon
the will of prostrate peoples; with another part I
thought that the greatest joy in the world would
be to drive a bayonet into a Buddhist priest's
guts. Feelings like these are the normal by-products of imperialism; ask any Anglo-Indian official, if you can catch him off duty.

One day something happened which in a
roundabout way was enlightening. It was a tiny
incident in itself, but it gave me a better glimpse
than I had had before of the real nature of imperialism—the real motives for which despotic governments act. Early one morning the subinspec-
tor at a police station the other end of the town
rang me up on the phone and said that an elephant was ravaging the bazaar. Would I please
come and do something about it? I did not know
what I could do, but I wanted to see what was
happening and I got on to a pony and started
out. I took my rifle, and old .44 Winchester and
much too small to kill an elephant, but I thought
the noise might be useful *in terrorem.* Various
Burmans stopped me on the way and told me
about the elephant's doings. It was not, of
course, a wild elephant, but a tame one which
had gone 'must'. It had been chained up as tame
elephants always are when their attack of 'must'
is due, but on the previous night it had broken
its chain and escaped. Its mahout, the only person who could manage it when it was in that

state, had set out in pursuit, but he had taken the wrong direction and was now twelve hours' journey away, and in the morning the elephant had suddenly reappeared in the town. The Burmese population had no weapons and were quite helpless against it. It had already destroyed somebody's bamboo hut, killed a cow and raided some fruit-stalls and devoured the stock; also it had met the municipal rubbish van, and, when the driver jumped out and took to his heels, had turned the van over and inflicted violence upon it.

The Burmese sub-inspector and some Indian constables were waiting for me in the quarter where the elephant had been seen. It was a very poor quarter, a labyrinth of squalid bamboo huts, thatched with palm-leaf, winding all over a steep hillside. I remember that it was a cloudy stuffy morning at the beginning of the rains. We began questioning the people as to where the elephant had gone, and, as usual, failed to get any definite information. That is invariably the case in the East; a story always sounds clear enough at a distance, but the nearer you get to the scene of events the vaguer it becomes. Some of the people said that the elephant had gone in one direction, some said that he had gone in another, some professed not even to have heard of any elephant. I had almost made up my mind that the whole story was a pack of lies, when we heard yells a little distance away. There was a loud, scandalized cry of 'Go away, child! Go away this instant!' and an old woman with a switch in her hand came round the corner of a hut, violently shooing away a crowd of naked children. Some more women followed, clicking their tongues and exclaiming; evidently there was something there that the children ought not to have seen. I rounded the hut and saw a man's dead body sprawling in the mud. He was an Indian, a black Dravidian coolie, almost naked, and he could not have been dead many minutes. The people said that the elephant had come suddenly upon him round the corner of the hut, caught him with his trunk, put its foot on his back and ground him into the earth. This was the rainy season and the ground was soft, and his face had

scored a trench a foot deep and a couple of yards long. He was lying on his belly with arms crucified and head sharply twisted to one side. His face was coated with mud, the eyes wide open, the teeth bared and grinning with an expression of unendurable agony. (Never tell me, by the way, that the dead look peaceful. Most of the corpses I have seen looked devilish.) The friction of the great beast's foot had stripped the skin from his back as neatly as one skins a rabbit. As soon as I saw the dead man I sent an orderly to a friend's house near by to borrow an elephant rifle. I had already sent back the pony, not wanting it to go mad with fright and throw me if it smelled the elephant.

The orderly came back in a few minutes with a rifle and five cartridges, and meanwhile some Burmans had arrived and told us that the elephant was in the paddy fields below, only a few hundred yards away. As I started forward practically the whole population of the quarter flocked out of their houses and followed me. They had seen the rifle and were all shouting excitedly that I was going to shoot the elephant. They had not shown much interest in the elephant when he was merely ravaging their homes, but it was different now that he was going to be shot. It was bit of fun to them, as it would be to an English crowd; besides, they wanted the meat. It made me vaguely uneasy, I had no intention of shooting the elephant—I had merely sent for the rifle to defend myself if necessary—and it is always unnerving to have a crowd following you. I marched down the hill, looking and feeling a fool, with the rifle over my shoulder and an ever-growing army of people jostling at my heels. At the bottom when you got away from the huts there was a metalled road and beyond that a miry waste of paddy fields a thousand yards across, not yet ploughed but soggy from the first rains and dotted with coarse grass. The elephant was standing eighty yards from the road, his left side towards us. He took not the slightest notice of the crowd's approach. He was tearing up bunches of grass, beating them against his knees to clean them and stuffing them into his mouth.

I had halted on the road. As soon as I saw the elephant I knew with perfect certainty that I ought not to shoot him. It is a serious matter to shoot a working elephant—it is comparable to destroying a huge and costly piece of machinery—and obviously one ought not to do it if it can possibly be avoided. And at that distance, peacefully eating, the elephant looked no more dangerous than a cow. I thought then and I think now that his attack of 'must' was already passing off; in which case he would merely wander harmlessly about until the mahout came back and caught him. Moreover, I did not in the least want to shoot him. I decided that I would watch him for a little while to make sure that he did not turn savage again, and then go home.

But at that moment I glanced round at the crowd that had followed me. It was an immense crowd, two thousand at the least and growing every minute. It blocked the road for a long distance on either side. I looked at the sea of yellow faces above the garish clothes—faces all happy and excited over this bit of fun, all certain that the elephant was going to be shot. They were watching me as they would watch a conjurer about to perform a trick. They did not like me, but with the magical rifle in my hands I was momentarily worth watching. And suddenly I realized that I should have to shoot the elephant after all. The people expected it of me and I had got to do it; I could feel their two thousand wills pressing me forward, irresistibly. And it was at this moment, as I stood there with the rifle in my hands, that I first grasped the hollowness, the futility of the white man's dominion in the East. Here was I, the white man with his gun, standing in front of the unarmed native crowd—seemingly the leading actor of the piece; but in reality I was only an absurd puppet pushed to and fro by the will of those yellow faces behind. I perceived in this moment that when the white man turns tyrant it is his own freedom that he destroys. He becomes a sort of hollow, posing dummy, the conventionalized figure of a sahib. For it is the condition of his rule that he shall spend his life in trying to impress the 'natives' and so in every crisis he has got to do what the 'natives' expect of

him. He wears a mask, and his face grows to fit it. I had got to shoot the elephant. I had committed myself to doing it when I sent for the rifle. A sahib has got to act like a sahib; he has got to appear resolute, to know his own mind and do definite things. To come all that way, rifle in hand, with two thousand people marching at my heels, and then to trail feebly away, having done nothing—no, that was impossible. The crowd would laugh at me. And my whole life, every white man's life in the East, was one long struggle not to be laughed at.

But I did not want to shoot the elephant. I watched him beating his bunch of grass against his knees, with that preoccupied grandmotherly air that elephants have. It seemed to me that it would be murder to shoot him. At that age I was not squeamish about killing animals, but I had never shot an elephant and never wanted to. (Somehow it always seems worse to kill a *large* animal.) Besides, there was the beast's owner to be considered. Alive, the elephant was worth at least a hundred pounds; dead, he would only be worth the value of his tusks—five pounds, possibly. But I had got to act quickly. I turned to some experienced-looking Burmans who had been there when we arrived, and asked them how the elephant had been behaving. They all said the same thing: he took no notice of you if you left him alone, but he might charge if you went too close to him.

It was perfectly clear to me what I ought to do. I ought to walk up to within, say, twenty-five yards of the elephant and test his behaviour. If he charged I could shoot, if he took no notice of me it would be safe to leave him until the mahout came back. But also I knew that I was going to do no such thing. I was a poor shot with a rifle and the ground was soft mud into which one would sink at every step. If the elephant charged and I missed him, I should have about as much chance as a toad under a steam-roller. But even then I was not thinking particularly of my own skin, only the watchful yellow faces behind. For at that moment, with the crowd watching me, I was not afraid in the ordinary sense, as I would have been if I had been alone.

A white man mustn't be frightened in front of 'natives'; and so, in general, he isn't frightened. The sole thought in my mind was that if anything went wrong those two thousand Burmans would see me pursued, caught, trampled on and reduced to a grinning corpse like that Indian up the hill. And if that happened it was quite probable that some of them would laugh. That would never do. There was only one alternative. I shoved the cartridges into the magazine and lay down on the road to get a better aim.

The crowd grew very still, and a deep, low, happy sigh, as of people who see the theatre curtain go up at last, breathed from innumerable throats. They were going to have their bit of fun after all. The rifle was a beautiful German thing with cross-hair sights. I did not then know that in shooting an elephant one should shoot to cut an imaginary bar running from ear-hole to ear-hole. I ought therefore, as the elephant was sideways on, to have aimed straight at his ear-hole; actually I aimed several inches in front of this, thinking the brain would be further forward.

When I pulled the trigger I did not hear the bang or feel the kick—one never does when a shot goes home—but I heard the devilish roar of glee that went up from the crowd. In that instant, in too short a time, one would have thought, even for the bullet to get there, a mysterious, terrible change had come over the elephant. He neither stirred nor fell, but every line of his body had altered. He looked suddenly stricken, shrunken, immensely old, as though the frightful impact of the bullet had paralysed him without knocking him down. At last, after what seemed a long time—it might have been five seconds, I dare say—he sagged flabbily to his knees. His mouth slobbered. An enormous senility seemed to have settled upon him. One could have imagined him thousands of years old. I fired again into the same spot. At the second shot he did not collapse but climbed with desperate slowness to his feet and stood weakly upright, with legs sagging and head drooping. I fired a third time. That was the shot that did for him. You could see the agony of it jolt his whole body and knock the last remnant of strength

from his legs. But in falling he seemed for a moment to rise, for as his hind legs collapsed beneath him he seemed to tower upwards like a huge rock toppling, his trunk reaching skyward like a tree. He trumpeted, for the first and only time. And then down he came, his belly towards me, with a crash that seemed to shake the ground even where I lay.

I got up. The Burmans were already racing past me across the mud. It was obvious that the elephant would never rise again, but he was not dead. He was breathing very rhythmically with long rattling gasps, his great mound of a side painfully rising and falling. His mouth was wide open—I could see far down into caverns of pale pink throat. I waited a long time for him to die, but his breathing did not weaken. Finally I fired my two remaining shots into the spot where I thought his heart must be. The thick blood welled out of him like red velvet, but still he did not die. His body did not even jerk when the shots hit him, the tortured breathing continued without a pause. He was dying, very slowly and in great agony, but in some world remote from me where not even a bullet could damage him further. I felt that I had got to put an end to that dreadful noise. It seemed dreadful to see the great beast lying there, powerless to move and yet powerless to die, and not even to be able to finish him. I sent back for my small rifle and poured shot after shot into his heart and down his throat. They seemed to make no impression. The tortured gasps continued as steadily as the ticking of a clock.

In the end I could not stand it any longer and went away. I heard later that it took him half an hour to die. Burmans were arriving with dahs and baskets even before I left, and I was told they had stripped his body almost to the bones by the afternoon.

Afterwards, of course, there were endless discussions about the shooting of the elephant. The owner was furious, but he was only an Indian and could do nothing. Besides, legally I had done the right thing, for a mad elephant has to be killed, like a mad dog, if its owner fails to control it. Among the Europeans opinion was divided. The older men said I was right, the younger men said it was a damn shame to shoot an elephant for killing a coolie, because an elephant was worth more than any damn Coringhee coolie. And afterwards I was very glad that the coolie had been killed; it put me legally in the right and it gave me a sufficient pretext for shooting an elephant. I often wondered whether any of the others grasped that I had done it solely to avoid looking a fool.

1. What were relations like between the Burmese and Europeans? Why were they so difficult?

2. What is the ambivalence Orwell feels about imperialism?

3. Why did Orwell shoot the elephant?

4. What did the incident reveal to Orwell about the nature of imperialism?

5. How does Orwell's experience in Burma fit with the views of Rhodes and Kipling?

·130·

Sayyid Jamal ad Din al-Afghani
A Commentary on the Commentator
(1881)

Sayyid Jamal ad Din al-Afghani (1839–1897), commonly known as "al-Afghani" (the Afghan), was born in Iran to a family that traced itself back to the Prophet Muhammed. He received a traditional Shi'ite education and went for further religious education in Iraq. After this, "al-Afghani" (as he called himself) began a period of travel throughout the Muslim world, disguising his origins and heritage for fear of persecution. He came to be influenced by those Muslims who, toward the end of the nineteenth century, argued against modernization and the acceptance of Western ways, especially Western science. Al-Afghani was himself attacked as unorthodox and after a period as a political advisor to both the shah of Iran and the sultan of Turkey, he was imprisoned in Istanbul, where he died in 1897.

While in India between 1880 and 1882 al-Afghani wrote against British colonialism and the Western domination of the Islamic world. He spoke out for Arab unity and an end to British domination of the Middle East. He also wrote against those Muslims who began to call into question ancient Islamic traditions. The *Commentary on the Commentator* (1881) was one such attack, written in response to *The Commentary on the Koran* of Ahmed Khan.

He who does not look upon things with the eye of insight is lost and to be blamed.

Man is man because of education. None of the peoples of mankind, not even the savage, is completely deprived of education. If one considers man at the time of his birth, one sees that his existence without education is impossible. Even if we assumed that his existence were possible without education, his life would in that state be more repulsive and vile than the life of animals. Education consists of a struggle with nature, and overcoming her, whether the education be in plants, animals, or men.

Education, if it is good, produces perfection from imperfection, and nobility from baseness. If it is not good it changes the basic state of nature and becomes the cause of decline and decadence. This appears clearly among agriculturalists, cattle raisers, teachers, civil rulers, and religious leaders. In general, good education in these three kingdoms [human, animal, and plant] is the cause of all perfections and virtues. Bad education is the source of all defects and evils.

When this is understood, one must realize that if a people receives a good education, all of its classes and ranks, in accord with the natural law of relationships, will flourish simultaneously and will progress. Each class and group among that people, according to its rank and degree, tries to acquire the perfections that are appropriate to it, and does obtain them. The classes of that people, according to their rank, will always be in a state of balance and equilibrium with each other. This means that just as great rulers will appear among such a people because of their good education, so there will also come into existence excellent philosophers, erudite scholars, skilled craftsmen, able agriculturalists, wealthy merchants, and other professions. If that people because of its good education reaches such a level that its rulers are distinguished beyond the rulers of other peoples, one can be certain that all its classes will be distinguished above the classes of other countries. This is because perfect progress in each class depends on the progress of the other classes. This is the general rule, the law of nature, and the divine practice.

When, however, corruption finds its way into that people's education, weakness will occur in all its classes in proportion to their rank and to the extent of the corruption. That is, if weakness appears in the ruling circles, this weakness will surely overtake the class of philosophers, scholars, craftsmen, agriculturalists, merchants, and the other professions. For their perfection is the effect of a good education. When weakness, disorder, and corruption are introduced into a good education, which is the causative factor, inevitably the same weakness, disorder, and corruption will enter into the effects of that education. When corruption enters a nation's education it sometimes happens that, because of the increase of corruption in education and the ruin of manners and customs, the various classes, which are the cause of stability, and especially the noble classes, are gradually destroyed. The individuals of that nation, after removing their former clothes and changing their name, become part of another nation and appear with new adornments. This happened to the

Chaldeans, the Phoenicians, the Copts, and similar people.

Sometimes Eternal Grace aids that people, and some men of high intelligence and pure souls appear among them and bring about a new life. They remove that corruption which was the cause of decline and destruction, and rescue souls and minds from the terrible malady of bad education. And through their own basic luster and brightness they return the good education and give back life once more to their people. They restore to them greatness, honor, and the progress of classes.

This is why every people who enter into decline, and whose classes are overtaken by weakness, are always, because of their expectation of Eternal Grace, waiting to see if perhaps there is to be found among them a wise renewer, experienced in policy, who can enlighten their minds and purify their souls through his wise management and fine efforts, and do away with the corrupt education. By the policies of that sage they could return to their former condition.

There is no doubt that in the present age, distress, misfortune, and weakness besiege all classes of Muslims from every side. Therefore every Muslim keeps his eyes and ears open in expectation—to the East, West, North, and South—to see from what corner of the earth the sage and renewer will appear and will reform the minds and souls of the Muslims, repel the unforeseen corruption, and again educate them with a virtuous education. Perhaps through that good education they may return to their former joyful condition.

Since I am certain that the Absolute Truth (ḥaqq-i muṭlaq) will not destroy this true religion and right sharīʿa, I more than others expect that the minds and souls of the Muslims will very soon be enlightened and rectified by the wisdom of a sage. For this reason I always want to keep abreast of the articles and treatises that are now appearing from the pens of Muslims, and be thoroughly acquainted with the views of their authors. I hope that in these readings I may discover the elevated ideas of a sage who could be the cause of good education, virtue, and prosperity for the Muslims. I would then hope, to the extent of my ability, to assist him in his elevated ideas and become a helper and associate in the reform of my people.

In the course of discussions and investigations about the ideas of the Muslims, I heard of one of them who, mature in years and rich in experience, took a trip to European countries. After much labor and effort he wrote a Commentary on the Koran in order to improve the Muslims. I said to myself, "Here is just what you wanted."

And as is customary with those who hear new things, I let my imagination wander, and formed various conceptions of that commentator and that commentary. I believed that this commentator, after all the commentaries written by Traditionists, jurists, orators, philosophers, Sufis, authors, grammarians, and heretics like *Ibn Rāwandī* and others, would have done justice to that subject, unveiled the truth, and achieved the precise goal. For he had followed the ideas of both Easterners and Westerners. I thought that this commentator would have explained in the introduction to his commentary, as wisdom requires, the truth and essence of religion for the improvement of his people. That he would have demonstrated the necessity of religion in the human world by rational proofs, and that he would have set up a general rule, satisfying the intellect, to distinguish between true and false religions. I imagined that this commentator had undoubtedly explained the influence of each of the prior, untrue religions on civilization and the social order and on men's souls and minds. I thought he would have explained in a philosophical way the reason for the divergence of religions on some matters, along with their agreement on many precepts, and the reason for the special relation of each age to a particular religion and prophet.

Since he claims to have written this commentary for the improvement of the community, I was certain he had in the introduction of his book described and explained in a new manner, with the light of wisdom, those divine policies and Koranic ethics that were the cause of the superiority and expansion of the Arabs in every human excellence. I was sure he had included in his introduction those precepts that were the cause of the unity of the Arabs, the transformation of their ideas, the enlightenment of their minds, and the purification of their souls; and all that when they were in the extremity of discord, savagery, and hardship.

When I read the commentary I saw that this commentator in no way raised a word about these matters or about divine policy. In no manner are Koranic ethics explained. He has not mentioned any of those great precepts that were the cause of the enlightenment of the minds and purification of the souls of the Arabs. He has left without commentary those verses that relate to divine policy, support the promulgation of virtuous ethics and good habits, rectify domestic and civil intercourse, and cause the enlightenment of minds. Only at the beginning of his commentary does he pronounce a few words on the meaning of "sura," "verse," and the separate letters at the beginning of the suras. After that all his effort is devoted to taking every verse in which there is mention of angels, or *jinns,* or the faithful spirit [Gabriel], revelation, paradise, hell, or the miracles of the prophets, and, lifting these verses from their external meaning, interpreting them according to the specious allegorical interpretations of the heretics of past Muslim centuries.

The difference is that the heretics of past Muslim centuries were scholars, whereas this unfortunate commentator is very ignorant. Therefore he cannot grasp their words correctly. Taking the subject of man's *nature* as a subject of discourse, he pronounces some vague and meaningless words, without rational demonstrations or natural proofs. He apparently does not know that man is man through education, and all his virtues and habits are acquired. The man who is nearest to his nature is the one who is the farthest from civilization and from acquired virtues and habits. If men abandoned the legal and intellectual virtues they have acquired with

the greatest difficulty and effort, and gave over control to the hands of nature, undoubtedly they would become lower than animals.

Even stranger is the fact that this commentator has lowered the divine, holy rank of prophecy and placed it on the level of the *reformer.* He has considered the prophets to be men like Washington, Napoleon, Palmerston, Garibaldi, Mister Gladstone, and Monsieur Gambetta.

When I saw the commentary to be of this kind, amazement overtook me, and I began to ask myself what was the purpose of this commentator in writing such a commentary. If the goal of this commentator is, as he says, the improvement of his community, then why does he try to end the belief of Muslims in the Islamic religion, especially in these times when other religions have opened their mouths to swallow this religion?

Does he not understand that if the Muslims, in their current state of weakness and misery, did not believe in miracles and hell-fire, and considered the Prophet to be like Gladstone, they undoubtedly would soon abandon their own weak and conquered camp, and attach themselves to a powerful conqueror? For in that event there would no longer remain anything to prevent this, nor any fear or anxiety. And from another standpoint the prerequisities for changing religion now exist, since being like the conqueror, and having the same religion as he, is attractive to everyone.

After these ideas and reflections, it first occurred to me that this commentator certainly believes that the cause of the decline of the Muslims and of their distressed condition is their religion itself, and that if they abandoned their beliefs they would restore their former greatness and honor. Therefore, he is trying to remove these beliefs, and because of his motivation he could be forgiven.

Having reflected further, however, I said to myself that the Jews, thanks to these same beliefs, rescued themselves from the humiliation of slavery to the pharoahs and rubbed in the dust the pride of the tyrants of Palestine. Has not the commentator heard of this?

And the Arabs, thanks to these same beliefs, came up from the desert lands of the Arabian peninsula, and became masters of the whole world in power, civilization, knowledge, manufacture, agriculture, and trade. The Europeans in their speeches referred aloud to those believing Arabs as their masters. Has not this fact reached the ears of this commentator? Of course it has.

After considering the great effects of these true beliefs and their followers, I looked at the followers of false beliefs. I saw that the Hindus at the same time that they made progress in the laws of civilization, and in science, knowledge, and the various crafts, believed in thousands of gods and idols. This commentator is not ignorant of this. The Egyptians at the times when they laid the foundations of civilization, science, and manufactures, and were the masters of the Greeks, believed in idols, cows, dogs, and cats. This commentator undoubtedly knows this. The Chaldeans, at the time that they founded observatories, manufactured astronomical instruments, built high castles, and composed books on agricultural science, were worshippers of the stars. This is not hidden from the commentator. The Phoenicians, in the age that they made manufacture and commerce on land and sea flourish, and colonized the lands of Britain, Spain, and Greece, presented their own children as sacrifices to idols. This is clear to the commentator.

The Greeks, in that century that they were rulers of the world, and at the time that great sages and revered philosophers appeared among them, believed in hundreds of gods and thousands of superstitions. This is known to the commentator. The Persians, at the time when they ruled from the regions of Kashgar to the frontiers of Istanbul, and were considered incomparable in civilization, had hundreds of absurdities engraved in their hearts. Of course the commentator remembers this. The modern Christians, at the same time as they acknowledged the Trinity, the cross, resurrection, baptism, purgatory, confession, and transubstantiation, assured their domination; progressed in the spheres of science, knowledge, and industry; and reached the

summit of civilization. Most of them still, with all their science and knowledge, follow the same beliefs. The commentator knows this well.

When I considered these matters I realized that the commentator never was of the opinion that faith in these true beliefs caused the decline of the Muslims. For religious beliefs, whether true or false, are in no way incompatible with civilization and worldly progress unless they forbid the acquisition of science, the earning of a livelihood, and progress in sound civilization. I do not believe that there is a religion in the world that forbids these things, as appears clearly from what has been said above. Rather I can say that the lack of faith results only in disorder and corruption in civil life, and in insecurity. Reflect— this is *Nihilism!*

If the lack of faith brought about the progress of peoples, then the Arabs of the Age of Ignorance would have had to have precedence in civilization. For they were mostly followers of the materialist path, and for this reason they used to say aloud: "Wombs push us forth, the earth swallows us up, and only time destroys us." They also always used to say: "Who can revive bones after they have decomposed?" This despite the fact that they lived in the utmost ignorance, like wild animals.

After all these various thoughts and considerations, I understood well that this commentator is not a reformer, nor was his commentary written for the improvement and education of the Muslims. Rather this commentator and this commentary are for the Islamic community at the present time like those terrible and dangerous illnesses that strike man when he is weak and decrepit. The aim of his modifications has been demonstrated above.

The goal of this commentator from this effort to remove the beliefs of the Muslims is to serve others and to prepare the way for conversion to their religion.

These few lines have been written hastily. Later, by the power of God, I will write in detail about this commentary and the aims of the commentator.

1. Does al-Afghani accept the class system?

2. What is the function of education?

3. What is al-Afghani's opinion of "the Commentator"?

4. What lessons does al-Afghani draw from studying non-Muslim cultures?

·131·

Robert Moffat
Missionary Labors and Scenes in Southern Africa
(1846)

Robert Moffat (1795–1883) was a Scottish missionary who spent most of his adult life in Africa. To further his work bringing Christianity to African tribes, he translated portions of the Bible into African dialects. He also traveled extensively through the southern part of Africa. He was present in the teens and twenties during the rise of the Zulu under their great chieftain Shaka and witnessed the beginnings of the fierce intertribal warfare that continued in southern Africa for nearly three decades.

Moffat's descriptions of the peoples he encountered and the events he witnessed defined European perceptions of African warrior tribes. His book went through nine editions in seven years. The section excerpted here recounts his meeting with Chief Moselekatse and the Matabeles, a fierce warrior society.

On a Sabbath morning I ascended a hill, at the base of which we had halted the preceding evening, to spend the day. I had scarcely reached the summit, and sat down, when I found that my intelligent companion had stolen away from the party, to answer some questions I had asked the day before, and to which he could not reply, because of the presence of his superiors. Happening to turn to the right, and seeing before me a large extent of level ground covered with ruins, I inquired what had become of the inhabitants.

He had just sat down, but rose, evidently with some feeling, and, stretching forth his arm in the direction of the ruins, said, "I, even I, beheld it!" and paused, as if in deep thought. "There lived the great chief of multitudes. He reigned among them like a king. He was the chief of the blue-coloured cattle. They were numerous as the dense mist on the mountain brow; his flocks covered the plain. He thought the number of his warriors would awe his enemies. His people boasted in their spears, and laughed at the cowardice of such as had fled from their towns. 'I shall slay them, and hang up their shields on my hill. Our race is a race of warriors. Who ever subdued our fathers? they were mighty in combat. We still possess the spoils of ancient times. Have not our dogs eaten the shields of their nobles? The vultures shall devour the slain of our enemies.' Thus they sang and thus they danced, till they beheld on yonder heights the approaching foe. The noise of their song was hushed in night, and their hearts were filled with dismay. They saw the clouds ascend from the plains. It was the smoke of burning towns. The confusion of a whirlwind was in the heart of the great chief of the blue-coloured cattle. This shout was raised, 'They are friends;' but they shouted again, 'They are foes,' till their near approach proclaimed them naked Matabele. The men seized their arms, and rushed out, as if to chase the antelope. The onset was as the voice of lightning, and their spears as the shaking of a forest in the autumn storm. The Matabele lions raised the shout of death, and flew upon their victims. It was the shout of victory. Their hissing and hollow groans told their progress among the dead. A few moments laid hundreds on the ground. The clash of shields was the signal of triumph. Our people fled with their cattle to the top of yonder mount. The Matabele entered the town with the roar of the lion; they pillaged and fired the houses, speared the mothers, and cast their infants to the flames. The sun went down. The victors emerged from the smoking plain, and pursued their course, surrounding the base of yonder hill. They slaughtered cattle; they danced and sang till the dawn of day; they ascended, and killed till their hands were weary of the spear." Stooping to the ground on which we stood, he took up a little dust in his hand; blowing it off, and holding out his naked palm, he added, "That is all that remains of the great chief of the blue-coloured cattle!" It is impossible for me to describe my

feelings while listening to this descriptive effusion of native eloquence; and I afterwards embraced opportunities of writing it down, of which the above is only an abridgment. I found also from other aborigines that his was no fabled song, but merely a compendious sketch of the catastrophe.

We were detained several days at this place by dreadful storms of thunder, which appeared to make the very mountains shake, and heavy rains which caused torrents of water to fall from the neighbouring heights, which deluged the plains. The luxuriance of every thing on hill and dale was great. The rich black soil being saturated with water, became so adhesive, that it was found impossible for either men or oxen to proceed. The wheels became one mass of clay, which nothing could detach, while the feet of the oxen became so large with the tenacious soil, that it was out of our power to move them from the spot. Though we could only see the smoke of distant villages, we had frequent visitors bringing us abundant supplies of milk and grain, borne on the heads of women belonging to the subjugated Bechuana tribes.

The dark cloudy weather and uncomfortable accommodations awoke gloomy forebodings in the minds of my people, some of whom would gladly have escaped, but the distance from home was too great. When the weather allowed us to proceed, two days more brought us through a fertile country to the banks of the Limpopo, called Uri, higher up, where the scaly crocodile may be seen protruding his ugly snout on the sedgy bank of the river.

. . . Two days more we proceeded eastward, over a hilly, trackless, and woody country, receiving every demonstration of the pleasure Moselekatse anticipated in welcoming us at his capital. In the early part of the day we came within sight of the long-looked-for spot under a range of hills. One of the Tunas had left us at the Limpopo, to appear in person before his king, and, as he expressed it, to make my path straight to the abode of his sovereign. "There," said 'Umbate, pointing to the town, "there dwells the great king Pezoolu, the Elephant, the Lion's paw," following up these titles with ascriptions of extravagant praise.

As the wagons had to make a circuit to arrive at a ford through the river, Entsabotluku, Mr. Archbell, myself, and two of our attendants, saddled our horses to go the direct road. When we reached the river, we found people bathing, who, seeing horsemen, scampered off in the greatest terror. We proceeded directly to the town, and on riding into the centre of the large fold, which was capable of holding ten thousand head of cattle, we were rather taken by surprise to find it lined by eight hundred warriors, besides two hundred which were concealed in each side of the entrance, as if in ambush. We were beckoned to dismount, which we did, holding our horses' bridles in our hands. The warriors at the gate instantly rushed in with hideous yells, and leaping from the earth with a kind of kilt around their bodies, hanging like loose tails, and their large shields, frightened our horses. They then joined the circle, falling into rank with as much order as if they had been accustomed to European tactics. Here we stood surrounded by warriors, whose kilts were of ape skins, and their legs and arms adorned with the hair and tails of oxen, their shields reaching to their chins, and their heads adorned with feathers.

Although in the centre of a town all was silent as the midnight hour, while the men were motionless as statues. Eyes only were seen to move, and there was a rich display of fine white teeth. After some minutes of profound silence, which was only interrupted by the breathing of our horses, the war song burst forth. There was harmony, it is true, and they beat time with their feet, producing a sound like hollow thunder, but some parts of it was music befitting the nether regions, especially when they imitated the groanings of the dying on the field of battle, and the yells and hissings of the conquerors. Another simultaneous pause ensued, and still we wondered what was intended, till out marched the monarch from behind the lines, followed by a number of men bearing baskets and bowls of food. He came up to us, and having been instructed in our mode of salutation, gave each a clumsy but hearty shake of the hand. He then politely turned to the food, which was placed at our feet, and invited us to partake. By this time the wagons were seen in the distance, and having intimated our wish to be directed to a place where we might encamp in the outskirts of the town, he accompanied us, keeping fast hold of my right arm, though not in the most graceful manner, yet with perfect familiarity. "The land is before you; you are come to your son. You must sleep where you please." When the "moving houses," as the wagons were called, drew near, he took a firmer grasp of my arm, and looked on them with unutterable surprise; and this man, the terror of thousands, drew back with fear, as one in doubt as to whether they were not living creatures. When the oxen were unyoked, he approached the wagon with the utmost caution, still holding me by one hand, and placing the other on his mouth, indicating his surprise. He looked at them very intently, particularly the wheels, and when told of how many pieces of wood each wheel was composed, his wonder was increased. After examining all very closely, one mystery yet remained, how the large band of iron surrounding the felloes of the wheel came to be in one piece without either end or joint. 'Umbate, my friend and fellow-traveller, whose visit to our station had made him much wiser than his master, took hold of my right hand, and related what he had seen. "My eyes," he said, "saw that very hand," pointing to mine, "cut these bars of iron, take a piece off one end, and then join them as you now see them." A minute inspection ensued to discover the welded part. "Does he give medicine to the iron?" was the monarch's inquiry. "No," said 'Umbate, "nothing is used but fire, a hammer, and a chisel." Moselekatse then returned to the town, where the warriors were still standing as he left them, who received him with immense bursts of applause.

Some thousands of the Matabele, composing several regiments, are distinguished by the colour of their shields, as well as the kind and profusion of feathers which generally adorn their heads, having also a long feather of the blue crane rising from their brows, all which has an imposing effect at their onset. Their arms consist of a shield, short spear, and club. The club, often made of the horn of a rhinoceros or hard wood, they throw with unerring precision, so as even to strike dead the smaller antelope. The spear is not intended for throwing, but for close combat, and such being their mode of warfare, the tribes accustomed to throw their light javelins to a distance, are overtaken by these organized soldiers and mowed down. They must conquer or die, and if one return without his shield or spear, at the frown of his sovereign he is instantly despatched by another. They look best in their war dress, which is only worn on great occasions, and without which they are like the Kafir tribes in a state of nudity. They rarely use a war axe, which distinguishes the Bechuana warrior, and which he only uses when brought into embarrassed circumstances, when his spears are expended, or when butchering the vanquished enemy. Their shields, made of the thickest part of the ox hide, are very different in size and shape. That of the Matabele is sufficiently large to cover the body, while the other is light, and easily manœuvred so as to throw off the missiles of the enemy. That of a Basuto is smaller still, and seems only capable of defending the left hand, which grasps the spears, and a rod bearing a plume of black ostrich feathers.

Moselekatse did not fail to supply us abundantly with meat, milk and a weak kind of beer, made from the native grain. He appeared anxious to please, and to exhibit himself and people to the best advantage. In accordance with savage notions of conferring honour, and all the inhabitants warriors of the neighbouring towns were ordered to congregate at head-quarters, and on the following day a public ball was given in compliment to the strangers. A smooth plain adjoining the town was selected for the purpose, where Moselekatse took his stand in the centre of an immense circle of his soldiers, numbers of women being present, who with their shrill voices and clapping of hands took part in the concert. About thirty ladies from his harem with long white wands marched to the song backward and forward on the outside of the ranks, their well lubricated shining bodies being too weighty for the agile movements which characterized the matrons and damsels of lower rank. They sang their war songs, and one composed on occasion of the visit of the strangers, gazing on and adoring with trembling fear and admiration the potentate in the centre, who stood and sometimes regulated the motions of thousands by the movement of his head, or the raising or depression of his hand. He then sat down on his shield of lion's skin, and asked me if it was not fine, and if we had such things in my country. I could not gratify his vanity by saying I did admire that which excited the most thrilling sensations in his martial bosom, and as to there being balls, public balls, in honour of the great and renowned, I did not choose to acknowledge.

This public entertainment or display of national glory occupied the greater part of the day, when the chief retired swollen with pride, amidst the deafening shouts of adoring applause, not only of the populace, but of his satraps, who followed at a distance to do him homage at his own abode. Whenever he arose or sat down, all within sight hailed him with a shout, *Baaite!* or *Aaite!* followed by a number of his high sounding titles, such as Great King, King of heaven, the Elephant, etc.

1. Why did the chief of the blue-colored cattle believe that he could defeat the Matabeles? On what arguments did he rely to convince his warriors?

2. Why did the Matabeles slaughter the cattle of their enemies?

3. Why did the Matabeles greet Moffat and his company with a war dance?

4. What most impressed Moffat about the Matabele warriors? What most impressed Moselekatse about Moffat?

·132·

Carl Veltin
Social Life of the Swahilis
(late 19th century)

Carl Veltin was a German professor of African and Oriental languages who spent a number of years as the official interpreter for the governor of the German East African territories. He worked among the Swahilis, mostly Bantu tribesman who lived in Mrima, the coast opposite Zanzibar. Veltin was interested in Swahili customs and folklore and appears to have interviewed village elders and recorded their responses. He also made transcripts of accounts of Swahili travelers, including an unusual diary of an ivory trader. When he returned to Berlin in 1896 he translated and published his notes. He published his accounts in the original Swahili so that his own (and subsequent) translations would not distort the experiences he tried to record.

The selections printed here are related to Swahili customs regarding the raising of children until marriage. They provide an intimate glimpse into the lives of ordinary Africans and demonstrate the importance of ceremony and ritual in a predominantly oral culture.

A child (baby) is fed on millet, and the millet is pounded into a flour and ladled into earthen pitchers to keep it from dust and sand. Each morning they draw out enough for the child's food, and it is cooked with sugar and the child is fed. As to the feeding, they put some gruel in a small cooking-pot and it is cooled off and then put on a small plate. Holding the child, the mother puts some gruel on the palm of her hand and feeds the child with her finger and the child swallows (the gruel). When it has eaten she gives it some water or suckles it. Then the child goes to sleep.

When he wakes up, the child has his face washed and antimony is applied to his face. Then *muru* medicine is ground and the child is given the *muru* water to drink by another person, and they anoint the child's whole body with it, for this is children's medicine for intestinal worms. And when he sleeps a knife is placed under his pillow and his feet are wrapped in asafoetida for fear of being possessed by a great bird. In a house where there is a small child a crab is hung up in the roof on the wood in the middle of the ridge pole for fear of evil diseases. . . .

And the person who comes with the medicine for convulsions agrees to place the child under a charm, that is he fastens medicine (a charm) on the child in case the child 'be broken in body' because of the people who commit adultery and the people who look at the child with 'the evil eye'. He brings *jimbo* medicine and it is placed on a large cooking-pot, and the water from it is used for washing the child morning and evening. Unless they do this, the adulterers will get hold of him, and he will have rickets.

When the child is about to grow teeth *fungo* medicine is made for him, this is to make the teeth firm so that they do not grow badly, in case the upper teeth come first. The old men and women make this medicine; they dig up the tubers of the nut-grass weed, and a charm is prepared for wearing round the (child's) neck until the teeth are grown.

If the teeth are slow in growing the child is treated by medicine-men; he is given *jimbo* medicines for bathing and anointing. Also *hoza* medicine is gathered; these are certain leaves from the forest, and the child is anointed. After a few days the teeth appear.

If the child grows his upper teeth (first), in the old days they would not bring the child up, and even now some people do not like to do so. Others say, 'I can't throw away my own blood, I will bring it up.' And some nurture the child, but have no joy in it. A child like this is called *kibi*, but afterwards he is given a name just like other children. Some people are afraid to give their hand to a child like this, because they fear death or illness (as a consequence). A child born with feet first is also called *kibi*. They do not bring him up, they will kill him or they will take him to the mosque and leave him inside. At day-break when the people who come to pray find him they know that this child was badly born. It may happen that someone will take him and bring him up, he will make him his son; the reason for refusing to nurture him is that they fear death. This custom amongst the Swahilis is held also among the Zaramu.

In Mrima country there are children who turn out very white, but their parents are black. They believe that such a child has been exchanged for a child of an evil spirit. During the first seven days his mother went to the toilet at night, and left him by himself; she did not put a necklace or a knife under the pillow nor fasten asafoetida on the child's arm. The evil one saw the child by itself and exchanged him; leaving the child of an evil spirit, he took away the human being.

Or others say, 'When his mother was pregnant she was possessed by an evil spirit, and so she bore a white child.' This is why Swahilis, when their children are small, fasten asafoetida on their arms; asafoetida has a bad smell, and an evil spirit does not like it. And these albino children, when Swahilis see them they are very startled and do not like them. Some want to kill them, but if they bring them up, when they are big, they (the albinos) do not shake hands with people, (it is) as if they had a skin disease or leprosy.

Up to the age of seven a girl is called *kigori*, and when she is fifteen she is called *mwari*. It is usual for these children to stay in the house. First their ears are pierced with thorns. And on the day of the piercing they rejoice with her just like at a wedding. The child is taught how to behave (lit. very good manners) at home; she washes the utensils, plates and bowls, and when she has finished she is given the beginning of a leaf-strip to plait. Each day her work is plaiting mats and being taught to cook. She is not allowed to go out, but at night she may go to visit people connected with her, but she does not go alone, she is chaperoned by a female slave or a woman elder. But if she is a gad-about, she is beaten by her parents, and she finds it difficult to get a husband, for people say, 'So-and-So's girl is a gad-about, she knows every place.'

When she is in the house and a visitor comes to the door, male or female, and her parents do not know about it, she must hide in another room without conversing with the visitor. If her parents hear her conversing they go for her, saying to her, 'When you hear someone at the door, do you peep out so that everyone can see your face?' And if people hear that she does not hide her face, they speak against her in the village, 'So-and-So's girl, her face has dried her up, she is not modest, she is not a suitable person to be married; she may possibly get a husband, but it will take a long time.'

And when the girl is ten there comes a woman who is her confidential adviser, and she puts a string of beads around the girl's loins. This woman is her special friend for always. A woman who has no string of beads, people say of her that her loins are withered.

When they bring up a child, especially when he gets to the age of six or seven, they teach him good manners. And he must listen carefully to the commands of his parents. If they have refused him something, he must obey.

They teach him to greet people; especially if he sees an important person with his parents, he should greet him. He is taught to approach adults with respect and good manners. If he begs ha'pennies from every person passing, he is beaten. When a child is in the company of adults, he should not sit down before the adults are seated. If he is in company, it is not customary (for him) to say this or that. When a young person goes with an elder in public or to a feast, and he is sitting with them as they converse, it is his duty to be perfectly quiet, listening to whatever command they wish to give him. It is not good manners to laugh now with this person and then with that. Unless of course he is with friends of his own age, then he can converse and laugh and make as much noise as he likes.

When a child accompanies his father, it is not right for that child to lead the way, but the father should be in front. Or if he goes out with his teacher, likewise the teacher should go in front. Unless the child does this he has insulted his father and his teacher, and he has abused his own reputation, for people will ask him, 'Did not your father teach you good manners, nor your teacher, that you should be so unmannerly?'

In the same way it is not right for a child to point out people's failings, for example, 'So-and-So's wife does not cook properly', or, 'Today they have gone to bed hungry, they have no food, their house is dark, they have no lamp.' If a child says things like this, people know that he has no manners. Then a child is often told by his parents, 'If ever you are told a secret, you must hide it, for it is not right to tell it to every Tom, Dick, and Harry.'

And when visitors are come to the house and they are eating together, a child is told not to wash his hands before the adults have done so. If there is no one in the house to serve at the meal, the child takes the water-jug and brings the people water to wash their hands. And when they are eating, it is not mannerly to take the meat all the time, but only when they give the child permission to eat the meat. When he is eating and takes a piece of meat with every ball of food, people look at him, and say afterwards, 'That child has no manners, another day, don't take him out in public, he brings shame.'

Every child must obey commands from three sources (lit. of three people) if he wants the blessing of God. First, the command of the ruler (lit. king), and secondly of his two parents, and thirdly of his teacher. Laws from these three he must closely obey. And if he scorns these commands, he has disobeyed the law of God.

A female child of seven years of age is called *kigori*, but when she is about thirteen years old people say, 'Such-and-such a *kigori* has become a *mwari*.' When her parents find that she has begun her puberty, news is sent at once to her *kungwi*, and she comes to the girl's house to take her to her own home for her to be confined there. And the girl does not appear before strangers, but (is seen) only by her *kungwi* and her relatives; she stays at her *kungwi*'s house for six months or a whole year, but some (girls) stay only a month and then return to their parents.

And at her *kungwi*'s house she is taught to look after herself properly, and to live properly, respecting people; she is taught to cook and to plait mats and when she is married to live properly with her husband. Her *kungwi* gives her a *msio* stone; this is a coral stone from the top of a reef on the coast, (which) is dressed by an expert so that it becomes soft and round. A young girl receives this stone to grind mixtures like *tibu* perfume, *dalia* powder, *maua maulidi* scent, and every kind of perfume with which she massages herself. The same stone is used on her wedding day, and when it is taken to the wedding, or when a woman goes to her friend to borrow it, the stone is not carried unless it is covered, it is covered with a cloth for people not to see it; but when it is kept in the house after being used it is not covered, everybody can see it.

When the time for staying at the *kungwi*'s is over, the *kungwi* tells her parents, 'We want to take the girl to the *muyombo* tree.' Her elders brew fermented and unfermented beer. At the *muyombo* tree many women gather together, and other young girls are there (lit. come). Sometimes they go into a house if it is big enough there in the country (i.e. away from the town), at other times they build a hut. And these girls are taken by night so that people should not see them; they are also carried pick-a-back by the women. The *kungwi* has her former clients, perhaps six or seven of them; she invites them, saying, 'Tomorrow we are going to the *muyombo* tree, so come along and carry your friend.' And they are obliged to go (lit. come), because a girl does not neglect (lit. leave) the bidding of her *kungwi;* she obeys the bidding of her *kungwi* more than that of her mother.

After they have taken the girl to the lodge, a dance takes place called *unyago*. And at the *unyago* dance the drums are played, and some women dance to show the girls, so that the girls may dance just as the grown-ups do, for unless they

know how to do it they must be taught. And they sing initiation-songs. Something is put down behind the girl's back, and she takes it up by her mouth bending backwards and moving her hips, while a drum is beaten and a song is sung.

If the *makungwi* have sung and the girl is unable to recognize the meaning of such-and-such a song, or if she is given instruction without being able to comprehend it, she is beaten, (but) also she is told the meaning of it. If she knows the instruction, all the women say with a loud voice, '*Chiriku, chiriku*', and this means, 'Oh my child, my beautiful child.'

On the seventh day the girls are taken to the *muyombo* tree. All the *makungwi* and the girls stay beating the drums and dancing, and if there is beer they drink it. In the evening the girls have their hair shaved, some of them have a tuft (left) on the crown, they have their eyes blackened, and on their heads they apply *dalia* powder, because of being shaven. Then they are dressed in new clothes and decked with silver ornaments. In the evening they are brought to the village; there is no singing as they are brought. The free-born children are given a present at home by their relatives, they bring them all sorts of things there. Some give them mats, others bracelets, others again rings, and some give them money. And the slave-girls are paraded round the villages, and they are dressed up just like the free-born girls; they are led around by their *makungwi*. If they see a man they know, they give him their hand, and he puts out money to give them as a present; and if they see a woman they know they fall down at her feet, that is the proper greeting, and the woman produces something to give them. And they are not allowed to speak with anyone except the person who has given a present. They are paraded for three days. The fine dress is taken off and they get everyday clothes.

When a man wants to marry first he makes a proposal of marriage, and for his proposal he sends someone, a relative of the bride-to-be (lit. that woman), to take a message to the girl's father, and the one who is sent is called a go-between or an ambassador. Some send the go-between to speak with the girl's father, and others write a letter. When they have agreed, the suitor and the go-between, the go-between replies, 'Give me a kerchief and I will write a letter.' So the suitor gives a kerchief, and the go-between writes a letter like this:

> My ancient one So-and-So son of So-and-So, I inform you that So-and-So's son has come and he wants to marry your daughter, and these are happy matters. A daughter (is) a perishable commodity (lit. rotten goods) like gunpowder and fire, or like cotton and fire, or like an onion. Please if you read this letter, I want a reply, and excuse me. Greetings, &c.

When the letter is finished the kerchief is its envelope, for that is great respect. When the girl's father has read the letter he will call his relatives, men and women, to advise them. Some will accept, others will refuse. Those who refuse want to be given a little something by the suitor, and he will produce something to give to the contentious ones. Then they will say, 'The matter is settled, this is indeed the man.'

The go-between will inform the suitor that his (future) in-laws are all content, and the suitor will buy every (kind of) gift to send to his sweetheart, like a nice cloth or nice just-ripe fruits, but they do not meet, from the day when money is sent to the wedding-day, whether it be a period of a month of a year.

The go-between will go back again to the in-laws and ask the father, 'How much will your marriage payments be?' The girl's father will reply, 'My *kilemba* will be so much and the dowry so much.' The go-between goes back, he gives the suitor the information from the in-laws, and if he accepts and has the money, at once he counts out the marriage payment to give it to the go-between to take to his in-law. If the in-law has died, his brother or his elder (the girl's grandparent) receives it, and if these are not (alive)

they look for people in the family (lit. house), connected with the girl, but one who is a man. If there is no one at all, the woman herself receives it.

When the father has received the money he calls his relatives to show them the money, and they divide it between them. The mother gets her *uweleko* and her *kondawi*. If there is an aunt, she receives a little, and if there is a grandmother, she gets a little. Every person amongst the relations get a little, because this is respect. All the money that is left the father takes. And this money is called 'the door shutter' or 'the courtship clincher', meaning that the girl may not be sought in marriage by another person.

After payment of the proposal money the in-laws will want the woman's marriage payment. If the man has no marriage payment they will agree about a period (for payments), like a year or more, so that he can give it to them afterwards. If they accept he must write a note to guarantee before witnesses that the agreement really is such.

After a few days the man will want his wife; he tells his go-between, 'At the new moon I want to get married.' The go-between takes the news to the in-laws', and they reply, 'Very well, we are ready.' The girl's father tells the people concerned, 'On such-and-such a day I have a cup of coffee.' This message is the responsibility of the girl's father, and if he is unable, if he is poor, the suitor does it, if he is a person of substance.

The wedding usually takes place in the house of the bride's parents until the seven days are over. On the morning of the wedding the house is decorated, it is arranged neatly with dishes and chairs and mirrors, and it is fumigated with aromatic aloe wood and (sprinkled) with a bottle of rose-water. At the beginning of the afternoon the women friends of the bride and others on her side come to make her ready; they take her to the toilet, bathe her, and comb her hair, and they massage her whole body with *tibu* perfume, then she is censed, they plait her hair and cut it, that is they cut the hair a little (in a small patch, but lit. on the face), this is called *denge*. They also apply antimony to the eyes (i.e. the eyebrows and the lashes) and a little on the face, and they sing as they do this.

When this toilet is finished the bridegroom is brought after sunset to the bride's house by her friends, with rejoicing and merriment. And he has adorned himself with a calico garment, a cloth cloak, a turban and shoes, a curved dagger and perhaps a sword or a stick in the hand. When he reaches the wedding-house and wants to go in, the women prevent him at the door, they want their *kingia* (due for entering), and he gives a certain amount of money. Or he tries (lit. wants) to deceive them, saying, 'Allow me to see my bride (lit. wife), and then I will give you your *kingia* gift.' But the women do not agree.

When he goes inside, the *makungwi* give him his wife (to-be), and she gives him her hand and greets him. And this is when they meet for the first time. The woman does not speak to the groom until he first gives the *kono* and *kipakasa* and *fichuo* gifts, the *kono* because she gave him her hand, she wants the gift due for this in (his) taking a new woman. And *kipakasa* is for (his) embracing (her), and the *fichuo* is for speaking with her, because formerly he had not seen her face nor heard her voice, this is why these dues are wanted. And the groom gives (the gifts); for example, he gives her a ring for her *kono*, or a bracelet for her *kipakasa*, and a metal chain for her *fichuo*, or else he gives her as much money as he can.

When he has made these customary gifts, the groom goes to the reception-hall, and his bride stays in her room, and the groom goes to partake of 'the wedding-dish'; he breaks off some cooked rice and puts it on a plate with some meat; his bride is sent this to eat; it is called 'the gift-rice'. Meanwhile, the young women play their small drums and cymbals, they sing their wedding-songs. And when the people have partaken of the wedding-dish, they read the first chapter of the Quran. The bridal pair, the man and the woman, have already been married by the Muslim teacher on the day preferred by the

bridegroom, but some are married by the teacher on the wedding-day itself in the morning.

The people at the wedding pray to God for the bridal couple, and they say:

> God grant you a good home for speaking and listening; may He greatly increase your prosperity, may He take away from you sickness in your home, may He give you male and female offspring. May God protect you from enemies, through His loving kindness.

When they have eaten, and read the first chapter of the Quran, the bridegroom undresses and puts on two cloths, because he is about to have his feet washed; one cloth he wears around the lower half of his body, and one he covers himself with (i.e. over the head). He sits on a chair, and his feet are in a tray or a flat wooden platter. The bride's *kungwi* will wash his feet, and a slave-girl holds a water-jug. The *kungwi* sings a song and the women respond, like this: 'Let us wash the master's feet with water from Zemzem', or, 'The dish-shaped gong of the song-leaders, let them enter the dance in pairs', or 'And let the money be placed on the Swahilis' gong.'

If the young people hear this song, everyone arranges to put something on the gong, everyone according as he is able. The *kungwi* will count the money obtained. Then she will call the parents of the bride for them to divide the money in three parts; one part for the *kungwi*, the second part the parents will receive, and the third goes to the bridal couple, but the money taken by the *kungwi* and the parents will not be used (i.e. for themselves), they will buy necessaries for the honeymoon period of six days.

When the honeymoon period is over, the wife is taken to her husband, and a screen is made for her, and this screen is a canopy. A big screen is made and the bride goes into it with other women. The slave-girls hold cymbals, and some have a buffalo horn, and they go along singing songs. When she gets to the house her husband invites the women relatives of both sides to show them the bride's kitchen. And they are shown this by having a lot of food made for them, and he invites anyone he likes to eat his food, and it is called 'The Kitchen Hint'. After this no further meal is prepared, for this is the end of the wedding.

1. How are children acculturated in a Swahili community?

2. What is the role of science and medicine in bringing up children? Why did the Swahili practice infanticide?

3. What is the role of the Kungwi in the education of women?

4. How are marriages arranged among the Swahili?

PART VI

The Modern World

World War I

Recruitment poster, World War I.

·133·
Ernst Jünger
Storm of Steel
(1920)

*E*rnst Jünger (b. 1895) left his middle-class German home in 1912 in search of adventure. Military life attracted him, so he enlisted in the renowned French Foreign Legion. At the outbreak of World War I, he returned to Germany, where at the age of 19 he enlisted in the forces and became a lieutenant on the Western front. Jünger served in the trenches throughout the war and received a medal for bravery. Afterward, he studied philosophy and natural science. When Jünger first began to write, his work brought him to the attention of the newly formed Nazi party, but he did not join and did not support many of the Nazi causes. He again enlisted when World War II began and was one of the officers involved in the abortive attempt on Hitler's life in 1944. After the war Jünger's militarist attitudes changed radically, and he became an active campaigner for peace and European unity.

   Storm of Steel was Jünger's first novel. A memoir of his days in the trenches, it graphically portrays the lives of the soldiers—both the privations they suffered and the bonds that they built up together.

THE AUTHOR'S PREFACE

I was a nineteen-year-old lieutenant in command of a platoon, and my part of the line was easily recognizable from the English side by a row of tall shell-stripped trees that rose from the ruins of Monchy. My left flank was bounded by the sunken road leading to Berles-au-Bois, which was in the hands of the English; my right was marked by a sap running out from our lines, one that helped us many a time to make our presence felt by means of bombs and rifle grenades.

   Today there is no secret about what those trenches concealed, and a book such as this may, like a trench map years after the event, be read with sympathy and interest by the other side. But here not only the blue and red lines of the trenches are shown, but the blood that beat and the life that lay hid in them.

   Time only strengthens my conviction that it was a good and strenuous life, and that the war, for all its destructiveness, was an incomparable schooling of the heart. The front-line soldier whose foot came down on the earth so grimly and harshly may claim this at least, that it came down cleanly. Warlike achievements are enhanced by the inherent worth of the enemy.

   On the 23d of August we were transported in lorries to Le Mesnil. Our spirits were excellent, though we knew we were going to be put in where the battle of Somme was at its worst. Chaff and laughter went from lorry to lorry. We marched from Le Mesnil at dusk to Sailly-Saillisel, and here the battalion dumped packs in a large meadow and paraded in battle order.

Artillery fire of a hitherto unimagined intensity rolled and thundered on our front. Thousands of twitching flashes turned the western horizon into a sea of flowers. All the while the wounded came trailing back with white, dejected faces, huddled into the ditches by the gun and ammunition columns that rattled past.

A man in a steel helmet reported to me as guide to conduct my platoon to the renowned Combles, where for the time we were to be in reserve. Sitting with him at the side of the road, I asked him, naturally enough, what it was like in the line. In reply I heard a monotonous tale of crouching all day in shell holes with no one on either flank and no trenches communicating with the rear, of unceasing attacks, of dead bodies littering the ground, of maddening thirst, of wounded and dying, and of a lot besides. The face half-framed by the steel rim of the helmet was unmoved; the voice accompanied by the sound of battle droned on, and the impression they made on me was one of unearthly solemnity. One could see that the man had been through horror to the limit of despair and there had learned to despise it. Nothing was left but supreme and superhuman indifference.

"Where you fall, there you lie. No one can help you. No one knows whether he will come back alive. They attack every day, but they can't get through. Everybody knows it is life and death."

As far as we could see in the darkness, Combles was utterly shot to bits. The damage seemed to be recent, judging from the amount of timber among the ruins and the contents of the houses slung over the road. We climbed over numerous heaps of débris—rather hurriedly, owing to a few shrapnel shells—and reached our quarters. They were in a large, shot-riddled house. Here I established myself with three sections. The other two occupied the cellar of a ruin opposite.

At 4 a.m. we were aroused from our rest on the fragments of bed we had collected, in order to receive steel helmets. It was also the occasion of discovering a sack of coffee beans in a corner of the cellar; whereupon there followed a great brewing of coffee.

After breakfast I went out to have a look round. Heavy artillery had turned a peaceful little billeting town into a scene of desolation in the course of a day or two. Whole houses had been flattened by single direct hits or blown up so that the interiors of the rooms hung over the chaos like the scenes on a stage. A sickly scent of dead bodies rose from many of the ruins, for many civilians had been caught in the bombardment and buried beneath the wreckage of their homes. A little girl lay dead in a pool of blood on the threshold of one of the doorways.

The square in front of the ruins of the church had been particularly hard hit. Here was the entrance to the catacombs, a very ancient underground passage with recesses here and there in which were crowded the staffs of all the units engaged. It was said that the civilians had opened up the entrance with pickaxes when the bombardment began. It had been walled up and kept secret from the Germans during the whole of their occupation. The streets were reduced to narrow paths winding circuitously round and over heaps of timber and masonry. Quantities of fruit and vegetables were going to waste in the churned-up gardens.

A plentiful supply of "iron rations" provided us with a dinner that we cooked in the kitchen, and concluded, needless to say, with strong coffee. I then settled myself in an armchair upstairs. From letters scattered about I saw that the house belonged to a brewer, Lesage. Cupboards and chests of drawers were thrown open; there was an overturned washstand, a sewing machine, and a perambulator. The pictures and the looking glasses on the walls were all broken. Drawers had been pulled out and emptied, and a yard deep all over the floor were underclothes, corsets, books, papers, bedroom tables, broken glass, bottles, notebooks, chair legs, coats, cloaks, lamps, curtains, window frames, doors torn from their hinges, lace, photographs, oil paintings, albums, broken boxes, hats, flower pots, and torn wall paper, all tangled up together in wild confusion.

In the course of the afternoon the firing increased to such a degree that single explosions were no longer audible. There was nothing but one terrific tornado of noise. From seven onward the square and the houses round were shelled at intervals of half a minute with fifteen-centimeter shells. There were many duds among them, which all the same made the houses rock. We sat all this while in our cellar, round a table, on armchairs covered in silk, with our heads propped on our hands, and counted the seconds between the explosions. Our jests became less frequent, till at last the foolhardiest of us fell silent, and at eight o'clock two direct hits brought down the next house.

From nine to ten the shelling was frantic. The earth rocked and the sky boiled like a gigantic cauldron.

Hundreds of heavy batteries were concentrated on and round Combles. Innumerable shells came howling and hurtling over us. Thick smoke, ominously lit up by Very lights, veiled everything. Head and ears ached violently, and we could only make ourselves understood by shouting a word at a time. The power of logical thought and the force of gravity seemed alike to be suspended. One had the sense of something as unescapable and as unconditionally fated as a catastrophe of nature. An N.C.O. of No. 3 platoon went mad.

At ten this carnival of hell gradually calmed down and passed into a steady drum fire. It was still certainly impossible to distinguish one shell from another.

At last we reached the front line. It was held by men cowering close in the shell holes, and their dead voices trembled with joy when they heard that we were the relief. A Bavarian sergeant major briefly handed over the sector and the Very-light pistol.

My platoon formed the right wing of the position held by the regiment. It consisted of a shallow sunken road which had been pounded by shells. It was a few hundred meters left of Guillemont and a rather shorter distance right

of Bois-de-Trônes. We were parted from the troops on our right, the Seventy-sixth Regiment of Infantry, by a space about five hundred meters wide. This space was shelled so violently that no troops could maintain themselves there.

As I had no idea how far off the enemy were, I warned my men to be ready for the worst. We all remained on guard. I spent the night with my batman and two orderlies in a hole perhaps one yard square and one yard deep.

When day dawned we were astonished to see, by degrees, what a sight surrounded us.

The sunken road now appeared as nothing but a series of enormous shell holes filled with pieces of uniform, weapons, and dead bodies. The ground all round, as far as the eye could see, was plowed by shells. You could search in vain for one wretched blade of grass. This churned-up battlefield was ghastly. Among the living lay the dead. As we dug ourselves in we found them in layers stacked one upon the top of another. One company after another had been shoved into the drum fire and steadily annihilated. The corpses were covered with the masses of soil turned up by the shells, and the next company advanced in the place of the fallen.

The sunken road and the ground behind were full of German dead; the ground in front, of English. Arms, legs, and heads stuck out stark above the lips of the craters. In front of our miserable defenses there were torn-off limbs and corpses over many of which cloaks and ground sheets had been thrown to hide the fixed stare of their distorted features. In spite of the heat no one thought for a moment of covering them with soil.

The village of Guillemont was distinguished from the landscape around it only because the shell holes there were of a whiter color by reason of the houses which had been ground to powder. Guillemont railway station lay in front of us. It was smashed to bits like a child's plaything. Delville Wood, reduced to matchwood, was farther behind.

Day had scarcely dawned when an English flying man descended on us in a steep spin and circled round incessantly like a bird of prey, while we made for our holes and cowered there. Nevertheless, the observer's sharp eyes must have spied us out, for a siren sounded its deep, long-drawn notes above us at short intervals. After a little while it appeared that a battery had received the signal. One heavy shell after another came at us on a flat trajectory with incredible fury. We crouched in our refuges and could do nothing. Now and then we lit a cigar and threw it away again. Every moment we expected a rush of earth to bury us. The sleeve of Schmidt's coat was torn by a big splinter.

At three in the afternoon the men came in from the left flank and said they could stick it no longer, as their shelters were shot to bits. It cost me all my callousness to get them back to their posts.

Just before ten at night the left flank of the regimental front was heavily shelled, and after twenty minutes we came in for it too. In a brief space we were completely covered in dust and smoke, and yet most of the hits were just in front or just behind. While this hurricane was raging I went along my platoon front. The men were standing, rifle in hand, as though carved in stone, their eyes fixed on the ground in front of them. Now and then by the light of a rocket I saw the gleam of helmet after helmet, bayonet after bayonet, and I was filled with pride at commanding this handful of men that might very likely be pounded into the earth but could not be conquered. It is in such moments that the human spirit triumphs over the mightiest demonstrations of material force. The fragile body, steeled by the will, stands up to the most terrific punishment.

1. When he wrote *Storm of Steel* Jünger believed that his experience had been a positive one. Why?

2. What was the average soldier's experience in the trenches like?

3. How did the war affect those caught up in it?

4. Judging from Jünger's account, why was World War I so devastating? How was it different?

5. Is this an antiwar novel?

·134·

Woodrow Wilson
The Fourteen Points
(1918)

Woodrow Wilson (1856–1924), twenty-eighth President of the United States, brought the United States into World War I on the side of the Allied powers. Wilson was born in Virginia, but he was educated in the north, where he later made his home. A brilliant student, he became a professor of political economy, first at Weslyan University and later at Princeton. His abilities led him into administration, and in 1902 he was named president of Princeton. Wilson's credentials as a reformer were impressive enough to win him the governorship of New Jersey in 1910. Two years later he was elected president on the Democratic ticket. He was reelected in 1916 on the platform that he had kept America out of the European conflict, but by the next year he was persuaded to throw the country's might behind Britain and France. Wilson's change of policy was founded on his idealism—on the belief that the war would make the world safe for democracy and would eliminate forever the need for war. His dream of a League of Nations to settle world problems by debate rather than gunfire was achieved; but the U.S. Senate refused to ratify the Treaty of Versailles, so the United States never joined the League of Nations.

The Fourteen Points neatly summarizes the principles for which Wilson believed World War I was fought.

We have entered this war because violations of right had occurred which touched us to the quick and made the life of our own people impossible, unless they were corrected, and the world secured once for all against their recurrence.

What we demand in this war, therefore, is nothing peculiar to ourselves. It is that the world be made fit and safe to live in, and particularly that it be made safe for every peace-loving nation which, like our own, wishes to live its own free life, determine its own institutions, be assured of justice and fair dealing by the other peoples of the world, as against force and selfish aggression. All the peoples of the world are in effect partners in this interest, and for our own part we see very clearly that unless justice be done to others it will not be done to us.

The program of the world's peace, therefore, is our program; and that program, the only possible one as we see it, is this:

I. Open covenants of peace, openly arrived at, after which there shall be no private international understandings of any kind, but diplomacy shall proceed always frankly and in the public view.

II. Absolute freedom of navigation upon the seas, outside territorial waters, alike in peace and in war, except as the seas may be closed in

Woodrow Wilson (1856–1924) served as the twenty-eighth president of the United States.

whole or in part by international action for the enforcement of international covenants.

III.   The removal, so far as possible, of all economic barriers and the establishment of an equality of trade conditions among all the nations consenting to the peace and associating themselves for its maintenance.

IV.   Adequate guarantees given and taken that national armaments will be reduced to the lowest point consistent with domestic safety.

V.   A free, open-minded, and absolutely impartial adjustment of all colonial claims, based upon a strict observance of the principle that in determining all such questions of sovereignty the interests of the populations concerned must have equal weight with the equitable claims of the Government whose title is to be determined.

VI.   The evacuation of all Russian territory, and such a settlement of all questions affecting Russia as will secure the best and freest cooperation of the other nations of the world in obtaining for her an unhampered and unembarrassed opportunity for the independent determination of her own political development and national policy, and assure her of a sincere welcome into the society of free nations under institutions of her own choosing; and, more than a welcome, assistance also of every kind that she may need and may herself desire. The treatment accorded Russia by her sister nations in the months to come will be the acid test of their good will, of their comprehension of her needs as distinguished from their own interests, and of their intelligent and unselfish sympathy.

VII.   Belgium, the whole world will agree, must be evacuated and restored without any attempt to limit the sovereignty which she enjoys in common with all other free nations. No other single act will serve as this will serve to restore confidence among the nations in the laws which they have themselves set and determined for the government of their relations with one another. Without this healing act the whole structure and validity of international law is forever impaired.

VIII.   All French territory should be freed and the invaded portions restored; and the wrong done to France by Prussia in 1871 in the matter of Alsace-Lorraine, which has unsettled the peace of the world for nearly fifty years, should be righted, in order that peace may once more be made secure in the interest of all.

IX.   A readjustment of the frontiers of Italy should be effected along clearly recognizable lines of nationality.

X.   The peoples of Austria-Hungary, whose place among the nations we wish to see safeguarded and assured, should be accorded the freest opportunity of autonomous development.

XI.   Rumania, Serbia, and Montenegro should be evacuated; occupied territories restored; Serbia accorded free and secure access to the sea; and the relations of the several Balkan states to one another determined by friendly counsel along historically established lines of allegiance and nationality; and international guarantees of the political and economic independence and territorial integrity of the several Balkan states should be entered into.

XII.   The Turkish portions of the present Ottoman Empire should be assured a secure sovereignty, but the other nationalities which are now under Turkish rule should be assured an undoubted security of life and an absolutely unmolested opportunity of autonomous development, and the Dardanelles should be permanently opened as a free passage to the ships and commerce of all nations under international guaranties.

XIII.   An independent Polish state should be erected which should include the territories inhabited by indisputably Polish populations, which should be assured a free and secure access to the sea, and whose political and economic independence and territorial integrity should be guaranteed by international covenant.

XIV.   A general association of nations must be formed, under specific covenants, for the purpose of affording mutual guaranties of political independence and territorial integrity to great and small states alike.

In regard to these essential rectifications of wrong and assertions of right we feel ourselves to be intimate partners of all the Governments and peoples associated together against the imperialists. We cannot be separated in interest or divided in purpose. We stand together until the end.

1. Why, according to Wilson, had the United States entered the war?

2. A number of the points of Wilson's plan touch on questions of national borders. Who, according to the president, should have the greatest role in deciding such questions?

3. What was to be the function of "general association of nations"?

4. The Fourteen Points was a masterful piece of political propaganda, but Wilson was less successful at translating them into reality. Why?

5. Does The Fourteen Points reflect any peculiarly American characteristics? Would the plan have been different if written by a French or British statesman?

·135·

Lenin
What Is to Be Done?
(1902)

Vladimir Ilich Ulyanov (1870–1924) took his famous pseudonym, Lenin, after he began his career as a professional revolutionary. Lenin was from a middle-class family and was strongly influenced by his older brother, who also was engaged in revolutionary politics. In 1887 his brother was captured by the tsarist regime and executed. From that moment, Lenin dedicated himself to the overthrow of the Russian government. He became a Marxist and joined the underground movement. In 1895 Lenin, too, was arrested and briefly imprisoned in Siberia. After 1900 he lived abroad, the exiled leader of the Bolshevik wing of the Social Democratic party. It was not until the outbreak of World War I that Lenin was able to return to Russia and begin the work of creating a Marxist revolution. In 1917 the feeble government of the tsar was overthrown and eventually replaced by a provisional government led by Alexander Kerensky. It was Kerensky's government that Lenin worked to remove, tirelessly advocating its replacement by a truly revolutionary Marxist workers' regime. He succeeded in November 1917 and spent the rest of his life consolidating power in the new Soviet Union.

What Is to Be Done? is an early statement of Lenin's belief in the need for a truly socialist revolution. Against those who advocated a democratic trade union movement, as had developed in the Western democracies, Lenin called for a socialist revolution led by a cadre of party professionals. Only these revolutionaries could create the fundamental change that Lenin believed was necessary for Russia.

We have said that *there could not yet be* Social-Democratic consciousness among the workers. It could only be brought to them from without. The history of all countries shows that the working class, exclusively by its own effort, is able to develop only trade union consciousness, i.e., the conviction that it is necessary to combine in unions, fight the employers and strive to compel the government to pass necessary labour legislation, etc. The theory of Socialism, however, grew out of the philosophic, historical and economic theories that were elaborated by the educated representatives of the propertied classes, the intellectuals. According to their social status, the founders of modern scientific Socialism, Marx and Engels, themselves belonged to the bourgeois intelligentsia.

Since there can be no talk of an independent ideology being developed the masses of the workers themselves in the process of their movement the *only* choice is: either the bourgeois or the socialist ideology. There is no middle course (for humanity has not created a "third" ideology, and, moreover, in a society torn by class antagonisms there can never be a non-class or above-class ideology). Hence, to belittle the socialist ideology *in any way,* to *turn away from it in the slightest degree* means to strengthen bourgeois ideology. There is a lot of talk about spontaneity, but the *spontaneous* development of the working-class movement leads to its becoming subordi-

nated to the bourgeois ideology, *leads to its developing according to the program* of the *Credo,* for the spontaneous working-class movement is trade unionism, and trade unionism means the ideological enslavement of the workers by the bourgeoisie. Hence, our task, the task of Social-Democracy, is to *combat spontaneity,* to *divert* the working-class movement from this spontaneous, trade-unionist striving to come under the wing of the bourgeoisie, and to bring it under the wing of revolutionary Social-Democracy.

As a matter of fact, it is possible to "raise the activity of the masses of the workers" *only* provided this activity *is not restricted* to "political agitation on an economic basis." And one of the fundamental conditions for the necessary expansion of political agitation is the organization of *comprehensive* political exposure. The masses *cannot* be trained in political consciousness and revolutionary activity in any other way except by means of such exposures. Hence, activity of this kind is one of the most important functions of international Social-Democracy as a whole, for even the existence of political liberty does not in the least remove the necessity for such exposures; it merely changes somewhat the sphere against which they are directed.

We are not children to be fed on the thin gruel of "economic" politics alone; we want to know everything that others know, we want to learn the details of *all* aspects of political life and to take part *actively* in every single political event. In order that we may do this, the intellectuals must talk to us less of what we already know, and tell us more about what we do not yet know and what we can never learn from our factory and "economic" experience, that is, you must give us political knowledge. You intellectuals can acquire this knowledge, and it is your *duty* to bring it to us in a hundred and a thousand times greater measure than you have done up to now; and you must bring it to us, not only in the form of arguments, pamphlets and articles which sometimes—excuse our frankness!—are rather dull, but precisely in the form of live *exposures* of what our government and our governing classes are doing at this very moment in all spheres of life. Just devote more zeal to carrying out this duty, and *talk less about "raising the activity of the masses of the workers!"* We are far more active than you think, and we are quite able to support, by open, street fighting, demands that do not promise any "palpable results" whatever! And it is not for you to "raise" our activity, because *activity is precisely the thing you yourselves lack!* Bow less in worship to spontaneity, and think more about raising *your own* activity, gentlemen!

A workers' organization must in the first place be a trade organization; secondly, it must be as broad as possible; and thirdly, it must be as little clandestine as possible (here, and further on, of course, I have only autocratic Russia in mind). On the other hand, the organizations of revolutionaries must consist first, foremost and mainly of people who make revolutionary activity their profession (that is why I speak of organizations of *revolutionaries,* meaning revolutionary Social-Democrats). In view of this common feature of the members of such an organization, *all distinctions as between workers and intellectuals,* and certainly distinctions of trade and profession, must be *utterly obliterated.* Such an organization must of necessity be not too extensive and as secret as possible.

As I have already said time and again that by "wise men," in connection with organization, I mean *professional revolutionaries,* irrespective of whether they are trained from among students or workingmen. I assert: 1) that no revolutionary movement can endure without a stable organization of leaders that maintains continuity; 2) that the wider the masses spontaneously drawn into the struggle, forming the basis of the movement and participating in it, the more urgent the need of such an organization, and the more solid this organization must be (for it is much easier for demagogues to sidetrack the more backward sections of the masses); 3) that such an organization must consist chiefly of people professionally engaged in revolutionary activity; 4) that in an autocratic state, the more we *confine* the membership of such an organization to people who are professionally engaged in revolutionary activity and who have been professionally trained in the art of combating the political police, the more difficult will it be to wipe out such an organization, and 5) the *greater* will be the number of people of the working class and of the other classes of society who will be able to join the movement and perform active work in it.

To concentrate all secret functions in the hands of as small a number of professional revolutionaries as possible does not mean that the latter will "do the thinking for all" and that the crowd will not take an active part in the *movement.* On the contrary, the crowd will advance from its ranks increasing numbers of professional revolutionaries; for it will know that it is not enough for a few students and for a few workingmen waging the economic struggle, to gather together and form a "committee," but that it takes years to train oneself to be a professional revolutionary; the crowd will "think" not of amateurish methods alone but of such training. The centralization of the secret functions of the *organization* by no means implies the centralization of all the functions of the *movement.* The active participation of the widest mass in the illegal press will not diminish because a "dozen" professional revolutionaries centralize the secret functions connected with this work; on the contrary, it will *increase* tenfold. In this way, and in this way alone, will we ensure that reading of illegal literature, writing for it, and to some extent even distributing it, will *almost cease to be secret work*, for the police will soon come to realize the folly and futility of setting the whole judicial and administrative machine into motion to intercept every copy of publication that is being broadcast in thousands. This applies not only to the press, but to every function of the movement, even to demonstrations. The active and widespread participation of the masses will not suffer; on the contrary, it will benefit by the fact that a "dozen" experienced revolutionaries, trained professionally no less than the police, will centralize all the secret aspects of the work—drawing up leaflets, working out approximate plans and appointing bodies of leaders for each urban district, for each factory district and for each educational institution, etc. (I know that exception will be taken to my "undemocratic" views, but I shall reply fully to this anything but intelligent objection later on.) The centralization of the most secret functions in an organization of revolutionaries will not diminish, but rather increase the extent and quality of the activity of a large number of other organizations which are intended for a broad public and are therefore as loose and as non-secret as possible, such as workers' trade unions, workers' self-education circles and circles for reading illegal literature, socialist and also democratic circles among *all* other sections of the population, etc., etc. We must have such circles, trade unions and organizations everywhere in *as large a number as possible* and with the widest variety of functions; but it would be absurd and dangerous to *confuse* them with the organization of *revolutionaries,* to obliterate the border line between them, to dim still more the masses' already incredibly hazy appreciation of the fact that in order to "serve" the mass movement we must have people who will devote themselves exclusively to Social-Democratic activities, and that such people must *train* themselves patiently and steadfastly to be professional revolutionaries.

1. What is Lenin's view of dissent? How closely must people adhere to socialist thought?

2. Why does Lenin reject trade unionism for the working class?

3. What must a revolutionary movement have to succeed?

4. Lenin argues that revolutionary activity must be centralized. Why? How does this reflect his own interests?

5. Lenin ultimately succeeded in his goal of overthrowing the Russian government. Is *What Is to Be Done?* an effective blueprint for would-be revolutionaries?

East Meets West

In the Meiji era in the late nineteenth century, Japanese women learned Western musical forms and how to play Western instruments.

·136·
Lin Tse-Hsü
Letter of Advice to Queen Victoria
(1839)

*L*in Tse-Hsü (1785–1850) was the Chinese Commissioner in Canton whose actions precipitated the Opium Wars (1839–1842). Although opium was used in China for centuries, it was not until the opening of the tea trade to Dutch and British merchants that China was able to import large quantities of the drug. By the early nineteenth century opium was the principal product that the English East India Company traded in China and opium addiction was becoming a widespread social problem. When the emperor's own son died of an overdose, he decided to put an end to the trade. Lin Tse-Hsü was sent to Canton, the chief trading port of the East India Company, with instructions to negotiate an end to the importation of opium into China. The English merchants were uncooperative, so he seized their stores of opium. This led to immediate military action. The Chinese were decisively defeated and had to concede to a humiliating treaty that legalized the opium trade. As a result, Commissioner Lin was dismissed from office and sent into exile.

Lin Tse-Hsü's "Letter of Advice to Queen Victoria" was written before the outbreak of the Opium Wars. It was a remarkably frank document, especially given the usual highly stylized language of Chinese diplomacy. There remains some question whether Queen Victoria ever read the letter.

A communication: magnificently our great Emperor soothes and pacifies China and the foreign countries, regarding all with the same kindness. If there is profit, then he shares it with the peoples of the world; if there is harm, then he removes it on behalf of the world. This is because he takes the mind of heaven and earth as his mind.

The kings of your honorable country by a tradition handed down from generation to generation have always been noted for their politeness and submissiveness. We have read your successive tributary memorials saying, "In general our countrymen who go to trade in China have always received His Majesty the Emperor's gracious treatment and equal justice," and so on. Privately we are delighted with the way in which the honorable rulers of your country deeply understand the grand principles and are grateful for the Celestial grace. For this reason the Celestial Court in soothing those from afar has redoubled its polite and kind treatment. The profit from trade has been enjoyed by them continuously for two hundred years. This is the source from which your country has become known for its wealth.

But after a long period of commercial intercourse, there appear among the crowd of barbarians both good persons and bad, unevenly. Consequently there are those who smuggle opium to seduce the Chinese people and so cause the spread of the poison to all provinces. Such persons who only care to profit themselves, and disregard their harm to others, are not tolerated by the laws of heaven and are unanimously hated by human beings. His Majesty the Emperor, upon hearing of this, is in a towering rage. He has especially sent me, his commissioner, to come to Kwangtung, and together with the governor-general and governor jointly to investigate and settle this matter.

All those people in China who sell opium or smoke opium should receive the death penalty. If we trace the crime of those barbarians who through the years have been selling opium, then the deep harm they have wrought and the great profit they have usurped should fundamentally justify their execution according to law. We take into consideration, however, the fact that the various barbarians have still known how to repent their crimes and return to their allegiance to us by taking the 20,183 chests of opium from their storeships and petitioning us, through their consular officer [superintendent of trade], Elliot, to receive it. It has been entirely destroyed and this has been faithfully reported to the Throne in several memorials by this commissioner and his colleagues.

Fortunately we have received a specially extended favor from His Majesty the Emperor, who considers that for those who voluntarily surrender there are still some circumstances to palliate their crime, and so for the time being he has magnanimously excused them from punishment. But as for those who again violate the opium prohibition, it is difficult for the law to pardon them repeatedly. Having established new regulations, we presume that the ruler of your honorable country, who takes delight in our culture and whose disposition is inclined towards us, must be able to instruct the various barbarians to observe the law with care. It is only necessary to explain to them the advantages and disadvantages and then they will know that the legal code of the Celestial Court must be absolutely obeyed with awe.

We find that your country is sixty or seventy thousand *li* [three *li* make one mile, ordinarily] from China. Yet there are barbarian ships that strive to come here for trade for the purpose of making a great profit. The wealth of China is used to profit the barbarians. That is to say, the great profit made by barbarians is all taken from the rightful share of China. By what right do they then in return use the poisonous drug to injure the Chinese people? Even though the barbarians may not necessarily intend to do us harm, yet in coveting profit to an extreme, they have no regard for injuring others. Let us ask, where is your conscience? I have heard that the smoking of opium is very strictly forbidden by your country; that is because the harm caused by opium is clearly understood. Since it is not permitted to do harm to your own country, then even less should you let it be passed on to the harm of other countries—how much less to China! Of all that China exports to foreign countries, there is not a single thing which is not beneficial to people: they are of benefit when eaten, or of benefit when used, or of benefit when resold: all are beneficial. Is there a single article from China which has done any harm to foreign countries? Take tea and rhubarb, for example; the foreign countries cannot get along for a single day without them. If China cuts off these benefits with no sympathy for those who are to suffer, then what can the barbarians rely upon to keep themselves alive? Moreover the woolens, camlets, and longells [i.e., textiles] of foreign countries cannot be woven unless they obtain Chinese silk. If China, again, cuts off this beneficial export, what profit can the barbarians expect to make? As for other foodstuffs, beginning with candy, ginger, cinnamon, and so forth, and articles for use, beginning with silk, satin, chinaware, and so on, all the things that must be had by foreign countries are innumerable. On the other hand, articles coming from the outside to China can only be used as toys. We can take them or get along without them. Since they are not needed by China, what difficulty would there be if we closed the frontier and stopped the trade? Nevertheless our Celestial Court lets tea, silk, and other goods be shipped without limit and circulated everywhere without begrudging it in the slightest. This is for no other reason but to share the benefit with the people of the whole world.

The goods from China carried away by your country not only supply your own consumption and use, but also can be divided up and sold to other countries, producing a triple profit. Even if you do not sell opium, you still have this threefold profit. How can you bear to go further, selling products injurious to others in order to fulfill your insatiable desire?

Suppose there were people from another country who carried opium for sale to England and seduced your people into buying and smoking it; certainly your honorable ruler would deeply hate it and be bitterly aroused. We have heard heretofore that your honorable ruler is kind and benevolent. Naturally you would not wish to give unto others what you yourself do not want. We have also heard that the ships coming to Canton have all had regulations promulgated and given to them in which it is stated that it is not permitted to carry contraband goods. This indicates that the administrative orders of your honorable rule have been originally strict and clear. Only because the trading ships are numerous, heretofore perhaps they have not been examined with care. Now after this communication has been dispatched and you have clearly understood the strictness of the prohibitory laws of the Celestial Court, certainly you will not let your subjects dare again to violate the law.

We have further learned that in London, the capital of your honorable rule, and in Scotland, Ireland, and other places, originally no opium has been produced. Only in several places of India under your control such as Bengal, Madras, Bombay, Patna, Benares, and Malwa has opium been planted from hill to hill, and ponds have been opened for its manufacture. For months and years work is continued in order to accumulate the poison. The obnoxious odor ascends, irritating heaven and frightening the spirits. Indeed you, O King, can eradicate the opium plant in these places, hoe over the fields

entirely, and sow in its stead the five grains [i.e., millet, barley, wheat, etc.]. Anyone who dares again attempt to plant and manufacture opium should be severely punished. This will really be a great, benevolent government policy that will increase the common weal and get rid of evil. For this, Heaven must support you and the spirits must bring you good fortune, prolonging your old age and extending your descendants. All will depend on this act.

As for the barbarian merchants who come to China, their food and drink and habitation are all received by the gracious favor of our Celestial Court. Their accumulated wealth is all benefit given with pleasure by our Celestial Court. They spend rather few days in their own country but more time in Canton. To digest clearly the legal penalties as an aid to instruction has been a valid principle in all ages. Suppose a man of another country comes to England to trade, he still has to obey the English laws; how much more should he obey in China the laws of the Celestial Dynasty?

Now we have set up regulations governing the Chinese people. He who sells opium shall receive the death penalty and he who smokes it also the death penalty. Now consider this: if the barbarians do not bring opium, then how can the Chinese people resell it, and how can they smoke it? The fact is that the wicked barbarians beguile the Chinese people into a death trap. How then can we grant life only to these barbarians? He who takes the life of even one person still has to atone for it with his own life; yet is the harm done by opium limited to the taking of one life only? Therefore in the new regulations, in regard to those barbarians who bring opium to China, the penalty is fixed at decapitation or strangulation. This is what is called getting rid of a harmful thing on behalf of mankind.

Moreover we have found that in the middle of the second month of this year [April 9] Consul [Superintendent] Elliot of your nation, because the opium prohibition law was very stern and severe, petitioned for an extension of the time limit. He requested a limit of five months for India and its adjacent harbors and related territories, and ten months for England proper, after which they would act in conformity with the new regulations. Now we, the commissioner and others, have memorialized and have received the extraordinary Celestial grace of His Majesty the Emperor, who has redoubled his consideration and compassion. All those who within the period of the coming one year (from England) or six months (from India) bring opium to China by mistake, but who voluntarily confess and completely surrender their opium, shall be exempt from their punishment. After this limit of time, if there are still those who bring opium to China then they will plainly have committed a wilful violation and shall at once be executed according to law, with absolutely no clemency or pardon. This may be called the height of kindness and the perfection of justice.

Our Celestial Dynasty rules over and supervises the myriad states, and surely possesses unfathomable spiritual dignity. Yet the Emperor cannot bear to execute people without having first tried to reform them by instruction. Therefore he especially promulgates these fixed regulations. The barbarian merchants of your country, if they wish to do business for a prolonged period, are required to obey our statues respectfully and to cut off permanently the source of opium. They must by no means try to test the effectiveness of the law with their lives. May you, O King, check your wicked and sift your vicious people before they come to China, in order to guarantee the peace of your nation, to show further the sincerity of your politeness and submissiveness, and to let the two countries enjoy together the blessings of peace. How fortunate, how fortunate indeed! After receiving this dispatch will you immediately give us a prompt reply regarding the details and circumstances of your cutting off the opium traffic. Be sure not to put this off. The above is what has to be communicated.

1. Why did Lin Tse-Hsü write this letter to Queen Victoria?

2. Why is he worried about the sale of opium in China?

3. What connection does he think Queen Victoria has to the opium trade? Do you think he is right?

4. What does this document tell us about the relations between China and the West in the nineteenth century?

·137·

Lafcadio Hearn
Of Women's Hair
(1894)

Lafcadio Hearn (1850–1904) traveled to Japan from the United States in 1890 to pursue his studies in Eastern religions. While he was there he spent several years teaching English to schoolboys and learning Japanese from them. From the moment he set foot in Japan, Hearn composed short essays about his experiences. Some were published in American magazines; others were collected into books. "Of Women's Hair" was published in a two-volume collection entitled *Glimpses of Unfamiliar Japan* (1894). He also published a number of more scholarly books on Eastern religions. Hearn ultimately became a Japanese citizen and was one of the most popular Western interpreters of Eastern culture.

"Of Women's Hair" describes the complex symbolism of hairstyling as it was practiced for generations. The ways in which hair was cut, arranged, and worn was a complex interaction between beauty, style, and social roles. Hairstyle was a symbolic language in which observers could read a woman's age, class, and marital status.

The hair of the younger daughter of the family is very long; and it is a spectacle of no small interest to see it dressed. It is dressed once in every three days; and the operation, which costs four sen, is acknowledged to require one hour. As a matter of fact it requires nearly two. The hairdresser (*kamiyui*) first sends her maiden apprentice, who cleans the hair, washes it, perfumes it, and combs it with extraordinary combs of at least five different kinds. So thoroughly is the hair cleansed that it remains for three days, or even four, immaculate beyond our Occidental conception of things. In the morning, during the dusting time, it is carefully covered with a handkerchief or a little blue towel; and the curious Japanese wooden pillow, which supports the neck, not the head, renders it possible to sleep at ease without disarranging the marvelous structure.

After the apprentice has finished her part of the work, the hairdresser herself appears, and begins to build the coiffure. For this task she uses, besides the extraordinary variety of combs, fine loops of gilt thread or colored paper twine, dainty bits of deliciously tinted crape-silk, delicate steel springs, and curious little basket-shaped things over which the hair is moulded into the required forms before being fixed in place.

The kamiyui also brings razors with her; for the Japanese girl is shaved,—cheeks, ears, brows, chin, even nose! What is there to shave? Only that peachy floss which is the velvet of the finest human skin, but which Japanese taste removes. There is, however, another use for the razor. All maidens bear the signs of their maidenhood in the form of a little round spot, about an inch in diameter, shaven clean upon the very top of the head. This is only partially concealed by a band of hair brought back from the forehead across it, and fastened to the back hair. The girl-baby's head is totally shaved. When a few years old the little creature's hair is allowed to grow except at the top of the head, where a large tonsure is maintained. But the size of the tonsure diminishes year by year, until it shrinks after childhood to the small spot above described; and this, too, vanishes after marriage, when a still more complicated fashion of wearing the hair is adopted.

Such absolutely straight dark hair as that of most Japanese women might seem, to Occidental ideas at least, ill-suited to the highest possibilities of the art of the *coiffeuse*. But the skill of the kamiyui has made it tractable to every aesthetic whim. Ringlets, indeed, are unknown, and curling irons. But what wonderful and beautiful shapes the hair of the girl is made to assume: volutes, jets, whirls, eddyings, foliations, each passing into the other blandly as a linking of brush-strokes in the writing of a Chinese master! Far beyond the skill of the Parisian *coiffeuse* is the art of the kamiyui. From the mythical era of the race, Japanese ingenuity has exhausted itself in the invention and the improvement of pretty devices for the dressing of woman's hair; and probably there have never been so many beautiful fashions of wearing it in any other country as there have been in Japan. These have changed through the centuries; sometimes becoming wondrously intricate of design, sometimes exquisitely simple,—as in that gracious custom, recorded for us in so many quaint drawings, of allowing the long black tresses to flow unconfined below the waist. But every mode of which we have any pictorial record had its own striking charm. Indian, Chinese, Malayan, Kōrean ideas of beauty found their way to the Land of the Gods, and were appropriated and transfigured by the finer native conceptions of comeliness. Buddhism, too, which so profoundly influenced all Japanese art and thought, may possibly have influenced fashions of wearing the hair; for its female divinities appear with the most beautiful coiffures. Notice the hair of a Kwannon or a Benten, and the tresses of the Tennin,—those angel-maidens who float in azure upon the ceilings of the great temples.

Not less than fourteen different ways of dressing the hair are practiced by the *coiffeuses* of Izumo; but doubtless in the capital, and in some of the larger cities of eastern Japan, the art is much more elaborately developed. The hairdressers (*kamiyui*) go from house to house to exercise their calling, visiting their clients upon fixed days at certain regular hours. The hair of little girls from seven to eight years old is in Matsue dressed usually after the style called O-tabako-bon, unless it be simply "banged." In the O-tabako-bon ("honorable smoking-box" style) the hair is cut to the length of about four inches all round except above the forehead, where it is clipped a little shorter; and on the summit of the head it is allowed to grow longer and is gathered up into a peculiarly shaped knot, which justifies the curious name of the coiffure. As soon as the girl becomes old enough to go to a female public day-school, her hair is dressed in the pretty, simple style called katsurashita, or perhaps in the new, ugly, semi-foreign "bundle-style" called sokuhatsu, which has become the regulation fashion in boarding-schools. For the daughters of the poor, and even for most of those of the middle classes, the public-school period is rather brief; their studies usually cease a few years before they are marriageable, and girls marry very early in Japan. The maiden's first elaborate coiffure is arranged for her when she reaches the age of fourteen or fifteen, at earliest. From twelve to fourteen her hair is dressed in the fashion called Omoyedzuki; then the style is changed to the beautiful coiffure called jorōwage. There are various forms of this style, more or less complex. A couple of years later, the jorōwage yields place in the turn to the shinjōchō ("new-butterfly" style), or the shimada, also called takawage. The shinjōchō style is common, is worn by women of various ages, and is not considered very genteel. The shimada, exquisitely elaborate, is; but the more respectable the family, the smaller the form of this coiffure; geisha and jorō wear a larger and loftier variety of it, which properly answers to the name takawage, or "high coiffure." Between eighteen and twenty years of age the maiden again exchanges this style for another termed Tenjingaeshi; between twenty and twenty-four years of age she adopts the fashion called mitsuwage, or the "triple coiffure" of three loops; and a somewhat similar but still more complicated coiffure, called mitsuwakudzushi is worn by young women of from twenty-five to twenty-eight. Up to that age every change in the fashion of wearing the hair has been in the direction of elaborateness and complexity. But after twenty-eight a Japanese woman is no longer considered young, and there is only one more coiffure for her,—the mochiriwage or bobai, the simple and rather ugly style adopted by old women.

But the girl who marries wears her hair in a fashion quite different from any of the preceding. The most beautiful, the most elaborate, and the most costly of all modes is the bride's coiffure, called hanayome, a word literally signifying "flower-wife." The structure is dainty as its name, and must be seen to be artistically appreciated. Afterwards the wife wears her hair in the styles called kumesa or maruwage, another name for which is katsuyama. The kumesa style is not genteel, and is the coiffure of the poor; the maruwage or katsuyama is refined. In former times the samurai women wore their hair in two particular styles: the maiden's coiffure was ichōgaeshi, and that of the married folk katahajishi. It is still possible to see in Matsue a few katahajishi coiffures.

The hair of dead women is arranged in the manner called tabanegami, somewhat resembling the shimada extremely simplified, and without ornaments of any kind. The name tabanegami signifies hair tied into a bunch, like a sheaf of rice. This style must also be worn by women during the period of mourning.

Ghosts, nevertheless, are represented with hair loose and long, falling weirdly over the face. And no doubt because of the melancholy suggestiveness of its drooping branches, the willow is believed to be the favorite tree of ghosts. Thereunder, 't is said, they mourn in the night, mingling their shadowy hair with the long disheveled tresses of the tree.

As the hair of the Japanese woman is her richest ornament, it is of all her possessions that which she would most suffer to lose; and in other days the man too manly to kill an erring wife deemed it vengeance enough to turn her away with all her hair shorn off. Only the greatest faith or the deepest love can prompt a woman to the voluntary sacrifice of her entire *chevelure,* though partial sacrifices, offerings of one or two long thick cuttings, may be seen suspended before many an Izumo shrine.

What faith can do in the way of such sacrifice, he best knows who has seen the great cables, woven of women's hair, that hang in the vast Hongwanji temple at Kyōto. And love is stronger than faith, though much less demonstrative. According to ancient custom a wife bereaved sacrifices a portion of her hair to be placed in the coffin of her husband, and buried with him. The quantity is not fixed: in the majority of cases it is very small, so that the appearance of the coiffure is thereby nowise affected. But she who resolves to remain forever loyal to the memory of the lost yields up all. With her own hand she cuts off her hair, and lays the whole glossy sacrifice— emblem of her youth and beauty—upon the knees of the dead.

It is never suffered to grow again.

1. Why is so much emphasis placed on women's hair?

2. What do the variations in the way different women wear their hair indicate?

3. What choice do women have in the way they wear their hair?

4. How do you think American women would have responded to Hearn's essay?

·138·

Fukuzawa Yukichi
On Japanese Women

(1885)

*F*ukuzawa Yukichi (1835–1901) was the most important social critic and educator of late imperial Japan. Though he came from a samurai family, it was not a prosperous one. He was the youngest child and his father died when he was only two. Fukuzawa was educated in Osaka, where he became fascinated with Dutch scientific works and Western culture in general. In the 1860s he traveled to the United States and Western Europe, and was struck by the differences in social customs and educational institutions. After returning to Japan, Fukuzawa founded a daily newspaper in Tokyo that helped introduce educated Japanese to Western ways. His attacks upon Japanese xenophobia helped change attitudes toward the West and ushered in an age of reform. He further disseminated his theories by founding a university and by writing and speaking tirelessly. He was one of the most controversial intellectuals of his day.

In 1885 Fukuzawa Yukichi published a series of essays on the status of women in Japan that were among the most radical of all of his writings. Adopting a viewpoint that was advanced even by Western standards, he challenged nearly every aspect of traditional Japanese gender relations. He had hoped to found a school for women in which he could put his ideas into practice, but his efforts were ultimately restricted to educating his five daughters.

Now, mixed marriages, the importing of new stocks of men and women from outside, should certainly be encouraged. This method I shall call the external aid method. Also, one must not neglect the self-aid method, too: that is, to improve the physique of the present Japanese men and women and thereby produce more perfect children. For this purpose, one can consider a number of ways. One of them is to rectify wrong customs concerning food and clothing; another is hygiene, or taking care of diseases and nourishment. Improvement in these important topics in eugenics will undoubtedly be effective.

Besides all these, there is one important topic which, in my opinion, is generally neglected by the whole of society, even by the upper and intellectual classes, which dismiss it lightly. Therefore, in this article, I propose to take this topic up exclusively without referring to the care of diseases and hygiene. The subject I am going to discuss concerns the intellectual and recreational activities of women, which I propose to encourage for the purpose of improving the physical condition of our women. The purpose of my discourse being solely on the improvement of the physical condition, when I discuss the pleasures, I shall at times be touching on the animal nature of human beings. My description may make us appear no different from beasts, and my words may seem dubious to the narrow-minded moralist. However, because the spiritual and the physical phenomena are perfectly distinct affairs, I pray earnestly that my readers will take in my argument without any undue misunderstanding.

My idea for the improvement of our race is to enliven our women's minds and encourage their physical vigor to grow with them, thus to obtain better health and physique for our posterity. In recent years in our country, there have been many discussions on women. But most of them have dwelt on the poor state of their education and their lack of good sense. Some have advocated making them read more or teaching them technical skills to improve their spiritual well-being or encouraged physical exercise for the improvement of their physical growth and the eventual stimulation of their minds, too. These are the common arguments of the advocates of the new civilization.

To me, these arguments are not sufficient to insure the true development of our women. Confucian education, the so-called *Greater Learning for Women* school of thought is simply out of the question, because the more one teaches it the more restricted women become. It is nothing but a philosophy to oppress the mind and, in the process, destroy the physical body too. I am not even satisfied with the so-called new education of civilized men. The reason is that even when women are taught to read and trained in other skills and given plenty of physical training, that education is confined to the school rooms. When they go home, they are treated as the daughters of the family, no different from the old times, and when they marry, they become traditional housewives.

All in all, men and women mold their lives out of the pains and pleasures of life. When their sufferings and pleasures are greater, their lives are that much more fulfilling. This leads to the idea that attempts to increase their sufferings and pleasures will result in heavier responsibilities. For instance, in politics and other worldly affairs, suppose there is a man whose every move influences national affairs, and another whose every utterance and action influences one village; the former person's responsibilities will be heavier than the latter's and his worries and satisfactions will be so much greater than the latter's.

The importance of responsibility being thus, let us examine the actual condition of women in Japan. They are given no responsibility at all. As in the saying "Women have no home of their own anywhere in the world," when she is born, she is brought up in the house which is her father's; when she is grown and married, she lives in a house which is her husband's; when she is old and is being cared for by her son, the house will be her son's. All the family property is her husband's property; women are only allowed to share in the benefits of that property. When the house is poor, the poverty is her husband's poverty; the wife simply follows her husband in the hardship.

It is natural that the work involving the raising and feeding of children falls to the wife, but too often it turns out that she is bringing up her husband's children and not her own. To give proof of this, during her pregnancy, if the husband prays for a male child, the wife too will pray for the same. This is nothing to be wondered at, but often because the husband wants a male child, the wife feels compelled to agree and suffers over it. In an extreme case, if a female baby comes, the husband is dissatisfied and the wife is embarrassed. When a male child comes, the husband praises his wife and he may even give her a present as an award for her performance. Whether the child is male or female is something determined by nature, and it is, after all, foolish to wish for either sex. But leaving that folly aside, what I wish to stress is that it is a true insult to one's consort to think of awarding her for bearing a male child. Through such an abominable act, the husband regards his wife as a mere instrument for producing children.

Women of our country have no responsibility either inside or outside their homes, and their position is very low. Consequently, their sufferings and pleasures are very small in scale. It has been the custom for hundreds and even thousands of years to make them as feeble as they are, and it is not an easy matter now to lead both their minds and bodies to activity and to vigorous health. There are animated discussions on the education of women. No doubt education will be effective. When taught, women will acquire knowledge and the arts. When the body is exercised, the body will develop. But those attempts will be nothing more than attacking limited areas in a life of confinement and feebleness. . . .

Disrespect for women is a common practice among all the nations of the East, and Japan alone should not be blamed. In neighboring China and Korea, particularly among the middle and upper classes, the women are confined like prisoners within their homes and they are not allowed out. The cruelty the women suffer there is even severer than that suffered by Japanese women. . . .

I by no means intend to advise Japanese women to copy the licentious ways of our neighboring countries. But I do long for the vigor and the freedom of the women of the West. However, looseness and arbitrariness are often unavoidable diseases which go with freedom and activity. I do not long for these diseases. In the West, women's behavior sometimes goes beyond control: they make light of men; their minds are sharp, but their thoughts may be tarnished and their personal behavior unchaste; they may neglect their own homes and flutter about society like butterflies. Such behavior is no model for Japanese women. To set women's force against men's rampancy is no more than brute force against brute force. If the scheme goes too well and women come out triumphant, the result will

be no more than one brute force exchanged for another. I offer no explanation here as my readers must have already appreciated my thoughts. In short, I am not demanding much of men nor any special advantage for women. What I aim at is simply equality between the sexes.

That freedom and pleasure ought to be common possessions of both men and women is a concept that cannot be refuted. When something in limited quantity belongs to two parties, if one party takes a larger share, the other party's share will decrease. This, too, is an irrefutable fact. In Japan today, who enjoys freedom and pleasure in greatest quantities? The answer is that men enjoy them in excessive proportions. As an illustration, let us examine the general customs of our society. There is practically nothing that women are allowed to do but that men cannot do. But there are many, truly countless, things that men are allowed but women not. From the right to possess property, as discussed previously, to all sorts of trivial everyday occurrences: behavior censured as overly forward in a woman is praised as nonchalant and masculine in men; things that are ugly for women are not ugly for men. While a man may play in the gay quarters and enjoy women and wine, his mate will be wasting her youth in the deep confines of a home and even her right to remarry is nullified.

All these are proof of the inequality of sexes. I am not advocating special privileges for women; I only seek to divide the happiness evenly so that both parties can share it evenly. For instance, if men monopolize 99 percent of the right to remarry while women have only 1 percent, I suggest the men give up 49 percent and make the shares even.

The basic purpose of my argument is not to side with women to contest their rights. My purpose is the improvement of the Japanese race. And because it will be impossible to expect women today to bring forth a posterity of better physique, our first necessity is to make our women more active mentally and physically. To make them more active, they must be given more responsibilities and more enjoyments. This is the general gist of my present discourse.

Without our mind, the human body is, after all, no more than an animal's. Suppose there is one male and one female dog, and the male dog is left free to play and roam about while the female dog is chained to a dog-house. Though she is given sufficient food, she is not allowed to play with other dogs or to run on the grass or to romp about on the snow. Furthermore, when the mating season comes, she is still tied to the dog-house with the least freedom. The result is an aggravation of her nerves and weakening of her body.

Suppose this female dog, after all these trials, happens to bear a pup—what kind of pup will it be? Even to me, a person entirely ignorant about the care of dogs, it is clear that the pup will not be a very healthy one. If it is so with a dog, why should it be any different with human beings? The leaders in the forefront of our social progress, if they cannot refute this illustration of the domestic dog, should quickly endeavor to unchain the women of Japan.

1. What role does Fukuzawa think formal education plays in defining gender roles? What does he think should define them?

2. How does he characterize the attitude of Japanese men toward their wives?

3. What does he see as the model for Japanese women? Is he entirely comfortable with it?

4. Why is Fukuzawa interested in seeing Japanese women liberated?

·139·

The Meiji Constitution

(1889)

*I*n 1868 centuries of decentralized rule in Japan were brought to a formal end by the restoration of imperial power under the Meiji emperor, Mutsuhito. It was under his aegis that a group of reformers began the process of modernizing Japan. Leading ministers were sent to the West to study political institutions and economic arrangements. They returned with new ideas and expertise that were to transform Japan into an industrial and commercial power in the East. Among the innovations that were brought from the West was the idea of a written constitution. Ito Hirobumi (1841–1909), prime minister from 1881, was placed in charge of a commission to produce a constitution. He was deeply impressed by the rise of Prussia and brought Herman Roesler (a German diplomat) to Japan to help draft a constitution along Prussian lines. It was promulgated by the emperor in 1889.

CHAPTER I: THE EMPEROR

Article I

The Empire of Japan shall be reigned over and governed by a line of Emperors unbroken for ages eternal.

Article II

The Imperial Throne shall be succeeded to by Imperial male descendants, according to the provisions of the Imperial House Law.

Article III

The Emperor is sacred and inviolable.

Article IV

The Emperor is the head of the Empire, combining in Himself the rights of sovereignty, and exercises them, according to the provisions of the present Constitutions.

Article V

The Emperor exercises the legislative power with the consent of the Imperial Diet.

Article VI

The Emperor gives sanction to laws and orders them to be promulgated and executed.

Article VII

The Emperor convokes the Imperial Diet, opens, closes, and prorogues it, and dissolves the House of Representatives.

Article VIII

The Emperor, in consequence of an urgent necessity to maintain public safety or to avert public calamities, issues, when the Imperial Diet is not sitting, Imperial Ordinances in the place of law.

Such Imperial Ordinances are to be laid before the Imperial Diet at its next session, and when the Diet does not approve the said Ordinances, the Government shall declare them to be invalid for the future.

Article X

The Emperor determines the organization of the different branches of the administration, and salaries of all civil and military officers, and appoints and dismisses the same. Exceptions especially provided for in the present Constitution or in other laws, shall be in accordance with the respective provisions (bearing thereon).

Article XI

The Emperor has the supreme command of the Army and Navy.

Article XII

The Emperor determines the organization and peace standing of the Army and Navy.

Article XIII

The Emperor declares war, makes peace, and concludes treaties.

Article XIV

The Emperor declares a state of siege. The conditions and effects of a state of siege shall be determined by law.

Article XV

The Emperor confers titles of nobility, rank, orders and other marks of honor.

Article XVI

The Emperor orders amnesty, pardon, commutation of punishments and rehabilitation.

CHAPTER II: RIGHTS AND DUTIES OF SUBJECTS

Article XVIII

The conditions necessary for being a Japanese subject shall be determined by law.

Article XIX

Japanese subjects may, according to qualifications determined in laws or Ordinances, be appointed to civil or military or any other public offices equally.

Article XX

Japanese subjects are amenable to service in the Army or Navy, according to the provisions of law.

Article XXI

Japanese subjects are amenable to the duty of paying taxes, according to the provisions of law.

Article XXII

Japanese subjects shall have the liberty of abode and of changing the same within the limits of the law.

Article XXIII

No Japanese subject shall be arrested, detained, tried or punished, unless according to law.

Article XXIV

No Japanese subject shall be deprived of his right of being tried by the judges determined by law.

Article XXV

Except in the cases provided for in the law, the house of no Japanese subject shall be entered or searched without his consent.

Article XXVI

Except in the cases mentioned in the law, the secrecy of the letters of every Japanese subject shall remain inviolate.

Article XXVII

The right of property of every Japanese subject shall remain inviolate.

Measures necessary to be taken for the public benefit shall be provided for by law.

Article XXVIII

Japanese subjects shall, within limits not prejudicial to peace and order, and not antagonistic to their duties as subjects, enjoy freedom of religious belief.

Article XXIX

Japanese subjects shall, within the limits of law, enjoy the liberty of speech, writing, publication, public meetings and associations.

Article XXX

Japanese subjects may present petitions, by observing the proper forms of respect, and by complying with the rules specially provided for the same.

Article XXXI

The provisions contained in the present Chapter shall not affect the exercises of the powers appertaining to the Emperor, in times of war or in cases of a national emergency.

CHAPTER III: THE IMPERIAL DIET

Article XXXIII

The Imperial Diet shall consist of two Houses, a House of Peers and a House of Representatives.

Article XXXIV

The House of Peers shall, in accordance with the Ordinance concerning the House of Peers, be composed of the members of the Imperial Family, of the orders of nobility, and of those who have been nominated thereto by the Emperor.

Article XXXV

The House of Representatives shall be composed of Members elected by the people, according to the provisions of the Law of Election.

Article XXXVI

No one can at one and the same time be a Member of both Houses.

Article XXXVII

Every law requires the consent of the Imperial Diet.

Article XXXVIII

Both Houses shall vote upon projects of law submitted to it by the Government, and may respectively initiate projects of law.

Article XL

Both Houses can make representations to the Government, as to laws or upon any other subject. When, however, such representations are not accepted, they cannot be made a second time during the same session.

Article XLI

The Imperial Diet shall be convoked every year.

Article XLII

A session of the Imperial Diet shall last during three months. In case of necessity, the duration of a session may be prolonged by the Imperial Order.

Article XLIII

When urgent necessity arises, an extraordinary session may be convoked in addition to the ordinary one. The duration of an extraordinary session shall be determined by Imperial Order.

Article XLV

When the House of Representatives has been ordered to dissolve, Members shall be caused by Imperial Order to be newly elected, and the new House shall be convoked within five months from the day of dissolution.

Article XLVII

Votes shall be taken in both Houses by absolute majority. In the case of a tie vote, the President shall have the casting vote.

Article XLVIII

The deliberations of both Houses shall be held in public. The deliberations may, however, upon demand of the Government or by resolution of the House, be held in secret sitting.

Article XLIX

Both Houses of the Imperial Diet may respectively present addresses to the Emperor.

Article LII

No Member of either House shall be held responsible outside the respective Houses, for any opinion uttered or for any vote given in the House. When, however, a Member himself has given publicity to his opinions by public speech, by documents in print or in writing, or by any other similar means, he shall, in the matter, be amenable to the general law.

Article LIII

The Members of both Houses shall, during the session, be free from arrest, unless with the consent of the House, except in cases of flagrant delicts, or of offenses connected with a state of internal commotion or with a foreign trouble.

Article LIV

The Ministers of State and the Delegates of the Government may, at any time, take seats and speak in either House.

CHAPTER VI: FINANCE

Article LXII

The imposition of a new tax or the modification of the rates (of an existing one) shall be determined by law.

However, all such administrative fees or other revenue having the nature of compensation shall not fall within the category of the above clause.

The raising of national loans and the contracting of other liabilities to the charge of the National Treasury, except those that are provided in the Budget, shall require the consent of the Imperial Diet.

Article LXIII

The taxes levied at present shall, in so far as they are not remodelled by a new law, be collected according to the old system.

Article LXIV

The expenditure and revenue of the State require the consent of the Imperial Diet by means of an annual Budget.

Any and all expenditures overpassing the appropriations set forth in the Titles and Paragraphs of the Budget, or that are not provided for in the Budget, shall subsequently require the approbation of the Imperial Diet.

Article LXV

The Budget shall be first laid before the House of Representatives.

Article LXVI

The expenditures of the Imperial House shall be defrayed every year out of the National Treasury, according to the present fixed amount for the same, and shall not require the consent thereto of the Imperial Diet, except in case an increase thereof is found necessary.

Article LXVII

Those already fixed expenditures based by the Constitution upon the powers appertaining to the Emperor, and such expenditures as may have arisen by the effect of law, or that appertain to the legal obligations of the Government, shall be neither rejected nor reduced by the Imperial Diet, without the concurrence of the Government.

Article LXXI

When the Imperial Diet has not voted on the Budget, or when the Budget has not been brought into actual existence, the Government shall carry out the Budget of the preceding year.

1.   Characterize the power of the emperor under the Constitution.

2.   What is the role of the Diet? How much power does it have?

3. Why is it significant that the expenditures of the imperial house do not require the consent of the Diet?

4. What would it have been like to be a subject under the Meiji Constitution?

·140·

Sun Yat-sen
Fundamentals of National Reconstruction
(1923)

*S*un Yat-sen (1866–1925) began life as the son of poor farmers, yet became father of modern China. A younger son, he was brought to Hawaii by an older brother who had immigrated there as a laborer. Sun studied at a missionary school and ultimately earned a medical degree in Hong Kong. His years in the West induced in him a dissatisfaction with the government of China and he began his political career by attempting to organize reform groups of Chinese exiles in Hong Kong. In 1895 a coup he plotted failed, and for the next 16 years Sun was an exile in Europe, the United States, and Japan. In Japan he joined dissident Chinese groups and soon became their leader. He was expelled from Japan and was in America when he learned of the successful rebellion against the Ching emperor. Sun immediately returned to China, headed the revolutionary movement for a time, and then went back into exile until 1923, when he finally emerged as president of China. He died two years later, having founded the Koumintang (Nationalist Party).

Fundamentals of National Reconstruction is Sun Yat-sen's most important political statement. It enunciates his famous three principles whereby he set China on the road to modernity.

HISTORY OF THE CHINESE REVOLUTION

Following China's war with France (1883–1884) I made up my mind to devote myself to the revolution. In 1895 I started the first insurrection in Canton and the revolution of 1911 culminated in the establishment of the Republic. Up to the present the task of revolution, however, has not

Sun Yat-sen, the father of modern China.

yet been completed. A span of thirty-seven years of my revolutionary work is to be chronicled by future historians from all manner of facts and incidents. An outline sketch is given below.

I. Principles of Revolution

The term *Kemin*, or revolution, was first used by Confucius. Incidents of a revolutionary nature repeatedly happened in Chinese history after Tang (founder of the Shang Dynasty, B.C. 1766) and Wu (founder of the Chou Dynasty, B.C. 1122). In Europe revolutionary tides surged in the seventeenth and eighteenth centuries and they have since spread over the whole world. In due course they created republics, they conferred constitutions on monarchies. The principles which I have held in promoting the Chinese

revolution were in some cases copied from our traditional ideals, in other cases modelled on European theory and experience and in still others formulated according to original and self-developed theories. They are described as follows:—

1. *Principle of Nationalism.* Revelations of Chinese history prove that the Chinese as a people are independent in spirit and in conduct. Coerced into touch with other peoples, they could at times live in peace with them by maintaining friendly relations and at others assimilate them as the result of propinquity. During the periods when their political and military prowess declined, they could not escape for the time from the fate of a conquered nation, but they could eventually vigorously reassert themselves. Thus the Mongol rule of China (A.D. 1260–1333), lasting for nearly a hundred years, was finally overthrown by Tai Tsu of the Ming Dynasty and his loyal followers. So in our own time was the Manchu yoke thrown off by the Chinese. Nationalistic ideas in China did not come from a foreign source; they were inherited from our remote forefathers. Upon this legacy is based my principle of nationalism, and where necessary, I have developed it, amplified it and improved upon it. No vengeance has been inflicted on the Manchus and we have endeavored to live side by side with them on an equal footing. This is the nationalistic policy toward the races within our national boundaries. Externally, we should strive to maintain independence in the family of nations, and to spread our indigenous civilization as well as to enrich it by absorbing what is best in world civilization, with the hope that we may forge ahead with other nations toward the goal of ideal brotherhood.

2. *Principle of Democracy.* In ancient China we had Emperor Yao (B.C. 2357–2258) and Emperor Shun (B.C. 2258–2206) who departed from the hereditary system and chose their successors. We also had Tang and Wu who overthrew kingdoms by revolution. Preserved in our books are such sayings as "Heaven sees as the

people see; Heaven hears as the people hear." "We have heard of a person named Chou having been slain, we have not heard of a monarch having been murdered." "The people are most important, while the king is of the least importance." All these sayings ring with democratic sentiments. Since we have had only ideas about popular rights, and no democratic system has been evolved, we have to go to Europe and America for a republican form of government. There some countries have become republics and others have adopted constitutional monarchism, under which royal power has shrunk in the face of the rising demand for popular rights. Though hereditary monarchs have not yet disappeared, they are but vestiges and shadows of their former selves.

All through my revolutionary career I have held the view that China must be made a republic. There are three reasons. First, from a theoretical point of view, there is no ground for preserving a monarchical form of government, since it is widely recognized that the people constitute the foundation of a nation and they are all equal in their own country. In the second place, under Manchu occupation the Chinese people were forced into the position of the vanquished, and suffered oppression for more than two hundred and sixty years. While a constitutional monarchy may not arouse deep resentment in other countries and can maintain itself for the time being, it will be an impossibility in China. This is from a historical point of view. A third reason may be advanced with an eye on the future of the nation. That in China prolonged period of disorder usually followed a revolution was due to the desire of every insurgent to be a king and to his subsequent contention for the throne. If a republican government is adopted, there will be no contention. For these three reasons, I have decided for the republican form of government in order to realize the principle of democracy.

My second decision is that a constitution must be adopted to ensure good government. The true meaning of constitutionalism was dis-

covered by Montesquieu. The threefold separation of the legislative, judicial, and executive powers as advocated by him was accepted in every constitutional country in Europe. On a tour of Europe and America I made a close study of their governments and laws and took note of their shortcomings as well as their advantages. The shortcomings of election, for instance, are not incurable. In the past China had two significant systems of examination and censoring and they can be of avail where the Western system of government and law falls short. I therefore advocate that the examinative and censorial powers should be placed on the same level with legislative, judicial and executive, thereby resulting in the fivefold separation of powers. On top of that, the system if the people's direct political powers should be adopted in order that the provision that the sovereign power is vested in the people may become a reality. In this way my principle of democracy may be carried out satisfactorily.

3. *Principle of Livelihood*. With the invention of modern machines, the phenomenon of uneven distribution of wealth in the West has become all the more marked. Intensified by cross-currents, economic revolution was flaring up more ferociously than political revolution. This situation was scarcely noticed by our fellow-countrymen thirty years ago. On my tour of Europe and America, I saw with my own eyes the instability of their economic structure and the deep concern of their leaders in groping for a solution. I felt that, although the disparity of wealth under our economic organization is not so great as in the West, the difference is only in degree, not in character. The situation will become more acute when the West extends its economic influence to China. We must form plans beforehand in order to cope with the situation. After comparing various schools of economic thought, I have come to the realization that the principle of state ownership is most profound, reliable and practical. Moreover, it will forestall in China difficulties which have already caused much anxiety in the West. I have therefore decided to enforce the principle of the peo-

ple's livelihood simultaneously with the principles of nationalism and democracy, with the hope to achieve our political objective and nip economic unrest in the bud.

To sum up, my revolutionary principles in a nutshell consist in the Three Principles of the People and the Five-Power Constitution. Those who have a clear knowledge of the general tendency of the world and the conditions in China will agree that my views are practical and must be put in practice.

II. Fundamentals of Revolution

In the age of autocracy, the masses of the people were fettered in spirit and body so that emancipation seemed impossible. Those who worked for the welfare of the people and were willing to sacrifice themselves for the success of revolution not only did not receive assistance from the people but were also ridiculed and disparaged. Much as they desired to be the guides of the people, they proceeded without followers. Much as they desired to be the vanguards, they advanced without reinforcement. It becomes necessary that, apart from destroying enemy influence, those engaged in revolution should take care to develop the constructive ability of the people. A revolutionary program is therefore indispensable.

According to my plan, the progress of our revolution should be regulated and divided into three stages: First, military rule; second, political tutelage; third, constitutional government. The first stage is a period of destruction, during which military rule is installed. The revolutionary army is to break down (as it did) Manchu despotism, sweep away official corruptions, and reform vicious customs.

The second stage is a transitional period, during which a provisional constitution (not the present one) will be promulgated. Its object is to build a local self-government system for the development of democracy. The *hsien* or district will be a unit of self-government. When disbanded troops are disposed of and fighting ceases,

every district should accept the provisional constitution, which will regulate the rights and duties of the people and the administrative powers of the revolutionary government. It will be in force for three years, at the end of which period the people will choose their district magistrates. Even before the expiration of the period, the people in a district may be empowered to choose their own magistrate and become a complete self-governing body on the following conditions: That the self-government bureau of the said district has already cleaned the district of its long standing corruptions; that it has succeeded in getting more than half of its population to understand the Three Principles of the People and devote themselves to the republic; that it has fulfilled the minimum requirements of the provisional constitution in regard to census-taking, residence registration, police, health, education and road-building. In reference to the self-government body, the revolutionary government may exercise the power of political tutelage only in accordance with the provisional constitution. Six years after the whole nation is restored to peace and order, each district which has attained complete self-government may elect one delegate, and these delegates will form the People's Congress to adopt the five-power constitution.

The central government will have five *yuan* or boards. The five *yuan* will be (1) The Executive Yuan, (2) The Legislative Yuan, (3) The Judicial Yuan, (4) The Examination Yuan, and (5) The Censor Yuan. Following the promulgation of the constitution, citizens of the various districts will elect the President by vote for the formation of the Executive Yuan, and elect representatives for the formation of the Legislative Yuan. The heads of the three other *yuan* will be appointed by the President with the consent of the Legislative Yuan, but they will not be responsible to the President and the Legislative Yuan. All the five *yuan* will be responsible to the People's Congress. Members of a *yuan*, in case of failure to discharge their duties, may be impeached before the People's Congress by the Censor Yuan. In case the members of the Censor Yuan fail in their duties, the Congress will directly impeach them and remove them. The duty of the Congress is solely to attend to the amendment of the constitution and the punishment of public servants. The qualification of the employees in the Congress and the five *yuan* as well as the high and junior officials of the whole nation will be determined by the Examination Yuan. Following the adoption of the five-power constitution and the election of the President and representatives, the revolutionary government will be turned over to the President elected by the people, whereupon the period of political tutelage will terminate.

The third stage, which marks the completion of national reconstruction, will usher in constitutional government. During this period the self-governing bodies in the various districts should exercise the direct political powers of the people. In district political affairs citizens should have the rights of universal suffrage, initiative, referendum and recall. In national political affairs they should, while directly exercising the right of election, delegate the three other rights to their representatives in the People's Congress. This period of constitutional government marks the completion of national reconstruction and the successful conclusion of the revolution.

If we can proceed according to the revolutionary fundamentals that have been briefly outlined, not only can we clean the Augean stable of autocracy and carry out the rights of the people, but we can also strengthen and safeguard the constructive power of the people against the manipulations of politicians and the unscrupulousness of militarists. It becomes obvious that the principles of revolution must depend upon the fundamentals of revolution for a thorough realization.

1. Why did Sun Yat-sen write his *Fundamentals of National Reconstruction*?

2. What did Sun Yat-sen learn from his time in Europe and the United States?

3. What does the author hope to achieve through revolution?

4. What does Sun Yat-sen mean by his three fundamental principles of nationalism, democracy, and livelihood?

The Soviet Union

Soviet troops parading through Red Square in the annual May Day ceremony, 1951. In the background are the walls of the Kremlin and the Spasskaya Tower.

·141·
Alexandra Kollontai
Theses on Communist Morality in the Sphere of Marital Relations
(1921)

Alexandra Kollontai (1872–1952) was the daughter of a tsarist general. Her father's lineage was of the ancient Russian nobility and even included a saint. Kollontai's youth was spent amid the glitter and splendor of country houses and palaces. Her first act of rebellion was to marry against her family's wishes; the next was to become a supporter of the Marxist worker's movement in Narva, near her home. She took up socialist causes and in 1908 fled to Germany to avoid arrest. She then became active in the international women's socialist movement and attended a number of conventions in Germany and Britain. In 1915, under the influence of Lenin, she joined the Bolshevik party. She returned to Russia to take part in the revolution and became a leader of the women's branch of the Communist party. She was subsequently assigned to the diplomatic corps and spent much of the rest of her life in Soviet embassies in Scandinavia.

Most of Kollontai's writings deal with women's issues on the personal, theoretical, and political planes. In *The Autobiography of a Sexually Emancipated Communist Woman,* her matter-of-fact discussion of the intimate details of sexual life was unusual and unsettling for her time. She was credited with the statement that sexual relations should be as uncomplicated as drinking a glass of water. These selections from a characteristic essay show the political dimension of her views on family life.

Family and marriage are historical categories, phenomena which develop in accordance with the economic relations that exist at the given level of production. The form of marriage and of the family is thus determined by the economic system of the given epoch, and it changes as the economic base of society changes. The family, in the same way as government, religion, science, morals, law and customs, is part of the superstructure which derives from the economic system of society.

Where economic functions are performed by the family rather than by society as a whole, family and marital relations are more stable and possess a vital capacity: "The less the development of labour, and the more limited its volume of production . . . the more preponderantly does the social order appear to be dominated by ties of sex" (Engels, *Origins of the Family*). In the period of natural economy the family formed an enclosed economic unit which was necessary for humankind and thus had a vital capacity. The family was at the time a unit of both production and consumption. Outside the family/economic unit the individual had no means, especially at the earliest levels of the development of society, of sustaining the conditions necessary for life. In some areas and in some countries where capitalism is weakly developed (among the peoples of the East, for example) the peasant family is still fundamentally, a family/economic union. With the transition, however, from a natural economy to a merchant capitalist economy based on trade and exchange, the family ceases to be necessary for the functioning of society and thus loses its strength and vital capacity.

The fact that with the consolidation of the capitalist system of production, the marital/family union develops from a production unit into a legal arrangement concerned only with consumption, leads inevitably to the weakening of marital/family ties. In the era of private property and the bourgeois-capitalist economic system, marriage and the family are grounded in (a) material and financial considerations, (b) economic dependence of the female sex on the family breadwinner—the husband—rather than the social collective, and (c) the need to care for the rising generation. Capitalism maintains a system of individual economies; the family has a role to play in performing economic tasks and functions within the national capitalist economy. Thus under capitalism the family does not merge with or dissolve into the national economy but continues to exist as an independent economic unit, concerned with production in the case of the peasant family and consumption in the case of the urban family. The individual economy which springs from private property is the basis of the bourgeois family.

The communist economy does away with the family. In the period of the dictatorship of the proletariat there is a transition to the single production plan and collective social consumption, and the family loses it significance as an economic unit. The external economic functions of the family disappear, and consumption ceases to be organised on an individual family basis; a network of social kitchens and canteens is established, and the making, mending and washing of clothes and other aspects of housework are integrated into the national economy. In the period of the dictatorship of the proletariat the family

economic unit should be recognised as being, from the point of view of the national economy, not only useless but harmful. The family economic unit involves (a) the uneconomic expenditure of products and fuel on the part of small domestic economies, and (b) unproductive labour, especially by women, in the home—and is therefore in conflict with the interest of the workers' republic in a single economic plan and the expedient use of the labour force (including women).

Under the dictatorship of the proletariat then, the material and economic considerations in which the family was grounded cease to exist. The economic dependence of women on men and the role of the family in the care of the younger generation also disappear, as the communist elements in the workers' republic grow stronger. With the introduction of the obligation of all citizens to work, woman has a value in the national economy which is independent of her family and marital status. The economic subjugation of women in marriage and the family is done away with, and responsibility for the care of the children and their physical and spiritual education is assumed by the social collective. The family teaches and instills egoism, thus weakening the ties of collective and hindering the construction of communism. However, in the new society relations between parents and children are freed from any element of material considerations and enter a new historic stage.

Once the family has been stripped of its economic functions and its responsibilities towards the younger generation and is no longer central to the existence of the woman, it has ceased to be a family. The family unit shrinks to a union of two people based on mutual agreement.

In the period of the dictatorship of the proletariat, the workers' state has to concern itself not with the economic and social unit of the family, since this unit dies as the bonds of communism are consolidated, but with the changing forms of marital relations. The family as an economic unit and as a union of parents and children based on the need to provide for the material welfare of the latter is doomed to disappear.

Thus the workers' collective has to establish its attitude not to economic relationships but to the form of relationships between the sexes. What kind of relations between the sexes are in the best interests of the workers' collective? What form of relations would strengthen, not weaken, the collective in the transitional stage between capitalism and communism and would thus assist the construction of the new society? The laws and the morality that the workers' system is evolving are beginning to give an answer to this question.

Once relations between the sexes cease to perform the economic and social function of the former family, they are no longer the concern of the workers' collective. It is not the relationships between the sexes but the result—the child—that concerns the collective. The workers' state recognises its responsibility to provide for maternity, *i.e.,* to guarantee the well-being of the woman and the child, but it does not recognise the couple as a legal unit separate from the workers' collective. The decrees on marriage issued by the workers' republic establishing the mutual rights of the married couple (the right to demand material support from the partner for yourself or the child), and thus giving legal encouragement to the separation of this unit and its interests from the general interests of the workers' social collective (the right of wives to be transferred to town or village where their husbands are working), are survivals of the past; they contradict the interests of the collective and weaken its bonds, and should therefore be reviewed and changed.

The law ought to emphasise the interest of the workers' collective in maternity and eliminate the situation where the child is dependent on the relationship between its parents. The law of the workers' collective replaces the right of the parents, and the workers' collective keeps a close watch, in the interests of the unified economy and of present and future labour resources. In the period of the dictatorship of the proletariat there must, instead of marriage law, be regulation of the relationship of the government to maternity, of the relationship between mother

and child and of the relationship between the mother and the workers' collective (i.e. legal norms must regulate the protection of female labour, the welfare of expectant and nursing mothers, the welfare of children and their social education). Legal norms must regulate the relationship between the mother and the socially educated child, and between the father and the child. Fatherhood should not be established through marriage or a relationship of a material nature. The man should be able to choose whether or not to accept the role of fatherhood (i.e. the right which he shares equally with the mother to decide on a social system of education for the child, and the right, where this does not conflict with the interests of the collective, of intellectual contact with the child and the opportunity to influence its development).

There are two grounds on which, in the interests of the workers' collective, the relationships between the sexes ought to be subject to legislative regulations: (a) the health and hygiene of the nation and the race, and (b) the increase or decrease of the population required by the national economic collective. In the period of the dictatorship of the proletariat, the regulation of relationships enters a new phase. Instead of laws and the threat of legal proceedings, the workers' collective must rely on agitational and educational influences, and on social measures to improve the relationships between the sexes and to guarantee the health of the children born from these relationships. For example, the Commissariats of Health and Education must carry out a broad campaign on the question of venereal and other infectious diseases, thereby reducing the danger of these diseases spreading through sexual intercourse and daily living. A person is guilty before the law not for having had sexual relations but for having consciously kept silent and hidden the fact that he or she has the disease from those with whom he or she lives and works, and thus for failing to observe the rule on precautions to be taken to reduce the likelihood of infection.

In the period of the dictatorship of the proletariat, communist morality—and not the law—

regulates sexual relationships in the interest of the workers' collective and of future generations.

Each historical (and therefore economic) epoch in the development of society has its own ideal of marriage and its own sexual morality. Under the tribal system, with its ties of kinship, the morality was different from that which developed with the establishment of private property and the rule of the husband and father (patriarchy). Different economic systems have different moral codes. Not only each stage in the development of society, but each class has its corresponding sexual morality (it is sufficient to compare the morals of the feudal landowning class and of the bourgeoisie in one and the same epoch to see that this is true). The more firmly established the principles of private property, the stricter the moral code. The importance of virginity before legal marriage sprang from the principles of private property and the unwillingness of men to pay for the children of others.

Hypocrisy (the outward observance of decorum and the actual practice of depravity), and the double code (one code of behavior for the man and another for the woman) are the twin pillars of bourgeois morality. Communist morality must, above all, resolutely spurn all the hypocrisy inherited from bourgeois society in relationships between the sexes, and reject the double standard of morality.

In the period of the dictatorship of the proletariat, relations between the sexes should be evaluated only according to the criteria mentioned above—the health of the working population and the development of inner bonds of solidarity within the collective. The sexual act must be seen not as something shameful and sinful but as something which is as natural as the other needs of healthy organism, such as hunger and thirst. Such phenomena cannot be judged as moral or immoral. The satisfaction of healthy and natural instincts only ceases to be normal when the boundaries of hygiene are overstepped. In such cases, not only the health of the person concerned but the interests of the work collective, which needs the strength and energy and health of its members, are threatened. Communist morality, therefore, while openly recognising the normality of sexual interests, condemns unhealthy and unnatural interest in sex (excesses, for example, or sexual relations before maturity has been reached, which exhaust the organism and lower the capacity of men and women for work).

As communist morality is concerned for the health of the population, it also criticises sexual restraint. The preservation of health includes the full and correct satisfaction of all man's needs; norms of hygiene should work to this end, and not artificially suppress such an important function of the organism as the sex drive (Bebel, *Woman and Socialism*). Thus both early sexual experience (before the body has developed and grown strong) and sexual restraint must be seen as equally harmful. This concern for the health of the human race does not establish either monogamy or polygamy as the obligatory form of relations between the sexes, for excesses may be committed in the bounds of the former, and a frequent change of partners by no means signifies sexual intemperance. Science has discovered that when a woman has relationships with many men at one time, her ability to have children is impaired; and relationships with a number of women drain the man and affect the health of his children negatively. Since the workers' collective needs strong and healthy men and women, such arrangements of sexual life are not in its interests.

It is accepted that the psychological state of parents at the moment of conception influences the health and life capacity of the child. Thus in the interests of human health, communist morality criticises sexual relations which are based on physical attraction alone and are not attended by love or fleeting passion. In the interests of the collective, communist morality also criticises persons whose sexual relationships are built not on physical attraction but on calculation, habit or even intellectual affinity.

In view of the need to encourage the development and growth of feelings of solidarity and to strengthen the bonds of the work collective, it should above all be established that the isolation of the "couple" as a special unit does not answer the interests of communism. Communist morality requires the education of the working class in comradeship and the fusion of the hearts and minds of the separate members of this collective. The needs and interests of the individual must be subordinated to the interests and aims of the collective. On the one hand, therefore, the bonds of family and marriage must be weakened, and on the other, men and women need to be educated in solidarity and the subordination of the will of the individual to the will of the collective. Even at this present, early stage, the workers' republic demands that mothers learn to be the mothers not only of their own child but of all workers' children; it does not recognise the couple as a self-sufficient unit, and does not therefore approve of wives deserting work for the sake of this unit.

As regards sexual relations, communist morality demands first of all an end to all relations based on financial or other economic considerations. The buying and selling of caresses destroys the sense of equality between the sexes, and thus undermines the basis of solidarity without which communist society cannot exist. Moral censure is consequently directed at prostitution in all its forms and at all types of marriage of convenience, even when recognised by Soviet law. The preservation of marriage regulations creates the illusion that the workers' collective can accept the "couple" with its special, exclusive interests. The stronger the ties between the members of the collective as a whole, the less the need to reinforce marital relations. Secondly, communist morality demands the education of the younger generation in responsibility to the collective and in the consciousness that love is not the only thing in life (this is especially important in the case of women, for they have been taught the opposite for centuries). Love is only one aspect of life, and must not be allowed to overshadow the other facets of the relationships between individual and collective. The ideal of the bourgeoisie was the married couple, where the partners complemented each other so com-

pletely that they had no need of contact with society. Communist morality demands, on the contrary, that the younger generation be educated in such a way that the personality of the individual is developed to the full, and the individual with his or her many interests has contact with a range of persons of both sexes. Communist morality encourages the development of many and varied bonds of love and friendship among people. The old ideal was "all for the loved one"; communist morality demands all for the collective.

Though sex love is seen in the context of the interests of the collective, communist morality demands that people are educated in sensitivity and understanding and are psychologically demanding both to themselves and to their partners. The bourgeois attitude to sexual relations as simply a matter of sex must be criticised and replaced by an understanding of the whole gamut of joyful love-experience that enriches life and makes for greater happiness. The greater the intellectual and emotional development of the individual the less place will there be in his or her relationship for the bare physiological side of love, and the brighter will be the love experience.

In the transitional period, relations between men and women must, in order to meet the interests of the workers' collective, be based on the following considerations. (1) All sexual relationships must be based on mutual inclination, love, infatuation or passion, and in no case on financial or material motivations. All calculation in relationships must be subject to merciless condemnation. (2) The form and length of the relationship are not regulated, but the hygiene of the race and communist morality require that relationships be based not on the sexual act alone, and that it should not be accompanied by any excesses that threaten health. (3) Those with illnesses etc. that might be inherited should not have children. (4) A jealous and proprietary attitude to the person loved must be replaced by a comradely understanding of the other and an acceptance of his or her freedom. Jealousy is a destructive force of which communist morality cannot approve. (5) The bonds between the members of the collective must be strengthened. The encouragement of the intellectual and political interests of the younger generation assists the development of healthy and bright emotions in love.

The stronger the collective, the more firmly established becomes the communist way of life. The closer the emotional ties between the members of the community, the less the need to seek a refuge from loneliness in marriage. Under communism the blind strength of matter is subjugated to the will of the strongly welded and thus unprecedentedly powerful workers' collective. The individual has the opportunity to develop intellectually and emotionally as never before. In this collective, new forms of relationships are maturing and the concept of love is extended and expanded.

1. How does the economy affect family organization?

2. Why will there be no families under communism? Why is the family harmful, in Kollontai's view?

3. How will children be raised in a true Communist society? What will be the responsibilities of parents?

4. What is Communist morality? How does it differ from bourgeois morality?

5. What is the role of emotion in Communist morality?

·142·

Alexander Solzhenitsyn
One Day in the Life of Ivan Denisovich
(1962)

Alexander Solzhenitsyn (b. 1918) is one of the most celebrated victims of Stalin's regime. A member of a family of intellectuals, Solzhenitsyn took a degree in mathematics just before the outbreak of World War II. He served in the Red Army and rose to the rank of captain of artillery. In 1945, however, he criticized Stalin and was sentenced to life imprisonment in Siberia, where he spent 11 years before being released upon Stalin's death. Solzhenitsyn then began the teaching career that he had planned as a student, and started to write. *One Day in the Life of Ivan Denisovich* was published at a time of liberalization in the Soviet Union and was an immediate international success. But, when Soviet policy changed, Solzhenitsyn was barred from any further publication. A number of his novels were smuggled to the West where they were published to critical acclaim. In 1970 Solzhenitsyn was awarded the Nobel Prize for literature. In 1973 he was accused of treason and exiled. He currently lives in Vermont.

One Day in the Life of Ivan Denisovich is a realistic depiction of life in the Siberian labor camps, a theme that dominates many of Solzhenitsyn's major works. He is interested in the ways in which his characters are able to maintain their dignity and humanity when faced with nearly unendurable conditions of deprivation.

Outside the moon shone brighter than ever. The lamps seemed to be paler now. The barracks cast deep shadows. The door to the mess hall lay beyond a broad porch with four steps. Now the porch too lay in shadows. But above it a small lamp was swaying, and creaking dismally in the cold. The light it cast was rainbow-hued, from the frost maybe, or the dirt on the glass.

The camp commandant had issued yet another strict order: the squads were to enter the mess hall in double file. To this he added: on reaching the steps they were to stay there and not climb onto the porch; they were to form up in fives and remain standing until the mess orderly gave them the go-ahead.

The post of mess orderly was firmly held by "the Limper." Because of his lameness he'd managed to get classed as disabled, but he was a hefty son-of-a-bitch. He'd got himself a birch club, and standing on the porch would hit anyone who came up the steps without his say-so. No, not anyone. He was smart, and could tell, even in the dark, when it was better to let a man alone—anyone who might give him as good as he got. He hit the down-and-outs. Once he hit Shukhov.

He was called an orderly. But, looking closer into it, he was a real prince—he palled around with the cooks.

Today all the squads may have turned up together or there may have been delay in getting things in order, but there was quite a crowd on the porch. Among them was the Limper, with his assistant. The mess chief himself was there too. They were handling the crowd without guards—the bruisers.

The mess chief was a fat pig with a head like a pumpkin and a broad pair of shoulders. He was bursting with energy and when he walked he seemed nothing but a lot of jerks, with springs for arms and legs. He wore a white lambskin hat without a number on it, finer than any civilian's. And his waistcoat was lambskin to match, with a number on it, true, but hardly bigger than a postage stamp. He bore no number at all on his back. He respected no one and all the zeks were afraid of him. He held the lives of thousands in his hands. Once they'd tried to beat him up but all the cooks—a prize bunch of thugs they were—had leaped to his defense.

Shukhov would be in hot water if the 104th had already gone in. The Limper knew everyone by sight and, with his chief present, wouldn't think of letting a man in with the wrong squad; he'd make a point of putting the finger on him.

Prisoners had been known to slip in behind the Limper's back by climbing over the porch railings. Shukhov had done it too. But tonight, under the chief's very nose, that was out of the question—he'd bust you so bad that you'd only just manage to drag yourself off to the doctor.

Get along to the porch and see whether, among all those identical black coats, the 104th was still there.

He got there just as the men began shoving (what could they do? it would soon be time to turn in) as though they were storming a stronghold—the first step, the second, the third, the fourth. Got there! They poured onto the porch.

"Stop, you fuckers," the Limper shouted and raised his stick at the men in front. "Get back or I'll bash your heads in."

"Form fives, blockheads," he shouted. "How many times have I told you I'll let you in when I'm ready?"

"Twenty-seventh," the Limper called, "go ahead."

The 27th bounded up and made a dash for the door, and the rest surged after them. Shukhov, among them, was shoving with all his might. The porch quivered, and the lamp overhead protested shrilly.

"What again, you shits?" the Limper shouted in rage. Down came his stick, on a shoulder, on a back, pushing the men off, toppling one after another.

Again he cleared the steps.

From below Shukhov saw Pavlo at the Limper's side. It was he who led the squad to the mess hall—Tiurin wouldn't lower himself by joining in the hullabaloo.

"Form fives, hundred and fourth," Pavlo called from the porch. "Make way for them, friends."

Friends—just see them making way, fuck 'em.

"Let me through, you in front. That's my squad," Shukhov grunted, shoving against a back.

The man would gladly have done so but others were squeezing him from every side.

The crowd heaved, pushing away so that no one could breathe. To get its stew. Its lawful stew.

Shukhov tried something else. He grasped the porch rail on his left, got his arms around a pillar, and heaved himself up. He kicked someone's knee and caught a blow in the ribs; a few curses, but he was through. He planted a foot on the edge of the porch floor, close to the top step, and waited. Some of his pals who were already there give him a hand.

The mess chief walked to the door and looked back.

"Come on, Limper, send in two more squads."

"One hundred and fourth," shouted the Limper. "Where d'you think *you're* crawling, shit?"

He slammed a man from another squad on the back of the neck with his stick.

"One hundred and fourth," shouted Pavlo, leading in his men.

"Whew!" gasped Shukhov in the mess hall. And, without waiting for Pavlo's instructions, he started looking for free trays.

The mess hall seemed as usual, with clouds of steam curling in through the door and the men sitting shoulder to shoulder—like seeds in a sunflower. Others pushed their way through the tables, and others were carrying loaded trays. Shukhov had grown used to it all over the years and his sharp eyes had noticed that S 208 had only five bowls on the tray he was carrying. This meant that it was the last tray-load for his squad. Otherwise the tray would have been full.

He went up to the man and whispered in his ear: "After you with that tray."

"Someone's waiting for it at the counter. I promised. . . ."

"Let him wait, the lazy bastard."

They came to an understanding.

S 208 carried his tray to the table and unloaded the bowls. Shukhov immediately grabbed it. At that moment the man it had been promised to ran up and tried to grab it. But he was punier than Shukhov. Shukhov shoved him off with the tray—what the hell are you pulling for?—and threw him against a post. Then putting the tray under his arm, he trotted off to the serving window.

Pavlo was standing in the line there, worried because there was no empty tray. He was delighted to see Shukhov. He pushed the man ahead of him out of the way: "Why are you standing here? Can't you see I've got a tray?"

Look, there was Gopchik—with another tray.

"They were arguing," he said with a laugh, "and I grabbed it."

Gopchik will do well. Give him another three years—he has still to grow up—and he'll become nothing less than a breadcutter. He's fated for it.

Pavlo told him to hand over the second of the trays to Yermolayev, a hefty Siberian who was serving a ten-year stretch, like Shukhov, for being caught by the Germans; then sent him to keep an eye on any table where the men might be finishing. Shukhov put his tray down and waited.

"One hundred and fourth," announced Pavlo at the counter.

In all there were five of these counters: three for serving regular food, one for zeks on special diets (ulcer victims, and bookkeeping personnel, as a favor), and one for the return of dirty dishes (that's where the dish-lickers gathered, sparring with one another). The counters were low—about waist level. The cooks themselves were out of sight; only their hands, and the ladles, could be seen.

The cook's hands were white and well cared for, but huge and hairy: a boxer's hands, not a cook's. He took a pencil and made a note on the wall—he kept his list there.

The cook took an enormous ladle and stirred, stirred, stirred. The soup kettle had just been refilled, almost up to the brim, and steam poured from it. Replacing the huge ladle with a smaller one he began serving the stew in twenty-ounce portions. He didn't go deep.

"One, two, three, four. . . ."

Some of the bowls had been filled while the stuff from the bottom of the kettle hadn't yet settled after the stirring, and some were duds—nothing but soup. Shukhov made a mental note of which was which. He put ten bowls on his tray and carried them off. Gopchik waved from the second row of posts.

"Over here, Ivan Denisovich, over here."

No horsing around with bowls of stew. Shukhov was careful not to stumble. He kept his throat busy too.

"Hey you, H 920. Gently, uncle. Out of the way, my boy."

It was hard enough, in a crowd like this, to carry a single bowl without slopping it. He was carrying ten. Just the same, he put the tray down safely, on the end of the table that Gopchik had cleared. No splashes. He managed, too, to maneuver the tray so that the two bowls with the thickest stew were just opposite the place he was about to sit down in.

Yermolayev brought another ten bowls. Gopchik ran off and came back with Pavlo, the last four in their hands.

Kilgas brought the bread tray. Tonight they were being fed in accordance with the work they had done. Some got six ounces, some nine, and Shukhov twelve. He took a piece with a crust for himself, and six ounces from the middle of the loaf for Tsezar.

Now from all over the mess hall Shukhov's squad began streaming up, to collect their supper and eat it where they could. As he handed out the bowls, there were two things he had to take care of: he had to remember whom he'd served, and he had to watch out for the tray—and for his own corner of it. (He put his spoon into a bowl—one of the "thick" ones. Reserved, that meant.) Fetiukov was among the first to arrive. But he soon walked off, figuring there was nothing to be scrounged that particular evening; better to wander around the mess, hunting for leftovers (if someone doesn't finish his stew and pushes his bowl back, there are always people hustling to pounce on it, like vultures).

The empty trays were handed in. Pavlo sat there with his double helping, Shukhov with his two bowls. And now they had nothing more to say to one another—the sacred moments had come.

Shukhov took off his hat and laid it on his knees. He tasted one bowl, he tasted the other. Not bad—there was some fish in it. Generally, the evening stew was much thinner than at breakfast: if they're to work, prisoners must be fed in the morning; in the evening they'll go to sleep anyway.

He dug in. First he only drank the broth, drank and drank. As it went down, filling his whole body with warmth, all his guts began to flutter inside him at their meeting with the stew. Goo-ood! There it comes, that brief moment for which a zek lives.

And now Shukhov complained about nothing: neither about the length of his stretch, nor about the length of the day, nor about their swiping another Sunday. This was all he thought about now: we'll survive. We'll stick it out, God willing, till it's over.

He drained the hot soup from both bowls, and then tipped what was left in the second into the first, scraping it clean with his spoon. That set his mind at ease. Now he didn't have to think about the second and keep an eye or a hand on it.

Now that he could look freely he glanced at his neighbors' bowls. The one on his left was little more than water. The dirty snakes. The tricks they play! And on their fellow zeks.

He began to eat the cabbage with what was left of the soup. A potato had found its way into one of the bowls. A medium-sized spud, frostbitten, hard and sweetish. There wasn't much fish, just a few stray bits of bare backbone. But you must chew every bone, every fin, to suck the juice out of them, for the juice is healthy. It takes time, of course, but he was in no hurry to go anywhere. Today was a red-letter day for him; two helpings for dinner, two helpings for supper. Everything else could wait.

Except, maybe, that visit to the Lett for tobacco. None might be left in the morning.

He ate his supper without bread. A double helping *and* bread—that was going too far. The bread would do for tomorrow. The belly is a demon. It doesn't remember how well you treated it yesterday; it'll cry out for more tomorrow.

He ate up his stew without taking much interest in what was happening around him. No need for that: he wasn't on the lookout for extras, he was eating his own lawful portions. All the same, he noticed that when the fellow opposite got up a tall old man—U 81—sat down in his place.

He'd been told that this old man had spent years without number in camps and prisons, and that he hadn't benefited from a single amnesty. Whenever one ten-year stretch had run out they shoved another onto him right away.

Now Shukhov looked closely at the man. He held himself straight—the other zeks sat all hunched up—and looked as if he'd put something extra on the bench to sit on. There was nothing left to crop on his head: his hair had dropped out long since—the result of high living, no doubt. His eyes didn't dart after everything going on in the mess hall. He kept them fixed in an unseeing gaze at some spot over Shukhov's head. His worn wooden spoon dipped rhythmically into the thin stew, but instead of lowering his head to the bowl like everybody else, he raised the spoon high to his lips. He'd lost all his teeth and chewed his bread with iron gums. All life had drained out of his face but it had been left, not sickly or feeble, but hard and dark like carved stone. And by his hands, big and cracked and blackened, you could see that he'd had little opportunity of doing soft jobs. But he wasn't going to give in, oh no! *He* wasn't going to put his nine ounces on the dirty, bespattered table—he put it on a well-washed bit of rag.

Shukhov came out with a full belly. He felt pleased with himself and decided that, although it was close to curfew, he'd run over to the Lett all the same. Instead of taking the bread to his barracks, he strode to Barracks 7.

The moon was high—clean and white, as if chiseled out of the sky. It was clear up there and there were some stars out—the brightest of them. But he had even less time for stargazing than for watching people in the mess hall. One thing he realized—the frost was no milder. One of the civilians had said, and this had been passed on, that it was likely to drop to −25° in the night, and as low as −40° toward morning.

1. Why do the cooks in the labor camp have such an enviable position? What is their standing among the other prisoners?

2. What are some of the strategies prisoners employ in the mess hall? What purpose do they serve?

3. Ivan considered his day a great success. Why?

4. How do the prisoners get along? How do they try to maintain their dignity?

·143·

Winston Churchill
The Iron Curtain
(1946)

Winston Churchill (1874–1965) was an artist, writer, historian, journalist, and twice prime minister of England (1940–1945; 1951–1955). He was a vigorous wartime leader, both in his aggressive military policies and in his inspirational speeches and public appearances. His ever-present cigar held between two raised fingers became a universal symbol of "V" for victory. Churchill led a coalition government and, as an allied victory in World War II grew near, the elements of his coalition came apart. He contested the 1945 general election as a Conservative, but the nation returned the Labor party. For the next six years Churchill was leader of the opposition.

Churchill had long been an outspoken critic of Soviet communism but had quickly embraced the Soviets as allies against Nazi Germany. Nevertheless, he was wary of the peace settlement that gave the Soviets control of Eastern Europe. Early in 1946 Churchill accepted an invitation to tour the United States. At Westminster College in Fulton, Missouri, he and President Harry Truman were both given honorary degrees and Churchill gave the speech that is said to have initiated the cold war between East and West. Churchill maintained that it was the duty of Britain and America to unite against the threat of Soviet communism.

I am glad to come to Westminster College this afternoon, and am complimented that you should give me a degree. The name "Westminster" is somehow familiar to me. I seem to have heard of it before. Indeed, it was at Westminster that I received a very large part of my education in politics, dialectic, rhetoric, and one or two other things. In fact we have both been educated at the same, or similar, or, at any rate, kindred establishments.

The United States stands at this time at the pinnacle of world power. It is a solemn moment for the American Democracy. For with primacy in power is also joined an awe-inspiring accountability to the future. If you look around you, you must feel not only the sense of duty done but also you must feel anxiety lest you fall below the level of achievement. Opportunity is here now, clear and shining for both our countries. To reject it or ignore it or fritter it away will bring upon us all the long reproaches of the after-time. It is necessary that constancy of mind, persistency of purpose, and the grand simplicity of decision shall guide and rule the conduct of the English-speaking peoples in peace as they did in war. We must, and I believe we shall, prove ourselves equal to this severe requirement.

I have a definite and practical proposal to make for action. Courts and magistrates may be set up but they cannot function without sheriffs and constables. The United Nations Organization must immediately begin to be equipped with an international armed force. In such a matter we can only go step by step, but we must begin now. I propose that each of the Powers and States should be invited to delegate a certain number of air squadrons to the service of the world organization. These squadrons would be trained and prepared in their own countries, but would move around in rotation from one country to another. They would wear the uniform of their own countries but with different badges. They would not be required to act against their own nation, but in other respects they would be directed by the world organization. This might be started on a modest scale and would grow as confidence grew. I wished to see this done after the first world war, and I devoutly trust it may be done forthwith.

It would nevertheless be wrong and imprudent to entrust the secret knowledge or experience of the atomic bomb, which the United States, Great Britain, and Canada now share, to the world organization, while it is still in its infancy. It would be criminal madness to cast it adrift in this still agitated and un-united world. No one in any country has slept less well in their beds because this knowledge and the method and the raw materials to apply it, are at present largely retained in American hands. I do not believe we should all have slept so soundly had the positions been reversed and if some Communist or neo-Fascist State monopolized for the time being

these dread agencies. The fear of them alone might easily have been used to enforce totalitarian systems upon the free democratic world, with consequences appalling to human imagination. God has willed that this shall not be and we have at least a breathing space to set our house in order before this peril has to be encountered: and even then, if no effort is spared, we should still possess so formidable a superiority as to impose effective deterrents upon its employment, or threat of employment, by others. Ultimately, when the essential brotherhood of man is truly embodied and expressed in a world organization with all the necessary practical safeguards to make it effective, these powers would naturally be confided to that world organization.

Now I come to the second danger of these two marauders which threatens the cottage, the home, and the ordinary people—namely, tyranny. We cannot be blind to the fact that the liberties enjoyed by individual citizens throughout the British Empire are not valid in a considerable number of countries, some of which are very powerful. In these States control is enforced upon the common people by various kinds of all-embracing police governments. The power of the State is exercised without restraint, either by dictators or by compact oligarchies operating through a privileged party and a political police. It is not our duty at this time when difficulties are so numerous to interfere forcibly in the internal affairs of countries which we have not conquered in war. But we must never cease to proclaim in fearless tones the great principles of freedom and the rights of man which are the joint inheritance of the English-speaking world and which through Magna Carta, the Bill of Rights, the Habeas Corpus, trial by jury, and the English common law find their most famous expression in the American Declaration of Independence.

All this means that the people of any country have the right, and should have the power by constitutional action, by free unfettered elections, with secret ballot, to choose or change the character or form of government under which they dwell; that freedom of speech and thought should reign; that courts of justice, independent of the executive, unbiased by any party, should administer laws which have received the broad assent of large majorities or are consecrated by time and custom. Here are the title deeds of freedom which should lie in every cottage home. Here is the message of the British and American peoples to mankind. Let us preach what we practice—let us practice what we preach. Neither the sure prevention of war, nor the continuous rise of world organization will be gained without what I have called the fraternal association of the English-speaking peoples. This means a special relationship between the British Commonwealth and Empire and the United States. Fraternal association requires not only the growing friendship and mutual understanding between our two vast but kindred systems of society, but the continuance of the intimate relationship between our military advisers, leading to common study of potential dangers, the similarity of weapons and manuals of instructions, and to the interchange of officers and cadets at technical colleges. It should carry with it the continuance of the present facilities for mutual security by the joint use of all Naval and Air Force bases in the possession of either country all over the world.

A shadow has fallen upon the scenes so lately lighted by the Allied victory. Nobody knows what Soviet Russia and its Communist international organization intends to do in the immediate future, or what are the limits, if any, to their expansive and proselytizing tendencies. I have a strong admiration and regard for the valiant Russian people and for my wartime comrade, Marshal Stalin. There is deep sympathy and goodwill in Britain—and I doubt not here also—towards the peoples of all the Russias and a resolve to persevere through many differences and rebuffs in establishing lasting friendships. We understand the Russian need to be secure on her western frontiers by the removal of all possibility of German aggression. We welcome Russia to her rightful place among the leading nations of the world. We welcome her flag upon the seas. Above all, we welcome constant, frequent and growing contacts between the Russian people and our own people on both sides of the Atlantic. It is my duty however, for I am sure you would wish me to state the facts as I see them to you, to place before you certain facts about the present position in Europe.

From Stettin in the Baltic to Trieste in the Adriatic, an iron curtain has descended across the Continent. Behind that line lie all the capitals of the ancient states of Central and Eastern Europe. Warsaw, Berlin, Prague, Vienna, Budapest, Belgrade, Bucharest and Sofia, all these famous cities and the populations around them lie in what I must call the Soviet sphere, and all are subject in one form or another, not only to Soviet influence but to a very high and, in many cases, increasing measure of control from Moscow. Athens alone—Greece with its immortal glories—is free to decide its future at an election under British, American and French observation. The Russian-dominated Polish Government has been encouraged to make enormous and wrongful inroads upon Germany, and mass expulsions of millions of Germans on a scale grievous and undreamed-of are now taking place. The Communist parties, which were very small in all these Eastern States of Europe, have been raised to preeminence and power far beyond their numbers and are seeking everywhere to obtain totalitarian control. Police governments are prevailing in nearly every case, and so far, except in Czechoslovakia, there is no true democracy.

The safety of the world requires a new unity in Europe, from which no nation should be permanently outcast. It is from the quarrels of the strong parent races in Europe that the world wars we have witnessed, or which occurred in former times, have sprung. Twice in our own lifetime we have seen the United States, against their wishes and their traditions, against arguments, the force of which it is impossible not to comprehend, drawn by irresistible forces into these wars in time to secure the victory of the good cause, but only after frightful slaughter and devastation had occurred. Twice the United States has had to send several millions of its young men across the Atlantic to find the war; but now war can find any nation, wherever it may dwell between dusk and dawn. Surely we should work with conscious purpose for a grand pacification of Europe, within the structure of the United Nations and in accordance with its Charter. That I feel is an open cause of policy of very great importance.

In front of the iron curtain which lies across Europe are other causes for anxiety. In Italy the Communist Party is seriously hampered by having to support the Communist-trained Marshal Tito's claims to former Italian territory at the head of the Adriatic. Nevertheless the future of Italy hangs in the balance. Again one cannot imagine a regenerated Europe without a strong France. All my public life I have worked for a strong France and I never lost faith in her destiny, even in the darkest hours. I will not lose faith now. However, in a great number of countries, far from the Russian frontiers and throughout the world, Communist fifth columns are established and work in complete unity and absolute obedience to the directions they receive from the Communist centre. Except in the British Commonwealth and in the United States where Communism is in its infancy, the Communist parties or fifth columns constitute a growing challenge and peril to Christian civilization. These are somber facts for anyone to have to recite on the morrow of a victory gained by so much splendid comradeship in arms and in the cause of freedom and democracy; but we should be most unwise not to face them squarely while time remains.

I have felt bound to portray the shadow which, alike in the west and in the east, falls upon the world. I was a high minister at the time of the Versailles Treaty and a close friend of Mr. Lloyd-George, who was the head of the British delegation at Versailles. I did not myself agree with many things that were done, but I have a very strong impression in my mind of that situation, and I find it painful to contrast it with that which prevails now. In those days there were high hopes and unbounded confidence that the wars were over, and that the League of Nations would become all-powerful. I do not see or feel that same confidence or even the same hopes in the haggard world at the present time.

On the other hand I repulse the idea that a new war is inevitable; still more that it is imminent. It is because I am sure that our fortunes are still in our own hands and that we hold the power to save the future, that I feel the duty to speak out now that I have the occasion and the opportunity to do so. I do not believe that Soviet Russia desires war. What they desire is the fruits of war and the indefinite expansion of their power and doctrines. But what we have to consider here today while time remains, is the permanent prevention of war and the establishment of conditions of freedom and democracy as rapidly as possible in all countries. Our difficulties and dangers will not be removed by closing our eyes to them. They will not be removed by mere waiting to see what happens; nor will they be removed by a policy of appeasement. What is needed is a settlement, and the longer this is delayed, the more difficult it will be and the greater our dangers will become.

From what I have seen of our Russian friends and Allies during the war, I am convinced that there is nothing they admire so much as strength, and there is nothing for which they have less respect than for weakness, especially military weakness. For that reason the old doctrine of a balance of power is unsound. We cannot afford, if we can help it, to work on narrow margins, offering temptations to a trial of strength. If the Western Democracies stand together in strict adherence to the principles of the United Nations Charter, their influence for furthering those principles will be immense and no one is likely to molest them. If however they become divided or falter in their duty and if these all-important years are allowed to slip away then indeed catastrophe may overwhelm us all.

Last time I saw it all coming and cried aloud to my own fellow-countrymen and to the world, but no one paid any attention. Up till the year 1933 or even 1935, Germany might have been saved from the awful fate which has overtaken her and we might all have been spared the miseries Hitler let loose upon mankind. There never was a war in all history easier to prevent by timely action than the one which has just desolated such great areas of the globe. It could have been prevented in my belief without the firing of a single shot, and Germany might be powerful, prosperous and honoured today; but no one would listen and one by one we were all sucked into the awful whirlpool. We surely must not let that happen again. This can only be achieved by reaching now, in 1946, a good understanding on all points with Russia under the general authority of the United Nations Organization and by the maintenance of that good understanding through many peaceful years, by the world instrument, supported by the whole strength of the English-speaking world and all its connections. There is the solution which I respectfully offer to you in this Address to which I have given the title "The Sinews of Peace?"

1. Britain emerged from the World War II much weaker than it had been before 1939. Does Churchill's speech acknowledge the new role his country was prepared to play?

2. What will the postwar relationship between the United States and Britain be like? How does Churchill envisage Anglo-American relations?

3. What is the principal threat to the postwar peace?

4. How does Churchill propose that Soviet aggression be met?

5. What, in Churchill's view, was the role of the newly founded United Nations?

·144·

Nikita Khrushchev
Report to the Communist Party Congress
(1961)

Nikita Khrushchev (1894–1971) came from a modest Russian background but rose rapidly in the ranks of the Communist party, which he joined in 1918. He fought in the civil war against the so-called Whites, and in 1925 became a full-time party official. Khrushchev was a loyal Stalinist and survived the worst of the party's purges in the 1930s. He emerged from World War II as a lieutenant general of the Red Army and a full member of the Politburo, the inner circle of the party. Khrushchev's great postwar achievement was rebuilding the Ukraine, one of the richest areas of the Soviet Union but one that had been devastated by the war. After Stalin's death, Khrushchev headed the Communist party in Moscow and then, after a bitter faction fight, was chosen first secretary of the party to succeed Stalin. In 1956 Khrushchev began a policy of de-Stalinization, criticizing the excesses of that regime. This was only partly successful, and when a number of foreign policy blunders became apparent, the old-line party leaders acted to depose Khrushchev. He died in obscurity in 1971.

Khrushchev will always be remembered in the West for his dramatic action in the United Nations when, in disagreement with a statement from the U.S. ambassador, Khrushchev removed his shoe and banged it on the table. Khrushchev's report to the Party Congress of 1961 is a sample of his personal style—long-winded and bombastic but shrewdly to the point. In this report he concentrates on the international competition between capitalism and communism and his own goals for the Soviet people.

Comrades! Some six years have passed since the 20th Congress of the Communist Party of the Soviet Union. For our party, for the Soviet people, for all mankind these years have been of extraordinary, one might say world-historic, significance.

Nikita Khrushchev, shown in 1960, demanding admittance of Red China to the United Nations.

The Soviet motherland has entered the period of full-scale construction of communism along a wide front of great projects. The economy and culture of the Soviet Union are advancing sharply. The seven-year plan, a plan of mighty development of the productive forces of our motherland, is being successfully fulfilled. The creative forces of the masses of people are pouring forth as from thousands of springs throughout the whole country. The triumphant flights of Soviet men into outer space, the first in human history, are like a crown of splendid victories, a banner of communist construction raised high.

The activity of our party and state has been conducted in a complex international situation. More than once the imperialists have tried to bring the world to the brink of war, to test the strength of the Soviet Union and the courage of its peoples. Many bourgeois politicians have comforted themselves with illusions that our plans would fail and that the socialist camp would disintegrate. They undertook many provocations and acts of subversion against us. The Party, the entire Soviet people, exposed the intrigues of enemies and emerged with honor from all trials. Today the Soviet Union is stronger and more powerful than ever! [*Prolonged applause.*]

THE PRESENT WORLD SITUATION AND THE INTERNATIONAL POSITION OF THE SOVIET UNION

Comrades! The competition of the two world social systems, the socialist and the capitalist, has been the chief content of the period since the 20th Party Congress. It has become the pivot, the foundation of world development at the present historical stage. Two lines, two historical trends, have manifested themselves more and more clearly in social development. One is the line of social progress, peace and constructive activity. The other is the line of reaction, oppression and war.

In the course of the peaceful competition of the two systems capitalism has suffered a profound moral defeat in the eyes of all peoples. The common people are daily convinced that capitalism is incapable of solving a single one of the urgent problems confronting mankind. It becomes more and more obvious that only on the paths to socialism can a solution to these problems be found. Faith in the capitalist system and the capitalist path of development is dwindling. Monopoly capital, losing its influence, resorts more and more to intimidating and suppressing the masses of the people, to methods of open dictatorship in carrying out its domestic policy and to aggressive acts against other countries. But the masses of the people offer increasing resistance to reaction's acts.

It is no secret to anyone that the methods of intimidation and threat are not a sign of strength but evidence of the weakening of capitalism, the deepening of its general crisis. As the saying goes, if you can't hang on by the mane, you won't hang on by the tail! [*Laughter in the hall.*] Reaction is still capable of dissolving parliaments in some countries in violation of their constitutions, of casting the best representatives of the people into prison, of sending cruisers and marines to subdue the "unruly." All this can put off for a time the approach of the fatal hour for the rule of capitalism. But such repressive measures still further expose the brigand nature of imperialism. The imperialists are sawing away at the branch on which they sit. There is no force in the world capable of stopping man's advance along the road of progress. [*Stormy applause.*]

The ruling circles of some imperialist powers have elevated subversive activities against the socialist countries to the level of state policy. With cynical frankness, the United States of America is spending hundreds of millions of dollars on espionage and subversion against the socialist countries and organizing so-called "guerilla units," assembling in them criminal elements and cut-throats prepared to undertake the vilest crimes for money. For several successive years the United States has been holding provocational "captive nations weeks." The hired agents of the monopolies call "captive" all those peoples who have liberated themselves from imperialist bondage and taken the path of free development. Truly, imperialist demagogy and hypocrisy know no bounds! The monopolists' howl about "captive peoples" is like the cry of the pickpocket who shouts "Stop, thief!" [*Stir in the hall. Applause.*]

The imperialists' intrigues must never be forgotten. Our tremendous successes in building a new life should not lead to complacency, to relaxation of vigilance. Of course, the greater the successes of socialism and the higher the living standard in each socialist country, the more the people rally around the Communist and Workers' Parties. This is one aspect of the matter, and a very gratifying aspect. But one must bear in mind another aspect also. As the solidarity of the peoples in all the socialist countries grows, the imperialists' hopes for the restoration of capitalist ways and for the degeneration of the socialist countries fade. World reaction therefore becomes more and more oriented toward striking a blow at the socialist states from outside in order through war to achieve the rule of capitalism throughout the world, or at least to check the development of the countries of socialism.

Our society is open to those people who come to us from abroad with open hearts. It is open to honest trade, to scientific, technical and cultural exchanges, to the exchange of truthful information. If it's an iron curtain we're talking about, where it really exists is in the world of capitalism, which, though dubbing itself the "free world," every now and then fearfully slams its gates shut to Soviet people, one moment to our cooks, the next to our chess players. There was a case where one state, which calls itself the "most open," was afraid to let in Soviet dancers. Can they really have feared that Russian folk dancing might shake the foundations of the capitalist world?! [*Stir in the hall.*]

We have long proposed to the capitalist world that we compete not in an arms race but in improving the working people's lives. We are confident that capitalism cannot stand up under that kind of competition! We are confident that in the end all peoples will make the correct choice, will give their preference to the truly free world of communism and turn their backs on the so-called "free world" of capitalism. [*Applause.*]

Comrades! When the Party mapped the major measures for expanding our country's economy, bourgeois politicians and economists had quite a good deal to say about how the Communists were sacrificing the people's vital interests to heavy industry, about how production in the Soviet Union exists only for production's sake. What a vicious libel on socialism! Production not for the sake of production but for the sake of man is the sacred principle governing the activities of the Party and the Soviet state. Now everyone, even the most incorrigible skeptic and doubter, can once more see for himself that our party always honors its pledges to the people. [*Applause.*]

In the area of domestic policy, our party is setting Communists and the Soviet people the following tasks for the next few years:

The entire effort of the people must be directed toward fulfillment and overfulfillment of the seven-year plan—an important stage in the creation of the material and technical base for communism. We must continue to raise the level of material production and to keep the country's defenses up to the mark. As we seize new heights in the economic development of the Soviet homeland, we should bear in mind that only steady progress will assure us complete superiority and bring closer the day of our victory in the peaceful economic competition with capitalism.

We must strive to accelerate technical progress in all branches of socialist industry without exception. We must move forward particularly in power engineering, chemistry, machine building, metallurgy and the fuel industry. We must specialize enterprises on a broader scale, see to the integrated mechanization and automation of production processes and apply the achievements of modern science and technology and the experience of innovators more rapidly in production. Steady growth of labor productivity and reduction of production costs and an improvement in the quality of output must become law for all Soviet enterprises.

We must strive for a level of industrial and agricultural development that will enable us to meet the public's demand for manufactured goods and foodstuffs ever more fully. Funds that accumulate as a result of overfulfillment of industrial output plans should be channeled primarily into agriculture, light industry, the food industry and other consumer goods industries.

We must advance along the entire front of cultural and social development. There must be continuous progress in Soviet science, public education, literature and art. We must raise the working people's living standards, complete the adjustment of wages and the planned measures for shortening the working day and week, maintain a rapid pace in housing construction, and improve the pension system, trade, public catering, and medical and everyday services for the working people.

Our country is experiencing a great upsurge of creative effort. All the many nationalities of the Soviet Union look upon the building of communism as a cause near and dear to them and are working hand in hand and making invaluable contributions toward our common victory. Consciousness of the grandeur of the tasks we pursue is multiplying the efforts of Soviet people tenfold, causing them to be more exacting of themselves and more intolerant of shortcomings, stagnation and inertia. We must take maximum advantage of the enormous motive forces inherent in the socialist system. [*Prolonged applause.*]

1. How does Khrushchev depict the state of the Soviet Union?

2. What is the Soviet view of the international situation?

3. Why does Khrushchev focus upon the iniquity of the Soviet Union's foreign enemies? How might such a focus be useful to him domestically?

4. What are the Communist party's plans for the future at home and abroad?

5. Khrushchev mentions Churchill's Iron Curtain in his address, a tribute to the power of the metaphor. Compare the oratorical styles of the two statesmen.

Generations of Cultural Protest

English suffragettes rioting in front of Buckingham Palace, 1914.

·145·
Virginia Woolf
A Room of One's Own
(1929)

Virginia Woolf (1882–1941) was born into a literary family and became one of the most important English writers of the early twentieth century. Her father was Sir Leslie Stephen, a distinguished critic and journalist, who educated young Virginia at home rather than at school so that she grew up surrounded by the leading intellectuals of the day. She lived in central London and became a member of the Bloomsbury group, which included Vanessa and Clive Bell, E. M. Forster, John Maynard Keynes, and also Leonard Woolf, whom she married in 1912 and with whom she established a publishing firm. Woolf worked as a publisher while beginning her own career as a novelist. Her work was characterized by experimentation in form and character. Her most creative period was in the 1920s, when she published three novels and more than a dozen short stories as well as the autobiographical *A Room of One's Own*. Despite her successes, Virginia Woolf suffered from severe depression. In 1941 she took her own life.

A Room of One's Own is an extended version of two lectures she gave to English university students. It is a brilliant example of her method of drawing meaning from everyday events as well as an evocative, provocative account of the difficulties faced by women writers throughout the centuries.

All I could do was to offer you an opinion upon one minor point—a woman must have money and a room of her own if she is to write fiction; and that, as you will see, leaves the great problem of the true nature of woman and the true nature of fiction unsolved. I have shirked the duty of coming to a conclusion upon these two questions—women and fiction remain, so far as I am concerned, unsolved problems. But in order to make some amends I am going to do what I can to show you how I arrived at this opinion about the room and the money. I am going to develop in your presence as fully and freely as I can the train of thought which led me to think this. Perhaps if I lay bare the ideas, the prejudices, that lie behind this statement you will find that they have some bearing upon women and some upon fiction. At any rate, when a subject is highly controversial—and any question about sex is that—one cannot hope to tell the truth. One can only show how one came to hold whatever opinion one does hold. One can only give one's audience the chance of drawing their own conclusions as they observe the limitations, the prejudices, the idiosyncrasies of the speaker. Fiction here is likely to contain more truth than fact.

My aunt, Mary Beton, I must tell you, died by a fall from her horse when she was riding out to take the air in Bombay. The news of my legacy reached me one night about the same time that the act was passed that gave votes to women. A solicitor's letter fell into the post-box and when I opened it I found that she had left me five hundred pounds a year for ever. Of the two—the vote and the money—the money, I own, seemed infinitely the more important. Before that I had made my living cadging odd jobs from newspapers, by reporting a donkey show here or a wedding there; I had earned a few pounds by addressing envelopes, reading to old ladies, making artificial flowers, teaching the alphabet to small children in a kindergarten. Such were the chief occupations that were open to women before 1918. I need not, I am afraid, describe in any detail the hardness of the work, for you know perhaps women who have done it; nor the difficulty of living on the money when it was earned, for you may have tried. But what still remains with me as a worse infliction than either was the poison of fear and bitterness which those days bred in me. To begin with, always to be doing work that one did not wish to do, and to do it like a slave, flattering and fawning, not always necessarily perhaps, but it seemed necessary and the stakes were too great to run risks; and then the thought of that one gift which it was death to hide—a small one but dear to the possessor—perishing and with it myself, my soul—all this became like a rust eating away the bloom of the spring, destroying the tree at its heart. However, as I say, my aunt died; and whenever I change a tenshilling note a little of that rust and corrosion is rubbed off; fear and bitterness go. Indeed, I thought, slipping the silver into my purse, it is remarkable, remembering the bitterness of those days, what a change of temper a fixed income will bring about. No force in the world can take from me my five hundred pounds. Food, house and clothing are mine for ever. Therefore not merely do effort and labour cease, but also hatred and bitterness. I need not hate any man; he cannot hurt me. I need not flatter any man; he has nothing to give me. So imperceptibly I found myself adopting a new attitude towards the other half of the human race.

What I find deplorable, I continued, looking about the bookshelves again, is that nothing is known about women before the eighteenth century. I have no model in my mind to turn about this way and that. Here am I asking why women did not write poetry in the Elizabethan age, and I am not sure how they were educated; whether they were taught to write; whether they had sitting-rooms to themselves; how many women had children before they were twenty-one; what, in short, they did from eight in the morning till eight at night. They had no money evidently; they were married whether they liked it or not before they were out of the nursery, at fifteen or sixteen very likely. It would have been extremely odd, even upon this showing, had one of them suddenly written the plays of Shakespeare, I concluded, and I thought of that old gentlemen, who is dead now, but was a bishop, I think, who declared that it was impossible for any woman, past, present, or to come, to have the genius of Shakespeare. He wrote to the papers about it. He also told a lady who applied to him for information that cats do not as a matter of fact go to heaven, though they have, he added, souls of a sort. How much thinking those old gentlemen used to save one! How the borders of ignorance shrank back at their approach! Cats do not go to heaven. Women cannot write the plays of Shakespeare.

Be that as it may, I could not help thinking, as I looked at the works of Shakespeare on the shelf, that the bishop was right at least in this; it would have been impossible, completely and entirely, for any woman to have written the plays of Shakespeare in the age of Shakespeare. Let me imagine, since facts are so hard to come by, what would have happened had Shakespeare had a wonderfully gifted sister, called Judith, let us say. Shakespeare himself went, very probably—his mother was an heiress—to the grammar school, where he may have learnt Latin—Ovid, Virgil and Horace—and the elements of grammar and logic. He was, it is well known, a wild boy who poached rabbits, perhaps shot a deer, and had, rather sooner than he should have done, to marry a woman in the neighbourhood, who bore him a child rather quicker than was right. That escapade sent him to seek his fortune in London. He had, it seemed, a taste for the theatre; he began by holding horses at the stage door. Very soon he got work in the theatre, became a successful actor, and lived at the hub of the universe, meeting everybody, knowing everybody, practising his art on the boards, exercising his wits in the streets, and even getting access to the palace of the queen. Meanwhile his extraordinarily gifted sister, let us suppose, remained at home. She was as adventurous, as imaginative, as agog to see the world as he was. But she was not sent to school. She had no chance of learning grammar and logic, let alone of reading Horace and Virgil. She picked up a book now and then, one of her brother's perhaps, and read a few pages. But then her parents came in and told her to mend the stockings or mind the stew and not moon about with books and papers. They would have spoken sharply but kindly, for they were substantial people who knew the conditions of life for a woman and loved their daughter—indeed, more likely than not she was the apple of her father's eye. Perhaps she scribbled some pages up in an apple loft on the sly, but was careful to hide them or set fire to them. Soon, however, before she was out of her teens, she was to be betrothed to the son of a neighbouring wool-stapler. She cried out that marriage was hateful to her, and for that she was severely beaten by her father. Then he ceased to scold her. He begged her instead not to hurt him, not to shame him in this matter of her marriage. He would give her a chain of beads or a fine petticoat, he said; and there were tears in his eyes. How could she disobey him? How could she break his heart? The force of her own gift alone drove her to it. She made up a small parcel of her belongings, let herself down by a rope one summer's night and took the road to London. She was not seventeen. The birds that sang in the hedge were not more musical than she was. She had the quickest fancy, a gift like her brother's,

for the tune of words. Like him, she had a taste for the theatre. She stood at the stage door; she wanted to act, she said. Men laughed in her face. The manager—a fat, loose-lipped man—guffawed. He bellowed something about poodles dancing and women acting—no woman, he said, could possibly be an actress. He hinted—you can imagine what. She could get no training in her craft. Could she even seek her dinner in a tavern or roam the streets at midnight? Yet her genius was for fiction and lusted to feed abundantly upon the lives of men and women and the study of their ways. At last—for she was very young, oddly like Shakespeare the poet in her face, with the same grey eyes and rounded brows—at last Nick Greene the actor-manager took pity on her; she found herself with child by that gentleman and so—who shall measure the heat and violence of the poet's heart when caught and tangled in a woman's body?—killed herself one winter's night and lies buried at some cross-roads where the omnibuses now stop outside the Elephant and Castle.

This may be true or it may be false—who can say?—but what is true in it, so it seemed to me, reviewing the story of Shakespeare's sister as I had made it, is that any woman born with a great gift in the sixteenth century would certainly have gone crazed, shot herself, or ended her days in some lonely cottage outside the village, half witch, half wizard, feared and mocked at. For it needs little skill in psychology to be sure that a highly gifted girl who had tried to use her gift for poetry would have been so thwarted and hindered by other people, so tortured and pulled asunder by her own contrary instincts, that she must have lost her health and sanity to a certainty. No girl could have walked to London and stood at a stage door and forced her way into the presence of actor-managers without doing herself a violence and suffering an anguish which may have been irrational—for chastity may be a fetish invented by certain societies for unknown reasons—but were none the less inevitable. Chastity had then, it has even now, a religious importance in a woman's life, and has so wrapped itself round with nerves and instincts that to cut it free and bring it to the light of day demands courage of the rarest.

Even so, the very first sentence that I would write here, I said, crossing over to the writing-table and taking up the page headed Women and Fiction, is that it is fatal for any one who writes to think of their sex. It is fatal to be a man or woman pure and simple; one must be woman-manly or man-womanly. It is fatal for a woman to lay the least stress on any grievance; to plead even with justice any cause; in any way to speak consciously as a woman. And fatal is no figure of speech; for anything written with that conscious bias is doomed to death. It ceases to be fertilised. Brilliant and effective, powerful and masterly, as it may appear for a day or two, it must wither at nightfall; it cannot grow in the minds of others. Some collaboration has to take place in the mind between the woman and the man before the act of creation can be accomplished. Some marriage of opposites has to be consummated. The whole of the mind must lie wide open if we are to get the sense that the writer is communicating his experience with perfect fullness. There must be freedom and there must be peace. Not a wheel must grate, not a light glimmer. The curtains must be close drawn. The writer, I thought, once his experience is over, must lie back and let his mind celebrate its nuptials in darkness. He must not look or question what is being done. Rather, he must pluck the petals from a rose or watch the swans float calmly down the river. . . .

How can I further encourage you to go about the business of life? Young women, I would say, and please attend, for the peroration is beginning, you are, in my opinion, disgracefully ignorant. You have never made a discovery of any sort of importance. You have never shaken an empire or led an army into battle. The plays of Shakespeare are not by you, and you have never introduced a barbarous race to the blessings of civilisation. What is your excuse? It is all very well for you to say, pointing to the streets and squares and forests of the globe swarming with black and white and coffee-coloured inhabitants, all busily engaged in traffic and enterprise and love-making, we have had other work on our hands. Without our doing, those seas would be unsailed and those fertile lands a desert. We have borne and bred and washed and taught, perhaps to the age of six or seven years, the one thousand six hundred and twenty-three million human beings who are, according to statistics, at present in existence, and that, allowing that some had help, takes time.

There is truth in what you say—I will not deny it. But at the same time may I remind you that there have been at least two colleges for women in existence in England since the year 1866; that after the year 1880 a married woman was allowed by law to possess her own property; and that in 1919—which is a whole nine years ago—she was given a vote? May I also remind you that the most of the professions have been open to you for close on ten years now? When you reflect upon these immense privileges and the length of time during which they have been enjoyed, and the fact that there must be at this moment some two thousand women capable of earning over five hundred a year in one way or another, you will agree that the excuse of lack of opportunity, training, encouragement, leisure and money no longer holds good. Moreover, the economists are telling us that Mrs. Seton has had too many children. You must, of course, go on bearing children, but, so they say, in twos and threes, not in tens and twelves.

Thus, with some time on your hands and with some book learning in your brains—you have had enough of the other kind, and are sent to college partly, I suspect, to be uneducated—surely you should embark upon another stage of your very long, very laborious and highly obscure career. A thousand pens are ready to suggest what you should do and what effect you will have.

My own suggestion is a little fantastic, I admit; I prefer, therefore, to put it in the form of fiction.

I told you in the course of this paper that Shakespeare had a sister; but do not look for her in Sir Sidney Lee's life of the poet. She died young—alas, she never wrote a word. She lies buried where the omnibuses now stop, opposite the Elephant and Castle. Now my belief is that this poet who never wrote a word and was buried at the crossroads still lives. She lives in you and in me, and in many other women who are not here tonight, for they are washing up the dishes and putting the children to bed. But she lives; for great poets do not die; they are continuing presences; they need only the opportunity to walk among us in the flesh. This opportunity, as I think, it is now coming within your power to give her. For my belief is that if we live another century or so—I am talking of the common life which is the real life and not of the little separate lives which we live as individuals—and have five hundred a year each of us and rooms of our own; if we have the habit of freedom and the courage to write exactly what we think; if we escape a lit-tle from the common sitting-room and see human beings not always in their relation to each other but in relation to reality; and the sky, too, and the trees or whatever it may be in themselves; if we look past Milton's bogey, for no human being should shut out the view; if we face the fact, for it is a fact, that there is no arm to cling to, but that we go alone and that our relation is to the world of reality and not only to the world of men and women, then the opportunity will come and the dead poet who was Shakespeare's sister will put on the body which she has so often laid down. Drawing her life from the lives of the unknown who were her forerunners, as her brother did before her, she will be born. As for her coming without that preparation, without that effort on our part, without that determination that when she is born again she shall find it possible to live and write her poetry, that we cannot expect, for that would be impossible. But I maintain that she would come if we worked for her, and that so to work, even in poverty and obscurity, is worth while.

1. What does a woman need to be able to write fiction?

2. What was Woolf's life as an independent middle-class woman like before she received her legacy? What options were available to women of her class at the time?

3. How have ideas of women's abilities changed from the days of Woolf's imaginary Judith Shakespeare to the late 1920s?

4. How should a writer approach the question of gender, according to Woolf? Would she say that men could write about women?

5. Is Woolf satisfied with the progress of women in the literary world?

·146·
Jean-Paul Sartre
Existentialism
(1946)

Jean-Paul Sartre (1905–1980) was born in Paris and grew up in the home of his grandfather, a professor at the Sorbonne. Sartre followed a traditional educational path, attending distinguished schools and finally studying at the Sorbonne. He worked as a high school teacher while beginning to develop the concept of existentialism. In 1938, he published his first novel, *Nausea,* a story of the extreme alienation of mankind. Even in his fiction, Sartre's philosophical inclinations were apparent, and he soon turned to writing directly theoretical works. *Being and Nothingness* (1943) was the most important statement of his views. During World War II he was interned in a German prison camp but continued to write, turning to drama as his medium—*The Flies* (1943) and *No Exit* (1944) were composed there. In 1964 he was awarded the Nobel Prize for literature, which, characteristically, he refused to accept.

Existentialism was an attempt to explain and defend his philosophical views. It is written in a very straightforward and simple manner, unlike his usual philosophical style, and explains the core of his doctrine. Compare it with the concept of existentialism that has become diluted and absorbed into the cultural mainstream, shorn of both its atheism and its radicalism.

I should like on this occasion to defend existentialism against some charges which have been brought against it.

First, it has been charged with inviting people to remain in a kind of desperate quietism because, since no solutions are possible, we should have to consider action in this world as quite impossible. We should then end up in a philosophy of contemplation; and since contemplation is a luxury, we come in the end to a bourgeois philosophy. The communists in particular have made these charges.

On the other hand, we have been charged with dwelling on human degradation, with pointing up everywhere the sordid, shady, and slimy, and neglecting the gracious and beautiful, the bright side of human nature; for example, according to Mlle. Mercier, a Catholic critic, with forgetting the smile of the child. Both sides charge us with having ignored human solidarity, with considering man as an isolated being. The communists say that the main reason for this is that we take pure subjectivity, the *Cartesian I think,* as our starting point; in other words, the moment in which man becomes fully aware of what it means to him to be an isolated being; as a result, we are unable to return to a state of solidarity with the men who are not ourselves, a state which we can never reach in the *cogito.*

From the Christian standpoint, we are charged with denying the reality and seriousness of human undertakings, since, if we reject God's commandments and the eternal verities, there no longer remains anything but pure caprice, with everyone permitted to do as he pleases and incapable, from his own point of view, of condemning the points of view and acts of others.

Actually, it is the least scandalous, the most austere of doctrines. It is intended strictly for specialists and philosophers. Yet it can be defined easily. What complicates matters is that there are two kinds of existentialist; first, those who are Christian, among whom I would include Jaspers and Gabriel Marcel, both Catholic; and on the other hand the atheistic existentialists, among whom I class Heidegger, and then the French existentialists and myself. What they have in common is that they think that existence precedes essence, or, if you prefer, that subjectivity must be the starting point.

Atheistic existentialism states that if God does not exist, there is at least one being in whom existence precedes essence, a being who exists before he can be defined by any concept, and that this being is man, or, as Heidegger says, human reality. What is meant here by saying that existence precedes essence? It means that, first of all, man exists, turns up, appears on the scene, and, only afterwards, defines himself. If man, as the existentialist conceives him, is indefinable, it is because at first he is nothing. Only afterward will he be something, and he himself will have made what he will be. Thus, there is no human nature, since there is no God to conceive it. Not only is man what he conceives himself to be, but he is also only what he wills himself to be after this thrust toward existence.

Man is nothing else but what he makes of himself. Such is the first principle of existentialism. It is also what is called subjectivity, the name we are labeled with when charges are brought against us. But what do we mean by this, if not that man has a greater dignity than a stone or table? For we mean that man first exists, that is, that man first of all is the being who hurls himself toward a future and who is conscious of imagining himself as being in the future. Man is at the start a plan which is aware of itself, rather than a patch of moss, a piece of garbage, or a cauliflower; nothing exists prior to this plan; there is nothing in heaven; man will be what he will have planned to be. Not what he will want to be. Because by the word "will" we generally mean a conscious decision, which is subsequent to what we have already made of ourselves. I may want to belong to a political party, write a book, get married; but all that is only a manifestation of an earlier, more spontaneous choice that is called "will." But if existence really does precede essence, man is responsible for what he is. Thus, existentialism's first move is to make every man aware of what he is and to make the full responsibility of his existence rest on him. And when we say that a man is responsible for himself, we do not only mean that he is responsible for his own individuality, but that he is responsible for all men.

If existence precedes essence, and if we grant that we exist and fashion our image at one and the same time, the image is valid for everybody and for our whole age. Thus, our responsibility is much greater than we might have supposed, because it involves all mankind. To take an individual matter, if I want to marry, to have children; even if this marriage depends solely on my own circumstances or passion or wish, I am involving all humanity in monogamy and not merely myself. Therefore, I am responsible for myself and for everyone else. I am creating a certain image of man of my own choosing. In choosing myself, I choose man.

This helps us understand what the actual content is of such rather grandiloquent words as anguish, forlornness, despair. As you will see, it's all quite simple.

First, what is meant by anguish? The existentialists say at once that man is anguish. What that means is this: The man who involves himself and who realizes that he is not only the person he chooses to be, but also a lawmaker who is, at the same time, choosing all mankind as well as himself, cannot help escape the feeling of his total and deep responsibility. Of course, there are many people who are not anxious; but we claim that they are hiding their anxiety, that they are fleeing from it. Certainly, many people believe that when they do something, they themselves are the only ones involved, and when someone says to them, "What if everyone acted that way?" they shrug their shoulders and answer, "Everyone doesn't act that way." But really, one should always ask himself, "What would happen if everybody looked at things that way?" There is no escaping this disturbing thought except by a kind of double-dealing. A man who lies and makes excuses for himself by saying "not everybody does that," is someone with an uneasy conscience, because the act of lying implies that a universal value is conferred upon the lie.

When we speak of forlornness, a term Heidegger was fond of, we mean only that God does not exist and that we have to face all the consequences of this.

The existentialist thinks it very distressing that God does not exist, because all possibility of finding values in a heaven of ideas disappears along with Him; there can no longer be an *a priori* Good, since there is no infinite and perfect consciousness to think it. Nowhere is it written that the Good exists, that we must be honest, that we must not lie; because the fact is we are on a plane where there are only men. Dostoievsky said, "If God didn't exist, everything would be possible." That is the very starting point of existentialism. Indeed, everything is permissible if God does not exist, and as a result man is forlorn, because neither within him nor without does he find anything to cling to. He can't start making excuses for himself.

If existence really does precede essence, there is no explaining things away by reference to a fixed and given human nature. In other words, there is no determinism, man is free, man is freedom. On the other hand, if God does not exist, we find no values or commands to turn to which legitimize our conduct. So, in the bright realm of values, we have no excuse behind us, nor justification before us. We are alone, with no excuses.

That is the idea I shall try to convey when I say that man is condemned to be free. Condemned, because he did not create himself, yet, in other respects is free; because, once thrown into the world, he is responsible for everything he does. The existentialist does not believe in the power of passion. He will never agree that a sweeping passion is a ravaging torrent which fatally leads a man to certain acts and is therefore an excuse. He thinks that man is responsible for his passion.

The existentialist does not think that man is going to help himself by finding in the world some omen by which to orient himself. Because he thinks that man will interpret the omen to suit himself. Therefore, he thinks that man, with no support and no aid, is condemned every moment to invent man. Ponge, in a very fine article, has said "Man is the future of man." That's exactly it.

From these few reflections it is evident that nothing is more unjust than the objections that have been raised against us. Existentialism is nothing else than an attempt to draw all the consequences of a coherent atheistic position. It isn't trying to plunge man into despair at all. But if one calls every attitude of unbelief despair, like the Christians, then the word is not being used in its original sense. Existentialism isn't so atheistic that it wears itself out showing that God doesn't exist. Rather, it declares that even if God did exist, that would change nothing. There you've got our point of view. Not that we believe that God exists, but we think that the problem of His existence is not the issue. In this sense existentialism is optimistic, a doctrine of action, and it is plain dishonesty for Christians to make no distinction between their own despair and ours and then to call us despairing.

1. Sartre's philosophy was attacked from both the left and the right. What did his critics say about his work?

2. What does Sartre mean when he says that existence precedes essence?

3. Sartre believes that there is no God. How does this affect his worldview?

4. What is Sartre's view of individual responsibility?

5. Sartre's philosophy has been characterized as extremely pessimistic. Would you agree? How might his personal experiences have affected his views?

·147·

Simone de Beauvoir
The Second Sex
(1949)

Simone de Beauvoir (1908–1986) grew up in Paris and was educated in private Catholic schools. She took a degree in philosophy from the Sorbonne and taught philosophy at a number of evening colleges during the early part of her career. At this time she met Jean-Paul Sartre; they began a lifelong association, though both rejected marriage as a bourgeois institution. In the 1930s de Beauvoir took up writing as a full-time occupation, alternating between existential novels and academic treatises. She was particularly adept at portraying the complexities of personal relationships in a world without fixed values and beliefs. She also edited the magazine *Modern Times*, an influential intellectual journal.

The Second Sex delves into the condition of modern women through a study of the subjugation of women throughout history. It is a bitter and incisive account and quickly became a seminal work in the developing women's liberation movement. It was widely translated; the first American edition appeared in 1953.

In a sense her whole existence is waiting, since she is confined in the limbo of immanence and contingence, and since her justification is always in the hands of others. She awaits the homage, the approval of men, she awaits love, she awaits the gratitude and praise of her husband or her lover. She awaits her support, which comes from man; whether she keeps the checkbook or merely gets a weekly or monthly allowance from her husband, it is necessary for him to have drawn his pay or obtained that raise if she is to be able to pay the grocer or buy a new dress. She waits for man to put in an appearance, since her economic dependence places her at his disposal; she is only one element in masculine life while man is her whole existence. The husband has his occupations outside the home, and the wife has to put up with his absence all day long; the lover—passionate as he may be—is the one who decides on their meetings and separations in accordance with his obligations. In bed, she awaits the male's desire, she awaits—sometimes anxiously—her own pleasure.

All she can do is arrive later at the rendezvous her lover has set, not be ready at the time designated by her husband; in that way she asserts the importance of her own occupations, she insists on her independence; and for the moment she becomes the essential subject to whose will the other passively submits. But these are timid attempts at revenge; however persistent she may be in keeping men waiting, she will never compensate for the interminable hours she has spent in watching and hoping, in awaiting the good pleasure of the male.

Woman is bound in a general way to contest foot by foot the rule of man, though recognizing his over-all supremacy and worshipping his idols. Hence that famous "contrariness" for which she has often been reproached. Having no independent domain, she cannot oppose positive truths and values of her own to those asserted and upheld by males; she can only deny them. Her negation is more or less thoroughgoing, according to the way respect and resentment are proportioned in her nature. But in fact she knows all the faults in the masculine system, and she has no hesitation in exposing them. . . .

It is understandable, in this perspective, that woman takes exception to masculine logic. Not only is it inapplicable to her experience, but in his hands, as she knows, masculine reasoning becomes an underhand form of force; men's undebatable pronouncements are intended to confuse her. The intention is to put her in a dilemma: either you agree or you do not. Out of respect for the whole system of accepted principles she should agree; if she refuses, she rejects the entire system. But she cannot venture to go so far; she lacks the means to reconstruct society in different form. Still, she does not accept it as it is. Halfway between revolt and slavery, she resigns herself reluctantly to masculine authority. On each occasion he has to force her to accept the consequences of her halfhearted yielding. Man pursues that chimera, a companion half slave, half free: in yielding to him, he would have her yield to the convincingness of an argument, but she knows that he has himself chosen the premises on which his rigorous deductions depend. As long as she avoids questioning them, he will easily reduce her to silence; nevertheless he will not convince her, for she senses his arbitrariness. And so, annoyed, he will accuse her of being obstinate and illogical; but she refuses to play the game because she knows the dice are loaded.

Woman does not entertain the positive belief that the truth is something *other* than men claim; she recognizes, rather, that there *is not* any fixed truth. It is not only the changing nature of life that makes her suspicious of the principle of constant identity, nor is it the magic phenomena with which she is surrounded that destroy the notion of causality. It is at the heart of the masculine world itself, it is in herself as belonging to this world that she comes upon the ambiguity of all principle, of all value, of everything that exists. She knows that masculine morality, as it concerns her, is a vast hoax. Man pompously thunders forth his code of virtue and honor; but in secret he invites her to disobey it, and he even counts on this disobedience; without it, all that splendid façade behind which he takes cover would collapse. . . .

Woman has the same faults because she is a victim of the same paternalistic oppression; she has the same cynicism because she sees man from top to toe, as a valet sees his master. But it is clear that none of woman's traits manifest an originally perverted essence or will: they reflect a situation. "There is dissimulation everywhere under a coercive regime," says Fourier. "Prohibition and contraband are inseparable in love as in trade." And men know that woman's faults indicate her situation so well that, anxious to maintain the hierarchy of sexes, they encourage in their companions the very traits that merit their contempt. No doubt the husband or lover is irritated by the faults of the particular woman he lives with, and yet when they extoll the charms of femininity in general, they believe it to be inseparable from its defects. If woman is not faithless, futile, cowardly, indolent, she loses her seductiveness. . . .

Not accepting logical principles and moral imperatives, skeptical about the laws of nature, woman lacks the sense of the universal; to her the world seems a confused conglomeration of special cases. This explains why she believes more readily in the tittle-tattle of a neighbor than in a scientific explanation. No doubt she respects the printed book, but she respectfully skims the pages of type without getting at the meaning; on the contrary, the anecdote told by some unknown in a waiting line or drawing-room at once takes on an overwhelming authority. Within her sphere all is magic; outside, all is mystery. She is unfamiliar with the criterion of plausibility; only immediate experience carries conviction—her own experience, or that of others if stated emphatically enough. As for her own self, she feels she is a special case because she is isolated in her home and hence does not come into active contact with other women; she is always expecting that destiny and men will make an exception in her favor. She believes in her intuitions much more firmly than in universally valid reasoning; she readily admits that they come from God or from some vague world-spirit; regarding some misfortune or accident she calmly thinks: "That will not happen to me." Regarding benefits, on the other hand, she

imagines that "an exception will be made in my case": she rather expects special favors. The storekeeper will give her a discount, the policeman will let her through without a pass; she has been taught to overestimate the value of her smile, and no one has told her that all women smile. It is not that she thinks herself more extraordinary than her neighbor: she does not make the comparison. And for the same reason experience rarely shows her how wrong she is: she meets with one failure after another, but she does not sum them up in a valid conclusion.

This shows why women do not succeed in building up a solid counter-universe whence they can challenge the males; now and then they rail at men in general, they tell what happens in the bedroom or at childbirth, they exchange horoscopes and beauty secrets. But they lack the conviction necessary to build this grievance-world their resentment calls for; their attitude toward man is too ambivalent. Doubtless he is a child, a necessitous and vulnerable body, he is a simpleton, a bothersome drone, a mean tyrant, a vain egotist; but he is also the liberating hero, the divinity who bestows values. His desire is gross appetite, his embrace a degrading duty; yet his fire and virile force seem like demiurgic power. When a woman says ecstatically: "He is a man!" she evokes at once the sexual vigor and the social effectiveness of the man she admires. In both he displays the same creative superiority; she does not conceive of his being a great artist, a great man of business, a general, a leader, without being a potent lover, and thus his social successes always have a sexual attractiveness; inversely, she is quick to see genius in the man who satisfies her desires. . . .

The ambiguity of woman's feelings toward man is found again in her general attitude toward herself and the world. The domain in which she is confined is surrounded by the masculine universe, but it is haunted by obscure forces of which men are themselves the playthings; if she allies herself with these magical forces, she will come to power in her turn. Society enslaves Nature; but Nature dominates it. The Spirit flames out beyond Life; but it ceases to burn when life no longer supports it. Woman is justified by this equivocation in finding more verity in a garden than in a city, in a malady than in an idea, in a birth than in a revolution; she endeavors to reestablish that reign of the earth, of the Mother, in order to become again the essential in face of the inessential. But as she, also, is an existent having transcendence, she can give value to that domain where she is confined only by transfiguring it: she lends it a transcendent dimension. Man lives in a consistent universe that is a reality conceivable in thought. Woman is at grips with a magical reality that defies thought, and she escapes from it through thoughts without real content. Instead of taking up her existence, she contemplates in the clouds the pure Idea of her destiny; instead of acting, she sets up her own image in the realm of imagination: that is, instead of reasoning, she dreams. Hence the fact that while being "physical," she is also artificial, and while being earthy, she makes herself ethereal. Her life is passed in washing pots and pans, and it is a glittering novel; man's vassal, she thinks she is his idol; carnally humiliated, she is all for Love. Because she is condemned to know only the factual contingence of life, she makes herself priestess of the Ideal.

This ambivalence is evident in the way woman regards her body. It is a burden: worn away in service to the species, bleeding each month, proliferating passively, it is not for her a pure instrument for getting a grip on the world but an opaque physical presence; it is no certain source of pleasure and it creates lacerating pains; it contains menaces: woman feels endangered by her "insides." It is a "hysteric" body, on account of the close connection of the endocrine secretions with the nervous and sympathetic systems that control the muscles and the viscera. Her body displays reactions for which the woman denies responsibility; in sobs, vomiting, convulsions, it escapes her control, it betrays her; it is her most intimate verity, but it is a shameful verity that she keeps hidden. And yet it is also her glorious double; she is dazzled in beholding it in the mirror; it is promised happiness, work of art, living statue; she shapes it, adorns it, puts it on show. When she smiles at herself in the glass, she forgets her carnal contingence; in the embrace of love, in maternity, her image is destroyed. But often, as she muses on herself, she is astonished to be at one and the same time that heroine and that flesh.

Nature similarly presents a double face to her, supplying the soup kettle and stimulating mystical effusions. When she became a housekeeper and a mother, woman renounced her free roaming of field and wood, she preferred the quiet cultivation of her kitchen garden, she tamed the flowers and put them in vases; yet she is still entranced with moonlight and sunset. In the terrestrial fauna and flora she sees food and ornament before all; but in them a sap circulates which is nobility and magic. Life is not merely immanence and repetition: it has also a dazzling face of light; in flowery meadows it is revealed as Beauty. Attuned to nature by the fertility of her womb, woman is also swept by its animating breeze, which is spirit. And to the extent that she remains unsatisfied and, like the young girl, feels unfulfilled and unlimited, her soul, too, will be lost to sight down roads stretching endlessly on, toward unbounded horizons. Enslaved as she is to her husband, her children, her home, it is ecstasy to find herself alone, sovereign on the hillsides; she is no longer mother, wife, housekeeper, but a human being; she contemplates the passive world, and she remembers that she is wholly a conscious being, an irreducible free individual. Before the mystery of water and the leap of summits, the male's supremacy fades away. Walking through the heather, dipping her hand in the stream, she is living not for others, but for herself. Any woman who has preserved her independence through all her servitudes will ardently love her own freedom in Nature. Others will find there only pretexts for refined raptures; and they will hesitate at twilight between the danger of catching cold and an ecstasy of the soul.

1. How do women traditionally struggle against male domination? What are their tactics?

2. Why are women "illogical" or "obstinate"?

3. De Beauvoir implies that men and women think differently. How? Do you think she is correct, or is she only reinforcing an old stereotype?

4. Women have ambiguous feelings toward men, de Beauvoir says. Is this a positive or a negative thing, in her view?

·148·

Bob Dylan
Songs

(1962–1965)

*B*ob Dylan (b. 1941) was born Robert Zimmerman in Hibbing, Minnesota. He became interested in music as a child and was especially influenced by blues and folk music traditions. After a year at the University of Minnesota, Dylan hitchhiked to New York, where he lived in Greenwich Village and began to perform folk music at a number of small clubs. His distinctive voice and unusual appearance attracted the attention of a number of music critics and ultimately brought him a record contract. Dylan's traditional folk music soon developed into a characteristic genre often described as "Protest Songs," especially after the production of "Blowin' in the Wind" (1962). His subsequent work brought him international attention; he was much admired by the Beatles, among other British rock bands. In 1965, Dylan took a further step when he merged his folk and protest poetry with rock music, synthesizing what had been two different traditions and bringing protest music to a vastly larger audience.

Dylan's songs reveal the central concerns of what later came to be called "The Movement." "Blowin' in the Wind" and "Only a Pawn in Their Game" grew out of agitation for civil rights; "A Hard Rain's A-Gonna Fall" over worries about nuclear extermination. "Subterranean Homesick Blues" marked the beginning of the period in which youth protest began to clash with established authority over drugs and politics. The radical underground group The Weathermen took their name from one of the lines in that song.

Blowin' in the Wind

How many roads must a man walk down
Before you call him a man?
Yes, 'n' how many seas must a white dove sail
Before she sleeps in the sand?
Yes, 'n' how many times must the cannon balls
    fly
Before they're forever banned?
The answer, my friend, is blowin' in the wind,
The answer is blowin' in the wind.

How many times must a man look up
Before he can see the sky?
Yes 'n' how many ears must one man have
Before he can hear people cry?
Yes, 'n' how many deaths will it take till he
    knows
That too many people have died?
The answer, my friend, is blowin' in the wind,
The answer is blowin' in the wind.

How many years can a mountain exist
Before it's washed to the sea?

Folk prophet Bob Dylan performing at a 1971 benefit concert at Madison Square Garden.

Yes, 'n' how many years can some people exist
Before they're allowed to be free?
Yes, 'n' how many times can a man turn his
    head,
Pretending he just doesn't see?
The answer, my friend, is blowin' in the wind,
The answer is blowin' in the wind.

A Hard Rain's A-Gonna Fall

Oh, where have you been my blue-eyed son?
Oh, where have you been, my darling young
    one?
I've stumbled on the side of twelve misty moun-
    tains,
I've walked and I've crawled on six crooked
    highways,
I've stepped in the middle of seven sad forests,
I've been out in front of a dozen dead oceans,
I've been ten thousand miles in the mouth of a
    graveyard,
And it's a hard, and it's a hard, it's a hard, and
    it's a hard,
And it's a hard rain's a-gonna fall.

Oh, what did you see, my blue-eyed son?
Oh, what did you see, my darling young one?
I saw a newborn baby with wild wolves all
    around it,
I saw a highway of diamonds with nobody on it,
I saw a black branch with blood that kept
    drippin',
I saw a room full of men with their hammers
    a-bleedin',
I saw a white ladder all covered with water,
I saw ten thousand talkers whose tongues were
    all broken,
I saw guns and sharp swords in the hands of
    young children,
And it's a hard, and it's a hard, it's a hard, it's a
    hard,
And it's a hard rain's a-gonna fall.

And what did you hear, my blue-eyed son?
And what did you hear, my darling young one?

I heard the sound of a thunder, it roared out a
    warnin',
Heard the roar of a wave that could drown the
    whole world,
Heard ten thousand whisperin' and nobody
    listenin',
Heard one person starve, I heard many people
    laughin',
Heard the song of a poet who died in the
    gutter,
Heard the sound of a clown who cried in the
    alley,
And it's a hard, and it's a hard, it's a hard, it's a
    hard,
And it's a hard rain's a-gonna fall.

Oh, who did you meet, my blue-eyed son?
Who did you meet, my darling young one?
I met a young child beside a dead pony,
I met a white man who walked a black dog,
I met a young woman whose body was burning,
I met a young girl, she gave me a rainbow,
I met one man who was wounded in love,
I met another man who was wounded with
    hatred,
And it's a hard, it's a hard, it's a hard, it's a
    hard,
It's a hard rain's a-gonna fall.

Oh, what'll you do now, my blue-eyed son?
Oh, what'll you do now, my darling young one?
I'm a-goin' back out 'fore the rain starts a-
    fallin',
I'll walk to the depths of the deepest black
    forest,
Where the people are many and their hands are
    all empty,
Where the pellets of poison are flooding their
    waters,
Where the home in the valley meets the damp
    dirty prison,
Where the executioner's face is always well
    hidden,
Where hunger is ugly, where souls are
    forgotten,
Where black is the color, where none is the
    number,

And I'll tell it and think it and speak it and
    breathe it,
And reflect it from the mountain so all souls
    can see it,
Then I'll stand on the ocean until I start sinkin',
But I'll know my song well before I start singin',
And it's a hard, it's a hard, it's a hard, it's a
    hard,
It's a hard rain's a-gonna fall.

Only a Pawn in Their Game

A bullet from the back of a bush took Medgar
    Evers' blood.
A finger fired the trigger to his name.
A handle hid out in the dark
A hand set the spark
Two eyes took the aim
Behind a man's brain
But he can't be blamed
He's only a pawn in their game.

A South politician preaches to the poor white
    man,
"You got more than the blacks, don't complain.
You're better than them, you been born with
    white skin," they explain.
And the Negro's name
Is used it is plain
For the politician's gain
As he rises to fame
And the poor white remains
On the caboose of the train
But it ain't him to blame
He's only a pawn in their game.

The deputy sheriffs, the soldiers, the governors
    get paid,
And the marshals and cops get the same,
But the poor white man's used in the hands of
    them all like a tool.
He's taught in his school
From the start by the rule
That the laws are with him
To protect his white skin
To keep up his hate

So he never thinks straight
'Bout the shape that he's in
But it ain't him to blame
He's only a pawn in their game.

From the poverty shacks, he looks from the
    cracks to the tracks,
And the hoof beats pound in his brain.
And he's taught how to walk in a pack
Shoot in the back
With his fist in a clinch
To hang and to lynch
To hide 'neath the hood
To kill with no pain
Like a dog on a chain
He ain't got no name
But it ain't him to blame
He's only a pawn in their game.

Today, Medgar Evers was buried from the bullet
    he caught.
They lowered him down as a king.
But when the shadowy sun sets on the one
That fired the gun
He'll see by his grave
On the stone that remains
Carved next to his name
His epitaph plain:
Only a pawn in their game.

Subterranean Homesick Blues

Johnny's in the basement
Mixing up the medicine
I'm on the pavement
Thinking about the government
The man in the trench coat
Badge out, laid off
Says he's got a bad cough
Wants to get it paid off
Look out kid
It's somethin' you did
God knows when
But you're doin' it again
You better duck down the alley way

Lookin' for a new friend
The man in the coon-skin cap
In the big pen
Wants eleven dollar bills
You only got ten

Maggie comes fleet foot
Face full of black soot
Talkin' that the heat put
Plants in the bed but
The phone's tapped anyway
Maggie says that many say
They must bust in early May
Orders from the D.A.
Look out kid
Don't matter what you did
Walk on your tip toes
Don't try "No Doz"
Better stay away from those
That carry around a fire hose
Keep a clean nose
Watch the plain clothes
You don't need a weather man
To know which way the wind blows

Get sick, get well
Hang around a ink well
Ring bell, hard to tell
If anything is goin' to sell
Try hard, get barred
Get back, write braille
Get jailed, jump bail
Join the army, if you fail
Look out kid
You're gonna get hit
But users, cheaters
Six-time losers
Hang around the theaters
Girl by the whirlpool
Lookin' for a new fool
Don't follow leaders
Watch the parkin' meters

Ah get born, keep warm
Short pants, romance, learn to dance

Get dressed, get blessed
Try to be a success
Please her, please him, buy gifts
Don't steal, don't lift
Twenty years of schoolin'
And they put you on the day shift
Look out kid
They keep it all hid

Better jump down a manhole
Light yourself a candle
Don't wear sandals
Try to avoid the scandals
Don't wanna be a bum
You better chew gum
The pump don't work
'Cause the vandals took the handles

1. Do you think there are answers to the questions Dylan poses in "Blowin' in the Wind"? Are they meant to be answered?

2. Who does Dylan identify as the villain in the struggle for civil rights?

3. What is "A Hard Rain's A-Gonna Fall" about? What is Dylan concerned with in this song?

4. What is the view of authority in "Subterranean Homesick Blues"?

5. Music was an important part of the politics of the 1960s. Why was it so important?

World War II

Mr. and Mrs. Winston Churchill, inspecting London air raid damage.

·149·
Adolf Hitler
Mein Kampf
(1923)

Adolf Hitler (1889–1945) was the leader of one of the most powerful and brutal dictatorships in Western history. His father was a minor customs official in Austria, so Adolf grew up in a provincial town on the German border. His early years were spent pursuing an unsuccessful career as an artist against his father's wishes. In 1913 he left Austria in order to avoid military conscription and settled in Munich where, paradoxically, he became so caught up in war fever that he joined the German army. Hitler served in France where he was wounded several times and eventually decorated for bravery. The war was the happiest period of his life; when he was demobilized after the German defeat, he joined and eventually led the right-wing National Socialist German Workers Party. His politics were a mixture of nationalism and racism, which appealed especially to former soldiers who shared Hitler's view that Germany had not lost World War I, but had been betrayed by its leaders. By 1932 the Nazi party was the largest in Germany; Hitler was named chancellor in 1933. Once in power, he began an economic and military recovery that restored Germany to its former position as one of the leading states in Europe. His territorial ambitions, however, led directly to World War II. When Germany's military situation became hopeless, Hitler committed suicide in Berlin in 1945.

Hitler wrote *Mein Kampf* (*My Struggle*) while he was in jail after an attempt to overthrow the German government; this very long and turgid work is a combination of a memoir and a statement of political philosophy. It includes some of Hitler's characteristic racist and anti-Semitic ideas.

It is a futile enterprise to argue which race or races were the original bearers of human culture and, with it, the actual founders of what we sum up with the word "mankind." It is simpler to put this question to oneself with regard to the present, and here the answer follows easily and distinctly. What we see before us of human culture today, the results of art, science, and techniques, is almost exclusively the creative product of the Aryan. But just this fact admits of the not unfounded conclusion that he alone was the founder of higher humanity as a whole, thus the prototype of what we understand by the word "man." He is the Prometheus of mankind, out of whose bright forehead springs the divine spark of genius at all times, forever rekindling that fire which in the form of knowledge lightened up the night of silent secrets and thus made man climb the path towards the position of master of the other beings on this earth. Exclude him—

German Chancellor and Führer Adolf Hitler (1889–1945).

and deep darkness will again fall upon the earth, perhaps even, after a few thousand years, human culture would perish and the world would turn into a desert.

If one were to divide mankind into three groups: culture-founders, culture-bearers, and culture-destroyers, then, as representative of the first kind, only the Aryan would come in question. It is from him that the foundation and the walls of all human creations originate, and only the external form and color depend on the characteristics of the various peoples involved. He furnishes the gigantic building-stones and also the plans for all human progress, and only the execution corresponds to the character of the people and races in the various instances. In a few decades, for instance, the entire east of Asia will call a culture its own, the ultimate bases of which will be Hellenic spirit and Germanic technique, just as is the case with us. Only the *external*

form will (at least partly) bear the features of Asiatic character. It is not the case, as some people claim, that Japan adds European techniques to her culture, but European science and techniques are trimmed with Japanese characteristics. But the basis of actual life is no longer the special Japanese culture, although it determines the color of life (because outwardly, in consequence of its inner difference, it is more visible to European eyes), but it is the enormous scientific and technical work of Europe and America, that is, of Aryan peoples. Based on these achievements alone the East is also able to follow general human progress. This creates the basis for the fight for daily bread, it furnishes weapons and tools for it, and only the external makeup is gradually adapted to Japanese life.

But if, starting today, all further Aryan influence upon Japan should stop, and supposing that Europe and America were to perish, then a further development of Japan's present rise in science and technology could take place for a little while longer; but in the time of a few years the source would dry out, Japanese life would gain, but its culture would stiffen and fall back into the sleep out of which it was startled seven decades ago by the Aryan wave of culture. Therefore, exactly as the present Japanese development owes its life to Aryan origin, thus also in the dim past foreign influence and foreign spirit were the awakener of the Japanese culture. The best proof of this is the fact that the latter stiffened and became completely paralyzed later on. This can only happen to a people when the originally creative race nucleus was lost, or when the external influence, which gave the impetus and the material for the first development in the cultural field, was lacking later on. But if it is ascertained that a people receives, takes in, and works over the essential basic elements of its culture from other races, and if then, when a further external influence is lacking, it stiffens again and again, then one can perhaps call such a race a "*culture-bearing*" one but never a "*culture-creating*" one.

We see this most clearly in that race that cannot help having been, and being, the supporter of the development of human culture—the Aryans. As soon as Fate leads them towards special conditions, their latent abilities begin to develop in a more and more rapid course and to mold themselves into tangible forms. The cultures which they found in such cases are nearly always decisively determined by the available soil, the climate, and—by the subjected people. The latter, however, is the most decisive of all factors. The more primitive the technical presumptions for a cultural activity are, the more necessary is the presence of human auxiliary forces which then, collected and applied with the object of organization, have to replace the force of the machine. Without this possibility of utilizing inferior men, the Aryan would never have been able to take the first steps towards his later culture; exactly as, without the help of various suitable animals which he knew how to tame, he would never have arrived at a technology which now allows him to do without these very animals. The words *Der Mohr hat seine Schuldigkeit getan, er kann gehen*" ["The Moor has done his duty, he may go"] has unfortunately too deep a meaning. For thousands of years the horse had to serve man and to help in laying the foundations of a development which now, through the motor-car, makes the horse itself superfluous. In a few years it will have ceased its activity, but without its former cooperation man would hardly have arrived at where he stands today.

Therefore, for the formation of higher cultures, the existence of inferior men was one of the most essential presumptions, because they alone were able to replace the lack of technical means without which a higher development is unthinkable. The first culture of mankind certainly depended less on the tamed animal, but rather on the use of inferior people.

Only after the enslavement of subjected races, the same fate began to meet the animals, and not *vice versa,* as many would like to believe. For first the conquered walked behind the plow—and after him, the horse. Only pacifist fools can again look upon this as a sign of human baseness, without making clear to themselves

that this development had to take place in order to arrive finally at that place from where today these apostles are able to sputter forth their drivel into the world.

The progress of mankind resembles the ascent on an endless ladder; one cannot arrive at the top without first having taken the lower steps. Thus the Aryan had to go the way which reality showed him and not that of which the imagination of a modern pacifist dreams. The way of reality, however, is hard and difficult, but it finally ends where the other wishes to bring mankind by dreaming, but unfortunately removes it from, rather than brings it nearer to, it.

Therefore, it is no accident that the first cultures originated in those places where the Aryan, by meeting lower peoples, subdued them and made them subject to his will. They, then, were the first technical instrument in the service of a growing culture.

With this the way that the Aryan had to go was clearly lined out. As a conqueror he subjected the lower peoples and then he regulated their practical ability according to his command and his will and for his aims. But while he thus led them towards a useful, though hard activity, he not only spared the lives of the subjected, but perhaps he even gave them a fate which was better than that of their former so-called "freedom." As long as he kept up ruthlessly the master's standpoint, he not only really remained "master" but also the preserver and propagator of the culture. For the latter was based exclusively on his abilities, and, with it, on his preservation in purity. But as soon as the subjected peoples themselves began to rise (probably) and approached the conqueror linguistically, the sharp separating wall between master and slave fell. The Aryan gave up the purity of his blood and therefore he also lost his place in the Paradise which he had created for himself. He became submerged in the race-mixture, he gradually lost his cultural ability more and more, till at last not only mentally but also physically he began to resemble more the subjected and aborigines than his ancestors. For some time he may still live on the existing cultural goods, but then petrifaction sets in, and finally oblivion.

In this way cultures and realms collapse in order to make room for new formations.

The blood-mixing, however, with the lowering of the racial level caused by it, is the sole cause of the dying-off of old cultures; for the people do not perish by lost wars, but by the loss of that force of resistance which is contained only in the pure blood.

All that is not race in this world is trash.

All world historical events, however, are only the expression of the races' instinct of self-preservation in its good or in its evil meaning.

The Jew forms the strongest contrast to the Aryan. Hardly in any people of the world is the instinct of self-preservation more strongly developed than in the so-called "chosen people." The fact of the existence of this race alone may be looked upon as the best proof of this. Where is the people that in the past two thousand years has been exposed to so small changes of the inner disposition, of character, etc., as the Jewish people? Which people finally has experienced greater changes than this one—and yet has always come forth the same from the most colossal catastrophes of mankind? What an infinitely persistent will for life, for preserving the race do these facts disclose!

Also the intellectual abilities were schooled in the course of centuries. Today the Jew is looked upon as "clever," and in a certain sense he has been so at all times. But his reason is not the result of his own development, but that of object lessons from without.

Never did the reverse process take place.

For, even if the Jewish people's instinct of self-preservation is not smaller, but rather greater, than that of other nations, and even if his spiritual abilities very easily create the impression as though they were equal to the intellectual disposition of the other races, yet the most essential presumption for a cultured people is completely lacking, the idealistic disposition.

But how far the Jew takes over foreign culture, only imitating, or rather destroying, it, may be seen from the fact that he is found most frequently in that art which also appears directed least of all towards invention of its own, the art of acting. But here, too, he is really only the "juggler," or rather the ape; for here, too, he lacks the ultimate touch of real greatness; here, too, he is not the ingenious creator, but the outward imitator, whereby all the turns and tricks he applies cannot deceive us concerning the inner lack of life of his creative ability. Here the Jewish press alone comes lovingly to his aid, because about every, even the most mediocre, bungler, provided that he is a Jew, it raises such a clamor of hosannas that the rest of the world finally actually believes that it sees a real artist before its eyes, whereas in reality it has only to deal with a wretched comedian.

No, the Jew possesses no culture-creating energy whatsoever, as the idealism, without which there can never exist a genuine development of man towards a higher level, does not and never did exist in him. His intellect, therefore, will never have a constructive effect, but only a destructive one.

A racially pure people, conscious of its blood, can never be enslaved by the Jew. It will forever only be the master of bastards in this world.

Thus he systematically tries to lower the racial level by a permanent poisoning of the individual.

In the political sphere, however, he begins to replace the idea of democracy by that of the dictatorship of the proletariat.

In the organized mass of Marxism he has found the weapon which makes him now dispense with democracy and which allows him, instead, to enslave and to "rule" the people dictatorially with the brutal fist.

He now works methodically towards the revolution in a twofold direction: economically and politically.

Thanks to his international influence, he ensnares with a net of enemies those peoples which put up a too violent resistance against the enemy from within, he drives them into war, and finally, if necessary, he plants the flag of revolution on the battlefield.

In the field of economics he undermines the States until the social organizations which have become unprofitable are taken from the State and submitted to his financial control.

Politically he denies to the State all means of self-preservation, he destroys the bases of any national self-dependence and defense, he destroys the confidence in the leaders, he derides history and the past, and he pulls down into the gutter everything which is truly great.

In the domain of culture he infects art, literature, theater, smites natural feeling, overthrows all conceptions of beauty and sublimity, of nobility and quality, and in turn he pulls the people down into the confines of his own swinish nature.

If we let all the causes of the German collapse pass before our eyes, there remains as the ultimate and decisive cause the non-recognition of the race problem and especially of the Jewish danger.

The defeats in the battlefield of August, 1918, would have been easily bearable. They were out of proportion to the victories of our people. Not the defeats have overthrown us, but we were overthrown by that power which prepared these defeats by robbing our people systematically, for many decades, of its political and moral instincts and forces which alone enable and entitle peoples to exist in this world.

The old Reich, by inattentively passing by the question of the preservation of the racial foundations of our nationality, disregarded also the sole right which alone gives life in this world. Peoples which bastardize themselves, or permit themselves to be bastardized, sin against the will of eternal Providence, and their ruin by the hand of a stronger nation is consequently not an injustice that is done to them, but only the restoration of right. If a people no longer wants to respect the qualities which Nature has given it and which root in its blood, then it has no longer the right to complain about the loss of its worldly existence.

Everything in this world can be improved. Any defeat can become the father of a later victory. Any lost war can become the cause of a later rise, every distress the fertilization of human energy, and from every suppression can come the forces of a new spiritual rebirth, as long as the blood remains preserved in purity.

Alone the loss of the purity of the blood destroys the inner happiness forever; it eternally lowers man, and never again can its consequences be removed from body and mind.

Only upon examining and comparing, in the face of this sole question, all the other problems of life, one will be able to judge how ridiculously small the latter are as compared with the former. How all of them are only temporal, while the question of the preservation of the blood is one of human eternity.

All really important symptoms of decay of the pre-War time ultimately go back to racial causes.

1. What is the role of the Aryan race in human history, according to Hitler?

2. Why are the Japanese, in Hitler's theories, a "culture-bearing" rather than a "culture-creating" people?

3. Hitler believed that cultural progress was necessarily aggressive. Why? How might these views have applied to his own policies in later years?

4. How are Jews said to destroy cultures?

5. Did Hitler view the defeat in World War I as inevitable? Was the Allied victory a good or a bad thing, in Hitler's view?

·150·
Winston Churchill
Speeches
(1940)

Winston Churchill (1874–1965), artist, writer, historian, journalist, and prime minister of England from 1940 to 1945 and again from 1951 to 1955, was born at Blenheim, the ancestral home of his family since the eighteenth century. His father was Lord Randolph Churchill, one of the rising stars in the Conservative party during the 1880s. Winston attended Harrow and the Royal Military Academy at Sandhurst, where he prepared for a career as an officer. He fought in India and Africa before returning to England to enter politics. First elected to Parliament in 1901, by 1911 he was first Lord of the Admiralty, where he was instrumental in rebuilding the British navy prior to World War I. After the war he abandoned his political career and turned to writing histories and to journalism. He opposed Chamberlain's policy of appeasement and did not return to government until the war broke out in 1939. The following year he became prime minister.

Churchill was one of the greatest orators of his day. His speeches in the House of Commons and those broadcast to the nation over the BBC provided encouragement to the British people during the darkest periods of the war. His familiar cigar and "V" for victory sign made him known throughout the world.

BLOOD, TOIL, TEARS AND SWEAT

May 13, 1940

On Friday evening last I received His Majesty's Commission to form a new Administration. It was the evident wish and will of Parliament and the nation that this should be conceived on the broadest possible basis and that it should include all parties, both those who supported the late Government and also the parties of the Opposition. I have completed the most important part of this task. A War Cabinet has been formed of five Members, representing, with the Opposition Liberals, the unity of the nation. The three party Leaders have agreed to serve, either in the War Cabinet or in high executive office. The three Fighting Services have been filled. It was necessary that this should be done in one single day, on account of the extreme urgency and rigour of events. A number of other positions, key positions, were filled yesterday, and I am submitting a further list to His Majesty tonight. I hope to complete the appointment of the principal Ministers during tomorrow. The appointment of the other Ministers usually takes a little longer, but I trust that, when Parliament meets again, this part of my task will be completed, and that the administration will be complete in all respects.

I considered it in the public interest to suggest that the House should be summoned to meet today. Mr. Speaker agreed, and took the necessary steps, in accordance with the powers conferred upon him by the Resolution of the House. At the end of the proceedings today, the Adjournment of the House will be proposed until Tuesday, 21st May, with, of course, provision for earlier meeting, if need be. The business to be considered during that week will be notified to Members at the earliest opportunity. I now invite the House, by the Motion which stands in my name, to record its approval of the steps taken and to declare its confidence in the new Government.

To form an Administration of this scale and complexity is a serious undertaking in itself, but it must be remembered that we are in the preliminary stage of one of the greatest battles in history, that we are in action at many other points in Norway and in Holland, that we have to be prepared in the Mediterranean, that the air battle is continuous and that many preparations, such as have been indicated by my hon. Friend below the Gangway, have to be made here at home. In this crisis I hope I may be pardoned if I do not address the House at any length today. I hope that any of my friends and colleagues, or former colleagues, who are affected by the political reconstruction, will make allowance, all allowance, for any lack of ceremony with which it has been necessary to act. I would say to the House, as I said to those who have joined this Government: "I have nothing to offer but blood, toil, tears and sweat."

We have before us an ordeal of the most grievous kind. We have before us many, many long months of struggle and of suffering. You ask, what is our policy? I can say: It is to wage war, by sea, land and air, with all our might and with all the strength that God can give us; to wage war against a monstrous tyranny, never surpassed in the dark, lamentable catalogue of human crime. That is our policy. You ask, what is our aim? I can answer in one word: It is victory, victory at all costs, victory in spite of all terror, victory, however long and hard the road may be; for without victory, there is no survival. Let that be realised; no survival for the British Empire, no survival for all that the British Empire has stood for, no sur-

vival for the urge and impulse of the ages, that mankind will move forward towards its goal. But I take up my task with buoyancy and hope. I feel sure that our cause will not be suffered to fail among men. At this time I feel entitled to claim the aid of all, and I say, "Come then, let us go forward together with our united strength."

WAR SITUATION

August 20, 1940

Almost a year has passed since the war began, and it is natural for us, I think, to pause on our journey at this milestone and survey the dark, wide field.

Rather more than a quarter of a year has passed since the new Government came into power in this country. What a cataract of disaster has poured out upon us since then. The trustful Dutch overwhelmed; their beloved and respected Sovereign driven into exile; the peaceful city of Rotterdam the scene of a massacre as hideous and brutal as anything in the Thirty Years' War. Belgium invaded and beaten down; our own fine Expeditionary Force, which King Leopold called to his rescue, cut off and almost captured, escaping as it seemed only by a miracle and with the loss of all its equipment; our Ally, France, out; Italy in against us; all France in the power of the enemy, all its arsenals and vast masses of military material converted or convertible to the enemy's use; a puppet Government set up at Vichy which may at any moment be forced to become our foe; the whole Western seaboard of Europe from the North Cape to the Spanish frontier in German hands; all the ports, all the airfields on this immense front, employed against us as potential springboards of invasion. Moreover, the German air power, numerically so far outstripping ours, has been brought so close to our Island that what we used to dread greatly has come to pass and the hostile bombers not only reach our shores in a few minutes and from many directions, but can be escorted by their fighting aircraft. Why Sir, if we had been confronted at the beginning of May with such a prospect, it would have seemed incredible that at the end of a period of horror and disaster, or at this point in a period of horror and disaster, we should stand erect, sure of ourselves, masters of our fate and with the conviction of final victory burning unquenchable in our hearts. Few would have believed we could survive; none would have believed that we should today not only feel stronger but should actually be stronger than we have ever been before.

Let us see what has happened on the other side of the scales. The British nation and the British Empire finding themselves alone, stood undismayed against disaster. No one flinched or wavered; nay, some who formerly thought of peace, now think only of war. Our people are united and resolved, as they have never been before. Death and ruin have become small things compared with the shame of defeat or failure in duty. We cannot tell what lies ahead. It may be that even greater ordeals lie before us. We shall face whatever is coming to us. We are sure of ourselves and of our cause and here then is the supreme fact which has emerged in these months of trial.

Meanwhile, we have not only fortified our hearts but our Island. We have rearmed and rebuilt our armies in a degree which would have been deemed impossible a few months ago. We have ferried across the Atlantic, in the month of July, thanks to our friends over there, an immense mass of munitions of all kinds, cannon, rifles, machine guns, cartridges and shells, all safely landed without the loss of a gun or a round. The output of our own factories, working as they have never worked before, has poured forth to the troops. The whole British Army is at home. More than 2,000,000 determined men have rifles and bayonets in their hands tonight and three-quarters of them are in regular military formations. We have never had armies like this in our Island in time of war. The whole Island bristles against invaders, from the sea or from the air.

Why do I say all this? Not assuredly to boast; not assuredly to give the slightest countenance to complacency. The dangers we face are still enormous, but so are our advantages and resources. I recount them because the people have a right to know that there are solid grounds for the confidence which we feel, and that we have good reason to believe ourselves capable, as I said in a very dark hour two months ago, of continuing the war "if necessary alone, if necessary for years." I say it also because the fact that the British Empire stands invincible, and that Nazidom is still being resisted, will kindle again the spark of hope in the breasts of hundreds of millions of down-trodden or despairing men and women throughout Europe, and far beyond its bounds, and that from these sparks there will presently come a cleansing and devouring flame.

The great air battle which has been in progress over this Island for the last few weeks has recently attained a high intensity. It is too soon to attempt to assign limits either to its scale or to its duration. We must certainly expect that greater efforts will be made by the enemy than any he has so far put forth. Hostile air fields are still being developed in France and the Low Countries, and the movement of squadrons and material for attacking us is still proceeding. It is quite plain that Herr Hitler could not admit defeat in his air attack on Great Britain without sustaining most serious injury. If, after all his boastings and blood-curdling threats and lurid accounts trumpeted round the world of the damage he has inflicted, of the vast numbers of our Air Force he has shot down, so he says, with so little loss to himself; if after tales of the panic-stricken British crouched in their holes cursing the plutocratic Parliament which has led them to such a plight; if after all this his whole air onslaught were forced after a while tamely to peter out, the Führer's reputation for veracity of statement might be seriously impugned. We may be sure, therefore, that he will continue as long as he has the strength to do so, and as long as any preoccupations he may have in respect of the Russian Air Force allow him to do so.

The gratitude of every home in our Island, in our Empire, and indeed throughout the world, except in the abodes of the guilty, goes out to the British airmen who, undaunted by odds, unwearied in their constant challenge and mortal danger, are turning the tide of world war by their prowess and by their devotion. Never in the field of human conflict was so much owed by so many to so few. All hearts go out to the fighter pilots, whose brilliant actions we see with our own eyes day after day, but we must never forget that all the time, night after night, month after month, our bomber squadrons travel far into Germany, find their targets in the darkness by the highest navigational skill, aim their attacks, often under the heaviest fire, often with serious loss, with deliberate, careful discrimination, and inflict shattering blows upon the whole of the technical and war-making structure of the Nazi power.

We are still toiling up the hill, we have not yet reached the crestline of it, we cannot survey the landscape or even imagine what its condition will be when that longed-for morning comes. The task which lies before us immediately is at once more practical, more simple and more stern. I hope—indeed I pray—that we shall not be found unworthy of our victory if after toil and tribulation it is granted to us. For the rest, we have to gain the victory. That is our task.

For my own part, looking out upon the future, I do not view the process with any misgivings. I could not stop it if I wished; no one can stop it. Like the Mississippi, it just keeps rolling along. Let it roll. Let it roll on full flood, inexorable, irresistible, benignant, to broader lands and better days.

1. What was the government's policy at the start of Churchill's premiership?

2. What was Britain's situation after a year of war against the Axis?

3. How does Churchill characterize Britain's military situation? Is he optimistic or pessimistic?

4. Churchill was very unpopular with many people in Britain before the war; yet he became an immensely effective wartime leader. Why? Do his speeches offer any clues to his success?

5. How does Churchill's style of oratory differ from that common among politicians today?

·151·
Charter of the United Nations
(1946)

Drawn closer together in their struggle to defeat fascism at the cost of millions of lives, the leaders of the Allied nations were determined to find an effective means to maintain international stability after World War II. The prewar League of Nations had been a failure, partly because the United States had refused to join and partly because the League had proven incapable of enforcing its decrees. The victorious Allies envisioned something more powerful and universal. In 1946 representatives from around the world met in San Francisco to hammer out a plan to produce a workable international organization. The result was the United Nations. Divided between a General Assembly and a Security Council, the United Nations was to have the responsibility of mediating disputes between nations and, in the last resort, to send its own peace-keeping forces into troubled areas. The Charter of the United Nations was considered the first step in the direction of world government and toward the end of war.

WE THE PEOPLES OF THE UNITED NATIONS DETERMINED

to save succeeding generations from the scourge of war, which twice in our lifetime has brought untold sorrow to mankind, and to reaffirm faith in fundamental human rights, in the dignity and worth of the human person, in the equal rights of men and women and of nations large and small, and

to establish conditions under which justice and respect for the obligations arising from treaties and other sources of international law can be maintained, and

to promote social progress and better standards of life in larger freedom,

AND FOR THESE ENDS

to practice tolerance and live together in peace with one another as good neighbors, and to unite our strength to maintain international peace and security, and

to ensure, by the acceptance of principles and the institution of methods, that armed force shall not be used, save in the common interest, and

to employ international machinery for the promotion of the economic and social advancement of all peoples,

HAVE RESOLVED TO COMBINE OUR EFFORTS TO ACCOMPLISH THESE AIMS.

Accordingly, our respective Governments, through representatives assembled in the city of San Francisco, who have exhibited their full powers found to be in good and due form, have agreed to the present Charter of the United Nations and do hereby establish an international organization to be known as the United Nations.

CHAPTER I: PURPOSES AND PRINCIPLES

Article 1

The Purposes of the United Nations are:

1. To maintain international peace and security, and to that end; to take effective collective measures for the prevention and removal of threats to the peace, and for the suppression of acts of aggression or other breaches of the peace, and to bring about by peaceful means, and in conformity with the principles of justice and international law, adjustment or settlement of international disputes or situations which might lead to a breach of the peace;

2. To develop friendly relations among nations based on respect for the principle of equal rights and self-determination of peoples,

and to take other appropriate measures to strengthen universal peace;

3. To achieve international cooperation in solving international problems of an economic, social, cultural, or humanitarian character, and in promoting and encouraging respect for human rights and for fundamental freedoms for all without distinction as to race, sex, language, or religion; and

4. To be a center for harmonizing the actions of nations in the attainment of these common ends.

Article 2

The Organization and its Members, in pursuit of the Purposes stated in Article 1, shall act in accordance with the following Principles.

1. The Organization is based on the principle of the sovereign equality of all its Members.

2. All Members, in order to ensure to all of them the rights and benefits resulting from membership, shall fulfill in good faith the obligations assumed by them in accordance with the present Charter.

3. All Members shall settle their international disputes by peaceful means in such a manner that international peace and security, and justice, are not endangered.

4. All Members shall refrain in their international relations from the threat of use of force against the territorial integrity or political independence of any state, or in any other manner inconsistent with the Purposes of the United Nations.

5. All Members shall give the United Nations every assistance in any action it takes in accordance with the present Charter, and shall refrain from giving assistance to any state against which the United Nations is taking preventive or enforcement action.

6. The Organization shall ensure that states which are not Members of the United Nations act in accordance with these Principles so far as may be necessary for the maintenance of international peace and security.

7. Nothing contained in the present Charter shall authorize the United Nations to intervene in matters which are essentially within the domestic jurisdiction of any state or shall require the Members to submit such matters to settlement under the present Charter; but this principle shall not prejudice the application of enforcement measures under Chapter VII.

CHAPTER II: MEMBERSHIP

Article 3

The original Members of the United Nations shall be the states which, having participated in the United Nations Conference on International Organization at San Francisco, or having previously signed the Declaration by United Nations of January 1, 1942, sign the present Charter and ratify it in accordance with Article 110.

Article 4

Membership in the United Nations is open to all other peace-loving states which accept the obligations contained in the present Charter and, in the judgment of the Organization, are able and willing to carry out these obligations.

Article 5

A Member of the United Nations against which preventive or enforcement action has been taken by the Security Council may be suspended from the exercise of the rights and privileges of membership by the General Assembly upon the recommendation of the Security Council. The exercise of these rights and privileges may be restored by the Security Council.

Article 6

A Member of the United Nations which has persistently violated the Principles contained in the present Charter may be expelled from the Organization by the General Assembly upon the recommendation of the Security Council.

CHAPTER III: ORGANS

Article 7

There are established as the principal organs of the United Nations: a General Assembly, a Security Council, an Economic and Social Council, a Trusteeship Council, an International Court of Justice, and a Secretariat.

Article 8

The United Nations shall place no restrictions on the eligibility of men and women to participate in any capacity and under conditions of equality in its principal and subsidiary organs.

CHAPTER VI: PACIFIC SETTLEMENT OF DISPUTES

Article 33

1. The parties to any dispute, the continuance of which is likely to endanger the maintenance of international peace and security, shall, first of all, seek a solution by negotiation, enquiry, mediation, conciliation, arbitration, judicial settlement, resort to regional agencies or arrangements, or other peaceful means of their own choice.

2. The Security Council shall, when it deems necessary, call upon the parties to settle their dispute by such means.

Article 34

The Security Council may investigate any dispute, or any situation which might lead to international friction or give rise to a dispute, in order to determine whether the continuance of the dispute or situation is likely to endanger the maintenance of international peace and security.

CHAPTER VII: ACTION WITH RESPECT TO THREATS TO THE PEACE, BREACHES OF THE PEACE, AND ACTS OF AGGRESSION

Article 39

The Security Council shall determine the existence of any threat to the peace, breach of the peace, or act of aggression and shall make recommendations, or decide what measures shall be taken in accordance with Articles 41 and 42, to maintain or restore international peace and security.

Article 41

The Security Council may decide what measures not involving the use of armed force are to be employed to give effect to its decisions, and it may call upon the Members of the United Nations to apply such measures. These may include complete or partial interruption of economic relations and of rail, sea, air, postal, telegraphic, radio, and other means of communication, and the severance of diplomatic relations.

Article 42

Should the Security Council consider that measures provided for in Article 41 would be inadequate or have proved to be inadequate, it may take such action by air, sea, or land forces as may be necessary to maintain or restore international peace and security. Such action may include demonstrations, blockade, and other operations by air, sea, or land forces of Members of the United Nations.

CHAPTER XI: DECLARATION REGARDING NON-SELF-GOVERNING TERRITORIES

Article 73

Members of the United Nations which have or assume responsibilities for the administration of territories whose peoples have not yet attained a full measure of self-government recognize the principle that the interests of the inhabitants of these territories are paramount, and accept as a sacred trust the obligation to promote to the utmost, within the system of international peace and security established by the present Charter, the well-being of the inhabitants of these territories, and, to this end:

a.   to ensure, with due respect for the culture of the peoples concerned, their political, economic, social, and educational advancement, their just treatment, and their protection against abuses;

b.   to develop self-government, to take due account of the political aspirations of the peoples, and to assist them in the progressive development of their free political institutions, according to the particular circumstances of each territory and its peoples and their varying stages of advancement;

c.   to further international peace and security;

d.   to promote constructive measures of development, to encourage research, and to cooperate with one another and, when and where appropriate, with specialized international bodies with a view to the practical achievement of the social, economic, and scientific purposes set forth in this Article.

1.   What is the mission of the United Nations?

2.   How are members of the United Nations supposed to behave toward one another? What are their relative rights within the organization?

3.   How are disputes between members to be resolved?

4.   Under what circumstances may force be used in international affairs?

5.   How does the Charter take into account the realities of postwar international relations?

Struggles for National Liberation

Ho Chi Minh, 1957.

·152·
Mohandas Gandhi
Hind Swaraj
(1938)

*M*ohandas Gandhi (1869–1948), the father of modern India, was trained as a lawyer in England and first practiced in South Africa where he was deeply disturbed by apartheid. He organized the Indian community against racial discrimination, wrote pamphlets attacking the South African government, and was subsequently jailed. He returned to India at the outbreak of World War I and began his political career by protesting British rule. He became head of the Indian National Congress, the political group that advocated independence from British rule. Gandhi was a pacifist and consistently opposed armed opposition to the British. In 1930 Gandhi led one of the central events in the independence movement: a march to the sea to protest the British tax on salt. The marchers sat down and refused to disperse even after being severely beaten by British soldiers. The moral pressure of nonviolent resistance weakened British resolve. In 1947 Gandhi, now known as Mahatma ("Great-Souled"), negotiated with the British for Indian independence. He was assassinated the following year.

Hind Swaraj (*Indian Home Rule*) is one of Gandhi's best-known works. In it Gandhi explains his creed of nonviolence. The piece is written in the form of a dialogue, one of the classic genres for philosophical discussion. Passive resistance became one of the most influential doctrines of the mid-twentieth century and was adopted by Martin Luther King in the struggle against racial discrimination in the United States.

PASSIVE RESISTANCE

READER.   Is there any historical evidence as to the success of what you have called soul-force or truth-force? No instance seems to have happened of any nation having risen through soul-force. I still think that the evil-doers will not cease doing evil without physical punishment.

EDITOR.   The poet Tulsidas has said: "Of religion, pity, or love, is the root, as egotism of the body. Therefore, we should not abandon pity so long as we are alive." This appears to me to be a scientific truth. I believe in it as much as I believe in two and two being four. The force of love is the same as the force of the soul or truth. We have evidence of its working at every step. The universe would disappear without the existence of that force. But you ask for historical evidence. It is, therefore, necessary to know what history means. The Gujarati equivalent means: "It so happened". If that is the meaning of history, it is possible to give copious evidence. But, if it means the doings of kings and emperors, there can be no evidence of soul-force or passive resistance in such history. You cannot expect silver ore in a tin mine. History, as we know it, is a record of the wars of the world, and so there is a proverb among Englishmen that a nation which has no history, that is, no wars, is a happy nation. How kings played, how they became enemies of one another, how they murdered one another, is found accurately recorded in history, and if this were all that had happened in the world, it would have been ended long ago. If the story of the universe had commenced with wars, not a man would have been found alive today. Those people who have been warred against have disappeared as, for instance, the natives of Australia of whom hardly a man was left alive by the intruders. Mark, please, that these natives did not use soul-force in self-defence, and it does not require much foresight to know that the Australians will share the same fate as their victims. "Those that take the sword shall perish by the sword." With us the proverb is that professional swimmers will find a watery grave.

The fact that there are so many men still alive in the world shows that it is based not on the force of arms but on the force of truth or love. Therefore, the greatest and most unimpeachable evidence of the success of this force is to be found in the fact that, in spite of the wars of the world, it still lives on.

Thousands, indeed tens of thousands, depend for their existence on a very active working of this force. Little quarrels of millions of families in their daily lives disappear before the exercise of this force. Hundreds of nations live in peace. History does not and cannot take note of this fact. History is really a record of every interruption of the even working of the force of love or of the soul. Two brothers quarrel; one of them repents and re-awakens the love that was lying dormant in him; the two again begin to live in peace; nobody takes note of this. But if the two brothers, through the intervention of solicitors or some other reason take up arms or go to law—which is another form of the exhibition of brute force,—their doings would be immediately noticed in the press, they would be the talk of

their neighbours and would probably go down to history. And what is true of families and communities is true of nations. There is no reason to believe that there is one law for families and another for nations. History, then, is a record of an interruption of the course of nature. Soul-force, being natural, is not noted in history.

READER. According to what you say, it is plain that instances of this kind of passive resistance are not to be found in history. It is necessary to understand this passive resistance more fully. It will be better, therefore, if you enlarge upon it.

EDITOR. Passive resistance is a method of securing rights by personal suffering; it is the reverse of resistance by arms. When I refuse to do a thing that is repugnant to my conscience, I use soul-force. For instance, the Government of the day has passed a law which is applicable to me. I do not like it. If by using violence I force the Government to repeal the law, I am employing what may be termed body-force. If I do not obey the law and accept the penalty for its breach, I use soul-force. It involves sacrifice of self.

Everybody admits that sacrifice of self is infinitely superior to sacrifice of others. Moreover, if this kind of force is used in a cause that is unjust, only the person using it suffers. He does not make others suffer for his mistakes. Men have before now done many things which were subsequently found to have been wrong. No man can claim that he is absolutely in the right or that a particular thing is wrong because he thinks so, but it is wrong for him so long as that is his deliberate judgment. It is therefore meet that he should not do that which he knows to be wrong, and suffer the consequence whatever it may be. This is the key to the use of soul-force.

READER. You would then disregard laws—this is rank disloyalty. We have always been considered a law-abiding nation. You seem to be going even beyond the extremists. They say that we must obey the laws that have been passed, but that if the laws be bad, we must drive out the law-givers even by force.

EDITOR. Whether I go beyond them or whether I do not is a matter of no consequence to either of us. We simply want to find out what is right and to act accordingly. The real meaning of the statement that we are a law-abiding nation is that we are passive resisters. When we do not like certain laws, we do not break the heads of law-givers but we suffer and do not submit to the laws. That we should obey laws whether good or bad is a new-fangled notion. There was no such thing in former days. The people disregarded those laws they did not like and suffered the penalties for their breach. It is contrary to our manhood if we obey laws repugnant to our conscience. Such teaching is opposed to religion and means slavery. If the Government were to ask us to go about without any clothing, should we do so? If I were a passive resister, I would say to them that I would have nothing to do with their law. But we have so forgotten ourselves and become so compliant that we do not mind any degrading law.

A man who has realized his manhood, who fears only God, will fear no one else. Man-made laws are not necessarily binding on him. Even the Government does not expect any such thing from us. They do not say: "You must do such and such a thing," but they say: "If you do not do it, we will punish you." We are sunk so low that we fancy that it is our duty and our religion to do what the law lays down. If man will only realize that it is unmanly to obey laws that are unjust, no man's tyranny will enslave him. This is the key to self-rule or home-rule.

It is a superstition and ungodly thing to believe that an act of a majority binds a minority. Many examples can be given in which acts of majorities will be found to have been wrong and those of minorities to have been right. All reforms owe their origin to the initiation of minorities in opposition to majorities. If among a band of robbers a knowledge of robbing is obligatory, is a pious man to accept the obligation? So long as the superstition that men should obey unjust laws exists, so long will their slavery exist. And a passive resister alone can remove such a superstition.

To use brute-force, to use gunpowder, is contrary to passive resistance, for it means that we want our opponent to do by force that which we desire but he does not. And if such a use of force is justifiable, surely he is entitled to do likewise by us. And so we should never come to an agreement. We may simply fancy, like the blind horse moving in a circle round a mill, that we are making progress. Those who believe that they are not bound to obey laws which are repugnant to their conscience have only the remedy of passive resistance open to them. Any other must lead to disaster.

READER. From what you say I deduce that passive resistance is a splendid weapon of the weak, but that when they are strong they may take up arms.

EDITOR. This is gross ignorance. Passive resistance, that is, soul-force, is matchless. It is superior to the force of arms. How, then, can it be considered only a weapon of the weak? Physical-force men are strangers to the courage that is requisite in a passive resister. Do you believe that a coward can ever disobey a law that he dislikes? Extremists are considered to be advocates of brute force. Why do they, then, talk about obeying laws? I do not blame them. They can say nothing else. When they succeed in driving out the English and they themselves become governors, they will want you and me to obey their laws. And that is a fitting thing for their constitution. But a passive resister will say he will not obey a law that is against his conscience, even though he may be blown to pieces at the mouth of a cannon.

What do you think? Wherein is courage required—in blowing others to pieces from behind a cannon, or with a smiling face to approach a cannon and be blown to pieces? Who is the true warrior—he who keeps death always as a bosom-friend, or he who controls the death of others? Believe me that a man devoid of courage and manhood can never be a passive resister.

This however, I will admit: that even a man weak in body is capable of offering this resistance. One man can offer it just as well as millions. Both men and women can indulge in it. It does not require the training of an army; it needs no jiu-jitsu. Control over the mind is alone necessary, and when that is attained, man is free like the king of the forest and his very glance withers the enemy.

Passive resistance is an all-sided sword, it can be used anyhow; it blesses him who uses it and him against whom it is used. Without drawing a drop of blood it produces far-reaching results. It never rusts and cannot be stolen. Competition between passive resisters does not exhaust. The sword of passive resistance does not require a scabbard. It is strange indeed that you should consider such a weapon to be a weapon merely of the weak.

READER.   You have said that passive resistance is a speciality of India. Have cannons never been used in India?

EDITOR.   Evidently, in your opinion, India means its few princes. To me it means its teeming millions on whom depends the existence of its princes and our own.

Kings will always use their kingly weapons. To use force is bred in them. They want to command, but those who have to obey commands do not want guns: and these are in a majority throughout the world. They have to learn either body-force or soul-force. Where they learn the former, both the rulers and the ruled become like so many madmen; but where they learn soul-force, the commands of the rulers do not go beyond the point of their swords, for true men disregard unjust commands. Peasants have never been subdued by the sword, and never will be. They do not know the use of the sword, and they are not frightened by the use of it by others. That nation is great which rests its head upon death as its pillow. Those who defy death are free from all fear. For those who are labouring under the delusive charms of brute-force, this picture is not overdrawn. The fact is that, in India, the nation at large has generally used passive resistance in all departments of life. We cease to co-operate with our rulers when they displease us. This is passive resistance.

I remember an instance when, in a small principality, the villagers were offended by some command issued by the prince. The former immediately, began vacating the village. The prince became nervous, apologized to his subjects and withdrew his command. Many such instances can be found in India. Real Home Rule is possible only where passive resistance is the guiding force of the people. Any other rule is foreign rule.

READER.   Then you will say that it is not at all necessary for us to train the body?

EDITOR.   I will certainly not say any such thing. It is difficult to become a passive resister unless the body is trained. As a rule, the mind, residing in a body that has become weakened by pampering, is also weak, and where there is no strength of mind there can be no strength of soul. We shall have to improve our physique by getting rid of infant marriages and luxurious living. If I were to ask a man with a shattered body to face a cannon's mouth I should make a laughing-stock of myself.

READER.   From what you say, then, it would appear that it is not a small thing to become a passive resister, and, if that is so, I should like you to explain how a man may become one.

EDITOR.   To become a passive resister is easy enough but it is also equally difficult. I have known a lad of fourteen years become a passive resister; I have known also sick people do likewise; and I have also known physically strong and otherwise happy people unable to take up passive resistance. After a great deal of experience it seems to me that those who want to become passive resisters for the service of the country have to observe perfect chastity, adopt poverty, follow truth, and cultivate fearlessness.

Chastity is one of the greatest disciplines without which the mind cannot attain requisite firmness. A man who is unchaste loses stamina, becomes emasculated and cowardly. He whose mind is given over to animal passions is not capable of any great effort. This can be proved by innumerable instances. What, then, is a married person to do is the question that arises naturally; and yet it need not. When a husband and wife gratify the passions, it is no less an animal indulgence on that account. Such an indulgence, except for perpetuating the race, is strictly prohibited. But a passive resister has to avoid even that very limited indulgence because he can have no desire for progeny. A married man, therefore, can observe perfect chastity. This subject is not capable of being treated at greater length. Several questions arise: How is one to carry one's wife with one, what are her rights, and other similar questions. Yet those who wish to take part in a great work are bound to solve these puzzles.

Just as there is necessity for chastity, so is there for poverty. Pecuniary ambition and passive resistance cannot well go together. Those who have money are not expected to throw it away, but they *are* expected to be indifferent about it. They must be prepared to lose every penny rather than give up passive resistance.

Passive resistance has been described in the course of our discussion as truth-force. Truth, therefore, has necessarily to be followed and that at any cost. In this connection, academic questions such as whether a man may not lie in order to save a life, etc., arise, but these questions occur only to those who wish to justify lying. Those who want to follow truth every time are not placed in such a quandary; and if they are, they are still saved from a false position.

Passive resistance cannot proceed a step without fearlessness. Those alone can follow the path of passive resistance who are free from fear, whether as to their possessions, false honour, their relatives, the government, bodily injuries or death.

These observances are not to be abandoned in the belief that they are difficult. Nature has implanted in the human breast ability to cope with any difficulty or suffering that may come to man unprovoked. These qualities are worth having, even for those who do not wish to serve the country. Let there be no mistake, as those who want to train themselves in the use of arms are also obliged to have these qualities more or less. Everybody does not become a warrior for the wish. A would-be warrior will have to observe chastity and to be satisfied with poverty as his lot. A warrior without fearlessness cannot be conceived of. It may be thought that he would not need to be exactly truthful, but that quality follows real fearlessness. When a man abandons truth, he does so owing to fear in some shape or form. The above four attributes, then, need not frighten anyone. It may be as well here to note that a physical-force man has to have many other useless qualities which a passive resister never needs. And you will find that whatever extra effort a swordsman needs is due to lack of fearlessness. If he is an embodiment of the latter, the sword will drop from his hand that very moment. He does not need its support. One who is free from hatred requires no sword. A man with a stick suddenly came face to face with a lion and instinctively raised his weapon in self-defence. The man saw that he had only prated about fearlessness when there was none in him. That moment he dropped the stick and found himself free from all fear.

1. How does passive resistance work?

2. Why does Gandhi call passive resistance "soul-force" or "truth-force?"

3. What are the attributes of a successful passive resister? Why are they necessary?

4. Why is *Hind Swaraj* written as a dialogue?

·153·
Mao Zedong
On Letting a Hundred Flowers Blossom
(1957)

Mao Zedong (1893–1976) was the leader of the Chinese Communist Revolution and chairman of the People's Republic of China and the Chinese Communist party. Mao began his political career as a soldier in the army of Sun Yat-sen, which overthrew the Manchu dynasty. He converted to Marxism in the early 1920s and organized a Communist movement, mostly of peasants. Mao led the Communists in a long war against the Nationalist forces under the command of Chiang Kai-shek. The victory of the Red Army, which Mao commanded, finally came in 1949. He was chairman of the People's Republic for the next decade, but the failure of his economic reforms led to his resignation in 1959. Nevertheless, Mao remained chairman of the Communist party and effective leader of the country, especially during the Cultural Revolution that began in 1966. After his death, most of Mao's policies were discredited but his cult status as father of modern China was stronger than ever.

In 1957 Mao announced a policy of self-criticism in a speech that came to be known as "The Hundred Flowers" speech. It initiated a brief period of free speech and appraisal of Communist rule in China. But criticism of the party and of Chairman Mao was so widespread that Mao reversed his position and suppressed the "hundred flowers" who had spoken and written against him.

"Let a hundred flowers blossom," and "let a hundred schools of thought contend," "long-term coexistence and mutual supervision"—how did these slogans come to be put forward?

They were put forward in the light of the specific conditions existing in China, on the basis of the recognition that various kinds of contradictions still exist in a socialist society, and in response to the country's urgent need to speed up its economic and cultural development.

The policy of letting a hundred flowers blossom and a hundred schools of thought contend is designed to promote the flourishing of the arts and the progress of science; it is designed to enable a socialist culture to thrive in our land. Different forms and styles in art can develop freely and different schools in science can contend freely. We think that it is harmful to the growth of art and science if administrative measures are used to impose one particular style of art or school of thought and to ban another. Questions of right and wrong in the arts and sciences should be settled through free discussion in artistic and scientific circles and in the course of practical work in the arts and sciences. They should not be settled in summary fashion. A period of trial is often needed to determine whether something is right or wrong. In the past, new and correct things often failed at the outset to win recognition from the majority of people and had to develop by twists and turns in struggle. Correct and good things have often at first been looked upon not as fragrant flowers but as poisonous weeds. Copernicus' theory of the solar system and Darwin's theory of evolution were once dismissed as erroneous and had to win through over bitter opposition. Chinese history offers many similar examples. In socialist society, conditions for the growth of new things are radically different from and far superior to those in the old society. Nevertheless, it still often happens that new, rising forces are held back and reasonable suggestions smothered.

The growth of new things can also be hindered, not because of deliberate suppression, but because of lack of discernment. That is why we should take a cautious attitude in regard to questions of right and wrong in the arts and sciences, encourage free discussion, and avoid hasty conclusions. We believe that this attitude will facilitate the growth of the arts and sciences.

Marxism has also developed through struggle. At the beginning, Marxism was subjected to all kinds of attack and regarded as a poisonous weed. It is still being attacked and regarded as a poisonous weed in many parts of the world. However, it enjoys a different position in the socialist countries. But even in these countries, there are non-Marxist as well as anti-Marxist ideologies. It is true that in China, socialist transformation, in so far as a change in the system of ownership is concerned, has in the main been completed, and the turbulent, large-scale, mass class struggles characteristic of the revolutionary periods have in the main concluded. But remnants of the overthrown landlord and comprador classes still exist, the bourgeoisie still exists, and the petty bourgeoisie has only just begun to remould itself. Class struggle is not yet over. The class struggle between the proletariat and the bourgeoisie, the class struggle between various political

cal forces, and the class struggle in the ideological field between the proletariat and the bourgeoisie will still be long and devious and at times may even become very acute. The proletariat seeks to transform the world according to its own world outlook, so does the bourgeoisie. In this respect, the question whether socialism or capitalism will win is still not really settled. Marxists are still a minority of the entire population as well as of the intellectuals. Marxism therefore must still develop through struggle. Marxism can only develop through struggle—this is true not only in the past and present, it is necessarily true in the future also. What is correct always develops in the course of struggle with what is wrong. The true, the good and the beautiful always exist in comparison with the false, the evil and the ugly, and grow in struggle with the latter. As mankind in general rejects an untruth and accepts a truth, a new truth will begin struggling with new erroneous ideas. Such struggles will never end. This is the law of development of truth and it is certainly also the law of development of Marxism.

It will take a considerable time to decide the issue in the ideological struggle between socialism and capitalism in our country. This is because the influence of the bourgeoisie and of the intellectuals who come from the old society will remain in our country as the ideology of a class for a long time to come. Failure to grasp this, or still worse, failure to understand it at all, can lead to the gravest mistakes—to ignoring the necessity of waging the struggle in the ideological field. Ideological struggle is not like other forms of struggle. Crude, coercive methods should not be used in this struggle, but only the method of painstaking reasoning. Today, socialism enjoys favourable conditions in the ideological struggle. The main power of the state is in the hands of the working people led by the proletariat. The Communist Party is strong and its prestige stands high. Although there are defects and mistakes in our work, every fair-minded person can see that we are loyal to the people, that we are both determined and able to build up our country together with the people, and that we have achieved great successes and will achieve still greater ones. The vast majority of the bourgeoisie and intellectuals who come from the old society are patriotic; they are willing to serve their flourishing socialist motherland, and they know that if they turn away from the socialist cause and the working people led by the Communist Party, they will have no one to rely on and no bright future to look forward to.

People may ask: Since Marxism is accepted by the majority of the people in our country as the guiding ideology, can it be criticized? Certainly it can. As a scientific truth, Marxism fears no criticism. If it did, and could be defeated in argument, it would be worthless. In fact, aren't the idealists criticizing Marxism every day and in all sorts of ways? As for those who harbour bourgeois and petty-bourgeois ideas and do not wish to change, aren't they also criticizing Marxism in all sorts of ways? Marxists should not be afraid of criticism from any quarter. Quite the contrary, they need to steel and improve themselves and win new positions in the teeth of criticism and the storm and stress of struggle. Fighting against wrong ideas is like being vaccinated—a man develops greater immunity from disease after the vaccine takes effect. Plants raised in hot-houses are not likely to be robust. Carrying out the policy of "letting a hundred flowers blossom and a hundred schools of thought contend" will not weaken but strengthen the leading position of Marxism in the ideological field.

What should our policy be towards non-Marxist ideas? As far as unmistakable counter-revolutionaries and wreckers of the socialist cause are concerned, the matter is easy: we simply deprive them of their freedom of speech. But it is quite a different matter when we are faced with incorrect ideas among the people. Will it do to ban such ideas and give them no opportunity to express themselves? Certainly not. It is not only futile but very harmful to use crude and summary methods to deal with ideological questions among the people, with questions relating to the spiritual life of man. You may ban the expression of wrong ideas, but the ideas will still be there. On the other hand, correct ideas, if

pampered in hot-houses without being exposed to the elements or immunized from disease, will not win out against wrong ones. That is why it is only by employing methods of discussion, criticism and reasoning that we can really foster correct ideas, overcome wrong ideas, and really settle issues.

The bourgeoisie and petty bourgeoisie are bound to give expression to their ideologies. It is inevitable that they should stubbornly persist in expressing themselves in every way possible on political and ideological questions. You can't expect them not to do so. We should not use methods of suppression to prevent them from expressing themselves, but should allow them to do so and at the same time argue with them and direct well-considered criticism at them.

There can be no doubt that we should criticize all kinds of wrong ideas. It certainly would not do to refrain from criticism and look on while wrong ideas spread unchecked and acquire their market. Mistakes should be criticized and poisonous weeds fought against wherever they crop up. But such criticism should not be doctrinaire. We should not use the metaphysical method, but strive to employ the dialectical method. What is needed is scientific analysis and fully convincing arguments. Doctrinaire criticism settles nothing. We don't want any kind of poisonous weeds, but we should carefully distinguish between what is really a poisonous weed and what is really a fragrant flower. We must learn together with the masses of the people how to make this careful distinction, and use the correct methods to fight poisonous weeds.

While criticizing doctrinairism, we should at the same time direct our attention to criticizing revisionism. Revisionism, or rightist opportunism, is a bourgeois trend of thought which is even more dangerous than doctrinairism. The revisionists, or right opportunists, pay lip-service to Marxism and also attack "doctrinairism". But the real target of their attack is actually the most fundamental elements of Marxism. They oppose or distort materialism and dialectics, oppose or try to weaken the people's democratic dictatorship and the leading role of the Communist

Party, oppose or try to weaken socialist transformation and socialist construction. Even after the basic victory of the socialist revolution in our country, there are still a number of people who vainly hope for a restoration of the capitalist system. They wage a struggle against the working class on every front, including the ideological front. In this struggle, their right-hand men are the revisionists.

On the surface, these two slogans—"let a hundred flowers blossom" and "let a hundred schools of thought contend"—have no class character: the proletariat can turn them to account, so can the bourgeoisie and other people. But different classes, strata and social groups each have their own views on what are fragrant flowers and what are poisonous weeds. So what, from the point of view of the broad masses of the people, should be the criteria today for distinguishing between fragrant flowers and poisonous weeds?

In the political life of our country, how are our people to determine what is right and what is wrong in our words and actions? Basing ourselves on the principles of our Constitution, the will of the overwhelming majority of our people and the political programmes jointly proclaimed on various occasions by our political parties and groups, we believe that, broadly speaking, words and actions can be judged right if they:

1.   Help to unite the people of our various nationalities, and do not divide them;

2.   Are beneficial, not harmful, to socialist transformation and socialist construction;

3.   Help to consolidate, not undermine or weaken, the people's democratic dictatorship;

4.   Help to consolidate, not undermine or weaken, democratic centralism;

5.   Tend to strengthen, not to cast off or weaken, the leadership of the Communist Party;

6.   Are beneficial, not harmful, to international socialist solidarity and the solidarity of the peace-loving peoples of the world.

Of these six criteria, the most important are the socialist path and the leadership of the Party. These criteria are put forward in order to foster, and not hinder, the free discussion of various questions among the people. Those who do not approve of these criteria can still put forward their own views and argue their case. When the majority of the people have clear-cut criteria to go by, criticism and self-criticism can be conducted along proper lines, and these criteria can be applied to people's words and actions to determine whether they are fragrant flowers or poisonous weeds. These are political criteria. Naturally, in judging the truthfulness of scientific theories or assessing the aesthetic value of works of art, other pertinent criteria are needed, but these six political criteria are also applicable to all activities in the arts or sciences. In a socialist country like ours, can there possibly be any useful scientific or artistic activity which runs counter to these political criteria?

All that is set out above stems from the specific historical conditions in our country. Since conditions vary in different socialist countries and with different Communist Parties, we do not think that other countries and Parties must or need to follow the Chinese way.

1.   What problem is Mao trying to address in this passage? What is his solution?

2.   What role does Mao envision for the Communist party in China?

3.   What does the slogan "Let a hundred flowers blossom" mean? Does Mao believe in the concept behind this slogan?

4.   Why does Mao think struggle is necessary for the development of Marxism?

·154·

Ho Chi Minh
Selected Writings
(1945, 1968)

*H*o Chi Minh (1890–1969), whose given name was Nguyen Tat Thanh, was the president of the Democratic Republic of Vietnam and the leader of the Vietnamese revolutionary movement. He was born in rural poverty, but his father was a scholar; thus, Ho received an education, and began his career as a school teacher. In 1917 he took passage to Europe and America as a ship's cook and spent six years in France. There he organized Vietnamese ex-patriots and studied politics. He was deeply impressed with the Russian Revolution, becoming a Communist convert and going to Moscow in 1923. For the next decade Ho organized a series of Indochinese revolutionary parties from bases in China and Europe. During World War II he took the name Ho Chi Minh ("He Who Enlightens") and began organizing against the Japanese occupation of Vietnam. After the war, Ho, in collaboration with the American secret service, moved his organization into Hanoi, where, in 1945, he issued the Vietnamese Declaration of Independence. For the rest of his life Ho Chi Minh led the Vietnamese nationalist struggle, first against France and then the United States. He died before the final liberation of his country was achieved.

The documents printed here come from the voluminous body of Ho's writings and speeches. The Vietnamese Declaration of Independence was issued after the Allied armies had expelled the Japanese from Indochina. His "Appeal to the Nation" in 1968 came after President Lyndon Johnson ended the bombing of North Vietnam.

DECLARATION OF INDEPENDENCE OF THE DEMOCRATIC REPUBLIC OF VIET NAM

"All men are created equal. They are endowed by their Creator with certain unalienable Rights; among these are Life, Liberty and the pursuit of Happiness."

This immortal statement appeared in the Declaration of Independence of the United States of America in 1776. In a broader sense, it means: All the peoples on the earth are equal from birth, all the peoples have a right to live and to be happy and free.

The Declaration of the Rights of Man and the Citizen, made at the time of the French Revolution, in 1791, also states: "All men are born free and with equal rights, and must always remain free and have equal rights."

Those are undeniable truths.

Nevertheless, for more than eighty years, the French imperialists, abusing the standard of Liberty, Equality and Fraternity, have violated our

Fatherland and oppressed our fellow-citizens. They have acted contrary to the ideals of humanity and justice.

Politically, they have deprived our people of every democratic liberty.

They have enforced inhuman laws; they have set up three different political regimes in the North, the Centre and the South of Viet Nam in order to wreck our country's oneness and prevent our people from being united.

They have built more prisons than schools. They have mercilessly massacred our patriots. They have drowned our uprisings in seas of blood.

They have fettered public opinion and practised obscurantism.

They have weakened our race with opium and alcohol.

In the field of economics, they have sucked us dry, driven our people to destitution and devastated our land.

They have robbed us of our ricefields, our mines, our forests and our natural resources. They have monopolized the issue of bank-notes and the import and export trade.

They have invented numerous unjustifiable taxes and reduced our people, especially our peasantry, to extreme poverty.

They have made it impossible for our national bourgeoisie to prosper; they have mercilessly exploited our workers.

In the autumn of 1940, when the Japanese fascists invaded Indochina to establish new bases against the Allies, the French colonialists went down on their bended knees and opened the doors of our country to welcome the Japanese in.

Thus, from that date, our people were subjected to the double yoke of the French and the Japanese. Their sufferings and miseries increased. The result was that towards the end of last year and the beginning of this year, from Quang Tri province to the North, more than two million of our fellow-citizens died from starvation.

On the 9th of March this year, the French troops were disarmed by the Japanese. The French colonialists either fled or surrendered, showing that not only were they incapable of "protecting" us, but that, in a period of five years, they had twice sold our country to the Japanese.

Before the 9th of March, how often the Viet Minh had urged the French to ally themselves with it against the Japanese! But instead of agreeing to this proposal, the French colonialists only intensified their terrorist activities against the Viet Minh. After their defeat and before fleeing, they massacred the political prisoners detained at Yen Bai and Cao Bang.

In spite of all this, our fellow-citizens have always manifested a lenient and humane attitude towards the French. After the Japanese putsch of March 9, 1945, the Viet Minh helped many Frenchmen to cross the frontier, rescued others from Japanese jails and protected French lives and property. In fact, since the autumn of 1940, our country had ceased to be a French colony and had become a Japanese possession.

When the Japanese surrendered to the Allies, our entire people rose to gain power and founded the Democratic Republic of Viet Nam.

The truth is that we have wrested our independence from the Japanese, not from the French.

The French have fled, the Japanese have capitulated, Emperor Bao Dai has abdicated. Our people have broken the chains which have fettered them for nearly a century and have won independence for Viet Nam. At the same time they have overthrown the centuries-old monarchic regime and established a democratic republican regime.

We, the Provisional Government of the new Viet Nam, representing the entire Vietnamese people, hereby declare that from now on we break off all relations of a colonial character with France; cancel all treaties signed by France on Viet Nam, and abolish all privileges held by France in our country.

The entire Vietnamese people are of one mind in their determination to oppose all wicked schemes by the French colonialists.

We are convinced that the Allies, which at the Teheran and San Francisco Conferences upheld the principle of equality among the nations, cannot fail to recognize the right of the Vietnamese people to independence.

A people who have courageously opposed French enslavement for more than eighty years, a people who have resolutely sided with the Allies against the fascists during these last years, such a people must be free, such a people must be independent.

For these reasons, we, the Provisional Government of the Democratic Republic of Viet Nam, solemnly make this declaration to the world:

Viet Nam has the right to enjoy freedom and independence and in fact has become a free and independent country. The entire Vietnamese people are determined to mobilize all their physical and mental strength, to sacrifice their lives and property in order to safeguard their freedom and independence.

APPEAL TO THE NATION

Fellow-countrymen and fighters all over the country,

Under the impact of the great victories won by our armed forces and people in both zones, especially in the South since early spring this year, the United States government was forced on Nov. 1st, 1968 to end unconditionally its bombing and shelling on the whole territory of the Democratic Republic of Viet Nam.

Indeed, four years of incredibly heroic fighting of our armed forces and people have yielded tremendous results: more than 3,200 aircraft shot down, hundreds of war vessels, big and small, set on fire, the US war of destruction against the North of our country brought to nothing.

This is a victory of momentous significance for our people's great resistance against American aggression, for national salvation.

The American imperialists had mistakenly expected that the savage destructive power of their bombs and shells would weaken the North, prevent the flow of support from the great rear area to the great fighting front and impair the fighting strength of the South. In fact, in the course of the fight against the American aggressors, the all-round strength of the North has never ceased growing, and its wholehearted assistance to the liberation struggle of our valiant Southern fellow-countrymen has been maintained. Similarly, our Southern compatriots' unity, force, and successes have been increasing as their struggle against US aggression grows in intensity.

Our victory can be ascribed to our Party's sound revolutionary line, our people's fervent patriotism, the strength of their oneness of mind and determination to win, and our fine socialist regime. It goes to the common credit of our armed forces and people in both zones, South and North. It is also a victory won by the people of the fraternal socialist countries and our friends on the five continents.

On this occasion, on behalf of the Party and the Government, I warmly praise our fellow-countrymen and fighters all over the country, and sincerely thank the fraternal socialist countries, friendly countries far and near, and the world peoples, including the progressives in the USA, for their great help and for their sympathy and support.

Dear fellow-countrymen and fighters,

We have defeated the war of destruction of the American imperialists in the North. But this is only an initial victory. The American imperialists are very obdurate and perfidious. They talk of "peace" and "negotiation" but still harbour dark aggressive designs. More than a million American, puppet and satellite troops are still daily committing untold crimes against our Southern compatriots.

Therefore, the sacred duty of our entire people at present is to stiffen our determination to fight and win, our resolve to liberate the South, defend the North and ultimately achieve peaceful national reunification.

So long as a single aggressor remains on our soil, we must continue our fight and wipe him out.

Let our gallant Southern people and fighters, under the glorious banner of the South Viet Nam National Front for Liberation, stage uninterrupted offensives and uprisings and resolutely advance towards complete victory.

Let the Northern armed forces and people bend all their efforts in patriotic emulation to build socialism and fulfil their duty towards their Southern kinsmen, constantly sharpen their watchfulness, practise self-reliance, increase their strength and preparedness, and frustrate all new schemes of the enemy.

We are confident that our people's resistance to American aggression, for national salvation, will enlist ever growing sympathy, support and help from the peoples of the fraternal countries and all over the world, including progressive Americans.

After nearly a hundred years under the yoke of colonial servitude and more than twenty years of resistance against imperialist aggressive wars, our people, more than any other people hold peace which is so badly needed for national construction deep in their hearts. But this must be genuine peace in independence and freedom.

That is why we firmly insist that:

—The United States government put an end to its war of aggression against Viet Nam and definitively abstain from all encroachments on the sovereignty and security of the Democratic Republic of Viet Nam;

—All American and satellite troops be withdrawn from South Viet Nam;

—The internal affairs of the South be settled by the Southern people themselves in accordance with the Political Programme of the South Viet Nam National Front for Liberation, without foreign interference;

—The question of the reunification of Viet Nam be settled by the people of the two zones, South and North, free from foreign intervention.

Dear fellow-countrymen and fighters,

Many hardships and sacrifices still lie ahead, but our people's great resistance against American aggression and for national salvation, is progressing at a brisk pace toward victory. The Fatherland is calling on us to march vigorously forward to defeat the American aggressors completely!

The American imperialists will certainly be defeated!

Our people will undoubtedly win!

1. What was Ho asserting independence from? On what grounds?

2. Why does Ho use the American and French declarations as models for his own? What does he see as the most important parts of these works?

3. What did Ho hope to achieve by delivering his "Appeal to the Nation"?

4. Why does Ho include references to "progressive Americans" in his "Appeal"?

·155·

Kwame Nkrumah
A Republican Form of Government
(1960)

Kwame Nkrumah (1909–1972) was the first prime minister of Ghana and became, in 1960, the first president of the Republic of Ghana. He was born in the British colony of the Gold Coast where he was first educated and later taught school. In 1939 he went to the United States to further his education, receiving a master's degree from the University of Pennsylvania; he also studied at the London School of Economics. Nkrumah was influenced by the ideas of the Black Nationalists and became one of the early spokesmen of the Pan-African movement, which promoted the liberation and unification of African colonies. He returned to the Gold Coast in 1947 and led a nonviolent resistance movement against British rule. Ten years later, he was elected the first prime minister of an independent Ghana.

In "A Republican Form of Government," Nkrumah argues for complete independence even from the status of a commonwealth nation, and when Ghana became a republic later that year, he was elected its first president. But Nkrumah could not rule as a democratic leader. His own authoritarian personality and several unsuccessful attempts to assassinate him led to the suppression of opposition political parties, the suspension of freedom of speech and of the press, and imprisonments without trial. In 1966 he was overthrown by the army and he died in exile.

On the third anniversary of our Independence I broadcast the news that the Government had drawn up proposals for a new Republican constitution, and that a plebiscite would be held to allow the people to decide whether or not to accept them:

The Convention People's Party and the Government believe that the authority to govern a state should spring from the people and that the people's right to exercise these powers is based on the principle of one man, one vote. In the first Article of the draft Constitution it is stated that 'without distinction of sex, race, tribe, religion or political belief, every person who, being by law a citizen of Ghana, has attained the age of twenty-one years and is not disqualified by law on grounds of absence, infirmity of mind or criminality, shall be entitled to one vote'. We realise that only when this principle of one man, one vote is adopted throughout the length and breadth of the continent of Africa, can the misery and oppression, which prevail in many parts of this continent, come to an end. It is our aim to strive with all our might to bring this about.

The Convention People's Party and the Government believe also that the people of Africa will never be truly great, happy and prosperous while they remain divided into a number of small states. In the new Constitution we advocate strongly the principle of African unity. So deep is our faith in African unity that we have declared our preparedness to surrender the sovereignty of Ghana, in whole or in part, in the interest of a Union of African States and Territories as soon as ever such a union becomes practicable. The keynote of the Constitution which we are putting before you is: One man, one vote and unity of Africa, namely, the political union of African countries.

I explained that while the system of a ceremonial head of state might be suitable in some countries, it was quite contrary to the historical tradition and true character of Ghana. In the draft constitution, therefore, it was proposed that the head of state would also be the actual head of government, in accordance with the cherished traditions of our country. This would mean that, as in the case of India and Pakistan, which are Republics, and Malaya, which has a Paramount Ruler, the Queen would be recognised by Ghana as Head of the Commonwealth, but not as Head of State. The first President of Ghana would be elected by a direct vote of the people:

The draft Constitution provides that the election of the President thereafter will be linked with the election of Members to the National Assembly in such a way that the President will be the leader of the party which commands a majority in Parliament.

Under this draft Constitution, the President will be assisted in administering the country by a Cabinet drawn from Members of Parliament. In this way both the National Assembly and the political party which wins the general election will be closely associated in the running of the state.

The sovereign law-making body will be Parliament which will consist of the President and the National Assembly. The President will not be a Member of the National Assembly, but he will have the same powers in relation to Parliament as the Head of State at present possesses.

Parliament is not, however, given direct power to alter the basic principles of the Constitution. Only the people can do this, and only after they have been consulted in a referendum ordered by the President will Parliament be entitled to make any law which alters these basic principles of the Constitution.

The essence of the Constitution which we are asking you to approve is that Ghana is a sovereign, unitary Republic, that there is a President responsible to the people and a Cabinet to assist him which is chosen from amongst Members of Parliament.

Equally essential is the existence and the legislative power of Parliament. This cannot be taken away unless the people are consulted, nor can Parliament's exclusive rights over what taxes are imposed be abrogated.

I outlined other features of the proposed Constitution, which I urged everyone to study at leisure the following day when the constitutional proposals and a Government White Paper explaining them would be on sale:

It is for you, people of Ghana, to decide on the form of constitution under which you wish to be governed. You cannot arrive at this decision until you have carefully studied and clearly understood the proposals which have been submitted to you.

In many ways this Constitution is unique and contains a number of features which are not found in the constitution of any other country. This is so because it is fashioned to fit in with our historical experience and circumstances and designed to meet our own needs. It guarantees chieftaincy, preserves the Houses of Chiefs and in other ways is fitted to the general system of government which we have evolved in Ghana.

The Convention People's Party and the Government commend the proposed Constitution when the plebiscite is held next month. In that plebiscite I ask all of you to come forward uninfluenced and unawed to vote in an orderly and disciplined manner. The Government, for its part, will see to it that the plebiscite is conducted with absolute fairness and that every citizen of Ghana has a free and unfettered right to express his opinion. Furthermore, the Government is determined to suppress intimidation, coercion, malicious rumours and violence from whatever quarter it might come. It is essential for the well-being and good government of Ghana that the Constitution is enacted by the free will of the people. Countrymen, Ghana depends on each one of you to do your duty and I feel sure that you will rise to the occasion and do it well.

During the weeks which followed, plans went ahead for the holding of the plebiscite. Dr. J. B. Danquah was named by the Opposition United Party as their candidate for the presidency.

My candidature was based on my leadership of the Convention People's Party. I made this point quite clear when I spoke at the opening of the Party Headquarters on 2 April. After reviewing the past work of the Party, I turned to the future:

Our Party is moving into what can become a most glorious chapter in the history of Africa. Our plans for the re-organisation of all sections of the community is to give everybody a chance to make his contribution to the development of our nation. The test of the future will be the amount of purchasing power we put into the hand of our workers and farmers, and the protection the Party and the Government can give to ensure a dignified existence and comfortable standard of living for all our people. There will be no place in that society for the exploitation of the labour of others for the enrichment of a minority. Our Party is great and strong because we aim for a socialist pattern of society. We are the Party of the workers, the farmers and all progressive elements in our community and we will remain faithful to the principles that guide us in evolving our own Ghanaian pattern of socialist society.

Everybody will be given equal opportunities for development whether it be in the fields of education or of cultural and economic advancement. Every worker and farmer will receive a fair share of the wealth of the country and their children will have the same opportunities as others for education, so that they can become doctors of medicine, engineers, barristers, professional workers and scientists. We want working-class intellectuals devoid of arrogance and an end to class distinctions based on privilege.

We want to give to the farmers, co-operators and workers equal status in our new society, and this explains our attachment to the Trade Union Congress, the United Ghana Farmers Council and the National Council of Co-operatives. These three Party organisations are the true and practical schools of our philosophy and those who go against them go against the Convention People's Party also.

The Convention People's Party is a powerful force; more powerful, indeed, than anything that has yet appeared in the history of Ghana. It is the uniting force that guides and pilots the nation and is the nerve centre of the positive operations in the struggle for African irredentism. Its supremacy cannot be challenged.

The Convention People's Party is Ghana, and Ghana is the Convention People's Party.

It was my firm belief that only the C.P.P. had the organisation necessary to build the new Ghana and safeguard its future:

It is on the basis of the Party's record that we contest the Presidential election and recommend our proposals for a Republican constitution. We have become convinced that it is only under a Republican form of government that the Ghanaian will realise his full sovereign stature and find the true expression of his aspirations. Our Party runs a stable government to guide us forward in planning an economy that will give us abundance of wealth for the improvement of our standards of living. The signs of what we can do for the country in the future can be seen around you everywhere. Hospitals are being built, highways modernised for communications, factories are springing up and modern townships are replacing the slums that we inherited. The Party's Government has accelerated the construction of schools and colleges. We have built the University College at Legon, Kumasi College of Technology, the Nautical College and Flying Training School, the School of Law and the School of Business Administration. In the field of health, considerable improvement has been made. Health clinics, maternity homes, and dispensaries can now be found in your own vicinity.

Today you yourselves are the State, and those of us who bear the responsibility of government do so on your behalf. Thus the State exists in the image of the people and operates confidently in the service of the people. When the Party and the Government take your interests to heart and fulfil their responsibilities towards you, it is your duty in return to help the Party and the Government by your devotion to our cause and your steadfast loyalty to all our ideals.

Our record for the past ten years stands before the country as an example of what we can do in the future. I am simply asking you, on my own behalf and on behalf of the Convention People's Party, under all circumstances and at all costs, to stand united with us and vote solidly for the Republican constitution. This is the duty the Party expects of you and when to-day I open the National Headquarters Secretariat of the Convention People's Party, I also have the pleasure to launch the Party's Campaign for the plebiscite and offer myself to you as the first President under the new constitution.

1. Why is the new Ghanian constitution different than other constitutions?

2. What form of government does Nkrumah advocate?

3. What does Nkrumah see as evidence of progress brought about in Ghana by the Convention People's Party?

4. What is Nkrumah's vision for the future of Africa?

·156·

Regis Debray
Revolution in the Revolution?
(1967)

*R*egis Debray (b. 1940) was born in Paris, the son of two attorneys. He was a brilliant student and studied philosophy with the distinguished Marxist philosopher Louis Althusser. He made his first trip to Cuba in 1959 as part of a high school graduation present from his parents. He was there just after the Communist Revolution put Fidel Castro in power. After his graduation from college, Debray returned to Cuba and in 1963–1964 traveled throughout Latin America making contact with various Marxist political parties and guerrilla organizations. It was on this trip that Debray began to develop a new theory of revolutionary struggle based on the success of Castro in organizing guerrilla warfare and in rejecting the orthodox dictates of Marxism-Leninism. Influenced by the activities of Ché Guevara, Debray went on to articulate this call to action without theory in *Revolution in the Revolution?*

Revolution in the Revolution? was one of the most influential works in the organization of Latin American Communist movements. To put his ideas into action, Debray accompanied Ché Guevara to Bolivia, where a Cuban-type guerrilla movement was being organized. It resulted in a disaster; Guevara was assassinated and Debray imprisoned for three years. Debray returned to France, where he continued writing and worked for the election of a socialist government. In 1981 he became an official in the Mitterrand government.

We are never completely contemporaneous with our present. History advances in disguise; it appears on stage wearing the mask of the preceding scene, and we tend to lose the meaning of the play. Each time the curtain rises, continuity has to be re-established. The blame, of course is not history's, but lies in our vision, encumbered with memory and images learned in the past. We see the past superimposed on the present, even when the present is a revolution.

The impact of the Cuban Revolution has been experienced and pondered, principally in Latin America, by methods and schemas already catalogued, enthroned, and consecrated by history. This is why, in spite of all the commotion it has provoked, the shock has been softened. Today the tumult has died down; Cuba's real significance and the scope of its lessons, which had been overlooked before, are being discovered. A new conception of guerrilla warfare is coming to light.

Among other things, Cuba remembered from the beginning that the socialist revolution is the result of an armed struggle against the armed power of the bourgeois state. This old historic law, of a strategic nature if you like, was at first given a known tactical content. One began by identifying the guerrilla struggle with insurrection because the archetype—1917—had taken this form, and because Lenin and later Stalin had developed several theoretical formulas based on it—formulas which have nothing to do with the present situation and which are periodically debated in vain, such as those which refer to conditions for the outbreak of an insurrection, meaning an immediate assault on the central power. But this disparity soon became evident. American guerrilla warfare was next virtually identified with Asian guerrilla warfare, since both are "irregular" wars of encirclement of cities from the countryside. This confusion is even more dangerous than the first.

The armed revolutionary struggle encounters specific conditions on each continent, in each country, but these are neither "natural" nor obvious. So true is this that in each case years of sacrifice are necessary in order to discover and acquire an awareness of them. The Russian Social Democrats instinctively thought in terms of repeating the Paris Commune in Petrograd; the Chinese Communists in terms of repeating the Russian October in the Canton of the twenties; and the Vietnamese comrades, a year after the foundation of their party, in terms of organizing insurrections of peasant soviets in the northern part of their country. It is now clear to us today that soviet-type insurrections could not triumph in prewar colonial Asia, but it was precisely here that the most genuine Communist activists had to begin their apprenticeship for victory.

One may well consider it a stroke of good luck that Fidel had not read the military writings of Mao Tse-tung before disembarking on the coast of Orient: he could thus invent, on the spot and out of his own experience, principles of a military doctrine in conformity with the terrain. It was only at the end of the war, when their tactics were already defined, that the rebels discovered the writings of Mao. . . .

Fidel once blamed certain failures of the guerrillas on a purely intellectual attitude toward war. The reason is understandable: aside from his physical weakness and lack of adjustment to rural life, the intellectual will try to grasp the present through preconceived ideological constructs and live it through books. He will be less able than others to invent, improvise, make do with available resources, decide instantly on bold moves when he is in a tight spot. Thinking that he already knows, he will learn more slowly, display less flexibility. And the irony of history has willed, by virtue of the social situation of many Latin American countries, the assignment of precisely this vanguard role to students and revolutionary intellectuals, who have had to unleash, or rather initiate, the highest forms of class struggle.

The guerrilla struggle has political motives and goals. It must have the support of the masses or disappear; before enlisting them directly, it must convince them that there are valid reasons for its existence so that the "rebellion" will truly be—by the manner of its recruitment and the origins of its fighters—a "war of the people." In order to convince the masses, it is necessary to address them, that is, to address speeches, proclama-

tions, explanations to them—in brief, to carry on political work, "mass work." Hence the first nucleus of fighters will be divided into small propaganda patrols which will cover the mountain areas, going into villages, holding meetings, speaking here and there, in order to explain the social goals of the Revolution, to denounce the enemies of the peasantry, to promise agrarian reform and punishment for traitors, etc. If the peasants are skeptical, their confidence in themselves must be restored by imbuing them with revolutionary faith; faith in the revolutionaries who are speaking to them. Cells, public or underground, will be organized in the villages; union struggles will be supported or initiated; and the program of the Revolution will be reiterated again and again. It is only at the end of this stage, having achieved active support by the masses, a solid rearguard, regular provisioning, a broad intelligence network, rapid mail service, and a recruiting center, that the guerrillas can pass over to direct action against the enemy.

In many countries of America the guerrilla force has frequently been called the "armed fist" of a liberation front, in order to indicate its dependence on a patriotic front or on a party. This expression, copied from models elaborated elsewhere—principally in Asia—is, at bottom, contrary to the maxim of Camilo Cienfuegos: "The rebel army is the people in uniform." In the absence of concrete knowledge of a concrete and different situation, and particularly if the differences themselves are not understood, it is dangerous to import organizational formulas, even if they are based on a known theory. Clearly, it is physically dangerous, since many military errors derive from a single political error, and a single military error can result in the total destruction of an incipient *foco*. Doubtless, the fact that the armed struggle in Latin America has not been buried under the weight of its many missteps, its fumblings and false starts, is a tribute to history's tolerance. Meanwhile, the penalty for a false theory is military defeat, and the cost of military defeat is the butchery of tens and hundreds of comrades and men of the people.

As Fidel once said, certain policies belong to the field of criminology.

Which should be strengthened today, the Party or the guerrillas, embryo of the people's army? Which is the decisive link? Where should the principal effort be made?

Such are the questions which divide militants today in those vanguard nations of Latin America where a guerrilla movement exists.

Tomorrow the militants of other nations will confront them.

Today they express a dilemma.

These questions have met with a standard response in the history of Marxism and in history as such. An answer so immutable that the mere asking of it in this form will seem a *heresy* to many. That answer is that the Party must be strengthened first, for it is the creator and the directive nucleus of the people's army. Only the Party of the working class can create a true army of the people—as the guarantor of a scientifically based political line—and win power in the interests of the workers.

In Cuba, military (operational) and political leadership have been combined in one man: Fidel Castro. Is this the result of mere chance, without significance, or is it an indication of an historically different situation? Is it an exception or does it foreshadow something fundamental? What light does it throw on the current Latin American experience? We must decipher this experience in time, and we must not rush to condemn history in the making because it does not conform to received principles. Fidel Castro said recently:

> I am accused of heresy. It is said that I am a heretic within the camp of Marxism-Leninism. Hmm! It is amusing that so-called Marx-

ist organizations, which fight like cats and dogs in their dispute over possession of revolutionary truth, accuse us of wanting to apply the Cuban formula mechanically. They reproach us with a lack of understanding of the Party's role; they reproach us as heretics within the camp of Marxism-Leninism.

The fact is that those who want mechanically to apply formulas to the Latin American reality are precisely these same "Marxists," since it is always in the interest of the man who commits a robbery to be the first to cry thief. But what does Fidel Castro say that causes him to be characterized as "a heretic," "subjective," and "petty bourgeois"? What explosive message of his causes people in the capitals of America and of the socialist countries of Europe and Asia, all those who "want to wage revolutionary war by telepathy," "the unprincipled ones," to join in the chorus against the Cuban Revolution?

"Who will make the revolution in Latin America? Who? The people, the revolutionaries, with or without a party." (Fidel)

Fidel Castro says simply that there is no revolution without a vanguard; that this vanguard is not necessarily the Marxist-Leninist party; and that those who want to make the revolution have the right and the duty to constitute themselves a vanguard, independently of these parties.

It takes courage to state the facts out loud when these facts contradict a tradition. There is, then, no metaphysical equation in which vanguard = Marxist-Leninist party; there are merely dialectical conjunctions between a given function—that of the vanguard in history—and a given form of organization—that of the Marxist-Leninist party. These conjunctions arise out of prior history and depend on it. Parties exist here on earth and are subject to the rigors of terrestrial dialectics. If they have been born, they can die and be reborn in other forms.

1. What is Debray's attitude toward traditional Marxist theory?

2. Why does he think revolutionary theorists retard Latin American revolutions?

3. What is the role of propaganda in the revolutionary struggle?

4. How does Debray characterize the originality of Fidel Castro?

·157·

The Arab–Israeli Conflict

(1967)

The late twentieth century has been wracked by bitter religious and nationalist conflicts. In Northern Ireland, India and Pakistan, Iraq, and in the
component parts of Yugoslavia, brutal terrorist warfare marked successionist
and sectarian movements. Perhaps no conflict in the late twentieth century
has been as fierce as that between the Palestinians and the Israelis over territorial rights and religious freedom. The struggles have been nearly continuous since the establishment of a Jewish homeland in Palestine after World
War I. They intensified after Israel proclaimed its statehood in 1948 and
reached its greatest crisis in the "Six Days War" of 1967.

The selections that follow present representative opinions from both
sides. United Nations Security Council Resolution 242 is still the operative
international position on the Arab–Israeli conflict. The speech of Israeli
Ambassador to the United Nations Abba Eban is a succinct and eloquent
expression of Israel's position in the wake of its military triumph. The Palestinian National Charter, the governing document of the Palestine Liberation
Organization (PLO), was drafted in 1968, a year after Resolution 242.

ABBA EBAN'S SPEECH AT THE SPECIAL ASSEMBLY OF THE UNITED NATIONS, JUNE 19, 1967

Our Watchword Is 'Forward to Peace'

The subject of our discussion is the Middle East,
its past agony and its future hope. We speak of a
region whose destiny has profoundly affected
the entire human experience. In the heart of
that region, at the very centre of its geography
and history, lives a very small nation called Israel.
This nation gave birth to the currents of thought
which have fashioned the life of the Mediterranean world and of vast regions beyond. It has
now been re-established as the home and sanctuary of a people which has seen six million of its
sons exterminated in the greatest catastrophe
ever endured by a family of the human race.

In recent weeks the Middle East has passed
through a crisis whose shadows darken the
world. This crisis has many consequences but
only one cause. Israel's rights to peace, security,
sovereignty, economic development and maritime freedom—indeed its very right to exist—
has been forcibly denied and aggressively
attacked. This is the true origin of the tension
which torments the Middle East. All the other

elements of the conflict are the consequences of this single cause. There has been danger, there is still peril in the Middle East because Israel's existence, sovereignty and vital interests have been and are violently assailed.

The threat to Israel's existence, its peace, security, sovereignty and development has been directed against her in the first instance by the neighbouring Arab states. But all the conditions of tension, all the impulses of aggression in the Middle East have been aggravated by the policy of one of the Great Powers which under our Charter bear primary responsibilities for the maintenance of international peace and security. I shall show how the Soviet Union has been unfaithful to that trust. The burden of responsibility lies heavy upon her.

I come to this rostrum to speak for a united people which, having faced danger to the national survival, is unshakably resolved to resist any course which would renew the perils from which it has emerged.

The General Assembly is chiefly pre-occupied by the situation against which Israel defended itself on the morning of June 5. I shall invite every peace-loving state represented here to ask itself how it would have acted on that day if it faced similar dangers. But if our discussion is to have any weight or depth, we must understand that great events are not born in a single instant of time. It is beyond all honest doubt that between May 14 and June 5, Arab governments led and directed by President Nasser, methodically prepared and mounted an aggressive assault designed to bring about Israel's immediate and total destruction. . . .

Nobody who lived through those days in Israel, between May 23 and June 5, will ever forget the air of doom that hovered over our country. Hemmed in by hostile armies ready to strike, affronted and beset by a flagrant act of war, bombarded day and night by predictions of her approaching extinction, forced into a total mobilization of all her manpower, her economy and commerce beating with feeble pulse, her main supplies of vital fuel choked by a belligerent act, Israel faced the greatest peril of her existence that she had known since her resistance against aggression 19 years before, at the hour of her birth. There was peril wherever she looked and she faced it in deepening solitude. On May 24 and on succeeding days, the Security Council conducted a desultory debate which sometimes reached a point of levity. The Soviet Representative asserted that he saw no reason for discussing the Middle Eastern situation at all. The Bulgarian delegate uttered these unbelievable words.

> At the present moment there is really no need for an urgent meeting of the Security Council.

A crushing siege bore down upon us. Multitudes throughout the world trembled for Israel's fate. The single consolation lay in the surge of public opinion which rose up in Israel's defence. . . .

On the fateful morning of June 5, when Egyptian forces moved by air and land against Israel's western coast and southern territory, our country's choice was plain. The choice was to live or perish, to defend the national existence or to forfeit it for all time.

From these dire moments Israel emerged in five heroic days from awful peril to successful and glorious resistance. Alone, unaided, neither seeking nor receiving help, our nation rose in self-defence. So long as men cherish freedom, so long as small states strive for the dignity of existence, the exploits of Israel's armies will be told from one generation to another with the deepest pride. The Soviet Union has described our resistance as aggression and sought to have it condemned. We reject this accusation with all our might. Here was armed force employed in a just and righteous cause, as righteous as the defenders at Valley Forge, as just as the expulsion of Hitler's bombers from the British skies, as noble as the protection of Stalingrad against the Nazi hordes, so was the defence of Israel's security and existence against those who sought our nation's destruction.

What should be condemned is not Israel's action, but the attempt to condemn it. Never have freedom, honour, justice, national interest and international morality been so righteously protected.

The Vision of Peace

In free negotiation with each of our neighbours we shall offer durable and just solutions redounding to our mutual advantage and honour. The Arab states can no longer be permitted to recognize Israel's existence only for the purpose of plotting its elimination. They have come face to face with us in conflict. Let them now come face to face with us in peace.

. . .The old prejudices could be replaced by a new comprehension and respect, born of a reciprocal dialogue in the intellectual domain. In such a Middle East, military budgets would spontaneously find a less exacting point of equilibrium. Excessive sums devoted to security could be diverted to development projects.

Thus, in full respect of the region's diversity, an entirely new story, never known or told before, would unfold across the Eastern Mediterranean. For the first time in history, no Mediterranean nation is in subjection. All are endowed with sovereign freedom. The challenge now is to use this freedom for creative growth. There is only one road to that end. It is the road of recognition, of direct contact, of true cooperation. It is the road of peaceful co-existence. This road, as the ancient prophets of Israel foretold, leads to Jerusalem.

Jerusalem, now united after her tragic division, is no longer an arena for gun emplacements and barbed wire. In our nation's long history there have been few hours more intensely moving than the hour of our reunion with the Western Wall. A people had come back to the cradle of its birth. It has renewed its link with the memories which that reunion evokes. For 20 years there has not been free access by men of all faiths to the shrines which they hold in unique reverence. This access now exists. Israel is resolved to give effective expression, in cooperation with the world's great religions, to the immunity and sanctity of all the Holy Places. The prospect of a negotiated peace is less remote than it may seem. Israel waged her defensive struggle in pursuit of two objectives—security and peace. Peace and security, with their territorial, economic and demographic implications, can only be built by the free negotiation which is the true essence of sovereign responsibility. A call to the recent combatants to negotiate the conditions of their future co-existence is the only constructive course which this Assembly could take.

We ask the great powers to remove our tormented region from the scope of global rivalries, to summon its governments to build their common future themselves, to assist it, if they will, to develop social and cultural levels worthy of its past.

We ask the developing countries to support a dynamic and forward-looking policy and not to drag the new future back into the out-worn past.

To the small nations, which form the bulk of the international family, we offer the experience which teaches us that small communities can best secure their interests by maximal self-reliance. Nobody will help those who will not help themselves; we ask the small nations in the solidarity of our smallness, to help us stand firm against intimidation and threat such as those by which we are now assailed. We ask world opinion, which rallied to us in our plight, to accompany us faithfully in our new opportunity. We ask the United Nations, which was prevented from offering us security in our recent peril, to respect our independent quest for the peace and security which are the Charter's higher ends. We shall do what the Security Council decided should be done—and reject the course which the Security Council emphatically and wisely rejected. It may seem that Israel stands alone against numerous and powerful adversaries. But we have faith in the undying forces in our nation's history which have so often given the final victory to spirit over matter, to inner truth over mere quantity. We believe in the vigilance of history which has guarded our steps. The Guardian of Israel neither slumbers nor sleeps.

The Middle East, tired of wars, is ripe for a new emergence of human vitality. Let the opportunity not fall again from our hands.

SECURITY COUNCIL RESOLUTION ON THE MIDDLE EAST, NOVEMBER 22, 1967

The Security Council,

Expressing its continuing concern with the grave situation in the Middle East,

Emphasizing the inadmissibility of the acquisition of territory by war and the need to work for a just and lasting peace in which every state in the area can live in security.

Emphasizing further that all member states in their acceptance of the Charter of the United Nations have undertaken a commitment to act in accordance with Article 2 of the Charter,

1. *Affirms* that the fulfillment of Charter principles requires the establishment of a just and lasting peace in the Middle East which should include the application of both the following principles:

(i) Withdrawal of Israeli armed forces from territories of recent conflict;

(ii) Termination of all claims or states of belligerency and respect for and acknowledgment of the sovereignty, territorial integrity and political independence of every state in the area and their right to live in peace within secure and recognized boundaries free from threats or acts of force;

2. *Affirms further* the necessity

(a) For guaranteeing freedom of navigation through international waterways in the area;

(b) For achieving a just settlement of the refugee problem;

(c) For guaranteeing the territorial inviolability and political independence of every state in the area, through measures including the establishment of demilitarized zones;

3. *Requests* the Secretary General to designate a special representative to proceed to the Middle East to establish and maintain contacts with the states concerned in order to promote agreement and assist efforts to achieve a peaceful and accepted settlement in accordance with the provisions and principles in this resolution.

4. *Requests* the Secretary General to report to the Security Council on the progress of the efforts of the special representative as soon as possible.

THE PALESTINIAN NATIONAL CHARTER: RESOLUTIONS OF THE PALESTINE NATIONAL COUNCIL

Charter

1. Palestine is the homeland of the Arab Palestinian people; it is an indivisible part of the Arab homeland, and the Palestinian people are an integral part of the Arab nation.

2. Palestine, with the boundaries it had during the British Mandate, is an indivisible territorial unit.

3. The Palestinian Arab people possess the legal right to their homeland and have the right to determine their destiny after achieving the liberation of their country in accordance with their wishes and entirely of their own accord and will.

4. The Palestinian identity is a genuine, essential, and inherent characteristic; it is transmitted from parents to children. The Zionist occupation and the dispersal of the Palestinian Arab people, through the disasters which befell them, do not make them lose their Palestinian identity and their membership in the Palestinian community, nor do they negate them.

5. The Palestinians are those Arab nationals who, until 1947, normally resided in Palestine regardless of whether they were evicted from it or have stayed there. Anyone born, after that date, of a Palestinian father—whether inside Palestine or outside it—is also a Palestinian.

7. That there is a Palestinian community and that it has material, spiritual, and historical connection with Palestine are indisputable facts. It is a national duty to bring up individual Palestinians in an Arab revolutionary manner. All means of information and education must be adopted in order to acquaint the Palestinian with his country in the most profound manner, both spiritual and material, that is possible. He must be prepared for the armed struggle and ready to sacrifice his wealth and his life in order to win back his homeland and bring about its liberation.

8. The phase in their history, through which the Palestinian people are now living, is that of national struggle for the liberation of Palestine. . . .

9. Armed struggle is the only way to liberate Palestine. Thus it is the overall strategy, not merely a tactical phase. The Palestinian Arab people assert their absolute determination and firm resolution to continue their armed struggle and to work for an armed popular revolution for the liberation of their country and their return to it. They also assert their right to normal life in Palestine and to exercise their right to self-determination and sovereignty over it.

13. Arab unity and the liberation of Palestine are two complementary objectives, the attainment of either of which facilitates the attainment of the other. Thus, Arab unity leads to the liberation of Palestine, the liberation of Palestine leads to Arab unity; and work toward the realization of one objective proceeds side by side with work toward the realization of the other.

14. The destiny of the Arab nation, and indeed Arab existence itself, depend upon the destiny of the Palestine cause. From this interdependence spring the Arab nation's pursuit of, and striving for, the liberation of Palestine. The people of Palestine play the role of the vanguard in the realization of this sacred national goal.

15. The liberation of Palestine, from an Arab viewpoint, is a national duty and it attempts to repel the Zionist and imperialist aggression against the Arab homeland, and aims at the elimination of Zionism in Palestine. Absolute responsibility for this falls upon the Arab nation—peoples and governments—with the Arab people of Palestine in the vanguard. Accordingly, the Arab nation must mobilize all its military, human, moral, and spiritual capabilities to participate actively with the Palestinian people in the liberation of Palestine. It must, particularly in the phase of the armed Palestinian revolution, offer and furnish the Palestinian people with all possible help, and material and human support, and make available to them the means and opportunities that will enable them to continue to carry out their leading role in the armed revolution, until they liberate their homeland.

22. Zionism is a political movement organically associated with international imperialism and antagonistic to all action for liberation and to progressive movements in the world. It is racist and fanatic in its nature, aggressive, expansionist, and colonial in its aims, and fascist in its methods. Israel is the instrument of the Zionist movement, and a geographical base for world imperialism placed strategically in the midst of the Arab homeland to combat the hopes of the Arab nation for liberation, unity, and progress. Israel is a constant source of threat *vis-à-vis* peace in the Middle East and the whole world. Since the liberation of Palestine will destroy the Zionist and imperialist presence and will contribute to the establishment of peace in the Middle East, the Palestinian people look for the support of all the progressive and peaceful forces and urge them all, irrespective of their affiliations and beliefs, to offer the Palestinian people all aid and support in their just struggle for the liberation of their homeland.

1. Why does Eban compare Israel's actions in the Six Days War to Valley Forge, the bombing of London, and the siege of Stalingrad?

2. Who is the intended audience of Eban's speech? How does he attempt to win their support?

3. What does U.N. Resolution 242 mean when it affirms "respect for and acknowledgment of the sovereignty, territorial integrity and political independence of every state in the area"?

4. What, according to the Palestinian National Charter, defines a Palestinian?

5. Who is the intended audience of the Palestinian National Charter? What arguments are used to win their support?

·158·

Athol Fugard
Sizwe Bansi Is Dead
(1972)

Athol Fugard (b. 1932) is one of South Africa's most prolific playwrights. He has worked as an actor and director and founded the experimental Space Theater in Cape Town, which presented plays with white and black actors to racially mixed audiences. Though his plays reflect his own lower-middle-class white background, they center upon the injustice of apartheid and the brutal dehumanization of South African blacks. He is best known in America for the award-winning play *Master Harold and the Boys. Sizwe Bansi Is Dead,* one of his earlier plays, was a sensation when it was performed in London in the mid-1970s.

Sizwe Bansi Is Dead is set in the context of the attempt by the South African government to establish native homelands for blacks. Residents were given identity cards that allowed them to live or work in one place only. In the play, Sizwe Bansi (called Man) has come to Port Elizabeth in search of work without the proper stamp on his identity card. While there he is introduced to Buntu, who is adept at circumventing bureaucratic regulations. His solution to Sizwe Bansi's problem raises profound personal and political questions.

BUNTU. Hi. Buntu.

[*They shake hands.*]

MAN. Sizwe Bansi.

BUNTU. Sit down.

[*They sit.*]

MAN. I've got no permit to stay in Port Elizabeth.

BUNTU. Where do you have a permit to stay?

MAN. King William's Town.

BUNTU. How did they find out?

MAN [*tells his story with the hesitation and uncertainty of the illiterate. When words fail him he tries to use his hands.*]

I was staying with Zola, as you know. I was very happy there. But one night . . . I was sleeping on the floor . . . I heard some noises and when I looked up I saw torches shining in through the window . . . then there was a loud knocking on the door. When I got up Zola was there in the dark . . . he was trying to whisper something. I think he was saying I must hide. So I crawled under the table. The headman came in and looked around and found me hiding under the table . . . and dragged me out.

BUNTU. Raid?

MAN. Yes, it was a raid. I was just wearing my pants. My shirt was lying on the other side. I just managed to grab it as they were pushing me out. . . . I finished dressing in the van. They drove straight to the administration office . . . and then from there they drove to the Labour Bureau. I was made to stand in the passage there, with everybody looking at me and shaking their heads like they knew I was in big trouble. Later I was taken into an office and made to stand next to the door. . . . The white man behind the desk had my book and he also looked at me and shook his head. Just then one other white man came in with a card. . . .

BUNTU. A card?

MAN. He was carrying a card.

BUNTU. Pink card?

MAN. Yes, the card was pink.

BUNTU. Record card. Your whole bloody life is written down on that. Go on.

MAN. Then the first white man started writing something on the card . . . and just then somebody came in carrying a. . . .

[*demonstrates what he means by banging a clenched fist on the table.*]

BUNTU. A stamp?

MAN. Yes, a stamp. [*Repeats the action.*] He was carrying a stamp.

BUNTU. And then?

MAN. He put it on my passbook.

BUNTU. Let me see your book?

[*Sizwe produces his passbook from the back-pocket of his trousers. Buntu examines it.*]

Shit! You know what this is? [*The stamp.*]

MAN. I can't read.

BUNTU. Listen . . . [*reads*]. 'You are required to report to the Bantu Affairs Commissioner, King William's Town, within three days of the above-mentioned date for the. . . .' You should have been home yesterday!. . . 'for the purpose of repatriation to home district.' Influx Control. You're in trouble, Sizwe.

MAN. I don't want to leave Port Elizabeth.

BUNTU. Maybe. But if that book says go, you go.

MAN. Can't I maybe burn this book and get a new one?

BUNTU. Burn that book? Stop kidding yourself, Sizwe! Anyway suppose you do. You must immediately go apply for a new one. Right? And until that new one comes, be careful the police don't stop you and ask for your book. Into the Courtroom, brother. Charge: Failing to produce Reference Book on Demand. Five rand or five days. Finally the new book comes. Down to the Labour Bureau for a stamp . . . it's got to be endorsed with permission to be in this area. White man at the Labour Bureau takes the book, looks at it—doesn't look at you!—goes to the big machine and feeds in your number. . .

[*Buntu goes through the motions of punching out a number on a computer.*]

. . . card jumps out, he reads: 'Sizwe Bansi. Endorsed to King William's Town. . . .' Takes your book, fetches that same stamp, and in it goes again. So you burn that book, or throw it away, and get another one. Same thing happens.

BUNTU.   Okay, Sizwe, I'll take over from here. But just hang on for a second I want to have a piss. Don't move!

[*Buntu disappears into the dark.*] [*Buntu comes running back.*]

BUNTU [*urgently*].   Let's get out of here.

MAN.   Wait, Mr Buntu.

BUNTU.   Come on! There's trouble there. . . [*pointing in the direction from which he has come*] . . . let's move.

MAN.   Wait, Mr Buntu, wait.

BUNTU.   There's a dead man lying there!

MAN.   Dead man?

BUNTU.   I thought I was just pissing on a pile of rubbish, but when I looked carefully I saw it was a man. Dead. Covered in blood. Tsotsis must have got him. Let's get the hell out of here before anybody sees us.

MAN.   Buntu . . . Buntu. . . .

BUNTU.   Listen to me, Sizwe! The Tsotsis might still be around.

MAN.   Buntu. . . .

BUNTU.   Do you want to join him?

MAN.   I don't want to join him.

BUNTU.   Then come.

MAN.   Wait, Buntu.

BUNTU.   Jesus!

MAN.   Buntu, . . . we must report that man to the police station.

BUNTU.   Police Station! Are you mad? You drunk, passbook not in order. . . 'We've come to report a dead man, Sergeant.' 'Grab them!' Case closed. We killed him.

MAN.   Mr Buntu, . . . we can't leave him. . . .

BUNTU.   Please, Sizwe!

MAN.   Wait. Let's carry him home.

BUNTU.   Just like that! Walk through New Brighton streets, at this hour, carrying a dead man. Anyway we don't know where he stays. Come.

MAN.   Wait, Buntu, . . . listen. . . .

BUNTU.   Sizwe!

MAN.   Buntu, we can know where he stays. That passbook of his will talk. It talks, friend, like mine. His passbook will tell you.

BUNTU [*after a moment's desperate hesitation*]. You really want to land me in the shit, hey.

[*Disappears into the dark again.*]

MAN.   It will tell you in good English where he stays. My passbook talks good English too . . . big words that Sizwe can't read and doesn't understand. Sizwe wants to stay here in New Brighton and find a job; passbook says, 'No! Report back.'

Sizwe wants to feed his wife and children; passbook says, 'No. Endorsed out.'

Sizwe wants to. . . .

[*Buntu reappears, a passbook in his hand. Looks around furtively and moves to the light under a lamp-post.*]

They never told us it would be like that when they introduced it. They said: Book of Life! Your friend! You'll never get lost! They told us lies.

[*He joins Buntu who is examining the book.*]

BUNTU.   *Haai!* Look at him [*the photograph in the book, reading*].

'Robert Zwelinzima. Tribe: Xhosa. Native Identification Number. . . .'

MAN.   Where does he stay, Buntu?

BUNTU [*paging through the book*].   Worked at Dorman Long seven years . . . Kilomet Engineering . . . eighteen months . . . Anderson Hardware two years . . . now unemployed. Hey, look, Sizwe! He's one up on you. He's got a work-seeker's permit.

MAN.   Where does he stay, Buntu?

BUNTU.   Lodger's Permit at 42 Mdala Street. From there to Sangocha Street . . . now at. . . .

[*Pause. Closes the book abruptly.*]

To hell with it I'm not going *there*. . . . I'm putting this book back and we're going home.

MAN.   Buntu!

BUNTU [*half-way back to the alleyway*].   What?

MAN.   Would you do that to me, friend? If the Tsotsis had stabbed Sizwe, and left him lying there, would you walk away from him as well?

[*The accusation stops Buntu.*]

Would you leave me lying there, wet with your piss? I wish I was dead. I wish I was dead because I don't care a damn about anything any more.

[*Turning away from Buntu to the audience.*]

What's happening in this world, good people? Who cares for who in this world? Who wants who?

Who wants me, friend? What's wrong with me? I'm a man.

I've got eyes to see. I've got ears to listen when people talk.

I've got a head to think good things. What's wrong with me?

[*Starts to tear off his clothes.*]

Look at me! I'm a man. I've got legs. I can run with a wheelbarrow full of cement! I'm strong! I'm a man. Look! I've got a wife. I've got four children. How many has he made, lady? [*The man sitting next to her.*] Is he a man? What has he got that I haven't. . . ?

[*A thoughtful Buntu rejoins them, the dead man's reference book still in his hand.*]

BUNTU.   Let me see your book?

[*Sizwe doesn't respond.*]

Give me your book!

MAN.   Are you a policeman now, Buntu?

BUNTU.   Give me your bloody book, Sizwe!

MAN [*handing it over*].   Take it, Buntu. Take this book and read it carefully, friend, and tell me what it says about me. Buntu, does that book tell you I'm a man?

[*Buntu studies the two books. Sizwe turns back to the audience.*]

That bloody book. . . ! People, do you know? No! Wherever you go . . . it's that bloody book. You go to school, it goes too. Go to work, it goes too. Go to church and pray and sing lovely hymns, it sits there with you. Go to hospital to die, it lies there too!

[*Buntu has collected Sizwe's discarded clothing.*]

BUNTU.   Come!

[*Buntu's house, as earlier. Table and two chairs. Buntu pushes Sizwe down into a chair. Sizwe still mut-tering, starts to struggle back into his clothes. Buntu opens the two reference books and places them side by side on the table. He produces a pot of glue, then very carefully tears out the photograph in each book. A dab of glue on the back of each and then Sizwe's goes back into Robert's book, and Robert's into Sizwe's. Sizwe watches this operation, at first uninterestedly, but when he realizes what Buntu is up to, with growing alarm. When he is finished, Buntu pushes the two books in front of Sizwe.*]

MAN [*shaking his head emphatically*].   Yo! Haai, haai. No, Buntu.

BUNTU.   It's a chance.

MAN.   *Haai, haai, haai* . . .

BUNTU.   It's your only chance!

MAN.   No, Buntu! What's it mean? That me, Sizwe Bansi. . . .

BUNTU.   Is dead.

MAN.   I'm not dead, friend.

BUNTU.   We burn this book. . . [*Sizwe's original*] . . . and Sizwe Bansi disappears off the face of the earth.

MAN.   What about the man we left lying in the alleyway?

BUNTU.   Tomorrow the Flying Squad passes there and finds him. Check in his pockets . . . no passbook. Mount Road Mortuary. After three days nobody has identified him. Pauper's Burial. Case closed.

MAN.   And then?

BUNTU.   Tomorrow I contact my friend Norman at Feltex. He's a boss-boy there. I tell him about another friend, Robert Zwelinzima, book in order, who's looking for a job. You roll up later, hand over the book to the white man. Who does Robert Zwelinzima look like? You! Who gets the pay on Friday? You, man!

MAN.   What about all that shit at the Labour Bureau, Buntu?

BUNTU.   You don't have to there. This chap had a work-seeker's permit, Sizwe. All you do is hand over the book to the white man. *He* checks at the Labour Bureau. They check with their big machine. 'Robert Zwelinzima has the right to be employed and stay in this town.'

MAN.   I don't want to lose my name, Buntu.

BUNTU.   You mean you don't want to lose your bloody passbook! You love it, hey?

MAN.   Buntu. I cannot lose my name.

BUNTU [*leaving the table*].   All right, I was only trying to help. As Robert Zwelinzima you could have stayed and worked in this town. As Sizwe Bansi. . .? Start walking, friend, King William's Town. Hundred and fifty miles. And don't waste any time! You've got to be there by yesterday. Hope you enjoy it.

MAN.   Buntu. . . .

BUNTU.   Lots of scenery in a hundred and fifty miles.

MAN.   Buntu!. . .

BUNTU.   Maybe a better idea is just to wait until they pick you up. Save yourself all that walking. Into the train with the escort! Smart stuff, hey. Hope it's not too crowded though. Hell of a lot of people being kicked out. I hear.

MAN.   Buntu!. . .

BUNTU.   But once you're back! Sit down on the side of the road next to your pondok with your family . . . the whole Bansi clan on leave . . . for life! Hey, that sounds okay. Watching all the cars passing, and as you say, friend, cough your bloody lungs out with Ciskeian Independence.

MAN [*now really desperate*].   Buntu!!!

BUNTU.   What you waiting for? Go!

MAN.   Buntu.

BUNTU.   What?

MAN.   What about my wife, Nowetu?

BUNTU.   What about her?

MAN [*maudlin tears*].   Her loving husband, Siwze Bansi, is dead!

BUNTU.   So what! She's going to marry a better man.

MAN [*bridling*].   Who?

BUNTU.   You . . . Robert Zwelinzima.

MAN [*thoroughly confused*].   How can I marry my wife, Buntu?

BUNTU.   Get her down here and I'll introduce you.

MAN.   Don't make jokes, Buntu. Robert . . . Sizwe . . . I'm all mixed up. Who am I?

BUNTU.   A fool who is not taking his chance.

MAN.   And my children! Their father is Sizwe Bansi. They're registered at school under Bansi. . . .

BUNTU.   Are you really worried about your children, friend, or are you just worried about yourself and your bloody name? Wake up, man! Use that book and with your pay on Friday you'll have a real chance to do something for them.

1.   How was it discovered that Man did not have a work permit?

2.   What is Man's attitude toward his identity card?

3.   Why does Man strip off his clothes?

4.   What is Buntu's solution to Man's problem? What is Man's reaction? What do you think is the outcome?

·159·

Desmond Tutu
My Vision for South Africa
(1979)

*D*esmond Tutu (b. 1931), the son of a teacher and a domestic servant, grew
up in the gold-mining town of Kierksdorp, South Africa. When he was 12
he moved to Johannesburg, where he met Father Trevor Huddleston, the anti-
apartheid activist who became his mentor and role model. After graduation
from college and a brief stint as a high-school teacher, he trained for the
Anglican priesthood. After serving as a curate in local South African parishes,
he traveled to England, where he became the associate director of the Theo-
logical Education Fund. In 1975 he returned to South Africa as the Anglican
dean of Johannesburg. There he led the anti-apartheid movement as the first
black secretary of the interdenominational South African Council of Churches. In 1984 he received the Nobel Peace Prize. He is currently the bishop of
Johannesburg.

In "My Vision for South Africa," Tutu presents his dream for the future of
South Africa. His eloquent statement demonstrates his firm belief in the
teachings of the Anglican church as well as his optimism in the possibilities for
positive political change in South Africa.

We should all have the freedom to become fully
human. That is basic to my understanding of
society—that God created us without any coercion, freely for freedom. Responsibility is a nonsense except in the context of freedom—freedom to accept or reject alternative options,
freedom to obey or disobey. God, who alone has
the perfect right to be a totalitarian, has such a
tremendous respect for our freedom to be
human, that he would much rather see us go
freely to hell than compel us to go to heaven.

According to the Bible, a human being can
be a human being only because he belongs to a
community. A person is a person through other
persons, as we say in our African idiom. And so
separation of persons because of biological accidents is reprehensible and blasphemous. A person is entitled to a stable community life, and the
first of these communities is the family. A stable

family life would be of paramount importance in
my South Africa.

There would be freedom of association, of
thought and of expression. This would involve
freedom of movement as well. One would be
free to go wherever one wanted, to associate with
whomsoever one wished. As adult humans we
would not be subject to draconian censorship
laws. We can surely decide for ourselves what we
want to read, what films to view and what views to
have. We must not be frogmarched into puri-
tanism.

Because we are created in the image of God
one of our attributes is creativity. South Africa is
starved of the great things many of her children
can create and do, because of artificial barriers,
and the refusal to let people develop to their
fullest potential. When one has been overseas
and seen for example the Black Alvin Abbey

Bishop Desmond Tutu condemning the violence of South African police and rioters during unrest in the Eastern Cape. An Anglican bishop from South Africa, Tutu won the Nobel Peace Prize in 1984.

dance group, which performed modern ballet to standing room only crowds at Covent Garden, then one weeps for how South Africa has allowed herself to be cheated of such performances by her own inhabitants. How many potentially outstanding people are being denied the opportunity to get on?

When I think of the splendid young people I have met, who despite some horrendous experiences at the hands of the system, have emerged quite unscathed with bitterness, and who have a tremendous humanity and compassion, then I weep because we are so wantonly wasteful of human resources. We need a course on human ecology.

I lay great stress on humaneness and being truly human. In our African understanding, part of Ubantu—being human—is the rare gift of sharing. This concept of sharing is exemplified at African feasts even to this day, when people eat together from a common dish, rather than from individual dishes. That means a meal is indeed to have communion with one's fellows. Blacks are beginning to lose this wonderful attribute, because we are being inveigled by the excessive individualism of the West. I loathe Capitalism because it gives far too great play to our inherent selfishness. We are told to be highly competitive, and our children start learning the attitudes of the ratrace quite early. They mustn't just do well at school—they must sweep the floor with their rivals. That's how you get on. We give prizes to such persons, not so far as I know to those who know how best to get on with others, or those who can coax the best out of others. We must delight in our ulcers, the symbols of our success.

So I would look for a socio-economic system that placed the emphasis on sharing and giving, rather than on self-aggrandisement and getting. Capitalism is exploitative and I can't stand that. We need to engage the resources that each person has. My vision includes a society that is more compassionate and caring, in which 'superfluous appendages' [*the government's way of describing families of black workers*] are unthinkable, where young and old are made to feel wanted, and that they belong and are not resented. It is a distorted community that trundles its aged off into soulless institutions. We need their accumulated wisdom and experience. They are splendid for helping the younger to feel cared for; certainly that has been the experience in the extended family.

I believe too that in a future South Africa we must be supportive of the family. The nuclear family is not geared to stand all the strains placed on it by modern day pressures. There are things we can survive better in a group than singly. I know there are pressures in the extended family, but I need to be persuaded that these are greater than those presently haunting the nuclear family.

Basically I long and work for a South Africa that is more open and more just; where people count and where they will have equal access to the good things of life, with equal opportunity to live, work, and learn. I long for a South Africa where there will be equal and untrammelled access to the courts of the land, where detention without trial will be a thing of the hoary past, where bannings and other such arbitrary acts will no longer be even so much as mentioned, and where the rule of law will hold sway in the fullest sense. In addition, all adults will participate fully in political decision making, and in other decisions which affect their lives. Consequently they will have the vote and be eligible for election to all public offices. This South Africa will have integrity of territory with a common citizenship, and all the rights and privileges that go with such a citizenship, belonging to all its inhabitants.

Clearly, for many people, what I have described is almost a Utopia, and we cannot reach that desired goal overnight. Black leaders would, I feel, be willing to go back to the black community, and say: 'Hold on—things are moving in the right direction' if certain minimum conditions were pledged and met, even in stages, by the white powers that be. These are:

(A)   Abolition of the Pass Laws.

(B)   The immediate halting of population removals.

(C)   The scrapping of Bantu Education, and a move towards a unitary educational system.

(D)   A commitment to call a National Convention.

These would be significant steps towards realising the vision.

1.   What is freedom to Tutu?

2.   Why doesn't Tutu like capitalism?

3.   What place does the family have in Tutu's vision of South Africa?

4.   Tutu describes his vision as "almost a Utopia." How would you characterize it?

The Japanese Miracle

A high-speed train crossing a bridge on the Tokaido line below Mt. Fuji.

·160·

The Constitution of Japan

(1947)

The Constitution of Japan was drafted in great secrecy by members of the military occupation force in 1946. No Japanese were included on the drafting team, which was appointed by General Douglas MacArthur under his authority as commander-in-chief of the occupation forces. Nevertheless, the Constitution was described as an amendment to the Meiji Constitution of 1889 and MacArthur required that the Japanese government sponsor it as such. It was submitted for ratification by the Diet as provided under the amendment clause of the Meiji Constitution. The Diet made minor modifications, all of which were approved by the occupation forces, and it was ratified on May 3, 1947.

Despite its Western origins and the fact that it was imposed upon the Japanese government, the Constitution of 1947 has been remarkably successful. The doctrine of popular sovereignty, which replaced that of the sovereignty of the emperor, struck a responsive chord within Japanese society. The guarantee of human rights and of equality before the law were essential ingredients in the postwar reorganization of Japan. The most controversial aspect of the Constitution of 1947 has been the renunciation of war and the implicit ban on the creation of a Japanese military.

We, the Japanese people, acting through our duly elected representatives in the National Diet, determined that we shall secure for ourselves and our posterity the fruits of peaceful cooperation with all nations and the blessings of liberty throughout this land, and resolved that never again shall we be visited with the horrors of war through the action of government, do proclaim that sovereign power resides with the people and do firmly establish this Constitution. Government is a sacred trust of the people, the authority for which is derived from the people, the powers of which are exercised by the representatives of the people, and the benefits of which are enjoyed by the people. This is a universal principle of mankind upon which this Constitution is founded. We reject and revoke all constitutions, laws, ordinances, and rescripts in conflict herewith.

We, the Japanese people, desire peace for all time and are deeply conscious of the high ideals controlling human relationship, and we have determined to preserve our security and existence, trusting in the justice and faith of the peace-loving peoples of the world. We desire to occupy an honored place in an international society striving for the preservation of peace, and the banishment of tyranny and slavery, oppression and intolerance for all time from the earth. We recognize that all peoples of the world have the right to live in peace, free from fear and want.

CHAPTER I. THE EMPEROR

Article 1

The Emperor shall be the symbol of the State and of the unity of the people, deriving his position from the will of the people, with whom resides sovereign power.

Article 2

The Imperial Throne shall be dynastic and succeeded to in accordance with the Imperial House Law passed by the Diet.

Article 3

The advice and approval of the Cabinet shall be required for all acts of the Emperor in matters of state, and the Cabinet shall be responsible therefor.

Article 4

The Emperor shall perform only such acts in matters of state as are provided for in this Constitution and he shall not have powers related to government.

2. The Emperor may delegate the performance of his acts in matters of state as may be provided by law.

Article 5

When, in accordance with the Imperial House Law, a Regency is established, the Regent shall perform his acts in matters of state in the Emperor's name. In this case, paragraph one of the preceding article will be applicable.

Article 6

The Emperor shall appoint the Prime Minister as designated by the Diet.

2. The Emperor shall appoint the Chief Judge of the Supreme Court as designated by the Cabinet.

CHAPTER II. RENUNCIATION OF WAR

Article 9

Aspiring sincerely to an international peace based on justice and order, the Japanese people

forever renounce war as a sovereign right of the nation and the threat or use of force as means of settling international disputes.

2. In order to accomplish the aim of the preceding paragraph, land, sea, and air forces, as well as other war potential, will never be maintained. The right of belligerency of the state will not be recognized.

CHAPTER III. RIGHTS AND DUTIES OF THE PEOPLE

Article 10

The conditions necessary for being a Japanese national shall be determined by law.

Article 11

The people shall not be prevented from enjoying any of the fundamental human rights. These fundamental human rights guaranteed to the people of this Constitution shall be conferred upon the people of this and future generations as eternal and inviolate rights.

Article 13

All of the people shall be respected as individuals. Their right to life, liberty, and the pursuit of happiness shall, to the extent that it does not interfere with the public welfare, be the supreme consideration in legislation and in other governmental affairs.

Article 14

All of the people are equal under the law and there shall be no discrimination in political, economic, or social relations because of race, creed, sex, social status, or family origin.

Article 15

The people have the inalienable right to choose their public officials and to dismiss them.

2. All public officials are servants of the whole community and not of any group thereof.

3. Universal adult suffrage is guaranteed with regard to the election of public officials.

4. In all elections, secrecy of the ballot shall not be violated. A voter shall not be answerable, publicly or privately, for the choice he has made.

Article 16

Every person shall have the right of peaceful petition for the redress of damage, for the removal of public officials, for the enactment, repeal, or amendment of laws, ordinances, or regulations, and for other matters, nor shall any person be in any way discriminated against for sponsoring such a petition.

Article 18

No person shall be held in bondage of any kind. Involuntary servitude, except as punishment for crime, is prohibited.

Article 19

Freedom of thought and conscience shall not be violated.

Article 20

Freedom of religion is guaranteed to all. No religious organization shall receive any privileges from the State nor exercise any political authority.

2. No person shall be compelled to take part in any religious acts, celebration, rite, or practice.

3. The State and its organs shall refrain from religious education or any other religious activity.

Article 21

Freedom of assembly and association as well as speech, press, and all other forms of expression are guaranteed.

2. No censorship shall be maintained, nor shall the secrecy of any means of communication be violated.

Article 23

Academic freedom is guaranteed.

Article 24

Marriage shall be based only on the mutual consent of both sexes and it shall be maintained through mutual cooperation with the equal rights of husband and wife as a basis.

2. With regard to choice of spouse, property rights, inheritance, choice of domicile, divorce, and other matters pertaining to marriage and the family, laws shall be enacted from the standpoint of individual dignity and the essential equality of the sexes.

Article 25

All people shall have the right to maintain the minimum standards of wholesome and cultured living.

Article 26

All people shall have the right to receive an equal education correspondent to their ability, as provided by law.

Article 27

All people shall have the right and the obligation to work.

Article 28

The right of workers to organize and to bargain and act collectively is guaranteed.

Article 29

The right to own or to hold property is inviolable.

Article 30

The people shall be liable to taxation as provided by law.

Article 31

No person shall be deprived of life or liberty, nor shall any other criminal penalty be imposed, except according to procedure established by law.

Article 32

No person shall be denied the right of access to the courts.

Article 33

No person shall be apprehended except upon warrant issued by a competent judicial officer which specifies the offense with which the person is charged, unless he is apprehended, the offense being committed.

Article 34

No person shall be arrested or detained without being at once informed of the charges against him or without the immediate privilege of counsel; nor shall he be detained without adequate cause; and upon demand of any person such cause must be immediately shown in open court in his presence and the presence of his counsel.

Article 35

The right of all persons to be secure in their homes, papers, and effects against entries, searches, and seizures shall not be impaired except upon warrant issued for adequate cause and particularly describing the place to be searched and things to be seized, or except as provided by Article 33.

2. Each search or seizure shall be made upon separate warrant issued by a competent judicial officer.

Article 36

The infliction of torture by any public officer and cruel punishments are absolutely forbidden.

Article 37

In all criminal cases the accused shall enjoy the right to a speedy and public trial by an impartial tribunal.

3. At all times the accused shall have the assistance of competent counsel who shall, if the accused is unable to secure the same by his own efforts, be assigned to his use by the State.

Article 38

No person shall be compelled to testify against himself.

Article 39

No person shall be held criminally liable for an act which was lawful at the time it was committed, or of which he has been acquitted, nor shall he be placed in double jeopardy.

Article 40

Any person, in case he is acquitted after he has been arrested or detained, may sue the State for redress as provided by law.

CHAPTER IV. THE DIET

Article 41

The Diet shall be the highest organ of state power, and shall be the sole law-making organ of the State.

Article 42

The Diet shall consist of two Houses, namely the House of Representatives and the House of Councillors.

Article 43

Both Houses shall consist of elected members, representative of all the people.

2.   The number of the members of each House shall be fixed by law.

Article 45

The term of office of members of the House of Representatives shall be four years. However, the term shall be terminated before the full term is up in case the House of Representatives is dissolved.

Article 46

The term of office of members of the House of Councillors shall be six years, and election for half the members shall take place every three years.

Article 50

Except in cases provided by law, members of both Houses shall be exempt from apprehension while the Diet is in session, and any members apprehended before the opening of the session shall be freed during the term of the session upon demand of the House.

Article 51

Members of both Houses shall not be held liable outside the House for speeches, debates, or votes cast inside the House.

Article 52

An ordinary session of the Diet shall be convoked once per year.

Article 54

When the House of Representatives is dissolved, there must be a general election of members of the House of Representatives within forty (40) days from the date of dissolution, and the Diet must be convoked within thirty (30) days from the date of the election.

2.   When the House of Representatives is dissolved, the House of Councillors is closed at the same time. However, the Cabinet may in time of national emergency convoke the House of Councillors in emergency session.

Article 57

Deliberation in each House shall be public. However, a secret meeting may be held where a majority of two-thirds or more of those members present passes a resolution therefor.

2.   Each House shall keep a record of proceedings. This record shall be published and given general circulation, excepting such parts of proceedings of secret session as may be deemed to require secrecy.

Article 59

A bill becomes a law on passage by both Houses, except as otherwise provided by the Constitution.

2.   A bill which is passed by the House of Representatives, and upon which the House of Councillors makes a decision different from that of the House of Representatives, becomes a law when passed a second time by the House of Representatives by a majority of two-thirds or more of the members present.

4.   Failure by the House of Councillors to take final action within sixty (60) days after receipt of a bill passed by the House of Representatives, time in recess excepted, may be determined by the House of Representatives to constitute a rejection of the said bill by the House of Councillors.

Article 60

The budget must first be submitted to the House of Representatives.

Article 63

The Prime Minister and other Ministers of State may, at any time, appear in either House for the purpose of speaking on bills, regardless of whether they are members of the House or not. They must appear when their presence is required in order to give answers or explanations.

Article 64

The Diet shall set up an impeachment court from among the members of both Houses for the purpose of trying those judges against whom removal proceedings have been instituted.

CHAPTER V. THE CABINET

Article 65

Executive power shall be vested in the Cabinet.

Article 66

The Cabinet shall consist of the Prime Minister, who shall be its head, and other Ministers of State, as provided for by law.

2. The Prime Minister and other Ministers of State must be civilians.

3. The Cabinet, in the exercise of executive power, shall be collectively responsible to the Diet.

Article 67

The Prime Minister shall be designated from among the members of the Diet by a resolution of the Diet. This designation shall precede all other business.

CHAPTER VI. JUDICIARY

Article 76

The whole judicial power is vested in a Supreme Court and in such inferior courts as are established by law.

Article 79

The Supreme Court shall consist of a Chief Judge and such number of judges as may be determined by law; all such judges excepting the Chief Judge shall be appointed by the Cabinet.

2. The appointment of the judges of the Supreme Court shall be reviewed by the people at the first general election of members of the House of Representatives following their appointment, and shall be reviewed again at the first general election of members of the House of Representatives after a lapse of ten (10) years, and in the same manner thereafter.

5. The judges of the Supreme Court shall be retired upon the attainment of the age as fixed by law.

CHAPTER IX. AMENDMENTS

Article 96

Amendments to this Constitution shall be initiated by the Diet, through a concurring vote of two-thirds or more of all the members of each House and shall thereupon be submitted to the people for ratification, which shall require the affirmative vote of a majority of all votes cast thereon, at a special referendum or at such election as the Diet shall specify.

2. Amendments when so ratified shall immediately be promulgated by the Emperor in the name of the people, as an integral part of this Constitution.

CHAPTER X. SUPREME LAW

Article 97

The fundamental human rights by this Constitution guaranteed to the people of Japan are fruits of the age-old struggle of man to be free; they have survived the many exacting tests for durability and are conferred upon this and future generations in trust, to be held for all time inviolate.

Article 98

This Constitution shall be the supreme law of the nation and no law, ordinance, imperial rescript, or other act of government, or part thereof, contrary to the provisions hereof, shall have legal force or validity.

1. What form of government is established by this constitution?

2. What ideals does this constitution embrace?

3. What are the differences between the rights and the duties of the people as outlined in Chapter III?

4. What impact did World War II have on the conceptualization of the Constitution of Japan? What other constitutions do you think influenced it?

·161·

Kamei Katsuichiro
An Ideal Portrait of Twentieth-Century Japan
(1954)

Kamei Katsuichiro (1907–1966) was an influential Japanese critic and author. Born in Hokkaido, he studied literature at Tokyo University. His early years were spent in association with a group of radical left-wing critics of Japanese culture, but gradually Kamei found intellectual inspiration from the early periods of Japanese culture, particularly Buddhism. His writings became more personal and more romantic. In 1951 he received the Yomiuri Prize for Literature. His best known work is *Literature and Faith.*

In 1954 Kamei published *An Ideal Portrait of Twentieth-Century Japan,* which opposed the continued Westernization of Japan. He argues for a return to traditional Japanese values and beliefs and for a resuscitation of pan-Asianism, the combination of Asian nations and cultures.

RETURN TO THE EAST

One of the problems with which Japanese have been burdened since the Meiji Era has been the necessity of examining Japan's place in Asia and our special fate as Asians. Japan, as everyone knows, was the first country in Asia to become "modernized," but it is not yet clear what meaning this modernization had for Asia. It is also a question whether Asian thought, which possesses strong traditions despite the repeated taste of defeat and a sense of inferiority before Western science, is doomed to perish without further struggle, or if it is capable of reviving in the twentieth century and contributing something which will enable us to surmount the present crisis. We must begin to consider these questions. In contrast with the fervor with which Europeanization has been pursued since the Meiji Era, this aspect of our lives has been extraordinarily neglected. I believe that the neglect—or perhaps one should say ingratitude—shown by Japanese towards Asia is the tragedy of modern Japan, and that to study it has become since the defeat the greatest responsibility incumbent on us.

It is true, of course, that "Asia" covers an immense area, and undoubtedly contains many "spiritual kingdoms" with which I am unfamiliar. I myself have never actually journeyed through Asia; I have not so much as glimpsed it with my own eyes. The best I have been able to do is to imagine what Asia is like by means of the books I have read. Nevertheless, looking back on Japanese history has revealed to me that in every age Asia has breathed in the minds of Japanese. We are all familiar with how Asian culture, transformed or more highly refined, became part of the flesh and blood of Japanese culture. However, like most young men of the past sixty or seventy years, I used not to consider Asia as being necessarily primary to us. My ignorance of and indifference to China and India did not trouble me in the least, and I was constantly fascinated by Europe. I thought that to learn from European knowledge was our first task, and I neglected the matter of learning from the wisdom of the East.

There was something even more seriously wrong with my attitude. My ignorance and indifference with respect to China and India might still have been pardoned if they had been no more than that, but to them in fact was joined a feeling of contempt for those countries. Since the defeat I have come to recognize the fact that it was a fatal error for us to have allowed such a feeling to attain the status of a deep-seated national prejudice. Japan, thanks to the fact that she was the first country in the Orient to become "modernized" (or perhaps on account of her modern military strength), began from about the time of the Russo-Japanese War to entertain attitudes of extreme superiority towards the peoples of Asia. This feeling, we must remember, was the reverse of the medal of our feeling of inferiority towards the Europeans, and it came to express itself in a kind of brutality towards the other Asian peoples. We cannot deny that we tended to look on them as our slaves. When and how the fate of Japanese as Asians went astray is the most significant problem of our modern history.

"Asia is one. The Himalayas divide, only to accentuate, two mighty civilizations, the Chinese with its communism of Confucius, and the Indian with its individualism of the Vedas. But not even the snowy barriers can interrupt for one moment that broad expanse of love for the Ultimate and Universal, which is the common thought-inheritance of every Asian race, enabling them to produce all the great religions of the world, and distinguishing them from those maritime peoples of the Mediterranean and the Baltic, who love to dwell on the Particular, and to search out the means, not the end, of life."

"[The average Westerner] was wont to regard Japan as barbarous while she indulged in the gentle arts of peace: he calls her civilized since she began to commit wholesale slaughter on Manchurian battlefields. Much comment has

been given lately to the Code of the Samurai—
the Art of Death which makes our soldiers exult
in self-sacrifice; but scarcely any attention has
been paid to Teaism,* which represents so much
of our Art of Life. Fain we would remain barbarians, if our claim to civilization were to be based
on the gruesome glory of war. Fain would we
await the time when due respect shall be paid to
our art and ideals."

"What mean these strange combinations
which Europe displays—the hospital and the tor-
pedo, the Christian missionary and imperialism,
the maintenance of vast armaments as a guarantee of peace? Such contradictions did not exist in
the ancient civilization of the East. Such were not
the ideals of the Japanese Restoration, such is
not the goal of her reformation. The night of the
Orient, which had hidden us in its folds, has
been lifted, but we find the world still in the dusk
of humanity, Europe has taught us war; when
shall she learn the blessings of peace?"

These words were pronounced about the
time of the Russo-Japanese War. They voice profound doubts and resistance on the part of one
Oriental to certain important aspects of the
modern European civilization which was then
penetrating eastwards. This situation was not
confined to Japan. There should have been common outcries made by men in India, China, and
Japan, as Orientals. There should at least have
been outcries which would have linked Gandhi
and Tagore, Sun Yat-sen and Lu Hsün, and
Okakura—outcries of surprise and alarm, or of
doubt, or of malediction, or of resistance to the
European conquest of Asia.

It should certainly be a matter of the pro-
foundest regret to the Orient that these outcries
uttered in the nineteenth and twentieth centuries as Asians, in inflections which varied with
the particular features of the different countries
of Asia, should never have achieved full expression, but should have died out without reinforcing one another. To us Japanese the most impor-

tant fact is that the responsibility for causing
these voices to die out rests with us. The cause of
the tragedy lies in our vigorous, precipitous
modernization. We tried with desperate efforts
to master European civilization, and in the act of
acquiring it we lost something very precious—
what I should like to call the characteristic "love"
of Asia.

We cannot ignore the fact that this responsibility is connected with the singularity of our
racial transformation. The period between the
appearance of Perry's "black ships" at the end of
the shogunate, and the completion of the battle-
ship *Yamato* was a period when Japan was changing with extraordinary rapidity into "the West
within the East." Indeed, if one were asked for
what Japan poured out her strength most lavishly, and to what she devoted the finest flower of
her scientific abilities during the years following
the Meiji Restoration, one would have to answer
that it was for warships. This emphasis on armaments must certainly have had its origins in the
profound anxiety of our grandfathers who had
seen before their eyes the nations of Asia being
colonized, one after the other.

It undoubtedly represented an astonishing
burst of energy displayed for the sake of national
independence and self-defense, but, as fate
would have it, the raw materials of the continent
were necessary to it. One gets the feeling that in
the matter of raw materials and the acquisition
of markets Japan was hastily and sometimes
crudely imitating the colonial policies of the
European nations. We, first among the Asians,
mastered the weapons which modern European
civilization had employed to invade Asia in pursuit of its colonial policies, and we turned the
points of these weapons on Asians. The modernization of Japan would have been impossible had
we not victimized China and estranged ourselves
from her. Japan has experienced this contradiction at least as a historical fact. The high development of the intellectual curiosity of the Japanese has often been mentioned, but this virtue has
been accompanied on the Asian mainland by
deadly vice.

The cult of the tea ceremony.

This is not the only contradiction. There were during this same period quite a few men like Okakura Kakuzō who preached love for Asia. Indeed, one thing which surprises us when we read the history of Japan during the past half-century is how often the phrase "to secure the peace of Asia" was used by statesmen. The invasion of China, in fact, was carried out in the name of this principle. In the midst of the so-called Greater East Asia War, I myself believed in Okakura's words and approved of the war because of them. What can this mean?

Every war, inevitably, has its fine slogans which serve as its intellectual adornment. But in my case this was not the whole story. As I have already mentioned, there was in me a deep-seated contempt for the other Asian peoples, a contempt nourished in Japan from about the time of the Russo-Japanese War; one may say that I had become imbued with the conqueror mentality. I could as an overlord of Asia preach with equanimity the love of Asia. And yet it was of course true that Okakura's words were meaningful only so long as Japan did not invade any Asian country.

Japan carried out the European method of conquest: confronting other countries with weapons in one hand and a gospel of love in the other. Warships and Christianity were indivisible elements in the European conquest of Asia; Japan slaughtered people while preaching the love of Asia and the Way of the Gods.

What was the result? Japan became in the East the stepchild of the West, and as a consequence seems now to be fated to become this time the stepchild of the East. The intellectual energy which the Japanese showed when once they had received the baptism of modern Europe was undoubtedly the wonder of Asia, but it imposed strange contradictions on Japan.

One of these, it may be imagined, results from the fact that Japan is an island nation. Japan is assuredly a part of Asia, but it is a special area separated from the continent and, perhaps, though Asian should not really be called Asian at all. Sometimes I have found myself wondering along these lines. Of course Japan is not the West either. While on the one hand preserving in a uniquely assimilated form the various systems of thought and arts of the East, she has an insatiable intellectual curiosity which would make all of the West her own. Has ever a people harbored such frantic contradictions: impetuosity and caution, confusion and harmony, division and unity—and all of them changing at every instant? I have sometimes wondered whether Japan may not be the unique example in the world of a kind of "nation in the experimental stage." It was this island nation's knowledge which, in response to a ceaseless impulse towards Europe, perpetrated the multi-sided betrayal of Asia.

At the same time—and one may also speak of this as a result—the defeat of Japan brought about the independence of the nations of Asia. The long European rule of Asia either collapsed or was shaken at its very roots. This, together with the revolution in China, represents the greatest event occasioned by the Second World War; one may indeed say that it effected an immense upheaval in world history. A further result, one can probably say, was the ironic one that European capitalism, after playing its part in Japan, should have met this fate in the other countries of Asia because of Japan. Japan, it needs hardly be mentioned, lost all the territory she had gained through aggression.

However, an important factor came into being at this juncture. Now, for the first time in modern Japanese history, Japan was furnished with the conditions of being able to deal with the nations of Asia on terms of equality—not as conquerors or as conquered, but on a genuinely equal footing. I should like to lay emphasis on this factor for which our defeat was responsible. The basis for Japanese independence is to be found here—by which I mean that it is the only ethical basis we have for independence.

The true meaning of what I am attempting to discuss under the theme of "return to the East" may be said in the final analysis to be the product of a sense of guilt towards the East. The only qualifications we have for a "return" is a sense of guilt, particularly towards China and

Korea. This is not a question of who holds political power in these countries. A more fundamental question is the recognition of guilt for former aggression towards the peoples of Asia. We must abandon completely the consciousness of being "leaders" in Asia. I should like to consider the return to Asia as an ethical rather than as a political question.

As a basis for this return Japanese traditions must be scrutinized afresh: how has what Okakura called the "common inheritance of every Asiatic race" been transmitted from ancient times to the present, and should it be passed on in the future? A re-examination of Buddhism, Confucianism, and Taoism as they exist in Japan, together with a general re-examination of the characteristically Japanese types of learning and art as they have been influenced by these teachings, must be undertaken. I should like to call attention to the steady achievements of men in the fields of anthropology, Japanese literature, Chinese studies, and Buddhist studies. It is a question of the *roots* of the tree onto which European culture has been grafted, and this re-examination is essential if we are to discover the "individuality" of modern Japan which gives a native character to all our thought.

At the same time there has never been a greater need than today for intellectual interchange among the nations of Asia. Some interchange, however slight, has been begun with India, but Japan must seek out opportunities throughout the whole of Asia to discover what the possibilities are of "Eastern spirit." However long it may take, I believe that a deepening of intellectual interchange should be made a basic policy. And, may we not say, the primary goal should be the discovery of a possibility of common spiritual association in the East. This is the prerequisite for the establishment of a new image of the Asian.

There are in Asia Buddhism, Mohammedanism, Christianity, Communism. European influence also remains powerful. Various systems of thinking thus exist, but they are backed by a characteristically Asian quality, and there is unquestionably one way of thought in which they are all unified through a process of "Asianization." This is what we must look for. However, in so doing we must free ourselves from any infantile notions such as the simple schematization formerly in vogue here, according to which the East stood for the spirit and the West for material things. Indeed, the return to the East must not be accompanied by prejudices directed against the West or any form of xenophobia. In fact, it should result in the destruction of the very sense of opposition between East and West which figured so prominently in our former ideas.

1. Does Kamei see Japan as part of Asia?

2. What does he consider to be Western influences in Japan? What is his opinion of these influences?

3. Why did the author have anti-Asian feelings?

4. What does he mean by his opinion that Japan needs to "return to the East"? How does he think this is possible?

·162·
Chitoshi Yanaga
Big Business in Japanese Politics
(1968)

Although Chitoshi Yanaga (1903–1985) was born in Hawaii and spent most of his academic career in the United States, he was sent as a child by his Japanese parents to study in Japan. He returned to America in his early twenties and earned a Ph. D. from the University of California at Berkeley. Yanaga taught political science at Berkeley and Yale. During World War II he worked in the U.S. Intelligence service and was involved with preserving documents seized from Japan afterward. He was a professor at Yale for 25 years before his retirement in 1971.

Chitoshi Yanaga's study of the relationship between Japanese business and politics is a classic work of scholarship that has helped shape the way American policymakers have responded to the "Japanese miracle." His penetrating analysis of the relationship between government and business has also led to calls for similar developments in the West.

One of the characteristics of Japanese society is the existence of a number of rather exclusive groupings.... Such cliques or groups provide the oasis of the power structure. In the prewar period, power was exercised by three distinct cliques, the financial (*zaibatsu*), bureaucratic (*kambatsu*), and military (*gumbatsu*), but in the postwar period the military and the financial cliques have ceased to exist. Only the bureaucratic clique has retained its power. Zaibatsu has been superseded by *zaikai* (the business leader clique). Two other groups, already mentioned, have come into prominence, namely, the extended family clique (*keibatsu*) and the university clique (*gakubatsu*).

... Although no longer recognized as a basic legal unit, the family is still the touchstone of social success. The importance of family background or connections in achieving success in almost any field has not diminished. On the contrary, it seems to have increased greatly. More than ever, family status (*iegara*) and pedigree (*kenami*) are necessary qualifications for membership in high society and for achieving a position of prestige and influence in business and politics, even in academic life.

Candidates for important posts are judged on the basis of family ties. When a new governor of the Bank of Japan was appointed in late 1964, press and public approval was on the basis of the appointee's family background rather than on his ability, which was widely recognized. If one's pedigree is not the best, it is always possible to improve it by marrying into the right family. Such ties are widely sought, especially in the business community. Chances for such marriages are greatly enhanced for men who have acquired a quality education, such as graduation from the prestigious Tokyo University, which is open to all solely on the basis of ability. Bright young graduates of the best universities are always in demand as husbands for daughters of influential business and political leaders. When one already has a good pedigree, it is possible to improve it socially and financially by acquiring a degree from an elite school. Marital ties are often established to enhance the position, prestige, and power of the families as well as the individuals involved. . . .

UNIVERSITY AND SCHOOL CLIQUES (*GAKUBATSU*)

The unique character of the university clique is responsible for the influence wielded by the graduates of Tokyo University in business, politics, and government as well as in higher education, science, technology, and medicine. Ever since its establishment in 1886, Tokyo University has inculcated in its students a strong sense of elitism and leadership. In light of the incredibly difficult entrance examinations, it is not surprising that its graduates feel superior, even though in many instances such an attitude is not justified in terms of academic achievement. The university was founded specifically for the purpose of training government officials. Upon graduation, its early graduates were given the privilege of immediate appointment, without examination, to the newly created higher civil service. This established a tradition of administrative elitism, and until the end of World War I the cream of the Tokyo Imperial University graduates went into government service. In no time the university had established undisputed supremacy in higher education. It attracted the best students from all over the nation, and students have been flocking to it ever since.

Tōdai—as Tokyo University is commonly known—is in a sense a most exclusive club, membership in which establishes eligibility for the highest positions in the realm. Of the ten postwar prime ministers between 1945 and 1965, seven were Tōdai graduates (Shidehara, Katayama, Ashida, Yoshida, Hatoyama, Kishi, and Satō). . . .

CONCENTRATION OF POWER IN TOKYO

One of the most distinctive features of Japan's power structure is the extraordinarily high concentration of power wielders in Tokyo. Here, in the world's largest city, a supermetropolis of over 11 million people and the seat of the national government, are located the main offices of practically all the major corporations, making it the business, banking, financial, transportation, communication, publishing, and mass media center of Japan. All political parties, labor unions, and trade associations have their national headquarters here. The leading universities, research institutes, museums, art galleries, theaters, radio and television broadcasting systems, and the country's six largest newspapers are located in Tokyo. All major political and economic decisions are made in this city. It is as if Washington, D.C., New York, Chicago, Philadelphia, Pittsburgh, Boston, and Detroit were rolled into one.

Such a concentration of power is unknown in the United States. To create an analogous situation, it would be necessary to locate the head offices of America's hundred largest corporations in Washington, D.C., together with their presidents, board chairmen, and directors, many of whom would be related by marriage not only to each other but to influential political leaders and government administrators. Furthermore these top-level executives would, for the most part, claim the same alma mater, belong to the same country clubs, have ready access to government offices, maintain daily contact with government officials by phone or over the luncheon table, enjoy intimate relations with influential senators and congressmen, and also serve on government advisory bodies and administrative commissions. The impact of this sort of concentration of political, economic, and social power on the governing process can indeed be far-reaching. . . .

. . . There are power groups representing different segments of society, to be sure, but they cannot be isolated easily. There seems to be general agreement among students of Japanese politics that the nation is governed jointly by organized business, the party government, and the administrative bureaucracy.

As to which of the three groups is most powerful, there is no agreement. Any judgment must necessarily be highly subjective and is likely to be biased. Professional politicians believe that the administrators are running the country. Businessmen are quick to assert that the party politicians determine national policies. Administrators are convinced that organized business, working through the party in power, is in control of national policies.

In terms of economic policies, it is easy to conclude that organized business rules supreme. The power of the administrative bureaucracy over organized business is quite apparent when it comes to power to regulate and control business, and to grant or withhold licenses, government loans, and subsidies. The party is no match against the power of organized business. Yet there have been instances where the party in power was able to exert a decisive influence over the bureaucracy. . . .

As presently constituted, organized business, the party government, and the administrative bureaucracy are the three legs of the tripod on which the Japanese political system rests. Functionally they are interdependent, even though they operate for the most part in distinct areas. Organized business initiates and proposes policies. It sponsors and supports the party in power. The party in turn forms the government and selects candidates for the Diet, who function as legitimatizers of government policy. The administrative bureaucracy proposes, drafts, modifies, interprets, and implements policies under the surveillance of the party and the government. The most important functions of the bureaucracy involve the protection and promotion of business and industry, in whose behalf it formulates long-term economic plans, makes forecasts, sets goals, and establishes priorities. Organized business provides members for the cabinet, the Diet, and government advisory councils and adminis-

trative commissions. It hires retired government officials as corporation executives and trade associations officials.

In return for political contributions by organized business, the party in power strives to create a political climate conducive to carrying on profitable business enterprises. In this role, the party in power is in effect the political arm of organized business in much the same manner that the Japan Socialist party is the political arm of labor. It is the party in power that selects the prime minister and the cabinet members who head the administrative departments and exercise decisive influence on budget formulation.

The spectacle of Japanese politics is in a sense a dramatic production, presented jointly by the business community, the ruling party, and the administrative bureaucracy. Organized business is the playwright as well as the financier. The ruling party, as producer, director, and stage manager, adapts the play and makes sure that the production meets with the approval of the playwright-financier. It is also responsible for picking the leading actor, who must be *persona grata* to the financier. The administrative bureaucracy utilizes its expertise in looking after the technical details as well as the business end of the production.

ENTERPRISE GROUPS

Unlike the old zaibatsu, which dominated the prewar economic scene under a system of highly centralized family control through holding companies, the new postwar big business structure is composed of enterprise groups. These groups are of two kinds: those organized around the former zaibatsu and using the old names (Mitsubishi with thirty-eight separate corporations and a research institute; Mitsui with twenty-two corporations; Sumitomo with fifteen corporations) and those held together by large banks (Fuji, formerly Yasuda; Dai Ichi; and the Industrial Bank of Japan, through which the enterprises in both groups manage their financing).

These groups, known as *keiretsu,* cannot be described in American business terms. They are not really monopolies, since they compete with each other strongly and no one group completely dominates a given field. Actually they are horizontal groups of companies, each group containing many varied industries as well as a bank, a trust company, insurance companies, a trade company (or companies), and a real estate company. Member companies tend to cooperate with other companies within the group and to compete with companies outside the group. When entering new fields such as atomic energy or petrochemicals, where investment requirements are beyond the capability of any one company in the group, several or most members will combine to finance the venture jointly. The groups vary in cohesiveness. Within each group, the bank is the primary though not the sole source of banking support. The group's trading company handles the sales, particularly export trading, and the purchase of raw materials, but not exclusively. Policy coordination is achieved through presidents' clubs, which meet periodically.

These enterprise groups represent the postwar restructuring of big business on the basis of common interests, the better to cope with common problems in such fields as production, sales, and financing. . . .

1. Who is the intended audience of *Big Business in Japanese Politics?*

2. Characterize the Japan described in these passages.

3. What do these passages imply about the role of women in post–World War II Japanese society?

4. According to Chitoshi Yanaga, what is the relationship between business and politics in Japan?

·163·

Donald Richie
Japanese Rhythms
(1984)

Donald Richie (b. 1924) has been one of the foremost Western interpreters of Japanese culture. He went to Japan at the end of the occupation in 1946 and has lived there ever since. He has written numerous books and countless essays and articles attempting to explain all aspects of Japanese culture and society to a Western audience. He is an authority on popular culture and has written extensively on the work of film director Akira Kurasawa as well as on Japanese popular music, literature, and television.

Japanese Rhythms is characteristic of Richie's sensitivity to the survival of traditional aspects of Japanese life within its modern framework. Concepts such as the group are to be seen in such everyday activities as who leaves an office first or who waits for someone on a street corner. Richie is quick to point to what seem to Westerners to be contradictions in Japanese customs and attitudes and to explain why they are coherent within their own cultural assumptions.

Cultures have their own rhythms: how they divide the days and the nights, when to go fast and when to go slow, in what manner to fragment time.

Some of the differences are familiar. A well-known temporal gulf exists between the global north and south. The latter have, for example, their famous siesta—night again in the middle of the day. The northern visitor is always surprised at this diurnal difference, and often irritated as well. What? The post office isn't open? Don't these people know it is two in the afternoon?

Another familiar gulf, this time a chasm, exists also between East and West, the Orient and the Occident. We speak of the slower pace, calling it leisurely if we like it, indolent if we do

Japanese girls dancing to rock music in Meiji Park, Tokyo.

not. Our travel brochures advise us to go and, specifically, *relax* in exotic such-and-such.

These various temporal differences are well known. Not so familiar are those cultures which blend the differences and bridge the gulfs. Among these, the most spectacular is Japan. Here the rhythms of the West have been rigorously applied and yet, under these, the old pulse of Asia is still strongly felt.

Seen from the outside, the way in which the Japanese structure time seems much closer to New York than, say, Kandy or Mandalay. Indeed, most of the Western temporal virtues—efficiency, promptness, get-up-and-go—are being flung in our faces by this seemingly industrious nation.

Yet, the view from the inside indicates that older, more purely Asian rhythms persist. There is the new way of arranging the day and then there is the old. And these two, as with so much else in Japan, coexist—strata in time.

Early to bed, early to rise, etc., has been the recipe for business success in the WASP world and this is the image (bright-eyed and bushy-tailed) that such have had of themselves. Thus, the Japanese, taking over this image and making it theirs, now insist that they are a hard-working people and are more flattered than wounded when called workaholics. Such a role means rising at dawn, rushing to the office, putting in long hours, racing home and going to bed early to rest for the next fulfilling day.

Since this is the official version, it is officially supported. And since everyone has nominally gone home, buses stop running at ten-thirty; the subways stop at midnight, and the trains shut down half an hour later. Unlike that of New York and Paris, shameless night-owl abodes, Japanese civic transportation does not run all night long.

Yet, the populace is no more off the streets at twelve now than it was in old Tokugawa Japan. The entertainment districts are filled with people long after midnight. These are not at home resting for the next busy day. They are getting around the night spots by taking taxis.

Nor do the Japanese actually get up at dawn. Indeed, nowadays, a majority does not get to work until ten o'clock, also the hour when the bazaar at Rangoon opens. To be sure, some attempt an earlier arrival. Being first into the office in the morning supports, and in part creates, the modern idea of the Japanese as being very hard workers.

And the last out as well. One is supposed to hang around even though one's work may be finished. Being one of the group is considered important and rushing out to conform to an egotistical timetable is bad modern form. Rather, one subscribes to the group timetable. This has nothing to do with working hard. It has to do merely with attendance.

Indeed, as one looks more closely at the manner in which modern Japan structures the business day, one becomes very aware of the differences between modern and traditional time-keeping and how these intermingle.

Once the modern rush to the office is over and the business day is actually begun, the time scheme becomes traditional. There is lots of discussion, lots of stopping to drink tea—and nowadays lots of visits to the ubiquitous coffee shop to talk some more. Nor is this talk confined to work in the narrow Western sense of the term. Rather, work is socialized, and social talk can serve as work because its larger purpose is the cementing of personal relations.

The amount of time spent at what we in the West would call work is much less than what one might expect. The notorious efficiency of Japan does not depend upon time spent. Rather, it depends upon absence of intermural conflict, lots of intramural competition, and an ideological solidarity which is almost beyond the comprehension of Europe and America. This is of use mainly (or merely) in the hours, days, years spent together—in the creation and continuation of the group. This is equally true when the office is left. It is often left as a group since no one wishes to break cohesion by leaving first. Then the group divides into sub-groups which then go out on the town, to favorite pubs and bars, to continue the social amelioration which has traditionally been so important to Japan.

Far from early-to-bed, the upwardly mobile Japanese male is fortunate if he catches the last train home. And often he will stay overnight with an office friend, an event that his wife back home will accept as a part of the normal rhythm of her spouse.

She may even encourage the event. I know of one young office worker who would like nothing better than to leave his company confreres and return to wife and child. But this she discourages because if he were seen by the neighbors coming home early they would certainly gossip, and the rumor would spread that he was not properly getting on in his company career.

In places where day and night are divided strictly according to the needs of actual work—I don't know, let's say, Chicago—the pattern may be closer to the ideal of which Japan brags. As it is, Japanese temporal reality is something different—far closer to that of Bangkok or Jakarta, the rest of Asia, places where time is almost by definition something which is spent together.

That a good deal of time in Japan is wasted (endless tea and coffee breaks, lots of after-hours in cabarets) is a Western, not a Japanese criticism. Japan never considers time together as time wasted. Rather, it is time invested.

Yet, for a culture as time-conscious as Japan (one sees mottos on office walls: Time is Money), the amount of real temporal waste is surprising. Here, too, the country shows its ancient Asian roots.

Take the matter of appointments for example. In the big business world of the West being punctual is sacrosanct. Again, actuality may be another matter, but all subscribe to the idea that to be on time is to be good.

In Asia, however, this is not so. One is frequently left cooling one's heels in the great capitals of the Orient. And here Japan, despite its Western temporal veneer, is no different. If you are meeting a member of your group, then he will wait and you can be late. If you are meeting a non-member you can also be late because it is not so important whether you meet or not.

Spatially, the Japanese are very efficient regarding rendezvous. There are known places to meet. In Tokyo one meets in front of Shinjuku's Kinokuniya Bookstore, in front of Ginza's Wako Department Store, in front of the Almond Coffee Shop at Roppongi, and at Shibuya in front of the statue of Hachiko, famous loyal dog who waited years there for its dead master.

Most waiting Japanese are in the position of Hachiko. It is rare to observe anyone being on time. Indeed, it appears as though one portion of the nation (smaller) is punctilious and that the rest (larger) is flagrantly errant.

Those who are on time and are doing the waiting are those in an inferior position (in Japan it is the girls who wait for the boys and not the other way about) or those who want something from the late arrival. Time is money, indeed—but then, come to think of it, the motto is written usually in English and in a Japanese situation only Japanese is operative. For all this show of making appointments, Japanese standards of punctuality are closer to those of Samarkand than of Paris or London.

Still, one wonders. With time so precious that it must be doled out in little pieces, must be compared to legal tender, how then can it be so wantonly wasted?

Well, it is not one's own time that is being wasted, to be sure. It is the other person's, he or she who is waiting. In fact, one's own time supply is somewhat short. That is why one is late, you see.

We in the West who make nothing like the fuss about time that the Japanese do, would be mortally insulted to be kept waiting, let us say, an hour. Yet many Japanese would wait an hour, standing by store, coffee shop or bronze dog.

And is this not perhaps then the largest difference between the time concept of East and West? Time is not moral in Asia; it cannot be used as a weapon. (Do you realize that you have kept me waiting for fifteen minutes?) And it cannot really be used to indicate virtue (hard-working, efficient) or vice (lax, late for appointments).

It is rather a seamless entity, an element like the air in which we live. To live naturally with time, says Asia, is to pay no attention to it. And Japan, despite its modernization, still subscribes to this ancient tradition. Dig down through company minutes and office hours and there, firm eternal, is time itself.

1. Why don't the subways run after midnight in Japan?

2. Why is time spent having tea, at coffee-breaks, and at bars not wasted?

3. Why don't boys wait for girls in Japan?

4. Can you identify some of the ways tradition has survived in modern Japanese culture?

Toward the Future

United States President Ronald Reagan and Soviet leader Mikhail Gorbachev met for a superpower summit in Geneva, 1985.

·164·

Charter of Economic Rights and Duties of States

(1974)

*B*eginning in the 1970s the leaders of underdeveloped states in the so-called Third World began to voice concerns about the relationship between foreign and domestic ownership of natural resources and about the obligations that industrialized nations owed to developing ones. These issues were becoming particularly troublesome in light of the energy crisis and the skyrocketing international indebtedness of Third-World nations. Third-World leaders called increasingly for programs that would guarantee world economic justice.

The Charter of Economic Rights and Duties of States was among the most visionary of the programs proposed. It was adopted by the General Assembly of the United Nations by a vote of 120 to 6 with 10 abstentions. Voting against the charter were the United States, Great Britain, West Germany, Belgium, Denmark, and Luxembourg. The most serious issues relating to the charter concerned the renationalization of resources and the obligation of underdeveloped states to pay compensation for reclaiming their own property.

PREAMBLE

The General Assembly,

Reaffirming the fundamental purposes of the United Nations, in particular the maintenance of international peace and security, the development of friendly relations among nations and the achievement of international co-operation in solving international problems in the economic and social fields,

Affirming the need for strengthening international co-operation in these fields,

Reaffirming further the need for strengthening international co-operation for development,

Declaring that it is a fundamental purpose of the present Charter to promote the establishment of the new international economic order, based on equity, sovereign equality, interdependence, common interest and co-operation among all States, irrespective of their economic and social systems,

Desirous of contributing to the creation of conditions for:

(a)   The attainment of wider prosperity among all countries and of higher standards of living for all peoples,

(b)   The promotion by the entire international community of the economic and social progress of all countries, especially developing countries,

(c)   The encouragement of co-operation, on the basis of mutual advantage and equitable benefits for all peace-loving States which are willing to carry out the provisions of the present Charter, in the economic, trade, scientific and technical fields, regardless of political, economic or social systems,

(d)   The overcoming of main obstacles in the way of the economic development of the developing countries,

The delegation of Senegal headed by Assane Seck, Minister for Foreign Affairs. United Nations, New York, 1974.

(e) The acceleration of the economic growth of developing countries with a view to bridging the economic gap between developing and developed countries,

(f) The protection, preservation and enhancement of the environment,

Mindful of the need to establish and maintain a just and equitable economic and social order through:

(a) The achievement of more rational and equitable international economic relations and the encouragement of structural changes in the world economy,

(b) The creation of conditions which permit the further expansion of trade and intensification of economic co-operation among all nations,

(c) The strengthening of the economic independence of developing countries,

(d) The establishment and promotion of international economic relations, taking into account the agreed differences in development of the developing countries and their specific needs,

Determined to promote collective economic security for development, in particular of the developing countries, with strict respect for the sovereign equality of each State and through the co-operation of the entire international community,

Considering that genuine co-operation among States, based on joint consideration of and concerted action regarding international economic problems, is essential for fulfilling the international community's common desire to achieve a just and rational development of all parts of the world,

Stressing the importance of ensuring appropriate conditions for the conduct of normal economic relations among all States, irrespective of differences in social and economic systems, and for the full respect of the rights of all peoples, as well as strengthening instruments of international economic co-operation as means for the consolidation of peace for the benefit of all,

Convinced of the need to develop a system of international economic relations on the basis of sovereign equality, mutual and equitable benefit and the close interrelationship of the interests of all States,

Reiterating that the responsibility for the development of every country rests primarily upon itself but that concomitant and effective international co-operation is an essential factor for the full achievement of its own development goals,

Firmly convinced of the urgent need to evolve a substantially improved system of international economic relations,

Solemnly adopts the present Charter of Economic Rights and Duties of States.

CHAPTER I. FUNDAMENTALS OF INTERNATIONAL ECONOMIC RELATIONS

Economic as well as political and other relations among States shall be governed, *inter alia,* by the following principles:

(a) Sovereignty, territorial integrity and political independence of States;

(b) Sovereign equality of all States;

(c) Non-aggression;

(d) Non-intervention;

(e) Mutual and equitable benefit;

(f) Peaceful coexistence;

(g) Equal rights and self-determination of peoples;

(h) Peaceful settlement of disputes;

(i) Remedying of injustices which have been brought about by force and which deprive a nation of the natural means necessary for its normal development;

(j) Fulfillment in good faith of international obligations;

(k) Respect for human rights and fundamental freedoms;

(l) No attempt to seek hegemony and spheres of influence;

(m) Promotion of international social justice;

(n) International co-operation for development;

(o) Free access to and from the sea by landlocked countries within the framework of the above principles.

CHAPTER II. ECONOMIC RIGHTS AND DUTIES OF STATES

Article 1

Every State has the sovereign and inalienable right to choose its economic system as well as its political, social and cultural systems in accordance with the will of its people, without outside interference, coercion or threat in any form whatsoever.

Article 2

1. Every State has and shall freely exercise full permanent sovereignty, including possession, use and disposal, over all its wealth, natural resources and economic activities.

2. Each State has the right:

(a) To regulate and exercise authority over foreign investment within its national jurisdiction in accordance with its laws and regulations and in conformity with its national objectives and priorities. No State shall be compelled to grant preferential treatment to foreign investment;

(b) To regulate and supervise the activities of transnational corporations within its national jurisdiction and take measures to ensure that such activities comply with its laws, rules and regulations and conform with its economic and social policies. Transnational corporations shall not intervene in the internal affairs of a host State. Every State should, with full regard for its sovereign rights, co-operate with other States in the exercise of the right set forth in this subparagraph;

(c)　To nationalize, expropriate or transfer ownership of foreign property, in which case appropriate compensation should be paid by the State adopting such measures, taking into account its relevant laws and regulations and all circumstances that the State considers pertinent. In any case where the question of compensation gives rise to a controversy, it shall be settled under the domestic law of the nationalizing State and by its tribunals, unless it is freely and mutually agreed by all States concerned that other peaceful means be sought on the basis of the sovereign equality of States and in accordance with the principle of free choice of means.

Article 4

Every State has the right to engage in international trade and other forms of economic cooperation irrespective of any differences in political, economic and social systems. No State shall be subjected to discrimination of any kind based solely on such differences. In the pursuit of international trade and other forms of economic co-operation, every State is free to choose the forms of organization of its foreign economic relations and to enter into bilateral and multilateral arrangements consistent with its international obligations and with the needs of international economic co-operation.

Article 5

All States have the right to associate in organizations of primary commodity producers in order to develop their national economies, to achieve stable financing for their development and, in pursuance of their aims, to assist in the promotion of sustained growth of the world economy, in particular accelerating the development of developing countries. Correspondingly all States have the duty to respect that right by refraining from applying economic and political measures that would limit it.

Article 7

Every State has the primary responsibility to pro-mote the economic, social and cultural development of its people. To this end, each State has the right and the responsibility to choose its means and goals of development, fully to mobilize and use its resources, to implement progressive economic and social reforms and to ensure the full participation of its people in the process and benefits of development. All States have the duty, individually and collectively, to co-operate in order to eliminate obstacles that hinder such mobilization and use.

Article 8

States should co-operate in facilitating more rational and equitable international economic relations and in encouraging structural changes in the context of a balanced world economy in harmony with the needs and interests of all countries, especially developing countries, and should take appropriate measures to this end.

Article 10

All States are juridically equal and, as equal members of the international community, have the right to participate fully and effectively in the international decision-making process in the solution of world economic, financial and monetary problems, *inter alia,* through the appropriate international organizations in accordance with their existing and evolving rules, and to share equitably in the benefits resulting therefrom.

Article 13

1.　Every State has the right to benefit from the advances and developments in science and technology for the acceleration of its economic and social development.

2.　All States should promote international scientific and technological co-operation and the transfer of technology, with proper regard for all legitimate interests including, *inter alia,* the rights and duties of holders, suppliers and recipients of technology. In particular, all States should facilitate the access of developing countries to the achievements of modern science and technology, the transfer of technology and the

creation of indigenous technology for the benefit of the developing countries in forms and in
accordance with procedures which are suited to
their economies and their needs.

3. Accordingly, developed countries
should co-operate with the developing countries
in the establishment, strengthening and development of their scientific and technological infra-
structures and their scientific research and technological activities so as to help to expand and
transform the economies of developing countries.

4. All States should co-operate in research
with a view to evolving further internationally
accepted guidelines or regulations for the transfer of technology, taking fully into account the
interests of developing countries.

Article 15

All States have the duty to promote the achievement of general and complete disarmament
under effective international control and to uti-
lize the resources released by effective disarmament measures for the economic and social development of countries, allocating a substantial
portion of such resources as additional means for
the development needs of developing countries.

Article 16

1. It is the right and duty of all States, individually and collectively, to eliminate colonialism, *apartheid,* racial discrimination, neo-colo-
nialism and all forms of foreign aggression,
occupation and domination, and the economic
and social consequences thereof, as a prerequisite for development. States which practice such
coercive policies are economically responsible to
the countries, territories and peoples affected
for the restitution and full compensation for the
exploitation and depletion of, and damages to,
the natural and all other resources of those
countries, territories and peoples. It is the duty
of all States to extend assistance to them.

2. No State has the right to promote or
encourage investments that may constitute an
obstacle to the liberation of a territory occupied
by force.

Article 19

With a view to accelerating the economic growth
of developing countries and bridging the economic gap between developed and developing
countries, developed countries should grant
generalized preferential, non-reciprocal and
non-discriminatory treatment to developing
countries in those fields of international economic cooperation where it may be feasible.

Article 20

Developing countries should, in their efforts to
increase their over-all trade, give due attention
to the possibility of expanding their trade with
socialist countries, by granting to these countries
conditions for trade not inferior to those granted normally to the developed market economy
countries.

CHAPTER III. COMMON RESPONSIBILITIES TOWARDS THE INTERNATIONAL COMMUNITY

Article 29

The sea-bed and ocean floor and the subsoil
thereof, beyond the limits of national jurisdiction, as well as the resources of the area, are the
common heritage of mankind.

Article 30

The protection, preservation and enhancement
of the environment for the present and future
generations is the responsibility of all States. All
States shall endeavor to establish their own envi-
ronmental and developmental policies in conformity with such responsibility. The environ-
mental policies of all States should enhance and
not adversely affect the present and future development potential of developing countries. All
States have the responsibility to ensure that activities within their jurisdiction or control do not
cause damage to the environment of other States
or of areas beyond the limits of national jurisdiction. All States should co-operate in evolving
international norms and regulations in the field
of the environment.

1. What is the new international economic order?

2. What seem to be the most important principles behind the creation of the new economic order?

3. Why do you think the Western powers opposed the adoption of the charter?

4. What is the responsibility of the developed countries towards the undeveloped?

5. How would the full implementation of the charter change the world economy?

·165·

E. P. Thompson
Questions for Mr. Weinberger
(1984)

*E*dward Palmer Thompson (1924–1993), historian and journalist, was one of the most powerful spokesmen for nuclear disarmament. He was educated at Cambridge University, where he was president of the University Socialist Club and a member of the British Communist party. After wartime service, Thompson began to teach adult education classes and to work on his first major piece of historical scholarship, a biography of William Morris. In 1956 Thompson broke with the British Communist party over the conduct of the Soviet Union and worked full-time as a journalist on the *New Left Review* and similar publications. In 1963 he published *The Making of the English Working Class,* one of the most influential works on modern British history. Thompson was briefly professor of history at the University of Warwick but retired to devote his time to writing and political activism. In the late 1970s he became a leader of the Campaign for Nuclear Disarmament (CND).

In 1984 Thompson was invited to Oxford University for an Oxford Union debate on the resolution: "That there is no moral difference between the foreign policies of the United States and the Union of Soviet Socialist Republics?" His opponent was Caspar Weinberger, U.S. Secretary of Defense.

Mr. President. Ladies and Gentlemen. I also wish to express my pleasure that Mr. Weinberger is here. I think that this is a recognition not only of the standing of this society but a recognition also of the depth of concern in Europe and in this country on the issues of peace. And I welcome it also as one of those signs of the openness to debate of the American system: an openness which I have myself often benefited from. I have been able to say in the United States what I wanted to say on behalf of the British or the European peace movement. I have been welcomed at the National Press Club in Washington, at campuses and churches in the United States, and I know very well that I would not be able to speak openly in the same way in the Soviet Union.

Without this tradition and vitality of openness in American intellectual life, humanity would not now know the perils in which it is placed. If it had not been for the tradition of the United States scientists, of "whistleblowers" like Daniel Ellsberg, or of arms controllers who have come out and made the most radical criticism of their own state policy—if it had not been for publications like the *Bulletin of the Atomic Scientists,* we would not even know about the nuclear winter that would follow even a medium exchange of weapons. We would not know this through Soviet sources, and we would not know it from British sources which are obsessed with "official secrecy."

This emphasizes that we are tonight not discussing the relative merits of the two political systems. We are not discussing whether we would prefer to live in the Soviet Union or in the United States. There is scarcely any room for choice in this for any serious intellectual worker who needs the tools of his trade, who needs to be able to consult the libraries or to publish without censorship.

We are discussing tonight the foreign policies, not the internal social systems, the foreign policies of the United States and the USSR and the moral differences between them. And I can find none. Today the world is dominated by two towering superpowers, locked in each others' nuclear arms, aggravating each other, inciting each other in their ideological postures, rendering and reducing to client status their lesser allies. . . .

By no means all the blame for the enhancement of deterrence in Europe lies with the United States. Our own political leaders have been throughout consenting adults in the corruption and subordination of this nation to the hegemony of United States' military policy. Now the first flight of these missiles, owned and operated by the United States, are here on our territory and they are supposed to be for our greater security. Do we really feel more secure because cruise and Pershing have come? No one feels more secure:

neither Europeans nor the Soviet people nor the people of the United States. . . .

[A] reason that we do not feel more secure lies in the predicted consequences of this action. The blocs have closed against each other. The counter-deployment is going on of SS21s, 22s or 23s, including deployment in Czechoslovakia and East Germany (which have hitherto been only very lightly, if at all, occupied by nuclear weapons). We have been saying up and down Europe for two years that the dragons' teeth sown in Comiso and Greenham Common would spring up as missiles on the other side. And so it has taken place. Any child could see that. Any child. Why can eminent statespersons not understand what Auden wrote in agony at the commencement of World War II?

> I and the public know
> What all schoolchildren learn:
> Those to whom evil is done
> Do evil in return.

The missiles are futile, of course. The Dutch women's peace movement have told me they have found out that the cruise missiles are actually cartons full of washing powder. It doesn't matter what they are: they are symbols and they are symbols of menace, of "posture," of clientage and subordination in the recipient nations, of NATO or Warsaw Pact "unity."

But they are not only symbols. Nor are they all that there is. We know what is coming on behind them. Thanks to the openness of the American system we know much more about what is coming on on the United States' side. MX, BI, Trident (there and here), the Iowa task force with its load of sea-launched cruise missiles, the air-launched cruise missiles: 1,300 are in production now and in the fiscal year '85. And beyond that the vista of space weapons and space scenarios for war. And there are other little bits of things in Mr. Weinberger's latest 1985 Fiscal Year *Report;* I think that there are five new short-range nuclear systems now being brought forward and two new chemical systems. There are (perhaps he will tell us?) plans for siting new ground-launched antiship missiles in the Western Isles and in Scotland.

I say that this is a condition of barbarism. And I put forward two documents, essential to my case. These are both part of the propaganda, that led us to this disastrous situation. One is called *Soviet Military Power* and it has a foreword by Mr. Weinberger. It is a "Sears, Roebuck" catalogue of all the deadly military equipment, whether naval or air or on the ground, possessed by the Soviet Union. And the other, which was produced in answer to it by the Soviet propagandists, is called *Whence the Threat to Peace?* This also is a catalogue—rather better illustrated, because they could get the illustrations more easily from the United States' press—of all the marvelous military equipment being developed in the United States. They have even copied each other in maps. Here is a power projection in the United States catalogue, with a *huge* Soviet Union, with arrows going in every direction around the world. And in the Soviet catalogue, the Soviet Union is rather smaller and all the arrows are spreading out from the United States towards the five continents of the world.

The usual half-lies and propaganda statements are made in both these books. But the tragedy is that *both* these books are largely *true*. William Hazlitt said about a philosophical radical, the Rev. Fawcett, in the 1790s that he had Thomas Paine's *Rights of Man* and Edmund Burke's *Reflections on the French Revolution* bound together in the same covers, and he said that, taken together, they made a very good book. But bind these two together and they make the most evil book known in the whole human record. They are a catalogue, an inventory of the matched evils of this accelerating system, a confession of absolute human failure. What moral difference is there between these two catalogues? What language of "ought" can be found there? Is this the product of our most advanced civilization? "Was it for this the clay grew tall?"

The globe has shrunk now to a little gourd. It is controlled by two vast, mutually-exacerbating military structures at the summit of which there is extraordinary centralized power in the functions of the President of the United States and the First Secretary of the Soviet Communist Party. We know now that throughout last autumn this power lay in the hands of two elderly men, one of whom was on a kidney-machine and half-dead from the neck down, and the other of whom (in the view of his critics) was on an autocue-machine and half-dead from the neck up.

The trouble with the statesmen and military leaders of both blocs is that they talk the same language. They both burn our taxes and our resources before the nostrils of the great Sacred Cow called the "balance" or "parity." We haven't, on this side in this debate, played the game of "snap." We haven't tried to list the offenses on one side and trade them against the offenses on the other. Vietnam—Afghanistan; Central Europe—Central America, the joint competition in the foul trade in arms. If anything, I would say, looking over the last 30 years, that the Gulag has been shrinking over on that side, and is tending to enlarge in the area of dependency on this side, the client or proxy states of the Western powers. There is now a formidable United States presence everywhere: Oman, Turkey, Iceland, South Korea, Egypt, Diego Garcia—what are you doing in Diego Garcia?—Somalia—what are you doing there?. . .

Let me end by being constructive. Am I speaking for "neutralism"? Am I saying "a plague on both your houses!"? Yes. But we—that is Europe—are also pretty plaguey. We are a source of the plague, we were the source of World War One and World War Two. And what we owe to ourselves, but also to the American and the Soviet people, is a more active strategy than mere neutrality. Neutrality isn't going to save us from the nuclear winter if the superpowers engage. We need to make a space between the two superpowers: a more tranquil space, maybe by nuclear-free zones in the Baltic and Balkans, a corridor in central Europe; by commencing a healing-process of citizens, of scholars, of doctors, of churches, a healing-process underneath the level of the states.

The European peace movement in the last three years has not just been about certain categories of missile. Underneath there has been a huge subterranean political-geological upheaval, the demand for greater autonomy both as individual nations and of Europe as a whole. I think Americans will understand when I say that we are on the edge of a moment that they might remember from their own history. We are in a place like 1771 or 1772. Europe is meditating now a declaration of independence.

I want to ask Mr. Weinberger what his solution is, beyond all the build-up of these missiles. What solution does he offer? I suggest that what we need is an "Austrian solution" for Europe, and then for the world. Yes, the problem as Mr. Shultz has said, is in effect "Yalta". But "Yalta" has got two sides: one side is the Soviet presence in Eastern and Central Europe, and the other side is the heavy American military hegemony in Western and Southern Europe. And you will never reach a settlement on one side without a settlement on the other. That is the strategy we have to look for. I am making no moral apologies for the presence of Soviet troops in Czechoslovakia or in Hungary, but as realists we must know that they will not withdraw unless there is some concession in the West and especially in West Germany. While West Germany is stashed with military forces will there be a withdrawal on the other side?. . .

But those who served in World War Two would not have believed it, they would have been amazed if they had been told that 39 years after the end of World War Two there would still be Soviet forces in East Europe and United States forces in West Europe. At that time we had a vision, and that vision extended also to the United States and the Soviet Union, of a socialist and democratic world. We have now to re-trace our steps back down to the point where "Yalta" was fixed and try and unscramble it.

When friends come to help us it's fine for them to stay in the house for three or four days, but when they stay for three weeks we get a little bit restive. After 39 years enough is enough. So it's now our duty to start this healing-process and it's yours, Mr. Weinberger, to assist us to this new objective whose end must be the withdrawal of these forces from both sides. This is not anti-Americanism—it is not anti-Sovietism. We'll send you home with flowers and we will welcome you back to our universities or to our countries as visitors with flowers once more. But it is in the interests of the people of both sides to be rid of the burden, the anguish, and the danger involved in this European connection.

The first moral difference that will appear will be when either superpower makes an actual *act* of disarmament. Then we can start to talk about morality. Until that happens I rest my case on these two odious books and I ask Oxford to support this motion in the name of a universalism at its very foundation in the Middle Ages: a universalism of scholarship which owed its duty to the skills of communication and learning and not to those of the armed state. As William Blake wrote:

> The strongest poison ever known
> Came from Caesar's laurel crown.

I support this motion in the confidence that this house will reject the poison of Caesar.

1. Why does Thompson liken the foreign policies of the United States and the Soviet Union?

2. Why does Thompson oppose deployment of nuclear weapons in Europe? What is wrong with the policy of deterrence?

3. What is Thompson's alternative to the superpower rivalry?

4. Thompson was speaking over 40 years after the foundation of the United Nations, which was designed to reduce tension in the world. Yet he never mentions it. Why?

5. What seem to be Thompson's views about states and governments in general?

Literary Credits

HOW TO READ A DOCUMENT

Thomas Wright, editor. *The Travels of Marco Polo, The Venetian.* (London: George Bell & Sons, 1880), pp. B, 171–179.

PART IV THE WORLD OF TRAVELERS AND TRADERS

Monarchy and Revolution

79. From *The Political Works of James* I, reprinted from the edition of 1616 with an introduction by Charles Howard McIlwain (Cambridge, Mass.: Harvard University Press, 1918), pp. 53–70. Reprinted by permission.
80. Excerpts from Philippe Duplessis-Mornay, *Vindiciae Contra Tyrannos* from *Readings in Western Civilization, Early Modern Europe: Crisis of Authority,* edited by Cochrane, Gray and Kishlansky. Copyright © 1987 by The University of Chicago. All rights reserved. Reprinted by permission of The University of Chicago Press.
81. William Clarke, *The Clarke Papers. Volume 1,* edited by C.H. Firth. (London: Royal Historical Society, 1891), pp. 299–307, 311–312, 315–317, 325–327.
82. Duc de Saint-Simon, *Memoirs,* translated by Bayle St. John. (London: Swan Sonnonschein & Co., 1900), pp. 357–365.

The New Science

83. From *Two New Sciences* by Galileo Galilei, translated by Stillman Drake. Copyright © 1989 by Stillman Drake. Reprinted with permission of Wall & Emerson, Inc., Toronto.
84. Rene Descartes, *Discourse on Method.* From *Descartes, Philosophical Writings,* selected and translated by Norman Kemp Smith. Reprinted by permission of Macmillan (London and Basingstoke).

Empires of Goods

85. Excerpt from *The Low Countries in Early Modern Times,* edited by Herbert H. Rowen. Copyright © 1972 by Herbert H. Rowen. Reprinted by permission of HarperCollins Publishers.

86.   Thomas Mun, England's Treasure by Foreign Trade. In *Early English Tracts on Commerce*, edited by J.R. McCulloch. (Cambridge: University Press, 1954), pp. 121–126, 134–141.

87.   Adam Smith, *An Inquiry into the Nature and Class of the Wealth of Nations*, edited by James E. Thorold Rogers. Volume I, 2nd Edition. (Oxford: Clarendon Press, 1880), pp. 59–65.

The Balance of Power in Europe

88.   From *Memoirs of Catherine the Great*, edited by Dominque Maroger, with an introduction by G. P. Gooch. Translated from the French by Moura Budberg. Reprinted by permission of Hachette.

89.   Excerpts from *The Hapsburg and Hohenzollern Dynasties in the Seventeenth and Eighteenth Centuries*, edited by C.A. Macartney. Copyright © 1970 by C.A. Macartney. Reprinted by permission of HarperCollins Publishers.

90.   Thomas Jefferson, The Declaration of Independence. In *Documents Illustrative of American History 1606–1863*, edited by Howard W. Preston. (New York: G.P. Putnam's Sons, 1893), pp. 210–215.

91.   Viscount Bolingbroke, *Letters on the Spirit of Patriotism: On the Idea of a Patriot King*. (London: T. Davies, 1775), pp. 76–81, 83–85, 111–114.

Asia Alone

92.   From *Hagakure*, published by Kodansha International Ltd. Copyright © 1979 by Kodansha International. Reprinted by permission. All rights reserved.

93.   From *The Japanese Discovery of Europe* by Donald Keene. Reprinted by permission of the author.

94.   *History of the Two Tartar Conquerors of China*, translated and edited by The Earl of Ellesmere. (New York: Burt Franklin, Publisher, 1854), pp. 12–130.

95.   From *The Scholars*, by Wu Ching-tzu, translated by Yang Hsien-yi and Gladys Yang. Foreign Languages Press, Peking, 1957. Reprinted by permission.

The European Enlightenment

96.   "Candide," from *Candide, Zadig and Selected Stories by Voltaire* by Françoise Voltaire, translated by Donald Murdoch Frame. Translation copyright © 1961 by Donald M. Frame. Used by permission of New American Library, a division of Penguin Books USA Inc.

97.   Jean-Jacques Rousseau, *The Social Contract*, translated by Rose M. Harrington. (New York: G.P. Putnam's Sons, 1906), pp. 19–22, 130–131, 158–162.

98.   Reprinted with the permission of Macmillan Publishing Company from *Beccaria's on Crimes and Punishments*, translated by Henry Paolucci. Copyright © 1985 by Macmillan Publishing Company.

99.   From *Sketch for a Historical Picture of the Progress of the Human Mind* by Marie-Jean de Condorcet, translated by June Barraclough. First published in this translation in this series 1955. Reprinted by permission of George Weidenfeld & Nicolson Limited.

100.   Montesquieu, *Spirit of Laws: A Compendium of the First English Edition,* translated by David Carrithers. Copyright © 1977 The Regents of the University of California. Reprinted by permission.

The French Revolution

101.   Reprinted with the permission of Macmillan Publishing Company from *A Documentary Survey of the French Revolution* by John Hall Stewart. Copyright © 1951 by Macmillan Publishing Company, renewed © 1979 by John Hall Stewart.

102   Declaration of the Rights of Man and Citizen. In *Readings in European History. Volume II: From the Opening of the Protestant Revolt to the Present Day,* edited by James Harvey Robinson. (Boston: Ginn & Company, 1906), pp. 409–411; Olympe de Gouges, Declaration of the Rights of Woman and the Female Citizen. In *Women in Revolutionary Paris 1789–1795,* translated by Darline Gay Levy, Harriet Branson Applewhite, and Mary Durham Johnson. (Urbana: University of Illinois Press, 1979), pp. 89–92.

103.   Edmund Burke, *Reflections on the Revolution in France.* (London: J. Dodsley, 1790), pp. 50–57, 70, 76–77, 95.

Travelers to the East and West

104.   J. Ovington, *A Voyage to Suratt in the Year 1689,* edited with an introduction by J.P. Guha. (New Delhi: Associated Publishing House, 1976), pp. 94–98, 100–104, 107–109.

105.   From *The Great Chinese Travelers,* edited and introduced by Jeannette Mirsky, 1964, pp. 266–271.

106.   Captain Vasilii Galownin, *Memoirs of a Captivity in Japan in the Years 1811, 1812, and 1813* (London: Henry C. Colburn Co., 1824), pp. 82–94, 202–203.

107.   *The East African Coast,* G.S.P. Freeman-Grenville. (London: Rex Collings Ltd., 1975), pp. 192–197.

108.   From *Prutky's Travels in Ethiopia and Other Countries,* translated and edited by J.H. Arrowsmith-Brown and annotated by Richard Pankhurst. Copyright © 1991 The Hakluyt Society. Reprinted by permission.

109.   *Equiano's Travels: His Autogiography,* abridged and edited by Paul Edwards. (Oxford: Heinemann International, 1967), pp. 1–5, 7–11.

110.   From *A Persian at the Court of King George 1809–10,* translated and edited by Margaret Morris Cloake. Copyright © Margaret Morris Cloake 1988. Reprinted by permission of Barrie & Jenkins.

PART V INDUSTRIALISM AND IMPERIALISM

The Industrial Revolution in Britain

111.   Arthur Young, *Political Arithmetic.* (London: W. Nicoll, 1774), pp. 4–6, 287–296.

112.   Samuel Smiles, *Self-Help.* (New York: A.L. Burt, n.d.), pp. 84–89.

113. Edwin Chadwick, *An Inquiry into the Sanitary Condition of the Labouring Population of Great Britain*. (London: W. Clowes and Sons, 1842), pp. 98–101, 111–112, 279.

114. Frederick Engels, *The Condition of the Working-Class in England in 1844,* translated by Florence Kelley Wischnewetsky. (London: George Allen and Unwin Ltd., 1892)

Critiquing Industrial Society

115. John Stuart Mill. *On Liberty*. (London: The Walter Scott Publishing Co., n.d.), pp. 17–18, 22–23, 225–226, 103–106, 140–143.

116. P.J. Proudhon, *What Is Property?* In *The Works of P.J. Proudhon. Volume I*. (Princeton, Mass.: Benjamin R. Tucker, 1876), pp. 269–272, 276–279, 286–288.

117. The Great Charter. In *Hansard's Parliamentary Debates. Volume LXII, Third Series*. (London: Thomas Hansard, 1842), pp. 1373–1381.

118. From *Manifesto of the Communist Party* by Karl Marx and Friedrich Engels. Authorized English translation edited and annotated by Friedrich Engels. All Rights Reserved, 1932. Reprinted by permission of International Publishers Co.

119. Charles Darwin, *On the Origin of Species by Means of Natural Selection*. (New York: D. Appleton and Company, 1883), pp. 48–51, 62–65, 70–71, 73.

120. From *The Basic Writings of Sigmund Freud,* translated and edited, with an introduction by Dr. A.A. Brill. Copyright 1938, renewed 1965, by Gioia B. Bernheim and Edmund Brill. Reprinted by permission.

Controlling Latin America

121. From *Selected Writings of Bolivar, Volume One,* compiled by Vicente Lecuna, edited by Harold A. Bierck, Jr., translation by Lewis Bertrand. Copyright 1951 by Banco de Venezuela. Reprinted by permission of Foundation Lecuna.

122. James D. Richardson, *A Compilation of the Messages and Papers of the Presidents 1789–1902, Volume II*. Published by Bureau of National Literature and Art, 1907, pp. 207–210, 217–220.

123. From *Latin American Civilization: History and Society 1492 to the Present, Fifth Edition,* edited by Benjamin Keen. Copyright © 1991 by Westview Press, Inc. Reprinted by permission of Westview Press, Boulder, Colorado.

Eastern Europe

124. Alexander II and Prince Kropotkin, "The Emancipation of the Serfs." From *A Source Book for Russian History from Early Times to 1917, Vol. 3,* edited by George Vernadsky et al., pp. 599–600, 604–605. Copyright © 1972 by Yale University Press. All rights reserved. Reprinted by permission.

125. Otto von Bismarck, "Professorial Politics." In *The German Classics: Masterpieces of German Literature. Volume 10,* translated by Edmund von Mach. (New York: The German Publication Society, 1914), pp. 175–176, 210, 219–220.

Imperialism

126. J.A. Hobson, *Imperialism*. (New York: James Pott & Company, 1902), pp. 377–379, 381–383, 389–390.

127. From *Cecil Rhodes* by John Flint. Copyright © 1974 by John Flint. By permission of Little, Brown and Company.

128. Rudyard Kipling, "The White Man's Burden" in *Rudyard Kipling's Verse 1885–1918*. (Garden City, N.Y.: Doubleday, 1920), pp. 371–372.

129. "Shooting an Elephant" from *Shooting an Elephant and Other Essays* by George Orwell, copyright 1950 by Sonia Brownell Orwell and renewed 1978 by Sonia Pitt-Rivers, reprinted by permission of Harcourt Brace Jovanovich, Inc. and The estate of the late Sonia Brownell Orwell.

130. Nikki Keddie. *Islamic Response to Imperlialism: Political and Religious Writings of Sayyid Jamal ad-Din*, pp. 123–129. Copyright © 1983 The Regents of the University of California. Reprinted by permission.

131. Robert Moffat, *Missionary Labours and Scenes in Southern Africa, Ninth Edition*. (New York: Robert Carter, 1846), pp. 347–352.

132. From Swahili Prose Texts, edited and translated by Lyndon Harries (1965). Copyright © 1965 Oxford University Press. Reprinted by permission.

PART VI THE MODERN WORLD

World War I

133. From *Storm of Steel* by Ernst Jünger, translated by Basil Creighton. Copyright 1929 by Doubleday, Doran & Company, Inc. Reprinted by permission of Chatto & Windus on behalf of Ernst Jünger.

134. Woodrow Wilson, The Fourteen Points.

135. V.I. Lenin, *What is to be Done?* Peking: Foreign Languages Press, 1975.

East Meets West

136. Reprinted by permission of the publishers from *China's Response to the West* by Ssu-yu Teng and John K. Fairbank. Cambridge, Mass.: Harvard University Press. Copyright © 1954, 1979 by the President and Fellows of Harvard College.

137. From "Of Women's Hair." Lafcadio Hearn, *Glimpses of Unfamiliar Japan, Volume II*. (Cambridge, Mass.: The Riverside Press, 1894).

138. From *Fukuzawa Yukichi on Japanese Women, Selected Works*, translated and edited by Eiichi Kiyooka. Copyright © 1988 University of Tokyo Press. Reprinted by permission.

139. From *The Making of the Meiji Constitution* by George M. Beckmann. Copyright © 1957 Committee on Social Science Studies, University of Kansas Publications. Reprinted by permission.

140. Sun Yat-sen, *Fundamentals of National Reconstruction*. (Taipei: China Cultural Service, 1953), pp. 76–87.

The Soviet Union

141. "Theses on Communist Morality in the Sphere of Marital Relations," Copyright © Alix Holt, 1977. Reprinted from *Selected Writings of Alexandra Kollontai*, translated with an introduction and commentaries by Alix Holt, by permission of the publisher, Lawrence Hill Books (Brooklyn, New York).

Generations of Cultural Protest

World War II

Struggles for National Liberation

152. From *Hind Swaraj or Indian Home Rule* by M.K. Gandhi, Navajivan Publishing House, 1938. Reprinted by permission of Navajivan Trust.

153. "On 'Letting a Hundred Flowers Blossom'" from *Mao Tse-Tung on Art and Literature.* Foreign Languages Press, Peking, 1960. Reprinted by permission.

154. *Ho Chi Minh, Selected Writings 1920–1969.* (Hanoi: Foreign Languages Publishing House, 1973), pp. 53–56, 346–349.

155. From *I Speak of Freedom* by Kwame Nkrumah. Copyright © 1961 Kwame Nkrumah. Reprinted by permission of Zed Press Ltd.

156. From *Revolution in the Revolution? Armed Struggle and Political Struggle in Latin America* by Regis Debray, translated by Bobbye Ortiz. Copyright © 1967 by Monthly Review Press. Reprinted by permission of Monthly Review Foundation.

157. Abba Eban's Speech at the Special Assembly of the United Nations, June 19, 1967. Reprinted from *The Jerusalem Post.*

158. From "Sizwe Bansi Is Dead" in *Statements,* Two Workshop Productions devised by Athol Fugard, John Kani, and Winston Ntshona. Copyright © Athol Fugard, John Kani, and Winston Ntshona 1973 and 1974. Reprinted by permission of Sheil Land Associates Ltd.

159. "My Vision for South Africa" from *Crying in the Wilderness* by Desmond Tutu, edited by John Webster. Introduction and notes Copyright © John Webster 1982. Text Copyright © Desmond Tutu. Reprinted by permission of Mowbray, a Cassell imprint.

The Japanese Miracle

160. From *The Constitution of Japan and Criminal Statutes* (Tokyo: Ministry of Justice, 1958).

161. From *Sources of Japanese Tradition, Volume II* by Wm. T. DeBary. Copyright © 1958 Columbia University Press, New York. Reprinted with the permission of the publisher.

162. From *Big Business in Japanese Politics* by Chitoshi Yanaga. Copyright © 1968 by Yale University Press. Reprinted by permission.

163. "Japanese Rhythms" from *A Lateral View: Essays on Culture and Style in Contemporary Japan* by Donald Richie. Copyright © 1987, 1991, 1992 by Donald Richie. Reprinted by permission of Stone Bridge Press.

Toward the Future

164. Charter of Economic Rights and Duties of States. *In Basic Documents in International Law,* edited by Ian Brownlie. (Oxford: Clarendon Press, 1983), pp. 236–248.

165. From *Heavy Dancers* by E.P. Thompson. Copyright © 1985 by E. P. Thompson. Reprinted by permission of Pantheon Books, a division of Random House, Inc. and The Merlin Press Ltd.

Photo
Acknowledgments

Unless otherwise acknowledged, all photographs are the property of ScottForesman.

PART IV THE WORLD OF TRAVELERS AND TRADERS

The Royal Collection © Her Majesty Queen Elizabeth II, p. 3. Reproduced by permission of the Trustees of the Wallace Collection, p. 20. Whipple Museum of the History of Science, University of Cambridge, p. 25. Giraudon/Art Resource, NY, p. 31. City of Bristol Museum and Art Gallery, p. 35. Copyright Yale University Art Gallery, p. 58. The Metropolitan Museum of Art, Rogers Fund, 1942 (42.141.2), p. 65. The Metropolitan Museum of Art, The Bashford Dean Memorial Collection, p. 67. The Mansell Collection, p. 85. Bulloz, p. 94. Giraudon/Art Resource, NY, p. 105. Giraudon/Art Resource, NY, p. 107.

PART V INDUSTRIALISM AND IMPERIALISM

Reproduced by permission of the Trustees of the Science Museum, London, p. 153. Weidonfeld & Nicolson Ltd., p. 173. The Bettman Archive, p. 175. By permission of the General Secretariat of the Organization of American States, p. 199. The Bettman Archive, p. 213. The Bettman Archive, p. 218. BBD Broadcasting House, London, p. 230.

PART VI THE MODERN WORLD

From copy in Bowman Gray Collection, Rare Book Collection, UNC Library, Chapel Hill, North Carolina, p. 253. Library of Congress, p. 258. The Granger Collection, NY, p. 265. AP/Wide World, p. 287. AP/Wide World, p. 303. UPI/Bettman, p. 307. UPI/Bettman, p. 321. Brown Brothers, p. 325. UPI/Bettman, p. 339. Reuters/Bettman, p. 371. United Nations, p. 373. J.P. Laffont/Sygma, p. 389. AP/Wide World, p. 393. United Nations/T. Chen, p. 395.